AWS®
Certified Developer
Official Study Guide
Associate (DVA-C01) Exam

AWS®
Certified Developer
Official Study Guide
Associate (DVA-C01) Exam

Nick Alteen   Jennifer Fisher   Casey Gerena

Wes Gruver   Asim Jalis   Heiwad Osman

Marife Pagan   Santosh Patlolla   Michael Roth

SYBEX®
A Wiley Brand

Published by John Wiley & Sons, Inc., Indianapolis, Indiana.

Published simultaneously in Canada

ISBN: 978-1-119-50819-9
ISBN: 978-1-119-50821-2 (ebk.)
ISBN: 978-1-119-50820-5 (ebk.)

Library of Congress Control Number: 2019943088

SKY10062927_121823

About the Authors

Nick Alteen, technical training architect, Amazon Web Services

Nick specializes in designing and building training labs that educate the U.S. intelligence community on AWS best practices and design patterns. Before this, Nick worked as a cloud support engineer, assisting customers in resolving any number of issues related to AWS DevOps services, with a specific focus on configuration management and infrastructure as code. In his free time, he enjoys building LEGO models with his daughter and watching horror movies with his wife.

Jennifer Fisher, senior technical curriculum developer, Amazon Web Services

Jennifer started at AWS in 2014 as a technical trainer and was the lead instructor for Big Data on AWS. She holds multiple AWS certifications and currently leads a curriculum development team and develops technical curriculum and labs to support public sector customers. Before that, Jennifer spent 20 years as a software and data engineer in the financial services, defense, and healthcare industries. She holds a BS in programming and an MS in software engineering management.

Jennifer grew up on a farm in Northern Maine and bought her first computer, a Tandy TRS-80, with her potato-picking money at the age of 12. She began writing basic programs and role-playing games, not realizing at the time that her passion for coding would turn into a lifelong career. She now mentors female engineers and volunteers for K-12 students in STEM.

Jennifer is based in Herndon, Virginia, and lives with her husband Steve. She is a doting stepmother to Kate, Sophie, and Mason. In her free time, Jennifer enjoys hiking, geocaching, kayaking, mountain biking, weight lifting, and competing in obstacle course races.

Casey Gerena, senior technical trainer, Amazon Web Services

Casey is passionate about helping others learn about the AWS Cloud. He enjoys teaching others new technical skills to help them solve problems using serverless technologies such as AWS Lambda. Casey holds a BS in management information systems from the University of Central Florida and an MS in logistics and global supply chain management from Embry-Riddle Aeronautical University. He is pursuing a second master's degree in computer science from the Georgia Institute of Technology. Casey holds several IT certifications, including the Certified Information Systems Security Professional (CISSP) and nine AWS certifications. Before joining Amazon, Casey was a software developer and cybersecurity consultant. In his free time, Casey enjoys spending time with his family, watching movies, playing video games, and running.

Wes Gruver, senior technical trainer, Amazon Web Services

Wes has been with AWS since 2015 and is a senior technical trainer with more than 20 years of experience and success in managing IT infrastructure and all aspects of application development and management. He is currently responsible for training AWS enterprise customers on how to use the AWS services best suited for their business and IT solutions. He teaches a broad range of classes, including basic to advanced architecture, DevOps on AWS, Big Data on AWS, and security operations. In his free time, Wes teaches scuba diving and loves to travel.

Asim Jalis, senior technical trainer, Amazon Web Services

Asim is a senior technical trainer at AWS. He has an MS in computer science from the University of Virginia and an MA in mathematics from the University of Wisconsin. When he is not working with AWS technologies, he likes to read and write fiction.

Heiwad Osman, senior manager, Solutions Builders, Amazon Web Services

Heiwad holds a BS in computer science and engineering from UCLA. In his role as an AWS trainer, he meets with AWS customers and teaches them to build resilient, scalable cloud applications. He has helped hundreds of software developers get started with AWS APIs through in-person training and online training videos. His current professional interests include user experience, web application development, and machine learning. In his free time, you can find him in New York City, trying new places to eat or relaxing in Central Park.

Marife Pagan, technical trainer, Amazon Web Services

Marife is a technical trainer for AWS, delivering training to AWS customers in North America. She has more than 15 years of experience in software and web development. Her experience brings a set of skills for multiple platforms, including .NET, Java, and Python. She holds a BS in information technology with a web design/development concentration from George Mason University, in addition to various leading industry certifications. She is currently working on her master's degree and pursuing higher studies in machine learning.

Before working at AWS, Marife worked for various government contracting firms, including Lockheed Martin. She also serves in the U.S. military as a signal officer working on the setup and maintenance of LAN and WAN signal network footprints, supporting voice and data for various military operations. She currently lives in the Washington, DC, metro area, and in her spare time enjoys fitness, travel, and gardening.

Santosh Patlolla, technical curriculum architect, Amazon Web Services

Santosh is a technical curriculum architect for AWS. He has more than 18 years of experience in developing software applications, automated solutions, and migration projects with complex data conversions. Santosh has been instrumental in providing production-support solutions and managing application delivery programs for enterprises. He also designed cost-effective technical and business solutions for the banking and insurance industries. Santosh is passionate about applying this experience in using the broad range of AWS services for developing business automations. Outside of work, he coaches elementary school robotics, and enjoys watching basketball games and playing with his kids.

Michael Roth, technical trainer, Amazon Web Services

Michael is a technical trainer having joined Amazon in 2015. He is one of the authors of the SysOps Administrator Study Guide (also by Wiley). He is a Certified Cisco Network Academy Instructor, and he has taught Linux. Michael graduated from the University of Michigan with a BS in zoology and a BA in urban planning. He also has an MS in telecommunications management from Golden Gate University. Michael would like to thank his coworkers in the AWS Training and Certification organization—he is very proud to be a part of this amazing group of people. Finally, he would like to thank his spouse, Betsy, and son, Robert. Without their support and love, this book would not have been possible.

Contents at a Glance

Contents

Table of Exercises

Foreword

Software development is changing. In today's competitive market, customers demand low-latency, highly scalable, responsive applications that work—all the time. Customers expect to receive the same level of performance and consistency of applications regardless of their device. Whether they are on a mobile device, desktop, laptop, or Amazon Fire tablet, they expect that applications will behave similarly across platforms.

The goal of building working applications that respond to increasing expectations means that building applications on highly available architecture is now more important than ever. As developers, you can use AWS Cloud computing to build highly available architectures and services on which to deploy and run your applications.

AWS provides you with a broad set of tools to build and develop your applications. We empower you by providing the best tools to achieve your goals. To that end, you'll learn about compute services, such as Amazon Elastic Compute Cloud (Amazon EC2), and file object storage services, such as Amazon Simple Storage Service (Amazon S3). You'll also learn about the many types of applications that you can build on top of these services.

Historically, developers have been responsible for designing, creating, and running their applications. In the AWS Cloud, you can create your compute resources with one click using AWS CloudFormation, or you can fully automate the running of your containers using AWS Fargate.

AWS continually listens to customer feedback to understand your workloads and changing needs better. AWS also monitors market trends, understanding that you want to build and run applications on the cloud, but you don't want to worry about managing the underlying infrastructure. You want infrastructure to scale automatically, you want services with a built-in high availability infrastructure, and you want to pay only for what you consume.

In response to these demands, AWS pioneered services such as AWS Lambda, which is based on serverless technology. It enables you to run compute programming logic in applications without having to worry about maintaining anything other than their code and core logic.

Today is the most exciting time to be a developer. With AWS services, you can focus on the core functionality of your application and allow the AWS Cloud to perform all of the administration of the resources, including server and operating system maintenance. This flexibility provides you with the unique ability to focus on what matters to you most—building, maintaining, and, most importantly, innovating your applications.

In this study guide, AWS experts coach you on how to develop and build applications that can run on and integrate with AWS services. This knowledge allows you, as a developer, to build your services and features quickly and get them running in the AWS Cloud for your customers to use. When you complete this guide and the test bank in the accompanying interactive online learning environment, you have gained the fundamental knowledge to succeed on the AWS Certified Developer – Associate certification exam.

So imagine, dream, and build, because on the AWS Cloud, the only limit is your imagination.

Werner Vogels
Vice President and Corporate Technology Officer
Amazon

Introduction

Developers are builders. They are responsible for imagining, designing, and building applications. This study guide is designed to help you develop, build, and create solutions by using AWS services and to provide you with the knowledge required to obtain the AWS Certified Developer – Associate certification.

The study guide covers relevant topics on the exam, with additional context to increase your understanding of how to build applications on AWS. This study guide references the exam blueprint throughout all of its chapters and content to provide a comprehensive view of the required knowledge to pass the exam. Furthermore, this study guide was designed to help you understand the key concepts required to earn the certification and for you to use as a reference for building highly available applications that run on the AWS Cloud. However, the study guide does not cover any prerequisite knowledge concerning software development; that is, the study guide does not cover how to program in Java, Python, .NET, and other platform languages. Instead, you will use these languages to build, manage, and deploy your resources on AWS.

The study guide begins with an introduction to the AWS Cloud and how you can interact with the AWS Cloud by using API calls. API calls are the heart of the AWS Cloud, as every interaction with AWS is an API call to the service. As such, the initial chapter provides you with the core knowledge on which the rest of the chapters are built. Because security is a top priority for all applications, the first chapter also describes how to create your API keys by using AWS Identity and Access Management (IAM). The rest of the chapters cover topics ranging from compute services, storage services, databases, encryption, and serverless-based applications.

The chapters were designed with the understanding that developers build. To enhance learning through hands-on experience, at the end of each chapter is an "Exercises" section with activities that help reinforce the main topic of the chapter. Each chapter also contains a "Review Questions" section to assess your understanding of the main concepts required to work with AWS. However, understand that the actual exam will test you on your ability to combine multiple concepts. The review questions at the end of each chapter focus only on the topics discussed in that chapter.

To help you determine the level of your AWS Cloud knowledge and aptitude before reading the guide, an assessment test with 50 questions is provided at the end of this introduction. Two practice exams with 75–100 questions each are also included to help you gauge your readiness to take the exam.

What Does This Book Cover?

This book covers topics that you need to know to prepare for the Amazon Web Services (AWS) Certified Developer – Associate Exam.

Chapter 1: Introduction to AWS Cloud API   This chapter provides an overview of how to use AWS Cloud API calls. The chapter includes an introduction to AWS software development kits (AWS SDKs) and the AWS global infrastructure. A review of AWS API keys and how to manage them using AWS Identity and Access Management (IAM) is also included.

Chapter 2: Introduction to Compute and Networking   This chapter reviews compute and networking environments in AWS. It provides an overview of resources, such as Amazon Elastice Compute Cloud (Amazon EC2), and the network controls exposed through Amazon Virtual Private Cloud (Amazon VPC).

Chapter 3: Hello, Storage   In this chapter, you will learn about cloud storage with AWS. It provides a review of storage fundamentals and the AWS storage portfolio of services, such as Amazon Simple Storage Service (Amazon S3) and Amazon S3 Glacier. The chapter also covers how to choose the right type of storage for a workload.

Chapter 4: Hello, Databases   This chapter provides an overview of the AWS database services. The chapter provides a baseline understanding of SQL versus NoSQL. It also introduces concepts such as caching with Amazon ElastiCache and business intelligence with Amazon Redshift. The chapter also covers Amazon Relational Database Service (Amazon RDS) and Amazon DynamoDB.

Chapter 5: Encryption on AWS   In this chapter, you will explore AWS services that enable you to perform encryption of data at rest using both customer and AWS managed solutions. An overview of each approach and the use case for each is provided. Example architectures are included that show the differences between a customer and an AWS managed infrastructure.

Chapter 6: Deployment Strategies   In this chapter, you will learn about automated application deployment, management, and maintenance by using AWS Elastic Beanstalk. You will also learn about the various deployment methodologies and options to determine the best approach for individual workloads.

Chapter 7: Deployment as Code   This chapter describes the AWS code services used to automate infrastructure and application deployments across AWS and on-premises resources. You will learn about the differences among continuous integration, continuous delivery, and continuous deployment, in addition to how AWS enables you to achieve each.

Chapter 8: Infrastructure as Code   This chapter focuses on AWS CloudFormation and how you can use the service to create flexible, repeatable templates for a cloud infrastructure. You will learn about the different AWS CloudFormation template components, supported resources, and how to integrate non-AWS resources into your templates using custom resources.

Chapter 9: Configuration as Code   In this chapter, you will learn about AWS OpsWorks Stacks and Amazon Elastic Container Service (Amazon ECS). OpsWorks Stacks enables you to perform automated configuration management on resources in your AWS account and on-premises instances using Chef cookbooks. You will learn how to add a Chef cookbook to your stack, associate it with an instance, and perform configuration changes. Using Amazon ECS, you will learn how to create clusters and services and how to deploy tasks to your cluster in response to changes in customer demand.

Chapter 10: Authentication and Authorization   This chapter explains the differences between authentication and authorization and how these differences apply to infrastructure and applications running on AWS. You will also learn about integrating third-party identity services, in addition to the differences between the control pane and data pane.

Chapter 11: Refactor to Microservices   In this chapter, you will learn about microservices and how to refactor large application stacks into small, portable containers. You will also learn how to implement messaging infrastructure to enable communication between microservices running in your environment.

Chapter 12: Serverless Compute   This chapter reviews AWS Lambda as a compute service that you can use to run code without provisioning or managing servers. In this chapter, you will learn about creating, triggering, and securing Lambda functions. You will also learn other features of Lambda, such as versioning and aliases.

Chapter 13: Serverless Applications   This chapter expands on the serverless concepts you learned in Chapter 12, "Serverless Compute," and shows you how to architect a full-stack serverless web application. You will learn how to map server-based application architectures to serverless application architectures.

Chapter 14: Stateless Application Patterns   This chapter expands on the concepts you learned in Chapter 13, "Serverless Applications," by explaining how to design stateless applications. You will learn how to develop applications that do not depend on state information stored on individual resources, allowing for additional portability and availability.

Chapter 15: Monitoring and Troubleshooting   This chapter discusses AWS services that you can use to monitor the health of your applications, in addition to changes to AWS resources over time. You will learn how to use Amazon CloudWatch to perform log analysis and create custom metrics for ingestion by other tools and for creating visualizations in the dashboard. You will also learn how to use AWS CloudTrail to monitor API activity for your AWS account to ensure that changes are appropriately audited over time. You will also learn how to use AWS X-Ray to create visual maps of application components for step-by-step analysis.

Chapter 16: Optimization   This chapter covers some of the best practices and considerations for designing systems to achieve business outcomes at a minimal cost and to maintain optimal performance efficiency. This chapter covers scenarios for compute and storage, how to use a serverless platform, and what to consider for efficient data transfer to optimize your solutions. The chapter describes key AWS tools for managing and monitoring the cost and performance of your infrastructure. It includes code snippets, samples, and exercises to develop monitoring solutions and designs that integrate other AWS services.

Interactive Online Learning Environment and Test Bank

The authors have worked hard to provide you with some great tools to help you with your certification process. The interactive online learning environment that accompanies the *AWS Certified Developer – Associate Official Study Guide* provides a test bank with study tools to help you prepare for the certification exam. This helps you increase your chances of passing it the first time! The test bank includes the following:

Sample Tests   All of the questions in this book, including the 50-question assessment test at the end of this introduction and the review questions that are provided at the end of each chapter are available online. In addition, there are two practice exams available online with 75–100 questions each. Use these questions to test your knowledge of the study guide material. The online test bank runs on multiple devices.

Flashcards   The online test banks include more than 200 flashcards specifically written to quiz your knowledge of AWS operations. After completing all the exercises, review questions, practice exams, and flashcards, you should be more than ready to take the exam. The flashcard questions are provided in a digital flashcard format (a question followed by a single correct answer). You can use the flashcards to reinforce your learning and provide last-minute test prep before the exam.

Glossary   A glossary of key terms from this book is available as a fully searchable PDF.

Go to www.wiley.com/go/sybextestprep to register and gain access to this interactive online learning environment and test bank with study tools.

Exam Objectives

The AWS Certified Developer – Associate Exam is intended for individuals who perform in a developer role. Exam concepts that you should understand for this exam include the following:

- Core AWS services, uses, and basic AWS architecture best practices
- Developing, deploying, and debugging cloud-based applications using AWS

   In general, certification candidates should understand the following:

- AWS APIs, AWS CLI, and AWS SDKs to write applications
- Key features of AWS services
- AWS shared responsibility model

- Application lifecycle management
- CI/CD pipeline to deploy applications on AWS
- Using or interacting with AWS services
- Using cloud-native applications to write code
- Writing code using AWS security best practices (for example, not using secret and access keys in the code, and instead using AWS Identity and Access Management (IAM) roles)
- Authoring, maintaining, and debugging code modules on AWS
- Writing code for serverless applications
- Using containers in the development process

The exam covers five different domains, with each domain broken down into objectives and subobjectives.

Objective Map

The following table lists each domain and its weighting in the exam, along with the chapters in this book where that domain's objectives and subobjectives are covered.

Domain	Percentage of Exam	Chapter
Domain 1: Deployment	**22%**	**6, 7, 8, 9, 12, 13, 14**
1.1 Deploy written code in AWS using existing CI/CD pipelines, processes, and patterns.		6, 7, 8, 9
1.2 Deploy applications using Elastic Beanstalk.		6, 8, 9
1.3 Prepare the application deployment package to be deployed to AWS.		7, 9, 12
1.4 Deploy serverless applications.		7, 12, 13, 14
Domain 2: Security	**26%**	**1, 3, 4, 5, 6, 10, 12, 14**
2.1 Make authenticated calls to AWS services.		1, 4, 10, 12, 13, 14
2.2 Implement encryption using AWS services.		3, 4, 5, 14
2.3 Implement application authentication and authorization.		3, 10, 13, 14

Domain 3: Development with AWS Services	**30%**	**1, 2, 3, 4, 5, 7, 9, 12, 13, 14, 16**
3.1 Write code for serverless applications.		9, 12, 13
3.2 Translate functional requirements into application design.		2, 3, 4, 13, 14
3.3 Implement application design into application code.		3, 4, 13, 14
3.4 Write code that interacts with AWS services by using APIs, SDKs, and AWS CLI.		1, 2, 3, 5, 7, 9, 12, 13, 14, 16
Domain 4: Refactoring	**10%**	**2, 3, 4, 11,16**
4.1 Optimize application to best use AWS services and features.		3, 4, 11, 16
4.2 Migrate existing application code to run on AWS.		2, 3, 11
Domain 5: Monitoring and Troubleshooting	**12%**	**2, 4, 6, 8, 11, 12, 13, 15, 16**
5.1 Write code that can be monitored.		8, 12, 13, 15, 16
5.2 Perform root cause analysis on faults found in testing or production.		2, 4, 12, 15

Assessment Test

1. You have an application running on Amazon Elastic Compute Cloud (Amazon EC2) that needs read-only access to several AWS services. What is the best way to grant that application permissions only to a specific set of resources within your account?

   A. Use API credentials derived based on the AWS account.

   B. Launch the EC2 instance into an AWS Identity and Access Management (IAM) role and attach the ReadOnlyAccess IAM-managed policy.

   C. Declare the necessary permissions as statements in the AWS SDK configuration file on the EC2 instance.

   D. Launch the EC2 instance into an IAM role with custom IAM policies for the permissions.

2. You have deployed a new application in the US West (Oregon) Region. However, you have accidentally deployed an Amazon Polly lexicon needed for your application in EU (London). How can you use your lexicon to synthesize speech while minimizing the changes to your application code and reducing cost?

   A. Point your SDK client to the EU (London) for all requests to Amazon Polly, but to US West (Oregon) for all other API calls.

   B. No action needed; the data is automatically available from all Regions.

   C. Upload a copy of the lexicon to US West (Oregon).

   D. Move the rest of the application resources to EU (London).

3. When you're placing subnets for a specific Amazon Virtual Private Cloud (Amazon VPC), you can place the subnets in which of the following?

   A. In any Availability Zone within the Region for the Amazon VPC

   B. In any Availability Zone in any Region

   C. In any AWS edge location

   D. In any specific AWS data center

4. You have identified two Amazon Elastic Compute Cloud (Amazon EC2) instances in your account that appear to have the same private IP address. What could be the cause?

   A. These instances are in different Amazon Virtual Private Cloud (Amazon VPCs).

   B. The instances are in different subnets.

   C. The instances have different network ACLs.

   D. The instances have different security groups.

5. You have a workload that requires 15,000 consistent IOPS for data that must be durable. What combination of the following do you need? (Select TWO.)

   A. Use an Amazon Elastic Block Store (Amazon EBS) optimized instance.

   B. Use an instance store.

   C. Use a Provisioned IOPS SSD volume.

   D. Use a previous-generation EBS volume.

6. Your company stores critical documents in Amazon Simple Storage Service (Amazon S3), but it wants to minimize cost. Most documents are used actively for only about one month and then used much less frequently after that. However, all data needs to be available within minutes when requested. How can you meet these requirements?

    A. Migrate the data to Amazon S3 Reduced Redundancy Storage (RRS) after 30 days.

    B. Migrate the data to Amazon S3 Glacier after 30 days.

    C. Migrate the data to Amazon S3 Standard – Infrequent Access (IA) after 30 days.

    D. Turn on versioning and then migrate the older version to Amazon S3 Glacier.

7. You are migrating your company's applications and data from on-premises to the AWS Cloud. You have performed a data inventory and discovered that you will need to transfer about 2 PB of data to AWS. Which migration option will be the best choice for your company with minimal cost and shortest time?

    A. AWS Snowball

    B. AWS Snowmobile

    C. Upload files directly to AWS over the internet using Amazon Simple Storage Service (Amazon S3) Transfer Acceleration.

    D. Amazon Kinesis Data Firehose

8. You are changing your application to take advantage of the elasticity and cost benefits provided by AWS Auto Scaling. To do this, you must move session state information from the individual Amazon Elastic Compute Cloud (Amazon EC2) instances. Which of the following AWS Cloud services is best suited as an alternative for storing session state information?

    A. Amazon DynamoDB

    B. Amazon Redshift

    C. AWS Storage Gateway

    D. Amazon Kinesis

9. Your company's senior management wants to query several data stores to obtain a "big picture" view of the business. The amount of data contained within the data stores is at least 2 TB in size. Which of the following is the best AWS service to deliver results to senior management?

    A. Amazon Elastic Block Store (Amazon EBS)

    B. Amazon Simple Storage Service (Amazon S3)

    C. Amazon Relational Database Service (Amazon RDS)

    D. Amazon Redshift

10. Your ecommerce application provides daily and ad hoc reporting to various business units on customer purchases. These operations result in a high level of read traffic to your MySQL Amazon Relational Database Service (Amazon RDS) instance. What can you do to scale up read traffic without impacting your database's performance?

    A. Increase the allocated storage for the Amazon RDS instance.

    B. Modify the Amazon RDS instance to be a Multi-AZ deployment.

   C. Create a read replica for an Amazon RDS instance.

   D. Change the Amazon RDS instance DB engine version.

11. Your company has refactored their application to use NoSQL instead of SQL. They would like to use a managed service for running the new NoSQL database. Which AWS service should you recommend?

   A. Amazon Relational Database Service (Amazon RDS)

   B. Amazon Elastic Compute Cloud (Amazon EC2)

   C. Amazon DynamoDB

   D. Amazon Redshift

12. A company is currently using Amazon Relational Database Service (Amazon RDS); however, they are retiring a database that is currently running. They have automatic backups enabled on the database. They want to make sure that they retain the last backup before deleting the Amazon RDS database. As the lead developer on the project, what should you do?

   A. Delete the database. Amazon RDS automatic backups are already enabled.

   B. Create a manual snapshot before deleting the database.

   C. Use the AWS Database Migration Service (AWS DMS) to back up the database.

   D. SSH into the Amazon RDS database and perform a SQL dump.

13. When using Amazon Redshift, which node do you use to run your SQL queries?

   A. Compute node

   B. Cluster node

   C. Master node

   D. Leader node

14. Your company is building a recommendation feature for their application. They would like to use an AWS managed graph database. Which service should you recommend?

   A. Amazon Relational Database Service (Amazon RDS)

   B. Amazon Neptune

   C. Amazon ElastiCache

   D. Amazon Redshift

15. You have an Amazon DynamoDB table that has a partition key and a sort key. However, a business analyst on your team wants to be able to query the DynamoDB table with a different partition key. What should you do?

   A. Create a local secondary index.

   B. Create a global secondary index.

   C. Create a new DynamoDB table.

   D. Advise the business analyst that this is not possible.

16. An application is using Amazon DynamoDB. Recently, a developer on your team has noticed that occasionally the application does not return the most up-to-date data after a read from the database. How can you solve this issue?

    A. Increase the number of read capacity units (RCUs) for the table.

    B. Increase the number of write capacity units (WCUs) for the table.

    C. Refactor the application to use a SQL database.

    D. Configure the application to perform a strongly consistent read.

17. A developer on your team would like to test a new idea and requires a NoSQL database. Your current applications are using Amazon DynamoDB. What should you recommend?

    A. Create a new table inside DynamoDB.

    B. Use DynamoDB Local.

    C. Use another NoSQL database on-premises.

    D. Create an Amazon Elastic Compute Cloud (Amazon EC2) instance, and install a NoSQL database.

18. The AWS Encryption SDK provides an encryption library that integrates with AWS Key Management Service (AWS KMS) as a master key provider. Which of the following operations does the AWS Encryption SDK perform to build on the AWS SDKs?

    A. Generates, encrypts, and decrypts data keys

    B. Uses the data keys to encrypt and decrypt your raw data

    C. Stores the encrypted data keys with the corresponding encrypted data in a single object

    D. All of the above

19. Of all the cryptographic algorithms that the AWS Encryption SDK supports, which one is the default algorithm?

    A. AES-256

    B. AES-192

    C. AES-128

    D. SSH-256

20. Amazon Elastic Block Store (Amazon EBS) volumes are encrypted by default.

    A. True

    B. False

21. Which of the following cannot be retained when deleting an AWS Elastic Beanstalk environment?

    A. Source code from the Git repository

    B. Data from the automatic backups of an Amazon Relational Database Service (Amazon RDS) instance

    C. Packaged code from the source bundle stored in an Amazon Simple Storage Service (Amazon S3) bucket

    D. Data from the snapshot of an Amazon RDS instance

22. Which of the following is not part of the AWS Elastic Beanstalk functionality?

  A. Notify the account user of language runtime platform changes

  B. Display events per environment

  C. Show instance statuses per environment

  D. Perform automatic changes to AWS Identity and Access Management (IAM) policies

23. What happens to AWS CodePipeline revisions that, upon reaching a manual approval gate, are rejected?

  A. The pipeline continues.

  B. A notification is sent to the account administrator.

  C. The revision is treated as failed.

  D. The pipeline creates a revision clone and continues.

24. Which of the following is an invalid strategy for migrating data to AWS CodeCommit?

  A. Incrementally committing files from a large repository

  B. Syncing the files from Amazon Simple Storage Service (Amazon S3) using the `sync` AWS CLI command

  C. Cloning an existing repository, updating the remote, and pushing

  D. Manually creating files in the AWS Management Console

25. You have an AWS CodeBuild task in your pipeline that requires large binary files that do not frequently change. What would be the best way to include these files in your build?

  A. Store the files in your source code repository. They will be passed in as part of the revision.

  B. Store the files in an Amazon Simple Storage Service (Amazon S3) bucket and copy them during the build.

  C. Create a custom build container that includes the files.

  D. It is not possible to include files above a certain size.

26. When you update an `AWS::S3::Bucket` resource, what is the expected behavior if the `Name` property is updated?

  A. The resource is updated with no interruption.

  B. The resource is updated with some interruption.

  C. The resource is replaced.

  D. The resource is deleted.

27. What is the preferred method for updating resources created by AWS CloudFormation?

  A. Updating the resource directly in the AWS Management Console

  B. Submitting an updated template to AWS CloudFormation to modify the stack

  C. Updating the resource using the AWS Command Line Interface (AWS CLI)

  D. Updating the resource using an AWS Software Development Kit (AWS SDK)

28. When does the AWS OpsWorks Stacks configure lifecycle event run?

    A. On individual instances immediately when they are first created

    B. On individual instances after a deploy lifecycle event

    C. On all instances in a stack when a single instance comes online or goes offline

    D. On all instances in a stack after a deploy lifecycle event

29. Which non-Amazon Elastic Compute Cloud (Amazon EC2) AWS resources can AWS OpsWorks Stacks manage? (Select THREE.)

    A. Elastic IP addresses

    B. Amazon Elastic Block Store (Amazon EBS) volumes

    C. Amazon Relational Database Service (Amazon RDS) database instances

    D. Amazon ElastiCache clusters

    E. Amazon Redshift data warehouses

30. Which AWS Cloud service can Simple Active Directory (Simple AD) use to authenticate users?

    A. Amazon WorkDocs

    B. Amazon Cognito

    C. Amazon Elastic Compute Cloud (Amazon EC2)

    D. Amazon Simple Storage Service (Amazon S3)

31. What is the best application of Amazon Cognito?

    A. Use instead of Active Directory for AWS Identity and Access Management (IAM) users.

    B. Provide authentication to third-party web applications.

    C. Use as an Amazon Aurora database.

    D. Use to access objects in an Amazon Simple Storage Service (Amazon S3) bucket.

32. You manage a sales tracking system in which point-of-sale devices send transactions of this form:

```
{"date":"2017-01-30", "amount":100.20, "product_id": "1012", "region":
"WA", "customer_id": "3382"}
```

You need to generate two real-time reports. The first reports on the total sales per day for each customer. The second reports on the total sales per day for each product. Which AWS offerings and services can you use to generate these real-time reports?

    A. Ingest the data through Amazon Kinesis Data Streams. Use Amazon Kinesis Data Analytics to query for sales per day for each product and sales per day for each customer using SQL queries. Feed the result into two new streams in Amazon Kinesis Data Firehose.

    B. Ingest the data through Kinesis Data Streams. Use Kinesis Data Firehose to query for sales per day for each product and sales per day for each customer with SQL queries. Feed the result into two new streams in Kinesis Data Firehose.

C. Ingest the data through Kinesis Data Analytics. Use Kinesis Data Streams to query for sales per day for each product and sales per day for each customer with SQL queries. Feed the result into two new streams in Kinesis Data Firehose.

D. Ingest the data in Amazon Simple Queue Service (Amazon SQS). Use Kinesis Data Firehose to query for sales per day for each product and sales per day for each customer with SQL queries. Feed the result into two new streams in Kinesis Data Firehose.

33. You design an application for selling toys online. Every time a customer orders a toy, you want to add an item into the orders table in Amazon DynamoDB and send an email to the customer acknowledging their order. The solution should be performant and cost-effective. How can you trigger this email?

A. Use an Amazon Simple Queue Service (Amazon SQS) queue.

B. Schedule an AWS Lambda function to check for changes to the orders table every minute.

C. Schedule an Lambda function to check for changes to the orders table every second.

D. Use Amazon DynamoDB Streams.

34. A company would like to use Amazon DynamoDB. They want to set up a NoSQL-style trigger. Is this something that can be accomplished? If so, how?

A. No. This cannot be done with DynamoDB and NoSQL.

B. Yes, but not with AWS Lambda.

C. No. DynamoDB is not a supported event source for Lambda.

D. Yes. You can use Amazon DynamoDB Streams and poll them with Lambda.

35. A company wants to access the infrastructure on which AWS Lambda runs. Is this possible?

A. No. Lambda is a managed service and runs the necessary infrastructure on your behalf.

B. Yes. They can access the infrastructure and make changes to the underlying OS.

C. Yes. They need to open a support ticket.

D. Yes, but they need to contact their Solutions Architect to provide access to the environment.

36. Using the smallest amount of memory possible for an AWS Lambda function, currently 128 MB, will result in the lowest bill.

A. True. Lambda bills based on the total memory allocated.

B. False. Lambda has a flat rate—memory allocation is not important for billing, only performance.

C. False. Lambda bills based on memory plus the number of times that you trigger the function.

D. False. Lambda bills based on memory, the amount of compute time spent on a function in 100-ms increments, and the number of times that you execute or trigger a function.

37. Which Amazon services can you use for caching? (Select TWO.)

  A. AWS CloudFormation

  B. Amazon Simple Storage Service (Amazon S3)

  C. Amazon CloudFront

  D. Amazon ElastiCache

38. Which Amazon API Gateway feature enables you to create a separate path that can be help-ful in creating a development endpoint and a production endpoint?

  A. Authorizers

  B. API keys

  C. Stages

  D. Cross-origin resource sharing (CORS)

39. Which of the following methods does Amazon API Gateway support?

  A. GET

  B. POST

  C. OPTIONS

  D. All of the above

40. Which authorization mechanisms does Amazon API Gateway support?

  A. AWS Identity and Access Management (IAM) policies

  B. AWS Lambda custom authorizers

  C. Amazon Cognito user pools

  D. All of the above

41. Which tool can you use to develop and test AWS Lambda functions locally?

  A. AWS Serverless Application Model (AWS SAM)

  B. AWS SAM CLI

  C. AWS CloudFormation

  D. None of the above

42. Which serverless AWS service can you use to store user session state?

  A. Amazon Elastic Compute Cloud (Amazon EC2)

  B. Amazon ElastiCache

  C. AWS Elastic Beanstalk

  D. Amazon DynamoDB

43. Which AWS service can you use to store user profile information?

  A. Amazon CloudFront

  B. Amazon Cognito

  C. Amazon Kinesis

  D. AWS Lambda

44. Which of the following objects are good candidates to store in a cache? (Select THREE.)

 A. Session state

 B. Shopping cart

 C. Product catalog

 D. Bank account balance

45. Which of the following cache engines does Amazon ElastiCache support? (Select TWO.)

 A. Redis

 B. MySQL

 C. Couchbase

 D. Memcached

46. How can you aggregate Amazon CloudWatch metrics across Regions?

 A. CloudWatch does not aggregate data across Regions.

 B. This is enabled by default.

 C. Send the metric data from other Regions to Amazon Simple Storage Service (Amazon S3) for retrieval by CloudWatch.

 D. Stream the metric data to Amazon Kinesis, and retrieve it using an AWS Lambda function.

47. Why would an Amazon CloudWatch alarm report as INSUFFICIENT_DATA instead of OK or ALARM? (Select THREE.)

 A. The alarm was just created.

 B. The metric is not available.

 C. There is an AWS Identity and Access Management (IAM) permission preventing the metric from receiving data.

 D. Not enough data is available for the metric to determine the alarm state.

 E. The alarm period is missing.

48. You were asked to develop an administrative web application that consumes low throughput and rarely receives high traffic. Which of the following instance type families will be the most optimized choice?

 A. Memory optimized

 B. Compute optimized

 C. General purpose

 D. Accelerated computing

49. Which of the following AWS Cost Management Tools can you use to view your costs and find ways to take advantage of elasticity?

 A. AWS Cost Explorer

 B. AWS Trusted Advisor

 C. Amazon CloudWatch

 D. Amazon EC2 Auto Scaling

50. Because cloud resources are easier to deploy and they incur usage-based costs, your organization is setting up good governance rules to manage costs. They are currently focusing on controlling and restricting Amazon Elastic Compute Cloud (Amazon EC2) instance deployments. Which of the following is an effective recommendation?

   A. Seek approval from Cost Engineering teams before deploying any EC2 instances.

   B. Use AWS Identity and Access Management (IAM) policies to enable engineers to deploy EC2 instances only when specific mandatory tags are used.

   C. Review Amazon CloudWatch metrics to optimize the resource utilization.

   D. Use AWS Cost Explorer usage and forecasting reports.

51. Because your applications are showing a consistent steady-state compute usage, you have decided to purchase Amazon Elastic Compute Cloud (Amazon EC2) Reserved Instances to gain significant pricing discounts. Which of the following is *not* the best purchase option?

   A. All Upfront

   B. Partial Upfront

   C. No Upfront

   D. Pay-as-you-go

52. Your application processes transaction-heavy and IOPS-intensive database workloads. You need to choose the right Amazon Elastic Block Store (Amazon EBS) volume so that application performance is not affected. Which of the following options would you suggest?

   A. HDD-backed storage (st1)

   B. SSD-backed storage (io1)

   C. Amazon Simple Storage Service (Amazon S3) Intelligent Tier class storage

   D. Cold HDD-backed storage (sc1)

53. A legacy financial institution is planning for a huge technical upgrade and planning to go global. The architecture depends heavily on using caching solutions. Which one of the following services does *not* fit into the caching solutions?

   A. Amazon ElastiCache for Redis

   B. Amazon ElastiCache for Memcached

   C. Amazon DynamoDB Accelerator

   D. Amazon Elastic Compute Cloud (Amazon EC2) memory-optimized

54. Which of the following characteristics separates Amazon DynamoDB from the Amazon Relational Database Service (Amazon RDS) design?

   A. Incurs the performance costs of an ACID-compliant transaction system

   B. Normalizes data and stores it on multiple tables

   C. Keeps related data together

   D. May require expensive joins

55. Which of the following partition key choices is an inefficient design that leads to poor distribution of the data in an Amazon DynamoDB table?

  A. User ID, where the application has many users

  B. Device ID, where each device accesses data at relatively similar intervals

  C. Status code, where there are only a few possible status codes

  D. Session ID, where the user session remains distinct

56. You are planning to build serverless backends by using AWS Lambda to handle web, mobile, Internet of Things (IoT), and third-party API requests. Which of the following are the main benefits in opting for a serverless architecture in this scenario? (Select THREE.)

  A. No need to manage servers

  B. No need to ensure application fault tolerance and fleet management

  C. No charge for idle capacity

  D. Flexible maintenance schedules

  E. Powered for high complex processing

57. Your enterprise infrastructure has recently migrated to the AWS Cloud. You are now trying to optimize the storage solutions. Which of the following are the appropriate storage management tools that you can use to review and analyze the storage classes and access patterns usage to help reduce costs? (Select TWO.)

  A. Amazon Simple Storage Service (Amazon S3) analytics

  B. Cost allocation Amazon S3 bucket tags

  C. Amazon S3 Transfer Acceleration

  D. Amazon Route 53

  E. AWS Budgets

Answers to Assessment Test

1. D. Use the custom IAM policy to configure the permissions to a specific set of resources in your account. The `ReadOnlyAccess` IAM policy restricts write access but grants access to all resources within your account. AWS account credentials are unrestricted. Policies do not go in an SDK configuration file. They are enforced by AWS on the backend.

2. C. This is the simplest approach because only a single resource is in the wrong Region. Option A is a possible approach, but it is not the simplest approach because it introduces cross-region calls that may increase latency and cross-region data transfer pricing.

3. A. Each Amazon VPC is placed in a specific Region and can span all the Availability Zones within that Region. Option B is incorrect because a subnet must be placed within the Region for the selected VPC. Option C is incorrect because edge locations are not available for subnets, and option D is incorrect because you cannot choose specific data centers.

4. A. Even though each instance in an Amazon VPC has a unique private IP address, you could assign the same private IP address ranges to multiple Amazon VPCs. Therefore, two instances in two different Amazon VPCs in your account could end up with the same private IP address. Options B, C, and D are incorrect because within the same Amazon VPC, there is no duplication of private IP addresses.

5. A, C. Amazon EBS optimized instances reserve network bandwidth on the instance for I/O, and Provisioned IOPS SSD volumes provide the highest consistent IOPS. Option B is incorrect because instance store is not durable. Option D is incorrect because a previous-generation EBS volume offers an average of 100 IOPS.

6. C. Migrating the data to Amazon S3 Standard-IA after 30 days using a lifecycle policy is correct. The lifecycle policy will automatically change the storage class for objects aged over 30 days. The Standard-IA storage class is for data that is accessed less frequently, but still requires rapid access when needed. It offers the same high durability, high throughput, and low latency of Standard, with a lower per gigabyte storage price and per gigabyte retrieval fee. Option A is incorrect because RRS provides a lower level of redundancy. The question did not state that the customer is willing to reduce the redundancy level of the data, and RRS does not replicate objects as many times as standard Amazon S3 storage. This storage option enables customers to store noncritical, reproducible data. Option B is incorrect because the fastest retrieval option for Amazon S3 Glacier is typically 3–5 hours. The customer requires retrieval in minutes. Option D is incorrect. Versioning will increase the number of files if new versions of files are being uploaded, which will increase cost. The question did not mention a need for multiple versions of files.

7. A. Option B is incorrect. You could use Snowmobile, but that would not be as cost effective because it is meant to be used for datasets of 10 PB or more. Option C is incorrect because uploading files directly over the internet to Amazon S3, even using Amazon S3 Transfer Accelerator, would take many months and would be using your on-premises bandwidth. Option D is incorrect because Amazon Kinesis Data Firehose would still be transferring over the internet and take months to complete while using your on-premises bandwidth.

8. A. DynamoDB is a NoSQL database store that is a good alternative because of its scalability, high availability, and durability characteristics. Many platforms provide open source, drop-in replacement libraries that enable you to store native sessions in DynamoDB. DynamoDB is a suitable candidate for a session storage solution in a share-nothing, distributed architecture.

9. D. Amazon Redshift is the best choice for data warehouse workloads that typically span multiple data repositories and are at least 2 TB in size.

10. C. Amazon RDS read replicas provide enhanced performance and durability for Amazon RDS instances. This replication feature makes it easy to scale out elastically beyond the capacity constraints of a single Amazon RDS instance for read-heavy database workloads. You can create one or more replicas of a given source Amazon RDS instance and serve high-volume application read traffic from multiple copies of your data, increasing aggregate read throughput.

11. C. DynamoDB is the best option. The question states a *managed service*, so this eliminates the Amazon EC2 service. Additionally, Amazon RDS and Amazon Redshift are SQL database products. The company is looking for a NoSQL product. DynamoDB is a managed NoSQL service.

12. B. Automatic backups do not retain the backup after the database is deleted. Therefore, option A is incorrect. Option C is incorrect. The AWS Database Migration Service is used to migrate databases from one source to another, which isn't what you are trying to accomplish here. Option D is incorrect because you cannot SSH into the Amazon RDS database, which is an AWS managed service.

13. D. The leader node acts as the SQL endpoint and receives queries from client applications, parses the queries, and develops query execution plans. Option A is incorrect because the compute nodes execute the query execution plan. However, the leader node is where you will submit the actual query. Options B and C are incorrect because there is no such thing as a cluster or master node in Amazon Redshift.

14. B. Amazon Neptune is a managed graph database service, which can be used to build recommendation applications. Option A is incorrect, because Amazon RDS is a managed database service and you are looking for a graph database. Option C is incorrect. Amazon ElastiCache is a caching managed database service. Option D is incorrect. Amazon Redshift is a data warehouse service.

15. B. A global secondary index enables you to use a different partition key or primary key in addition to a different sort key. Option A is incorrect because a local secondary index can only have a different sort key. Option C is incorrect. A new DynamoDB table would not solve the issue. Option D is incorrect because it is possible to accomplish this.

16. D. The application is configured to perform an eventually consistent read, which may not return the most up-to-date data. Option A is incorrect—increasing RCUs does not solve the underlying issue. Option B is incorrect because this is a read issue, not a write issue. Option C is incorrect. There is no need to refactor the entire application, because the issue is solvable.

17. B. DynamoDB Local is the downloadable version of DynamoDB that enables you to write and test applications without accessing the web service. Option A is incorrect. Although you can create a new table, there is a cost associated with this option, so it is not the best option. Option C is incorrect. Even though you can use another NoSQL database, your team is already using DynamoDB. This strategy would require them to learn a new database platform. Additionally, you would have to migrate the database to DynamoDB after development is done. Option D is incorrect for the same reasons as option C.

18. D. The AWS Encryption SDK is a client-side library designed to streamline data security operations so that customers can follow encryption best practices. It supports the management of data keys, encryption and decryption activities, and the storage of encrypted data. Thus, option D is correct.

19. A. Options B, C, and D refer to more outdated encryption algorithms. By default, the AWS Encryption SDK uses the industry-recommended AES-256 algorithm.

20. B. Encryption of Amazon EBS volumes is optional.

21. B. Elastic Beanstalk automatically deletes your Amazon RDS instance when your environment is deleted and does not automatically retain the data. You must create a snapshot of the Amazon RDS instance to retain the data.

22. D. Elastic Beanstalk cannot make automated changes to the policies attached to the service roles and instance roles.

23. C. Option C is correct because if a revision does not pass a manual approval transition (either by expiring or by being rejected), it is treated as a failed revision. Successive revisions can then progress past this approval gate (if they are approved). Pipeline actions for a specific revision will not continue past a rejected approval gate, so option A is incorrect. A notification can be sent to an Amazon Simple Notification Service (Amazon SNS) topic that you specify when a revision reaches a manual approval gate, but no additional notification is sent if a change is rejected; therefore, option B is incorrect. Option D is incorrect, as AWS CodePipeline does not have a concept of "cloning" revisions.

24. B. Though option D would be time-consuming, it is still possible to create files in the AWS CodeCommit console. Option A is a recommended strategy for migrating a repository containing a large number of files. Option C is also a valid strategy for smaller repositories. However, there is no way to sync files directly from an Amazon S3 bucket to an AWS Code-Commit repository. Thus, option B is correct.

25. C. Option A is not recommended, because storing binary files in a Git-based repository incurs significant storage costs. Option B can work. However, you would have to pay additional data transfer costs any time a build is started. Option C is the most appropriate choice, because you can update the build container any time you need to change the files. Option D is incorrect, as AWS CodeBuild does not limit the size of files that can be used.

26. C. Amazon Simple Storage Service (Amazon S3) bucket names are globally unique and cannot be changed after a bucket is created. Thus, options A and B are incorrect. Option D is incorrect because the resource is not being deleted, only updated. Option C is correct because you must create a replacement bucket when changing this property in AWS CloudFormation.

27. B. Option B is correct because you can manage resources declared in a stack entirely within AWS CloudFormation by performing stack updates. Manually updating the resource outside of AWS CloudFormation (using the AWS Management Console, AWS CLI, or AWS SDK) will result in inconsistencies between the state expected by AWS CloudFormation and the actual resource state. This can cause future stack operations to fail. Thus, options A, C, and D are incorrect.

28. C. Option A is incorrect because this is not the only time configure events run on instances in a stack. Options B and D are incorrect because the configure event does not run after a deploy event. AWS OpsWorks Stacks issues a configure lifecycle event on all instances in a stack any time a single instance goes offline or comes online. This is so that all instances in a stack can be made "aware" of the instance's status. Thus, option C is correct.

29. A, B, C. AWS OpsWorks Stacks includes the ability to manage AWS resources such as Elastic IP addresses, EBS volumes, and Amazon RDS instances. Thus, options A, B, and C are correct. Options D and E are incorrect because OpsWorks Stacks does not include any automatic integrations with Amazon ElastiCache or Amazon Redshift.

30. A. Option A is correct because Simple Active Directory (Simple AD) can be used to authenticate users of Amazon WorkDocs. Options B, C, and D are incorrect because Amazon Cognito is an identity provider (IdP), and you cannot use Simple AD to authenticate users of Amazon EC2 or Amazon S3.

31. B. Amazon Cognito acts as an identity provider (IdP) to mobile applications, eliminating the need to embed credentials into the web application itself. Option A is incorrect because if a customer is currently using Active Directory as their IdP, it is not good practice to create another IdP to operate and manage. Option C is incorrect because an Amazon Aurora database that is used to track data does not assign policies. Option D is incorrect because you can use Amazon Cognito to control an application's access to either an S3 bucket or an Amazon S3 object. You don't use it to directly control access to that bucket or object.

32. A. Option A is correct because you want to ingest into Amazon Kinesis Data Streams, pass that into Amazon Kinesis Data Analytics, and finally feed that data into Amazon Kinesis Data Firehose. Option B is incorrect because Kinesis Data Firehose cannot run SQL queries. Option C is incorrect because Kinesis Data Streams cannot run SQL queries. Option D is incorrect because Kinesis Data Analytics cannot run SQL queries against data in Amazon SQS.

33. D. Option D is correct because Amazon DynamoDB Streams allows Amazon DynamoDB to publish a message every time there is a change in a table. This solution is performant and cost-effective. Option A is incorrect because if you add an item to the orders table in DynamoDB, it does not automatically produce messages in Amazon Simple Queue Service (Amazon SQS). Options B and C are incorrect because if you check the orders table every minute or every second, it will degrade performance and increase costs.

34. D. AWS Lambda supports Amazon DynamoDB event streams as an event source, which can be polled. You can configure Lambda to poll this stream, look for changes, and create a trigger. Option A is incorrect because this can be accomplished with DynamoDB event streams. Option B is incorrect because this can be accomplished with Lambda. Option C DynamoDB is a supported event source for Lambda.

35. A. AWS Lambda uses containers to operate and is a managed service—you cannot access the underlying infrastructure. This is a benefit because your organization does not need to worry about security patching and other system maintenance. Option B is incorrect—you cannot access the infrastructure. Recall that Lambda is serverless. Option C is incorrect. AWS Support cannot provide access to the direct environment. Option D is incorrect—the Solutions Architect cannot provide direct access to the environment.

36. D. AWS Lambda uses three factors when determining cost: the amount of memory allocated, the amount of compute time spent on a function (in 100-ms increments), and the number of times you execute or trigger a function. Options A, B, and C are all incorrect because Lambda is billed based on memory allocated, compute time spent on a function in 100-ms increments, and the number of times that you execute or trigger a function.

37. C, D. Option A is incorrect because AWS CloudFormation is a service that helps you model and set up your AWS resources. Option B is incorrect because you use Amazon S3 as a storage tool for the internet. Options C and D are correct because they are both caching tools.

38. C. Option A is incorrect, as authorizers enable you to control access to your APIs by using Amazon Cognito or an AWS Lambda function. Option B is incorrect because API keys are used to provide customers to your API, which is useful for selling your API. Option C is the correct answer. You can use stages to create a separate path with multiple endpoints, such as development and production. Option D is incorrect, as CORS is used to allow one service to call another service.

39. D. API Gateway supports all of the methods listed. GET, POST, PUT, PATCH, DELETE, HEAD, and OPTIONS are all supported methods.

40. D. With Amazon API Gateway, you can enable authorization for a particular method with IAM policies, AWS Lambda custom authorizers, and Amazon Cognito user pools. Options A, B, and C are all correct, but option D is the best option because it combines all of them.

41. B. Option A is incorrect. Though AWS SAM is needed for the YAML/JSON template defining the function, it does not allow for testing the AWS Lambda function locally. Option B is the correct answer. AWS SAM CLI allows you to test the Lambda function locally. Option C is incorrect. AWS CloudFormation is used to deploy resources to the AWS Cloud. Option D is incorrect because AWS SAM CLI is the tool to test Lambda functions locally.

42. D. Option A is incorrect. Amazon EC2 is a virtual machine service. Option B is incorrect because Amazon ElastiCache deploys clusters of machines, which you are then responsible for scaling. Option C is incorrect because Elastic Beanstalk deploys full stack applications by using Amazon EC2. Option D is correct because ElastiCache can store session state in a NoSQL database. This option is also serverless.

43. B. With Amazon Cognito, you can create user pools to store user profile information and store attributes such as user name, phone number, address, and so on. Option A is incorrect. Amazon CloudFront is a content delivery network (CDN). Option C is incorrect. Amazon Kinesis is a service that you can implement to collect, process, and analyze streaming data in real time. Option D is incorrect. By using AWS Lambda, you can create custom programming functions for compute processing.

44. A, B, C. Option D is incorrect because when compared to the other options, a bank balance is not likely to be stored in a cache; it is probably not data that is retrieved as frequently as the others. Options A, B, and C are all better data candidates to cache because multiple users are more likely to access them repeatedly. However, you could also cache the bank account balance for shorter periods if the database query is not performing well.

45. A, D. Options A and D are correct because Amazon ElastiCache supports both the Redis and Memcached open source caching engines. Option B is incorrect because MySQL is not a caching engine—it is a relational database engine. Option C is incorrect because Couchbase is a NoSQL database and not one of the caching engines that ElastiCache supports.

46. A. Amazon CloudWatch does not aggregate data across Regions; therefore, option A is correct.

47. A, B, D. Amazon CloudWatch alarms changes to a state other than INSUFFICIENT_DATA only when the alarm resource has had sufficient time to initialize and there is sufficient data available for the specified metric and period. Option C is incorrect because permissions for sending metrics to CloudWatch are the responsibility of the resource sending the data. Option D is incorrect because the alarm does not create successfully unless it has a valid period.

48. C. General-purpose instances provide a balance of compute, memory, and networking resources. T2 instances are a low-cost option that provides a small amount of CPU resources that can be increased in short bursts when additional cycles are available. They are well suited for lower-throughput applications, such as administrative applications or low-traffic websites. For more details on the instance types, see https://aws.amazon.com/ec2/instance-types/.

49. A. AWS Cost Explorer reflects the cost and usage of Amazon Elastic Compute Cloud (Amazon EC2) instances over the most recent 13 months and forecasts potential spending for the next 3 months. By using Cost Explorer, you can examine patterns on how much you spend on AWS resources over time, identify areas that need further inquiry, and view trends that help you understand your costs. In addition, you can specify time ranges for the data and view time data by day or by month. Option D is incorrect because Amazon EC2 Auto Scaling helps you to maintain application availability and enables you to add or remove EC2 instances automatically according to conditions that you define. It does not give you insights into costs incurred.

50. B. You can use tags to control permissions. Using IAM policies, you can enforce the tag to gain precise control over access to resources, ownership, and accurate cost allocation. Option A is incorrect because eventually deployments become unmanageable, given the scale and rate at which resources get deployed in a successful organization. Options C and D are incorrect because Amazon CloudWatch and AWS Cost Explorer are unrelated to access controls and measures, and these tools monitor resources after they are created.

51. D. You can choose among the three payment options when you purchase a Standard or Convertible Reserved Instance. With the All Upfront option, you pay for the entire Reserved Instance term with one upfront payment. This option provides you with the largest discount compared to On-Demand Instance pricing. With the Partial Upfront option, you make a low upfront payment and then are charged a discounted hourly rate for the instance for the duration of the Reserved Instance term. The No Upfront option requires no upfront payment and provides a discounted hourly rate for the duration of the term.

52. B. The performance of the transaction-heavy workloads depends primarily on IOPS; SSD-backed volumes are designed for transactional, IOPS-intensive database workloads, boot volumes, and workloads that require high IOPS. For more information, see `https://docs.aws.amazon.com/AWSEC2/latest/UserGuide/AmazonEBS.html`.

53. D. Options A, B, and C help in building a high-speed data storage layer that stores a subset of data. This data is typically transient in nature so that future requests for that data are served up faster than is possible by accessing the data's primary storage location. Option D only supplements the setup of your own caching mechanism, and that is not the preferred solution for this scenario. For more information, see `https://aws.amazon.com/caching/aws-caching/`.

54. C. Keeping data together is a basic characteristic of a NoSQL database such as Amazon DynamoDB. Keeping related data in proximity has a major impact on cost and performance. Instead of distributing related data items across multiple tables, keep related items in your NoSQL system as close together as possible. Options A, B, and D are typical characteristics of a relational database.

55. C. The status code option suggests an inefficient partition key, because few possible status codes lead to uneven distribution of data and cause request throttling. Options A, B, and D suggest the efficient partition keys because of their distinct nature, which leads to an even distribution of the data. For more information, see:

```
https://docs.aws.amazon.com/amazondynamodb/latest/developerguide/
bp-partition-key-design.html
```

56. A, B, C. Using a serverless approach means not having to manage servers and not incurring compute costs when there is no user traffic. This is achieved while still offering instant scale to meet high demand, such as a flash sale on an ecommerce site or a social media mention that drives a sudden wave of traffic. Option D is incorrect because AWS Lambda runs your code on a high-availability compute infrastructure and performs all the administration of the compute resources, including server and operating system maintenance, capacity provisioning and automatic scaling, code and security patch deployment, and code monitoring and logging. Option E is incorrect because you can configure Lambda functions to run up to 15 minutes per execution. As a best practice, set the timeout value based on your expected execution time to prevent your function from running longer than intended.

57. A, B. Use this feature to analyze storage access patterns to help you decide when to transition the right data to the right storage class. This feature observes data access patterns to help you determine when to transition less frequently accessed STANDARD storage to the STANDARD_IA storage class. Option B is correct. A cost allocation tag is a key-value pair that you associate with an Amazon S3 bucket. To manage storage data most effectively, you can use these tags to categorize your Amazon S3 objects and filter on these tags in your data lifecycle policies. Options C and D are incorrect. These options focus on establishing a solution with an efficient data transfer. Option E is incorrect. With AWS Budgets, you can set custom budgets that alert you when your costs or usage exceed (or are forecasted to exceed) your budgeted amount.

Chapter

1

Introduction to AWS Cloud API

**THE AWS CERTIFIED DEVELOPER –
ASSOCIATE EXAM TOPICS COVERED IN
THIS CHAPTER MAY INCLUDE, BUT ARE
NOT LIMITED TO, THE FOLLOWING:**

Domain 2: Security

✓ **2.1** Make authenticated calls to AWS services.

Domain 3: Development with AWS Services

✓ **3.4** Write code that interacts with AWS services by
using APIs, SDKs, and AWS CLI.

Introduction to AWS

The AWS Cloud provides infrastructure services, such as compute, storage, networking, and databases, and a broad set of platform capabilities such as mobile services, analytics, and machine learning (ML). These services are available on demand, through the internet, and with pay-as-you-go pricing.

Think of AWS as a programmable data center. Rather than making a phone call or sending email to provision servers or other resources, you can manage all of your resources programmatically, via *application programming interfaces* (APIs). For example, you can provision virtual servers on demand in minutes and pay only for the compute capacity you use. The same is true for de-provisioning those servers; make a single API call to stop paying for resources that you no longer need. AWS operates many data centers worldwide, so you are not limited to a single data center.

In this chapter, you are introduced to AWS and shown how to make your first API calls. The AWS infrastructure behind the API calls follows. Afterward, you will learn how to manage the API credentials and permissions that you need to make API calls.

Getting Started with an AWS Account

The AWS Certified Developer – Associate is designed for developers who have hands-on experience working with AWS services. To help you prepare, this book has recommended exercises at the end of each chapter.

To work with AWS, you'll need an account. While you must provide contact and payment information to sign up for an account, you can test many of these services through the *AWS Free Tier*. The AWS Free Tier limits allow you to become familiar with the APIs for the included services without incurring charges.

The AWS Free Tier automatically provides usage alerts to help you stay in control of usage and identify possible charges. You can define additional alerts with AWS Budgets. To best take advantage of the AWS Free Tier and reduce costs, take some time to review the AWS Free Tier limits, and make sure to shut down or delete resources when you are done using them.

To create an account, sign up at https://aws.amazon.com/free.

AWS Management Console

After you have created an account, you will be prompted to sign in to the *AWS Management Console*. As part of the sign-up process, you define an email address and password to sign in to the console as the root user for the account.

The console is a web interface where you can create, configure, and monitor AWS resources in your account. You can quickly identify the AWS services that are available to you and explore the functionality of those services. Links are also provided to learning materials to help you get started.

Sign in to the console, as shown in Figure 1.1, at `https://signin.aws.amazon.com/console`.

FIGURE 1.1   AWS Management Console

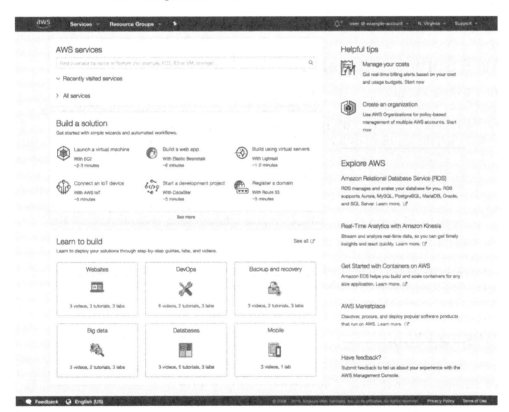

Because all the functionality of AWS is exposed through APIs, AWS provides more than only the web interface for managing resources. For example, the console is also available as a mobile app for iOS and for Android.

After you become familiar with a service, you can manage AWS resources programmatically through either the AWS Command Line Interface (AWS CLI) or the AWS software development kits (AWS SDKs), as shown in Figure 1.2.

FIGURE 1.2   Options for managing AWS resources

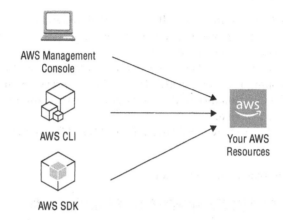

AWS Software Development Kits

AWS SDKs are available in many popular programming languages such as Java, .NET, JavaScript, PHP, Python, Ruby, Go, and C++. AWS also provides specialty SDKs such as the AWS Mobile SDK and AWS Internet of Things (IoT) Device SDK.

Although the instructions for installing and using an AWS SDK vary depending on the operating system and programming language, they share many similarities. In this chapter, the examples are provided in Python.

The Python SDK for AWS is called AWS SDK for Python (Boto). If Python 2 or Python 3 is already installed on your machine, install boto3 using pip, the Python package manager.

To install boto3, open a terminal and run the following command:

```
pip install boto3 --upgrade -user
```

For documentation on the Python SDK, see http://boto3.readthedocs.io/.

For more information on SDKs for other programming languages or platforms, see https://aws.amazon.com/tools/#sdk.

AWS CLI Tools

In addition to the AWS Management Console and SDKs, AWS provides tools to manage AWS resources from the command line. One such tool is the *AWS CLI*, which is available on Windows, Linux/Unix, and macOS.

The AWS CLI allows you to perform actions similar to those from the SDKs but in an interactive scripting environment. Because the AWS CLI is interactive, it is a good environment for experimenting with AWS features. Also, the AWS CLI and the SDK on the same server can share configuration settings.

If you prefer to manage your resources using PowerShell, use the AWS Tools for PowerShell instead of the AWS CLI. Other specialty command line tools are also provided, such as the Elastic Beanstalk command line interface and AWS SAM Local. For more information about these tools and installation, see https://aws.amazon.com/tools/#cli.

Calling an AWS Cloud Service

The functionality of AWS is powered by web services that are agnostic to the programming language and SDK. In this section, you use the AWS Python SDK to make an API request.

This is an overview of both making an API call and the parameters to configure the SDK. Subsequent sections will describe those parameters.

 Locate the API reference documentation about the underlying web services and programming language–specific documentation for each SDK at https://aws.amazon.com/documentation.

API Example: Hello World

In the following example, you will make a request to Amazon Polly. *Amazon Polly* provides text-to-speech service with natural-sounding speech, and it is able to provide speech in multiple languages with a variety of male and female voices. Furthermore, you can modify attributes, such as pronunciation, volume, pitch, or speed, by defining *lexicons* or supplying *Speech Synthesis Markup Language* (SSML).

This Python code example uses the AWS SDK for Python (Boto) and Amazon Polly to generate an audio clip that says, "Hello World."

```
import boto3

#Explicit Client Configuration
polly = boto3.client('polly',
        region_name='us-west-2',
        aws_access_key_id='AKIAIO5FODNN7EXAMPLE',
        aws_secret_access_key='ABCDEF+c2L7yXeGvUyrPgYsDnWRRC1AYEXAMPLE'
        )
result = polly.synthesize_speech(Text='Hello World!',
                                OutputFormat='mp3',
                                VoiceId='Aditi')

# Save the Audio from the response
audio = result['AudioStream'].read()
with open("helloworld.mp3","wb") as file:
    file.write(audio)
```

The AWS SDK maps the function call to an HTTPS request to an Amazon Polly API endpoint that is determined by the region name (region_name) parameter.

The SDK also adds authorization information to your request by signing the request using a key derived from the AWS secret access key.

When your request is received at the Amazon Polly API endpoint, AWS authenticates the signature and evaluates *AWS Identity and Access Management* (IAM) policies to authorize the API action.

If authorization succeeds, Amazon Polly processes the request, generates an MP3 audio file, and then returns it to the SDK client as part of the response to the HTTPS request, as shown in Figure 1.3.

FIGURE 1.3   API request and authorization

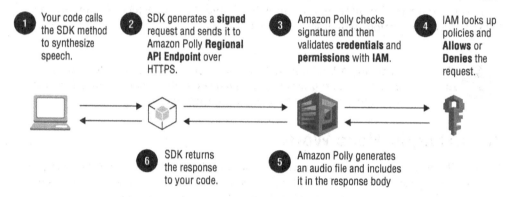

API Requests

Examine the request that is being transmitted in step 2 of Figure 1.3. When the SDK makes the request to Amazon Polly, it submits a JSON body using a standard HTTP POST to https://polly.us-west-2.amazonaws.com/v1/speech.

The SDK sets the following properties in the request:

```
POST /v1/speech HTTP/1.1
host: polly.us-west-2.amazonaws.com
content-Type: application/json
x-amz-date: 20180411T051402Z
authorization: AWS4-HMAC-SHA256 Credential=AKIAIO5FODNN7EXAMPLE/20180411/
us-west-2/polly/aws4_request, SignedHeaders=content-length;content-type;host;x-
amz-date, Signature=d968197e88a6a8de69d1a7bcab414669eecd5f841e13dc90e4a7852
c2c428038

{
        "OutputFormat": "mp3",
        "Text" : "Hello World!",
        "VoiceId": "Aditi"
}
```

Notice that the API endpoint or host URL includes the AWS Region parameter (us-west-2). The SDK also generates an authorization header by taking in the AWS access key credentials and applying the AWS Signature Version 4 signing process to the request.

API Responses

The API response corresponds to step 5 of Figure 1.3. For the example API request, the following headers are set in the response:

```
HTTP/1.1 200
status: 200
content-type: audio/mpeg
date: Wed, 11 Apr 2018 05:14:02 GMT
x-amzn-requestcharacters: 12
x-amzn-requestid: 924141bb-b0a6-11e8-b565-b1fabccdcbd9
transfer-encoding: chunked
connection: keep-alive
```

The headers include a standard HTTP response code. In this case, the status is 200. In general, AWS responds with standard HTTP response codes, such as the following:

- HTTP/200, if successful
- HTTP/403, if authorization is denied

You can also use an *x-amzn-requestid* header to troubleshoot when contacting AWS Support. The response body includes the audio stream; in this case, the audio stream is in MP3 format.

The AWS SDK wraps the web response and returns an object to the application. This step corresponds to step 6 of Figure 1.3. If the HTTP status code is not HTTP/200, the SDK generates an exception that your code can handle.

 The *AWS Signature Version 4* signing process incorporates the current date into the process to sign API requests, so make sure that the clock on the computer making API requests is accurate. AWS API requests must be received within 15 minutes of the timestamp in the request to be valid.

SDK Configuration

In the previous example, the AWS Region and AWS credentials are provided explicitly in the code. The SDK client initialization code from the earlier example is shown again here:

```
# Explicit Client Configuration
polly = boto3.client('polly',
      region_name='us-west-2',
      aws_access_key_id='AKIAIO5FODNN7EXAMPLE',
      aws_secret_access_key='ABCDEF+c2L7yXeGvUyrPgYsDnWRRC1AYEXAMPLE'
      )
```

This explicit approach of hardcoding credentials into the code is not recommended, because it carries the risk of checking the credentials into a source-control repository. This would expose the keys to everyone who has access to the repository and could even result in public disclosure. To prevent this, configure the SDK credentials separately from the application source code.

The SDK and AWS CLI automatically check several locations for credentials, and for the region if they are not explicitly provided in the code. These locations include environment variables, programming language–specific parameter stores, and local files.

To configure an AWS access key on your local machine in a local file, create a credentials file in the .aws folder in the home folder for the current user. Within this file, specify credentials for the default profile. You may optionally include additional named profiles beyond the default as needed.

```
[default]
aws_access_key id=AKIAIO5FODNN7EXAMPLE
aws_secret_access_key=ABCDEF+c2L7yXeGvUyrPgYsDnWRRC1AYEXAMPLE
```

From File: ~/.aws/credentials

Furthermore, hardcoding the AWS Region into the code makes it difficult to deploy your application in different AWS Regions. Instead, create a config file also within the .aws folder within your current user's home directory. Within this file, specify a region to use with the default profile.

```
[default]
region = us-west-2
```

From File: ~/.aws/config

As an alternative to creating the credentials and config files manually, you can use the AWS CLI to generate the credentials and config files for the default profile as follows:

```
aws configure
```

This command prompts for *credentials* and *region* settings. When the command completes, the config and credentials files are generated, as shown in Figure 1.4.

FIGURE 1.4   Configuring API credentials

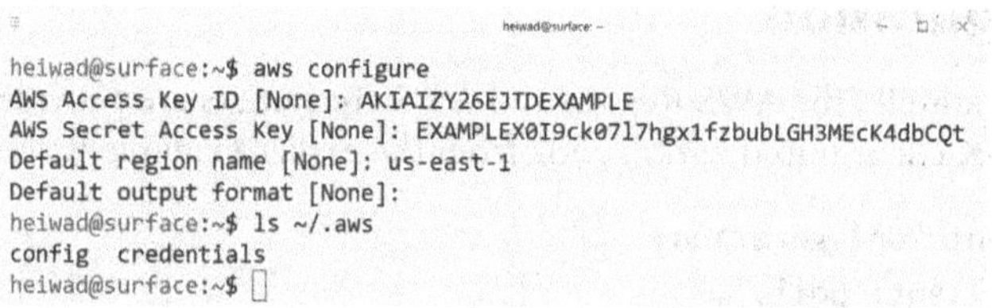

```
heiwad@surface:~$ aws configure
AWS Access Key ID [None]: AKIAIZY26EJTDEXAMPLE
AWS Secret Access Key [None]: EXAMPLEX0I9ck07l7hgx1fzbubLGH3MEcK4dbCQt
Default region name [None]: us-east-1
Default output format [None]:
heiwad@surface:~$ ls ~/.aws
config  credentials
heiwad@surface:~$ []
```

When the configuration is complete, replace this snippet of code:

```
# Explicit Client Configuration
polly = boto3.client('polly',
      region_name='us-west-2',
      aws_access_key_id='AKIAIO5FODNN7EXAMPLE',
      aws_secret_access_key='ABCDEF+c2L7yXeGvUyrPgYsDnWRRC1AYEXAMPLE'
      )
```

with this line of code:

```
# Implicit Client Configuration
polly = boto3.client('polly')
```

By separating your code from the credentials, you make it easier to collaborate with other developers while making sure that your credentials are not inadvertently disclosed to others.

For code running on an AWS compute environment, such as Amazon Elastic Compute Cloud (Amazon EC2) or AWS Lambda, instead of using local files, assign an IAM role to the environment. This enables the SDK to load the credentials automatically from the role and to refresh the credentials as they are automatically rotated.

Working with Regions

Now take a closer look at what it means to configure the AWS SDK with an *AWS Region*. AWS operates facilities in multiple regions across the world, as shown in Figure 1.5. Each AWS Region is located in a separate geographic area and maintains its own, isolated copies of AWS services. For many AWS services, you are required to select a specific region to process API requests and in which to provision your resources.

FIGURE 1.5 AWS Regions, Availability Zones, and planned regions (as of February 2019)

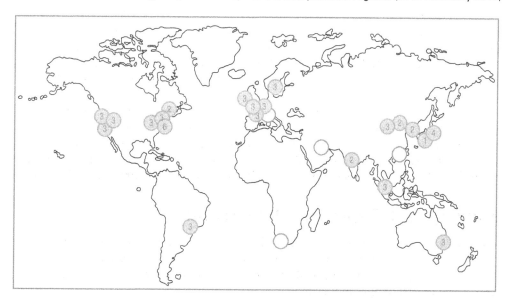

Customers expect that their data is durably held and that services remain highly available. In this section, you will explore how the structure of a region lends itself to providing reliable service and how to choose an appropriate region for your application.

Regions Are Highly Available

Each *AWS Region* contains multiple data centers, grouped together to form *Availability Zones*. Regions are composed of multiple Availability Zones, which allows AWS to provide highly available services in a way that differentiates them from traditional architectures with single or multiple data centers.

Availability Zones are physically separated from each other and are designed to operate independently from each other in the case of a fault or natural disaster, as shown in Figure 1.6. Even though they are physically separated, Availability Zones are connected via low-latency, high-throughput redundant networking.

FIGURE 1.6   Regions and Availability Zones

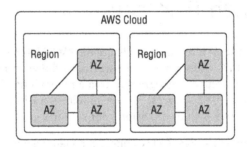

AWS customers can improve the resilience of their applications by deploying a copy of each application to a second Availability Zone within the same region. This allows the application to remain available to customers even in the face of events that could disrupt an entire data center. Similarly, many of the AWS services automatically replicate data across multiple Availability Zones within an AWS Region to provide high availability and durability of the data.

An example of an AWS service that replicates data across Availability Zones within a region is Amazon Simple Storage Service (Amazon S3). Amazon S3 enable you to upload files and store those files as objects within a bucket. By default, Amazon S3 automatically replicates objects across a minimum of three Availability Zones within the region hosting the bucket. This design protects data even against the loss of one entire Availability Zone.

Working with Regional API Endpoints

Many AWS services expose regional API endpoints. When making web service calls to regional endpoints, the region can typically be identified in the URL that you invoke. API calls to a regional endpoint usually affect only the resources within the specific AWS Region that corresponds to that endpoint.

To explore this concept, revisit the previous example of making a request to Amazon Polly to synthesize speech from text.

```
# Initializing SDK Client with Explicit Region Configuration
polly = boto3.client('polly', region_name='us-west-2')
result = polly.synthesize_speech(Text='Hello World!',
                                 OutputFormat='mp3',
                                 VoiceId='Aditi')
```

To explicitly configure the AWS SDK to use the US West (Oregon) Region, set the region_name parameter to us-west-2 when initializing the SDK client, as in the previous example.

This configuration results in the SDK computing the following URL for the API request, as shown in Figure 1.7.

FIGURE 1.7   A regional API endpoint and API action

You can see regional isolation in practice by uploading a lexicon to Amazon Polly. A *lexicon* stores custom pronunciation information that can be used when synthesizing speech from text. For example, you can require Amazon Polly to expand the acronym AWS to "Amazon Web Services" in the generated audio file by providing the following XML lexicon. The file tells Amazon Polly to speak the *alias* "Amazon Web Services" when it encounters the *grapheme* "AWS" in text.

```
<?xml version="1.0" encoding="UTF-8"?>
<lexicon version="1.0"
    xmlns="http://www.w3.org/2005/01/pronunciation-lexicon"
    xmlns:xsi="http://www.w3.org/2001/XMLSchema-instance"
    xsi:schemaLocation="http://www.w3.org/2005/01/pronunciation-lexicon
      http://www.w3.org/TR/2007/CR-pronunciation-lexicon-20071212/pls.xsd"
    alphabet="ipa"
    xml:lang="en-US">
  <lexeme>
    <grapheme>AWS</grapheme>
    <alias>Amazon Web Services</alias>
  </lexeme>
</lexicon>
File: aws-lexicon.xml
```

To use this lexicon when you synthesize speech, you must first upload it to Amazon Polly. The following shell snippet uses the AWS CLI to upload to the lexicon to the specified region:

```
aws polly put-lexicon --name awsLexicon --content file://aws-lexicon.xml
--region us-west-2
```

You can use the awsLexicon after it is uploaded. The following example generates a speech request that will be customized by the lexicon. This request is also being made to the us-west-2 API endpoint.

```
# Synthesizing speech with custom lexicon in the same region
aws polly synthesize-speech --text 'Hello AWS World!' --voice-id Joanna
--output-format mp3 hello.mp3 --lexicon-names="awsLexicon" --region us-west-2
{
    "ContentType": "audio/mpeg",
    "RequestCharacters": "15"
}
```

Assuming that the CLI is configured correctly with an appropriate access key, this request succeeds. In the downloaded audio file, you will hear Joanna say "Hello Amazon Web Services World," confirming that the lexicon is in effect.

However, if you run the same API request again, but change the region to the US East (N. Virginia) Region, as in the following example, you will get a different result:

```
# Trying again against a different Regional API endpoint
aws polly synthesize-speech --text 'Hello AWS World' --voice-id Joanna --output-
format mp3 hello-custom.mp3 --lexicon-names="awsLexicon" --region us-east-1
```

```
An error occurred (LexiconNotFoundException) when calling the SynthesizeSpeech
operation: Lexicon not found
```

In this case, an error occurs because the awsLexicon resides only in the US West (Oregon) Region where you placed it. When working with AWS services that are regional in scope, you are in control over where the data resides—AWS does not automatically copy your data for these services to other regions without an explicit action on your part. If you must use the lexicon in regions other than US West (Oregon), you could upload the lexicon to each region in which you plan to use it.

Identifying AWS Regions

When working with AWS services, the AWS Management Console refers to regions differently from the parameters used in the AWS CLI and SDK.

Table 1.1 lists several region names and the corresponding parameters for the AWS CLI and SDK.

TABLE 1.1   Sample of Region Names and Regions

Region Name	Region
US East (N. Virginia)	us-east-1
US West (Oregon)	us-west-2
EU (Frankfurt)	eu-central-1
EU (London)	eu-west-2
EU (Paris)	eu-west-3
Asia Pacific (Tokyo)	ap-northeast-1
Asia Pacific (Mumbai)	ap-south-1
Asia Pacific (Singapore)	ap-southeast-1

There are other AWS services, such as *IAM*, that are not limited to a single region. When you interact with these services in the console, the region selector in the upper-right corner of the console displays "Global." The API endpoint for IAM is the same regardless of the region. Table 1.2 lists some API endpoints.

TABLE 1.2   Selected IAM Service API Endpoints

Region Name	API Endpoint
US East (N. Virginia)	iam.amazonaws.com
US East (Ohio)	iam.amazonaws.com
US West (N. California)	iam.amazonaws.com

In the case of IAM, having IAM resources available in multiple regions is a useful strategy. IAM provides a way to create API credentials, and this means you can use the same set of API credentials to access resources in different AWS Regions.

For each AWS service, you can find the regions in which that service is available, along with the corresponding API endpoints, in the AWS General Reference documentation. The following link provides a comprehensive list of AWS services and their regional API endpoints: https://docs.aws.amazon.com/general/latest/gr/rande.html.

The exam may ask you to identify a URL or endpoint for an AWS resource, such as an Amazon S3 bucket, that has been deployed to a specific region. While the test does not require memorization of the region list, AWS recommends that you become familiar with the naming convention for regions and how it is related to the naming convention for Availability Zones.

Choosing a Region

One factor for choosing an AWS Region is the availability of the services required by your application. Other aspects to consider when choosing a region include latency, price, and data residency. Table 1.3 describes selection criteria to include when choosing an AWS Region.

TABLE 1.3   Selecting an AWS Region

Selection Criteria	Description
Service availability	Choose a region that has all or most of the services you intend to use. Each region exposes its own AWS Cloud service endpoints, and not all AWS services are available in all regions.
Proximity and latency	Choose a region closer to application users, on-premises servers, or your other workloads. This allows you to decrease the latency of API calls.
Data residency	Choose a region that allows you to stay compliant with regulatory or contractual requirements to store data within a specific geographic region.
Business continuity	Choose a pair of regions based on any specific requirements regarding data replication for disaster recovery. For example, you may select a second AWS Region as a target for replicating data based on its distance from the primary AWS Region.
Price	AWS service prices are set per region. Consider cost when service availability and latency are similar between candidate regions.

API Credentials and AWS Identity and Access Management

Now that you have seen how to make API calls and identified the infrastructure provided by the AWS Cloud, take a closer look at the access keys needed to make API calls. In AWS, an *access key* is a type of security credential that is associated with an identity. So, to make API calls, first you will create an identity in AWS Identity and Access Management (IAM).

To manage authentication and authorization for people or applications, IAM provides users, groups, and roles as identities that you can manage. IAM authenticates the security credentials used to sign an API call to verify that the request is coming from a known identity. Then, IAM authorizes the request by evaluating the policies associated with the identity and resources affected by the request. This section provides reviews users, groups, roles, and policies.

When you first create an account and sign in with your email address and password, you are authenticating as the root user for your account. Few AWS operations require root user permissions. To protect your account, do not generate an access key based on the root user. Instead, create an IAM user and generate an access key for that user. To provide administrator access, add that user to a group that provides administrator permissions.

Users

IAM users can be assigned long-term security credentials. You might create an IAM user when you have a new team member or application that needs to make AWS API calls. Manage the API permissions of the user by associating permissions policies with the user or adding the user to a group that has permissions policies associated with it.

After you create an IAM user, you can assign credentials to allow AWS Management Console access, programmatic access, or both, as shown in Figure 1.8.

FIGURE 1.8 IAM user long-term credentials

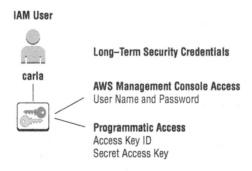

AWS Management Console Access

To sign in to the console, IAM users authenticate with an IAM user name and password. As part of the sign-in process, IAM users are prompted to provide either the account ID or alias so that IAM user names only need to be unique within your account. If *multi-factor authentication* (MFA) is enabled for an IAM user, they must provide their MFA code when they attempt to sign in.

To simplify sign-in, use the special sign-in link in the IAM dashboard that prefills the account field in the console sign-in form.

AWS IAM User API Access Keys

For *programmatic access to AWS*, create an access key for the IAM user. An *AWS access key* is composed of the following two distinct parts:

1. Access key ID

2. Secret access key

Here is an example of an AWS access key:

```
aws_access_key_id = AKIAJXR7IOGGTEIVNX7Q
aws_secret_access_key: oe/H0e2Ptj/fvwrdj6Wedo43Vsm05DHDADZ+tnP5
```

Each user may have up to two active access keys at any time. These access keys are *long-term* credentials and remain valid until you explicitly revoke them.

Given the importance of the secret access key, you can view or download it only once. If you forget the secret access key, create a new access key and then revoke the earlier key.

Other Credentials for IAM Users

In addition to passwords, multifactor devices, and access keys, IAM users can have other types of security credentials. You can have X.509 certificates, which are used with SOAP APIs, or you can have GIT credentials as either Secure Shell (SSH) keys or passwords to interact with the AWS CodeCommit service.

Groups

To help you manage the permissions of collections of IAM users, IAM provides *IAM groups*. IAM groups do not have their own credentials, but when an IAM user makes an API call with their access key, AWS looks up that user's group memberships and finds the relevant permissions policies. Associate users who need the same permissions with a group and then assign policies to the group instead of associating the permissions directly to each user.

For example, all developers working on a specific project could each have their own IAM user. Each of these users can be added to a group, named *developers*, to manage their permissions collectively. In this way, each team member has unique credentials while they are also given the same permissions.

You may create additional groups. For example, you may create a second group for the team members responsible for changing the build and deployment pipeline to which you can assign a name such as *devtools*.

The relationship between IAM users and IAM groups is *many-to-many*. An individual IAM user can be a member of many IAM groups, and each IAM group can have many

IAM users associated with the group. IAM users within an IAM group inherit permissions from the policies attached to their group, plus any permissions from policies that are associated directly with that IAM user.

In the example shown in Figure 1.9, *carla* inherits permissions from the IAM user *carla* and from the group *developers*, and *takumi* inherits the union of all of the policies from *developers* and from *devtools*, in addition to any policies directly associated with *takumi*.

FIGURE 1.9 IAM groups and IAM users

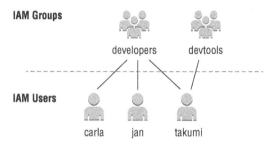

In the case that multiple permissions policies apply to the same API action, any policy that has the effect *deny* will take precedence over any policy that has the effect *allow*. This order of precedence is applied regardless of whether the policies are associated with the user, group, or resource.

Roles

There are situations in which you might not want to create and manage new sets of long-term credentials for team members or applications.

In a large company with many employees, you can use your existing corporate identity store instead of creating new identities and credentials for each team member who manages AWS.

Alternatively, you may delegate permissions to an AWS service to perform actions on your behalf. One common example of this is when application code running on an *AWS compute* service, such as Amazon EC2, needs permissions to make AWS API calls. In this case, AWS recommends allowing Amazon EC2 to manage the credentials for each instance.

In both situations, rather than creating new IAM users, create an *IAM role* to assign permissions. IAM roles can be assumed for short-term sessions, as shown in Figure 1.10.

FIGURE 1.10 IAM roles

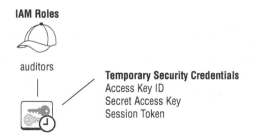

To control access to an IAM role, define a *trust policy* that specifies which *principals* can assume a role. Potential principals include AWS services and also users who have authenticated using identity federation. Principals could also include users who authenticate with web identity federation, IAM users, IAM groups, or IAM roles from *other* accounts.

This example trust policy allows Amazon EC2 to request short-term credentials associated with an IAM role:

```
{
  "Version": "2012-10-17",
  "Statement": [
    {
      "Effect": "Allow",
      "Principal": {
        "Service": "ec2.amazonaws.com"
      },
      "Action": "sts:AssumeRole"
    }
  ]
}
```

When a principal assumes a role, AWS provides new short-term security credentials that are valid for a time-limited session through the *AWS Security Token Service* (AWS STS). These credentials are composed of an access key ID, secret access key, and, additionally, a session token with a known expiration date.

This example displays the credentials that are generated when the role is assumed:

```
{
    "AccessKeyId": "ASIAJHP2KG65VIKQU2XQ",
    "SecretAccessKey": "zkvPEbYxCLVVD0seWdRnesc8krNDPHEX1cFMyI5W",
    "SessionToken":
"FQoDYXdzEMf//////////wEaDL1b0Wd7VTA3J25cNyL4ARzNSRczH4U3f8gJwi1W8XiDLWJIE9EdX
4l4KXTiST40gPoWc9Do9QkcN2xRHk6/qVT6W23d0u6+5YFY9C2wnoEeTTmiQBT5SMjqku5MYlhrCDy
FQAVbo6RKUeOZXXSG8REshuFGBtaCNmv95lFF6srCT1b4FZtTtULE7WV3LMcDs6Z2XuN+6aGTawhY5
0RMnlKRL1w6yHq++RysQWbBHkuNeK/VqjueDINFODPOje9ZnYePVjR5uLmL8ZARWYVBFrB2tpxG07/
dseUS9O2q1hMP8DJuEfsbaiK2ASsmXSRA8vOZnuu4AsBq6ERasBw5EcpICP/Ne8zdKO/93tYF",
    "Expiration": "2018-04-18T22:55:59Z"
}
```

When these short-term credentials are used, AWS looks up the permissions policies associated with the IAM role that was assumed. This is true even if the principal that assumed the role was an IAM user—policies that were associated with the IAM user or their groups are not evaluated when the role credentials are used to make a request. The IAM role is a distinct identity with its own permissions. Furthermore, you cannot nest IAM roles or add IAM roles to IAM groups, as shown in Figure 1.11.

FIGURE 1.11   IAM roles are distinct from IAM users and groups.

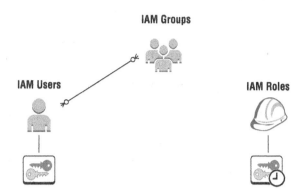

Choosing IAM Identities

Consider the following to determine how to define authorization and authentication.

Scenario: During Development

IAM users can be a convenient way to share access to an account with your team members or for application code that is running locally. The associated long-term credentials are easy to work with on a local development laptop, or on other hardware in your control, such as on-premises servers. To manage the permissions of collections of IAM users more simply, add those users to IAM groups.

Scenario: When Deploying Code to AWS

Use IAM roles. AWS compute services can be configured to distribute and rotate the role credentials automatically on your behalf, making it easier for you to manage credentials securely.

Scenario: When You Have an Existing External Identity Provider

When you have an external identity provider, such Active Directory, use IAM roles. That way, team members can use the single sign-on they already use to access AWS without needing to remember an extra password. Also, if a team member leaves, you disable their corporate access in only one place—the external directory.

Use roles in cases in which you need to make AWS API calls from untrusted machines because role credentials automatically expire. For example, use IAM roles for client-side code that must upload data to Amazon S3 or interact with Amazon DynamoDB.

Table 1.4 describes the use cases for IAM identities.

TABLE 1.4   IAM Users and IAM Roles Usage

For Code Running on...	Suggestion
A local development laptop or on-premises server	IAM user
An AWS compute environment such as Amazon EC2	IAM role
An IAM user mobile device	IAM role
Enterprise environments with an external identity provider	IAM role

The exam tests your knowledge of the recommended practices for distributing AWS credentials to your code depending on where that code is
running.

Managing Authorization with Policies

Manage the permissions for each user, group, or role by assigning *IAM policies* that either
allow or *deny* permissions to specific API actions, as shown in Figure 1.12. Any API action
is *implicitly denied* unless there is a policy that explicitly allows it. If there is a policy that
explicitly denies an action, that policy always takes precedence. In this way, AWS defaults
to secure operation and errs on the side of protecting the resources in cases where there are
conflicting policies.

FIGURE 1.12   IAM policies and IAM identities

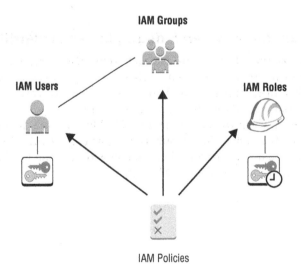

One method of granting permissions is to use AWS managed policies. AWS provides these policies to support common tasks and are automatically updated as new services and API operations are added.

When choosing permissions policies, AWS recommends that you adopt the principle of *least privilege* and grant someone the minimum permissions they need to complete a task. If they need more access later, they can ask for it, and you can update the permissions then.

Take the example of an application that uses Amazon Polly. If the application uses only Amazon Polly to synthesize speech, use the *AmazonPollyReadOnlyAccess* policy, which grants permissions to Amazon Polly actions that do not store any data or modify data stored in AWS. The policy is represented as a JSON document and shown here:

```
{
    "Version": "2012-10-17",
    "Statement": [
        {
            "Effect": "Allow",
            "Action": [
                "polly:DescribeVoices",
                "polly:GetLexicon",
                "polly:ListLexicons",
                "polly:SynthesizeSpeech"
            ],
            "Resource": [
                "*"
            ]
        }
    ]
}
```

If the application needs permission to upload (or delete) a custom lexicon, this operation modifies a state in Amazon Polly. To grant permissions to these actions, use the *AmazonPollyFullAccess* policy. The policy is shown here. Notice that the actions granted by the policy shown here are represented as "polly:*", where the * provides access to all Amazon Polly API actions.

```
{
    "Version": "2012-10-17",
    "Statement": [
        {
            "Effect": "Allow",
            "Action": [
                "polly:*"
            ],
            "Resource": [
```

```
            "*"
        ]
    }i
  ]
}
```

Custom Policies

AWS recommends that you use the AWS managed policies whenever possible. However, when you need more control, you can define custom policies.

As shown in the earlier examples, an *IAM policy* is a JSON-style document composed of one or more statements. Each statement has an effect that will either allow or deny access to specific API actions on AWS resources. *A deny statement takes precedence over any allow statements.* Use an *Amazon Resource Name* (ARN) to specify precisely the resource or resources to which a custom policy applies.

For example, the following policy authorizes access to the DeleteLexicon action in Amazon Polly on the resource specified by the ARN. In this case, the resource is a particular lexicon within a specific account and within a specific region.

```
{
  "Version": "2012-10-17",
  "Statement": [{
      "Sid": "AllowDeleteForSpecifiedLexicon",
      "Effect": "Allow",
      "Action": [
          "polly:DeleteLexicon"],
      "Resource": "arn:aws:polly:us-west-2:123456789012:lexicon/awsLexicon"
      }
  ]
}
```

To allow slightly broader permissions in a similar policy, use *wildcards* in the ARN. For example, to allow a user to delete any lexicon within the specified region and account, replace awsLexicon with an * in the ARN, as shown here:

```
{
  "Version": "2012-10-17",
  "Statement": [{
      "Sid": "AllowDeleteSpecifiedRegion",
      "Effect": "Allow",
      "Action": [
          "polly:DeleteLexicon"],
```

```
        "Resource": "arn:aws:polly:us-east-2:123456789012:lexicon/*"
    }
  ]
}
```

An ARN always starts with `arn:` and can include the following components to identify a particular AWS resource uniquely:

Partition   Usually aws. For some regions, such as in China, this can have a different value.

Service   Namespace of the AWS service.

Region   The region in which the resource is located. Some resources do not require a region to be specified.

Account ID   The account in which the resource resides. Some resources do not require an account ID to be specified.

Resource   The specific resource within the namespace of the AWS service. For services that have multiple types of resources, there may also be a resource type.

These are example formats for an ARN:

```
arn:partition:service:region:account-id:resource
arn:partition:service:region:account-id:resourcetype/resource
arn:partition:service:region:account-id:resourcetype:resource
```

Here are some examples of ARNs for various AWS resources:

```
<!-- Amazon Polly Lexicon -->
arn:aws:polly:us-west-2:123456789012:lexicon/awsLexicon

<!-- IAM user name -->
arn:aws:iam::123456789012:user/carla


<!-- Object in an Amazon S3 bucket -->
arn:aws:s3:::bucket-name/exampleobject.png
```

A single policy document can have multiple statements. Additional components to a statement may include an optional *statement ID* (Sid) and condition blocks to restrict when the policy applies. If the policy is attached to a resource rather than to an IAM identity, then the policy must also specify a principal (to whom the policy applies), as shown in Figure 1.13.

FIGURE 1.13   IAM policy elements

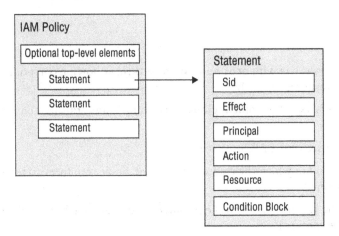

Write custom policies manually or use tools like the *Visual Policy Editor* in the AWS Management Console to generate policies more easily. To help you test the effects of policies, you can also use the IAM policy simulator at https://policysim.aws.amazon.com.

Summary

In this chapter, you learned about the AWS Management Console, the AWS CLI, and the AWS SDKs that AWS uses to configure and manage your resources. You learned how to make API request calls to the AWS Cloud, use configuration files, select an AWS Region, manage AWS API credentials, and identify regional API endpoints. The chapter also discussed AWS account root users, IAM, IAM policies, IAM groups, IAM roles, long-term and short-term credentials, the access key ID, and the secret access key.

Exam Essentials

Know the ways to manage AWS resources.   Recall that the AWS SDK, AWS CLI, and the AWS Management Console are options for managing the AWS resources within your account.

Know the importance of AWS Regions.   Be able to identify the impact of AWS Region selection on your application code, such as the relationship between region selection and user latency. Also recognize how region selection impacts API calls and API endpoints.

Know about IAM users and IAM roles.   Know when it is appropriate to use IAM users or IAM roles for a given application that needs to make AWS API calls.

Know how to recognize valid IAM policies.   Identify valid IAM policies and predict the effects of policy statements.

Resources to Review

AWS Free Tier:

    `https://aws.amazon.com/free`

Getting Started Resource Center: Create an AWS Account:

    `https://aws.amazon.com/getting-started`

Tracking Your Free Tier Usage:

    `https://docs.aws.amazon.com/awsaccountbilling/latest/aboutv2/`
    `tracking-free-tier-usage.html`

AWS Documentation:

    `https://aws.amazon.com/documentation`

AWS Management Console:

    `https://signin.aws.amazon.com/console`

AWS Command Line Interface (AWS CLI):

    `https://docs.aws.amazon.com/cli/latest/userguide/cli-chap-welcome.html`

SDKs, Toolkits, and Installation Directions:

    `https://aws.amazon.com/tools/#sdk`

Amazon Polly:

    `https://docs.aws.amazon.com/polly/latest/dg/what-is.html`

AWS Regions and Regional API Endpoints:

    `https://docs.aws.amazon.com/general/latest/gr/rande.html`

AWS IAM Documentation:

    `https://docs.aws.amazon.com/IAM/latest/UserGuide/getting-started.html`

AWS IAM Best Practices:

    `https://docs.aws.amazon.com/IAM/latest/UserGuide/best-practices.html`

AWS IAM FAQs:

    `https://aws.amazon.com/iam/faqs/`

AWS Signature Version 4 Signing Process:

    `https://docs.aws.amazon.com/general/latest/gr/signature-version-4.html`

AWS Whitepapers (Introduction to AWS):

   https://aws.amazon.com/whitepapers/

AWS Training and Certification:

   https://aws.amazon.com/training

AWS Events and Webinars:

   https://aws.amazon.com/about-aws/events

AWS Glossary:

   https://docs.aws.amazon.com/general/latest/gr/glos-chap.html

Exercises

EXERCISE 1.1

Sign Up for an Account

In this exercise, you'll sign up for an account.

1. Open your browser and go to https://aws.amazon.com/free/.

2. Choose **Create a Free Account**.

3. Provide personal information.

4. Provide payment Information.

5. Verify your phone number.

6. Select a support plan.

7. Choose **Sign in to the Console**.

8. Sign in to the console.

You are now signed in to the AWS Management Console.

EXERCISE 1.2

Create an IAM Administrators Group and User

In this exercise, you'll define an Administrators group and then add a user to that group. Generate API keys for this user and call this user DevAdmin.

1. Sign in to the AWS Management Console (at signin.aws.amazon.com/console).

2. Select **All Services**.

3. To open the IAM dashboard, select **IAM**.

4. To view the list of IAM groups, select **Groups**.

    If this is a new account, the list is empty.

5. Choose **Create New Group**.

6. For **Group Name**, enter **Administrators**.

7. Choose **Next Step**.

8. On the **Attach Policy** page, select the AdministratorAccess policy.

9. Choose **Next Step**.

10. On the **Review** page, choose **Create Group** to create the Administrators group.

11. To view the list of IAM users, select **Users**.

    If this is a new account, the list is empty.

12. Choose **Add user**.

13. Set the user name to **DevAdmin**.

14. Select both Access type check boxes: **Programmatic access** and **AWS Management Console access**.

15. Choose **Next: Permissions**.

16. To add this user to the Administrators group, select the **Administrators group** check box.

17. Clear the **Require password reset** check box.

18. Choose **Next: Tags**.

19. Provide a tag with a key of **project** and a value of **dev-study-guide**.

    Use tags to add customizable key-value pairs to resources so that you can more easily track and manage them.

20. Choose **Next: Review**.

21. Choose **Create user**.

22. Download the credentials.csv file.

23. Rename the file to **devadmin-credentials.csv**, and move the file to a folder where you would like to keep it.

24. Sign out of the AWS Management Console by clicking your name in the top bar and selecting **Sign Out**.

You now have a .csv file that contains a user name, password, access key ID, secret access key, and console login link. Use the DevAdmin user name, password, and console sign-in link to sign in to the AWS Management Console for all future exercises unless otherwise noted. Use the access key to configure the SDK in the following exercises.

Install and Configure the AWS CLI

In this exercise, you'll install and configure the AWS Command Line Interface (AWS CLI). The AWS CLI requires Python2 or Python3. Install Python using pip, the Python installer.

1. Install Python from https://www.python.org/downloads/.

2. Open a terminal window.

3. To install the AWS CLI, run the following command:

    `pip install aws-cli --upgrade --user`

4. (Optional) If you encounter issues with step 3, review the AWS CLI Installation guide for alternative installation options here:

    https://docs.aws.amazon.com/cli/latest/userguide/installing.html

5. To configure the AWS CLI with a default profile for credentials, run the following command:

    `aws configure`

6. Enter the following values when prompted:

    ▪ `AWS Access Key ID`: Paste the value from the CSV you downloaded in Exercise 1.2.

    ▪ `AWS Secret Access Key`: Paste the value from the CSV you downloaded in Exercise 1.2.

    ▪ `Default region name`: Enter us-east-1.

    ▪ `Default output format`: Press Enter to leave this blank.

7. Run the CLI command to verify that your CLI is working correctly, and view the available voices for Amazon Polly.

    `aws polly describe-voices --language en-US --output table`

A table in the terminal lists the available voices for Amazon Polly for the language US English.

Download the Code Samples

In this exercise, you'll download the code snippets to execute future exercises.

1. If you haven't downloaded the Chapter Resources from the online test bank, go to http://www.wiley.com/go/sybextestprep.

2. Register to get an access code.

3. Login and then redeem the access code. The book will be added to the online test bank.

4. Next to "Course Dashboard," click Resources.

5. Click "Chapter Resources" to download the code files.

You can also download the code files from the book page at https://www.wiley.com/ en-us/AWS+Certified+Developer+Official+Study+Guide%3A+Associate+%28DVA+C01% 29+Exam-p-9781119508199. Click Downloads to access the Online Materials for Chapters 1, 2, 11, and 12.

EXERCISE 1.5

Run a Python Script that Makes AWS API Calls

In this exercise, you'll run the Python script to make an AWS API call.

1. Open a terminal window and navigate to the folder with the book sample code.

2. To install the AWS SDK for Python (Boto), run the following command:

    `pip install boto3`

3. Navigate to the chapter-01 folder where you downloaded the sample code.

4. To generate an MP3 in the chapter-01 folder, run the helloworld.py program.

    `python helloworld.py`

5. To hear the audio, open the generated file, helloworld.mp3.

6. (Optional) Modify the Python code to use a different voice. See Exercise 1.3 for an AWS CLI command that provides the list of available voices.

You hear "Hello World" when you play the generated audio file. If you completed the optional challenge, you also hear the audio spoken in a different voice from the first audio.

EXERCISE 1.6

Working with Multiple Regions

In this exercise, you'll use Amazon Polly to understand the effects of working with different AWS Regions.

1. Open a terminal window and navigate to the folder with the book sample code.

2. Navigate to chapter-01 in the folder where you downloaded the sample code.

3. Verify that the region is us-east-1 by running the following command:

    `aws configure get region`

(continued)

EXERCISE 1.6 *(continued)*

4. Upload aws-lexicon.xml to the Amazon Polly service in the default region, which is US East (N. Virginia).

   ```
   aws polly put-lexicon --name awsLexicon --content file://aws-lexicon.xml
   ```

5. The file helloaws.py is currently overriding the region to be EU (London). Run the Python code and observe the LexiconNotFoundException that returns.

   ```
   python.helloaws.py
   ```

6. Upload the lexicon to EU (London) by setting the region to eu-west-2.

   ```
   aws polly put-lexicon --name awsLexicon --content
   file://aws-lexicon.xml --region eu-west-2
   ```

7. Run the following Python script again:

   ```
   python helloaws.py
   ```

   Observe that it executes successfully this time and generates an MP3 file in the current folder.

8. Play the generated helloaws.mp3 file to confirm that it says, "Hello Amazon Web Services."

9. (Optional) Delete the lexicons with the following commands:

   ```
   aws polly delete-lexicon --name awsLexicon
   aws polly delete-lexicon --name awsLexicon --region eu-west-2
   ```

Even though the text supplied by the API call to synthesize speech was "Hello AWS!," the generated audio file uses the lexicon you uploaded to pronounce it as "Hello Amazon Web Services."

EXERCISE 1.7

Working with Additional Profiles

In this exercise, you define a limited user for the account and configure a new profile in the SDK to use these credentials. Notice that the permissions are restrictive and that you need to update the permissions for that user to be more permissive.

1. Sign in to the AWS Management Console (at aws.amazon.com) using the credentials for DevAdmin from Exercise 1.2.

2. Select **Services**.

3. Select **IAM** to open the IAM dashboard.

4. Select **Users** to view the list of IAM users.

---

5. Choose **Add user**.

6. Set the user name to `DevRestricted`.

7. For **Access type**, select **Programmatic access**.

8. Choose **Next Permissions**.

9. Select **Attach existing policies directly**.

10. Select the **AmazonPollyReadOnlyAccess** policy.

11. To narrow the options, in **Filter**, enter `polly`.

12. Choose **Next: Tags**.

13. Define a tag as follows:

- Key: `project`
- Value: `dev-study-guide`

14. Choose **Next: Review**.

15. Choose **Create User**.

16. To configure the SDK in the following steps, download the `credentials.csv` file.

17. Rename the downloaded file to `devrestricted-credentials.csv` and move it to the same folder where you put the CSV file from Exercise 1.2.

18. Open a terminal window and navigate to the folder with the sample code.

19. Navigate to the `chapter-01` folder.

20. (Optional) Review the code in `upload-restricted.py`.

21. Configure the AWS CLI with a new profile called `restricted`. Run the following command:

`aws configure --profile restricted`

When prompted, enter the following values:

- `AWS Access Key ID`: Copy the value from the CSV you downloaded.
- `AWS Secret Access Key`: Copy the value from the CSV you downloaded.
- `Default region name`: Enter **us-east-1**.
- `Default output format`: Press Enter to retain the default setting.

22. Upload the lexicon.

The upload operation is expected to fail because of the restricted permissions associated with the profile specified in the script. Run the following Python script:

`python upload-restricted.py`

(*continued*)

23. Return to the AWS Management Console for IAM, and in the left navigation, select **Users**.

24. To view a user summary page, select **DevRestricted user**.

25. Choose **Add permissions**.

26. Select **Attach existing policies directly**.

27. To filter out other policies, in the search box, enter **polly**, and select the **AmazonPollyFullAccess** policy.

28. Choose **Next: Review**.

29. Choose **Add permissions**.

30. Repeat step 22 to upload the lexicon.

The upload is successful. After the change in permissions, you did not have to modify the credentials. After a short delay, the new policy automatically takes effect on new API calls from DevRestricted.

31. Delete the lexicon by running the following command:

```
aws polly delete-lexicon --name awsLexicon --region eu-west-2
```

In this exercise, you have configured the SDK and AWS CLI to refer to a secondary credentials profile and have tested the distinction between the AWS managed IAM policies related to Amazon Polly. You have also confirmed that it is possible to change the permissions of an IAM user without changing the access key used by that user.

Review Questions

1. Which of the following is typically used to sign API calls to AWS services?
   A. Customer master key (CMK)
   B. AWS access key
   C. IAM user name and password
   D. Account number

2. When you make API calls to AWS services, for most services those requests are directed at a specific endpoint that corresponds to which of the following?
   A. AWS facility
   B. AWS Availability Zone
   C. AWS Region
   D. AWS edge location

3. When you're configuring a local development machine to make AWS API calls, which of the following is the simplest secure method of obtaining an API credential?
   A. Create an IAM user, assign permissions by adding the user to an IAM group with IAM policies attached, and generate an access key for programmatic access.
   B. Sign in with your email and password, and visit My Security Credentials to generate an access key.
   C. Generate long-term credentials for a built-in IAM role.
   D. Use your existing user name and password by configuring local environment variables.

4. You have a large number of employees, and each employee already has an identity in an external directory. How might you manage AWS API credentials for each employee so that they can interact with AWS for short-term sessions?
   A. Create an IAM user and credentials for each member of your organization.
   B. Share a single password through a file stored in an encrypted Amazon S3 bucket.
   C. Define a set of IAM roles, and establish a trust relationship between your directory and AWS.
   D. Configure the AWS Key Management Service (AWS KMS) to store credentials for each user.

5. You have a team member who needs access to write records to an existing Amazon DynamoDB table within your account. How might you grant write permission to this specific table and only this table?
   A. Write a custom IAM policy that specifies the table as the resource, and attach that policy to the IAM user for the team member.
   B. Attach the `DynamoDBFullAccess` managed policy to the IAM role used by the team member.
   C. Delete the table and recreate it. Permissions are set when the DynamoDB table is created.
   D. Create a new user within DynamoDB, and assign table write permissions.

6. You created a `Movies` DynamoDB table in the AWS Management Console, but when you try to list your DynamoDB tables by using the Java SDK, you do not see this table. Why?

   A. DynamoDB tables created in the AWS Management Console are not accessible from the API.

   B. Your SDK may be listing your resources from a different AWS Region in which the table does not exist.

   C. The security group applied to the `Movies` table is keeping it hidden.

   D. Listing tables is supported only in C# and not in the Java SDK.

7. You make an API request to describe voices offered by Amazon Polly by using the AWS CLI, and you receive the following error message:

```
Could not connect to the endpoint URL:
https://polly.us-east-1a.amazonaws.com/v1/voices
```

What went wrong?

   A. Your API credentials have been rejected.

   B. You have incorrectly configured the AWS Region for your API call.

   C. Amazon Polly does not offer a feature to describe the list of available voices.

   D. Amazon Polly is not accessible from the AWS CLI because it is only in the AWS SDK.

8. To what resource does this IAM policy grant access, and for which actions?

```
{
"Version": "2012-10-17",
"Statement": {
  "Effect": "Allow",
  "Action": "s3:ListBucket",
  "Resource": "arn:aws:s3:::example_bucket"
}
}
```

   A. The policy grants full access to read the objects in the Amazon S3 bucket.

   B. The policy grants the holder the permission to list the contents of the Amazon S3 bucket called `example_bucket`.

   C. Nothing. The policy was valid only until October 17, 2012 (`2012-10-17`), and is now expired.

   D. The policy grants the user access to list the contents of all Amazon S3 buckets within the current account.

9. When an IAM user makes an API call, that user's long-term credentials are valid in which context?

   A. Only in the AWS Region in which their identity resides

   B. Only in the Availability Zone in which their identity resides

C. Only in the edge location in which their identity resides

D. Across multiple AWS Regions

10. When you use identity federation to assume a role, where are the credentials you use to make AWS API calls generated?

A. Access key ID and secret access key are generated locally on the client.

B. The AWS Security Token Service (AWS STS) generates the access key ID, secret access key, and session token.

C. The AWS Key Management Service (AWS KMS) generates a customer master key (CMK).

D. Your Security Assertion Markup Language (SAML) identity provider generates the access key ID, secret access key, and session token.

11. You have an on-premises application that needs to sample data from all your Amazon DynamoDB tables. You have defined an IAM user for your application called `TableAuditor`. How can you give the `TableAuditor` user read access to new DynamoDB tables as soon they are created in your account?

A. Define a custom IAM policy that lists each DynamoDB table. Revoke the access key, and issue a new access key for `TableAuditor` when tables are created.

B. Create an IAM user and attach one custom IAM policy per AWS Region that has DynamoDB tables.

C. Add the `TableAuditor` user to the IAM role `DynamoDBReadOnlyAccess`.

D. Attach the AWS managed IAM policy `AmazonDynamoDBReadOnlyAccess` to the `TableAuditor` user.

12. The principals who have access to assume an IAM role are defined in which document?

A. IAM access policy

B. IAM trust policy

C. MS grant token

D. AWS credentials file

13. A new developer has joined your small team. You would like to help your team member set up a development computer for access to the team account quickly and securely. How do you proceed?

A. Generate an access key based on your IAM user, and share it with your team member.

B. Create a new directory with AWS Directory Service, and assign permissions in the AWS Key Management Service (AWS KMS).

C. Create an IAM user, add it to an IAM group that has the appropriate permissions, and generate a long-term access key.

D. Create a new IAM role for this team member, assign permissions to the role, and generate a long-term access key.

14. You have been working with the Amazon Polly service in your application by using the Python SDK for Linux. You are building a second application in C#, and you would like to run that application on a separate Windows Server with .NET. How can you proceed?

    A. Migrate all your code for all applications to C#, and modify your account to a Windows account.

    B. Go to the Amazon Polly service, and change the supported languages to include .NET.

    C. Install the AWS SDK for .NET on your Windows Server, and leave your existing application unchanged.

    D. Implement a proxy service that accepts your API requests, and translate them to Python.

15. You are a Virginia-based company, and you have been asked to implement a custom application exclusively for customers in Australia. This application has no dependencies on any of your existing applications. What is a method you use to keep the customer latency to this new application low?

    A. Set up an AWS Direct Connect (DX) between your on-premises environment and US East (N Virginia), and host the application from your own data center in Virginia.

    B. Create all resources for this application in the Asia Pacific (Sydney) Region, and manage them from your current account.

    C. Deploy the application to the US East (N Virginia) Region, and select Amazon EC2 instances with enhanced networking.

    D. It does not matter which region you select, because all resources are automatically replicated globally.

Chapter

2

Introduction to Compute and Networking

THE AWS CERTIFIED DEVELOPER – ASSOCIATE EXAM TOPICS COVERED IN THIS CHAPTER MAY INCLUDE, BUT ARE NOT LIMITED TO, THE FOLLOWING:

Domain 3: Development with AWS Services

✓ 3.2 Translate functional requirements into application design.

✓ 3.4 Write code that interacts with AWS services by using APIs, SDKs, and AWS CLI.

Domain 4: Refactoring

✓ 4.2 Migrate existing application code to run on AWS.

Domain 5: Monitoring and Troubleshooting

✓ 5.2 Perform root cause analysis on faults found in testing or production.

Now that you have an AWS account and you can make application programming interface (API) calls from your local machine, it is time to explore how to run code on the AWS Cloud. AWS provides a broad set of compute options through the following services:

- Amazon Elastic Compute Cloud (Amazon EC2)
- Amazon Lightsail
- AWS Elastic Beanstalk
- Amazon Elastic Container Service (Amazon ECS)
- Amazon Elastic Container Service for Kubernetes (Amazon EKS)
- AWS Lambda

In this chapter, you will explore Amazon EC2, which provides you with environments called *instances*. You will learn about the components of an Amazon EC2 instance and explore an example of customizing an instance to run an application. Then, to learn how to customize the network environment for your instances, you will explore the network controls of Amazon Virtual Private Cloud (Amazon VPC). Finally, you will review some of the concerns related to managing your compute and networking environments.

Amazon EC2 and Amazon VPC are foundational services, and many of the concepts introduced in this chapter are transferrable to working with other AWS services.

Amazon Elastic Compute Cloud

Amazon Elastic Compute Cloud (Amazon EC2) enables you to provision computing environments called *instances*. With Amazon EC2, you have the flexibility to choose the hardware resources you need. You are in control of the operating system and any other software that will run on the instance.

An Amazon EC2 instance runs on a host machine within a specific AWS Availability Zone. Typically, Amazon EC2 instances provide virtualized access to the underlying host machine resources. Using a combination of hardware and software components, instances present a virtualized interface to machine resources to the operating system. This virtualization enables multiple, different isolated guest environments to share the same underlying host machine. In addition to virtualized environments, some EC2 instance types offer *bare-metal access*. Bare-metal instances provide your applications with direct access to the processor and memory resources of the underlying server.

Instance Types

With Amazon EC2, you choose your hardware resources from a broad set of preconfig-ured options by selecting a specific instance type and instance size. For example, your instance has a number of virtual CPUs (vCPUs) and a specific amount of RAM. The *instance type* is rated for a certain level of network throughput. Some instance types also include other hardware resources such as high-performance local disks, graphics cards, or even field-programmable gate arrays (FPGAs). The details of how the instance accesses the host resources, such as the specific hypervisor in use, also depend on the instance type that you select.

Even though AWS presets the hardware allocation for an instance type, a wide variety of instance types and sizes are available so that you can select the right level of resources for your application. For example, a t2.nano instance type allocates a fraction of a virtual CPU and 0.5 GiB of RAM to your instance. On the other end of the size spectrum, an x1e.32xlarge instance type provides 128 virtual CPUs and 3,904 GiB of RAM.

Instance types are also grouped into *instance families* to help you choose the appropriate instance for your application. Instances within a given family share similar characteristics, such as the ratio of vCPU to RAM or access to different types of storage options.

For an overview of the different instance families and their use cases, see Table 2.1.

TABLE 2.1   Amazon EC2 Instance Families

Amazon EC2 Instance Family	For Applications That Require...
General purpose	A balanced mix of CPU, RAM, and other resources
Compute optimized	A high amount of CPU, such as high-performance web servers, scientific modeling, and video encoding
Memory optimized	A large amount of RAM, such as in-memory databases and distributed web scale in-memory caches
Storage optimized	A large amount of storage and input/output (I/O) throughput, such as data warehousing, analytics, and big data distributed computing
Accelerated computing	Dedicated Graphics Processing Unit (GPU) or Field Program-mable Gate Array (FPGA) resources, such as 3D rendering, deep learning, genomics research, and real-time video processing

When you select an instance, choose a size that is appropriate for your current workload because Amazon EC2 instances are resizable. To change the hardware allocation, stop the instance, modify the instance type attribute, and then start the instance again.

Storage

Your instance requires storage volumes for both the root volume and any additional storage volumes that you want to configure. You can create persistent storage volumes with the *Amazon Elastic Block Store (Amazon EBS)* service to provide block storage devices for Amazon EC2 instances. Certain instance types enable you to mount volumes based on an *instance store*, which is temporary storage local to the host machine.

For an overview of the relationship between Amazon EBS volumes, instance store volumes, and the Amazon EC2 instance, see Figure 2.1.

FIGURE 2.1   Amazon EC2 storage

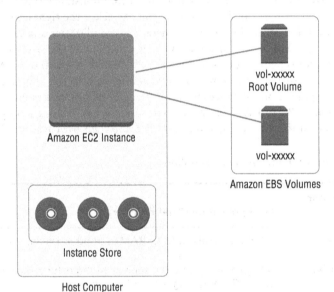

Persistent Storage

For Amazon EC2 instances, Amazon EBS provides persistent block storage. Similar to a hard drive, block storage volumes provide read/write access at a block level and can be formatted with a file system. Also similar to a hard drive, you can attach each EBS volume to a single instance at a time. Amazon EBS is suitable for installing operating systems and applications and for data that you want to store persistently. You can also encrypt the volumes.

When you create an EBS volume, you provision a specific size for the storage volume. You choose from several types of volumes with different underlying storage technologies and performance options. You can increase the size of the volume later, even while it is being used by a running instance.

While an EBS volume is attached to a particular instance, only that instance can access the data on that volume. However, you can detach an EBS volume from one instance and then attach that volume to another instance in the same Availability Zone.

EBS volumes are decoupled from the underlying physical host running the instance. The decoupling of the storage volume from the host machine enables you to persist data even if your instance is no longer running on the physical host. Although the EC2 instance treats the EBS volume as a local disk, the underlying host machine reads and writes to the EBS volume over the network. To maintain peak performance for this connection, you can use EBS-optimized instance types. EBS-optimized instances reserve dedicated network bandwidth specifically for traffic to the EBS volume.

EBS volumes automatically replicate the data for a particular volume within the same Availability Zone as your Amazon EC2 instance. To increase durability of your data, you can use Amazon EBS to make point-in-time snapshots of an EBS volume. Data for Amazon EBS snapshots is automatically replicated across multiple Availability Zones within a region, and these snapshots can be used to create new volumes. If there's an accidental delete or other application error, snapshots enable you to recover your data.

Temporary Storage

Certain Amazon EC2 instance types also allow you to mount *instance store* volumes—storage local to the physical host that runs your Amazon EC2 instance. An instance store volume is a good fit for high-performance storage of caches or temporary files and for use cases in which your application is already replicating the data to other locations.

This storage can have a high read/write performance because it is physically attached to the host machine that runs the instance. However, because this storage is local to the host machine, your data persists only while the instance is running on that host machine. The data persists if the instance reboots; however, AWS deletes the data on the instance store whenever you stop or terminate the instance.

Software Images

When the server first boots, it requires an operating system (OS) and the configuration of the attached storage volumes. An *Amazon Machine Image (AMI)* provides the template for the OS and applications on the root volume of your instance. AMIs also provide a block device mapping that can specify additional volumes to mount when an instance launches, as shown in Figure 2.2.

AWS provides a variety of AMIs. Paid AMIs are available through the AWS Marketplace.

You can create your own AMIs from an Amazon EC2 instance that you have previously customized or by importing your own virtual machine (VM) images. *Each AWS Region maintains its own listing of AMIs. Any AMIs that you create are available only within a specific region unless you copy them to other regions.* You can share AMIs between AWS accounts. To control which AWS accounts can use your AMIs, define the launch permissions for your AMI.

Depending on the source of the AMI and the type of software license required, the cost of the software licensing may be included in the hourly rate of the instance (such as Windows Server). For instances from the AWS Marketplace, charges are incurred for software licensing in addition to the Amazon EC2 infrastructure.

FIGURE 2.2   Amazon Machine Images

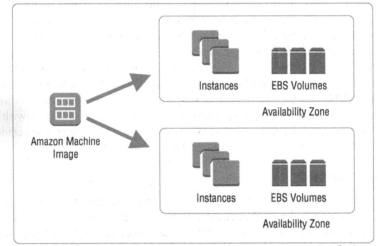

Network Interfaces

Virtual network interfaces called *elastic network interfaces* provide networking for your Amazon EC2 instances. Elastic network interfaces are associated with a software-defined network provided by Amazon VPC. Each Amazon EC2 instance is assigned a *primary network interface* that is associated with a subnet within an Amazon VPC. By default, if you omit the network configuration, Amazon EC2 assigns the instance to one of the subnets within the *default* VPC. The instance receives both a *private IP* address to communicate with instances inside the Amazon VPC and a *public IP* address to communicate with the internet. A *security group* protects the traffic entering and exiting the network interface. Security groups act as a stateful firewall. To make network connections to your instance, you must set security group rules to allow the connection.

You can attach additional network interfaces to an EC2 instance. Each network interface has its own MAC addresses and IP address associations. Unlike the primary network interface, you can detach secondary network interfaces from one Amazon EC2 instance and then attach it to another instance.

The number of network interfaces that you can attach to an instance and the network throughput depends on the specific instance type and size that you select. The number of network interfaces that you attach does not affect the network throughput of the instance; the bandwidth available to the instance depends on the instance type and size, not the number of network interfaces.

Accessing Instances

By default, Linux Amazon EC2 instances provide remote access through SSH, and Windows Amazon EC2 instances provide remote access through the Remote Desktop Protocol (RDP). To connect to these services, you must have the appropriate inbound rules on the security group for the instance.

Depending on the operating system and AMI that you use to launch the instance, a default administrator is provided for your initial sign-in. To acquire the credentials needed to sign in as the default user, you must specify an Amazon EC2 key pair when you launch the instance. After you sign in, you can create additional users with the appropriate Linux or Windows tools.

Default User

The default user for Amazon Linux instances is ec2-user. For other Linux operating systems, this default user may vary depending on the AMI provider. For example, the default user for Ubuntu Linux is ubuntu.

For Windows instances, the default user is Administrator. This account may have a different name depending on the language of the server. For example, if the server is configured with French as the language, the administrator account is localized to Administrateur.

Amazon EC2 Key Pairs

An *Amazon EC2 key pair* has a name, and it is composed of a public key and a private key. AWS retains the public key, and it is your responsibility to store the private key securely. If you specify an Amazon EC2 key pair when you launch the instance, it secures the sign-in credentials as part of the Amazon EC2 instance provisioning process. For a Linux instance, the public key from the key pair is added to the ~/.ssh/authorized_keys file for the default user. For a Windows instance, the password for the default administrator account is encrypted with the public key and can be decrypted with the private key.

When you create a new key pair, you can import a key pair that you generated locally, or you can have AWS generate a key pair for you. If you request that AWS generate the key pair, you can download the private key only at the time the key pair is generated. You are responsible for storing the private key file securely. You will not be able to download it again after it is created.

If you do not specify a key pair when you launch the instance, you are unable to sign in to that instance. Amazon EC2 key pairs are regional in scope, so you need key pairs in each region where you launch EC2 instances.

Instance Lifecycle

An Amazon EC2 instance has three primary states: running, stopped, and terminated. Additionally, there are intermediate states of pending, stopping, and shutting down. An Amazon EC2 instance accrues charges for the compute resources only when it is in the running state. However, EBS volumes persist data even when an instance is stopped, so the charges for persistent storage from any EBS volumes accrue independently from the state of the instance.

When you first launch an instance from an AMI, it goes into the pending state until it enters the running state on a host machine.

After an instance is running, for instances with EBS-backed storage, you can stop the instance. If you stop the instance, it enters the stopping state. Any data on instance store drives on that host are erased.

When an instance is stopped, you can modify attributes that cannot be changed, such as instance type, while the instance is running. You can also start stopped instances. When you start an instance, it enters the pending state until it is running again.

Typically, each time an instance is started, it is launched on a different physical host machine than before. If the underlying physical host is impaired and requires maintenance, stopping and then starting the Amazon EC2 instance moves the instance to a healthy host.

You can also terminate an instance. It first goes through shutting down; then eventually it is terminated. The default behavior is to delete the EBS volumes associated with the instance on termination.

To view the lifecycle of an Amazon EC2 instance, see Figure 2.3.

FIGURE 2.3   Amazon EC2 instance lifecycle

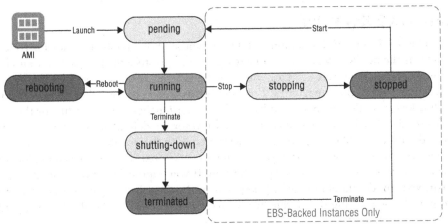

Running Applications on Instances

This section reviews how to connect to an EC2 instance and explores some features that are useful when you run applications or custom code on an instance. These features include ways of customizing the software on an instance, how your code can discover properties about the instance, and how to provide API credentials to your code running on an instance. An example that ties these features together is provided. Finally, the section describes how you can monitor the status of the instance.

Connecting to Amazon EC2 Instances

With EC2 instances, you have full administrative control to install software packages on your instance and create additional user accounts as needed. By default, to connect to a Linux instance, you can directly use the private key from the Amazon EC2 key pair with an SSH client, as shown in Figure 2.4.

FIGURE 2.4 Using SSH with an Amazon EC2 instance

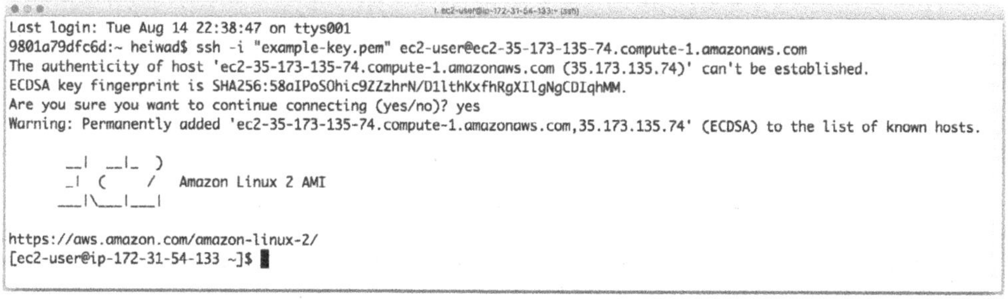

```
Last login: Tue Aug 14 22:38:47 on ttys001
9801a79dfc6d:~ heiwad$ ssh -i "example-key.pem" ec2-user@ec2-35-173-135-74.compute-1.amazonaws.com
The authenticity of host 'ec2-35-173-135-74.compute-1.amazonaws.com (35.173.135.74)' can't be established.
ECDSA key fingerprint is SHA256:58aIPoSOhic9ZZzhrN/D1lthKxfhRgXIlgNgCDIqhMM.
Are you sure you want to continue connecting (yes/no)? yes
Warning: Permanently added 'ec2-35-173-135-74.compute-1.amazonaws.com,35.173.135.74' (ECDSA) to the list of known hosts.


       __|  __|_  )
       _|  (     /   Amazon Linux 2 AMI
      ___|\___|___|

https://aws.amazon.com/amazon-linux-2/
[ec2-user@ip-172-31-54-133 ~]$ ▐
```

For a Windows instance, the password for the Administrator account is encrypted with the public key. You can decrypt the password by using the associated private key, as illustrated in Figure 2.5 and Figure 2.6.

FIGURE 2.5 Decrypting a Windows password

FIGURE 2.6   Viewing a Windows password

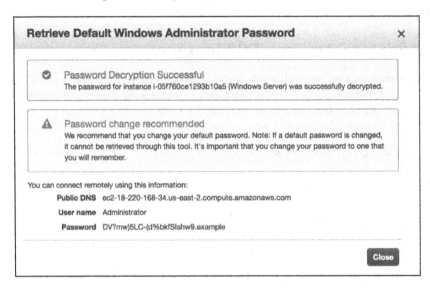

After you have decrypted the password, you can use Microsoft Remote Desktop to connect to the instance, as shown in Figure 2.7.

FIGURE 2.7   Connecting to a Windows instance

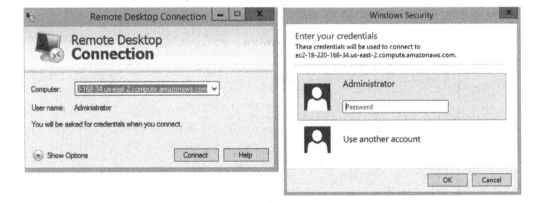

Customizing Software with User Data

You can connect to your instance and install any applications you want from an interactive session. However, one of the advantages of moving to the cloud is to automate previously manual steps. Instead of logging in to the instance, another way to customize the software on your instance is to provide *user data* as part of the request to launch the instance. For Linux instances, user data can be a shell script or a *cloud-init* directive. On Windows instances, depending on the version of Windows Server, either EC2Config or EC2Launch processes the user data. By default, commands supplied to user data execute only at first boot of the instance.

Here is an example of installing an Apache web server on an Amazon Linux 2 instance with a shell script that is provided as the user data:

```
#!/bin/bash
yum update -y
yum install httpd -y
systemctl start httpd
systemctl enable httpd
```

Discovering Instance Metadata

With the *instance metadata service* (IMDS), code running on an Amazon EC2 instance can discover properties about that instance. The instance metadata service exposes a special IP address, 169.254.169.254, which you can query using HTTP to perform lookups. You can query a broad range of metadata attributes, as shown in Figure 2.8 These attributes can include the instance ID and credentials derived from an Identity and Access Management (IAM) role.

FIGURE 2.8   Amazon EC2 metadata attributes

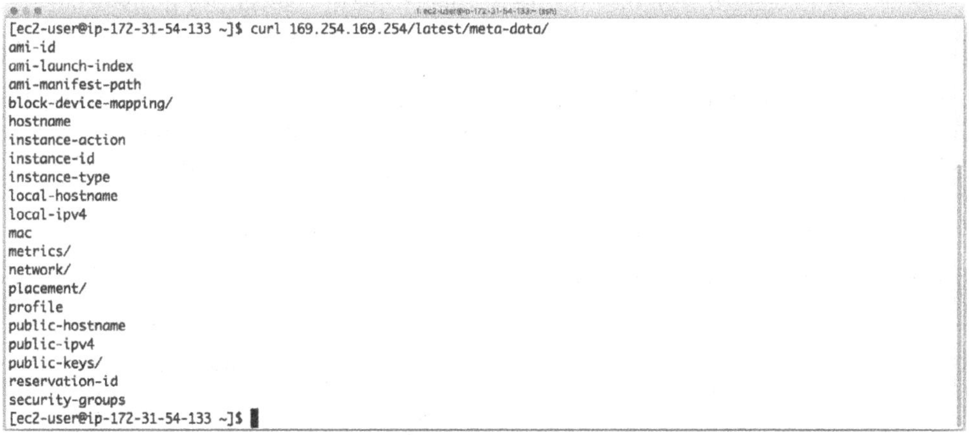

```
[ec2-user@ip-172-31-54-133 ~]$ curl 169.254.169.254/latest/meta-data/
ami-id
ami-launch-index
ami-manifest-path
block-device-mapping/
hostname
instance-action
instance-id
instance-type
local-hostname
local-ipv4
mac
metrics/
network/
placement/
profile
public-hostname
public-ipv4
public-keys/
reservation-id
security-groups
[ec2-user@ip-172-31-54-133 ~]$
```

With IMDS, it also possible to retrieve the user data that was used to bootstrap an instance, as shown in Figure 2.9.

FIGURE 2.9   Querying Amazon EC2 user data

```
[ec2-user@ip-172-31-54-133 ~]$ curl 169.254.169.254/latest/user-data/
#!/bin/bash
yum update -y
yum install httpd -y
systemctl start httpd
systemctl enable httpd
[ec2-user@ip-172-31-54-133 ~]$ 
```

Anyone who can access an instance can view its metadata and user data. Do not store sensitive data, such as passwords or access keys, as user data.

Assigning AWS API Credentials

You can assign an IAM role to an Amazon EC2 instance. The AWS Software Development Kit (SDK) and AWS Command Line Interface (AWS CLI) can automatically discover these credentials through the Amazon EC2 metadata service. You can skip the task of explicitly configuring credentials files on your instances during bootstrapping.

When you assign an IAM role to an instance, it is assigned indirectly, through an *instance profile,* which is a container for an IAM role. You can associate a particular instance profile with many Amazon EC2 instances. However, a particular Amazon EC2 instance can be associated with one instance profile at a time, and an instance profile can be associated with only one IAM role. You can associate or disassociate Amazon EC2 instances with an instance profile at launch or even when the instances are running.

When an instance profile with an IAM role is associated with an instance, the Amazon EC2 service makes the necessary calls to the *AWS Security Token Service (AWS STS)* automatically to generate short-term credentials for that instance. These credentials are based on the IAM role associated with the instance profile. The credentials are exposed to the instance through the Amazon EC2 metadata service, as shown in Figure 2.10.

FIGURE 2.10   Instance profile and IAM role credentials

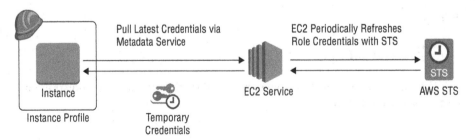

Serving a Custom Webpage

This example combines Amazon EC2 user data, the Amazon EC2 metadata service, and IAM roles to configure an Amazon EC2 instance. In the example, a web server displays a static webpage that shows custom information.

The following is a bootstrapping script that enables you to configure an Amazon EC2 instance running Amazon Linux 2. At first boot of the instance, the script generates a static page that displays the instance ID, instance type, Availability Zone, and public IP address of the instance at the time the script was executed.

The first line of the script declares the type of script. Then the script installs the Apache web server and configures it to run as a service. Because the script is running as the root user, there is no requirement to preface the commands with sudo.

Next, the script makes several calls to the Amazon EC2 metadata service and saves the results into environment variables to be used later in the script.

To generate an MP3 file that speaks out the instance ID, the script makes an API call to Amazon Polly. For this API call to succeed, you must assign the instance an IAM role that allows permissions to the Amazon Polly SynthesizeSpeech action. The managed AmazonPollyReadOnlyAccess policy can grant these permissions.

Next, the script generates a static HTML page. This page references the values that were previously stored as environment variables. After this script completes, your Amazon EC2 instance can respond to HTTP requests and show the customized page. To see this page, you must verify that the Amazon EC2 instance has port 80 open in its security group and is assigned a public IP address.

```
#!/bin/bash

# Install Apache Web Server
yum update -y
yum install httpd -y
systemctl start httpd
systemctl enable httpd

# Discover configuration using the EC2 metadata service
ID=$(curl 169.254.169.254/latest/meta-data/instance-id)
TYPE=$(curl 169.254.169.254/latest/meta-data/instance-type)
AZ=$(curl 169.254.169.254/latest/meta-data/placement/availability-zone)
IPV4=$(curl -f 169.254.169.254/latest/meta-data/public-ipv4)

# Set up the Web Site
cd /var/www/html

## Make AWS Cloud API calls to generate an audio file
VOICE=$(aws polly describe-voices --language-code en-US \
--region us-west-2 --query Voices[0].Id --output text)
aws polly synthesize-speech --region us-west-2 --voice-id $VOICE \
--text "Hello from EC2 instance $ID." --output-format mp3 instance.mp3
```

```
## Generate customized index.html for this instance
echo "<html><body><H1>Welcome to your EC2 Instance</H1><p><p>" > ./index.html
echo "<audio controls>" >> ./index.html
echo '<source src="instance.mp3" type="audio/mp3">' >> ./index.html
echo 'Here is an <a href="instance.mp3"> audio greeting.</a> ' >> ./index.html
echo "</audio><p><p>" >> ./index.html
echo "There are many other instances, but" >> ./index.html
echo "<strong>$ID</strong> is yours.<p><p>" >> ./index.html
echo "This is a <strong>$TYPE</strong> instance" >> ./index.html
echo " in <strong>$AZ</strong>. <p><p>" >> ./index.html
if [ "$IPV4" ];
then
    echo "The public IP is <strong>$IPV4</strong>.<p><p>" >> ./index.html
else
    echo "This instance does <strong>NOT</strong> have" >> ./index.html
    echo "a public IP address.<p><p>" >> ./index.html
fi
echo "--Audio provided by the $VOICE voice.<p><p>" >> ./index.html
echo "</body></html>" >> ./index.html
```

Monitoring Instances

Now that you have an application running on your instance, you may be interested in understanding how that application performs, or if it is still running at all. Amazon EC2 performs automated status checks of the software and hardware of the underlying host machine every minute. These status checks are to verify that the instance can connect to the network and can run successfully on the host machine. If the status checks find no underlying issues, they return the status OK. If an issue is detected that prevents normal operation of the Amazon EC2 instance, the status checks return the status as impaired. The results of these status checks are available in Amazon CloudWatch.

For each of your instances, the Amazon EC2 service automatically collects metrics related to CPU utilization, disk reads and writes, and network utilization and makes them available in *CloudWatch*. You can supplement these built-in metrics with data from the guest operating system on your instance, such as memory utilization and logs from your application, by installing and configuring the CloudWatch agent on the instance.

Using CloudWatch, you can automate actions based on a metric through CloudWatch alarms. For example, you can configure an CloudWatch alarm that applies the recover instance action if status checks show that the host running the instance is impaired.

Customizing the Network

While the default Amazon VPC service provides a quick way to start with Amazon EC2 instances, it is important to understand how multiple Amazon EC2 instances communicate within an Amazon VPC network. The AWS Certified Developer – Associate exam may test your knowledge of Amazon VPC by asking troubleshooting questions related to the network. In this section, you'll explore the Amazon VPC that enables you to create software-defined networks within an AWS Region.

Amazon Virtual Private Cloud

Amazon Virtual Private Cloud (Amazon VPC) provides logically isolated networks within your AWS account. These networks are software defined and can span all of the Availability Zones within a specific AWS Region. For each VPC, you have full control over whether the Amazon VPC is connected to the internet, to a private on-premises network, or to other Amazon VPCs. Until you explicitly create these connections, instances in your VPC are able to communicate with other instances in the same VPC only.

You define an Amazon VPC with one or more blocks of addresses specified in the Classless Inter-Domain Routing (CIDR) notation. If, for example, you specified 10.0.0.0/16 as the block for a VPC, this means that the VPC includes IP addresses in the range from 10.0.0.0 through 10.0.255.255. For an example of an Amazon VPC spanning multiple Availability Zones in a region, see Figure 2.11.

FIGURE 2.11   Amazon VPC overview

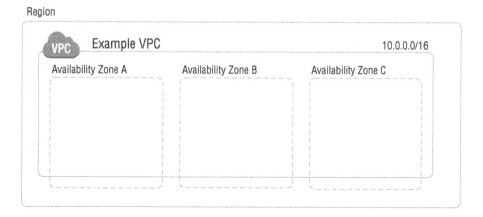

Connecting to Other Networks

By default, an Amazon VPC is an isolated network. Instances within an Amazon VPC cannot communicate with the internet or other networks until you explicitly create connections. Table 2.2 provides an overview of various types of connections that you can establish between an Amazon VPC and other networks.

TABLE 2.2 Amazon VPC Connection Types

Connection Type	Description
Internet Gateway	A highly available connection that allows outbound and inbound requests to the internet from your Amazon VPC
Egress Only Internet Gateway	A special type of internet gateway for IPv6 that allows outbound traffic and corresponding responses but blocks inbound connections
Virtual Private Gateway	Allows you to establish a private connection to your corporate network by using a VPN connection or through Direct Connect (DX)
Amazon VPC Endpoints	Allows traffic from your Amazon VPC to go to specific AWS services or third-party SaaS services without traversing an internet gateway
Amazon VPC Peering	Privately routes traffic from one Amazon VPC to another Amazon VPC by establishing a peer relationship between this VPC and another VPC
AWS Transit Gateway	Allows you to centrally manage connectivity between many VPCs and an on-premises environment using a single gateway

For an example of an Amazon VPC with a connection to an internet gateway and a VPN connection to an on-premises network provided by a virtual private gateway, see Figure 2.12.

FIGURE 2.12 Amazon VPC with gateway connections

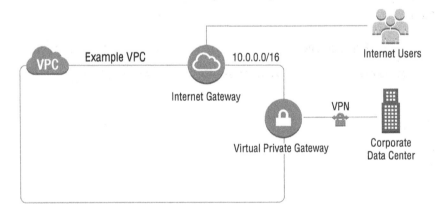

IP Addresses

When working with Amazon VPC, all instances placed within a particular VPC are assigned one or more IP addresses. There are four different types of IP addresses available for use with Amazon VPC. Primarily, these IP addresses are based on IPv4; however, you can enable support for IPv6.

Private IP Addresses

Private IP addresses are IPv4 addresses that are not reachable from the internet. These addresses are unique within a VPC and used for traffic that is to be routed internally within the VPC, for private communication with corporate networks, or for private communication with other VPCs.

When you create a VPC, you assign one or more blocks of addresses to the VPC, and typically these blocks will be within the range of IPv4 addresses reserved for private networks as specified in RFC1918. When an instance is launched, it is launched into a subnet within the VPC, and the instance is assigned a private IP address automatically from the block of addresses assigned to that particular subnet. When an instance is assigned a private IPv4 address, this association persists for the lifecycle of the instance—even when the instance is stopped.

Public IP Addresses

Whether an EC2 instance is assigned public IP addresses automatically, in addition to the private IP address, depends on the following factors:

- Configuration passed when launching the instance
- Options for the subnet in which that instance is launched

Unlike the private IP address, the public IP address is an IPv4 address that is reachable from the internet.

AWS manages the association between an instance and a public IPv4 address, and the association persists only while the instance is running. You cannot manually associate or disassociate public IP addresses from an instance.

Elastic IP Addresses

An *Elastic IP address* is similar to a public IP address in that it is an IPv4 address that is reachable from the internet. However, unlike public IP addresses, you manage the association between instances and Elastic IP addresses. You control when these addresses are allocated, and you can associate, disassociate, or move these addresses between instances as needed.

You may also assign Elastic IP addresses to infrastructure such as NAT gateways. These addresses can come from a pool of IP addresses that AWS manages or from blocks of IPv4 addresses you have brought to your AWS account.

IPv6 Addresses

In addition to IPv4 addresses, you can associate an Amazon-provided block of IPv6 addresses to your VPC. When you enable IPv6 in your VPC, the network operates in *dual-stack mode*, meaning that IPv4 and IPv6 commutations are independent of each other. Your resources can communicate over IPv4, IPv6, or both.

Subnets

Within an Amazon VPC, you define one or more subnets. A subnet is associated with a specific Availability Zone within the region containing the Amazon VPC. Each subnet has its own block of private IP addresses defined using CIDR notation. This block is a subset of the overall IP address range assigned to the Amazon VPC and does not overlap with any other subnet in the same Amazon VPC.

For example, a subnet may be assigned the CIDR block range 10.0.0.0/24, which would include addresses in the range 10.0.0.0–10.0.0.255. Out of the 256 possible addresses, Amazon VPC reserves the first four IP addresses and the last IP address in the range, leaving 251 IP addresses in the subnet.

When you launch an Amazon EC2 instance into a subnet, its primary network interface assigns a private IPv4 address automatically from the CIDR range assigned to the subnet.

Typically, you create at least two types of configurations for subnets in a VPC. The first is for subnets in which you place instances that you want to reach directly from the internet. This could be an instance running as a web server, for example. Subnets of this type are known as *public subnets*.

The second type of configuration is usually a subnet that backend instances use that must be accessible to your other instances but should not be directly accessible from the internet. Subnets of this type are known as *private subnets*. For example, if you had an instance that was dedicated to running a database, such as MySQL, you could place that instance in a private subnet. It would be accessible from the web server in the public subnet, but it would not accept traffic from the internet.

For an example of an Amazon VPC with a public and a private subnet, see Figure 2.13.

FIGURE 2.13   Amazon VPC with public and private subnets

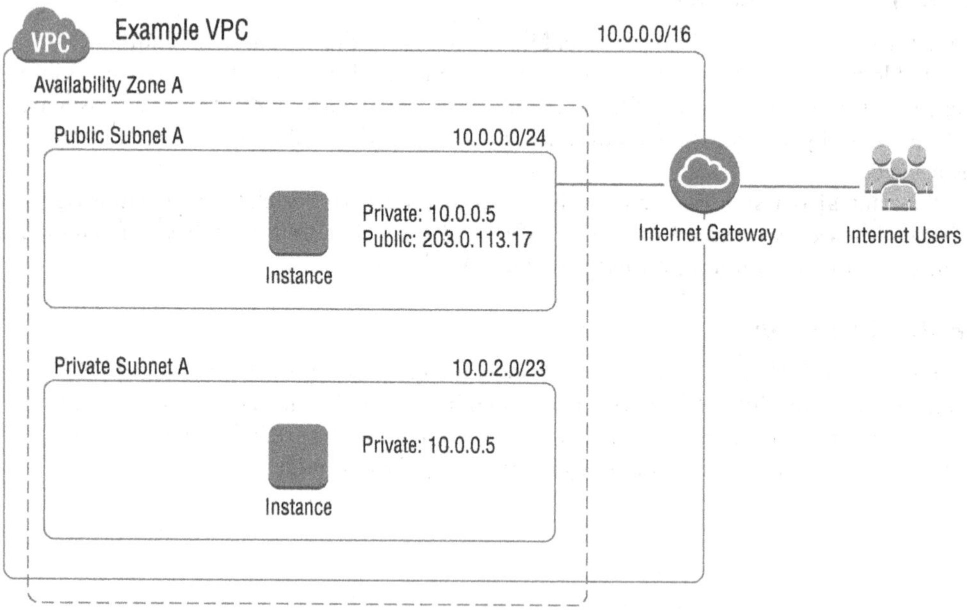

In addition to Amazon EC2 instances, many AWS managed services, such as Amazon Relational Database Service (Amazon RDS) or Amazon ElastiCache, also enable you to expose your resources in specific subnets and, in particular, into private subnets. You can create these resources and access them privately from instances within your Amazon VPC.

Route Tables

Network traffic exiting a subnet is controlled with routes that are defined in a route table. Routes define how the implicit router in the Amazon VPC routes IP traffic from a subnet to destinations outside that subnet. Each route table includes a rule called the *local route*. This rule or *route* is what allows traffic from instances in one subnet within the Amazon VPC to send traffic to instances in any other subnets within the same Amazon VPC. A route is composed of two parts: a destination and a target for the network traffic.

Unless explicitly associated with a specific route table, subnets associate with a default route table called the *main route table*. By default, the main route table includes only the local route. This means that subnets that are associated with the default route table have no connection to the internet. They can route traffic privately only within the Amazon VPC. However, you can modify this table or define additional route tables and rules as required.

For an example of the main route table for an Amazon VPC, see Table 2.3.

TABLE 2.3   Main Route Table Example

Destination	Target
10.0.0.0/16	local

Route tables and the configured rules differentiate public subnets from private subnets. For example, you might create a public subnet by associating the subnet with a route table that includes a rule to route internet-bound traffic through an internet gateway. To represent any IP address on the internet in the rule, you can use the 0.0.0.0/0 CIDR block. Table 2.4 is an example of a route table that contains the defined rules.

TABLE 2.4   Public Route Table Example

Destination	Target
10.0.0.0/16	local
0.0.0.0/0	igw-example123

When you launch an Amazon EC2 instance into a public subnet, assign a public IP address to the instance. Even though the subnet has a route to an internet gateway, the instance is not able to communicate with the internet without a public IP address. Route table rules are evaluated in order of specificity.

To review a diagram of an Amazon VPC that has a public and a private subnet configured with the route table rules, see Figure 2.14.

FIGURE 2.14   Amazon VPC with public and private subnets with rules

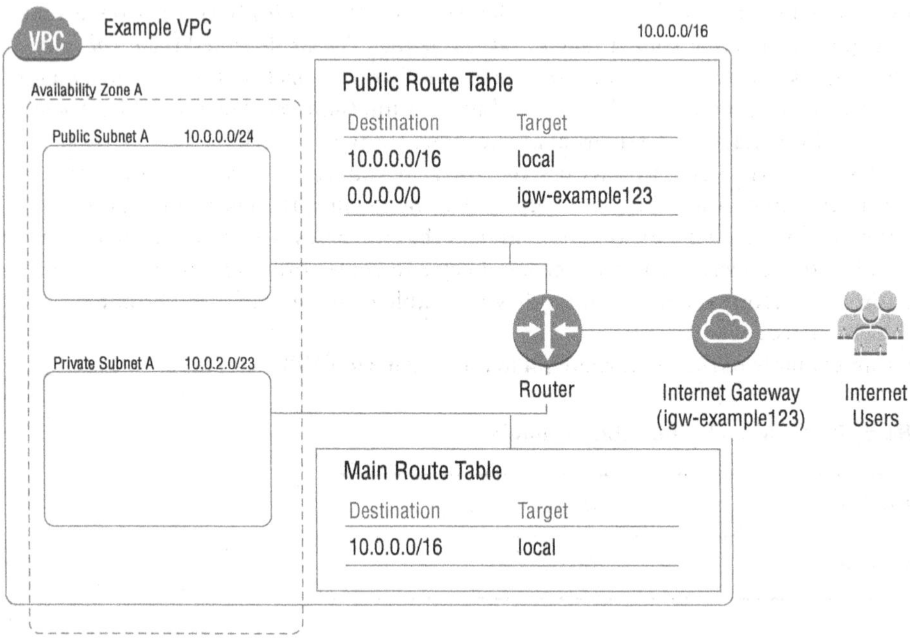

Security Groups

Security groups act as a stateful firewall for your Amazon EC2 instances. When you define security group rules, you specify the source or destination of the network traffic in addition to the protocols and ports that you allow. If you change the security group rules, that change propagates to any instances associated with that security group.

By using inbound security group rules, you can control the source, protocols, and ports of allowed network traffic. For example, you could allow TCP connections that originate from the IPv4 address of your home network so that you can administer an Amazon EC2 instance using SSH.

Outbound rules enable you to control destination, protocols, and ports of allowed network traffic. Security groups include a default outbound rule that allows all outbound requests on all protocols and ports to all destinations. To control outbound requests more tightly, you can remove this default rule and add specific outbound rules in its place.

When you specify a source or destination for a security group rule, you can use IPv4 or IPv6 address ranges. Alternatively, you can use an identifier for a security group as a source or destination.

Assume that you have two EC2 instances—one instance is running a web server, and a second instance is running a database application. To allow network connections to these instances, you create two security groups: a security group for your web server instances called websg and a second security group for your database instances called databasesg.

For websg, you set inbound rules that allow web requests from anywhere. You also allow inbound SSH but only from a specific IP address that your administrator uses. You have not yet modified the default outbound rule for websg, so all outgoing connections are allowed.

For databasesg, you write an inbound rule that allows incoming traffic on TCP port 3306 originating from websg. Remove the default outbound rule and instead add rules to allow outbound connections to download software updates over HTTP and HTTPS. All other outbound connections from databasesg will be blocked.

To view the diagram of the security groups and rules for this scenario, see Figure 2.15. Also, see Table 2.5, Table 2.6, Table 2.7, and Table 2.8 for the corresponding inbound and outbound rules for these security groups.

FIGURE 2.15 Security groups

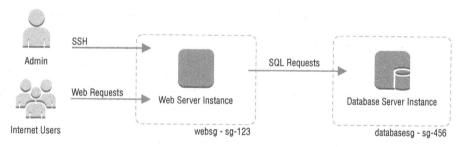

TABLE 2.5 Inbound Rules for websg

Protocol	Port	Source	Comments
TCP	80	0.0.0.0/0	Allow incoming HTTP requests from internet users
TCP	443	0.0.0.0/0	Allow incoming HTTPS requests from internet users
TCP	22	10.10.0.6/32	Allow incoming SSH only from the administrator's computer

TABLE 2.6   Outbound Rule for websg

Protocol	Port	Destination	Comments
All	All	0.0.0.0/0	Allow all outbound IPv4 traffic

TABLE 2.7   Inbound Rule for databasesg

Protocol	Port	Source	Comments
TCP	3306	sg-123	Allow inbound SQL queries from websg

TABLE 2.8   Outbound Rules for databasesg

Protocol	Port	Destination	Comments
TCP	80	0.0.0.0/0	Allow all outbound HTTP for updates
TCP	443	0.0.0.0/0	Allow outbound HTTPS requests for updates

If you specify an inbound rule, replies to that incoming connection are permitted. Similarly, if you specify an outbound rule, the replies to the outbound request are permitted. In the previous example, when a web server instance makes a connection to a database, only the outbound rule for the web server and the inbound rule for the database must allow the flow. The inbound rule for the web server and the outbound rule for the database will not be evaluated for this flow.

*Security groups only support rules to **allow** traffic.* Therefore, if you assign multiple security groups to your instance, the security group rules combine in the most permissive way; each group contributes to opening up more access to the instance.

If you fail to specify a security group when you launch the Amazon EC2 instance, the instance associates with the default security group for the Amazon VPC. If your Amazon EC2 instance has more than one network interface, you can manage the security groups for each network interface independently from the others.

Network Access Control Lists

In addition to routes, *network access control lists* (network ACLs) allow an administrator to control traffic that enters and leaves a subnet. A network ACL consists of inbound and outbound rules that you can associate with multiple subnets within a specific Amazon VPC. Network ACLs act as a stateless firewall for traffic to or from a specific subnet.

Whereas security group rules provide only the capability to allow traffic, network ACL rules support the ability to allow specific types of traffic and to deny specific traffic.

However, unlike security groups, network ACLs are stateless and do not track connections and their replies. This means that to allow for a particular traffic flow, both inbound and outbound rules must allow it for that network ACL. For inbound rules, you can specify the protocol, port range, and source IP address range. For outbound rules, you specify the protocol, port range, and destination IP address range. For each rule, you also choose whether the rule allows or denies traffic. Rules in a network ACL are numbered and evaluated in order from the smallest to largest rule number.

If you do not specify a network ACL, the subnet is associated with the default network ACL for the Amazon VPC. This network ACL comes with rules that allow all inbound and outbound traffic. Table 2.9 shows an example of the inbound rules for a default network ACL. The final rule for the network ACL, rule 100, is a universal rule that explicitly denies traffic that does not match any other rule. Because there is a rule to allow all traffic and rules are evaluated in order, this universal rule has no effect. However, if you remove or modify rule 100, then the final rule would apply to any traffic that did not match any of the other rules.

TABLE 2.9   Default Network ACL Inbound Rules

Rule Number	Type	Protocol	Port Range	Source	Allow/Deny
100	All traffic	All	All	0.0.0.0/0	Allow
*	All traffic	All	All	0.0.0.0/0	Deny

Table 2.10 shows an example of the outbound rules for the default network ACL for an Amazon VPC. As before, the final rule is a universal rule that denies traffic unless it has been explicitly allowed by a preceding rule.

TABLE 2.10   Default Network ACL Outbound Rules

Rule Number	Type	Protocol	Port Range	Destination	Allow/Deny
100	All traffic	All	All	0.0.0.0/0	Allow
*	All traffic	All	All	0.0.0.0/0	Deny

Figure 2.16 shows an example of an Amazon VPC with security groups protecting Amazon EC2 instances and network ACLs protecting subnets.

FIGURE 2.16 Network ACLs and security groups

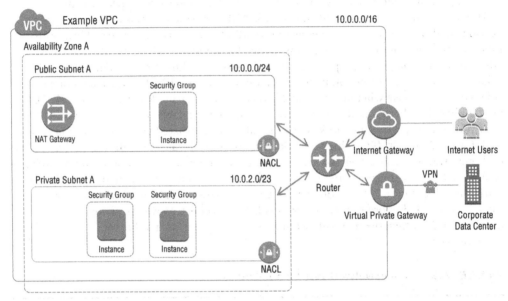

Figure 2.17 shows the same Amazon VPC, represented in a different way to highlight the features that control network traffic within an Amazon VPC.

FIGURE 2.17 Controlling network traffic within an Amazon VPC

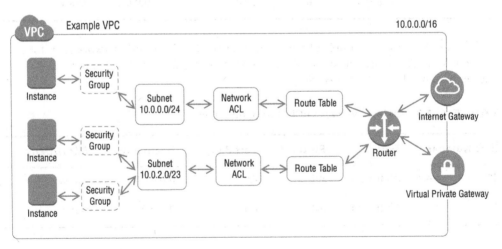

Table 2.11 summarizes key aspects of security groups and network ACLs.

TABLE 2.11 Security Groups and Network ACLs

Feature	Security Group	Network ACL
Applies to	Amazon EC2 instance or elastic network interface.	Subnet
Type of firewall	Stateful: Replies to an allowed traffic flow are automatically allowed.	Stateless: Must provide both inbound and outbound rules to allow a specific traffic flow.
Rules	Only allow traffic.	Allow or deny traffic.

Network Address Translation

Network address translation (NAT) allows for instances in a private subnet to make outbound requests to the internet without exposing those instances to inbound connections from internet users. To provide NAT for outbound requests from private subnets, you can use an Amazon EC2 instance configured to perform NAT or a NAT gateway. The instances in the private subnet maintain their own private IP addresses and effectively share the public IP address of the NAT when making internet requests.

For the NAT to perform its job, you must place the NAT instance or a NAT gateway in a correctly configured public subnet to forward traffic to the internet. Make sure that the public subnet has a route to an internet gateway, as previously shown in Table 2.4. To support outbound network requests, you can associate the private subnet with a route table, similar to the one shown in Table 2.12.

TABLE 2.12 Private Route Table Example

Destination	Target
10.0.0.0/16	local
0.0.0.0/0	nat-example456

For the Amazon VPC configuration example, Figure 2.18 shows the corresponding route tables for the public and private subnets using the NAT gateway.

FIGURE 2.18   Example of Amazon VPC with NAT

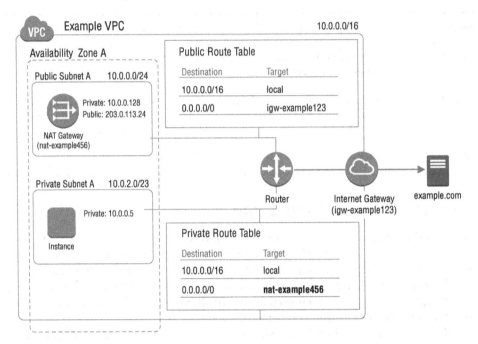

Internet-bound requests route to the NAT gateway through the route table of the private subnet. The NAT, located in a public subnet, then makes a corresponding request out to the internet. This second outbound request appears to have originated from the public IP address of the NAT when the external website received it. When the website responds, NAT receives the reply and forwards it to the instance that initiated the original request. Figure 2.19 shows the network flow.

Using an Amazon EC2 instance for NAT instead of a NAT gateway requires you to disable the *source/destination check* setting for the NAT instance.

This setting protects Amazon EC2 instances by requiring that the instance be the source or destination of any network traffic it receives. In the case of the NAT instance, while the packets are routed to the instance via a route table, they are addressed to destinations on the internet rather than the NAT. Disabling this setting allows the network traffic to be delivered to the NAT instance.

FIGURE 2.19   NAT gateway in Amazon VPC

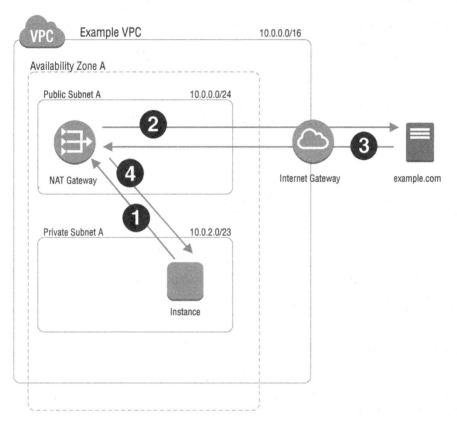

DHCP Option Sets

The *Dynamic Host Configuration Protocol* (DHCP) provides a standard for passing configuration information to hosts on a TCP/IP network. The options field of a DHCP message contains the configuration parameters.

Some of those parameters are the address of domain name servers (DNS), the domain names of the instances, and the addresses of Network Time Protocol (NTP) servers. By default, the Amazon VPC uses the DNS that AWS provides. However, you can override these settings by specifying a custom set of DHCP options.

Monitoring Amazon VPC Network Traffic

You can monitor the network flows within your Amazon VPC by enabling Amazon VPC Flow Logs. You can then publish these logs to Amazon CloudWatch Logs or store them as log files in Amazon Simple Storage Service (Amazon S3). Enable Amazon VPC Flow Logs on a particular Amazon VPC, on a subnet, or on a specific elastic network interface, such as for an Amazon EC2 instance.

For each network session, the Flow Logs capture metadata, such as the source, destination, protocol, port, packet count, byte count, and time interval. The log entry specifies whether the traffic was accepted or rejected. This information helps you debug the network configuration.

Managing Your Resources

You now know that you can customize the software running on your Amazon EC2 instances. Additionally, with Amazon VPC, you can control the virtual network for those instances through security groups, network ACLs, subnets, and route tables. Because you can configure your operating environment in AWS, you share the responsibility for securing your applications running in the AWS Cloud with AWS.

Shared Responsibility Security Model

AWS is responsible for the security *of* the cloud. This involves securing physical access to the underlying infrastructure, such as the AWS Regions and Availability Zones. This responsibility includes procedures for restricting access to the servers, physical networks, and decommissioning of hardware that is no longer useful. As part of securing the cloud infrastructure, AWS is also responsible for maintaining the underlying software for each service provided.

As the AWS customer, you are responsible for security *on* the cloud. This responsibility includes making secure choices when configuring your infrastructure and developing your applications. These responsibilities can include configuring the relevant encryption options and configuring your firewall rules. Even though this is your responsibility, you can simplify this task by taking advantage of AWS tools for encryption, defining firewall rules, and managing access and authorization to your AWS resources. For a summary of AWS and customer responsibilities, see Figure 2.20.

FIGURE 2.20   Shared responsibility security model

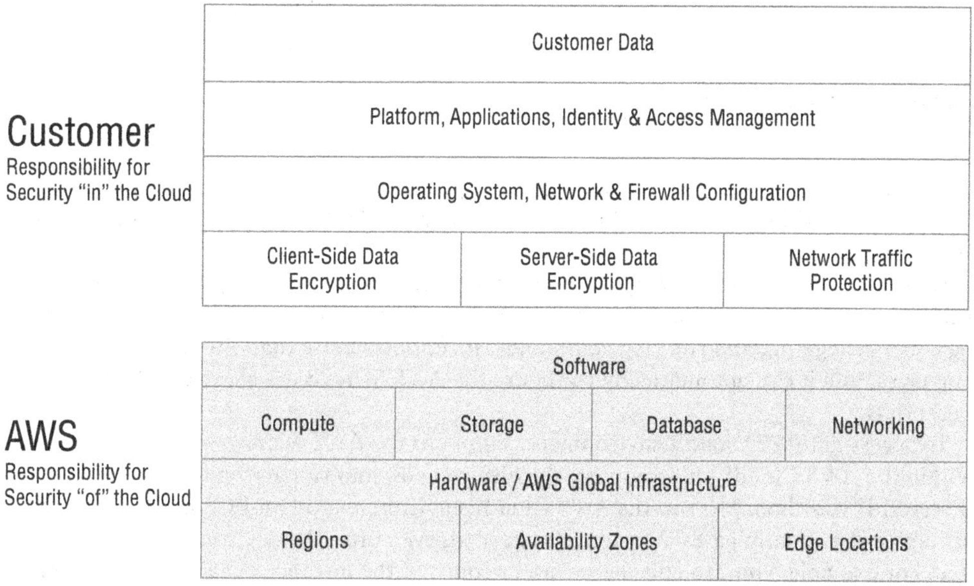

Customer	Customer Data		
Responsibility for Security "in" the Cloud	Platform, Applications, Identity & Access Management		
	Operating System, Network & Firewall Configuration		
	Client-Side Data Encryption	Server-Side Data Encryption	Network Traffic Protection

AWS	Software			
Responsibility for Security "of" the Cloud	Compute	Storage	Database	Networking
	Hardware / AWS Global Infrastructure			
	Regions	Availability Zones		Edge Locations

For example, with Amazon EC2, AWS is responsible for the software on the physical host machines up through maintaining the virtualization layer. However, beyond that, it is your responsibility to ensure that the guest operating system and everything running on it are secured. Your responsibilities include the following tasks:

- Making sure that any sensitive data is secured
- Making sure that the guest operating system is patched regularly
- Managing the guest operating system's user accounts
- Securing any applications that are installed on that instance

AWS provides tools to help you manage these concerns. For example, use AWS Systems Manager to automate the patching of instances on your behalf. You can also use network controls, such as security groups, to restrict access to the instance. However, it is your responsibility to configure these features in a way that meets the security requirements for your specific application.

Comparing Managed and Unmanaged Services

Even though services such as Amazon EC2 provide many low-level customizations, other AWS services provide a managed experience. When you use AWS managed services, you may find that you have less responsibility. For example, for Amazon RDS, AWS manages the software installed on the underlying database instance. You interact with the database using your SQL client rather than a shell session, and you do not install your own software on the database instance. In this case, parts of your operational burden for security are reduced—AWS manages the operating system and software on the database instance.

Developer Tools

In addition to providing the low-level infrastructure pieces, such as Amazon EC2 instances and VPC networking components, the AWS Cloud provides higher-level services to help developers be more productive.

With AWS Cloud9, you can create developer environments that execute on either an Amazon EC2 instance or another server. AWS Cloud9 provides a web interface for editing code, debugging, and running commands. It supports more than 40 programming languages, and it can automatically configure the AWS SDK to use short-term managed credentials.

To access an AWS Cloud9 environment, sign in to the AWS Management Console. Within the AWS Cloud9 environment, the files you edit and run are on the remote instance or server. If you choose to run the AWS Cloud9 environment on an EC2 instance, you can customize the underlying EC2 instance as needed, even after the environment has been created. For example, you can edit the security groups of the instance or increase the size of the Amazon EBS volume attached to the instance.

This service simplifies the common task of developing code, running it on Amazon EC2, and collaborating with other developers. If you want to reduce cost, one advantage of AWS Cloud9 is that it can automatically stop the underlying instance a short time after you close your browser window, and it automatically starts the instance the next time you try to connect. You can further explore EC2 instances, VPCs, and AWS Cloud9 environments in the exercises that accompany this chapter.

Summary

Amazon Elastic Compute Cloud (Amazon EC2) instances are compute environments that provide you with full control over the operating system and software. The instance type and instance size determine the hardware available to an instance. This includes properties such as vCPU, RAM, access to local storage, and network bandwidth. Amazon Elastic Block Store (Amazon EBS) provides persistent storage for EC2 instances. An Amazon Machine Image (AMI) provides the template for the software on the instance. Additionally, user data allows you to run a script on the instance to automatically update the software on the instance. To make AWS API calls from code running on an EC2 instance, assign an AWS Identity and Access Management (IAM) role to the instance by way of an instance profile. Use Amazon CloudWatch to collect instance monitoring and utilization metrics.

Amazon Virtual Private Cloud (Amazon VPC) enables your EC2 instances to be placed into isolated networks where you have control over the connectivity to other networks, such as the internet, on-premises networks, or other VPCs. Within a VPC, the network is segmented into subnets. Instances within a subnet in a VPC are assigned private IPv4 addresses. They can be assigned public IPv4 addresses, Elastic IP addresses, or IPv6 addresses.

Routing between the instances in the VPC and other networks is controlled on a subnet level using routes and route tables. This configuration enables you to define some subnets as public and others as private. In addition to routing, network traffic can also be controlled by two sets of controls that act as firewalls in a VPC. Network access control lists (network ACLs) act as a stateless firewall on all traffic that leaves or enters a subnet. Security groups act as a stateful firewall that protects individual traffic flows at an instance level.

The responsibility for keeping your instances secure is shared between AWS and you, the customer. AWS is responsible for securing access to the infrastructure and providing you with controls that you can use to secure your instances. As an AWS customer, you are responsible for configuring your resources in a way that is secure and meets your application needs.

Exam Essentials

Know the basics of Amazon EC2, such as resource types, instance types, AMIs, and storage. Be familiar with launching and connecting to Amazon EC2 instances. Understand the resource types of Amazon EC2 instance types. Be familiar with the purpose of an AMI in relation to launching an instance. Understand the distinction between persistent and ephemeral storage related to a particular Amazon EC2 instance.

Know about user data, instance metadata, and credentials. Be familiar with using user data to customize the software by executing scripts on instances. Any scripts or code running on an instance can use the Amazon EC2 metadata service to discover the instance configuration. Use IAM roles to provide AWS Cloud API credentials automatically to code running on an Amazon EC2 instance.

Know how Amazon EC2 communicates with Amazon VPC. Understand the relationship between an EC2 instance and the Amazon VPC network. There may be questions that ask you to troubleshoot issues related to connecting to an Amazon EC2 instance. Be familiar with how Amazon VPC enables communication between Amazon EC2 instances within the same Amazon VPC and isolates those instances from other Amazon VPCs. Recognize how route tables, network access control lists, and security groups control network traffic.

Know about public and private subnets. Within an Amazon VPC, you must be able to distinguish between public and private subnets. Public subnets allow you to assign public IPv4 addresses to Amazon EC2 instances. By contrast, instances in a private subnet have only private IP addresses. The key distinction is that public subnets have a route table entry that forwards internet-bound traffic to an internet gateway. Private subnets do not have a direct route to the internet. Instead, these subnets have a route that forwards internet-bound traffic through a NAT gateway or NAT instance.

Know about security groups and network ACLs.   Be familiar with security groups and network ACLs. Security groups are used with Amazon EC2 instances, acting as stateful firewalls. They provide only rules that allow traffic. In comparison, network ACLs allow traffic between subnets and are stateless. They can allow or deny specific types of traffic.

Know about responsibilities shared between you and AWS.   Be familiar with the separation between AWS responsibility and your responsibility concerning Amazon EC2 instances. AWS is responsible for providing secure building blocks up until the hypervisor layer for the Amazon EC2 instance. This includes securing the physical facilities and machines and any hardware decommissioning. You are responsible for patching the guest operating system and applications. You are also responsible for configuring firewall rules, encryption, and access to the instance in a way that meets their requirements.

Resources to Review

Amazon EC2 Instance Types:

   https://aws.amazon.com/ec2/instance-types/

Amazon EC2 User Guide for Linux Instances:

   https://docs.aws.amazon.com/AWSEC2/latest/UserGuide/index.html

Amazon EC2 User Guide for Windows Instances:

   https://docs.aws.amazon.com/AWSEC2/latest/WindowsGuide/index.html

Amazon EC2 Foundations on YouTube:

   https://www.youtube.com/watch?v=bgoPfn-Ppd8

Amazon EC2 Instance Metadata and User Data:

   https://docs.aws.amazon.com/AWSEC2/latest/UserGuide/
   ec2-instance-metadata.html

Amazon EC2 FAQs:

   https://aws.amazon.com/ec2/faqs/

Amazon VPC User Guide:

   https://docs.aws.amazon.com/vpc/latest/userguide/what-is-amazon-vpc.html

Amazon VPC Fundamentals and Connectivity on YouTube:

   https://www.youtube.com/watch?v=Tff1mekxOJ4

Amazon VPC Security:

   https://docs.aws.amazon.com/vpc/latest/userguide/VPC_Security.html

IP Addressing in Your VPC:

   https://docs.aws.amazon.com/vpc/latest/userguide/vpc-ip-addressing.html

Amazon VPC FAQs:

https://aws.amazon.com/vpc/faqs/

AWS Cloud9 User Guide:

https://docs.aws.amazon.com/cloud9/latest/user-guide/welcome.html

Exercises

These exercises provide hands-on experience with the fundamentals of working with Amazon EC2 and Amazon VPC. You will create an isolated network in the AWS Cloud and then launch Amazon EC2 instances into that network. The exam has questions that test your knowledge of how to troubleshoot common network-connectivity issues relating to Amazon EC2 instances.

For the following exercises, verify that the region is US West (Oregon). The directions for these exercises assume that you have already completed Exercises 1.1, 1.2, 1.3, and 1.4 in Chapter 1, "Introduction to AWS Cloud API."

You can complete these exercises within the AWS Free Tier, provided that you follow the steps to clean up resources promptly.

 The results from these exercises are used in a later chapter, so follow all the activities and directions exactly.

EXERCISE 2.1

Create an Amazon EC2 Key Pair

In this exercise, you'll generate and save an Amazon EC2 key pair. You are responsible for saving the private key and using it when you want to connect to your Amazon EC2 instances.

1. Sign in to the AWS Management Console using the **DevAdmin** IAM user you created in Exercise 1.2.

2. To open the Amazon EC2 console, select **Services ➢ EC2**.

3. Select **Network & Security ➢ Key Pairs**.

4. Select **Create Key Pair**.

5. For **Key pair name**, enter **devassoc**, and then choose **Create**.

    The key pair automatically downloads to your Downloads folder.

6. Move this key to a safe location on your computer. You need it to connect to your Amazon EC2 instances using Secure Shell (SSH) or Remote Desktop Protocol (RDP).

EXERCISE 2.2

Create an Amazon VPC with Public and Private Subnets

In this exercise, you'll create an Amazon Virtual Private Cloud (Amazon VPC). Within that Amazon VPC, you will have a public subnet directly connected to the internet through an internet gateway. You will also have a private subnet that only has an indirect connection to the internet using network address translation (NAT).

1. To display the Amazon VPC dashboard, select **Services ≻ VPC**.

2. Select **Launch VPC Wizard**.

    If a field does not contain an explicit value in these directions, retain the default value.

3. Select **VPC with Public and Private Subnets** and then click **Select**.

4. Enter the following details for Amazon VPC:

    a. For **Amazon VPC name**, enter **devassoc**.

    b. In the public and private subnets drop-down lists, select the first **AZ**.

    c. In the **Elastic IP Allocation ID** prompt, select **Use a NAT instance instead**.

    d. For the Amazon EC2 **Key Pair Name**, select **devassoc**.

5. Choose **Create VPC**.

6. When the Amazon VPC is created, choose **OK**.

7. Copy the VPC ID of the Amazon VPC named devassoc to a text document.

8. To view the list of subnets, select **Subnets**. In the filter box, paste the VPC ID you copied and then press the **Enter** key to filter the results.

    Two subnets are listed: **Public subnet** and **Private subnet**.

9. Copy the **Subnet ID** of the public and private subnet to the text file.

    After you have created Amazon VPC, your text document will look like the following:

    VPC ID: VPC-06bb2198eaexample
    Public subnet ID: subnet-0625e239a2example
    Private subnet ID: subnet-0e78325d9eexample

EXERCISE 2.3

Use an IAM Role for API Calls from Amazon EC2 Instances

In this exercise, you'll create an IAM role for the web server. This role enables you to make AWS Cloud API calls from code running on the Amazon EC2 instance of the web server. You are not required to save IAM credentials in a file on the instance. To do this, create a new IAM role and call it the devassoc-webserver role. The role provides permissions needed for the API calls.

1. Select **Services ≫ IAM**.

2. Select **Roles** and choose **Create Role**.

3. Under **Choose the service that will use this role**, select the option that allows Amazon EC2 instances to call AWS services on your behalf, and then choose **Next: Permissions**.

4. Select the following AWS managed policies to attach them to the devassoc-webserver role and then choose **Next: Tags**:

    AmazonPollyReadOnlyAccess: Grant read-only access to resources, list lexicons, fetch lexicons, list available voices, and synthesize speech to apply lexicons to the synthesized speech.

    TranslateReadOnly: Allow permissions to detect the dominant language in text, translate text, and list and retrieve custom terminologies.

 These permissions are required to complete future exercises.

5. Enter the following tag details and then choose **Next: Review**:

    Key: **project**

    Value: **devassoc**

6. For the **Role name**, enter **devassoc-webserver** and then choose **Create Role**.

EXERCISE 2.4

Launch an Amazon EC2 Instance as a Web Server

In this exercise, you'll launch an Amazon EC2 instance as a web server and connect to it.

1. Select **Services ≫ EC2**.

2. Select **Launch Instance**.

3. Select **Amazon Linux 2 AMI** and then choose **Next**.

4. Select **t2.micro** and then choose **Next: Configure Instance Details**.

(continued)

EXERCISE 2.4 *(continued)*

5. On the **Configure Instance Details** page, set the instance:

   ▪ Select **Network ≻ devassoc**.

   ▪ Select **Subnet ≻ Public Subnet**.

   ▪ Select **Auto-assign Public IP ≻ Enable**.

   ▪ Select **IAM Role ≻ devassoc-webserver**.

6. Expand **Advanced Details** and then paste the **User Data** script.

   ```
   #!/bin/bash
   yum install httpd -y
   systemctl start httpd
   systemctl enable httpd
   ```

 Paste this snippet from chapter-02/server-short.txt, located in the folder in which you downloaded the sample code for this guide.

7. Select **Next: Add Storage**.

8. Select **Next: Add Tags**.

9. On the **Add Tags** page, choose Add Tag and then enter the following:

   Key: Name

   Value: webserver

10. Choose **Next: Configure Security Group**.

11. On the **Configure Security Group** page:

    ▪ For **Security group name**, enter **restricted-http-ssh**.

    ▪ For **Description**, enter **HTTP and SSH from my IP address only**.

12. For the existing SSH rule, select **Source ≻ My IP**.

13. Select **Add Rule**, and then configure the second rule:

    ▪ For **Type**, select **HTTP**.

    ▪ For **Source**, select **My IP**.

14. Choose **Review and Launch**.

15. On the **Review Instance Launch** page, verify the settings and then choose **Launch**.

16. Under **Select a key pair**, select **devassoc** and select the box acknowledging that you have access to the key pair.

17. To launch your EC2 instance, choose **Launch Instances**.

18. To find your instance, choose **View Instances**.

19. From the list of instances, select **webserver**. Wait until **Instance Status** for your instance reads as running and **Status Checks** changes to 2/2 checks passed.

20. Copy the **Public IPv4 address** of the instance to a text document.

21. Paste the **IP address** of the **webserver** instance into a browser window.

   A test webpage is displayed. If you do not see a page, wait 30 seconds and then refresh the page.

22. Disable your mobile phone's Wi-Fi and then attempt to access the IP address of the **webserver** instance from your mobile phone with mobile data.

The page fails to load because the security group rule allows HTTP access from only a particular IP address.

EXERCISE 2.5

Connect to the Amazon EC2 Instance

In this exercise, you'll connect to the Amazon EC2 Instance using SSH.

1. Select **Services** ➤ **EC2**.

2. Select **Instances**.

3. Select the **webserver** instance from the list of instances.

4. Select **Actions** ➤ **Connect**.

5. In the **Connect to Your Instance** dialog box, follow the directions to establish an SSH connection.

6. From within your SSH session, run this command to view the available metadata fields from the Amazon EC2 metadata service:

   ```
   curl 169.254.169.254/latest/meta-data/
   ```

7. Run this command to query the Amazon EC2 instance ID:

   ```
   curl 169.254.169.254/latest/meta-data/instance-id
   ```

8. Call **AWS Cloud API** using the AWS CLI. This command translates text from English to French and uses credentials from the AWS role you assigned to the instance. Enter the following command as a single line:

   ```
   aws translate translate-text --text "Hello world." --source-language-code
   en --target-language-code fr --region us-west-2
   ```

9. To review the credentials that are being passed to the instance, query the Amazon EC2 Metadata service:

   ```
   curl 169.254.169.254/latest/meta-data/iam/security-credentials/
   devassoc-webserver
   ```

Configure NAT for Instances in the Private Subnet

In this exercise, you'll create a security group for the NAT instance. NAT allows Amazon EC2 instances in the private subnet to make web requests to the internet, to update software packages, and to make API calls.

1. Select **Services ➢ VPC**.

2. From the **Security** section, select **Security Groups**.

3. Select **Create Security Group** and configure the properties as follows:

    - Set the **Name** tag to nat-sg.

    - Set the **Group name** to nat-sg.

    - Set the **Description** to Allow NAT instance to forward internet traffic.

    - Set **Amazon VPC** to devassoc.

4. Choose **Create** to save the group, and then choose **Close** to return to the list of security groups.

5. Select the **nat-sg** security group.

6. To modify the inbound rules, select the **Inbound Rules** tab and select **Edit rules**.

7. Select **Add Rule**, and set the following properties for the first rule:

    - From **Type**, select **HTTP (80)**.

    - For **Source**, enter **10.0.0.0/16**.

    - For **Description**, enter **Enable internet bound HTTP requests from VPC instances**.

8. Select **Add Rule**, and set the following properties for this rule:

    - From **Type**, select **HTTPS (443)**.

    - For **Source**, enter **10.0.0.0/16**.

    - For **Description**, enter **Enable internet bound HTTPS. requests from VPC instances**.

9. Select **Add Rule**, and set the following properties for this rule:

    - From **Type**, select **All ICMP – IPv4**.

    - For **Source**, enter **10.0.0.0/16**.

    - For **Description**, **Enable outbound PING requests from VPC instances**.

10. Choose **Save rules**.

11. Select **Services > EC2**.

12. Select **Instances**.

13. Paste the **Public subnet ID** into the filter box.

    Two results are displayed. The result with an empty name is your **NAT instance**.

14. To edit the name of the NAT instance, hover over the **name** field and select the **pencil** icon.

15. Enter the name **devassoc-nat** and press **Enter**.

16. Modify the security groups for **devassoc-nat** to include the **nat-sg** group as follows:

    - Select the **devassoc-nat** instance and select **Actions**.

    - Select **Networking > Change Security Groups**.

    - Select **nat-sg**. You can clear the default.

    - Select **Assign Security Group**.

EXERCISE 2.7

Launch an Amazon EC2 Instance into the Private Subnet

In this exercise, you'll launch an Amazon EC2 instance into the private subnet and then verify that the security group allows HTTP from anywhere. Because this instance is in the private subnet, it does not have a public IP address. Even though the instance can make outbound requests to the internet through the NAT instance, it is not reachable for inbound connections from the internet.

1. Select **Services > EC2**.

2. Choose **Launch Instance**.

3. Select **Amazon Linux 2 AMI**.

4. Select **t2.micro** and then choose **Next: Configure Instance Details**.

5. On the **Instance Details** page, provide the following values:

   - Select **Network > devassoc** VPC.

   - Select **Subnet > Private Subnet**.

   - Select **IAM Role > devassoc-webserver**.

   - Select **Advanced Details > User Data > As File**.

   - Download the code files from the book page at https://www.wiley.com/en-us/ AWS+Certified+Developer+Official+Study+Guide%3A+Associate+%28DVA+C01 %29+Exam-p-9781119508199. Click Downloads to access the Online Materials for Chapter 2..

(continued)

6. Choose **Next: Add Storage**.

7. Choose **Next: Add Tags**.

8. Select **Tags ➢ Add tag** and set the following values:

   ▪ For **Key**, enter **Name**.

   ▪ For **Value**, enter **private-instance**.

9. Choose **Next: Configure Security Group**.

10. For **Security Group**, set the following values:

    ▪ For **Security group name**, enter **open-http-ssh**.

    ▪ For **Description**: enter **HTTP and SSH from Anywhere**.

11. For the SSH rule, select **Source ➢ Anywhere**.

12. Select **Add Rule** and then configure the second rule:

    ▪ For **Type**, select HTTP.

    ▪ For **Source**, select Anywhere.

13. Choose **Review and Launch**.

14. Choose **Launch**.

15. Under **Select a key pair**, choose **devassoc** and select the check box acknowledging that you have access to the key pair.

16. Choose **Launch Instances**.

17. Select **View Instances**.

18. Select **private-instance**.

19. Copy the **Private IP** of the instance to the text document.

    Notice that the instance has no public IP address.

Make Requests to Private Instance

In this exercise, you will explore connectivity to the private instance.

1. From your web browser, navigate to the private IP of the instance. Though the security group is open to requests from anywhere, this will fail because the private IP address is not routable over the internet.

2. Select **Services ≻ EC2**.

3. From the list of instances, select **webserver**.

4. Select **Connect** and then follow the directions to establish an SSH connection.

5. From within the SSH session, make an HTTP request to the private server with curl. Replace the variable `private-ip-address` with the private IP address of **private-instance** address that you copied earlier.

    `curl private-ip-address`

6. Download the MP3 audio from the **private-instance** to **webserver** using curl as follows:

    `curl private-ip-address/instance.mp3 --output instance.mp3`

7. Make the file available for download from **webserver**:

    `sudo cp instance.mp3 /var/www/html/instance.mp3`

8. In your web browser, enter the following address. Substitute `public-ip-of-webserver` with the public IPv4 address of **webserver**, and listen to the MP3.

    `http://public-ip-of-webserver/instance.mp3`

Though the private web server is not reachable from the internet, you have confirmed that it is reachable to other instances within the same Amazon VPC. As part of the bootstrapping, the private instance made AWS API calls, which require the ability to make both web requests via the NAT gateway and credentials from an IAM role. You have confirmed that these requests succeeded by downloading the resulting MP3 file from **private-instance** and placing it on **webserver**.

EXERCISE 2.9

Launch an AWS Cloud9 Instance

In this exercise, you'll launch an Amazon EC2 instance that you will create in the AWS Cloud9 service. You will connect to this Amazon EC2 instance from the AWS Cloud9 console. You will then use the AWS Cloud9 IDE to edit files, build software, and execute commands on the terminal from your web browser.

1. To display the AWS Cloud9 dashboard, select **Services ≻ Cloud9**.

2. Select **Create Environment**.

3. For **Name**, enter **devassoc-c9** and then select **Next step**.

4. Select **Network settings ≻ Advanced**.

5. Select **Network (VPC) ≻ Amazon VPC ID** (copied earlier).

(continued)

6. Select **Subnet ➤ Subnet ID for the Public VPC** (copied earlier).

7. Select **Next step ➤ Create environment**.

8. When the AWS Cloud9 environment loads, run the following in the AWS Cloud9 terminal. Make sure to replace the IP address in the example command with the address you copied earlier for **private-instance**.

   ```
   curl private-ip
   ```

9. From the **private-instance,** download the MP3 audio to **devassoc-c9** using curl as follows:

   ```
   curl private-ip-address/instance.mp3 --output instance.mp3
   ```

10. To preview the file, in the navigation pane, double-click **instance.mp3**.

11. Open **README.md** in a text editor.

You now have a managed development environment in AWS that is connected to your isolated VPC.

EXERCISE 2.10

Perform Partial Cleanup

In this exercise, you will clean up unused instances and keep this Amazon VPC for future use. This partial cleanup reduces costs while providing an environment to complete future exercises. After partial cleanup, you may generate charges related to the Elastic IP address that was allocated for devassoc-nat but is not in use while that instance is stopped.

Complete the following tasks as part of the cleanup:

webserver: Terminate.

private-instance: Terminate.

devassoc-nat: Stop. You must start this instance again before completing any exercises that require Amazon EC2 to launch or interact with instances in the private subnet.

devassoc-c9: No action. The AWS Cloud9 service will automatically stop and start this instance.

1. Navigate to the **Services ➤ EC2**.

2. To view your Amazon EC2 instances, select **Instances**. Clear any filters if they are present.

3. Select **webserver** and **private-instance**.

4. Select **Actions ➢ Instance-State** and **Terminate**.

5. Clear **public-webserver** and **private-webserver**.

6. Select **devassoc-nat**.

7. Select **Actions ➢ Instance-State** and **Stop**.

EXERCISE 2.11

(Optional) Complete Cleanup

If you plan to perform future exercises in this guide, this exercise is optional.

In this exercise, you will remove all of the EC2 and VPC resources that remain after Exercise 2.10.

1. Navigate to the Amazon EC2 console, and view the list of running instances.

2. Select **devassoc-nat**.

3. Select **Actions ➢ Instance-State** and **Terminate**.

4. In the **Terminate Instances** dialog box, expand **Release attached Elastic IPs** and select **Release Elastic IPs**.

5. Select **Yes, Terminate**.

6. Navigate to the AWS Cloud9 dashboard (**Services ➢ Cloud9**).

7. Select the **devassoc-c9** environment.

8. On the **Environment Details** page, select **Delete** and follow the on-screen directions to delete the instance.

9. To view the Amazon VPC dashboard, select **Services ➢ VPC**.

10. Navigate to the **Elastic IPs** list.

11. Select any Elastic IPs that are *not associated with an instance*.

12. To release the Elastic IPs, select **Actions and Release Addresses**.

13. Select **Release**.

14. Select **Your VPCs**.

15. Select **devassoc**.

16. Select **Actions ➢ Delete VPC**.

17. Select **Delete VPC**.

If the Amazon VPC deletion fails, wait up to 30 minutes after deleting the Amazon EC2 instances and then try again.

Review Questions

1. When you launch an Amazon Elastic Compute Cloud (Amazon EC2) instance, which of the following is the most specific type of AWS entity in which you can place it?

   A. Region

   B. Availability Zone

   C. Edge location

   D. Data center

2. You have saved SSH connection information for an Amazon Elastic Compute Cloud (Amazon EC2) instance that you launched in a public subnet. You previously stopped the instance the last time you used it. Now that you have started the instance, you are unable to connect to the instance using the saved information. Which of the following could be the cause?

   A. Your SSH key pair has automatically expired.

   B. The public IP of the instance has changed.

   C. The security group rules have expired.

   D. SSH is enabled only for the first boot of an Amazon EC2 instance.

3. You are working from a new location today. You are unable to initiate a Remote Desktop Protocol (RDP) to your Windows instance, which is located in a public subnet. What could be the cause?

   A. Your new IP address may not match the inbound security group rules.

   B. Your new IP address may not match the outbound security group rules.

   C. RDP is not available for Windows instances, only SSH.

   D. RDP is enabled only for the first 24 hours of your instance runtime.

4. You have a backend Amazon EC2 instance providing a web service to your web server instances. Your web servers are in a public subnet. You would like to block inbound requests from the internet to your backend instance but still allow the instance to make API requests over the public internet. What steps must you take? (Select TWO.)

   A. Launch the instance in a private subnet and rely on a NAT gateway in a public subnet to forward outbound internet requests.

   B. Configure the security group for the instance to explicitly deny inbound requests from the internet.

   C. Configure the network access control list (network ACL) for the public subnet to explicitly deny inbound web requests from the internet.

   D. Modify the inbound security group rules for the instance to allow only inbound requests from your web servers.

5. You have launched an Amazon Elastic Compute Cloud (Amazon EC2) instance and loaded your application code on it. You have now discovered that the instance is missing applications on which your code depends. How can you resolve this issue?

   A. Modify the instance profile to include the software dependencies.

   B. Create an AWS Identity and Access Management (IAM) user, and sign in to the instance to install the dependencies.

   C. Sign in to the instance as the default user, and install any additional dependencies that you need.

   D. File an AWS Support ticket, and request to install the software on your instance.

6. How can code running on an Amazon Elastic Compute Cloud (Amazon EC2) instance automatically discover its public IP address?

   A. The public IP address is presented to the OS on the instance automatically. No extra steps are required.

   B. The instance can query another Amazon EC2 instance in the same Amazon Virtual Private Cloud (Amazon VPC).

   C. You must use a third-party service to look up the public IP.

   D. The instance can make an HTTP query to the Amazon EC2 metadata service at 169.254.169.254.

7. How can you customize the software of your Amazon Elastic Compute Cloud (Amazon EC2) instance beyond what the Amazon Machine Image (AMI) provides?

   A. Provide a user data attribute at launch that contains a script or directives to install additional packages.

   B. Additional packages are installed automatically by placing them in a special Amazon Simple Storage Service (Amazon S3) bucket in your account.

   C. You do not have permissions to install new software on Amazon EC2 aside from what is in the AMI.

   D. Unlock the instance using the AWS Key Management Service (AWS KMS) and then sign in to install new packages.

8. You have a process running on an Amazon Elastic Compute Cloud (Amazon EC2) instance that exceeds the 2 GB of RAM allocated to the instance. This is causing the process to run slowly. How can you resolve the issue?

   A. Stop the instance, change the instance type to one with more RAM, and then start the instance.

   B. Modify the RAM allocation for the instance while it is running.

   C. Take a snapshot of the data and then launch a new instance. You cannot change the RAM allocation.

   D. Send an email to AWS Support to install additional RAM on the server.

9. You have launched an Amazon Elastic Compute Cloud (Amazon EC2) Windows instance, and you would like to connect to it using the Remote Desktop Protocol. The instance is in a public subnet and has a public IP address. How do you find the password to the Administrator account?

    A. Decrypt the password by using the private key from the Amazon EC2 key pair that you used to launch the instance.

    B. Use the password that you provided when you launched the instance.

    C. Create a new AWS Identity and Access Management (IAM) role, and use the password for that role.

    D. Create an IAM user, and use the password for that user.

10. What steps must you take to ensure that an Amazon EC2 instance can receive web requests from customers on the internet? (Select THREE.)

    A. Assign a public IP address to the instance.

    B. Launch the instance in a subnet where the route table routes internet-bound traffic to an internet gateway.

    C. Launch the instance in a subnet where the route table rules send internet-bound traffic to a NAT gateway.

    D. Set the outbound rules for the security group to allow HTTP and HTTPS traffic.

    E. Set the inbound rules for the security group to allow HTTP and HTTPS traffic.

11. Which of the following are true about Amazon Machine Images (AMI)? (Select TWO.)

    A. AMI can be used to launch one or multiple Amazon EC2 instances.

    B. AMI is automatically available in all AWS Regions.

    C. All AMIs are created and maintained by AWS.

    D. AMIs are available for both Windows and Linux instances.

12. Which of the following are true about Amazon Elastic Compute Cloud (Amazon EC2) instance types? (Select TWO.)

    A. All Amazon EC2 instance types include instance store for ephemeral storage.

    B. All Amazon EC2 instance types can use EBS volumes for persistent storage.

    C. Amazon EC2 instances cannot be resized once launched.

    D. Some Amazon EC2 instances may have access to GPUs or other hardware accelerators.

13. Which of the following actions are valid based on the Amazon Elastic Compute Cloud (Amazon EC2) instance lifecycle? (Select TWO.)

    A. Starting a previously terminated instance

    B. Starting a previously stopped instance

    C. Rebooting a stopped instance

    D. Stopping a running instance

14. You have a development Amazon Elastic Compute Cloud (Amazon EC2) instance where you have installed Apache Web Server and MySQL. How do you verify that the web server application can communicate with the database given that they are both running on the same instance?

  A. Modify the security group for the instance.

  B. Assign the instance a public IP address.

  C. Modify the network access control list (network ACL) for the instance.

  D. No extra configuration is required.

15. What type of route must exist in the associated route table for a subnet to be a public subnet?

  A. A route to a VPN gateway

  B. Only the local route is required.

  C. A route to an internet gateway

  D. A route to a NAT gateway or NAT instance

  E. A route to an Amazon VPC endpoint

16. What type of route must exist in the associated route table for a subnet to be a private subnet that allows outbound internet access?

  A. A route to a VPN gateway

  B. Only the local route is required.

  C. A route to an internet gateway

  D. A route to a NAT gateway or NAT instance

  E. A route to an Amazon Virtual Private Cloud (Amazon VPC) endpoint

17. Which feature of Amazon Virtual Private Cloud (Amazon VPC) enables you to see which network requests are being accepted or rejected in your Amazon VPC?

  A. Internet gateway

  B. NAT gateway

  C. Route table

  D. Amazon VPC Flow Log

18. Which AWS service enables you to track the CPU utilization of an Amazon Elastic Compute Cloud (Amazon EC2) instance?

  A. AWS Config

  B. AWS Lambda

  C. Amazon CloudWatch

  D. Amazon Virtual Private Cloud (Amazon VPC)

19. What happens to the data stored on an Amazon Elastic Block Store (Amazon EBS) volume when you stop an Amazon Elastic Compute Cloud (Amazon EC2) instance?

  A. The data is moved to Amazon Simple Storage Service (Amazon S3).

  B. The data persists in the EBS volume.

  C. The volume is deleted.

  D. An EBS-backed instance cannot be stopped.

20. Which programming language can you use to write the code that runs on an Amazon EC2 instance?

    A. C++

    B. Java

    C. Ruby

    D. JavaScript

    E. Python

    F. All of the above

21. You have launched an Amazon EC2 instance in a public subnet. The instance has a public IP address, and you have confirmed that the Apache web server is running. However, your internet users are unable to make web requests to the instance. How can you resolve the issue? (Select TWO.)

    A. Modify the security group to allow outbound traffic on port 80 to anywhere.

    B. Modify the security group for the web server to allow inbound traffic port 80 from anywhere.

    C. Modify the security group for the web server to allow inbound traffic on port 443 from anywhere.

    D. Modify the security group to allow outbound traffic from port 443 to anywhere.

22. Which of the following are the customer's responsibility concerning Amazon EC2 instances? (Select TWO.)

    A. Decommissioning storage hardware

    B. Patching the guest operating system

    C. Securing physical access to the host machine

    D. Managing the sign-in accounts and credentials on the guest operating system

    E. Maintaining the software that runs on the underlying host machine

Chapter

3

Hello, Storage

**THE AWS CERTIFIED DEVELOPER –
ASSOCIATE EXAM TOPICS COVERED IN
THIS CHAPTER MAY INCLUDE, BUT ARE
NOT LIMITED TO, THE FOLLOWING:**

Domain 2: Security

✓ 2.2   Implement encryption using AWS services.

✓ 2.3   Implement application authentication and
authorization.

Domain 3: Development with AWS Services

✓ 3.2   Translate functional requirements into application
design.

✓ 3.3   Implement application design into application code.

✓ 3.4   Write code that interacts with AWS services by using
APIs, SDKs, and AWS CLI.

Domain 4: Refactoring

✓ 4.1   Optimize application to best use AWS services and
features.

Domain 5: Monitoring and Troubleshooting

✓ 5.2   Perform root cause analysis on faults found in
testing or production.

Introduction to AWS Storage

Cloud storage is a critical component of cloud computing, holding the information used by applications built by developers. In this chapter, we will walk you through the portfolio of storage services that AWS offers and decompose some phrases that you might have heard, such as *data lake*.

The internet era brought about new challenges for data storage and processing, which prompted the creation of new technologies. The latest generation of data stores are no longer multipurpose, single-box systems. Instead, they are complex, distributed systems optimized for a particular type of task at a particular scale. Because no single data store is ideal for all workloads, choosing a data store for the entire system will no longer serve you well. Instead, you need to consider each individual workload or component within the system and choose a data store that is right for it.

The AWS Cloud is a reliable, scalable, and secure location for your data. Cloud storage is typically more reliable, scalable, and secure than traditional, on-premises storage systems. AWS offers *object storage*, *file storage*, *block storage*, and data transfer services, which we will explore in this chapter. Figure 3.1 shows the storage and data transfer options on AWS.

FIGURE 3.1   The AWS storage portfolio

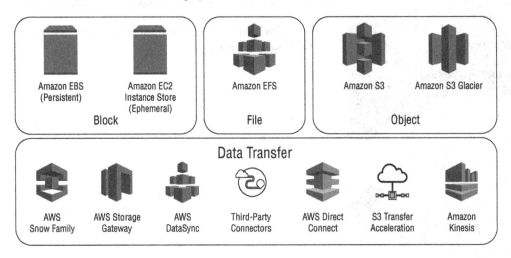

This chapter covers how to provision storage using just-in-time purchasing, which helps you avoid overprovisioning and paying for unused storage into which you expect to grow eventually.

Storage Fundamentals

Before we explore the various AWS storage services, let's review a few storage fundamentals. As a developer, you are likely already familiar with block storage and the differences between hot and cold storage. Cloud storage introduces some new concepts such as object storage, and we will compare these new concepts with the traditional storage concepts with which you are already familiar. If you have been working on the cloud already, these fundamentals are likely a refresher for you.

The goal of this chapter is to produce a mental model that will allow you, as a developer, to make the right decisions for choosing and implementing the best storage options for your applications. With the right mental model, people can usually make the best decisions for their solutions.

The AWS storage portfolio mental model starts with the core data building blocks, which include block, file, and object storage. For block storage, AWS has *Amazon Elastic Block Store* (Amazon EBS). For file storage, AWS has *Amazon Elastic File System* (Amazon EFS). For object storage, AWS has *Amazon Simple Storage Service* (Amazon S3) and Amazon S3 Glacier. Figure 3.2 illustrates this set of storage building blocks.

FIGURE 3.2   A complete set of storage building blocks

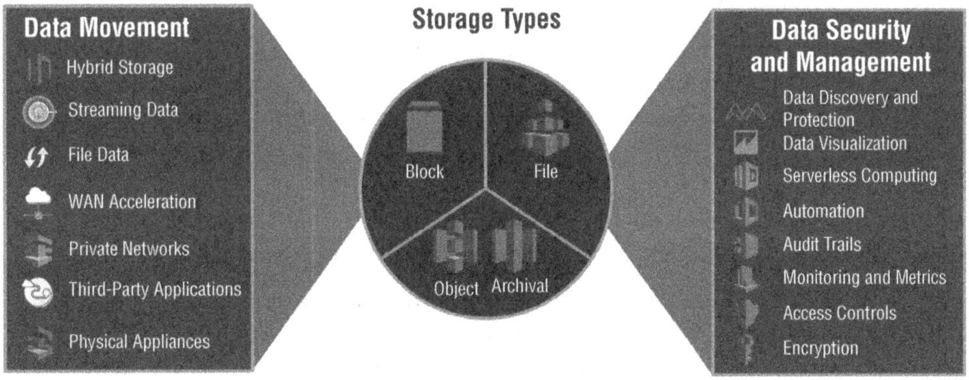

Data Dimensions

When investigating which storage options to use for your applications, consider the different dimensions of your data first. In other words, find the right tool for your data instead of squeezing your data into a tool that might not be the best fit.

So, before you start considering storage options, take time to evaluate your data and decide under which of these dimensions your data falls. This will help you make the correct decisions about what type of storage is best for your data.

> Think in terms of a data storage mechanism that is most suitable for a particular workload—not a single data store for the entire system. Choose the right tool for the job.

Velocity, Variety, and Volume

The first dimension to consider comprises the three Vs of big data: velocity, variety, and volume. These concepts are applicable to more than big data. It is important to identify these traits for any data that you are using in your applications.

Velocity   *Velocity* is the speed at which data is being read or written, measured in *reads per second* (RPS) or *writes per second* (WPS). The velocity can be based on batch processing, periodic, near-real-time, or real-time speeds.

Variety   *Variety* determines how structured the data is and how many different structures exist in the data. This can range from highly structured to loosely structured, unstructured, or *binary large object* (BLOB) data.

Highly structured data has a predefined schema, such as data stored in relational databases, which we will discuss in Chapter 4, "Hello, Databases." In highly structured data, each entity of the same type has the same number and type of attributes, and the domain of allowed values for an attribute can be further constrained. The advantage of highly structured data is its self-described nature.

Loosely structured data has entities, which have attributes/fields. Aside from the field uniquely identifying an entity, however, the attributes are not required to be the same in every entity. This data is more difficult to analyze and process in an automated fashion, putting more of the burden of reasoning about the data on the consumer or application.

Unstructured data does not have any sense or structure. It has no entities or attributes. It can contain useful information, but it must be extracted by the consumer of the data.

BLOB data is useful as a whole, but there is often little benefit in trying to extract value from a piece or attribute of a BLOB. Therefore, the systems that store this data typically treat it as a black box and only need to be able to store and retrieve a BLOB as a whole.

Volume   *Volume* is the total size of the dataset. There are two main uses for data: developing valuable insight and storage for later use. When getting valuable insights from data, having more data is often preferable to using better models. When keeping data for later use, be it for digital assets or backups, the more data that you can store, the less you need to guess what data to keep and what to throw away. These two uses prompt you to collect as much data as you can store, process, and afford to keep.

Typical metrics that measure the ability of a data store to support volume are maximum storage capacity and cost (such as $/GB).

Storage Temperature

Data temperature is another useful way of looking at data to determine the right storage for your application. It helps us understand how "lively" the data is: how much is being written or read and how soon it needs to be available.

Hot   *Hot data* is being worked on actively; that is, new ingests, updates, and transformations are actively contributing to it. Both reads and writes tend to be single-item. Items tend to be small (up to hundreds of kilobytes). Speed of access is essential. Hot data tends to be high-velocity and low-volume.

Warm   *Warm data* is still being actively accessed, but less frequently than hot data. Often, items can be as small as in hot workloads but are updated and read in sets. Speed of access, while important, is not as crucial as with hot data. Warm data is more balanced across the velocity and volume dimensions.

Cold   *Cold data* still needs to be accessed occasionally, but updates to this data are rare, so reads can tolerate higher latency. Items tend to be large (tens of hundreds of megabytes or gigabytes). Items are often written and read individually. High durability and low cost are essential. Cold data tends to be high-volume and low-velocity.

Frozen   *Frozen data* needs to be preserved for business continuity or for archival or regulatory reasons, but it is not being worked on actively. While new data is regularly added to this data store, existing data is never updated. Reads are extremely infrequent (known as "write once, read never") and can tolerate very high latency. Frozen data tends to be extremely high-volume and extremely low-velocity.

The same data can start as hot and gradually cool down. As it does, the tolerance of read latency increases, as does the total size of the dataset. Later in this chapter, we explore individual AWS services and discuss which services are optimized for the dimensions that we have discussed so far.

Data Value

Although we would like to extract useful information from all of the data we collect, not all data is equally important to us. Some data has to be preserved at all costs, and other data can be easily regenerated as needed or even lost without significant impact on the business. Depending on the value of data, we are more or less willing to invest in additional durability.

To optimize cost and/or performance further, segment data within each workload by value and temperature, and consider different data storage options for different segments.

Transient data *Transient data* is often short-lived. The loss of some subset of transient data does not have significant impact on the system as a whole. Examples include clickstream or Twitter data. We often do not need high durability of this data, because we expect it to be quickly consumed and transformed further, yielding higher-value data. If we lose a tweet or a few clicks, this is unlikely to affect our sentiment analysis or user behavior analysis.

Not all streaming data is transient, however. For example, for an *intrusion detection system* (IDS), every record representing network communication can be valuable because every log record can be valuable for a monitoring/alarming system.

Reproducible data *Reproducible data* contains a copy of useful information that is often created to improve performance or simplify consumption, such as adding more structure or altering a structure to match consumption patterns. Although the loss of some or all of this data may affect a system's performance or availability, this will not result in data loss, because the data can be reproduced from other data sources.

Examples include data warehouse data, read replicas of OLTP (online transaction processing) systems, and many types of caches. For this data, we may invest a bit in durability to reduce the impact on system's performance and availability, but only to a point.

Authoritative data *Authoritative data* is the source of truth. Losing this data will have significant business impact because it will be difficult, or even impossible, to restore or replace it. For this data, we are willing to invest in additional durability. The greater the value of this data, the more durability we will want.

Critical/Regulated data *Critical or regulated data* is data that a business must retain at almost any cost. This data tends to be stored for long periods of time and needs to be protected from accidental and malicious changes—not just data loss or corruption. Therefore, in addition to durability, cost and security are equally important factors.

One Tool Does Not Fit All

Despite the many applications of a hammer, it cannot replace a screwdriver or a pair of pliers. Likewise, there is no one-size-fits-all solution for data storage. Analyze your data and understand the dimensions that we have discussed. Once you have done that, then you can move on to reviewing the different storage options available on AWS to find the right tool to store and access your files.

For the exam, know the availability, level of durability, and cost factors for each storage option and how they compare.

Block, Object, and File Storage

There are three types of cloud storage: object, file, and block. Each offers its own unique advantages.

Block Storage

Some enterprise applications, like databases or *enterprise resource planning systems* (ERP systems), can require dedicated, low-latency storage for each host. This is analogous to *direct-attached storage* (DAS) or a *storage area network* (SAN). Block-based cloud storage solutions like Amazon EBS are provisioned with each Amazon Elastic Compute Cloud (Amazon EC2) instance and offer the ultra-low latency required for high-performance workloads.

Object Storage

Applications developed on the cloud often take advantage of object storage's vast scalability and metadata characteristics. Object storage solutions like Amazon S3 are ideal for building modern applications from scratch that require scale and flexibility and can also be used to import existing data stores for analytics, backup, or archive.

Cloud object storage makes it possible to store virtually limitless amounts of data in its native format.

File Storage

Many applications need to access shared files and require a file system. This type of storage is often supported with a *network-attached storage* (NAS) server. File storage solutions like Amazon EFS are ideal for use cases such as large content repositories, development environments, media stores, or user home directories.

AWS Shared Responsibility Model and Storage

The AWS shared responsibility model is important to understand as it relates to cloud storage. AWS is responsible for securing the storage services. As a developer and customer, you are responsible for securing access to and using encryption on the artifacts you create or objects you store.

AWS makes this model simpler for you by allowing you to inherit certain compliance factors and controls, but you must still ensure that you are securing your data and files on the cloud. It is a best practice always to use the principle of least privilege as part of your responsibility for using AWS Cloud storage. For example, ensure that only those who need access to the file have access and ensure that read and write access are separated and controlled.

Confidentiality, Integrity, Availability Model

The *confidentiality, integrity, availability model* (CIA model) forms the fundamentals of information security, and you can apply the principles of the CIA model to AWS storage.

Confidentiality can be equated to the privacy level of your data. It refers to levels of encryption or access policies for your storage or individual files. With this principle, you will limit access to prevent accidental information disclosure by restricting permissions and enabling encryption.

Integrity refers to whether your data is trustworthy and accurate. For example, can you trust that the file you generated has not been changed when it is audited later?

> Restrict permission of who can modify data and enable backup and versioning.

Availability refers to the availability of a service on AWS for storage, where an authorized party can gain reliable access to the resource.

> Restrict permission of who can delete data, enable multi-factor authentication (MFA) for Amazon S3 delete operation, and enable backup and versioning.

Figure 3.3 shows the CIA model.

FIGURE 3.3   The CIA model

AWS storage services provide many features for maintaining the desired level of confidentiality, integrity, and availability. Each of these features is discussed under its corresponding storage-option section in this chapter.

AWS Block Storage Services

Let's begin with the storage to which you are most likely already accustomed as a developer; that is, block storage.

Amazon Elastic Block Store

Amazon EBS presents your data to your Amazon EC2 instance as a disk volume, providing the lowest-latency access to your data from single Amazon EC2 instances.

Amazon EBS provides durable and persistent block storage volumes for use with Amazon EC2 instances. Each Amazon EBS volume is automatically replicated within its Availability Zone to protect your information from component failure, offering high availability and durability. Amazon EBS volumes offer the consistent and low-latency performance needed to run your workloads. With Amazon EBS, you can scale your usage up or down within minutes, while paying only for what you provision.

Typical use cases for Amazon EBS include the following:

- Boot volumes on Amazon EC2 instances
- Relational and NoSQL databases
- Stream and log processing applications
- Data warehousing applications.
- Big data analytics engines (like the Hadoop/HDFS (Hadoop Distributed File System) ecosystem and Amazon EMR clusters)

Amazon EBS is designed to achieve the following:

- Availability of 99.999 percent
- Durability of replication within a single availability zone
- *Annual failure rate* (AFR) of between 0.1 and 0.2 percent

Amazon EBS volumes are 20 times more reliable than typical commodity disk drives, which fail with an AFR of around 4 percent.

Amazon EBS Volumes

Amazon EBS volumes persist independently from the running life of an Amazon EC2 instance. After a volume is attached to an instance, use it like any other physical hard drive.

Amazon EBS volumes are flexible. For current-generation volumes attached to current-generation instance types, you can dynamically increase size, modify provisioned input/output operations per second (IOPS) capacity, and change the volume type on live production volumes without service interruptions.

Amazon EBS provides the following volume types, which differ in performance characteristics and price so that you can tailor your storage performance and cost to the needs of your applications.

SSD-backed volumes   *Solid-state drive (SSD)–backed volumes* are optimized for transactional workloads involving frequent read/write operations with small I/O size, where the dominant performance attribute is IOPS.

HDD-backed volumes   *Hard disk drive (HDD)–backed volumes* are optimized for large streaming workloads where throughput (measured in MiB/s) is a better performance measure than IOPS.

SSD vs. HDD Comparison

Table 3.1 shows a comparison of Amazon EBS HDD-backed and SSD-backed volumes.

TABLE 3.1   Volume Comparison

	SSD		HDD	
	General Purpose	Provisioned IOPS	Throughput-Optimized	Cold
Max volume size	16 TiB			
Max IOPS/volume	10,000	32,000	500	250
Max throughput/volume	160 MiB/s	500 MiB/s		250 MiB/s

Table 3.2 shows the most common use cases for the different types of Amazon EBS volumes.

TABLE 3.2   EBS Volume Use Cases

SSD		HDD	
General Purpose	Provisioned IOPS	Throughput-Optimized	Cold
▪ Recommended for most workloads ▪ System boot volumes ▪ Virtual desktops ▪ Low-latency interactive ▪ Apps ▪ Development and test environments	▪ I/O-intensive workloads ▪ Relational DBs ▪ NoSQL DBs	▪ Streaming workloads requiring consistent, fast throughput at a low price ▪ Big data ▪ Data warehouses ▪ Log processing ▪ Cannot be a boot volume	▪ Throughput-oriented storage for large volumes of data that is infrequently accessed ▪ Scenarios where the lowest storage cost is important ▪ Cannot be a boot volume

Elastic Volumes

Elastic Volumes is a feature of Amazon EBS that allows you to increase capacity dynamically, tune performance, and change the type of volume live. This can be done with no downtime or performance impact and with no changes to your application. Create a volume with the capacity and performance needed when you are ready to deploy your application, knowing that you have the ability to modify your volume configuration in the future and saving hours of planning cycles and preventing overprovisioning.

Amazon EBS Snapshots

You can protect your data by creating point-in-time snapshots of Amazon EBS volumes, which are backed up to Amazon S3 for long-term durability. The volume does not need to be attached to a running instance to take a *snapshot*.

As you continue to write data to a volume, periodically create a snapshot of the volume to use as a baseline for new volumes. These snapshots can be used to create multiple new Amazon EBS volumes or move volumes across Availability Zones.

When you create a new volume from a snapshot, it is an exact copy of the original volume at the time the snapshot was taken.

If you are taking snapshots at regular intervals, such as once per day, you may be concerned about the cost of the storage. Snapshots are incremental backups, meaning that only the blocks on the volume that have changed after your most recent snapshot are saved, making this a cost-effective way to back up your block data. For example, if you have a volume with 100 GiB of data, but only 5 GiB of data have changed since your last snapshot, only the 5 GiB of modified data is written to Amazon S3.

If you need to delete a snapshot, how do you know which snapshot to delete? Amazon EBS handles this for you. Even though snapshots are saved incrementally, the snapshot deletion process is designed so that you need to retain only the most recent snapshot to restore the volume. Amazon EBS will determine which dependent snapshots can be deleted to ensure that all other snapshots continue working.

Amazon EBS Optimization

Recall that Amazon EBS volumes are network-attached and not directly attached to the host like instance stores. On instances without support for Amazon EBS–optimized throughput, network traffic can contend with traffic between your instance and your Amazon EBS volumes. On *Amazon EBS–optimized instances*, the two types of traffic are kept separate. Some instance configurations incur an extra cost for using Amazon EBS–optimized, while others are always Amazon EBS–optimized at no extra cost.

Amazon EBS Encryption

For simplified *data* encryption, create encrypted Amazon EBS volumes with the Amazon EBS encryption feature. All Amazon EBS volume types support encryption, and you can use encrypted Amazon EBS volumes to meet a wide range of data-at-rest encryption requirements for regulated/audited data and applications.

Amazon EBS encryption uses 256-bit *Advanced Encryption Standard* (AES-256) algorithms and an Amazon-managed key infrastructure called *AWS Key Management Service* (AWS KMS). The encryption occurs on the server that hosts the Amazon EC2 instance, providing encryption of data in transit from the Amazon EC2 instance to Amazon EBS storage.

You can encrypt using an AWS KMS–generated key, or you can choose to select a *customer master key* (CMK) that you create separately using AWS KMS.

You can also encrypt your files prior to placing them on the volume. Snapshots of encrypted Amazon EBS volumes are automatically encrypted. Amazon EBS volumes that are restored from encrypted snapshots are also automatically encrypted.

Amazon EBS Performance

To achieve optimal performance from your Amazon EBS volumes in a variety of scenarios, use the following best practices:

Use Amazon EBS-optimized instances   The dedicated network throughput that you get when you request Amazon EBS–optimized support will make volume performance more predictable and consistent, and your Amazon EBS volume network traffic will not have to contend with your other instance traffic because they are kept separate.

Understand how performance is calculated   When you measure the performance of your Amazon EBS volumes, it is important to understand the units of measure involved and how performance is calculated.

Understand your workload   There is a relationship between the maximum performance of your Amazon EBS volumes, the size and number of I/O operations, and the time it takes for each action to complete. Each of these factors affects the others, and different applications are more sensitive to one factor or another.

On a given volume configuration, certain I/O characteristics drive the performance behavior for your Amazon EBS volumes. *SSD-backed volumes, General-Purpose SSD,* and *Provisioned IOPS SSD* deliver consistent performance whether an I/O operation is random or sequential. *HDD-backed volumes, Throughput-Optimized HDD,* and *Cold HDD* deliver optimal performance only when I/O operations are large and sequential.

To understand how SSD and HDD volumes will perform in your application, it is important to understand the connection between demand on the volume, the quantity of IOPS available to it, the time it takes for an I/O operation to complete, and the volume's throughput limits.

Be aware of the performance penalty when initializing volumes from snapshots   New Amazon EBS volumes receive their maximum performance the moment that they are available and do not require initialization (formerly known as *pre-warming*).

Storage blocks on volumes that were restored from snapshots, however, must be initialized (pulled down from Amazon S3 and written to the volume) before you can access the block. This preliminary action takes time and can cause a significant increase in the latency of an I/O operation the first time each block is accessed. Performance is restored after the data is accessed once.

For most applications, amortizing this cost over the lifetime of the volume is acceptable. For some applications, however, this performance hit is not acceptable. If that is the case, avoid a performance hit by accessing each block prior to putting the volume into production. This process is called *initialization*.

Factors that can degrade HDD performance   When you create a snapshot of a Throughput-Optimized HDD or Cold HDD volume, performance may drop as far as the volume's baseline value while the snapshot is in progress. This behavior is specific only to these volume types.

Other factors that can limit performance include the following:

- Driving more throughput than the instance can support
- The performance penalty encountered when initializing volumes restored from a snapshot
- Excessive amounts of small, random I/O on the volume

Increase read-ahead for high-throughput, read-heavy workloads   Some workloads are read-heavy and access the block device through the operating system *page cache* (for example, from a file system). In this case, to achieve the maximum throughput, we recommend that you configure the read-ahead setting to 1 MiB. This is a per-block-device setting that should be applied only to your HDD volumes.

Use RAID 0 to maximize utilization of instance resources   Some instance types can drive more I/O throughput than what you can provision for a single Amazon EBS volume. You can join multiple volumes of certain instance types together in a *RAID 0* configuration to use the available bandwidth for these instances.

Track performance with Amazon CloudWatch   *Amazon CloudWatch*, a monitoring and management service, provides performance metrics and status checks for your Amazon EBS volumes.

Amazon EBS Troubleshooting

If you are using an Amazon EBS volume as a boot volume, your instance is no longer accessible, and you cannot use *SSH* or *Remote Desktop Protocol* (RDP) to access that boot volume. There are some steps that you can take, however, to access the volume.

If you have an Amazon EC2 instance based on an *Amazon Machine Image* (AMI), you may just choose to terminate the instance and create a new one.

If you do need access to that Amazon EBS boot volume, perform the following steps to make it accessible:

1. Create a new Amazon EC2 instance with its own boot volume (a micro instance is great for this purpose).
2. Detach the root Amazon EBS volume from the troubled instance.
3. Attach the root Amazon EBS volume from the troubled instance to your new Amazon EC2 instance as a secondary volume.
4. Connect to the new Amazon EC2 instance, and access the files on the secondary volume.

Instance Store

Amazon EC2 *instance store* is another type of block storage available to your Amazon EC2 instances. It provides *temporary* block-level storage, and the storage is located on disks that are physically attached to the host computer (unlike Amazon EBS volumes, which are network-attached).

> If your data does not need to be resilient to *reboots*, *restarts*, or *auto recovery*, then your data may be a candidate for using instance store, but you should exercise caution.

Instance Store Volumes

Instance store should not be used for persistent storage needs. It is a type of ephemeral (short-lived) storage that does not persist if the instance fails or is terminated.

Because instance store is on the host of your Amazon EC2 instance, it will provide the lowest-latency storage to your instance other than RAM. Instance store volumes can be used when incurring large amounts of I/O for your application at the lowest possible latency. You need to ensure that you have another source of truth of your data, however, and that the only copy is not placed on instance store. For data that needs to be durable, we recommend using Amazon EBS volumes instead.

Not all instance types come with available instance store volume(s), and the size and type of volumes vary by instance type. When you launch an instance, the instance store is available at no additional cost, depending on the particular instance type. However, you must enable these volumes when you launch an Amazon EC2 instance, as you cannot add instance store volumes to an Amazon EC2 instance once it has been launched.

After you launch an instance, the instance store volumes are available to the instance, but you cannot access them until they are mounted. Refer to the AWS documentation for Amazon EBS to learn more about mounting these volumes on different operating systems.

Many customers use a combination of instance store and Amazon EBS volumes with their instances. For example, you may choose to place your scratch data, *tempdb*, or other temporary files on instance store while your root volume is on Amazon EBS.

> Do not use instance store for any production data.

Instance Store–Backed Amazon EC2 Instances

With Amazon EC2, you can use both instance store–backed storage volumes and Amazon EBS–backed storage volumes with your instances, meaning you can have your instance boot off instance store; however, you would want this configured so that you are using an AMI and that new instances will be created if one fails. This is not recommended for your primary instances where it would cause an issue for users if the instance fails. This configuration can save money on storage costs instead of using Amazon EBS as your boot volume in cases where your system is configured to be resilient to instances re-launching. It is critical to understand your application and infrastructure needs before choosing to use instance store-backed Amazon EC2 instances, so choose carefully.

Instance store–backed Amazon EC2 instances cannot be stopped and cannot take advantage of the auto recovery feature for Amazon EC2 instances.

Some AWS customers build instances on the fly that are completely resilient to reboot, relaunch, or failure and use instance store as their root volumes. This requires important due diligence regarding your application and infrastructure to ensure that this type of scenario would be right for you.

AWS Object Storage Services

Now we are going to dive into object storage. An *object* is a piece of data like a document, image, or video that is stored with some *metadata* in a flat structure. Object storage provides that data to applications via *application programming interfaces* (APIs) over the internet.

Amazon Simple Storage Service

Building a web application, which delivers content to users by retrieving data via making API calls over the internet, is not a difficult task with Amazon S3. Amazon Simple Storage Service (Amazon S3) is storage for the internet. It is a simple storage service that offers software developers a highly scalable, reliable, and low-latency data storage infrastructure at low cost. AWS has seen enormous growth with Amazon S3, and AWS currently has customers who store terabytes and exabytes of data.

Amazon S3 is featured in many AWS certifications because it is a core enabling service for many applications and use cases.

To begin developing with Amazon S3, it is important to understand a few basic concepts.

Buckets

A *bucket* is a container for objects stored in Amazon S3. Every object is contained in a bucket. You can think of a bucket in traditional terminology similar to a drive or volume.

Limitations

The following are limitations of which you should be aware when using Amazon S3 buckets:

- Do not use buckets as folders, because there is a maximum limit of 100 buckets per account.

- You cannot create a bucket within another bucket.

- A bucket is owned by the AWS account that created it, and bucket ownership is not transferable.

- A bucket must be empty before you can delete it.

- After a bucket is deleted, that name becomes available to reuse, but the name might not be available for you to reuse for various reasons, such as someone else taking the name after you release it when deleting the bucket. If you expect to use same bucket name, do not delete the bucket.

You can only create up to 100 buckets per account. Do not use buckets as folders or design your application in a way that could result in more than 100 buckets as your application or data grows.

Universal Namespace

A bucket name must be unique across all existing bucket names in Amazon S3 across all of AWS—not just within your account or within your chosen AWS Region. You must comply with *Domain Name System* (DNS) naming conventions when choosing a bucket name.

The rules for DNS-compliant bucket names are as follows:

- Bucket names must be at least 3 and no more than 63 characters long.

- A bucket name must consist of a series of one or more labels, with adjacent labels separated by a single period (.).

- A bucket name must contain lowercase letters, numbers, and hyphens.

- Each label must start and end with a lowercase letter or number.

- Bucket names must not be formatted like *IP addresses* (for example, 192.168.5.4).

- AWS recommends that you do not use periods (.) in bucket names. When using virtual hosted-style buckets with *Secure Sockets Layer* (SSL), the SSL wildcard certificate only matches buckets that do not contain periods. To work around this, use HTTP or write your own certificate verification logic.

Amazon S3 bucket names must be universally unique.

Table 3.3 shows examples of invalid bucket names.

TABLE 3.3   Invalid Bucket Names

Bucket Name	Reason
.myawsbucket	The bucket name cannot start with a period (.).
myawsbucket.	The bucket name cannot end with a period (.).
my..examplebucket	There can be only one period between labels.

The following code snippet is an example of creating a bucket using Java:

```java
private static String bucketName     = "*** bucket name ***";
public static void main(String[] args) throws IOException {
AmazonS3 s3client = new AmazonS3Client(new ProfileCredentialsProvider());
s3client.setRegion(Region.getRegion(Regions.US_WEST_1));
if(!(s3client.doesBucketExist(bucketName))){
    // Note that CreateBucketRequest does not specify region. So bucket is
    // created in the region specified in the client.
    s3client.createBucket(new CreateBucketRequest(bucketName));
    }

// Get location.
String bucketLocation = s3client.getBucketLocation(new GetBucketLocationRequest
(bucketName));
System.out.println("bucket location = " + bucketLocation);
```

Versioning

Versioning is a means of keeping multiple variants of an object in the same bucket. You can use versioning to preserve, retrieve, and restore every version of every object stored in your Amazon S3 bucket, including recovering deleted objects. With versioning, you can easily recover from both unintended user actions and application failures.

There are several reasons that developers will turn on versioning of files in Amazon S3, including the following:

- Protecting from accidental deletion
- Recovering an earlier version
- Retrieving deleted objects

Versioning is turned off by default. When you turn on versioning, Amazon S3 will create new versions of your object every time you overwrite a particular object key. Every time you update an object with the same key, Amazon S3 will maintain a new version of it.

In Figure 3.4, you can see that we have uploaded the same image multiple times, and all of the previous versions of those files have been maintained.

FIGURE 3.4 Amazon S3 versioning

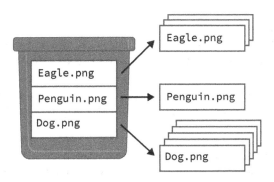

As those additional writes apply to a bucket, you can retrieve any of the particular objects that you need using GET on the object key name and the particular version. Amazon S3 versioning *tracks the changes over time.*

Amazon S3 versioning also protects against unintended deletes. If you issue a delete command against an object in a versioned bucket, AWS places a delete marker on top of that object, which means that if you perform a GET on it, you will receive an error as if the object does not exist. However, an administrator, or anyone else with the necessary permissions, could remove the delete marker and access the data.

When a delete request is issued against a versioned bucket on a particular object, Amazon S3 still retains the data, but it removes access for users to retrieve that data.

Versioning-enabled buckets let you recover objects from accidental deletion or overwrite. Your bucket's versioning configuration can also be MFA Delete–enabled for an additional layer of security. MFA Delete is discussed later in this chapter.

If you overwrite an object, it results in a new object version in the bucket. You can always restore from any previous versions.

In one bucket, for example, you can have two objects with the same key, but different version IDs, such as photo.gif (version 111111) and photo.gif (version 121212). This is illustrated in Figure 3.5.

FIGURE 3.5   Amazon S3 object version IDs

Key = photo.gif
ID = 121212

Key = photo.gif
ID = 111111

Versioning Enabled

Later in this chapter, we will cover *lifecycle policies*. You can use versioning in combination with lifecycle policies to implement them if the object is the current or previous version. If you are concerned about building up many versions and using space for a particular object, configure a lifecycle policy that will delete the old version of the object after a certain period of time.

 It is easy to set up a lifecycle policy to control the amount of data that's being retained when you use versioning on a bucket.

If you need to discontinue versioning on a bucket, copy all of your objects to a new bucket that has versioning disabled and use that bucket going forward.

 Once you enable versioning on a bucket, it can never return to an unversioned state. You can, however, suspend versioning on that bucket.

It is important to be aware of the cost implications of the bucket that is versioning-enabled. When calculating cost for your bucket, you must calculate as though every version is a completely separate object that takes up the same space as the object itself. As you can probably guess, this option might be cost prohibitive for things like large media files or performing many updates on objects.

Region

Amazon S3 creates buckets in a region that you specify. You can choose any AWS Region that is geographically close to you to optimize latency, minimize costs, or address regulatory requirements.

Objects belonging to a bucket that you create in a specific AWS Region never leave that region unless you explicitly transfer them to another region.

Operations on Buckets

There are a number of different operations (API calls) that you can perform on Amazon S3 buckets. We will summarize a few of the most basic operations in this section. For more comprehensive information on all of the different operations that you can perform, refer to the Amazon S3 API Reference document available in the AWS Documentation repository. In this section, we show you how to create a bucket, list buckets, and delete a bucket.

CREATE A BUCKET

This sample Python code shows how to create a bucket:

```
import boto3

s3 = boto3.client('s3')
s3.create_bucket(Bucket='my-bucket')
```

LIST BUCKETS

This sample Python code demonstrates getting a list of all of the bucket names available:

```
import boto3

# Create an S3 client
s3 = boto3.client('s3')

# Call S3 to list current buckets
response = s3.list_buckets()

# Get a list of all bucket names from the response
buckets = [bucket['Name'] for bucket in response['Buckets']]

# Print out the bucket list
print("Bucket List: %s" % buckets)
```

DELETE A BUCKET

The following sample Java code shows you how to delete a bucket. Buckets must be empty before you can delete them, unless you use a force parameter.

```java
import java.io.IOException;

import com.amazonaws.AmazonServiceException;
import com.amazonaws.SdkClientException;
import com.amazonaws.auth.profile.ProfileCredentialsProvider;
import com.amazonaws.services.s3.AmazonS3;
import com.amazonaws.services.s3.AmazonS3ClientBuilder;
import com.amazonaws.services.s3.model.DeleteObjectRequest;

public class DeleteObjectNonVersionedBucket {

    public static void main(String[] args) throws IOException {
        String clientRegion = "*** Client region ***";
        String bucketName = "*** Bucket name ***";
        String keyName = "*** Key name ****";

        try {
            AmazonS3 s3Client = AmazonS3ClientBuilder.standard()
                    .withCredentials(new ProfileCredentialsProvider())
                    .withRegion(clientRegion)
                    .build();

            s3Client.deleteObject(new DeleteObjectRequest(bucketName, keyName));
        }
        catch(AmazonServiceException e) {
            // The call was transmitted successfully, but Amazon S3 couldn't process
            // it, so it returned an error response.
            e.printStackTrace();
        }
        catch(SdkClientException e) {
            // Amazon S3 couldn't be contacted for a response, or the client
            // couldn't parse the response from Amazon S3.
            e.printStackTrace();
        }
    }
}
```

AWS COMMAND LINE INTERFACE

The following is a sample AWS Command Line Interface (AWS CLI) command that will delete a bucket and will use the `--force` parameter to remove a nonempty bucket. This command deletes all objects first and then deletes the bucket.

```
$ aws s3 rb s3://bucket-name --force
```

Objects

You can store an unlimited number of objects within Amazon S3, but an object can only be between 1 byte to 5 TB in size. If you have objects larger than 5 TB, use a file splitter and upload the file in chunks to Amazon S3. Then reassemble them if you download the file parts for later use.

The largest object that can be uploaded in a single PUT is 5 GB. For objects larger than 100 MB, you should consider using multipart upload (discussed later in this chapter). For any objects larger than 5 GB, you must use multipart upload.

Object Facets

An object consists of the following facets:

Key   The *key* is the name that you assign to an object, which may include a simulated folder structure. Each key must be unique within a bucket (unless the bucket has versioning turned on).

Amazon S3 URLs can be thought of as a basic data map between "bucket + key + version" and the web service endpoint. For example, in the URL `http://doc.s3.amazonaws.com/2006-03-01/AmazonS3.wsdl`, doc is the name of the bucket and `2006-03-01/AmazonS3.wsdl` is the key.

Version ID   Within a bucket, a key and *version ID* uniquely identify an object. If versioning is turned off, you have only a single version. If versioning is turned on, you may have multiple versions of a stored object.

Value   The *value* is the actual content that you are storing. An object value can be any sequence of bytes, and objects can range in size from 1 byte up to 5 TB.

Metadata   *Metadata* is a set of name-value pairs with which you can store information regarding the object. You can assign metadata, referred to as *user-defined metadata*, to your objects in Amazon S3. Amazon S3 also assigns system metadata to these objects, which it uses for managing objects.

Subresources   Amazon S3 uses the *subresource* mechanism to store additional object-specific information. Because subresources are subordinates to objects, they are always associated with some other entity such as an object or a bucket. The subresources associated with Amazon S3 objects can include the following:

Access control list (ACL)   A list of grants identifying the grantees and the permissions granted.

Torrent   Returns the torrent file associated with the specific object.

Access Control Information   You can control access to the objects you store in Amazon S3. Amazon S3 supports both *resource-based access control*, such as an ACL and *bucket policies*, and *user-based access control*.

Object Tagging

Object tagging enables you to categorize storage. Each tag is a key-value pair. Consider the following tagging examples.

Suppose an object contains *protected health information* (PHI) data. You can tag the object using the following key-value pair:

```
PHI=True
```

or

```
Classification=PHI
```

> While it is acceptable to use tags to label objects containing confidential data (such as personally identifiable information (PII) or PHI), the tags themselves should not contain any confidential information.

Suppose that you store project files in your Amazon S3 bucket. You can tag these objects with a key called `Project` and a value, as shown here:

```
Project=Blue
```

You can add multiple tags to a single object, such as the following:

```
Project=SalesForecast2018
Classification=confidential
```

You can tag new objects when you upload them, or you can add them to existing objects. Note the following limitations when working with tagging:

- You can associate 10 tags with an object, and each tag associated with an object must have unique tag keys.
- A tag key can be up to 128 Unicode characters in length, and tag values can be up to 256 Unicode characters in length.

Keys and values are case sensitive.

Developers commonly categorize their files in a folder-like structure in the key name (remember, Amazon S3 has a flat file structure), such as the following:

```
photos/photo1.jpg
project/projectx/document.pdf
project/projecty/document2.pdf
```

This allows you to have only one-dimensional categorization, meaning that everything under a prefix is one category.

With tagging, you now have another dimension. If your *photo1* is in *project x* category, tag the object accordingly. In addition to data classification, tagging offers the following benefits:

- Object tags enable fine-grained access control of permissions. For example, you could grant an AWS Identity and Access Management (IAM) user permissions to read-only objects with specific tags.

- Object tags enable fine-grained object lifecycle management in which you can specify a tag-based filter, in addition to key name prefix, in a lifecycle rule.

- When using Amazon S3 analytics, you can configure filters to group objects together for analysis by object tags, by key name prefix, or by both prefix and tags.

- You can also customize Amazon CloudWatch metrics to display information by specific tag filters. The following sections provide details.

Cross-Origin Resource Sharing

Cross-Origin Resource Sharing (CORS) defines a way for client web applications that are loaded in one domain to interact with resources in a different domain. With CORS support in Amazon S3, you can build client-side web applications with Amazon S3 and selectively allow cross-origin access to your Amazon S3 resources while avoiding the need to use a proxy.

Cross-Origin Request Scenario

Suppose that you are hosting a website in an Amazon S3 bucket named *website* on Amazon S3. Your users load the website endpoint: `http://website.s3-website-us-east-1.amazonaws.com`.

Your website will use JavaScript on the web pages that are stored in this bucket to be able to make authenticated GET and PUT requests against the same bucket by using the Amazon S3 API endpoint for the bucket: `website.s3.amazonaws.com`.

A browser would normally block JavaScript from allowing those requests, but with CORS, you can configure your bucket to enable cross-origin requests explicitly from `website.s3-website-us-east-1.amazonaws.com`.

 Suppose that you host a web font from your Amazon S3 bucket. Browsers require a CORS check (also referred as a *preflight check*) for loading web fonts, so you would configure the bucket that is hosting the web font to allow any origin to make these requests.

There are no coding exercises as part of the exam, but these case studies can help you visualize how to use Amazon S3 and CORS.

Operations on Objects

There are a number of different operations (API calls) that you can perform on Amazon S3 buckets. We will summarize a few of the most basic operations in this section. For more comprehensive information on all of the different operations that you can perform, refer to the Amazon S3 API Reference document available in the AWS Documentation repository.

WRITE AN OBJECT

This sample Java code shows how to add an object to a bucket:

```
import boto3

# Create an S3 client
s3 = boto3.client('s3')

filename = 'file.txt'
bucket_name = 'my-bucket'

# Uploads the given file using a managed uploader, which will split up large
# files automatically and upload parts in parallel.
s3.upload_file(filename, bucket_name, filename)
```

READING OBJECTS

The following Java code example demonstrates getting a stream on the object data of a particular object and processing the response:

```
AmazonS3 s3Client = new AmazonS3Client(new ProfileCredentialsProvider());
S3Object object = s3Client.getObject(
                new GetObjectRequest(bucketName, key));
InputStream objectData = object.getObjectContent();
// Process the objectData stream.
objectData.close();
```

DELETING OBJECTS

You can delete one or more objects directly from Amazon S3. You have the following options when deleting an object:

Delete a Single Object   Amazon S3 provides the DELETE API to delete one object in a single HTTP request.

Delete Multiple Objects   Amazon S3 also provides the Multi-Object Delete API to delete up to 1,000 objects in a single HTTP request.

The following Java sample demonstrates deleting an object by providing the bucket name and key name:

```
AmazonS3 s3client = new AmazonS3Client(new ProfileCredentialsProvider());
s3client.deleteObject(new DeleteObjectRequest(bucketName, keyName));
```

This next Java sample demonstrates deleting a versioned object by providing a bucket name, object key, and a version ID:

```
AmazonS3 s3client = new AmazonS3Client(new ProfileCredentialsProvider());
s3client.deleteObject(new DeleteVersionRequest(bucketName, keyName,
versionId));
```

List Keys   The following Java code example lists object keys in a bucket:

```
private static String bucketName = "***bucket name***";
AmazonS3 s3client = new AmazonS3Client(new ProfileCredentialsProvider());
System.out.println("Listing objects");
        final ListObjectsV2Request req = new ListObjectsV2Request().
withBucketName(bucketName).withMaxKeys(2);
        ListObjectsV2Result result;
        do {
            result = s3client.listObjectsV2(req);

            for (S3ObjectSummary objectSummary :
                result.getObjectSummaries()) {
                System.out.println(" - " + objectSummary.getKey() + "  " +
                    "(size = " + objectSummary.getSize() +
                    ")");
            }
System.out.println("Next Continuation Token : " +
result.getNextContinuationToken());

req.setContinuationToken(result.getNextContinuationToken());
        } while(result.isTruncated() == true );
```

Storage Classes

There are several different storage classes from which to choose when using Amazon S3. Your choice will depend on your level of need for durability, availability, and performance for your application.

Amazon S3 Standard

Amazon S3 Standard offers high-durability, high-availability, and performance-object storage for frequently accessed data. Because it delivers low latency and high throughput, Amazon S3 Standard is ideal for a wide variety of use cases, including the following:

- Cloud applications
- Dynamic websites
- Content distribution
- Mobile and gaming applications
- Big data analytics

Amazon S3 Standard is designed to achieve durability of 99.999999999 percent of objects (designed to sustain the loss of data in two facilities) and availability of 99.99 percent over a given year (which is backed by the Amazon S3 Service Level Agreement).

Essentially, the data in Amazon S3 is spread out over multiple facilities within a region. You can lose access to two facilities and still have access to your files.

Reduced Redundancy Storage

Reduced Redundancy Storage (RRS) (or Reduced_Redundancy) is an Amazon S3 storage option that enables customers to store noncritical, reproducible data at lower levels of redundancy than Amazon S3 Standard storage. It provides a highly available solution for distributing or sharing content that is durably stored elsewhere or for objects that can easily be regenerated, such as thumbnails or transcoded media.

The RRS option stores objects on multiple devices across multiple facilities, providing 400 times the durability of a typical disk drive, but it does not replicate objects as many times as Amazon S3 Standard storage.

RRS is designed to achieve availability of 99.99 percent (same as Amazon S3 Standard) and durability of 99.99 percent (designed to sustain the loss of data in a single facility).

Amazon S3 Standard-Infrequent Access

Amazon S3 Standard-Infrequent Access (Standard_IA) is an Amazon S3 storage class for data that is accessed less frequently but requires rapid access when needed. It offers the same high durability, throughput, and low latency of Amazon S3 Standard, but it has a lower per-gigabyte storage price and per-gigabyte retrieval fee.

The ideal use cases for using Standard_IA include the following:

- Long-term storage
- Backups
- Data stores for disaster recovery

Standard_IA is set at the object level and can exist in the same bucket as Amazon S3 Standard, allowing you to use lifecycle policies to transition objects automatically between storage classes without any application changes.

Standard_IA is designed to achieve availability of 99.9 percent (but low retrieval time) and durability of 99.999999999 percent of objects over a given year (same as Amazon S3 Standard).

Amazon S3 One Zone-Infrequent Access

Amazon S3 One Zone-Infrequent Access (OneZone_IA) is similar to Amazon S3 Standard-IA. The difference is that the data is stored only in a single Availability Zone instead of a minimum of three Availability Zones. Because of this, storing data in OneZone_IA costs 20 percent less than storing it in Standard_IA. Because of this approach, however, any data stored in this storage class will be permanently lost in the event of an Availability Zone destruction.

Amazon Simple Storage Service Glacier

Amazon Simple Storage Service Glacier (Amazon S3 Glacier) is a secure, durable, and extremely low-cost storage service for data archiving that offers the same high durability as Amazon S3. Unlike Amazon S3 Standard's immediate retrieval times, Amazon S3 Glacier's retrieval times run from a few minutes to several hours.

To keep costs low, Amazon S3 Glacier provides three archive access speeds, ranging from minutes to hours. This allows you to choose an option that will meet your *recovery time objective* (RTO) for backups in your disaster recovery plan.

Amazon S3 Glacier can also be used to secure archives that need to be kept due to a compliance policy. For example, you may need to keep certain records for seven years before deletion and only need access during an audit. Amazon S3 Glacier allows redundancy in your files when audits do occur, but at an extremely low cost in exchange for slower access.

VAULTS

Amazon S3 Glacier uses *vaults* as containers to store archives. You can view a list of your vaults in the *AWS Management Console* and use the *AWS software development kits* (SDKs) to perform a variety of vault operations, such as the following:

- Create vault
- Delete vault
- Lock vault
- List vault metadata
- Retrieve vault inventory
- Tag vaults for filtering
- Configure vault notifications

You can also set access policies for each vault to grant or deny specific activities to users. You can have up to 1,000 vaults per AWS account.

Amazon S3 Glacier provides a management console to create and delete vaults. All other interactions with Amazon S3 Glacier, however, require that you use the AWS CLI or write code.

VAULT LOCK

Amazon S3 Glacier Vault Lock allows you to deploy and enforce compliance controls easily on individual Amazon S3 Glacier vaults via a lockable policy. You can specify controls such as *Write Once Read Many* (WORM) in a Vault Lock policy and lock the policy from future edits. Once locked, the policy becomes immutable, and Amazon S3 Glacier will enforce the prescribed controls to help achieve your compliance objectives.

Once you initiate a lock, you have 24 hours to validate your lock policy to ensure that it is working as you intended. Until that 24 hours is up, you can abort the lock and make changes. After 24 hours, that Vault Lock is permanent, and you will not be able to change it.

ARCHIVES

An *archive* is any object, such as a photo, video, or document that you store in a vault. It is a base unit of storage in Amazon S3 Glacier. Each archive has a unique ID and optional description. When you upload an archive, Amazon S3 Glacier returns a response that includes an archive ID. This archive ID is unique in the region in which the archive is stored. You can retrieve an archive using its ID, but not its description.

Amazon S3 Glacier provides a management console to create and delete vaults. However, all other interactions with Amazon S3 Glacier require that you use the AWS CLI or write code.

To upload archives into your vaults, you must either use the AWS CLI or write code to make requests, using either the *REST API* directly or the AWS SDKs.

MAINTAINING CLIENT-SIDE ARCHIVE METADATA

Except for the optional archive description, Amazon S3 Glacier does not support any additional metadata for the archives. When you upload an archive, Amazon S3 Glacier assigns an ID—an opaque sequence of characters—from which you cannot infer any meaning about the archive. Metadata about the archives can be maintained on the client side. The metadata can include identifying archive information such as the archive name.

If you use Amazon S3, when you upload an object to a bucket, you can assign the object an object key such as MyDocument.txt or SomePhoto.jpg. In Amazon S3 Glacier, you cannot assign a key name to the archives you upload.

If you maintain client-side archive metadata, note that Amazon S3 Glacier maintains a vault inventory that includes archive IDs and any descriptions that you provided during the archive upload. We recommend that you occasionally download the vault inventory to reconcile any issues in the client-side database that you maintain for the archive metadata. Amazon S3 Glacier takes vault inventory approximately once a day. When you request a vault inventory, Amazon S3 Glacier returns the last inventory it prepared, which is a point-in-time snapshot.

USING THE AWS SDKS WITH AMAZON S3 GLACIER

AWS provides SDKs for you to develop applications for Amazon S3 Glacier in various programming languages.

The AWS SDKs for Java and .NET offer both high-level and low-level wrapper libraries. The SDK libraries wrap the underlying Amazon S3 Glacier API, simplifying your programming tasks. The low-level wrapper libraries map closely to the underlying REST API supported by Amazon S3 Glacier. To simplify application development further, these SDKs also offer a higher-level abstraction for some of the operations in the high-level API. For example, when uploading an archive using the low-level API, if you need to provide a checksum of the payload, the high-level API computes the checksum for you.

ENCRYPTION

All data in Amazon S3 Glacier will be encrypted on the server side using key management and key protection, which Amazon S3 Glacier handles using AES-256 encryption. If you want, you can manage your own keys and encrypt the data prior to uploading.

RESTORING OBJECTS FROM AMAZON S3 GLACIER

Objects in the Amazon S3 Glacier storage class are not immediately accessible and cannot be retrieved via copy/paste once they have been moved to Amazon S3 Glacier.

Remember that Amazon S3 Glacier charges a retrieval fee for retrieving objects. When you restore an archive, you pay for both the archive and the restored copy. Because there is a storage cost for the copy, restore objects only for the duration that you need them. If you need a permanent copy of the object, create a copy of it in your Amazon S3 bucket.

ARCHIVE RETRIEVAL OPTIONS

There are several different options for restoring archived objects from Amazon S3 Glacier to Amazon S3, as shown in Table 3.4.

TABLE 3.4   Amazon S3 Glacier Archive Retrieval Options

Retrieval Option	Retrieval Time	Note
Expedited retrieval	1–5 minutes	
On-Demand		Processed immediately the vast majority of the time. During high demand, may fail to process, and you will be required to repeat the request.
Provisioned		Guaranteed to process immediately. After purchasing provisioned capacity, all of your retrievals are processed in this manner.
Standard retrieval	3–5 hours	
Bulk retrieval	5–12 hours	Lowest-cost option

Do not use Amazon S3 Glacier for backups if your RTO is shorter than the lowest Amazon S3 Glacier retrieval time for your chosen retrieval option. For example, if your RTO requires data retrieval of two hours in a disaster recovery scenario, then Amazon S3 Glacier standard retrieval will not meet your RTO.

Storage Class Comparison

Table 3.5 shows a comparison of the Amazon S3 storage classes. This is an important table for the certification exam. Many storage decision questions on the exam center on the level of durability, availability, and cost. The table's comparisons can help you make the right choice for a question, in addition to understanding trade-offs when choosing a data store for an application.

TABLE 3.5   Amazon S3 Storage Class Comparison

	Standard	Standard_IA	OneZone_IA	Amazon S3 Glacier
Designed for durability	99.999999999%*			
Designed for availability	99.99%	99.9%	99.%%	N/A
Availability SLAs	99.9%	99%		N/A
Availability zones	≥3		1	≥3
Minimum capacity charge per object	N/A	128 KB*		N/A
Minimum storage duration charge	N/A	30 days		90 days
Retrieval fee	N/A	Per GB retrieved*		
First byte latency	milliseconds			Minutes or hours*
Storage type	Object			
Lifecycle transitions	Yes			

* Because One Zone_IA stores data in a single Availability Zone, data stored in this storage class will be lost in the event of Availability Zone destruction. Standard_IA has a minimum object size of 128 KB. Smaller objects will be charged for 128 KB of storage. Amazon S3 Glacier allows you to select from multiple retrieval tiers based upon your needs.

Data Consistency Model

When deciding whether to choose Amazon S3 or Amazon EBS for your application, one important aspect to consider is the *consistency model* of the storage option. Amazon EBS provides read-after-write consistency for all operations, whereas Amazon S3 provides read-after-write consistency only for PUTs of new objects.

Amazon S3 offers eventual consistency for overwrite PUTs and DELETEs in all regions, and updates to a single key are atomic. For example, if you PUT an object to update an existing object and immediately attempt to read that object, you may read either the old data or the new data.

For PUT operations with new objects not yet in Amazon S3, you will experience read-after-write consistency. For PUT updates when you are overwriting an existing file or DELETE operations, you will experience eventual consistency.

Amazon S3 does not currently support object locking. If two PUT requests are simultaneously made to the same key, the request with the latest time stamp wins. If this is an issue, you will be required to build an object locking mechanism into your application.

You may be wondering why Amazon S3 was designed with this style of consistency. The *consistency, availability, and partition tolerance* theorem (CAP theorem) states that you can highly achieve only two out of the three dimensions for a particular storage design. The CAP theorem is shown in Figure 3.6.

FIGURE 3.6   CAP theorem

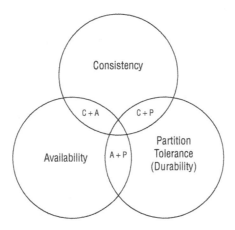

Think of partition tolerance in this equation as the storage durability. Amazon S3 was designed for high availability and high durability (multiple copies across multiple facilities), so the design trade-off is the consistency. When you PUT an object, you are not only putting the object into one location but into three, meaning that there is either a slightly increased latency on the read-after-write consistency of a PUT or eventual consistency on the PUT update or DELETE operations while Amazon S3 reconciles all copies. You do not know, for instance, which facility a file is coming from when you GET an object. If you had recently written an object, it may have propagated to only two facilities, so when you try to read the object right after your PUT, you may receive the old object or the new object.

Concurrent Applications

As a developer, it is critical to consider the way your application works and the consistency needs of your files. If your application requires read-after-write consistency on all operations, then Amazon S3 is not going to be the right choice for that application. If you are working with concurrent applications, it is important to know how your application performs PUT, GET, and DELETE operations *concurrently* to know whether eventual consistency will not be the right choice for your application.

In Figure 3.7, Amazon S3, both W1 (write 1) and W2 (write 2) complete before the start of R1 (read 1) and R2 (read 2). For a consistent read, R1 and R2 both return color = ruby. For an eventually consistent read, R1 and R2 might return color = red, color = ruby, or no results, depending on the amount of time that has elapsed.

FIGURE 3.7   Consistency example 1

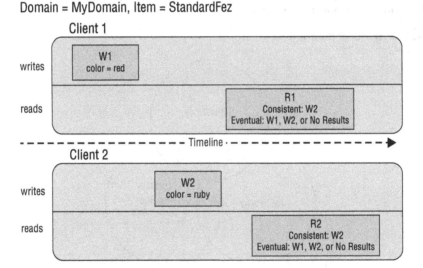

In Figure 3.8, W2 does not complete before the start of R1. Therefore, R1 might return color = ruby or color = garnet for either a consistent read or an eventually consistent read. Depending on the amount of time that has elapsed, an eventually consistent read might also return no results.

FIGURE 3.8   Consistency example 2

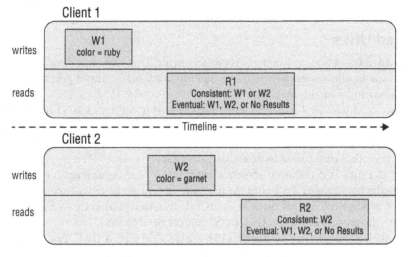

For a consistent read, R2 returns color = garnet. For an eventually consistent read, R2 might return color = ruby, color = garnet, or no results depending on the amount of time that has elapsed.

In Figure 3.9, client 2 performs W2 before Amazon S3 returns a success for W1, so the outcome of the final value is unknown (color = garnet or color = brick). Any subsequent reads (consistent read or eventually consistent) might return either value. Depending on the amount of time that has elapsed, an eventually consistent read might also return no results.

FIGURE 3.9   Consistency example 3

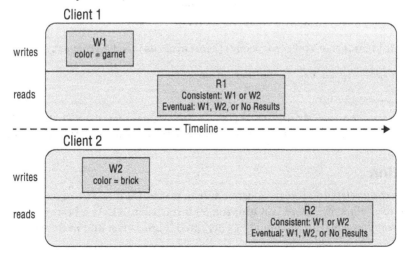

If you need a strongly consistent data store, choose a different data store than Amazon S3 or code consistency checks into your application.

Presigned URLs

A *presigned URL* is a way to grant access to an object. One way that developers use presigned URLs is to allow users to upload or download objects without granting them direct access to Amazon S3 or the account.

For example, if you need to send a document hosted in an Amazon S3 bucket to an external reviewer who is outside of your organization, you do not want to grant them access using IAM to your bucket or objects. Instead, generate a presigned URL to the object and send that to the user to download your file.

Another example is if you need someone external to your organization to upload a file. Maybe a media company is designing the graphics for the website you are developing. You can create a presigned URL for them to upload their artifacts directly to Amazon S3 without granting them access to your Amazon S3 bucket or account.

Anyone with valid security credentials can create a presigned URL. For you to upload an object successfully, however, the presigned URL must be created by someone who has permission to perform the operation upon which the presigned URL is based.

The following Java code example demonstrates generating a presigned URL:

```java
AmazonS3 s3Client = new AmazonS3Client(new ProfileCredentialsProvider());

java.util.Date expiration = new java.util.Date();
long msec = expiration.getTime();
msec += 1000 * 60 * 60; // Add 1 hour.
expiration.setTime(msec);

GeneratePresignedUrlRequest generatePresignedUrlRequest = new
GeneratePresignedUrlRequest(bucketName, objectKey);
generatePresignedUrlRequest.setMethod(HttpMethod.PUT);
generatePresignedUrlRequest.setExpiration(expiration);

URL s = s3client.generatePresignedUrl(generatePresignedUrlRequest);

// Use the pre-signed URL to upload an object.
```

Amazon S3 presigned URLs cannot be generated within the AWS Management Console, but they can be generated using the AWS CLI or AWS SDKs.

Encryption

Data protection refers to protecting data while in transit (as it travels to and from Amazon S3) and at rest (while it is stored on Amazon S3 infrastructure). As a best practice, all sensitive data stored in Amazon S3 should be encrypted, both at rest and in transit.

You can protect *data in transit* by using Amazon S3 SSL API endpoints, which ensures that all data sent to and from Amazon S3 is encrypted using the *HTTPS protocol* while in transit.

For *data at rest* in Amazon S3, you can encrypt it using different options of *Server-Side Encryption (SSE)*. Your objects in Amazon S3 are encrypted at the object level as they are written to disk in the data centers and then decrypted for you when you access the objects using AES-256.

You can also use client-side encryption, with which you encrypt the objects before uploading to Amazon S3 and then decrypt them after you have downloaded them. Some customers, for some workloads, will use a combination of both server-side and client-side encryption for extra protection.

Envelope Encryption Concepts

Before examining the different types of encryption available, we will review *envelope encryption*, which several AWS services use to provide a balance between performance and security.

The following steps describe how envelope encryption works:

1. A data key is generated by the AWS service at the time you request your data to be encrypted, as shown in Figure 3.10.

FIGURE 3.10   Generating a data key

Key
Generator

Data Key

2. The data key generated in step 1 is used to encrypt your data, as shown in Figure 3.11.

FIGURE 3.11   Encrypting the data

Plaintext
Data

Data Key

Encrypted
Data

3. The data key is then encrypted with a key-encrypting key unique to the service storing your data, as shown in Figure 3.12.

FIGURE 3.12   Encrypted data key

Data Key

Existing Key
Encrypting Key

Encrypted Data
Key

4. The encrypted data key and the encrypted data are then stored by the AWS storage service (such as Amazon S3 or Amazon EBS) on your behalf. This is shown in Figure 3.13.

FIGURE 3.13   Encrypted data and key storage

Encrypted Data
Key

Encrypted
Data

AWS Storage
Services

When you need access to your plain-text data, this process is reversed. The encrypted data key is decrypted using the key-encrypting key, and the data key is then used to decrypt your data.

The important point to remember regarding envelope encryption is that the key-encrypting keys used to encrypt data keys are stored and managed separately from the data and the data keys.

Server-Side Encryption (SSE)

You have three, mutually exclusive options for how you choose to manage your encryption keys when using SSE with Amazon S3.

SSE-S3 (Amazon S3 managed keys)   You can set an API flag or check a box in the AWS Management Console to have data encrypted before it is written to disk in Amazon S3. Each object is encrypted with a unique data key. As an additional safeguard, this key is encrypted with a periodically-rotated master key managed by Amazon S3. AES-256 is used for both object and master keys. This feature is offered at no additional cost beyond what you pay for using Amazon S3.

SSE-C (Customer-provided keys)   You can use your own encryption key while uploading an object to Amazon S3. This encryption key is used by Amazon S3 to encrypt your data using AES-256. After the object is encrypted, the encryption key you supplied is deleted from the Amazon S3 system that used it to encrypt your data. When you retrieve this object from Amazon S3, you must provide the same encryption key in your request. Amazon S3 verifies that the encryption key matches, decrypts the object, and returns the object to you. This feature is also offered at no additional cost beyond what you pay for using Amazon S3.

SSE-KMS (AWS KMS managed encryption keys)   You can encrypt your data in Amazon S3 by defining an AWS KMS master key within your account to encrypt the unique object key (referred to as a *data key*) that will ultimately encrypt your object. When you upload your object, a request is sent to AWS KMS to create an object key. AWS KMS generates this object key and encrypts it using the master key that you specified earlier. Then, AWS KMS returns this encrypted object key along with the plaintext object key to Amazon S3. The Amazon S3 web server encrypts your object using the plaintext object key and stores the now encrypted object (with the encrypted object key) and deletes the plaintext object key from memory.

To retrieve this encrypted object, Amazon S3 sends the encrypted object key to AWS KMS, which then decrypts the object key using the correct master key and returns the decrypted (plaintext) object key to Amazon S3. With the plaintext object key, Amazon S3 decrypts the encrypted object and returns it to you. Unlike SSE-S3 and SSE-C, using SSE-KMS does incur an additional charge. Refer to the AWS KMS pricing page on the AWS website for more information.

 For maximum simplicity and ease of use, use SSE with AWS managed keys (SSE-S3 or SSE-KMS). Also, know the difference between SSE-S3, SSE-KMS, and SSE-C for SSE.

Client-Side Encryption

Client-side encryption refers to encrypting your data before sending it to Amazon S3. You have two options for using data encryption keys.

CLIENT-SIDE MASTER KEY

The first option is to use a client-side master key of your own. When uploading an object, you provide a client-side master key to the Amazon S3 encryption client (for example, *AmazonS3EncryptionClient* when using the AWS SDK for Java). The client uses this master key only to encrypt the data encryption key that it generates randomly. When downloading an object, the client first downloads the encrypted object from Amazon S3 along with the metadata. Using the material description in the metadata, the client first determines which master key to use to decrypt the encrypted data key. Then the client uses that master key to decrypt the data key and uses it to decrypt the object. The client-side master key that you provide can be either a symmetric key or a public/private key pair.

The process works as follows:

1. The Amazon S3 encryption client locally generates a one-time-use symmetric key (also known as a *data encryption key* or *data key*) and uses this data key to encrypt the data of a single Amazon S3 object (for each object, the client generates a separate data key).

2. The client encrypts the data encryption key using the master key that you provide.

3. The client uploads the encrypted data key and its material description as part of the object metadata. The material description helps the client later determine which client-side master key to use for decryption (when you download the object, the client decrypts it).

4. The client then uploads the encrypted data to Amazon S3 and also saves the encrypted data key as object metadata (x-amz-meta-x-amz-key) in Amazon S3 by default.

AWS KMS-MANAGED CUSTOMER MASTER KEY (CMK)

The second option is to use an AWS KMS managed customer master key (CMK). This process is similar to the process described earlier for using KMS-SSE, except that it is used for data at rest instead of data in transit. There is an Amazon S3 encryption client in the AWS SDK for Java.

Using an AWS KMS Managed CMK (AWS SDK for Java)

```java
import java.io.ByteArrayInputStream;
import java.util.Arrays;

import junit.framework.Assert;

import org.apache.commons.io.IOUtils;

import com.amazonaws.auth.profile.ProfileCredentialsProvider;
import com.amazonaws.regions.Region;
import com.amazonaws.regions.Regions;
import com.amazonaws.services.s3.AmazonS3EncryptionClient;
import com.amazonaws.services.s3.model.CryptoConfiguration;
import com.amazonaws.services.s3.model.KMSEncryptionMaterialsProvider;
import com.amazonaws.services.s3.model.ObjectMetadata;
import com.amazonaws.services.s3.model.PutObjectRequest;
import com.amazonaws.services.s3.model.S3Object;

public class testKMSkeyUploadObject {

    private static AmazonS3EncryptionClient encryptionClient;

    public static void main(String[] args) throws Exception {
        String bucketName = "***bucket name***";
        String objectKey  = "ExampleKMSEncryptedObject";
        String kms_cmk_id = "***AWS KMS customer master key ID***";

        KMSEncryptionMaterialsProvider materialProvider = new
KMSEncryptionMaterialsProvider(kms_cmk_id);

        encryptionClient = new AmazonS3EncryptionClient(new ProfileCredentials
Provider(), materialProvider,
                new CryptoConfiguration().withKmsRegion(Regions.US_EAST_1))
            .withRegion(Region.getRegion(Regions.US_EAST_1));

        // Upload object using the encryption client.

        byte[] plaintext = "Hello World, S3 Client-side Encryption Using
Asymmetric Master Key!"
                .getBytes();
```

```
    System.out.println("plaintext's length: " + plaintext.length);
    encryptionClient.putObject(new PutObjectRequest(bucketName, objectKey,
            new ByteArrayInputStream(plaintext), new ObjectMetadata()));

// Download the object.
    S3Object downloadedObject = encryptionClient.getObject(bucketName,
            objectKey);
    byte[] decrypted = IOUtils.toByteArray(downloadedObject
        .getObjectContent());

// Verify same data.
    Assert.assertTrue(Arrays.equals(plaintext, decrypted));
  }
}
```

Know the difference between CMK and client-side master keys for client-side encryption.

Access Control

By default, all Amazon S3 resources—buckets, objects, and related sub-resources (for example, lifecycle configuration and website configuration)—are private. Only the resource owner, an account that created it, can access the resource. The resource owner can optionally grant access permissions to others by writing an access policy.

Amazon S3 offers access policy options broadly categorized as resource-based policies and user policies. Access policies that you attach to your resources (buckets and objects) are referred to as *resource-based policies*. For example, bucket policies and ACLs are resource-based policies. You can also attach access policies to users in your account. These are called *user policies*. You can choose to use resource-based policies, user policies, or some combination of both to manage permissions to your Amazon S3 resources. The following sections provide general guidelines for managing permissions.

Using Bucket Policies and User Policies

Bucket policy and user policy are two of the access policy options available for you to grant permissions to your Amazon S3 resources. Both use a JSON-based access policy language, as do all AWS services that use policies.

A *bucket policy* is attached only to Amazon S3 buckets, and it specifies what actions are allowed or denied for whichever principals on the bucket to which the bucket policy is attached (for instance, allow user Alice to PUT but not DELETE objects in the bucket).

A *user policy* is attached to IAM users to perform or not perform actions on your AWS resources. For example, you may choose to grant an IAM user in your account access to one of your buckets and allow the user to add, update, and delete objects. You can grant them access with a user policy.

Now we will discuss the differences between IAM policies and Amazon S3 bucket policies. Both are used for access control, and they are both written in JSON using the AWS access policy language. However, unlike Amazon S3 bucket policies, IAM policies specify what actions are allowed or denied on what AWS resources (such as, allow ec2:TerminateInstance on the Amazon EC2 instance with instance_id=i8b3620ec). You attach IAM policies to IAM users, groups, or roles, which are then subject to the permissions that you have defined. Instead of attaching policies to the users, groups, or roles, bucket policies are attached to a specific resource, such as an Amazon S3 bucket.

Managing Access with Access Control Lists

Access with access control lists (ACLs) are resource-based access policies that you can use to manage access to your buckets and objects, including granting basic read/write permissions to other accounts.

There are limits to managing permissions using ACLs. For example, you can grant permissions only to other accounts; you cannot grant permissions to users in your account. You cannot grant conditional permissions, nor can you explicitly deny permissions using ACLs.

ACLs are suitable only for specific scenarios (for example, if a bucket owner allows other accounts to upload objects), and permissions to these objects can be managed only using an object ACL by the account that owns the object.

You can only grant access to other accounts using ACLs—not users in your own account.

Defense in Depth—Amazon S3 Security

Amazon S3 provides comprehensive security and compliance capabilities that meet the most stringent regulatory requirements, and it gives you flexibility in the way that you manage data for cost optimization, access control, and compliance. With this flexibility, however, comes the responsibility of ensuring that your content is secure.

You can use an approach known as *defense in depth* in Amazon S3 to secure your data. This approach uses multiple layers of security to ensure redundancy if one of the multiple layers of security fails.

Figure 3.14 represents defense in depth visually. It contains several Amazon S3 objects (A) in a single Amazon S3 bucket (B). You can encrypt these objects on the server side or the client side, and you can also configure the bucket policy such that objects are accessible only through Amazon CloudFront, which you can accomplish through an origin access identity (C). You can then configure Amazon CloudFront to deliver content only over HTTPS in addition to using your own domain name (D).

FIGURE 3.14   Defense in depth on Amazon S3

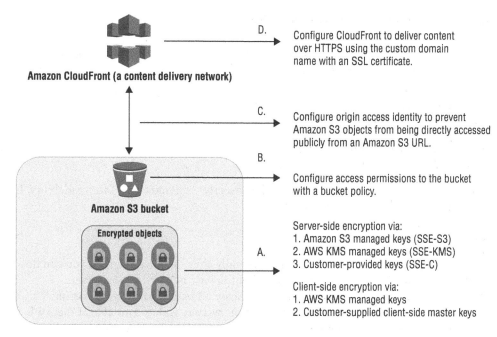

To meet defense in depth requirements on Amazon S3:

- Data must be encrypted at rest and during transit.
- Data must be accessible only by a limited set of public IP addresses.
- Data must not be publicly accessible directly from an Amazon S3 URL.
- A domain name is required to consume the content.

You can apply policies to Amazon S3 buckets so that only users with appropriate permissions are allowed to access the buckets. Anonymous users (with public-read/public-read-write permissions) and authenticated users without the appropriate permissions are prevented from accessing the buckets.

You can also secure access to objects in Amazon S3 buckets. The objects in Amazon S3 buckets can be encrypted at rest and during transit to provide end-to-end security from the source (in this case, Amazon S3) to your users.

Query String Authentication

You can provide authentication information using *query string parameters*. Using query parameters to authenticate requests is useful when expressing a request entirely in a URL. This method is also referred to as *presigning* a URL.

With presigned URLs, you can grant temporary access to your Amazon S3 resources. For example, you can embed a presigned URL on your website, or alternatively use it in a command line client (such as Curl), to download objects.

The following is an example presigned URL:

```
https://s3.amazonaws.com/examplebucket/test.txt
?X-Amz-Algorithm=AWS4-HMAC-SHA256
&X-Amz-Credential=<your-access-key-id>/20130721/us-east-1/s3/aws4_request
&X-Amz-Date=20130721T201207Z
&X-Amz-Expires=86400
&X-Amz-SignedHeaders=host
&X-Amz-Signature=<signature-value>
```

In the example URL, note the following:

- The line feeds are added for readability.
- The X-Amz-Credential value in the URL shows the / character only for readability. In practice, it should be encoded as %2F.

Hosting a Static Website

If your website contains static content and optionally client-side scripts, then you can host your *static website* directly in Amazon S3 without the use of web-hosting servers.

To host a static website, you configure an Amazon S3 bucket for website hosting and upload your website content to the bucket. The website is then available at the AWS Region–specific website endpoint of the bucket in one of the following formats:

```
<bucket-name>.s3-website-<AWS-region>.amazonaws.com
<bucket-name>.s3-website.<AWS-region>.amazonaws.com
```

Instead of accessing the website by using an Amazon S3 website endpoint, use your own domain (for instance, example.com) to serve your content. The following steps allow you to configure your own domain:

1. Register your domain with the registrar of your choice. You can use Amazon Route 53 to register your domain name or any other third-party domain registrar.

2. Create your bucket in Amazon S3 and upload your static website content.

3. Point your domain to your Amazon S3 bucket using either of the following as your DNS provider:
   - Amazon Route 53
   - Your third-party domain name registrar

Amazon S3 does not support server-side scripting or dynamic content. We discuss other AWS options for that throughout this study guide.

 Static websites can be hosted in Amazon S3.

MFA Delete

MFA is another way to control deletes on your objects in Amazon S3. It does so by adding another layer of protection against unintentional or malicious deletes, requiring an authorized request against Amazon S3 to delete the object. MFA also requires a unique code from a token or an authentication device (virtual or hardware). These devices provide a unique code that will then allow you to delete the object. Figure 3.15 shows what would be required for a user to execute a delete operation on an object when MFA is enabled.

FIGURE 3.15   MFA Delete

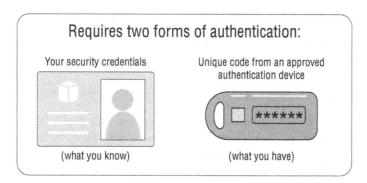

Cross-Region Replication

Cross-region replication (CRR) is a bucket-level configuration that enables automatic, asynchronous copying of objects across buckets in different AWS Regions. We refer to these buckets as the *source* bucket and *destination* bucket. These buckets can be owned by different accounts.

To activate this feature, add a replication configuration to your source bucket to direct Amazon S3 to replicate objects according to the configuration. In the replication configuration, provide information including the following:

- The destination bucket
- The objects that need to be replicated
- Optionally, the destination storage class (otherwise the source storage class will be used)

The replicas that are created in the destination bucket will have these same characteristics as the source objects:

- Key names
- Metadata
- Storage class (unless otherwise specified)
- Object ACL

All data is encrypted in transit across AWS Regions using SSL.

You can replicate objects from a source bucket to only one destination bucket. After Amazon S3 replicates an object, the object cannot be replicated again. For example, even after you change the destination bucket in an existing replication configuration, Amazon S3 will not replicate it again.

 After Amazon S3 replicates an object using CRR, the object cannot be replicated again (such as to another destination bucket).

Requirements for CRR include the following:

- Versioning is enabled for both the source and destination buckets.
- Source and destination buckets must be in different AWS Regions.
- Amazon S3 must be granted appropriate permissions to replicate files.

VPC Endpoints

A *virtual private cloud (VPC) endpoint* enables you to connect your VPC privately to Amazon S3 without requiring an internet gateway, *network address translation (NAT)* device, *virtual private network (VPN)* connection, or *AWS Direct Connect* connection. Instances in your VPC do not require public IP addresses to communicate with the resources in the service. Traffic between your VPC and Amazon S3 does not leave the Amazon network.

Amazon S3 uses a gateway type of VPC endpoint. The gateway is a target for a specified route in your route table, used for traffic destined for a supported AWS service. These endpoints are easy to configure, are highly reliable, and provide a secure connection to Amazon S3 that does not require a gateway or NAT instance.

Amazon EC2 instances running in private subnets of a VPC can have controlled access to Amazon S3 buckets, objects, and API functions that are in the same region as the VPC. You can use an Amazon S3 bucket policy to indicate which VPCs and which VPC endpoints have access to your Amazon S3 buckets.

Using the AWS SDKs, AWS CLI, and AWS Explorers

You can use the AWS SDKs when developing applications with Amazon S3. The AWS SDKs simplify your programming tasks by wrapping the underlying REST API. The AWS Mobile SDKs and the AWS Amplify JavaScript library are also available for building connected mobile and web applications using AWS. In addition to AWS SDKs, AWS explorers are available for Visual Studio and Eclipse for *Java Integrated Development Environment* (IDE). In this case, the SDKs and AWS explorers are available bundled together as AWS Toolkits. You can also use the AWS CLI to manage Amazon S3 buckets and objects.

AWS has deprecated SOAP support over HTTP, but it is still available over HTTPS. New Amazon S3 features will not be supported over SOAP. We recommend that you use either the REST API or the AWS SDKs for any new development and migrate any existing SOAP calls when you are able.

Making Requests

Every interaction with Amazon S3 is either authenticated or anonymous. *Authentication* is the process of verifying the identity of the requester trying to access an AWS product (you are who you say you are, and you are allowed to do what you are asking to do). Authenticated requests must include a signature value that authenticates the request sender, generated in part from the requester's AWS access keys. If you are using the AWS SDK, the libraries compute the signature from the keys that you provide. If you make direct REST API calls in your application, however, you must write code to compute the signature and add it to the request.

Stateless and Serverless Applications

Amazon S3 provides developers with secure, durable, and highly scalable object storage that can be used to decouple storage for use in *serverless applications*. Developers can also use Amazon S3 for storing and sharing state in *stateless applications*.

Developers on AWS are regularly moving shared file storage to Amazon S3 for stateless applications. This is a common method for decoupling your compute and storage and increasing the ability to scale your application by decoupling that storage. We will discuss stateless and serverless applications throughout this study guide.

Data Lake

Traditional data storage can no longer provide the agility and flexibility required to handle the volume, velocity, and variety of data used by today's applications. Because of this, many organizations are shifting to a *data lake* architecture.

A *data lake* is an architectural approach that allows you to store massive amounts of data in a central location for consumption by multiple applications. Because data can be stored as is, there is no need to convert it to a predefined schema, and you no longer need to know what questions to ask of your data beforehand.

Amazon S3 is a common component of a data lake solution on the cloud, and it can complement your other storage solutions. If you move to a data lake, you are essentially separating compute and storage, meaning that you are going to build and scale your storage and compute separately. You can take storage that you currently have on premises or in your data center and instead use Amazon S3, which then allows you to scale and build your compute in any desired configuration, regardless of your storage.

That design pattern is different from most applications available today, where the storage is tied to the compute. When you separate those two features and instead use a data lake, you achieve an agility that allows you to invent new types of applications while you are managing your storage as an independent entity.

In addition, Amazon S3 lets you grow and scale in a virtually unlimited fashion. You do not have to take specific actions to expand your storage capacity—it grows automatically with your data.

In the data lake diagram shown in Figure 3.16, you will see how to use Amazon S3 as a highly available and durable central storage repository. From there, a virtually unlimited number of services and applications, both on premises and in the cloud, can take advantage of using Amazon S3 as a data lake.

FIGURE 3.16 Data lakes

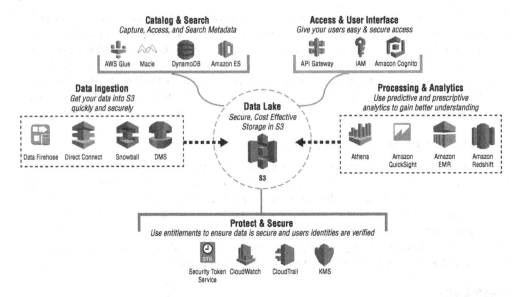

Customers often set up a data lake as part of their migration to the cloud so that they can access their data from new applications on the cloud, migrated applications to the cloud, and applications that have not yet been migrated to the cloud.

Performance

There are a number of actions that Amazon S3 takes by default to help you achieve high levels of performance. Amazon S3 automatically scales to thousands of requests per second per prefix based on your steady state traffic. Amazon S3 will automatically partition your prefixes within hours, adjusting to increases in request rates.

Consideration for Workloads

To optimize the use of Amazon S3 mixed or GET-intensive workloads, you must become familiar with best practices for performance optimization.

Mixed request types If your requests are typically a mix of GET, PUT, DELETE, and GET Bucket (list objects), choosing appropriate key names for your objects ensures better performance by providing low-latency access to the Amazon S3 index.

GET-intensive workloads If the bulk of your workload consists of GET requests, you may want to use Amazon CloudFront, a content delivery service (discussed later in this chapter).

Tips for Object Key Naming

The way that you name your keys in Amazon S3 can affect the data access patterns, which may directly impact the performance of your application.

It is a best practice at AWS to design for performance from the start. Even though you may be developing a new application, that application is likely to grow over time. If you anticipate your application growing to more than approximately 1,000 requests per second (including both PUTs and GETs on your object), you will want to consider using a three- or four-character hash in your key names.

If you anticipate your application receiving fewer than 1,000 requests per second and you don't see a lot of traffic in your storage, then you do not need to implement this best practice. Your application will still benefit from Amazon S3's default performance.

In the past, customers would also add entropy in their key names. Because of recent Amazon S3 performance enhancements, most customers no longer need to worry about introducing entropy in key names.

Example 1: Random Hash

```
examplebucket/232a-2017-26-05-15-00-00/cust1234234/photo1.jpg
examplebucket/7b54-2017-26-05-15-00-00/cust3857422/photo2.jpg
examplebucket/921c-2017-26-05-15-00-00/cust1248473/photo2.jpg
```

A random hash should come before patterns, such as dates and sequential IDs.

Using a *naming hash* can improve the performance of heavy-traffic applications. Object keys are stored in an index in all regions. If you're constantly writing the same key prefix over and over again (for example, a key with the current year), all of your objects will be close to each other within the same partition in the index. When your application experiences an increase in traffic, it will be trying to read from the same section of the index, resulting in decreased performance as Amazon S3 tries to spread out your data to achieve higher levels of throughput.

Always first ensure that your application can accommodate a naming hash.

By putting the hash at the beginning of your key name, you are adding randomness. You could hash the key name and place it at the beginning of your object right after the bucket name. This will ensure that your data will be spread across different partitions and allow you to grow to a higher level of throughput without experiencing a re-indexing slowdown if you go above peak traffic volumes.

Example 2: Naming Hash

```
examplebucket/animations/232a-2017-26-05-15-00/cust1234234/animation1.obj
examplebucket/videos/ba65-2017-26-05-15-00/cust8474937/video2.mpg
examplebucket/photos/8761-2017-26-05-15-00/cust1248473/photo3.jpg
```

In this second example, imagine that you are storing a lot of animations, videos, and photos in Amazon S3. If you know that you are going to have a lot of traffic to those individual prefixes, you can add your hash after the prefix. That allows you to write prefixes into your lifecycle policies or perform *list API* calls against a particular prefix. You are still getting the performance benefit by adding the hash to your key name, but now you can also use the prefix as necessary.

This example allows you to balance the need to list your objects and organize them against the need to spread your data across different partitions for performance.

Amazon S3 Transfer Acceleration

Amazon S3 Transfer Acceleration is a feature that optimizes throughput when transferring larger objects across larger geographic distances. Amazon S3 Transfer Acceleration uses Amazon CloudFront edge locations to assist you in uploading your objects more quickly in cases where you are closer to an edge location than to the region to which you are transferring your files.

Instead of using the public internet to upload objects from Southeast Asia, across the globe to Northern Virginia, take advantage of the global *Amazon content delivery network* (CDN). AWS has edge locations around the world, and you upload your data to the edge location closest to your location. This way, you are traveling across the AWS network backbone to your destination region, instead of across the public internet. This option might give you a significant performance improvement and better network consistency than the public internet.

To implement Amazon S3 Transfer Acceleration, you do not need to make any changes to your application. It is enabled by performing the following steps:

1. Enable Transfer Acceleration on a bucket that conforms to DNS naming requirements and does not contain periods (.).

2. Transfer data to and from the acceleration-enabled bucket by using one of the s3-accelerate endpoint domain names.

There is a small fee for using Transfer Acceleration. If your speed using Transfer Acceleration is no faster than it would have been going over the public internet, however, there is no additional charge.

The further you are from a particular region, the more benefit you will derive from transferring your files more quickly by uploading to a closer edge location. Figure 3.17 shows how accessing an edge location can reduce the latency for your users, as opposed to accessing content from a region that is farther away.

FIGURE 3.17   Using an AWS edge location

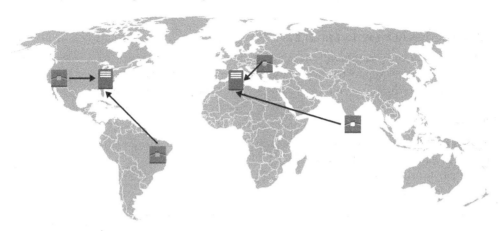

Multipart Uploads

When uploading a large object to Amazon S3 in a single-threaded manner, it can take a significant amount of time to complete. The multipart upload API enables you to upload large objects in parts to speed up your upload by doing so in parallel.

To use multipart upload, you first break the object into smaller parts, parallelize the upload, and then submit a manifest file telling Amazon S3 that all parts of the object have been uploaded. Amazon S3 will then assemble all of those individual pieces to a single Amazon S3 object.

Multipart upload can be used for objects ranging from 5 MB to 5 TB in size.

Range GETs

Range GETs are similar to multipart uploads, but in reverse. If you are downloading a large object and tracking the offsets, use range GETs to download the object as multiple parts instead of a single part. You can then download those parts in parallel and potentially see an improvement in performance.

Amazon CloudFront

Using a CDN like Amazon CloudFront, you may achieve lower latency and higher-throughput performance. You also will not experience as many requests to Amazon S3 because your content will be cached at the edge location. Your users will also experience the performance improvement of having cached storage through Amazon CloudFront versus going back to Amazon S3 for each new GET on an object.

TCP Window Scaling

Transmission Control Protocol (TCP) window scaling allows you to improve network throughput performance between your operating system, application layer, and Amazon S3 by supporting window sizes larger than 64 KB. Although it can improve performance, it can be challenging to set up correctly, so refer to the AWS Documentation repository for details.

TCP Selective Acknowledgment

TCP selective acknowledgment is designed to improve recovery time after a large number of packet losses. It is supported by most newer operating systems, but it might have to be enabled. Refer to the Amazon S3 Developer Guide for more information.

Pricing

With Amazon S3, you pay only for what you use. There is no minimum fee, and there is no charge for data transfer into Amazon S3.

You pay for the following:

- The storage that you use

- The API calls that you make (PUT, COPY, POST, LIST, GET)

- Data transfer out of Amazon S3

Data transfer out pricing is tiered, so the more you use, the lower your cost per gigabyte. Refer to the AWS website for the latest pricing.

 Amazon S3 pricing differs from the pricing of Amazon EBS volumes in that if you create an Amazon EBS volume and store nothing on it, you are still paying for the storage space of the volume that you have allocated. With Amazon S3, you pay for the storage space that is being used—not allocated.

Object Lifecycle Management

To manage your objects so that they are stored cost effectively throughout their lifecycle, use a *lifecycle configuration*. A lifecycle configuration is a set of rules that defines actions that Amazon S3 applies to a group of objects.

There are two types of actions:

Transition actions   *Transition actions* define when objects transition to another storage class. For example, you might choose to transition objects to the STANDARD_IA storage class 30 days after you created them or archive objects to the GLACIER storage class one year after creating them.

Expiration actions   *Expiration actions* define when objects expire. Amazon S3 deletes expired objects on your behalf.

When Should You Use Lifecycle Configuration?

You should use lifecycle configuration rules for objects that have a well-defined lifecycle. The following are some examples:

- If you upload periodic logs to a bucket, your application might need them for a week or a month. After that, you may delete them.

- Some documents are frequently accessed for a limited period of time. After that, they are infrequently accessed. At some point, you might not need real-time access to them, but your organization or regulations might require you to archive them for a specific period. After that, you may delete them.

- You can upload some data to Amazon S3 primarily for archival purposes. For example, archiving digital media, financial, and healthcare records; raw genomics sequence data, long-term database backups; and data that must be retained for regulatory compliance.

With lifecycle configuration rules, you can tell Amazon S3 to transition objects to less expensive storage classes or archive or delete them.

Configuring a Lifecycle

A *lifecycle configuration* (an XML file) comprises a set of rules with predefined actions that you need Amazon S3 to perform on objects during their lifetime. Amazon S3 provides a set of API operations for managing lifecycle configuration on a bucket, and it is stored by Amazon S3 as a *lifecycle subresource* that is attached to your bucket.

You can also configure the lifecycle by using the Amazon S3 console, the AWS SDKs, or the REST API.

The following lifecycle configuration specifies a rule that applies to objects with key name prefix logs/. The rule specifies the following actions:

- Two transition actions
  - Transition objects to the STANDARD_IA storage class 30 days after creation
  - Transition objects to the GLACIER storage class 90 days after creation

- One expiration action that directs Amazon S3 to delete objects a year after creation

```
<LifecycleConfiguration>
  <Rule>
    <ID>example-id</ID>
    <Filter>
       <Prefix>logs/</Prefix>
    </Filter>
    <Status>Enabled</Status>
    <Transition>
      <Days>30</Days>
      <StorageClass>STANDARD_IA</StorageClass>
    </Transition>
```

```
  <Transition>
    <Days>90</Days>
    <StorageClass>GLACIER</StorageClass>
  </Transition>
  <Expiration>
    <Days>365</Days>
  </Expiration>
</Rule>
</LifecycleConfiguration>
```

Figure 3.18 shows a set of Amazon S3 lifecycle policies in place. These policies move files automatically from one storage class to another as they age out at certain points in time.

FIGURE 3.18   Amazon S3 lifecycle policies

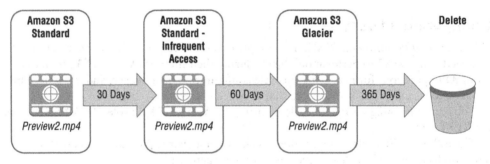

AWS File Storage Services

AWS offers Amazon Elastic File System (Amazon EFS) for file storage to enable you to share access to files that reside on the cloud.

Amazon Elastic File System

Amazon Elastic File System (Amazon EFS) provides scalable file storage and a standard file system interface for use with Amazon EC2. You can create an Amazon EFS file system, configure your instances to mount the file system, and then use an Amazon EFS file system as a common data source for workloads and application running on multiple instances.

Amazon EFS can be mounted to multiple Amazon EC2 instances simultaneously, where it can continue to expand up to petabytes while providing low latency and high throughput.

Consider using Amazon EFS instead of Amazon S3 or Amazon EBS if you have an application (Amazon EC2 or on premises) or a use case that requires a file system and any of the following:

- Multi-attach
- GB/s throughput
- Multi-AZ availability/durability
- Automatic scaling (growing/shrinking of storage)

Customers use Amazon EFS for the following use cases today:

- Web serving
- Database backups
- Container storage
- Home directories
- Content management
- Analytics
- Media and entertainment workflows
- Workflow management
- Shared state management

   Amazon EFS is not supported on Windows instances.

Creating your Amazon EFS File System

File System

The *Amazon EFS file system* is the primary resource in Amazon EFS, and it is where you store your files and directories. You can create up to 125 file systems per account.

Mount Target

To access your file system from within a VPC, create mount targets in the VPC. A *mount target* is a Network File System (NFS) endpoint within your VPC that includes an IP address and a DNS name, both of which you use in your mount command. A mount target is highly available, and it is illustrated in Figure 3.19.

Accessing an Amazon EFS File System

There are several different ways that you can access an Amazon EFS file system, including using Amazon EC2 and AWS Direct Connect.

FIGURE 3.19   Mount target

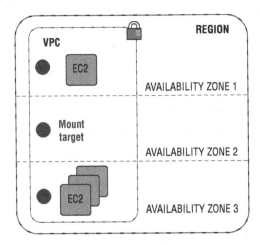

Using Amazon Elastic Compute Cloud

To access a file system from an *Amazon Elastic Compute Cloud* (Amazon EC2) instance, you must mount the file system by using the standard Linux mount command, as shown in Figure 3.20. The file system will then appear as a local set of directories and files. An NFS v4.1 client is standard on Amazon Linux AMI distributions.

FIGURE 3.20   Mounting the file system

```
mount -t nfs4 -o nfsvers=4.1
       [file system DNS name]:/
       /[user's target directory]
```

In your command, specify the file system type (nfs4), the version (4.1), the file system DNS name or IP address, and the user's target directory.

A file system belongs to a region, and your Amazon EFS file system spans all Availability Zones in that region. Once you have mounted your file system, data can be accessed from any Availability Zone in the region within your VPC while maintaining full consistency. Figure 3.21 shows how you communicate with Amazon EC2 instances within a VPC.

Using AWS Direct Connect

You can also mount your on-premises servers to Amazon EFS in your Amazon VPC using AWS Direct Connect. With *AWS Direct Connect*, you can mount your on-premises servers to Amazon EFS using the same mount command used to mount in Amazon EC2. Figure 3.22 shows how to use AWS Direct Connect with Amazon EFS.

FIGURE 3.21   Using Amazon EFS

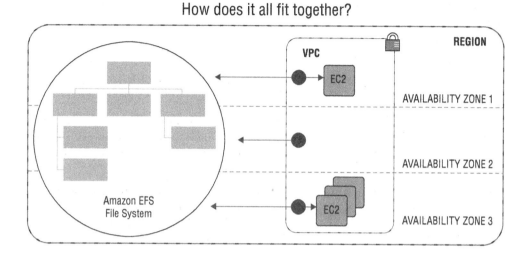

FIGURE 3.22   Using AWS Direct Connect with Amazon EFS

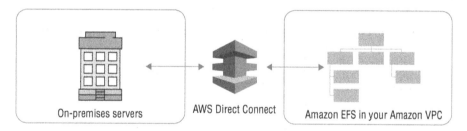

Customers can use Amazon EFS combined with AWS Direct Connect for migration, bursting, or backup and disaster recovery.

Syncing Files Using AWS DataSync

Now that you have a functioning Amazon EFS file system, you can use *AWS DataSync* to synchronize files from an existing file system to Amazon EFS. AWS DataSync can synchronize your file data and also file system metadata such as ownership, time stamps, and access permissions.

To do this, download and deploy a sync agent from the Amazon EFS console as either a *virtual machine* (VM) image or an AMI.

Next, create a sync tack and configure your source and destination file systems. Then start your task to begin syncing the files and monitor the progress of the file sync using Amazon CloudWatch.

Performance

Amazon EFS is designed for a wide spectrum of performance needs, including the following:

- High throughput and parallel I/O
- Low latency and serial I/O

To support those two sets of workloads, Amazon EFS offers two different performance modes, as described here:

General purpose (default)   General-purpose mode is the default mode, and it is used for latency-sensitive applications and general-purpose workloads, offering the lowest latencies for file operations. While there is a trade-off of limiting operations to 7,000 per second, general-purpose mode is the best choice for most workloads.

Max I/O   If you are running large-scale and data-heavy applications, then choose the max I/O performance option, which provides you with a virtually unlimited ability to scale out throughput and IOPS, but with a trade-off of slightly higher latencies. Use max I/O when you have 10 or more instances accessing your file system concurrently, as shown in Table 3.6.

TABLE 3.6   I/O Performance Options

Mode	What's It For?	Advantages	Trade-Offs	When to Use
General purpose (default)	Latency-sensitive applications and general-purpose workloads	Lowest latencies for file operations	Limit of 7,000 ops/sec	Best choice for most workloads
Max I/O	Large-scale and data-heavy applications	Virtually unlimited ability to scale out throughput/ IOPS	Slightly higher latencies	Consider if 10 (or more) instances are accessing your file system concurrently

If you are not sure which mode is best for your usage pattern, use the PercentIOLimit Amazon CloudWatch metric to determine whether you are constrained by general-purpose mode. If you are regularly hitting the 7,000 IOPS limit in general-purpose mode, then you will likely benefit from max I/O performance mode.

As discussed with the CAP theorem earlier in this study guide, there are differences in both performance and trade-off decisions when you're designing systems that use Amazon EFS and Amazon EBS. The distributed architecture of Amazon EFS results in a small increase in latency for each operation, as the data that you are storing gets pushed across multiple servers in multiple Availability Zones. Amazon EBS can provide lower latency than Amazon EFS, but at the cost of some durability. With Amazon EBS, you provision the size of the device, and if you reach its maximum limit, you must increase its size or add more volumes, whereas Amazon EFS scales automatically. Table 3.7 shows the various performance and other characteristics for Amazon EFS as related to Amazon EBS Provisioned IOPS.

TABLE 3.7 Amazon EBS Performance Relative to Amazon EFS

		Amazon EFS	Amazon EBS Provisioned IOPS
Performance	Per-operation latency	Low, consistent	Lowest, consistent
	Throughput scale	Multiple GBs per second	Single GB per second
Characteristics	Data availability/ durability	Stored redundantly across multiple Availability Zones	Stored redundantly in a single Availability Zone
	Access	1 to 1000s of EC2 instances, from multiple Availability Zones, concurrently	Single Amazon EC2 instance in a single Availability Zone
	Use cases	Big Data and analytics, media processing workflows, content management, web serving, home directories	Boot volumes, transactional and NoSQL databases, data warehousing, ETL

Security

You can implement security in multiple layers with Amazon EFS by controlling the following:

- Network traffic to and from file systems (mount targets) using the following:
  - VPC security groups
  - Network ACLs
- File and directory access by using POSIX permissions
- Administrative access (API access) to file systems by using IAM. Amazon EFS supports:
  - Action-level permissions
  - Resource-level permissions

Familiarize yourself with the Amazon EFS product, details, and FAQ pages. Some exam questions may be answered by components from those pages.

Storage Comparisons

This section provides valuable charts that can serve as a quick reference if you are tasked with choosing a storage system for a particular project or application.

Use Case Comparison

Table 3.8 will help you understand the main properties and use cases for each of the cloud storage products on AWS.

TABLE 3.8   AWS Cloud Storage Products

If You Need:	Consider Using:
Persistent local storage for Amazon EC2, relational and NoSQL databases, data warehousing, enterprise applications, big data processing, or backup and recovery	Amazon EBS
A file system interface and file system access semantics to make data available to one or more Amazon EC2 instances for content serving, enterprise applications, media processing workflows, big data storage, or backup and recovery	Amazon EFS
A scalable, durable platform to make data accessible from any internet location for user-generated content, active archive, serverless computing, Big Data storage, or backup and recovery	Amazon S3
Highly affordable, long-term storage that can replace tape for archive and regulatory compliance	Amazon S3 Glacier
A hybrid storage cloud augmenting your on-premises environment with AWS cloud storage for bursting, tiering, or migration	AWS Storage Gateway
A portfolio of services to help simplify and accelerate moving data of all types and sizes into and out of the AWS Cloud	AWS Cloud Data Migration Services

Storage Temperature Comparison

Table 3.9 shows a comparison of instance store, Amazon EBS, Amazon S3, and Amazon S3 Glacier.

 Understanding Table 3.9 will help you make decisions about latency, size, durability, and cost during the exam.

TABLE 3.9   Storage Comparison

	Instance Store	Amazon EBS	Amazon S3	Amazon S3 Glacier
Average latency	ms		ms, sec, min (~ size)	hrs
Data volume	4 GB to 48 TB	1 GiB to 1 TiB	No limit	
Item size	Block storage		5 TB max	40 TB max
Request rate	Very high		Low to very high (no limit)	Very low (no limit)
Cost/GB per month	Amazon EC2 instance cost	¢¢	¢	
Durability	Low	High	Very high	Very high
Temperature	Hot <— — — — — — — — — — — — — — — — — — — —> Cold			

Comparison of Amazon EBS and Instance Store

Before considering Amazon EC2 instance store as a storage option, make sure that your data does *not* meet any of these criteria:

- Must persist through instance stops, terminations, or hardware failures
- Needs to be encrypted at the full volume level
- Needs to be backed up with Amazon EBS snapshots
- Needs to be removed from instances and reattached to another

If your data meets any of the previous four criteria, use an Amazon EBS volume. Otherwise, compare instance store and Amazon EBS for storage.

Because instance store is directly attached to the host computer, it will have lower latency than an Amazon EBS volume attached to the Amazon EC2 instance. Instance store is provided at no additional cost beyond the price of the Amazon EC2 instance you choose (if the instance has instance store[s] available), whereas Amazon EBS volumes incur an additional cost.

Comparison of Amazon S3, Amazon EBS, and Amazon EFS

Table 3.10 is a useful in helping you to compare performance and storage characteristics for Amazon's highest-performing file, object, and block cloud storage offerings. This comparison will also be helpful when choosing the right data store for the applications that you are developing. It is also important for the exam.

TABLE 3.10   Storage Service Comparison (EFS, S3, and EBS)

		File Amazon EFS	Object Amazon S3	Block Amazon EBS
Performance	Per-operation latency	Low, consistent	Low, for mixed request types, and integration with CloudFront	Low, consistent
	Throughput scale	Multiple GB per second		Single GB per second
Characteristics	Data Availability/ Durability	Stored redundantly across multiple Availability Zones		Stored redundantly in a single Availability Zone
	Access	One to thousands of Amazon EC2 instances or on-premises servers, from multiple Availability Zones, concurrently	One to millions of connections over the web	Single Amazon EC2 instance in a single Availability Zone
	Use Cases	Web serving and content management, enterprise applications, media and entertainment, home directories, database backups, developer tools, container storage, Big Data analytics	Web serving and content management, media and entertainment, backups, Big Data analytics, data lake	Boot volumes, transactional and NoSQL databases, data warehousing, ETL

Cloud Data Migration

Data is the cornerstone of successful cloud application deployments. Your evaluation and planning process may highlight the physical limitations inherent to migrating data from on-premises locations into the cloud. To assist you with that process, AWS offers a suite of tools to help you move data via networks, roads, and technology partners in and out of the cloud through offline, online, or streaming models.

The daunting realities of data transport apply to most projects: Knowing how to move to the cloud with minimal disruption, cost, and time, and knowing what is the most efficient way to move your data.

To determine the best-case scenario for efficiently moving your data, use this formula:

```
Number of Days = (Total Bytes)/(Megabits per second * 125 * 1000 * Network
Utilization * 60 seconds * 60 minutes * 24 hours)
```

For example, if you have a T1 connection (1.544 Mbps) and 1 TB (1024 × 1024 × 1024 × 1024 bytes) to move in or out of AWS, the theoretical minimum time that it would take to load over your network connection at 80 percent network utilization is 82 days.

Instead of using up bandwidth and taking a long time to migrate, many AWS customers are choosing one of the *data migration* options that are discussed next.

Multiple-choice questions that ask you to choose two or three true answers require that all of your answers be correct. There is no partial credit for getting a fraction correct. Pay extra attention to those questions when doing your review.

AWS Storage Gateway

AWS Storage Gateway is a hybrid cloud storage service that enables your on-premises applications to use AWS cloud storage seamlessly. You can use this service for the following:

- Backup and archiving
- Disaster recovery
- Cloud bursting
- Storage tiering
- Migration

Your applications connect to the service through a gateway appliance using standard storage protocols, such as NFS and *internet Small Computer System Interface* (iSCSI). The gateway connects to AWS storage services, such as Amazon S3, Amazon S3 Glacier, and Amazon EBS, providing storage for files, volumes, and virtual tapes in AWS.

File Gateway

A *file gateway* supports a file interface into Amazon S3, and it combines a cloud service with a virtual software appliance that is deployed into your on-premises environment as a VM. You can think of file gateway as an NFS mount on Amazon S3, allowing you to access your data directly in Amazon S3 from on premises as a file share.

Volume Gateway

A *volume gateway* provides cloud-based storage volumes that you can mount as iSCSI devices from your on-premises application servers. A volume gateway supports cached mode and stored volume mode configurations.

Note that the volume gateway represents the family of gateways that support block-based volumes, previously referred to as *gateway-cached volumes* and *gateway-stored volumes*.

Cached Mode

In the *cached volume mode*, your data is stored in Amazon S3, and a cache of the frequently accessed data is maintained locally by the gateway. This enables you to achieve cost savings on primary storage and minimize the need to scale your storage on premises while retaining low-latency access to your most used data.

Stored Volume Mode

In the *stored volume mode*, data is stored on your local storage with volumes backed up asynchronously as Amazon EBS snapshots stored in Amazon S3. This provides durable off-site backups.

Tape Gateway

A *tape gateway* can be used for backup to migrate off of physical tapes and onto a cost-effective and durable archive backup such as Amazon S3 Glacier. For a tape gateway, you store and archive your data on virtual tapes in AWS. A tape gateway eliminates some of the challenges associated with owning and operating an on-premises physical tape infrastructure. It can also be used for migrating data off of tapes, which are nearing end of life, into a more durable type of storage that still acts like tape.

AWS Import/Export

AWS Import/Export accelerates moving large amounts of data into and out of the AWS Cloud using portable storage devices for transport. It transfers your data directly onto and off of storage devices using Amazon's high-speed internal network and bypassing the internet.

For significant datasets, AWS Import/Export is often faster than internet transfer and more cost-effective than upgrading your connectivity. You load your data onto your devices and then create a job in the AWS Management Console to schedule shipping of your devices.

You are responsible for providing your own storage devices and the shipping charges to AWS.

It supports (in a limited number of regions) the following:

- Importing and exporting of data in Amazon S3 buckets
- Importing data into Amazon EBS snapshots

You cannot export directly from Amazon S3 Glacier. You must first restore your objects to Amazon S3 before exporting using AWS Import/Export.

AWS Snowball

AWS Snowball is a petabyte-scale data transport solution that uses physical storage appliances, bypassing the internet, to transfer large amounts of data into and out of Amazon S3.

AWS Snowball addresses common challenges with large-scale data transfers, including the following:

- High network costs
- Long transfer times
- Security concerns

Figure 3.23 shows a physical AWS Snowball device.

FIGURE 3.23   AWS Snowball

When you transfer your data with AWS Snowball, you do not need to write any code or purchase any hardware. To transfer data using AWS Snowball, perform the following steps:

1. Create a job in the AWS Management Console. The AWS Snowball appliance is shipped to you automatically.

2. When the appliance arrives, attach it to your local network.

3. Download and run the AWS Snowball client to establish a connection.

4. Use the client to select the file directories that you need to transfer to the appliance. The client will then encrypt and transfer the files to the appliance at high speed.

5. Once the transfer is complete and the appliance is ready to be returned, the E Ink shipping label automatically updates and you can track the job status via Amazon Simple Notification Service (Amazon SNS), text messages, or directly in the console.

Table 3.11 shows some common AWS Snowball use cases.

TABLE 3.11   AWS Snowball Use Cases

Use Case	Description
Cloud migration	If you have large quantities of data that you need to migrate into AWS, AWS Snowball is often much faster and more cost-effective than transferring that data over the internet.
Disaster recovery	In the event that you need to retrieve a large quantity of data stored in Amazon S3 quickly, AWS Snowball appliances can help retrieve the data much quicker than high-speed internet.
Data center decommission	There are many steps involved in decommissioning a data center to make sure that valuable data is not lost. Snowball can help ensure that your data is securely and cost-effectively transferred to AWS during this process.
Content distribution	Use Snowball appliances if you regularly receive or need to share large amounts of data with clients, customers, or business associates. Snowball appliances can be sent directly from AWS to client or customer locations.

AWS Snowball Edge

AWS Snowball Edge is a 100-TB data transfer service with on-board storage and compute power for select AWS capabilities. In addition to transferring data to AWS, AWS Snowball Edge can undertake local processing and edge computing workloads. Figure 3.24 shows a physical AWS Snowball Edge device.

FIGURE 3.24   AWS Snowball Edge

Features of AWS Snowball Edge include the following:

- An endpoint on the device that is compatible with Amazon S3
- A file interface with NFS support
- A cluster mode where multiple AWS Snowball Edge devices can act as a single, scalable storage pool with increased durability
- The ability to run AWS Lambda powered by AWS IoT Greengrass functions as data is copied to the device
- Encryption taking place on the appliance itself

The transport of data is done by shipping the data in the appliances through a regional carrier. The appliance differs from the standard AWS Snowball because it can bring the power of the AWS Cloud to your local environment, with local storage and compute functionality.

There are three types of jobs that can be performed with Snowball Edge appliances:

- Import jobs into Amazon S3
- Export jobs from Amazon S3
- Local compute and storage-only jobs

Use AWS Snowball Edge when you need the following:

- Local storage and compute in an environment that might or might not have an internet connection
- To transfer large amounts of data into and out of Amazon S3, bypassing the internet

Table 3.12 shows the different use cases for the different AWS Snowball devices.

TABLE 3.12 AWS Snowball Device Use Cases

Use Case	AWS Snowball	AWS Snowball Edge
Import data into Amazon S3	✓	✓
Copy data directly from HDFS	✓	
Export from Amazon S3	✓	✓
Durable local storage		✓
Use in a cluster of devices		✓
Use with AWS IoT Greengrass		✓
Transfer files through NFS with a GUI		✓

AWS Snowmobile

AWS Snowmobile is an exabyte-scale data transfer service used to move extremely large amounts of data from on premises to AWS. You can transfer up to 100 PB per AWS Snowmobile, a 45-foot long ruggedized shipping container pulled by a semi-trailer truck.

AWS Snowmobile makes it easy to move massive volumes of data to the cloud, including video libraries, image repositories, or even a complete data center migration. In 2017, one AWS customer moved 8,700 tapes with 54 million files to Amazon S3 using AWS Snowmobile. Figure 3.25 shows an AWS Snowmobile shipping container being pulled by a semi-trailer truck.

FIGURE 3.25 AWS Snowmobile

How do you choose between AWS Snowmobile and AWS Snowball? To migrate large datasets of 10 PB or more in a single location, you should use AWS Snowmobile. For datasets that are less than 10 PB or distributed in multiple locations, you should use AWS Snowball.

Amazon Kinesis Data Firehose

Amazon Kinesis Data Firehose lets you prepare and load real-time data streams into data stores and analytics tools. Although it has much broader uses for loading data continuously for data streaming and analytics, it can be used as a one-time tool for data migration into the cloud.

Amazon Kinesis Data Firehose can capture, transform, and load streaming data into Amazon S3 and Amazon Redshift, which will be discussed further in Chapter 4, "Hello, Databases." With Amazon Kinesis Data Firehose, you can avoid writing applications or managing resources. When you configure your data producers to send data to Amazon Kinesis Data Firehose, as shown in Figure 3.26, it automatically delivers the data to the destination that you specified. This is an efficient option to transform and deliver data from on premises to the cloud.

FIGURE 3.26   Amazon Kinesis Data Firehose

Input	Amazon Kinesis Data Firehose	Data stores
Capture and send data to Kinesis Data Firehose	Prepares and loads the data continuously to the destinations you choose	Durably store the data for analytics

Destinations include the following:

- Amazon S3
- Amazon Redshift
- Amazon Elasticsearch Service
- Splunk

Key Concepts

As you get started with Amazon Kinesis Data Firehose, you will benefit from understanding the concepts described next.

Kinesis Data Delivery Stream

You use Amazon Kinesis Data Firehose by creating an Amazon Kinesis *data delivery stream* and then sending data to it.

Record

A *record* is the data that your producer sends to a Kinesis data delivery stream, with a maximum size of 1,000 KB.

Data Producer

Data producers send records to Amazon Kinesis data delivery streams. For example, your web server could be configured as a data producer that sends log data to an Amazon Kinesis delivery stream.

Buffer Size and Buffer Interval

Amazon Kinesis Data Firehose buffers incoming data to a certain size or for a certain period of time before delivering it to destinations. Buffer size is in megabytes, and buffer interval is in seconds.

Data Flow

You can stream data to your Amazon S3 bucket, as shown in Figure 3.27. If data transformation is enabled, you can optionally back up source data to another Amazon S3 bucket.

FIGURE 3.27   Streaming to Amazon S3

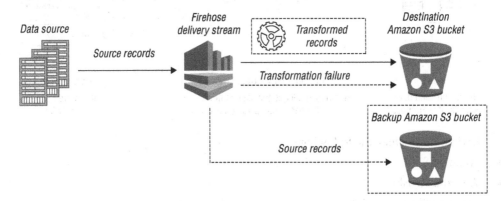

AWS Direct Connect

Using *AWS Direct Connect*, you can establish private connectivity between AWS and your data center, office, or colocation environment, which in many cases can reduce your network costs, increase bandwidth throughput, and provide a more consistent network experience than internet-based connections.

These benefits can then be applied to storage migration. Transferring large datasets over the internet can be time-consuming and expensive. When you use the cloud, you may find that transferring large datasets can be slow because your business-critical network traffic is contending for bandwidth with your other internet usage. To decrease the amount of time required to transfer your data, increase the bandwidth to your internet service provider. Be aware that this frequently requires a costly contract renewal and minimum commitment.

More details on using AWS Direct Connect will be provided in Chapter 4.

VPN Connection

You can connect your Amazon VPC to remote networks by using a VPN connection. Table 3.13 shows some of the connectivity options available to you.

TABLE 3.13   Amazon VPC Connectivity Options

VPN Connectivity Option	Description
AWS managed VPN	Create an IP Security (IPsec) VPN connection between your VPC and your remote network. On the AWS side of the VPN connection, a virtual private gateway provides two VPN endpoints (tunnels) for automatic failover. You configure your customer gateway on the remote side of the VPN connection.
AWS VPN CloudHub	If you have more than one remote network (for example, multiple branch offices), create multiple AWS managed VPN connections via your virtual private gateway to enable communication between these networks.
Third-party software VPN appliance	Create a VPN connection to your remote network by using an Amazon EC2 instance in your VPC that's running a third-party software VPN appliance. AWS does not provide or maintain third-party software VPN appliances; however, you can choose from a range of products provided by partners and open-source communities.

You can also use AWS Direct Connect to create a dedicated private connection from a remote network to your VPC. You can combine this connection with an AWS managed VPN connection to create an IPsec-encrypted connection.

You will learn more about VPN connections in subsequent chapters.

Summary

AWS cloud computing provides a reliable, scalable, and secure place for your data. Cloud storage is a critical component of cloud computing, holding the information used by applications. Big Data analytics, data warehouses, Internet of Things, databases, and backup and archive applications all rely on some form of data storage architecture. Cloud storage is typically more reliable, scalable, and secure than traditional on-premises storage systems.

AWS offers a complete range of cloud storage services to support both application and archival compliance requirements. You may choose from object, file, and block storage services and cloud data migration options to start designing the foundation of your cloud IT environment.

Amazon EBS provides highly available, consistent, low-latency, persistent local block storage for Amazon EC2. It helps you to tune applications with the right storage capacity, performance, and cost.

Amazon EFS provides a simple, scalable file system interface and file system access semantics to make data available to one or more EC2 instances as block storage. Amazon EFS grows and shrinks capacity automatically, and it provides high throughput with consistent low latencies. Amazon EFS is designed for high availability and durability, and it provides performance for a broad spectrum of workloads and applications.

Amazon S3 is a form of object storage that provides a scalable, durable platform to make data accessible from any internet location, and it allows you to store and access any type of data over the internet. Amazon S3 is secure, 99.999999999 percent durable, and scales past tens of trillions of objects.

Amazon S3 Glacier provides extremely low-cost and highly durable object storage for long-term backup and archiving of any type of data. Amazon S3 Glacier is a solution for customers who want low-cost storage for infrequently accessed data. It can replace tape, and assist with compliance in highly regulated organizations.

Amazon offers a full portfolio of cloud data migration services to help simplify and accelerate moving data of all types and sizes into and out of the AWS Cloud. These include AWS Storage Gateway, AWS Import/Export Disk, AWS Snowball, AWS Snowball Edge, AWS Snowmobile, Amazon Kinesis Data Firehose, AWS Direct Connect, and a VPN connection.

Understanding when to use the right tool for your data storage and data migration options is a key component of the exam, including data dimension, block versus object versus file storage, data structure, and storage temperature. Be ready to compare and contrast the durability, availability, latency, means of access, and cost of different storage options for a given use case.

Exam Essentials

Know the different data dimensions. Consider the different data dimensions when choosing which storage option and storage class will be most appropriate for your data. This includes velocity, variety, volume, storage temperature (hot, warm, cold, frozen), data value, transient, reproducible, authoritative, and critical/regulated data.

Know the difference between block, object, and file storage.   Block storage is commonly dedicated, low-latency storage for each host and is provisioned with each instance. Object storage is developed for the cloud, has vast scalability, is accessed over the Web, and is not directly attached to an instance. File storage enables accessing shared files as a file system.

Know the AWS shared responsibility model and how it applies to storage.   AWS is responsible for securing the storage services. You are responsible for securing access to the artifacts that you create or objects that you store.

Know what Amazon EBS is and for what it is commonly used.   Amazon EBS provides persistent block storage volumes for use with Amazon EC2 instances. It is designed for application workloads that benefit from fine tuning for performance, cost, and capacity. Typical use cases include Big Data analytics engines, relational and NoSQL databases, stream and log processing applications, and data warehousing applications. Amazon EBS volumes also serve as root volumes for Amazon EC2 instances.

Know what Amazon EC2 instance store is and what it is commonly used for.   An instance store provides temporary block-level storage for your instance. It is located on disks that are physically attached to the host computer. Instance store is ideal for temporary storage of information that changes frequently, such as buffers, caches, scratch data, and other temporary content, or for data that is replicated across a fleet of instances, such as a load-balanced pool of web servers. In some cases, you can use instance-store backed volumes. Do not use instance store (also known as ephemeral storage) for either production data or data that must be kept durable.

Know what Amazon S3 is and what it is commonly used for.   Amazon S3 is object storage built to store and retrieve any amount of data from anywhere. It is secure, durable, and highly scalable cloud storage using a simple web services interface. Amazon S3 is commonly used for backup and archiving, content storage and distribution, Big Data analytics, static website hosting, cloud-native application hosting, and disaster recovery, and as a data lake.

Know the basic concepts of Amazon S3.   Amazon S3 stores data as objects within resources called *buckets*. You can store as many objects as desired within a bucket, and write, read, and delete objects in your bucket. Objects contain data and metadata and are identified by a user-defined key in a flat file structure. Interfaces to Amazon S3 include a native REST interface, SDKs for many languages, the AWS CLI, and the AWS Management Console.

Know how to create a bucket, how to upload, download, and delete objects, how to make objects public, and how to open an object URL.

Understand how security works in Amazon S3.   By default, new buckets are private and nothing is publicly accessible. When you add an object to a bucket, it is private by default.

Know how much data you can store in Amazon S3.   The total volume of data and number of objects that you can store in Amazon S3 are unlimited. Individual Amazon S3 objects can range in size from a minimum of 0 bytes to a maximum of 5 TB. The largest object that can be uploaded in a single PUT is 5 GB. For objects larger than 100 MB, consider using the Multipart Upload capability.

Know the Amazon S3 service limit for buckets per account.   One hundred buckets are allowed per account.

Understand the durability and availability of Amazon S3.   Amazon S3 standard storage is designed for 11 nines of durability and four nines of availability of objects over a given year. Other storage classes differ. Reduced Redundancy Storage (RRS) storage class is less durable than Standard, and it is intended for noncritical, reproducible data.

Know the data consistency model of Amazon S3.   Amazon S3 is eventually consistent, but it offers read-after-write consistency (read after write consistency for PUT of new objects and eventual consistency for overwrite PUT and DELETE).

Know the Amazon S3 storage classes and use cases for each.   Standard is used to store general-purpose data that needs high durability, high performance, and low latency access. Standard_IA is used for data that is less frequently accessed but that needs the same performance and availability when accessed. OneZone_IA is similar to Standard_IA, but it is stored only in a single Availability Zone, costing 20 percent less. However, data stored with OneZone_IA will be permanently lost in the event of an Availability Zone destruction. Reduced_Redundancy offers lower durability at lower cost for easily-reproducible data. Amazon S3 Glacier is used to store rarely accessed archival data at an extremely low cost, when three- to five-hour retrieval time is acceptable under the standard retrieval option. There are other retrieval options for higher and lower cost at shorter and longer retrieval times, including expedited retrieval (on-demand or provisioned, 1–5 minutes) and bulk retrieval (5–12 hours).

Every object within a bucket can be designated to a different storage class.

Know how to enable static web hosting on Amazon S3.   The steps to enable static web hosting on Amazon S3 require you to do the following:

- Create a bucket with the website hostname.
- Upload your static content and make it public.
- Enable static website hosting on the bucket.
- Indicate the index and error page objects.

Know how to encrypt your data on Amazon S3.   For server-side encryption, use SSE-SE (Amazon S3 Managed Keys), SSE-C (Customer-Provided Keys), and SSE-KMS (KMS-Managed Keys). For client-side encryption, choose from a client-side master key or an AWS KMS managed customer master key.

Know how to protect your data on Amazon S3.   Know the different options for protecting your data in flight and in transit. Encrypt data in flight using HTTPS and at rest using server-side or client-side encryption. Enable versioning to keep multiple versions of an object in a bucket. Enable MFA Delete to protect against accidental deletion. Use ACLs,

Amazon S3 bucket policies, and IAM policies for access control. Use presigned URLs for time-limited download access. Use cross-region replication to replicate data to another region automatically.

Know how to use lifecycle configuration rules. Lifecycle rules can be used to manage your objects so that they are stored cost-effectively throughout their lifecycle. There are two types of actions. Transition actions define when an object transitions to another storage class. Expiration actions define when objects expire and will be deleted on your behalf.

Know what Amazon EFS is and what it is commonly used for. Amazon EFS provides simple, scalable, elastic file storage for use with AWS services and on-premises resources. Amazon EFS is easy to use and offers a simple interface that allows you to create and configure file systems quickly and easily. Amazon EFS is built to scale elastically on demand without disrupting applications, growing and shrinking automatically as you add and remove files, so your applications have the storage that they need, when they need it. Amazon EFS is designed for high availability and durability. Amazon EFS can be mounted to multiple Amazon EC2 instances at the same time.

Know the basics of Amazon S3 Glacier as a stand-alone service. Data is stored in encrypted archives that can be as large as 40 TB. Archives typically contain TAR and ZIP files. Vaults are containers for archives, and vaults can be locked for compliance.

Know which storage option to choose based on storage temperature. For hot to warm storage, use Amazon EC2 instance store, Amazon EBS, or Amazon S3. For cold storage, choose Amazon S3 Glacier.

Know which storage option to choose based on latency. Amazon EC2 instance store and Amazon EBS are designed for millisecond latency. Amazon S3 depends on size, anywhere from milliseconds to seconds to minutes. Amazon S3 Glacier is minutes to hours depending on retrieval option.

Know which storage option to choose based on data volume. Amazon EC2 instance store can be from 4 GB to 48 TB. Amazon EBS can be from 1 GiB to 16 TiB. Amazon S3 and Amazon S3 Glacier have no limit.

Know which storage option to choose based on item size. Amazon EC2 instance store and Amazon EBS depend on the size of the block storage and operating system limits. Amazon S3 has a 5 TB max size per object, but objects may be split. Amazon S3 Glacier has a 40 TB maximum.

Know when you should use Amazon EBS, Amazon EFS, Amazon S3, Amazon S3 Glacier, or AWS Storage Gateway for your data. For persistent local storage for Amazon EC2, use Amazon EBS. For a file system interface and file system access semantics to make data available to one or more Amazon EC2 instances, use Amazon EFS. For a scalable, durable platform to make data accessible from any internet location, use Amazon S3. For highly affordable, long-term cold storage, use Amazon S3 Glacier. For a hybrid storage cloud augmenting your on-premises environment with Amazon cloud storage, use AWS Storage Gateway.

Know when to choose Amazon EBS or Amazon EC2 instance store.   Amazon EBS is most often the default option. However, Amazon EC2 instance store may be an option if your data does not meet any of the following criteria:

- Must persist through instance stops, terminations, or hardware failures
- Needs to be encrypted at the full volume level
- Needs to be backed up with EBS snapshots
- Needs to be removed from one instance and reattached to another

Know the different cloud data migration options.   There are a number of options for migrating your data to the AWS Cloud, or having a hybrid data solution between AWS and your data center or on premises. These include (but are not limited to) AWS Storage Gateway, AWS Import/Export, AWS Snowball, AWS Snowball Edge, AWS Snowmobile, Amazon Kinesis Data Firehose, AWS Direct Connect, and AWS VPN connections. Know when to choose one over the other based on time, cost, or volume.

Know what AWS Storage Gateway is and how it is used for cloud data migration.   AWS Storage Gateway is a hybrid cloud storage service that enables your on-premises applications to use AWS cloud storage seamlessly. Use this for data migration by means of a gateway that connects to AWS storage services, such as Amazon S3, Amazon S3 Glacier, and Amazon EBS.

Know what AWS Import/Export Disk is and how it is used for cloud data migration.   AWS Import/Export Disk accelerates moving large amounts of data into and out of the AWS Cloud using portable storage devices for transport. It transfers your data directly onto and off of storage devices using Amazon's high-speed internal network and bypassing the internet. For significant data sets, it is often much faster than transferring the data via the internet. You provide the hardware.

Know what AWS Snowball is and how it is used for cloud data migration.   Snowball is a petabyte-scale data transport solution that uses devices designed to be secure to transfer large amounts of data into and out of the AWS Cloud. Using Snowball addresses common challenges with large-scale data transfers including high network costs, long transfer times, and security concerns. You can transfer data at as little as one-fifth the cost of transferring data via high-speed internet. AWS provides the hardware.

Know what AWS Snowball Edge is and how it is used for cloud data migration.   AWS Snowball Edge is a 100-TB data transfer device with on-board storage and compute capabilities. Use it to move large amounts of data into and out of AWS, as a temporary storage tier for large local datasets, or to support local workloads in remote or offline locations. AWS Snowball Edge is a fast and inexpensive way to transfer large amounts of data when migrating to AWS.

Know what AWS Snowmobile is and how it is used for cloud data migration.   AWS Snowmobile is an exabyte-scale data transfer service used to move extremely large amounts of data to AWS. You can transfer up to 100 PB per Snowmobile, a 45-foot long ruggedized shipping container pulled by a semi-trailer truck. Snowmobile makes it easy to move massive volumes of data to the cloud, even a complete data center migration.

Know what Amazon Kinesis Data Firehose is and how it is used for cloud data migration. Amazon Kinesis Data Firehose is the easiest way to load streaming data reliably into data stores and analytics tools. It can capture, transform, and load streaming data into Amazon S3, Amazon Redshift, Amazon Elasticsearch Service, and Splunk. Kinesis Data Firehose can be used to transform and migrate data from on premises into the cloud.

Know what AWS Direct Connect is and how it is used for cloud data migration. Use AWS Direct Connect to establish private connectivity between AWS and your data center, office, or colocation environment, which in many cases can reduce your network costs, increase bandwidth throughput, and provide a more consistent network experience than internet-based connections.

Know what a VPN connection is and how it is used for cloud data migration. Connect your Amazon VPC to remote networks by using a VPN connection to increase privacy while migrating your data.

Know which tool to use for migrating storage to the AWS Cloud based on data size, time-line, and cost. There are two ways to migrate data: online and offline.

Online   Use AWS Direct Connect to connect your data center privately and directly to an AWS Region. Use AWS Snowball to transport petabytes of data physically in batches to the cloud. Use Snowball Edge to build hybrid storage that preserves existing on-premises investment and adds AWS services. Use AWS Snowmobile to migrate exabytes of data in batches to the cloud. Use Amazon S3 Transfer Acceleration to work with Amazon S3 over long geographic distances.

Offline   Use AWS Storage Gateway to integrate existing on-premises resources with the cloud. Use AWS Snowball Edge to transport petabytes of data physically in an appliance with on-board storage and compute capabilities. Use Amazon Kinesis Data Firehose to collect and ingest multiple streaming data sources or perform ETL on data while migrating to the AWS Cloud.

Resources to Review

Cloud Storage with AWS:

https://aws.amazon.com/products/storage/

AWS Storage Optimization (Whitepaper):

https://docs.aws.amazon.com/aws-technical-content/latest/
cost-optimization-storage-optimization/cost-optimization-storage-
optimization.pdf

AWS Storage Services Overview (Whitepaper):

https://aws.amazon.com/whitepapers/storage-options-aws-cloud/

Overview of AWS Security—Storage Services (Whitepaper):

https://d1.awsstatic.com/whitepapers/Security/Security_Storage_
Services_Whitepaper.pdf

Writing IAM Policies—How to Grant Access to an Amazon S3 Bucket
(AWS Security Blog):

> https://aws.amazon.com/blogs/security/writing-iam-policies-how-to-
> grant-access-to-an-amazon-s3-bucket/

Leveraging the Breadth of Storage Services and the Ecosystem at AWS—Unlock the
Full Potential of Public Cloud IaaS:

> https://d0.awsstatic.com/analyst-reports/US41693416.pdf

Cloud Data Migration Services:

> https://aws.amazon.com/cloud-data-migration/

AWS Migration (Whitepaper):

> https://d1.awsstatic.com/whitepapers/Migration/aws-migration-
> whitepaper.pdf

AWS Storage Gateway (Whitepaper):

> https://d1.awsstatic.com/whitepapers/aws-storage-gateway-file-gateway-
> for-hybrid-architectures.pdf

Hosting Static Websites on AWS (Whitepaper):

> https://d1.awsstatic.com/whitepapers/Building%20Static%20Websites%20
> on%20AWS.pdf

Encrypting Data at Rest (Whitepaper):

> https://d0.awsstatic.com/whitepapers/AWS_Securing_Data_at_Rest_with_
> Encryption.pdf

Building Big Data Storage Solutions (Data Lakes) for Maximum Flexibility
(Whitepaper):

> https://docs.aws.amazon.com/aws-technical-content/latest/building-data-
> lakes/building-data-lakes-on-aws.pdf

What Is Cloud Object Storage?

> https://aws.amazon.com/what-is-cloud-object-storage/

Amazon Simple Storage Service—Getting Started Guide:

> http://docs.aws.amazon.com/AmazonS3/latest/gsg/

Amazon Simple Storage Service—Developer Guide:

> https://docs.aws.amazon.com/AmazonS3/latest/dev/Welcome.html

VPC Endpoints:

> https://docs.aws.amazon.com/AmazonVPC/latest/UserGuide/vpc-endpoints
> .html

Amazon S3 Glacier—Developer Guide:

> https://docs.aws.amazon.com/amazonglacier/latest/dev/introduction.html

Amazon Elastic File System—User Guide:

    https://docs.aws.amazon.com/efs/latest/ug/

Deep Dive on Elastic File System—2017 AWS Online Tech Talks (Video):

    https://youtu.be/NhI0g8vI5M0

AWS re:Invent 2017: Deep Dive on Amazon Elastic File System (Amazon EFS)
(STG307) (Video):

    https://www.youtube.com/watch?v=VffbHp34UzQ

Amazon Elastic Block Store—Linux:

    https://docs.aws.amazon.com/AWSEC2/latest/UserGuide/AmazonEBS.html

Amazon Elastic Block Store—Windows:

    https://docs.aws.amazon.com/AWSEC2/latest/WindowsGuide/AmazonEBS.html

Amazon EC2 Instance Storage:

    https://docs.aws.amazon.com/AWSEC2/latest/UserGuide/InstanceStorage.html

AWS Storage Gateway—User Guide:

    https://docs.aws.amazon.com/storagegateway/latest/userguide/
    WhatIsStorageGateway.html

AWS Import/Export Disk:

    https://aws.amazon.com/snowball/disk/

AWS Snowball—User Guide:

    http://docs.aws.amazon.com/snowball/latest/ug/whatissnowball.html

AWS Snowball Edge—Developer Guide:

    http://docs.aws.amazon.com/snowball/latest/developer-guide/whatisedge
    .html

AWS Snowmobile:

    https://aws.amazon.com/snowmobile/

Amazon Kinesis Data Firehose—Developer Guide:

    https://docs.aws.amazon.com/firehose/latest/dev/what-is-this-service.html

AWS Direct Connect—User Guide:

    http://docs.aws.amazon.com/directconnect/latest/UserGuide/

VPN Connections:

    https://docs.aws.amazon.com/AmazonVPC/latest/UserGuide/vpn-connections
    .html

How to Use Bucket Policies and Apply Defense-in-Depth to Help Secure Your
Amazon S3 Data:

    https://aws.amazon.com/blogs/security/how-to-use-bucket-policies-and-
    apply-defense-in-depth-to-help-secure-your-amazon-s3-data/

IAM Policies and Bucket Policies and ACLs! Oh, My! (Controlling Access to S3 Resources):

> https://aws.amazon.com/blogs/security/iam-policies-and-bucket-policies-and-acls-oh-my-controlling-access-to-s3-resources/

AWS re:Invent Storage State of the Union (Video):

> https://www.youtube.com/watch?v=U-flt95opTw

AWS re:Invent Best Practices for Amazon S3 (STG302) (Video):

> https://www.youtube.com/watch?v=UKuL1K3oWuo

What Is a Data Lake?

> https://aws.amazon.com/big-data/data-lake-on-aws/

Amazon S3 Service Level Agreement:

> https://aws.amazon.com/s3/sla/

Protecting Data Using Server-Side Encryption with Amazon S3-Managed Encryption Keys (SSE-S3):

> https://docs.aws.amazon.com/AmazonS3/latest/dev/serv-side-encryption.html

Picking the Right Data Store for Your Workload:

> https://aws.amazon.com/blogs/startups/picking-the-right-data-store-for-your-workload/

Demystifying Storage on AWS (Video):

> https://www.youtube.com/watch?v=6UWmN2RbsnY

Exercises

For assistance in completing the following exercises, refer to the Amazon Simple Storage Service Developer Guide:

> https://docs.aws.amazon.com/AmazonS3/latest/dev/Welcome.html

We assume that you have performed the Exercises in Chapter 1 and Chapter 2 to set up your development environment in AWS Cloud9, or have done so on your own system with the AWS SDK.

For instructions on creating and testing a working sample, see Testing the Amazon S3 Java Code Examples here:

> https://docs.aws.amazon.com/AmazonS3/latest/dev/UsingTheMPJavaAPI.html#TestingJavaSamples

EXERCISE 3.1

Create an Amazon Simple Storage Service (Amazon S3) Bucket

In this exercise, you will create an Amazon S3 bucket using the AWS SDK for Java. You will use this bucket in the exercises that follow.

For assistance in completing this exercise, copying this code, or for code in other languages, see the following documentation:

https://docs.aws.amazon.com/AmazonS3/latest/dev/create-bucket-get-location-example.html

1. Enter the following code in your preferred development environment for Java:

```java
import java.io.IOException;

import com.amazonaws.AmazonServiceException;
import com.amazonaws.SdkClientException;
import com.amazonaws.auth.profile.ProfileCredentialsProvider;
import com.amazonaws.services.s3.AmazonS3;
import com.amazonaws.services.s3.AmazonS3ClientBuilder;
import com.amazonaws.services.s3.model.CreateBucketRequest;
import com.amazonaws.services.s3.model.GetBucketLocationRequest;

public class CreateBucket {

    public static void main(String[] args) throws IOException {
        String clientRegion = "*** Client region ***";
        String bucketName = "*** Bucket name ***";

        try {
            AmazonS3 s3Client = AmazonS3ClientBuilder.standard()
                    .withCredentials(new ProfileCredentialsProvider())
                    .withRegion(clientRegion)
                    .build();

            if (!s3Client.doesBucketExistV2(bucketName)) {
                // Because the CreateBucketRequest object doesn't specify a
                region, the
                // bucket is created in the region specified in the client.
                s3Client.createBucket(new CreateBucketRequest(bucketName));
```

(continued)

```
                    // Verify that the bucket was created by retrieving it and
                    checking its location.
                    String bucketLocation = s3Client.getBucketLocation(new
                    GetBucketLocationRequest(bucketName));
                    System.out.println("Bucket location: " + bucketLocation);
                }
            }
            catch(AmazonServiceException e) {
                // The call was transmitted successfully, but Amazon S3 couldn't
                process
                // it and returned an error response.
                e.printStackTrace();
            }
            catch(SdkClientException e) {
                // Amazon S3 couldn't be contacted for a response, or the client
                // couldn't parse the response from Amazon S3.
                e.printStackTrace();
            }
        }
    }
```

2. Replace the static variable values for clientRegion and bucketName. Note that bucket names must be unique across all of AWS. Make a note of these two values; you will use the same region and bucket name for the exercises that follow in this chapter.

3. Execute the code. Your bucket gets created with the name you specified in the region you specified. A successful result shows the following output:

```
Bucket Location: [bucketLocation]
```

Upload an Object to a Bucket

Now that you have a bucket, you can add objects to it. In this example, you will create two objects. The first object has a text string as data, and the second object is a file. This example creates the first object by specifying the bucket name, object key, and text data directly in a call to AmazonS3Client.putObject(). The example creates a second object by using a PutObjectRequest that specifies the bucket name, object key, and file path. The PutObjectRequest also specifies the ContentType header and title metadata.

For assistance in completing this exercise, copying this code, or for code in other languages, see the following documentation:

> https://docs.aws.amazon.com/AmazonS3/latest/dev/UploadObjSingleOpJava .html

1. Enter the following code in your preferred development environment for Java:

```java
import java.io.File;
import java.io.IOException;

import com.amazonaws.AmazonServiceException;
import com.amazonaws.SdkClientException;
import com.amazonaws.auth.profile.ProfileCredentialsProvider;
import com.amazonaws.services.s3.AmazonS3;
import com.amazonaws.services.s3.AmazonS3ClientBuilder;
import com.amazonaws.services.s3.model.ObjectMetadata;
import com.amazonaws.services.s3.model.PutObjectRequest;

public class UploadObject {

    public static void main(String[] args) throws IOException {
        String clientRegion = "*** Client region ***";
        String bucketName = "*** Bucket name ***";
        String stringObjKeyName = "*** String object key name ***";
        String fileObjKeyName = "*** File object key name ***";
        String fileName = "*** Path to file to upload ***";

        try {
            AmazonS3 s3Client = AmazonS3ClientBuilder.standard()
                    .withRegion(clientRegion)
                    .withCredentials(new ProfileCredentialsProvider())
                    .build();

            // Upload a text string as a new object.
            s3Client.putObject(bucketName, stringObjKeyName, "Uploaded
            String Object");

            // Upload a file as a new object with ContentType and title
            specified.
```

(continued)

```
            PutObjectRequest request = new PutObjectRequest(bucketName,
            fileObjKeyName, new File(fileName));
            ObjectMetadata metadata = new ObjectMetadata();
            metadata.setContentType("plain/text");
            metadata.addUserMetadata("x-amz-meta-title", "someTitle");
            request.setMetadata(metadata);
            s3Client.putObject(request);
        }
        catch(AmazonServiceException e) {
            // The call was transmitted successfully, but Amazon S3 couldn't
            process
            // it, so it returned an error response.
            e.printStackTrace();
        }
        catch(SdkClientException e) {
            // Amazon S3 couldn't be contacted for a response, or the client
            // couldn't parse the response from Amazon S3.
            e.printStackTrace();
        }
    }
}
```

2. Replace the static variable values for clientRegion and bucketName used in the previous exercise.

3. Replace the value for stringObjKeyName with the name of the key that you intend to create in your Amazon S3 bucket, which will upload a text string as a new object.

4. Replace the Uploaded String Object text with the text being placed inside the object that you are generating.

5. Replace the someTitle text in the code with your own metadata title for the object that you are uploading.

6. Create a local file on your machine and then replace the value for fileName with the full path and filename of the file that you created.

7. Replace the fileObjKeyName with the key name that you want for the file that you will be uploading. A file can be uploaded with a different name than the filename that's used locally.

8. Execute the code. Your bucket gets created with the name that you specified in the region that you specified. A successful result without errors will create two objects in your bucket.

EXERCISE 3.3

Emptying and Deleting a Bucket

Now that you have finished with the Amazon S3 exercises, you will want to clean up your environment by deleting all the files and the bucket you created. It is easy to delete an empty bucket. However, in some situations, you may need to delete or empty a bucket that contains objects. In this exercise, we show you how to delete objects and then delete the bucket.

For assistance in completing this exercise, copying this code, or for code in other languages, see the following documentation:

> https://docs.aws.amazon.com/AmazonS3/latest/dev/delete-or-empty-bucket.html

> https://docs.aws.amazon.com/AmazonS3/latest/dev/delete-or-empty-bucket
> .html#delete-bucket-sdk-java

1. Enter the following code in your preferred development environment for Java:

```java
import java.util.Iterator;

import com.amazonaws.AmazonServiceException;
import com.amazonaws.SdkClientException;
import com.amazonaws.auth.profile.ProfileCredentialsProvider;
import com.amazonaws.services.s3.AmazonS3;
import com.amazonaws.services.s3.AmazonS3ClientBuilder;
import com.amazonaws.services.s3.model.ListVersionsRequest;
import com.amazonaws.services.s3.model.ObjectListing;
import com.amazonaws.services.s3.model.S3ObjectSummary;
import com.amazonaws.services.s3.model.S3VersionSummary;
import com.amazonaws.services.s3.model.VersionListing;

public class DeleteBucket {

    public static void main(String[] args) {
        String clientRegion = "*** Client region ***";
        String bucketName = "*** Bucket name ***";

        try {
            AmazonS3 s3Client = AmazonS3ClientBuilder.standard()
                    .withCredentials(new ProfileCredentialsProvider())
                    .withRegion(clientRegion)
                    .build();
```

(continued)

```
// Delete all objects from the bucket. This is sufficient
// for unversioned buckets. For versioned buckets, when you
attempt to delete objects, Amazon S3 inserts
// delete markers for all objects, but doesn't delete the object
versions.
// To delete objects from versioned buckets, delete all of the
object versions before deleting
// the bucket (see below for an example).
ObjectListing objectListing = s3Client.listObjects(bucketName);
while (true) {
    Iterator<S3ObjectSummary> objIter = objectListing.
    getObjectSummaries().iterator();
    while (objIter.hasNext()) {
        s3Client.deleteObject(bucketName, objIter.next().
        getKey());
    }

    // If the bucket contains many objects, the listObjects()
    call
    // might not return all of the objects in the first listing.
    Check to
    // see whether the listing was truncated. If so, retrieve
    the next page of objects
    // and delete them.
    if (objectListing.isTruncated()) {
        objectListing = s3Client.listNextBatchOfObjects
        (objectListing);
    } else {
        break;
    }
}

// Delete all object versions (required for versioned buckets).
VersionListing versionList = s3Client.listVersions(new
ListVersionsRequest().withBucketName(bucketName));
while (true) {
    Iterator<S3VersionSummary> versionIter = versionList.
    getVersionSummaries().iterator();
    while (versionIter.hasNext()) {
        S3VersionSummary vs = versionIter.next();
        s3Client.deleteVersion(bucketName, vs.getKey(),
        vs.getVersionId());
    }
```

```
                    if (versionList.isTruncated()) {
                        versionList = s3Client.listNextBatchOfVersions
                        (versionList);
                    } else {
                        break;
                    }
                }

                // After all objects and object versions are deleted, delete the
                bucket.
                s3Client.deleteBucket(bucketName);
            }
            catch(AmazonServiceException e) {
                // The call was transmitted successfully, but Amazon S3 couldn't
                process
                // it, so it returned an error response.
                e.printStackTrace();
            }
            catch(SdkClientException e) {
                // Amazon S3 couldn't be contacted for a response, or the client
                couldn't
                // parse the response from Amazon S3.
                e.printStackTrace();
            }
        }
    }
}
```

2. Replace the static variable values for clientRegion and bucketName with the values that you used in the previous steps.

3. Execute the code.

4. When execution is complete without errors, both of your objects and your bucket will have been deleted.

Review Questions

1. You are developing an application that will run across dozens of instances. It uses some components from a legacy application that requires some configuration files to be copied from a central location and be held on a volume local to each of the instances. You plan to modify your application with a new component in the future that will hold this configuration in Amazon DynamoDB. However, in the interim, which storage option should you use that will provide the lowest cost and the lowest latency for your application to access the configuration files?

    A. Amazon S3

    B. Amazon EBS

    C. Amazon EFS

    D. Amazon EC2 instance store

2. In what ways does Amazon Simple Storage Service (Amazon S3) object storage differ from block and file storage? (Select TWO.)

    A. Amazon S3 stores data in fixed size blocks.

    B. Objects are identified by a numbered address.

    C. Object can be any size.

    D. Objects contain both data and metadata.

    E. Objects are stored in buckets.

3. You are restoring an Amazon Elastic Block Store (Amazon EBS) volume from a snapshot. How long will it take before the data is available?

    A. It depends on the provisioned size of the volume.

    B. The data will be available immediately.

    C. It depends on the amount of data stored on the volume.

    D. It depends on whether the attached instance is an Amazon EBS–optimized instance.

4. What are some of the key characteristics of Amazon Simple Storage Service (Amazon S3)? (Select THREE.)

    A. All objects have a URL.

    B. Amazon S3 can store unlimited amounts of data.

    C. Buckets can be mounted to the file system of multiple Amazon EC2 instances.

    D. Amazon S3 uses a Representational State Transfer (REST) application program interface (API).

    E. You must pre-allocate the storage in a bucket.

5. Amazon S3 Glacier is well-suited to data that is which of the following? (Select TWO.)

   A. Infrequently or rarely accessed

   B. Must be immediately available when needed

   C. Is available after a three- to five-hour restore period

   D. Is frequently erased within 30 days

6. You have valuable media files hosted on AWS and want them to be served only to authenticated users of your web application. You are concerned that your content could be stolen and distributed for free. How can you protect your content?

   A. Use static web hosting.

   B. Generate presigned URLs for content in the web application.

   C. Use AWS Identity and Access Management (IAM) policies to restrict access.

   D. Use logging to track your content.

7. Which of the following are features of Amazon Elastic Block Store (Amazon EBS)? (Select TWO.)

   A. Data stored on Amazon EBS is automatically replicated within an Availability Zone.

   B. Amazon EBS data is automatically backed up to tape.

   C. Amazon EBS volumes can be encrypted transparently to workloads on the attached instance.

   D. Data on an Amazon EBS volume is lost when the attached instance is stopped.

8. Which option should you choose for Amazon EFS when tens, hundreds, or thousands of Amazon EC2 instances will be accessing the file system concurrently?

   A. General-Purpose performance mode

   B. RAID 0

   C. Max I/O performance mode

   D. Change to a larger instance

9. Which of the following must be performed to host a static website in an Amazon Simple Storage Service (Amazon S3) bucket? (Select THREE.)

   A. Configure the bucket for static hosting, and specify an index and error document.

   B. Create a bucket with the same name as the website.

   C. Enable File Transfer Protocol (FTP) on the bucket.

   D. Make the objects in the bucket world-readable.

   E. Enable HTTP on the bucket.

10. You have a workload that requires 1 TB of durable block storage at 1,500 IOPS during normal use. Every night there is an extract, transform, load (ETL) task that requires 3,000 IOPS for 15 minutes. What is the most appropriate volume type for this workload?

    A. Use a Provisioned IOPS SSD volume at 3,000 IOPS.

    B. Use an instance store.

    C. Use a general-purpose SSD volume.

    D. Use a magnetic volume.

11. Which statements about Amazon S3 Glacier are true? (Select THREE.)

    A. It stores data in objects that live in buckets.

    B. Archives are identified by user-specified key names.

    C. Archives take 3–5 hours to restore.

    D. Vaults can be locked.

    E. It can be used as a standalone service and as an Amazon S3 storage class.

12. You are developing an application that will be running on several hundred Amazon EC2 instances. The application on each instance will be required to reach out through a file system protocol concurrently to a file system holding the files. Which storage option should you choose?

    A. Amazon EFS

    B. Amazon EBS

    C. Amazon EC2 instance store

    D. Amazon S3

13. You need to take a snapshot of an Amazon Elastic Block Store (Amazon EBS) volume. How long will the volume be unavailable?

    A. It depends on the provisioned size of the volume.

    B. The volume will be available immediately.

    C. It depends on the amount of data stored on the volume.

    D. It depends on whether the attached instance is an Amazon EBS–optimized instance.

14. Amazon Simple Storage Service (S3) bucket policies can restrict access to an Amazon S3 bucket and objects by which of the following? (Select THREE.)

    A. Company name

    B. IP address range

    C. AWS account

    D. Country of origin

    E. Objects with a specific prefix

15. Which of the following are *not* appropriate use cases for Amazon Simple Storage Service (Amazon S3)? (Select TWO.)

A. Storing static web content or hosting a static website

B. Storing a file system mounted to an Amazon Elastic Compute Cloud (Amazon EC2) instance

C. Storing backups for a relational database

D. Primary storage for a database

E. Storing logs for analytics

16. Which features enable you to manage access to Amazon Simple Storage Service (Amazon S3) buckets or objects? (Select THREE.)

A. Enable static website hosting on the bucket.

B. Create a presigned URL for an object.

C. Use an Amazon S3 Access Control List (ACL) on a bucket or object.

D. Use a lifecycle policy.

E. Use an Amazon S3 bucket policy.

17. Your application stores critical data in Amazon Simple Storage Service (Amazon S3), which must be protected against inadvertent or intentional deletion. How can this data be protected? (Select TWO.)

A. Use cross-region replication to copy data to another bucket automatically.

B. Set a vault lock.

C. Enable versioning on the bucket.

D. Use a lifecycle policy to migrate data to Amazon S3 Glacier.

E. Enable MFA Delete on the bucket.

18. You have a set of users that have been granted access to your Amazon S3 bucket. For compliance purposes, you need to keep track of all files accessed in that bucket. To have a record of who accessed your Amazon Simple Storage Service (Amazon S3) data and from where, what should you do?

A. Enable versioning on the bucket.

B. Enable website hosting on the bucket.

C. Enable server access logging on the bucket.

D. Create an AWS Identity and Access Management (IAM) bucket policy.

E. Enable Amazon CloudWatch logs.

19. What are some reasons to enable cross-region replication on an Amazon Simple Storage Service (Amazon S3) bucket? (Select THREE.)

A. Your compliance requirements dictate that you store data at an even further distance than Availability Zones, which are tens of miles apart.

B. Minimize latency when your customers are in two geographic regions.

C. You need a backup of your data in case of accidental deletion.

D. You have compute clusters in two different AWS Regions that analyze the same set of objects.

E. Your data requires at least five nines of durability.

20. Your company requires that all data sent to external storage be encrypted before being sent. You will be sending company data to Amazon S3. Which Amazon Simple Storage Service (Amazon S3) encryption solution will meet this requirement?

   A.   Server-Side Encryption with AWS managed keys (SSE-S3)

   B.   Server-Side Encryption with customer-provided keys (SSE-C)

   C.   Client-side encryption with customer-managed keys

   D.   Server-side encryption with AWS Key Management Service (AWS KMS) keys (SSE-KMS)

21. How is data stored in Amazon Simple Storage Service (Amazon S3) for high durability?

   A.   Data is automatically replicated to other regions.

   B.   Data is automatically replicated within a region.

   C.   Data is replicated only if versioning is enabled on the bucket.

   D.   Data is automatically backed up on tape and restored if needed.

Chapter

4

Hello, Databases

**THE AWS CERTIFIED DEVELOPER –
ASSOCIATE EXAM TOPICS COVERED IN
THIS CHAPTER MAY INCLUDE, BUT ARE
NOT LIMITED TO, THE FOLLOWING:**

Domain 2: Security

✓ 2.1 Make authenticated calls to AWS services.

✓ 2.2 Implement encryption using AWS services.

Domain 3: Development with AWS Services

✓ 3.2 Translate functional requirements into application
design.

✓ 3.3 Write code that interacts with AWS services by using
APIs, SDKs, and AWS CLI.

Domain 4: Refactoring

✓ 4.1 Optimize application to best use AWS services and
features.

Domain 5: Monitoring and Troubleshooting

✓ 5.2 Perform root cause analysis on faults found in
testing or production.

Introduction to Databases

In addition to the storage options discussed in the previous chapters, AWS offers a broad range of databases purposely built for your specific application use cases. You can also set up your own database platform on the Amazon Elastic Compute Cloud (Amazon EC2). You can easily migrate your existing databases with the AWS Database Migration Service (AWS DMS) in a cost-effective manner.

AWS Cloud offerings include the following databases:

Managed relational databases—For transactional applications

Nonrelational databases—For internet-scale applications

Data warehouse databases—For analytics

In-memory data store databases—For caching and real-time workloads

Time-series databases—For efficiently collecting, synthesizing, and deriving insights from time-series data

Ledger databases—For when you need a centralized, trusted authority to maintain a scalable, complete, and cryptographically verifiable record of transactions

Graph databases—For building applications with highly connected data

Depending on your use case, you can choose from an AWS database that closely aligns with your needs. Table 4.1 describes each database service that AWS offers and indicates the database type.

TABLE 4.1 AWS Database Service Mapping to Database Type

Product	Type	Description
Amazon Aurora	Relational database	A MySQL- and PostgreSQL-compatible relational database built for the cloud that combines the performance and availability of traditional enterprise databases with the simplicity and cost-effectiveness of open source databases.

Product	Type	Description
Amazon Relational Database Service (Amazon RDS)	Relational database	A managed relational database for MySQL, PostgreSQL, Oracle, SQL Server, and MariaDB. Easy to set up, operate, and scale a relational database in the cloud quickly.
Amazon DynamoDB	NoSQL database	A serverless, managed NoSQL database that delivers consistent single-digit millisecond latency at any scale. Pay only for the throughput and storage you use.
Amazon Redshift	Data warehouse	A fast, fully managed, petabyte-scale data warehouse at one-tenth the cost of traditional solutions. Simple and cost-effective solution to analyze data by using standard SQL and your existing business intelligence (BI) tools.
Amazon ElastiCache	In-memory data store	To deploy, operate, and scale an in-memory data store based on Memcached or Redis in the cloud.
Amazon Neptune	Graph database	A fast, reliable, fully managed graph database to store and manage highly connected datasets.
Amazon Document DB (with MongoDB compatibility)	Nonrelational database	A fast, scalable, highly available, and fully managed document database service that supports MongoDB workloads.
Amazon Timestream	Time series database	A fast, scalable, fully managed time series database service for IoT and operational applications that makes it easy to store and analyze trillions of events per day at one-tenth the cost of relational databases.
Amazon Quantum Ledger Database (Amazon QLDB)	Ledger database	A fully managed ledger database that provides a transparent, immutable, and cryptographically verifiable transaction log owned by a central trusted authority.
AWS Database Migration Service (AWS DMS)	Database migration	Help migrate your databases to AWS easily and inexpensively with minimal downtime.

Now that you know the purpose of these database services and what they can do, review the type of applications that can be used for each AWS database service. Refer to the application type mappings shown in Table 4.2.

TABLE 4.2   Application Mapping to AWS Database Service

Applications	Product
Transactional applications, such as ERP, CRM, and ecommerce to log transactions and store structured data.	Aurora or Amazon RDS
Internet-scale applications, such as hospitality, dating, and ride sharing, to serve content and store structured and unstructured data.	DynamoDB or Amazon DocumentDB
Analytic applications for operational reporting and querying terabyte- to exabyte-scale data.	Amazon Redshift
Real-time application use cases that require submillisecond latency such as gaming leaderboards, chat, messaging, streaming, and Internet of Things (IoT).	ElastiCache
Applications with use cases that require navigation of highly connected data such as social news feeds, recommendations, and fraud detection.	Neptune
Applications that collect data at millions of inserts per second in a time-series fashion, for example clickstream data and IoT devices.	Timestream
Applications that require an accurate history of their application data; for example, tracking the history of credits and debits in banking transactions or verifying the audit trails created in relational databases.	Amazon QLDB

Relational Databases

Many developers have had to interact with relational databases in their applications. This section describes first what a relational database is. Then, it covers how you can run a relational database in the AWS Cloud with Amazon RDS or on Amazon EC2.

A *relational database* is a collection of data items with predefined relationships between them. These items are organized as a set of tables with columns and rows. Tables store information about the *objects* to be represented in the database. Each *column* in a table holds certain data, and a *field* stores the actual value of an attribute. The *rows* in the table represent a collection of related values of one object or entity. Each row in a table contains a unique identifier called a *primary key*, and rows among multiple tables can be linked by using *foreign keys*. You can access data in many different ways without reorganizing the database tables.

Characteristics of Relational Databases

Relational databases include four important characteristics: Structured Query Language, data integrity, transactions, and atomic, consistent, isolated, and durable compliance.

Structured Query Language

Structured query language (SQL) is the primary interface that you use to communicate with relational databases. The standard American National Standards Institute (ANSI) SQL is supported by all popular relational database engines. Some of these engines have extensions to ANSI SQL to support functionality that is specific to that engine. You use SQL to add, update, or delete data rows; to retrieve subsets of data for transaction processing and analytics applications; and to manage all aspects of the database.

Data Integrity

Data integrity is the overall completeness, accuracy, and consistency of data. Relational databases use a set of constraints to enforce data integrity in the database. These include primary keys, foreign keys, NOT NULL constraints, unique constraint, default constraints, and check constraints. These integrity constraints help enforce business rules in the tables to ensure the accuracy and reliability of the data. In addition, most relational databases enable you to embed custom code triggers that execute based on an action on the database.

Transactions

A database *transaction* is one or more SQL statements that execute as a sequence of operations to form a single logical unit of work. Transactions provide an all-or-nothing proposition, meaning that the entire transaction must complete as a single unit and be written to the database, or none of the individual components of the transaction will continue. In relational database terminology, a transaction results in a COMMIT or a ROLLBACK. Each transaction is treated in a coherent and reliable way, independent of other transactions.

ACID Compliance

All database transactions must be *atomic, consistent, isolated, and durable (ACID)–* compliant or be atomic, consistent, isolated, and durable to ensure data integrity.

Atomicity   *Atomicity* requires that the transaction as a whole executes successfully, or if a part of the transaction fails, then the entire transaction is invalid.

Consistency *Consistency* mandates that the data written to the database as part of the transaction must adhere to all defined rules and restrictions, including constraints, cascades, and triggers.

Isolation *Isolation* is critical to achieving concurrency control, and it makes sure that each transaction is independent unto itself.

Durability *Durability* requires that all of the changes made to the database be permanent when a transaction is successfully completed.

Managed vs. Unmanaged Databases

Managed database services on AWS, such as Amazon RDS, enable you to offload the administrative burdens of operating and scaling distributed databases to AWS so that you don't have to worry about the following tasks:

- Hardware provisioning
- Setup and configuration
- Throughput capacity planning
- Replication
- Software patching
- Cluster scaling

AWS provides a number of database alternatives for developers. As a managed database, Amazon RDS enables you to run a fully featured relational database while offloading database administration. By contrast, you can run unmanaged databases on Amazon EC2, which gives you more flexibility on the types of databases that you can deploy and configure; however, you are responsible for the administration of the unmanaged databases.

Amazon Relational Database Service

With *Amazon Relational Database Service (Amazon RDS)*, you can set up, operate, and scale a relational database in the AWS Cloud. It provides cost-efficient, resizable capacity for open-standard relational database engines. Amazon RDS is easy to administer, and you do not need to install the database software. Amazon RDS manages time-consuming database administration tasks, which frees you up to focus on your applications and business. For example, Amazon RDS automatically patches the database software and backs up your database. The Amazon RDS managed relational database service works with the popular database engines depicted in Figure 4.1.

FIGURE 4.1 Amazon RDS database engines

Amazon RDS assumes many of the difficult or tedious management tasks of a relational database:

Procurement, configuration, and backup tasks

- When you buy a server, you get a central processing unit (CPU), memory, storage, and input/output operations per second (IOPS) all bundled together. With Amazon RDS, these are split apart so that you can scale them independently and allocate your resources as you need them.

- Amazon RDS manages backups, software patches, automatic failure detection, and recovery.

- You can configure automated backups or manually create your own backup snapshot and use these backups to restore a database. The Amazon RDS restore process works reliably and efficiently.

- You can use familiar database products: MySQL, MariaDB, PostgreSQL, Oracle, Microsoft SQL Server, and the MySQL- and PostgreSQL-compatible Amazon Aurora DB engine.

Security and availability

- You can enable the encryption option for your Amazon RDS DB instance.

- You can get high availability with a primary instance and a synchronous secondary instance that you can fail over to when problems occur. You can also use MySQL, MariaDB, or PostgreSQL read replicas to increase read scaling.

- In addition to the security in your database package, you can use AWS Identity and Access Management (IAM) to define users, and permissions help control who can access your Amazon RDS databases. You can also help protect your databases by storing them in a virtual private cloud (VPC).

- To deliver a managed service experience, Amazon RDS does not provide shell access to DB instances, and it restricts access to certain system procedures and tables that require advanced permissions.

When you host databases on Amazon RDS, AWS is responsible for the items in Figure 4.2.

FIGURE 4.2   Amazon RDS host responsibilities

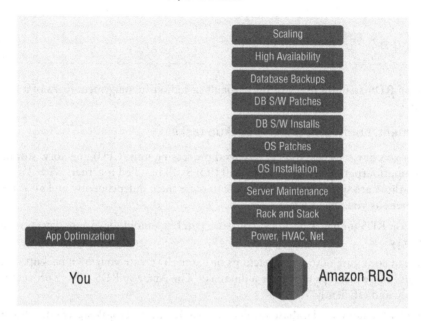

Relational Database Engines on Amazon RDS

Amazon RDS provides six familiar database engines: Amazon Aurora, Oracle, Microsoft SQL Server, PostgreSQL, MySQL, and MariaDB. Because Amazon RDS is a managed service, you gain a number of benefits and features built right into the Amazon RDS service. These features include, but are not limited to, the following:

- Automatic software patching
- Easy vertical scaling
- Easy storage scaling
- Read replicas
- Automatic backups
- Database snapshots
- Multi-AZ deployments
- Encryption
- IAM DB authentication
- Monitoring and metrics with Amazon CloudWatch

To create an Amazon RDS instance, you can run the following command from the AWS CLI:

```
aws rds create-db-instance \
--db-instance-class db.t2.micro \
--allocated-storage 30 \
--db-instance-identifier my-cool-rds-db --engine mysql \
--master-username masteruser --master-user-password masterpassword1!
```

Depending on the configurations chosen, the database can take several minutes before it is active and ready for use. You can monitor the Amazon RDS Databases console to view the status. When the status states Available, it is ready to be used, as shown in Figure 4.3.

FIGURE 4.3   Amazon RDS Databases console

Automatic Software Patching

Periodically, Amazon RDS performs maintenance on Amazon RDS resources. Maintenance mostly involves patching the Amazon RDS database underlying operating system (OS) or database engine version. Because this is a managed service, Amazon RDS handles the patching for you.

When you create an Amazon RDS database instance, you can define a maintenance window. A *maintenance window* is where you can define a period of time when you want to apply any updates or downtime to your database instance. You also can enable the automatic minor version upgrade feature, which automatically applies any new minor versions of the database as they are released (see Figure 4.4).

FIGURE 4.4   Maintenance window

You can select a maintenance window by using the AWS Management Console, AWS CLI, or Amazon RDS API. After selecting the maintenance window, the Amazon RDS instance is upgraded (if upgrades are available) during that time window. You can also modify the maintenance window by running the following AWS CLI command:

```
aws rds modify-db-instance --db-instance-identifer your-db-instance-identifer
--preferred-maintenance-window Mon:07:00-Mon:07:30
```

Vertical Scaling

If your database needs to handle a bigger load, you can vertically scale your Amazon RDS instance. At the time of this writing, there are 40 available DB instance classes, which enable you to choose the number of virtual CPUs and memory available. This gives you flexibility over the performance and cost of your Amazon RDS database. To scale the Amazon RDS instance, you can use the console, AWS CLI, or AWS SDK.

If you are in a Single-AZ configuration for your Amazon RDS instance, the database is unavailable during the scaling operation. However, if you are in a Multi-AZ configuration, the standby database is upgraded first and then a failover occurs to the newly configured database. You can also apply the change during the next maintenance window. This way, your upgrade can occur during your normal outage windows.

To scale the Amazon RDS database by using the AWS CLI, run the following command:

```
aws rds modify-db-instance --db-instance-identifer your-db-instance-identifer
--db-instance-class db.t2.medium
```

Easy Storage Scaling

Storage is a critical component for any database. Amazon RDS has the following three storage types:

General Purpose SSD (gp2)   This storage type is for cost-effective storage that is ideal for a broad range of workloads. Gp2 volumes deliver single-digit millisecond latencies and the ability to burst to 3,000 IOPS for extended periods of time. The volume's size determines the performance of gp2 volumes.

Provisioned IOPS (io1)   This storage type is for input/output-intensive workloads that require low input/output (I/O) latency and consistent I/O throughput.

Magnetic Storage   This storage type is designed for backward compatibility, and AWS recommends that you use General Purpose SSD or Provisioned IOPS for any new Amazon RDS workloads.

To scale your storage, you must modify the Amazon RDS DB instance by executing the following AWS CLI command:

```
aws rds modify-db-instance --db-instance-identifer your-db-instance-identifer
--allocated-storage 50 --storage-type io1 --iops 3000
```

This command modifies your storage to 50 GB in size, with a Provisioned IOPS storage drive and a dedicated IOPS of 3000. While modifying the Amazon RDS DB instance, consider the potential downtime.

Read Replicas (Horizontal Scaling)

There are two ways to scale your database tier with Amazon RDS: vertical scaling and horizontal scaling. Vertical scaling takes the primary database and increases the amount of memory and vCPUs allocated for the primary database. Alternatively, use horizontal scaling (add another server) to your database tier to improve the performance of applications that are read-heavy as opposed to write-heavy.

Read replicas create read-only copies of your master database, which allow you to offload any reads (or SQL SELECT statements) to the read replica. The replication from the master database to the read replica is asynchronous. As a result, the data queried from the read replica is not the latest data. If your application requires strongly consistent reads, consider an alternative option.

At the time of this writing, Amazon RDS MySQL, PostgreSQL, and MariaDB support up to five read replicas, and Amazon Aurora supports up to 15 read replicas. Microsoft SQL Server and Oracle do not support read replicas.

To create a read replica by using AWS CLI, run the following command:

```
aws rds create-db-instance-read-replica --db-instance-identifier your-db-instance-identifier --source-db-instance-identifier your-source-db
```

Backing Up Data with Amazon RDS

Amazon RDS has two different ways of backing up data of your database instance: automated backups and database snapshots (DB snapshots).

Automated Backups (Point-in-Time)

With Amazon RDS, automated backups offer a point-in-time recovery of your database. When enabled, Amazon RDS performs a full daily snapshot of your data that is taken during your preferred backup window. After the initial backup is taken (each day), then Amazon RDS captures transaction logs as changes are made to the database.

After you initiate a point-in-time recovery, to restore your database instance, the transaction logs are applied to the most appropriate daily backup. You can perform a restore up to the specific second, as long as it's within your retention period. The default retention period is seven days, but it can be a maximum of up to 35 days.

To perform a restore, you must choose the Latest Restorable Time, which is typically within the last 5 minutes. For example, suppose that the current date is February 14 at 10 p.m., and you would like to do a point-in-time restore of February 14 at 9 p.m. This restore would succeed because the Latest Restorable Time is a maximum of February 14 at 9:55 p.m. (which is the last 5-minute window). However, a point-in-time restore of February 14 at 9:58 p.m. would fail, because it is within the 5-minute window.

Automated backups are kept until the source database is deleted. After the source Amazon RDS instance is removed, the automated backups are also removed.

Database Snapshots (Manual)

Unlike automated backups, database snapshots with Amazon RDS are user-initiated and enable you to back up your database instance in a known state at any time. You can also restore to that specific snapshot at any time.

Similar to the other Amazon RDS features, you can create the snapshots through the AWS Management Console, with the CreateDBSnapshot API, or with the AWS CLI.

With DB snapshots, the backups are kept until you explicitly delete them; therefore, before removing any Amazon RDS instance, take a final snapshot before removing it. Regardless of the backup taken, storage I/O may be briefly suspended while the backup process initializes (typically a few seconds), and you may experience a brief period of elevated latency. A way to avoid these types of suspensions is to deploy in a Multi-AZ configuration. With such a deployment, the backup is taken from the standby instead of the primary database.

To create a snapshot of the database, from the Amazon RDS Databases console, under Actions, select the Take snapshot option (see Figure 4.5). After a snapshot is taken, you can view all of your snaps from the Snapshots console.

FIGURE 4.5 Taking an Amazon RDS snapshot

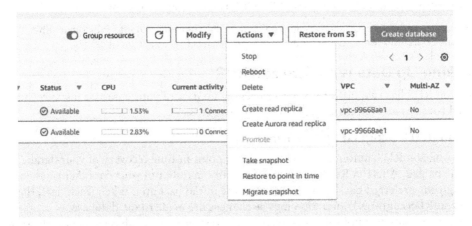

Multi-AZ Deployments

By using Amazon RDS, you can run in a Multi-AZ configuration. In a Multi-AZ configuration, you have a primary and a standby DB instance. Updates to the primary database replicate synchronously to the standby replica in a different Availability Zone. The primary benefit of Multi-AZ is realized during certain types of planned maintenance, or in the unlikely event of a DB instance failure or an Availability Zone failure. Amazon RDS automatically fails over to the standby so that you can resume your workload as soon as the standby is promoted to the primary. This means that you can reduce your downtime in the event of a failure.

Because Amazon RDS is a managed service, Amazon RDS handles the fail to the standby. When there is a DB instance failure, Amazon RDS automatically promotes the standby to the primary—you will not interact with the standby directly. In other words, you will receive one endpoint connection for the Amazon RDS cluster, and Amazon RDS handles the failover.

Amazon RDS Multi-AZ configuration provides the following benefits:

- Automatic failover; no administration required
- Increased durability in the unlikely event of component failure
- Increased availability in the unlikely event of an Availability Zone failure
- Increased availability for planned maintenance (automated backups; I/O activity is no longer suspended)

To create an Amazon RDS instance in a Multi-AZ configuration, you must specify a subnet group that has two different Availability Zones specified. You can specify a Multi-AZ configuration by using AWS CLI by adding the `--multi-az` flag to the AWS CLI command, as follows:

```
aws rds create-db-instance \
--db-instance-class db.t2.micro \
--allocated-storage 30 \
--db-instance-identifier multi-az-rds-db --engine mysql \
--master-username masteruser \
--master-user-password masterpassword1! \
--multi-az
```

Encryption

For encryption at rest, Amazon RDS uses the AWS Key Management Service (AWS KMS) for AES-256 encryption. You can use a default master key or specify your own for the Amazon RDS DB instance. Encryption is one of the few options that must be configured when the DB instance is created. You cannot modify an Amazon RDS database to enable encryption. You can, however, create a DB snapshot and then restore to an encrypted DB instance or cluster.

Amazon RDS supports using the Transparent Data Encryption (TDE) for Oracle and SQL Server. For more information on TDE with Oracle and Microsoft SQL Server, see the following:

- Microsoft SQL Server Transparent Data Encryption Support at:

    https://docs.aws.amazon.com/AmazonRDS/latest/UserGuide/Appendix.SQLServer.Options.TDE.html

- Options for Oracle DB Instances:

    https://docs.aws.amazon.com/AmazonRDS/latest/UserGuide/Appendix.Oracle.Options.html#Appendix.Oracle.Options.AdvSecurity

At the time of this writing, the following Amazon RDS DB instance types are not supported for encryption at rest:

- Db.m1.small
- Db.m1.medium
- Db.m1.large
- Db.m1.xlarge
- Db.m2.xlarge
- Db.m2.2xlarge
- Db.m2.4xlarge
- Db.t2.micro

For encryption in transit, Amazon RDS generates an SSL certificate for each database instance that can be used to connect your application and the Amazon RDS instance. However, encryption is a compute-intensive operation that increases the latency of your database connection. For more information, see the documentation for the specific database engine.

IAM DB Authentication

You can authenticate to your DB instance by using IAM. By using IAM, you can manage access to your database resources centrally instead of storing the user credentials in each database. The IAM feature also encrypts network traffic to and from the database by using SSL.

IAM DB authentication is supported only for MySQL and PostgreSQL. At the time of this writing, the following MySQL versions are supported:

- MySQL 5.6.34 or later
- MySQL 5.7.16 or later

There's no support for the following:

- IAM DB Authentication for MySQL 5.5 or MySQL 8.0
- db.t2.small and db.m1.small instances

The following PostgreSQL versions are supported:

- PostgreSQL versions 10.6 or later
- PostgreSQL 9.6.11 or later
- PostgreSQL 9.5.15 or later

To enable IAM DB authentication for your Amazon RDS instance, run the following command:

```
aws rds modify-db-instance --db-instance-identifier my-rds-db --enable-iam-
database-authentication --apply-immediately
```

Because downtime is associated with this action, you can enable this feature during the next maintenance window. You can do so by changing the last parameter to `--no-apply-immediately`.

Monitoring with Amazon CloudWatch

Use Amazon CloudWatch to monitor your database tier. You can create alarms to notify database administrators when there is a failure.

By default, CloudWatch provides some built-in metrics for Amazon RDS with a granularity of 5 minutes (600 seconds). If you want to gather metrics in a smaller window of granularity, such as 1 second, enable enhanced monitoring, which is similar to how you enable these features in Amazon EC2.

To view all the Amazon RDS metrics that are provided through CloudWatch, select the Monitoring tab from the Amazon RDS console (see Figure 4.6).

FIGURE 4.6   Amazon RDS with CloudWatch metrics

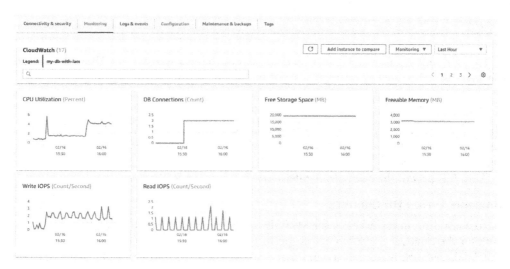

Amazon RDS integrates with CloudWatch to send it the following database logs:

- Audit log
- Error log
- General log
- Slow query log

From the Amazon RDS console, select the Logs & events tab to view and download the specified logs, as shown in Figure 4.7.

FIGURE 4.7   Amazon RDS with CloudWatch Logs

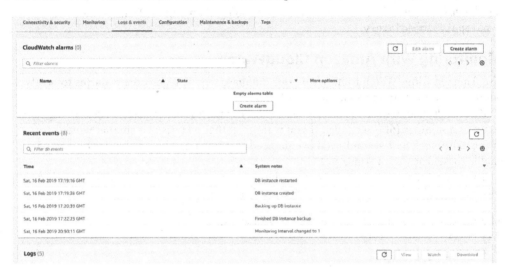

For more information on CloudWatch and its capabilities across other AWS services, see Chapter 15, "Monitoring and Troubleshooting."

Amazon Aurora

Amazon Aurora is a MySQL- and PostgreSQL-compatible relational database engine that combines the speed and availability of high-end commercial databases with the simplicity and cost-effectiveness of open source databases.

Aurora is part of the managed database service Amazon RDS.

Amazon Aurora DB Clusters

Aurora is a drop-in replacement for MySQL and PostgreSQL relational databases. It is built for the cloud, and it combines the performance and availability of high-end commercial databases with the simplicity and cost-effectiveness of open source databases. You can use the code, tools, and applications that you use today with your existing MySQL and PostgreSQL databases with Aurora.

The integration of Aurora with Amazon RDS means that time-consuming administration tasks, such as hardware provisioning, database setup, patching, and backups, are automated.

Aurora features a distributed, fault-tolerant, self-healing storage system that automatically scales up to 64 TiB per database instance. (In comparison, other Amazon RDS options allow for a maximum of 32 TiB.) Aurora delivers high performance and availability with up to 15 low-latency read replicas, point-in-time recovery, continuous backup to Amazon Simple Storage Service (Amazon S3), and replication across three Availability Zones. When you create an Aurora instance, you create a DB cluster. A *DB cluster* consists of one or more DB instances and a cluster volume that manages the data for those instances. An Aurora *cluster volume* is a virtual database storage volume that spans multiple Availability Zones, and each Availability Zone has a copy of the DB cluster data.

An Aurora DB cluster has two types of DB instances:

Primary Instance   Supports read and write operations and performs all of the data modifications to the cluster volume. Each Aurora DB cluster has one primary instance.

Amazon Aurora Replica   Supports read-only operations. Each Aurora DB cluster can have up to 15 *Amazon Aurora Replicas* in addition to the primary instance. Multiple Aurora Replicas distribute the read workload, and if you locate Aurora Replicas in separate Availability Zones, you can also increase database availability.

Figure 4.8 illustrates the relationship between the cluster volume, the primary instance, and Aurora Replicas in an Aurora DB cluster.

FIGURE 4.8   Amazon Aurora DB cluster

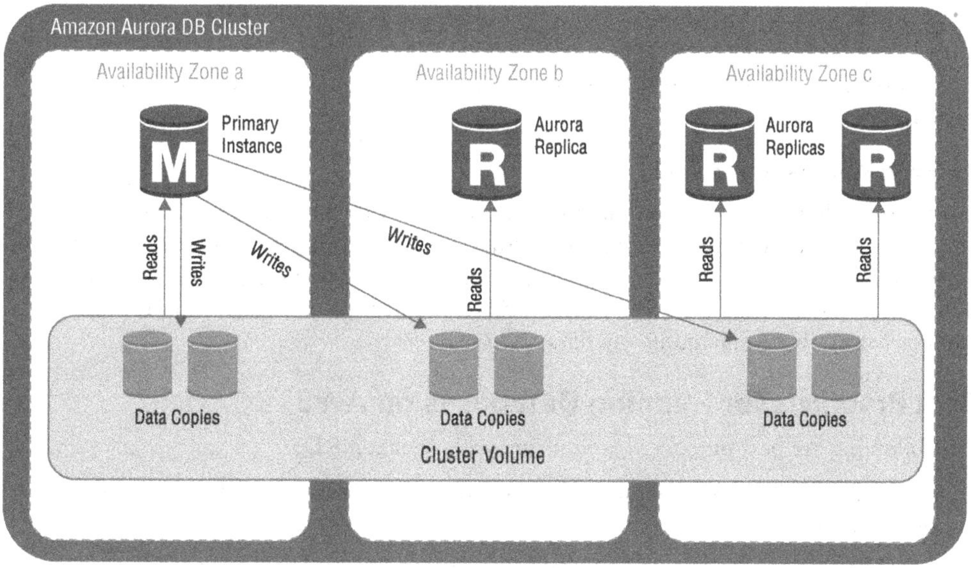

As you can see from Figure 4.8, this architecture is vastly different from the other Amazon RDS databases. Aurora is engineered and architected for the cloud. The primary difference is that there is a separate storage layer, called the *cluster volume*, which is spread across multiple Availability Zones in a single AWS Region. This means that the durability of your data is increased.

Additionally, Aurora has one primary instance that writes across the cluster volume. This means that Aurora replicas can be spun up quickly, because they don't have to copy and store their own storage layer; they connect to it. Because the cluster volume is separated in this architecture, the cluster volume can grow automatically as your data increases. This is in contrast to how other Amazon RDS databases are built, whereby you must define the allocated storage in advance.

Amazon Aurora Global Databases

With Aurora, you can also create a multiregional deployment for your database tier. In this configuration, the primary AWS Region is where your data is written (you may also do reads from the primary AWS Region). Any application performing writes must write to the primary AWS Region where the cluster is operating.

The secondary AWS Region is used for *reading* data only. Aurora replicates the data to the secondary AWS Region with typical latency of less than a second. Furthermore, you can use the secondary AWS Region for disaster recovery purposes. You can promote the secondary cluster and make it available as the primary typically in less than a minute. At the time of this writing, Aurora global databases are available in the following AWS Regions only:

- US East (N. Virginia)
- US East (Ohio)
- US West (Oregon)
- EU (Ireland)

Additionally, at the time of this writing, Aurora global databases are available only for MySQL 5.6.

Amazon Aurora Serverless

Aurora Serverless is an on-demand, automatic scaling configuration for Aurora. (It is available only for MySQL at the time of this writing.) With Aurora Serverless, the database will *automatically* start up, shut down, and scale capacity up or down based on your application's needs. This means that, as a developer, you can run your database in the AWS Cloud and not worry about managing any database instances.

Best Practices for Running Databases on AWS

The following are best practices for working with Amazon RDS:

Follow Amazon RDS basic operational guidelines.   The Amazon RDS Service Level Agreement requires that you follow these guidelines:

- Monitor your memory, CPU, and storage usage. Amazon CloudWatch can notify you when usage patterns change or when you approach the capacity of your deployment so that you can maintain system performance and availability.

- Scale up your DB instance when you approach storage capacity limits. Have some buffer in storage and memory to accommodate unforeseen increases in demand from your applications.

- Enable automatic backups, and set the backup window to occur during the daily low in write IOPS.

- If your database workload requires more I/O than you have provisioned, recovery after a failover or database failure will be slow. To increase the I/O capacity of a DB instance, do any or all of the following:
  - Migrate to a DB instance class with high I/O capacity.
  - Convert from standard storage either to General Purpose or Provisioned IOPS storage, depending on how much of an increase you need. If you convert to Provisioned IOPS storage, make sure that you also use a DB instance class that is optimized for Provisioned IOPS.
  - If you are already using Provisioned IOPS storage, provision additional throughput capacity.
- If your client application is caching the Domain Name Service (DNS) data of your DB instances, set a time-to-live (TTL) value of less than 30 seconds. Because the underlying IP address of a DB instance can change after a failover, caching the DNS data for an extended time can lead to connection failures if your application tries to connect to an IP address that no longer is in service.
- Test failover for your DB instance to understand how long the process takes for your use case and to ensure that the application that accesses your DB instance can automatically connect to the new DB instance after failover.

Allocate sufficient RAM to the DB instance.   An Amazon RDS performance best practice is to allocate enough RAM so that your working set resides almost completely in memory. Check the ReadIOPS metric by using CloudWatch while the DB instance is under load to view the working set. The value of ReadIOPS should be small and stable. Scale up the DB instance class until ReadIOPS no longer drops dramatically after a scaling operation or when ReadIOPS is reduced to a small amount.

Implement Amazon RDS security.   Use IAM accounts to control access to Amazon RDS API actions, especially actions that create, modify, or delete Amazon RDS resources, such as DB instances, security groups, option groups, or parameter groups, and actions that perform common administrative actions, such as backing up and restoring DB instances, or configuring Provisioned IOPS storage.

- Assign an individual IAM account to each person who manages Amazon RDS resources. Do not use an AWS account user to manage Amazon RDS resources; create an IAM user for everyone, including yourself.
- Grant each user the minimum set of permissions required to perform his or her duties.
- Use IAM groups to manage permissions effectively for multiple users.
- Rotate your IAM credentials regularly.

Use the AWS Management Console, the AWS CLI, or the Amazon RDS API to change the password for your master user. If you use another tool, such as a SQL client, to change the master user password, it might result in permissions being revoked for the user unintentionally.

Use enhanced monitoring to identify OS issues.   Amazon RDS provides metrics in real time for the OS on which your DB instance runs. You can view the metrics for your DB instance by using the console or consume the Enhanced Monitoring JSON output from CloudWatch Logs in a monitoring system of your choice. Enhanced Monitoring is available for the following database engines:

- MariaDB
- Microsoft SQL Server
- MySQL version 5.5 or later
- Oracle
- PostgreSQL

Enhanced Monitoring is available for all DB instance classes except for db.m1.small. Enhanced Monitoring is available in all regions except for AWS GovCloud (US).

Use metrics to identify performance issues.   To identify performance issues caused by insufficient resources and other common bottlenecks, you can monitor the metrics available for your Amazon RDS DB instance.

Monitor performance metrics regularly to see the average, maximum, and minimum values for a variety of time ranges. If you do so, you can identify when performance is degraded. You can also set CloudWatch alarms for particular metric thresholds.

To troubleshoot performance issues, it's important to understand the baseline performance of the system. When you set up a new DB instance and get it running with a typical work-load, you should capture the average, maximum, and minimum values of all the perfor-mance metrics at a number of different intervals (for example, 1 hour, 24 hours, 1 week, or 2 weeks) to get an idea of what is normal. It helps to get comparisons for both peak and off-peak hours of operation. You can then use this information to identify when perfor-mance is dropping below standard levels.

Tune queries.   One of the best ways to improve DB instance performance is to tune your most commonly used and most resource-intensive queries to make them less expensive to run.

A common aspect of query tuning is creating effective indexes. You can use the Database Engine Tuning Advisor to get potential index improvements for your DB instance.

Use DB parameter groups.   AWS recommends that you apply changes to the DB parameter group on a test DB instance before you apply parameter group changes to your production DB instances. Improperly setting DB engine parameters in a DB parameter group can have unintended adverse effects, including degraded performance and system instability. Always exercise caution when modifying DB engine parameters, and back up your DB instance before modifying a DB parameter group.

Use read replicas.   Use read replicas to relieve pressure on your master node with addi-tional read capacity. You can bring your data closer to applications in different regions and promote a read replica to a master for faster recovery in the event of a disaster.

 You can use the AWS Database Migration Service (AWS DMS) to migrate or replicate your existing databases easily to Amazon RDS.

Nonrelational Databases

Nonrelational databases are commonly used for internet-scale applications that do not require any complex queries.

NoSQL Database

NoSQL databases are nonrelational databases optimized for scalable performance and schema-less data models. NoSQL databases are also widely recognized for their ease of development, low latency, and resilience.

NoSQL database systems use a variety of models for data management, such as in-memory key-value stores, graph data models, and document stores. These types of databases are optimized for applications that require large data volume, low latency, and flexible data models, which are achieved by relaxing some of the data consistency restrictions of traditional relational databases.

When to Use a NoSQL Database

NoSQL databases are a great fit for many big data, mobile, and web applications that require greater scale and higher responsiveness than traditional relational databases. Because of simpler data structures and horizontal scaling, NoSQL databases typically respond faster and are easier to scale than relational databases.

Comparison of SQL and NoSQL Databases

Many developers are familiar with SQL databases but might be new to working with NoSQL databases. Relational database management systems (RDBMS) and nonrelational (NoSQL) databases have different strengths and weaknesses. In a RDBMS, data can be queried flexibly, but queries are relatively expensive and do not scale well in high-traffic situations. In a NoSQL database, you can query data efficiently in a limited number of ways. Table 4.3 shows a comparison of different characteristics of SQL and NoSQL databases.

TABLE 4.3 SQL vs. NoSQL Database Characteristics

Type	SQL	NoSQL
Data Storage	Rows and columns	Key-value, document, wide-column, graph
Schemas	Fixed	Dynamic
Querying	Using SQL	Focused on collection of documents
Scalability	Vertical	Horizontal
Transactions	Supported	Support varies
Consistency	Strong	Eventual and strong

The storage format for SQL versus NoSQL databases also differs. As shown in Figure 4.9, SQL databases are often stored in a row and column format, whereas NoSQL databases, such as Amazon DynamoDB, have a key-value format that could be in a JSON format, as shown in this example.

FIGURE 4.9   SQL versus NoSQL format comparison

SQL

ISBN	Title	Edition	Format
1119138558	AWS Certified Solutions Architect Study Guide	1	Paperback

NoSQL

```
{
    ISBN: 9182932465265,
    Title: "AWS Certified Solutions Architect Study Guide",
    Edition: "1",
    Format: "Paperback"
}
```

NoSQL Database Types

There are four types of NoSQL databases: columnar, document, graph, and in-memory key-value. Generally, these databases differ in how the data is stored, accessed, and structured, and they are optimized for different use cases and applications.

Columnar databases   Columnar databases are optimized for reading and writing columns of data as opposed to rows of data. Column-oriented storage for database tables is an important factor in analytic query performance because it drastically reduces the overall disk I/O requirements and reduces the amount of data that you must load from disk.

Document databases   Document databases are designed to store semi-structured data as documents, typically in JSON or XML format. Unlike traditional relational databases, the schema for each NoSQL document can vary, giving you more flexibility in organizing and storing application data and reducing storage required for optional values.

Graph databases   Graph databases store vertices and directed links called *edges*. Graph databases can be built on both SQL and NoSQL databases. Vertices and edges can each have properties associated with them.

In-memory key-value stores   In-memory key-value stores are NoSQL databases optimized for read-heavy application workloads (such as social networking, gaming, media sharing, and Q&A portals) or compute-intensive workloads (such as a recommendation engine). In-memory caching improves application performance by storing critical pieces of data in memory for low-latency access.

Amazon DynamoDB

Amazon DynamoDB is a fast and flexible NoSQL database service for all applications that need consistent, single-digit millisecond latency at any scale. It is a fully managed cloud database, and it supports both document and key-value store models. Its flexible data model, reliable performance, and automatic scaling of throughput capacity make it a great fit for the following:

- Mobile
- Gaming
- Adtech
- Internet of Things (IoT)
- Applications that do not require complex queries

With DynamoDB, you can create database tables that can store and retrieve any amount of data and serve any level of request traffic. You can scale up or scale down your table throughput capacity without downtime or performance degradation. DynamoDB automatically spreads the data and traffic for your tables over a sufficient number of servers to handle your throughput and storage requirements while maintaining consistent and fast performance. All of your data is stored on solid-state drives (SSDs) and automatically replicated across multiple Availability Zones in an AWS Region, providing built-in high availability and data durability. You can use global tables to keep DynamoDB tables in sync across AWS Regions.

Core Components of Amazon DynamoDB

In DynamoDB, tables, items, and attributes are the core components with which you work. A *table* is a collection of items, and each item is a collection of *attributes*. DynamoDB uses partition keys to identify uniquely each item in a table. Secondary indexes can be used to provide more querying flexibility. You can use DynamoDB Streams to capture data modification events in DynamoDB tables.

Figure 4.10 shows the DynamoDB data model, including a table, items, attributes, a required partition key, an optional sort key, and an example of data being stored in partitions.

FIGURE 4.10 Amazon DynamoDB tables and partitions

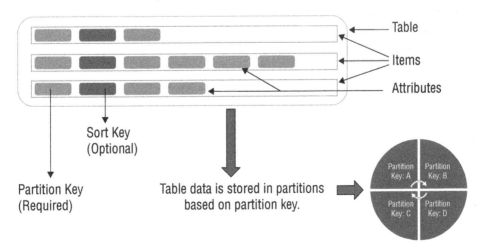

Tables

Similar to other database systems, DynamoDB stores data in tables. A table is a collection of items. For example, a table called *People* could be used to store personal contact information about friends, family, or anyone else of interest.

Items

An item in DynamoDB is similar in many ways to rows, records, or tuples in other database systems. Each DynamoDB table contains zero or more items. An *item* is a collection of attributes that is uniquely identifiable for each record in that table. For a *People* table, each item represents a person. There is no limit to the number of items that you can store in a table.

Attributes

Each item is composed of one or more attributes. Attributes in DynamoDB are similar in many ways to fields or columns in other database systems. An attribute is a fundamental data element, something that does not need to be broken down any further. You can think of an attribute as similar to columns in a relational database. For example, an item in a *People* table contains attributes called *PersonID*, *Last Name*, *First Name*, and so on.

Figure 4.11 shows a table named *People* with items and attributes. Each block represents an item, and within those blocks you have attributes that define the overall item:

- Each item in the table has a unique identifier, a primary key, or a partition key that distinguishes the item from all of the others in the table. The primary key consists of one attribute (`PersonID`).

- Other than the primary key, the *People* table is schemaless, which means that you do not have to define the attributes or their data types beforehand. Each item can have its own distinct attributes. This is where the contrast begins to show between NoSQL and SQL. In SQL, you would have to define a schema for each person, and every person would need to have the same data points or attributes. As you can see in Figure 4.11, with NoSQL and DynamoDB, each person can have different attributes.

- Most of the attributes are scalar, so they can have only one value. Strings and numbers are common examples of scalars.

- Some of the items have a nested attribute (`Address`). DynamoDB supports nested attributes up to 32 levels deep.

FIGURE 4.11   Amazon DynamoDB table with items and attributes

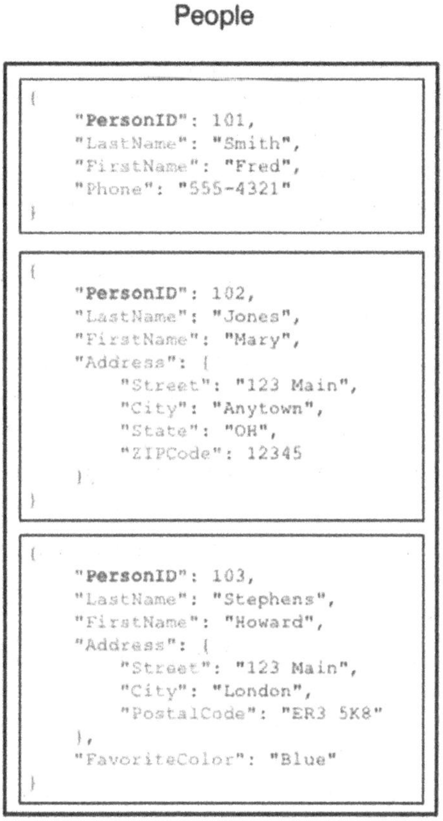

People

```
{
    "PersonID": 101,
    "LastName": "Smith",
    "FirstName": "Fred",
    "Phone": "555-4321"
}

{
    "PersonID": 102,
    "LastName": "Jones",
    "FirstName": "Mary",
    "Address": {
        "Street": "123 Main",
        "City": "Anytown",
        "State": "OH",
        "ZIPCode": 12345
    }
}

{
    "PersonID": 103,
    "LastName": "Stephens",
    "FirstName": "Howard",
    "Address": {
        "Street": "123 Main",
        "City": "London",
        "PostalCode": "ER3 5K8"
    },
    "FavoriteColor": "Blue"
}
```

Primary Key

When you create a table, at a minimum, you are required to specify the table name and primary key of the table. The primary key uniquely identifies each item in the table. No two items can have the same key within a table.

DynamoDB supports two different kinds of primary keys: partition key and partition key and sort key.

Partition key (hash key)   A simple primary key, composed of one attribute, is known as the *partition key*. DynamoDB uses the partition key's value as an input to an internal hash function. The output from the hash function determines the partition (physical storage internal to DynamoDB) in which the item is stored.

In a table that has only a partition key, no two items can have the same partition key value. For example, in the *People* table, with a simple primary key of PersonID, you cannot have two items with PersonID of 000-07-1075.

The partition key of an item is also known as its *hash attribute*. The term *hash attribute* derives from the use of an internal hash function in DynamoDB that evenly distributes data items across partitions based on their partition key values.

Each primary key attribute must be a scalar (meaning that it can hold only a single value). The only data types allowed for primary key attributes are string, number, or binary. There are no such restrictions for other, nonkey attributes.

Partition key and sort key (range attribute)   A *composite primary key* is composed of two attributes: *partition key* and the *sort key*.

The *sort key* of an item is also known as its *range attribute*. The term *range attribute* derives from the way that DynamoDB stores items with the same partition key physically close together, in sorted order, by the sort key value.

The *partition key* acts the same as the sort key, but in addition to also using a sort key, the items with the same partition key are stored together, in sorted order, by sort key value.

In a table that has a partition key and a sort key, it's possible for two items to have the same partition key value, but those two items must have different sort key values. You cannot have two items in the table that have identical partition key and sort key values.

For example, if you have a *Music* table with a composite primary key (*Artist* and *SongTitle*), you can access any item in the *Music* table directly if you provide the *Artist* and *SongTitle* values for that item.

A composite primary key gives you additional flexibility when querying data. For example, if you provide only the value for *Artist*, DynamoDB retrieves all of the songs by that artist. To retrieve only a subset of songs by a particular artist, you can provide a value for *Artist* with a range of values for *SongTitle*.

As a developer, the attribute you choose for your application has important implications. If there is little differentiation among partition keys, all of your data is stored together in the same physical location.

Figure 4.12 shows an example of these two types of keys. In the *SensorLocation* table, the primary key is the `SensorId` attribute. This means that every item (or row) in this table has a unique `SensorId`, meaning that each sensor has exactly one location or latitude and longitude value.

FIGURE 4.12   Amazon DynamoDB primary keys

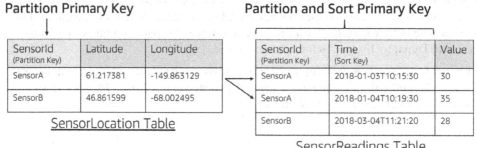

Conversely, the *SensorReadings* table has a partition key and a sort key. The SensorId attribute is the partition key and the Time attribute is the sort key, which combined make it a *composite key*. For each SensorId, there may be multiple items corresponding to sensor readings at different times. The combination of SensorId and Time uniquely identifies items in the table. This design enables you to query the table for all readings related to a particular sensor.

Secondary Indexes

If you want to perform queries on attributes that are not part of the table's primary key, you can create a *secondary index*. By using a secondary index, you can query the data in the table by using an alternate key, in addition to querying against the primary key. DynamoDB does not require that you use indexes, but doing so may give you more flexibility when querying your data depending on your application and table design.

After you create a secondary index on a table, you can then read data from the index in much the same way as you do from the table. DynamoDB automatically creates indexes based on the primary key of a table and automatically updates all indexes whenever a table changes.

A secondary index contains the following:

- Primary key attributes
- Alternate key attributes
- (Optional) A subset of other attributes from the base table (*projected attributes*)

DynamoDB provides fast access to the items in a table by specifying primary key values. However, many applications might benefit from having one or more secondary (or alternate) keys available. This allows efficient access to data with attributes other than the primary key.

DynamoDB supports two types of secondary indexes: *local secondary indexes* and *global secondary indexes*. You can define up to five global secondary indexes and five local secondary indexes per table.

Local Secondary Index

A *local secondary index* is an index that has the same partition key as the base table, but a different sort key (see Figure 4.13). It is "local" in the sense that every partition of a local secondary index is scoped to a base table partition that has the same partition key value. You can construct only one while creating the table, but you cannot add, remove, or modify it later.

FIGURE 4.13   Local secondary index

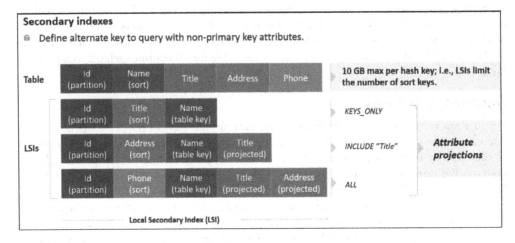

Global Secondary Index

A *global secondary index* is an index with a partition key and a sort key that can be different from those on the base table (see Figure 4.14). It is considered "global" because queries on the index can span all of the data in the base table across all partitions. You can create one during table creation, and you can add, remove, or modify it later.

FIGURE 4.14   Global secondary index

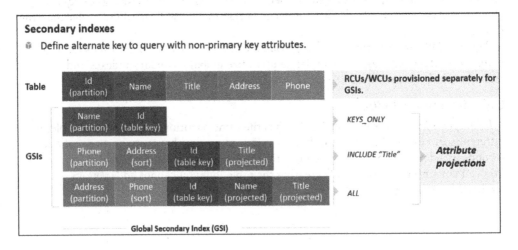

You can create a global secondary index, not a local secondary index, after table creation.

For example, by using a *Music* table, you can query data items by *Artist* (partition key) or by *Artist* and *SongTitle* (partition key and sort key). Suppose that you also wanted to query the data by *Genre* and *Album Title*. To do this, you could create a global secondary index on *Genre* and *AlbumTitle* and then query the index in much the same way as you'd query the *Music* table.

Figure 4.15 shows the example *Music* table with a new index called *GenreAlbumTitle*. In the index, *Genre* is the partition key, and *AlbumTitle* is the sort key.

FIGURE 4.15 Amazon DynamoDB table and secondary index

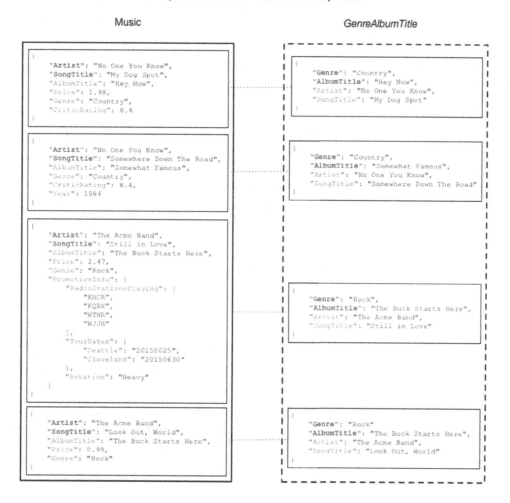

Note the following about the `GenreAlbumTitle` index:

- Every index belongs to a table, which is called the *base table* for the index. In the preceding example, *Music* is the base table for the `GenreAlbumTitle` index.

- DynamoDB maintains indexes automatically. When you add, update, or delete an item in the base table, DynamoDB adds, updates, or deletes the corresponding item in any indexes that belong to that table.

- When you create an index, you specify which attributes will be copied, or *projected*, from the base table to the index. At a minimum, DynamoDB projects the key attributes from the base table into the index. This is the case with `GenreAlbumTitle`, wherein only the key attributes from the *Music* table are projected into the index.

You can query the `GenreAlbumTitle` index to find all albums of a particular genre (for example, all *Hard Rock* albums). You can also query the index to find all albums within a particular genre that have certain album titles (for example, all *Heavy Metal* albums with titles that start with the letter *M*).

Comparison of Local Secondary Indexes and Global Secondary Indexes

To determine which type of index to use, consider your application's requirements. Table 4.4 shows the main differences between a global secondary index and a local secondary index.

TABLE 4.4   Comparison of Local and Global Secondary Indexes

Characteristic	Global Secondary Index	Local Secondary Index
Query Scope	Entire table, across all partitions.	Single partition, as specified by the partition key value in the query.
Key Attributes	▪ Partition key, or partition and sort key. ▪ Can be any scalar attribute in the table.	▪ Partition and sort key. ▪ Partition key of index must be the same attribute as base table.
Projected Attributes	Only projected attributes can be queried.	Can query attributes that are not projected. Attributes are retrieved from the base table.
Read Consistency	Eventual consistency only.	Eventual consistency or strong consistency.

Characteristic	Global Secondary Index	Local Secondary Index
Provisioned Throughput	▪ Separate throughput settings from base table. ▪ Consumes separate capacity units.	▪ Same throughput settings as base table. ▪ Consumes base table capacity units.
Lifecycle Considerations	Can be created or deleted at any time.	▪ Must be created when the table is created. ▪ Can be deleted only when the table is deleted.

Amazon DynamoDB Streams

Amazon DynamoDB Streams is an optional feature that captures data modification events in DynamoDB tables. The data about these events appears in the stream in near real time and in the order that the events occurred.

Each event is represented by a *stream record*. If you enable a stream on a table, DynamoDB Streams writes a stream record whenever one of the following events occurs:

A new item is added to the table—The stream captures an image of the entire item, including all of its attributes.

An item is updated—The stream captures the "before" and "after" images of any attributes that were modified in the item.

An item is deleted from the table—The stream captures an image of the entire item before it was deleted.

Each stream record also contains the name of the table, the event timestamp, and other metadata. Stream records have a lifetime of 24 hours; after that, they are automatically removed from the stream.

Figure 4.16 shows how you can use DynamoDB Streams together with AWS Lambda to create a *trigger*—code that executes automatically whenever an event of interest appears in a stream. For example, consider a *Customers* table that contains customer information for a company. Suppose that you want to send a "welcome" email to each new customer. You could enable a stream on that table and then associate the stream with a Lambda function. The Lambda function would execute whenever a new stream record appears, but only process new items added to the *Customers* table. For any item that has an EmailAddress attribute, the Lambda function could invoke Amazon Simple Email Service (Amazon SES) to send an email to that address.

FIGURE 4.16   Example of Amazon DynamoDB Streams and AWS Lambda

Customers

In addition to triggers, DynamoDB Streams enables other powerful solutions that developers can create, such as the following:

- Data replication within and across AWS regions
- Materialized views of data in DynamoDB tables
- Data analysis by using Amazon Kinesis materialized views

Read Consistency

DynamoDB replicates data among multiple Availability Zones in a region. When your application writes data to a DynamoDB table and receives an HTTP 200 response (OK), all copies of the data are updated. The data is eventually consistent across all storage locations, usually within 1 second or less. DynamoDB supports both *eventually consistent* and *strongly consistent* reads.

Eventually Consistent Reads

When you read data from a DynamoDB table immediately after a write operation, the response might not reflect the results of a recently completed write operation. The response might include some stale data. If you repeat your read request after a short time, the response should return the latest data. DynamoDB uses *eventually consistent reads*, unless you specify otherwise.

Strongly Consistent Reads

When querying data, you can specify whether DynamoDB should return *strongly consistent reads*. When you request a strongly consistent read, DynamoDB returns a response with the most up-to-date data, reflecting updates from all prior write operations that were successful. A strongly consistent read might not be available if there is a network delay or outage.

Comparison of Consistent Reads

As a developer, it is important to understand the needs of your application. In some applications, eventually consistent reads might be fine, such as a high-score dashboard. In other applications or parts of an application, however, such as a financial or medical system, an eventually consistent read could be an issue. You will want to evaluate your data usage patterns to ensure that you are choosing the right type of reads for each part of your application.

There is an additional cost for strongly consistent reads, and they will have more latency in returning data than an eventually consistent read. So, that cost and timing should also play into your decision.

Read and Write Throughput

When you create a table or index in DynamoDB, you must specify your capacity requirements for read and write activity. By defining your throughput capacity in advance, DynamoDB can reserve the necessary resources to meet the read and write activity your application requires, while ensuring consistent, low-latency performance. Specify your required throughput value by setting the ProvisionedThroughput parameter when you create or update a table.

You specify throughput capacity in terms of read capacity units and write capacity units:

- One *read capacity unit* (RCU) represents one strongly consistent read per second, or two eventually consistent reads per second, for an item up to 4 KB in size. If you need to read an item that is larger than 4 KB, DynamoDB will need to consume additional read capacity units. The total number of read capacity units required depends on the item size and whether you want an eventually consistent or strongly consistent read.

- One *write capacity unit* (WCU) represents one write per second for an item up to 1 KB in size. If you need to write an item that is larger than 1 KB, DynamoDB must consume additional write capacity units. The total number of write capacity units required depends on the item size.

For example, suppose that you create a table with five read capacity units and five write capacity units. With these settings, your application could do the following:

- Perform strongly consistent reads of up to 20 KB per second (4 KB × 5 read capacity units).

- Perform eventually consistent reads of up to 40 KB per second (twice as much read throughput).

- Write up to 5 KB per second (1 KB × 5 write capacity units).

If your application reads or writes larger items (up to the DynamoDB maximum item size of 400 KB), it consumes more capacity units.

If your read or write requests exceed the throughput settings for a table, DynamoDB can throttle that request. DynamoDB can also throttle read requests excess for an index. Throttling prevents your application from consuming too many capacity units. When a request is throttled, it fails with an HTTP 400 code (Bad Request) and a ProvisionedThroughputExceededException. The AWS SDKs have built-in support for retrying throttled requests, so you do not need to write this logic yourself.

DynamoDB provides the following mechanisms for managing throughput as it changes:

Amazon DynamoDB Auto Scaling DynamoDB automatic scaling actively manages throughput capacity for tables and global secondary indexes. With automatic scaling, you define a range (upper and lower limits) for read and write capacity units. You also define a target utilization percentage within that range. DynamoDB auto scaling seeks to maintain your target utilization, even as your application workload increases or decreases.

Provisioned throughput If you aren't using DynamoDB auto scaling, you have to define your throughput requirements manually. As discussed, with this setting you may run into a ProvisionedThroughputExceededException if you are throttled. But you can change your throughput with a few clicks.

Reserved capacity You can purchase *reserved capacity* in advance, where you pay a one-time upfront fee and commit to a minimum usage level over a period of time. You may realize significant cost savings compared to on-demand provisioned throughput settings.

On-demand It can be difficult to plan capacity, especially if you aren't collecting metrics or perhaps are developing a new application and you aren't sure what type of performance you require. With On-Demand mode, your DynamoDB table will automatically scale up or down to any previously reached traffic level. If a workload's traffic level reaches a new peak, DynamoDB rapidly adapts to accommodate the workload. As a developer, focus on making improvements to your application and offload scaling activities to AWS.

Partitions and Data Distribution

When you are using a table in DynamoDB, the data is placed on multiple partitions (depending on the amount of data and the amount of throughput allocated to it; recall that throughput is determined by RCUs and WCUs). When you allocate RCUs and

WCUs to a table, those RCUs and WCUs are split evenly among all partitions for your table.

For example, suppose that you have allocated 1,000 RCUs and 1,000 WCUs to a table, and this table has 10 partitions allocated to it. Then each partition would have 100 RCUs and 100 WCUs for it to use. If one of your partitions consumes all the RCUs and WCUs for the table, you may receive a `ProvisionedThroughputExceededException` error because one of your partitions is hot. To deal with hot partitions, DynamoDB has two features: burst capacity and adaptive capacity.

Burst Capacity

The previous example discussed how you had 10 partitions, each with 100 RCUs and 100 WCUs allocated to them. One of your partitions begins to become hot and now needs to consume more than 100 RCUs. Under normal circumstances, you may receive the `ProvisionedThroughputExceededException` error. However, with burst capacity, whenever your partition is not using all of its total capacity, DynamoDB reserves a portion of that unused capacity for later *bursts* of throughput to handle any spike your partition may experience.

At the time of this writing, DynamoDB currently reserves up to 300 seconds (5 minutes) of unused read and write capacity, which means that your partition can handle a peak load for 5 minutes over its normal expected load. Burst capacity is enabled and runs in the background.

Adaptive Capacity

Adaptive capacity is when it is not always possible to distribute read and write activity to a partition evenly. In the example, a partition is experiencing not only peak demand but also consistent demand over and above its normal 100 RCU and 100 WCUs. Suppose that now this partition requires 200 RCUs instead of 100 RCUs.

DynamoDB adaptive capacity enables your application to continue reading and writing to hot partitions without being throttled, provided that the total provisioned capacity for the table is not exceeded. DynamoDB allocates additional RCUs to the hot partition; in this case, 100 more. With adaptive capacity, you will still be throttled for a period of time, typically between 5–30 minutes, before adaptive capacity turns on or activates. So, for a portion of time, your application will be throttled; however, after adaptive capacity allocates the RCUs to the partition, DynamoDB is able to sustain the new higher throughput for your partition and table. Adaptive capacity is on by default, and there is no need to enable or disable it.

Retrieving Data from DynamoDB

Two primary methods are used to retrieve data from DynamoDB: Query and Scan.

Query

In DynamoDB, you perform `Query` operations directly on the table or index. To run the `Query` command, you must specify, at a minimum, a primary key. If you are querying an index, you must specify both `TableName` and `IndexName`.

The following is a query on a *Music* table in DynamoDB using the Python SDK:

```python
import boto3
import json
import decimal

# Helper class to convert a DynamoDB item to JSON.
class DecimalEncoder(json.JSONEncoder):
    def default(self, o):
        if isinstance(o, decimal.Decimal):
            if o % 1 > 0:
                return float(o)
            else:
                return int(o)
        return super(DecimalEncoder, self).default(o)

dynamodb = boto3.resource('dynamodb', region_name='us-east-1')

table = dynamodb.Table('Music')

print("A query with DynamoDB")

response = table.query(
    KeyConditionExpression=Key('Artist').eq('Sam Samuel')
)

for i in response['Items']:
    print(i['SongTitle'], "-", i['Genre'], i['Price'])
```

The query returns all of the songs by the artist Sam Samuel in the *Music* table.

Scan

You can also perform Scan operations on a table or index. The Scan operation returns one or more items and item attributes by accessing every item in a table or a secondary index. To have DynamoDB return fewer items, you can provide a FilterExpression operation.

If the total number of scanned items exceeds the maximum dataset size limit of 1 MB, the scan stops, and the results are returned to the user as a LastEvaluatedKey value to continue the scan in a subsequent operation. The results also include the number of items exceeding the limit. A scan can result in no table data meeting the filter criteria.

A single Scan operation reads up to the maximum number of items set (if you're using the Limit parameter) or a maximum of 1 MB of data and then applies any filtering to the results by using FilterExpression. If LastEvaluatedKey is present in the response, you must paginate the result set.

Scan operations proceed sequentially; however, for faster performance on a large table or secondary index, applications can request a parallel Scan operation by providing the Segment and TotalSegments parameters.

Scan uses eventually consistent reads when accessing the data in a table; therefore, the result set might not include the changes to data in the table immediately before the operation began. If you need a consistent copy of the data, as of the time that the Scan begins, you can set the ConsistentRead parameter to true.

The following is a scan on a *Movies* table with the Python SDK:

```python
// Return all of the data in the index
import boto3
import json
import decimal

# Create the DynamoDB Resource
dynamodb = boto3.resource('dynamodb', region_name='us-east-1')

# Use the Music Table
table = dynamodb.Table('Music')

# Helper class to convert a DynamoDB decimal/item to JSON.
class DecimalEncoder(json.JSONEncoder):
    def default(self, o):
        if isinstance(o, decimal.Decimal):
            if o % 1 > 0:
                return float(o)
            else:
                return int(o)
        return super(DecimalEncoder, self).default(o)

# Specify some filters for the scan
# Here we are stating that the Price must be between 12 - 30
fe = Key('Price').between(12, 30)
pe = "#g, Price"
# Expression Attribute Names for Projection Expression only.
ean = { "#g": "Genre", }

#
response_scan = table.scan(
    FilterExpression=fe,
    ProjectionExpression=pe,
    ExpressionAttributeNames=ean
    )

# Print all the items
for i in response_scan['Items']:
    print(json.dumps(i, cls=DecimalEncoder))
```

```
while 'LastEvaluatedKey' in response:
    response = table.scan(
        ProjectionExpression=pe,
        FilterExpression=fe,
        ExpressionAttributeNames= ean,
        ExclusiveStartKey=response['LastEvaluatedKey']
        )
    for i in response['Items']:
        print(json.dumps(i)
```

As you can see from the Python code, the scan returns all records with a price of between 12 and 30 and the genre and the price. The LastEvaluatedKey property is included to continue to loop through the entire table.

Global Tables

Global tables build upon the DynamoDB global footprint to provide you with a fully managed, multiregion, and multimaster database that provides fast, local, read-and-write performance for massively scaled, global applications. DynamoDB performs all the necessary tasks to create identical tables in these regions and propagate ongoing data changes to all of them. Figure 4.17 shows an example of how global tables can work with a global application and globally dispersed users.

FIGURE 4.17 Global tables

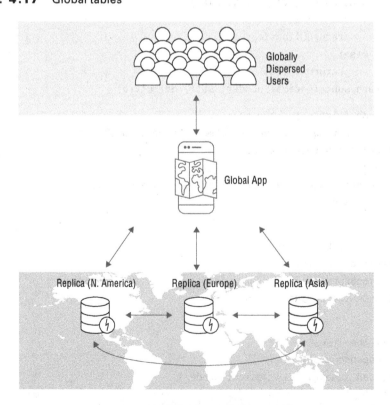

A *global table* is a collection of one or more DynamoDB tables, all owned by a single AWS account, identified as replica tables. A *replica table* (or replica, for short) is a single DynamoDB table that functions as a part of a global table. Each replica stores the same set of data items. Any given global table can have only one replica table per region, and every replica has the same table name and the same primary key schema. Changes made in one replica are recorded in a stream and propagated to other replicas, as shown in Figure 4.18.

FIGURE 4.18   Replication flow in global tables

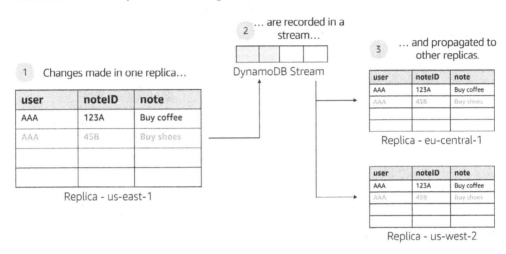

If your application requires strongly consistent reads, then it must perform all of its strongly consistent reads and writes in the same region. DynamoDB does not support strongly consistent reads across AWS Regions.

Conflicts can arise if applications update the same item in different regions at about the same time (concurrent updates). To ensure eventual consistency, DynamoDB global tables use a "last writer wins" reconciliation between concurrent updates whereby DynamoDB makes a best effort to determine the last writer. With this conflict resolution mechanism, all replicas agree on the latest update and converge toward a state in which they all have identical data.

To create a DynamoDB global table, perform the following steps:

1. Create an ordinary DynamoDB table, with DynamoDB Streams enabled, in an AWS Region.

2. Repeat step 1 for every other AWS Region where you want to replicate your data.

3. Define a DynamoDB global table based on the tables that you have created.

The AWS Management Console automates these tasks so that you can create a global table quickly and easily.

Object Persistence Model

The DynamoDB object persistence model enables you to map client-side classes to DynamoDB tables. The instances of these classes (objects) map to items in a DynamoDB table.

You can use the object persistence programming interface to connect to DynamoDB; perform create, read, update, and delete operations (CRUD); execute queries; and implement optimistic locking with a version number. Figure 4.19 shows an example of using the object persistence model to map client-side objects in DynamoDB.

FIGURE 4.19   Object persistence model

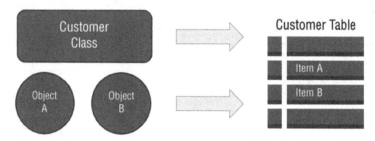

Support for the object persistence model is available in the Java and .NET SDKs.

Amazon DynamoDB Local

DynamoDB Local is the downloadable version of DynamoDB that lets you write and test applications by using the Amazon DynamoDB API without accessing the DynamoDB web service. Instead, the database is self-contained on your computer. When you're ready to deploy your application in production, you can make a few minor changes to the code so that it uses the DynamoDB web service.

Having this local version helps you save on provisioned throughput, data storage, and data transfer fees. In addition, you don't need an internet connection while you're developing your application.

IAM and Fine-Grained Access Control

You can use AWS IAM to grant or restrict access to DynamoDB resources and API actions. For example, you could allow a user to execute the GetItem operation on a *Books* table. DynamoDB also supports fine-grained access control so that you can control access to individual data items and attributes. This means that perhaps you have a *Users* table and you want the specific user to have access only to his or her data. You can accomplish this with fine-grained access control. Use a *condition* inside an IAM policy with the dynamodb:LeadingKeys property.

By using LeadingKeys, you can limit the user so that they can access only the items where the partition key matches the userID. In the following example in the *Users* table, you want to restrict who can view the profile information to only the user to which the data or profile information belongs:

```
{
    "Version": "2012-10-17",
    "Statement": [
        {
            "Sid": "LeadingKeysExample",
            "Effect": "Allow",
            "Action": [
                "dynamodb:GetItem",
                "dynamodb:BatchGetItem",
                "dynamodb:Query",
                "dynamodb:PutItem",
                "dynamodb:UpdateItem",
                "dynamodb:DeleteItem",
                "dynamodb:BatchWriteItem"
            ],
            "Resource": [
                "arn:aws:dynamodb:us-east-1:accountnumber:table/UserProfiles"
            ],
            "Condition": {
                "ForAllValues:StringEquals": {
                    "dynamodb:LeadingKeys": [
                        "${www.amazon.com:user_id}"

                    ],
                    "dynamodb:Attributes": [
                        "UserId",
                        "FirstName",
                        "LastName",
                        "Email",
                        "Birthday"
                    ]
                },
                "StringEqualsIfExists": {
                    "dynamodb:Select": "SPECIFIC_ATTRIBUTES"
                }
            }
        }
    ]
}
```

As you can see in the IAM policy, only the specific user is allowed to access a subset of the total attributes that are defined in the Attributes section of the policy. Furthermore, the SELECT statement specifies that the application must provide a list of specific attributes to act upon, preventing the application from requesting all attributes.

Backup and Restore

You can create on-demand backups and enable point-in-time recovery for your DynamoDB tables.

On-demand backups create full backups of your tables or restore them on-demand at any time. These actions execute with zero impact on table performance or availability and without consuming any provisioned throughput on the table.

Point-in-time recovery helps protect your DynamoDB tables from accidental write or delete operations. For example, suppose that a test script accidentally writes to a production DynamoDB table. With point-in-time recovery, you can restore that table to any point in time during the last 35 days. DynamoDB maintains incremental backups of your table. These operations will not affect performance or latency.

Encryption with Amazon DynamoDB

DynamoDB offers fully managed encryption at rest, and it is enabled by default. DynamoDB uses AWS KMS for encrypting the objects at rest. By default, DynamoDB uses the AWS-owned customer master key (CMK); however, you can also specify your own AWS KMS CMK key that you have created. For more information on AWS KMS, see Chapter 5, "Encryption on AWS."

Amazon DynamoDB Best Practices

Now that you understand what DynamoDB is and how you can use it to create a scalable database for your application, review some best practices for using DynamoDB.

Distribute Workload Evenly

The primary key or partition key portion of a table's primary key determines the logical partitions in which the table's data is stored. These logical partitions also affect the under-lying physical partitions. As a result, you want to distribute your workload across the parti-tions as evenly as possible, reducing the number of "hot" partition issues that may arise.

Table 4.5 compares the more common partition key schemas and whether they are good for DynamoDB.

TABLE 4.5 Amazon DynamoDB Partition Key Recommended Strategies

Partition Key Value	Uniformity
User ID, where the application has many users	Good
Status code, where there are only a few possible status codes	Bad

Partition Key Value	Uniformity
Item creation date, rounded to the nearest time period (for example, day, hour, or minute)	Bad
Device ID, where each device accesses data at relatively similar intervals	Good
Device ID, where even if there are many devices being tracked, one is by far more popular than all the others	Bad

Comparison of Query and Scan Operations

The Query operation finds items in a table based on primary key values. You must provide the name of the partition key attribute and the value of that attribute. You can provide a sort key attribute name and value to refine the search results (for example, all of the forums with this ID in the last seven days). By default, Query returns all of the data attributes for those items with specified primary keys. The results are sorted by the sort key in ascending order, which can be reversed. Additionally, queries are set to be Eventually Consistent, with an option to change to Strongly Consistent, if necessary.

The Scan operation returns all of the item attributes by accessing every item in the table. It is for this reason that Query is more efficient than the Scan operation.

Data Warehouse

If you are performing analytics, you may want to use a data warehouse. A *data warehouse* is a central repository of information that you can analyze to make better-informed decisions. Data flows into a data warehouse from transactional systems, relational databases, and other sources, typically on a regular cadence. Business analysts, data scientists, and decision-makers access the data through BI tools, SQL clients, and other analytics applications.

Data Warehouse Architecture

A data warehouse architecture consists of three tiers. The bottom tier of the architecture is the database server, where data is loaded and stored. The middle tier consists of the analytics engine that is used to access and analyze the data. The top tier is the front-end client that presents results through reporting, analysis, and data mining tools.

A data warehouse works by organizing data into a schema that describes the layout and type of data, such as integer, data field, or string. When data is ingested, it is stored in various tables described by the schema. Query tools use the schema to determine which data tables to access and analyze.

Data Warehouse Benefits

Benefits of using a data warehouse include the following:

- Better decision-making
- Consolidation of data from many sources
- Data quality, consistency, and accuracy
- Historical intelligence
- Analytics processing that is separate from transactional databases, improving the performance of both systems

The data warehousing landscape has changed dramatically in recent years with the emergence of cloud-based services that offer high performance, simple deployment, near-infinite scaling, and easy administration at a fraction of the cost of on-premises solutions.

Comparison of Data Warehouses and Databases

A data warehouse is specially designed for data analytics, which involves reading large amounts of data to understand relationships and trends across the data. A database is used to capture and store data, such as recording details of a transaction. Table 4.6 is useful in comparing the characteristics of data warehouses and databases.

TABLE 4.6   Comparison of Data Warehouse and Database Characteristics

Characteristics	Data Warehouse	Transactional Database
Suitable Workloads	Analytics, reporting, big data	Transaction processing
Data Source	Data collected and normalized from many sources	Data captured as-is from a single source, such as a transactional system
Data Capture	Bulk write operations typically on a predetermined batch schedule	Optimized for continuous write operations as new data is available to maximize transaction throughput
Data Normalization	Denormalized schemas, such as the star schema or snowflake schema	Highly normalized, static schemas
Data Storage	Optimized for simplicity of access and high-speed query performance by using columnar storage	Optimized for high-throughout write operations to a single row-oriented physical block
Data Access	Optimized to minimize I/O and maximize data throughput	High volumes of small read operations

Comparison of Data Warehouses and Data Lakes

Unlike a data warehouse, a data lake, as described in Chapter 3, "Hello, Storage," is a centralized repository for all data, including structured and unstructured. A data warehouse uses a predefined schema that is optimized for analytics. In a data lake, the schema is not defined, enabling additional types of analytics, such as big data analytics, full text search, real-time analytics, and machine learning. Table 4.7 compares the characteristics of a data warehouse and a data lake.

TABLE 4.7 Comparison of Data Warehouse and Data Lake Characteristics

Characteristics	Data Warehouse	Data Lake
Data	Relational data from transactional systems, operational databases, and line-of-business applications	Nonrelational and relational data from IoT devices, websites, mobile apps, social media, and corporate applications
Schema	Designed before the data warehouse implementation (schema-on-write)	Written at the time of analysis (schema-on-read)
Price/Performance	Fastest query results by using higher-cost storage	Query results getting faster by using low-cost storage
Data Quality	Highly curated data that serves as the central version of the truth	Any data that may or may not be curated (in other words, raw data)
Users	Business analysts, data scientists, and data developers	Data scientists, data developers, and business analysts (using curated data)
Analytics	Batch reporting, BI, and visualizations	Machine learning, predictive analytics, data discovery, and profiling

Comparison of Data Warehouses and Data Marts

A *data mart* is a data warehouse that serves the needs of a specific team or business unit, such as finance, marketing, or sales. It is smaller, is more focused, and may contain summaries of data that best serve its community of users. Table 4.8 compares the characteristics of a data warehouse and a data mart.

TABLE 4.8   Comparison of Data Warehouse and Data Mart Characteristics

Characteristics	Data Warehouse	Transactional Database
Scope	Centralized, multiple subject areas integrated together	Decentralized, specific subject area
Users	Organization-wide	A single community or department
Data Source	Many sources	A single or a few sources, or a portion of data already collected in a data warehouse
Size	Large—can be 100s of gigabytes to petabytes	Small, generally up to 10s of gigabytes
Design	Top-down	Bottom-up
Data Detail	Complete, detailed data	May hold summarized data

Amazon Redshift

Amazon Redshift is a fast, fully managed, petabyte-scale data warehouse that makes it simple and cost-effective to analyze all your data by using standard SQL and your existing BI tools. With Amazon Redshift, you can run complex analytic queries against petabytes of structured data using sophisticated query optimization, columnar storage on high-performance local disks, and massively parallel query execution. Most results come back in seconds. Amazon Redshift is up to 10 times faster than traditional on-premises data warehouses at 1/10 the cost.

Architecture

An Amazon Redshift data warehouse is a collection of computing resources called *nodes*, which are organized into a group called a *cluster*. Each cluster runs an Amazon Redshift engine and contains one or more databases. After you provision your cluster, you can upload your dataset and then perform data analysis queries. Each cluster has a leader node and one or more compute nodes, and you have a choice of a hardware platform for your cluster.

Client Applications

Amazon Redshift integrates with various data loading and extract, transform, and load (ETL) tools and BI reporting, data mining, and analytics tools. It is based on open standard PostgreSQL, so most existing SQL client applications will integrate with Amazon Redshift with only minimal changes. For important differences between Amazon Redshift SQL and PostgreSQL, see the Amazon Redshift documentation.

Leader Node

The *leader node* acts as the SQL endpoint and receives queries from client applications, parses the queries, and develops query execution plans. The leader node then coordinates a parallel execution of these plans with the compute nodes and aggregates the intermediate results from these nodes. Finally, it returns the results to the client applications. The leader node also stores metadata about the cluster. Amazon Redshift communicates with client applications by using open standard PostgreSQL, JDBC, and ODBC drivers.

Compute Nodes

Compute nodes execute the query execution plan and transmit data among themselves to serve these queries. The intermediate results are sent to the leader node for aggregation before being sent back to the client applications.

Node Slices

A compute node is partitioned into slices. Each slice is allocated a portion of the node's memory and disk space, where it processes a portion of the workload assigned to the node. The leader node manages distributing data to the slices and allocates the workload for any queries or other database operations to the slices. The slices then work in parallel to complete the operation. The node size of the cluster determines the number of slices per node.

Figure 4.20 shows the Amazon Redshift data warehouse architecture, including the client applications, JDBC and ODBC connections, leader node, compute nodes, and node slices.

FIGURE 4.20   Amazon Redshift architecture

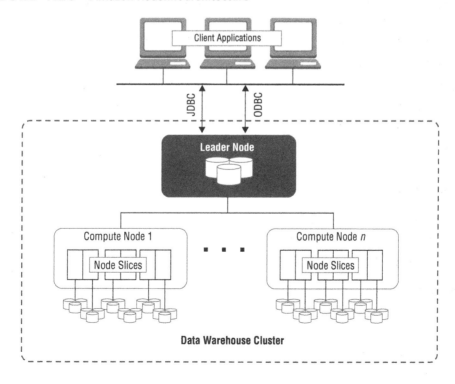

Databases

A cluster contains one or more databases. User data is stored on the compute nodes.

Hardware Platform Options

When you launch a cluster, one option you specify is the node type. The *node type* determines the CPU, RAM, storage capacity, and storage drive type for each node. There are two categories for node types. The *dense storage* (DS) node types are storage-optimized using large magnetic disks and can provide up to 2 PB of storage capacity. The *dense compute* (DC) node types are compute-optimized. Because they use solid state drive (SSD) storage, they deliver much faster I/O compared to DS node types but provide less storage space at a maximum of 326 TB.

Table Design

Each database within an Amazon Redshift cluster can support many tables. Like most SQL-based databases, you can create a table using the CREATE TABLE command. This command specifies the name of the table, the columns, and their data types. This command also supports specifying compression encodings, distribution strategy, and sort keys in Amazon Redshift.

Data Types

Each value that Amazon Redshift stores or retrieves has a data type with a fixed set of associated properties. Data types are declared when tables are created. Additional columns can be added to a table by using the ALTER TABLE command, but you cannot change the data type on an existing column.

Many familiar data types are available, including the following:

Numeric data types

- BIGINT
- DECIMAL
- DOUBLE PRECISION
- INTEGER
- REAL
- SMALLINT

Text data types

- CHAR
- VARCHAR

Date data types

- DATE
- TIMESTAMP
- TIMESTAMPTZ

Logical data type

- BOOLEAN

Compression Encoding

Amazon Redshift uses data compression as one of the key performance optimizations. When you load data for the first time into an empty table, Amazon Redshift samples your data automatically and selects the best compression scheme for each column. Alternatively, you can specify your preferred compression encoding on a per-column basis as part of the CREATE TABLE command.

Distribution Strategy

When you load data into a table, Amazon Redshift distributes the rows of the table to each of the compute nodes according to the table's distribution style. When you execute a query, the query optimizer redistributes the rows to the compute nodes as needed to perform any joins and aggregations. The goal in selecting a table distribution style is to minimize the impact of the redistribution step by locating the data where it needs to be before the query is executed.

This is one of the primary decisions when you're creating a table in Amazon Redshift. You can configure the distribution style of a table to give Amazon Redshift hints as to how the data should be partitioned to meet your query patterns. The style you select for your database affects query performance, storage requirements, data loading, and maintenance. By choosing the best distribution strategy for each table, you can balance your data distribution and significantly improve overall system performance.

When creating a table, you can choose among one of the three distribution styles: EVEN, KEY, or ALL.

EVEN distribution   Rows are distributed across the slices in a round-robin fashion, regardless of the values in any particular column. It is an appropriate choice when a table does not participate in joins or when there is not a clear choice between KEY distribution or ALL distribution. EVEN is the default distribution type.

KEY distribution   Rows are distributed according to the values in one column. The leader node attempts to place matching values on the same node slice. Use this style when you will be querying heavily against values of a specific column.

ALL distribution   A copy of the entire table is distributed to every node. This ensures that every row is collocated for every join in which the table participates. This multiplies the storage required by the number of nodes in the cluster, and it takes much longer to load, update, or insert data into multiple tables. Use this style only for relatively slow-moving tables that are not updated frequently or extensively.

Sort Keys

Another important decision to make during table creation is choosing the appropriate sort key. Amazon Redshift stores your data on disk in sorted order according to the sort key, and the query optimizer uses sort order when it determines the optimal query plans. Specify an appropriate sort key for the way that your data will be queried, filtered, or joined.

The following are some general guidelines for choosing the best sort key:

- If recent data is queried most frequently, specify the timestamp column as the leading column for the sort key.
- If you do frequent range filtering or equality filtering on one column, specify that column as the sort key.
- If you frequently join a table, specify the join column as both the sort key and the distribution key.

Loading Data

Loading large datasets can take a long time and consume many computing resources. How your data is loaded can also affect query performance. You can reduce these impacts by using COPY commands, bulk inserts, and staging tables when loading data into Amazon Redshift.

 The COPY command loads data in parallel from Amazon S3 or other data sources in a more efficient manner than INSERT commands.

Querying Data

You can query Amazon Redshift tables by using standard SQL commands, such as using SELECT statements, to query and join tables. For complex queries, you are able to analyze the query plan to choose better optimizations for your specific access patterns.

For large clusters supporting many users, you can configure workload management (WLM) to queue and prioritize queries.

Snapshots

Amazon Redshift supports snapshots, similar to Amazon RDS. You can create automated and manual snapshots, which are stored in Amazon S3 by using an encrypted Secure Socket Layer (SSL) connection. If you need to restore from a snapshot, Amazon Redshift creates a new cluster and imports data from the snapshot that you specify.

When you restore from a snapshot, Amazon Redshift creates a new cluster and makes it available before all of the data is loaded so that you can begin querying the new cluster immediately. Amazon Redshift will stream data on demand from the snapshot in response to active queries and load all the remaining data in the background.

Achieving proper durability for a database requires more effort and more attention. Even when using Amazon Elastic Block Store (Amazon EBS) volumes, take snapshots on a frozen file system to be consistent. Also, restoring a database might require additional operations other than restoring a volume from a snapshot and attaching it to an Amazon EC2 instance.

Security

Securing your Amazon Redshift cluster is similar to securing other databases running in the AWS Cloud. To meet your needs, you will use a combination of IAM policies, security groups, and encryption to secure the cluster.

Encryption

Protecting the data stored in Amazon Redshift is an important aspect of your security design. Amazon Redshift supports encryption of data in transit using SSL-encrypted connections.

You can also enable database encryption for your clusters to help protect data at rest. AWS recommends enabling encryption for clusters that contain sensitive data. You might be required to use encryption depending on the compliance guidelines or regulations that govern your data. Encryption is an optional setting, and it must be configured during the cluster launch. To change encryption on a cluster, you need to create a new cluster and migrate the data.

Amazon Redshift automatically integrates with AWS KMS.

 Implement security at every level of your Amazon Redshift architecture, including the infrastructure resources, database schema, data, and network access.

Access to Amazon Redshift resources is controlled at three levels: cluster management, cluster connectivity, and database access. For details on the controls available to help you manage each of these areas, see the Amazon Redshift Cluster Management Guide at https://docs.aws.amazon.com/redshift/latest/mgmt/welcome.html.

The following are some best practices for securing your Amazon Redshift deployments:

- Enable and use SSL when connecting to the Amazon Redshift database port.

- Ensure that your data is available only via SSL by setting the require_ssl parameter to true in the parameter group that is associated with the cluster.

- Use long, random database passwords generated by Amazon Redshift and store them by using a secret management system.

- Enable cluster encryption.

- Secure the S3 bucket by enabling Amazon S3 encryption and configuring access control for Amazon S3.

- Secure the ETL system by enacting access control, auditing/logging, patch management, disk encryption/secure deletion, and SSL connectivity to Amazon S3.

- Secure the BI system by enacting access control, auditing, patching, SSL connectivity to Amazon Redshift, and SSL UI (if applicable).

- Use cluster or VPC security groups to limit Amazon Redshift access only to the necessary IP addresses (for both inbound and outbound flows).

- Enable cluster encryption.

Amazon Redshift Spectrum

Amazon Redshift also includes *Redshift Spectrum*, allowing you to run SQL queries directly against exabytes of unstructured data in Amazon S3. No loading or transformation is required.

You can use many open data formats, including Apache Avro, CSV, Grok, Ion, JSON, Optimized Row Columnar (ORC), Apache Parquet, RCFile, RegexSerDe, SequenceFile, TextFile, and TSV. Redshift Spectrum automatically scales query compute capacity based on the data being retrieved, so queries against Amazon S3 run fast, regardless of dataset size.

To use Redshift Spectrum, you need an Amazon Redshift cluster and a SQL client that's connected to your cluster so that you can execute SQL commands. The cluster and the data files in Amazon S3 must be in the same AWS Region.

In-Memory Data Stores

In-memory data stores are used for caching and real-time workloads. AWS provides a variety of in-memory, key-value database options. You can operate your own nonrelational key-value data store in the cloud on Amazon EC2 and Amazon EBS, work with AWS solution providers, or take advantage of fully managed nonrelational services such as *Amazon ElastiCache*.

Caching

In computing, the data in a *cache* is generally stored in fast-access hardware, such as random-access memory (RAM), and may also be used in correlation with a software component. A cache's primary purpose is to increase data retrieval performance by reducing the need to access the underlying slower storage layer.

Trading off capacity for speed, a cache typically stores a subset of data transiently, in contrast to databases whose data is usually complete and durable.

Benefits of Caching

A cache provides high-throughput, low-latency access to commonly accessed application data by storing the data in memory. Caching can improve the speed of your application. Caching reduces the response latency, which improves a user's experience with your application.

Time-consuming database queries and complex queries often create bottlenecks in applications. In read-intensive applications, caching can provide large performance gains by reducing application processing time and database access time. Write-intensive applications typically do not see as great a benefit to caching. However, even write-intensive applications normally have a read/write ratio greater than 1, which implies that read caching can be beneficial. In summary, the benefits of caching include the following:

- Improve application performance
- Reduce database cost
- Reduce load on the backend database tier
- Facilitate predictable performance

- Eliminate database hotspots
- Increase read throughput (IOPS)

The following types of information or applications can often benefit from caching:

- Results of database queries
- Results of intensive calculations
- Results of remote API calls
- Compute-intensive workloads that manipulate large datasets, such as high-performance computing simulations and recommendation engines

Consider caching your data if the following conditions apply:

- It is slow or expensive to acquire when compared to cache retrieval.
- It is accessed with sufficient frequency.
- Your data or information for your application is relatively static
- Your data or information for your application is rapidly changing and staleness is not significant.

Caching Strategies

You can implement different caching strategies for your application. Two primary methods are lazy loading and write through. A *cache hit* occurs when the cache contains the information requested. A *cache miss* occurs when the cache does not contain the information requested.

Lazy loading   *Lazy loading* is a caching strategy that loads data into the cache only when necessary. When your application requests data, it first makes the request to the cache. If the data exists in the cache (a cache hit), it is retrieved; but if it does not or has expired (a cache miss), then the data is retrieved from your data store and then stored in the cache. The advantage of lazy loading is that only the requested data is cached. The disadvantage is that there is a cache miss penalty resulting in three trips:

1. The application requests data from the cache.
2. If there is a cache miss, you must query the database.
3. After data retrieval, the cache is updated.

Write through   The *write-through* strategy adds data or updates in the cache whenever data is written to the database. The advantage of write through is that the data in the cache is never stale. The disadvantage is that there is a write penalty because every write involves two trips: a write to the cache and a write to the database. Another disadvantage is that because most data is never read in many applications, the data or information that is stored in the cluster is never used. This storage incurs a cost for space and overhead due to the duplicate data. In addition, if your data is updated frequently, the cache may be updating often, causing cache churn.

In-Memory Key-Value Store

An *in-memory key-value store* is a NoSQL database optimized for read-heavy application workloads (such as social networking, gaming, media sharing, and Q&A portals) or compute-intensive workloads (such as a recommendation engine). In-memory caching improves application performance by storing critical pieces of data in memory for low-latency access. Cached information may include the results of I/O-intensive database queries or the results of computationally intensive calculations.

Benefits of In-Memory Data Stores

The strict performance requirements imposed by real-time applications mandate more efficient databases. Traditional databases rely on disk-based storage. A single user action may consist of multiple database calls. As they accumulate, latency increases. However, by accessing data in memory, in-memory data stores provide higher throughput and lower latency. In fact, in-memory data stores can be one to two orders of magnitude faster than disk-based databases.

As a NoSQL data store, an in-memory data store does not share the architectural limitations found in traditional relational databases. NoSQL data stores are built to be scalable. Traditional relational databases use a rigid table-based architecture. Some NoSQL data stores use a key-value store and therefore don't enforce a structure on the data. This enables scalability and makes it easier to grow, partition, or shard data as data stores grow. When consumed as a cloud-based service, an in-memory data store also provides availability and cost benefits. On-demand access allows organizations to scale their applications as needed in response to demand spikes and at a lower cost than disk-based stores. Using managed cloud services also eliminates the need to administer infrastructure. Database hotspots are reduced, and performance becomes more predictable. Some cloud-based services also offer the benefit of high availability with replicas and support for multiple Availability Zones.

Benefits of Distributed Cache

A caching layer helps further drive throughput for read-heavy applications. A *caching layer* is a high-speed storage layer that stores a subset of data. When a read request is sent, the caching layer checks to determine whether it has the answer. If it doesn't, the request is sent on to the database. Meeting read requests through the caching layer in this manner is more efficient and delivers higher performance than what can be had from a traditional database alone.

It is also more cost-effective. A single node of in-memory cache can deliver the same read throughput as several database nodes. Instead of provisioning additional instances of your traditional database to accommodate a demand spike, you can drive more throughput by adding one node of distributed cache, replacing several database nodes. The caching layer saves you money because you're paying for one node instead of multiple database nodes, and you get the added benefit of dramatically faster performance for reads.

Amazon ElastiCache

Developers need a way to maintain super-low latency, even as they accommodate spikes in demand and while controlling infrastructure and database costs and load.

Amazon ElastiCache is a web service that makes it easy to deploy, operate, and scale an in-memory cache in the AWS Cloud. The service improves the performance of web applications by allowing you to retrieve information from fast, managed, in-memory caches instead of relying entirely on slower disk-based databases.

ElastiCache automatically detects and replaces failed nodes, reducing the overhead associated with self-managed infrastructures and also provides a resilient system that mitigates the risk of overloaded cloud databases, which slow website and application load times.

ElastiCache currently supports two different open-source, in-memory, key-value caching engines: Redis and Memcached. Each engine provides some advantages.

Redis

Redis is an increasingly popular open-source, key-value store that supports more advanced data structures, such as sorted sets, hashes, and lists. Unlike Memcached, Redis has disk persistence built in, meaning that you can use it for long-lived data. Redis also supports replication, which can be used to achieve Multi-AZ redundancy, similar to Amazon RDS.

Memcached

Memcached is a widely adopted in-memory key store. It is historically the gold standard of web caching. ElastiCache is protocol-compliant with Memcached, and it is designed to work with popular tools that you use today with existing Memcached environments. Memcached is also multithreaded, meaning that it makes good use of larger Amazon EC2 instance sizes with multiple cores.

Comparison of Memcached and Redis

Although both Memcached and Redis appear similar on the surface, in that they are both in-memory key stores, they are quite different in practice. Because of the replication and persistence features of Redis, ElastiCache manages Redis more as a relational database. Redis ElastiCache clusters are managed as stateful entities that include failover, similar to how Amazon RDS manages database failover.

Conversely, because Memcached is designed as a pure caching solution with no persistence, ElastiCache manages Memcached nodes as a pool that can grow and shrink, similar to an Amazon EC2 Auto Scaling group. Individual nodes are expendable, and ElastiCache provides additional capabilities here, such as automatic node replacement and Auto Discovery.

Consider the following requirements when deciding between Memcached and Redis. Use Memcached if you require one or more of the following:

- Object caching is your primary goal, for example, to offload your database.
- You are interested in as simple a caching model as possible.

- You plan to run large cache nodes and require multithreaded performance with the use of multiple cores.
- You want to scale your cache horizontally as you grow.

Use Redis if you require one or more of the following:

- You are looking for more advanced data types, such as lists, hashes, and sets.
- Sorting and ranking datasets in memory help you, such as with leaderboards.
- Your application requires publish and subscribe (pub/sub) capabilities.
- Persistence of your key store is important.
- You want to run in multiple Availability Zones (Multi-AZ) with failover.
- You want transactional support, which lets you execute a group of commands as an isolated and atomic operation.

Amazon DynamoDB Accelerator

Amazon DynamoDB Accelerator (DAX) is a fully managed, highly available, in-memory cache for DynamoDB that delivers up to 10 times the performance improvement—from milliseconds to microseconds—even at millions of requests per second. DAX does all of the heavy lifting required to add in-memory acceleration to your DynamoDB tables, without requiring developers to manage cache invalidation, data population, or cluster management.

With DAX, you can focus on building great applications for your customers without worrying about performance at scale. You do not need to modify application logic, because DAX is compatible with existing DynamoDB API calls. You can enable DAX with a few clicks in the AWS Management Console or by using the AWS SDK, and you pay only for the capacity you provision.

Graph Databases

AWS provides a variety of graph database options, such as Amazon Neptune, or you can operate your own graph database in the cloud on Amazon EC2 and Amazon EBS. This section takes a closer look at what exactly is a graph database and when you would want to use one.

Many applications being built today must understand and navigate relationships between highly connected data. This can enable use cases like the following:

- Social applications
- Recommendation engines
- Fraud detection
- Knowledge graphs
- Life sciences
- IT/network

Because the data is highly connected, it is easily represented as a graph, which is a data structure that consists of *vertices* and directed links called *edges*. Vertices and edges can each have properties associated with them. Figure 4.21 depicts a simple graph of relationships between friends and their interests—or social network—that could be stored and queried by using a graph database. A *graph database* is optimized to store and process graph data.

FIGURE 4.21   Example of a social network diagram

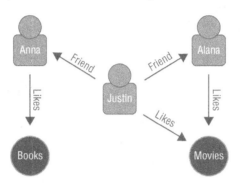

AWS provides a variety of graph database options. You can operate your own graph database in the cloud on Amazon EC2 and Amazon EBS. You can also use Neptune, a fully managed graph database service.

Amazon Neptune

Amazon Neptune is a fast, reliable, fully managed graph database service that makes it easy to build and run applications that work with highly connected datasets. The core of Neptune is a purpose-built, high-performance graph database engine optimized for storing billions of relationships and querying the graph with milliseconds latency.

Neptune is highly available and provides the following features:

- Read replicas
- Point-in-time recovery
- Continuous backup to Amazon S3
- Replication across Availability Zones
- Encryption at rest and in transit

Figure 4.22 shows a knowledge graph that can be powered by Neptune.

FIGURE 4.22   Example of a graph database architecture running on Amazon Neptune

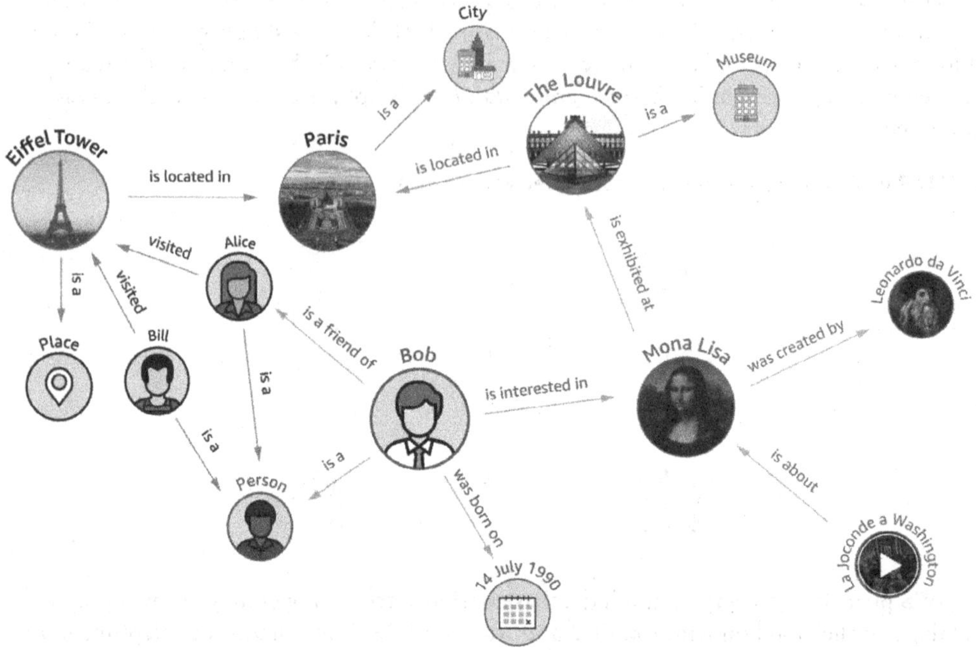

Neptune supports the popular graph models Property Graph and W3C's RDS and their respective query languages Apache TinkerPop Gremlin and SPARQL. With these models, you can easily build queries that efficiently navigate highly connected datasets. Neptune graph databases include the following use cases:

- Recommendation engines
- Fraud detection
- Knowledge graphs
- Drug discovery
- Network security

Cloud Database Migration

Data is the cornerstone of successful cloud application deployments. Your evaluation and planning process may highlight the physical limitations inherent to migrating data from on-premises locations into the cloud. Amazon offers a suite of tools to help you move data via networks, roads, and technology partners.

This chapter focuses on the AWS Database Migration Service (AWS DMS) and the AWS Schema Conversion Tool (AWS SCT). Customers also use other AWS services and features that are discussed in Chapter 3, "Hello, Storage," for cloud data migration, including the following:

- AWS Direct Connect (DX)
- AWS Snowball
- AWS Snowball Edge
- AWS Snowmobile
- AWS Import/Export Disk
- AWS Storage Gateway
- Amazon Kinesis Data Firehose
- Amazon S3 Transfer Acceleration
- Virtual private network (VPN) connections

AWS Database Migration Service

AWS Database Migration Service (AWS DMS) helps you migrate databases to AWS quickly and securely. The source database remains fully operational during the migration, minimizing downtime to applications that rely on the database. AWS DMS can migrate your data to and from the most widely used commercial and open-source databases.

The service supports *homogenous database migrations*, such as Oracle to Oracle, in addition to *heterogeneous migrations* between different database platforms, such as Oracle to Amazon Aurora or Microsoft SQL Server to MySQL. You can also stream data to Amazon Redshift, Amazon DynamoDB, and Amazon S3 from any of the supported sources, such as Amazon Aurora, PostgreSQL, MySQL, MariaDB, Oracle Database, SAP ASE, SQL Server, IBM DB2 LUW, and MongoDB, enabling consolidation and easy analysis of data in a petabyte-scale data warehouse. You can also use AWS DMS for continuous data replication with high availability.

Figure 4.23 shows an example of both heterogeneous and homogenous database migrations.

FIGURE 4.23   Homogenous database migrations using AWS DMS

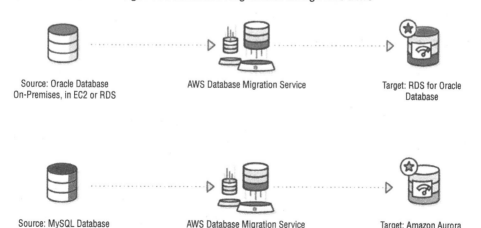

Source: Oracle Database On-Premises, in EC2 or RDS   AWS Database Migration Service   Target: RDS for Oracle Database

Source: MySQL Database On-Premises, in EC2 or RDS   AWS Database Migration Service   Target: Amazon Aurora Database

To perform a database migration, AWS DMS connects to the source data store, reads the source data, and formats the data for consumption by the target data store. It then loads the data into the target data store. Most of this processing happens in memory, though large transactions might require some buffering to disk. Cached transactions and log files are also written to disk.

At a high level, when you're using AWS DMS, complete the following tasks:

- Create a replication server.
- Create source and target endpoints that have connection information about your data stores.
- Create one or more tasks to migrate data between the source and target data stores.

A task can consist of three major phases:

- The full load of existing data
- The application of cached changes
- Ongoing replication

AWS Schema Conversion Tool

For heterogeneous database migrations, AWS DMS uses the *AWS Schema Conversion Tool* (AWS SCT). AWS SCT makes heterogeneous database migrations predictable by automatically converting the source database schema and a majority of the database code objects, including views, stored procedures, and functions, to a format compatible with the target database. Any objects that cannot be automatically converted are clearly marked so that they can be manually converted to complete the migration.

AWS SCT can also scan your application source code for embedded SQL statements and convert them as part of a database schema conversion project. During this process, AWS SCT performs cloud-native code optimization by converting legacy Oracle and SQL Server functions to their equivalent AWS service, thus helping you modernize the applications at the same time as database migration.

Figure 4.24 is snapshot of the Action Items tab in the AWS SCT report, which shows the items that the tool could not convert automatically. These are the items that you would need to evaluate and adjust manually as needed. The report helps you to determine how much work you would need to do to complete a conversion.

FIGURE 4.24 AWS SCT action items

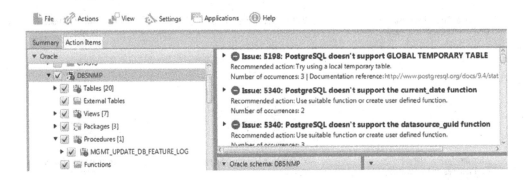

After the schema conversion is complete, AWS SCT can help migrate data from a range of data warehouses to Amazon Redshift by using built-in data migration agents.

Your source database can be on-premises, in Amazon RDS, or in Amazon EC2, and the target database can be in either Amazon RDS or Amazon EC2. AWS SCT supports a number of different heterogeneous conversions. Table 4.9 lists the source and target databases that are supported at the time of this writing.

TABLE 4.9   Source and Target Databases Supported by AWS SCT

Source Database	Target Database on Amazon RDS
Oracle Database	Amazon Aurora, MySQL, PostgreSQL, Oracle
Oracle Data Warehouse	Amazon Redshift
Azure SQL	Amazon Aurora, MySQL, PostgreSQL
Microsoft SQL Server	Amazon Aurora, Amazon Redshift, MySQL, PostgreSQL
Teradata	Amazon Redshift
IBM Netezza	Amazon Redshift
IBM DB2 LUW	Amazon Aurora, MySQL, PostgreSQL
HPE Vertica	Amazon Redshift
MySQL and MariaDB	PostgreSQL
PostgreSQL	Amazon Aurora, MySQL
Amazon Aurora	PostgreSQL
Greenplum	Amazon Redshift
Apache Cassandra	Amazon DynamoDB

Running Your Own Database on Amazon Elastic Compute Cloud

This chapter focused heavily on the AWS services that are available from a managed database perspective. However, it is important to know that you can also run your own unmanaged database on Amazon EC2, not only for the exam but for managing projects in the real world. For example, if you want to run MongoDB on Amazon EC2, this is perfectly within the realm of possibility. However, by doing so, you lose the many benefits of using a managed database service.

Compliance and Security

AWS includes various methods to provide security for your databases and meet the strictest of compliance standards. You can use the following:

- Network isolation through virtual private cloud (VPC)
- Security groups
- AWS resource-level permission controls that are IAM-based.
- Encryption at rest by using AWS KMS or Oracle/Microsoft Transparent Data Encryption (TDE)
- Secure Sockets Layer (SSL) protection for data in transit
- Assurance programs for finance, healthcare, government, and more

AWS Identity and Access Management

You can use *Identity and Access Management* (IAM) to perform governed access to control who can perform actions with Amazon Aurora MySQL and Amazon RDS for MySQL. Here's an example:

```
{
    "Version": "2012-10-17",
    "Statement": [
        {
            "Sid": "AllowCreateDBInstanceOnly",
            "Effect": "Allow",
            "Action": [
                "rds:CreateDBInstance"
            ],
            "Resource": [
                "arn:aws:rds:*:123456789012:db:test*",
                "arn:aws:rds: * : 123456789012:og:default*",
                "arn:aws:rds:*:123456789012:pg:default*",
                "arn:aws:rds: * : 1234 56789012 :subgrp: default"
            ],
```

```
        "Condition": {
            "StringEquals": {
            "rds:DatabaseEngine": "mysql",
            "rds:DatabaseClass": "db.t2.micro"
            }
        }
    }
  }
}
```

Summary

In this chapter, you learned the basic concepts of different types of databases, including relational, nonrelational, data warehouse, in-memory, and graph databases. From there, you learned about the various managed database services available on AWS. These included Amazon RDS, Amazon DynamoDB, Amazon Redshift, Amazon ElastiCache, and Amazon Neptune. You also saw how you can run your own database on Amazon EC2. Finally, you looked at how to perform homogenous database migrations using the AWS Database Migration Service (AWS DMS). For heterogeneous database migrations, you learned that AWS DMS can use the AWS Schema Conversion Tool (AWS SCT).

Exam Essentials

Know what a relational database is.   A relational database consists of one or more tables. Communication to and from relational databases usually involves simple SQL queries, such as "Add a new record" or "What is the cost of product x?" These simple queries are often referred to as online transaction processing (OLTP).

Know what a nonrelational database is.   Nonrelational databases do not have a hard-defined data schema. They can use a variety of models for data management, such as in-memory key-value stores, graph data models, and document stores. These databases are optimized for applications that have a large data volume, require low latency, and have flexible data models. In nonrelational databases, there is no concept of foreign keys.

Understand the database options available on AWS.   You can run all types of databases on AWS. You should understand that there are managed and unmanaged options available, in addition to relational, nonrelational, caching, graph, and data warehouses.

Understand which databases Amazon RDS supports.   Amazon RDS currently supports six relational database engines:

- Microsoft SQL Server
- MySQL
- Oracle
- PostgreSQL
- MariaDB
- Amazon Aurora

Understand the operational benefits of using Amazon RDS.   Amazon RDS is an AWS managed service. AWS is responsible for patching, antivirus, and the management of the underlying guest OS for Amazon RDS. Amazon RDS greatly simplifies the process of setting a secondary slave with replication for failover and setting up read replicas to offload queries.

Remember that you cannot access the underlying OS for Amazon RDS DB instances.   You cannot use Remote Desktop Protocol (RDP) or SSH to connect to the underlying OS. If you need to access the OS, install custom software or agents. If you want to use a database engine that Amazon RDS does not support, consider running your database on an Amazon EC2 instance instead.

Understand that Amazon RDS handles Multi-AZ failover for you.   If your primary Amazon RDS instance becomes unavailable, AWS fails over to your secondary instance in another Availability Zone automatically. This failover is done by pointing your existing database endpoint to a new IP address. You do not have to change the connection string manually; AWS handles the DNS changes automatically.

Remember that Amazon RDS read replicas are used for scaling out and increased performance.   This replication feature makes it easy to scale out your read-intensive databases. Read replicas are currently supported in Amazon RDS for MySQL, PostgreSQL, and Amazon Aurora. You can create one or more replicas of a database within a single AWS Region or across multiple AWS Regions. Amazon RDS uses native replication to propagate changes made to a source DB instance to any associated read replicas. Amazon RDS also supports cross-region read replicas to replicate changes asynchronously to another geography or AWS Region.

Know how to calculate throughput for Amazon DynamoDB.   Remember that one read capacity unit (RCU) represents one strongly consistent read per second or two eventually consistent reads per second for an item up to 4 KB in size. For writing data, know that one write capacity unit (WCU) represents one write per second for an item up to 1 KB in size. Be comfortable performing calculations to determine the appropriate setting for the RCU and WCU for a table.

Know that DynamoDB spreads RCUs and WCUs across partitions evenly.   Recall that when you allocate your total RCUs and WCUs to a table, DynamoDB spreads these across your partitions evenly. For example, if you have 1,000 RCUs and you have 10 partitions, then you have 100 RCUs allocated to each partition.

Know the differences between a local secondary index and a global secondary index. Remember that you can create local secondary indexes only when you initially create the table; additionally, know that local secondary indexes must share the same partition key as the parent or source table. Conversely, you can create global secondary indexes at any time, with different partitions keys or sort keys.

Know the difference between eventually consistent and strongly consistent reads. Know that with eventually consistent reads, your application may retrieve data that is stale; but with strongly consistent reads, the data is always up-to-date.

Understand the purpose of caching data and which related services are available. Know why caching is important for your database tier and how it helps to improve your application performance. Additionally, understand the differences between the caching methods (lazy loading and write-through) and the corresponding AWS services (Amazon DynamoDB Accelerator (DAX), ElastiCache for Redis, and ElastiCache for Memcached).

Resources to Review

What Is a Relational Database?

> https://aws.amazon.com/relational-database/

AWS Databases:

> https://aws.amazon.com/products/databases/

AWS Database Blog:

> https://aws.amazon.com/blogs/database/

A One Size Fits All Database Doesn't Fit Anyone:

> https://www.allthingsdistributed.com/2018/06/purpose-built-databases-in-aws.html

Amazon Relational Database Service (Amazon RDS) User Guide:

> https://docs.aws.amazon.com/AmazonRDS/latest/UserGuide/Welcome.html

Amazon RDS FAQs:

> https://aws.amazon.com/rds/faqs/

Development and Test on Amazon Web Services:

> https://d1.awsstatic.com/whitepapers/aws-development-test-environments.pdf

Amazon Redshift Snapshots:

> https://docs.aws.amazon.com/redshift/latest/mgmt/working-with-snapshots.html

Amazon Aurora:

    https://aws.amazon.com/rds/aurora/

Amazon Aurora Overview:

    https://docs.aws.amazon.com/AmazonRDS/latest/AuroraUserGuide/
    CHAP_AuroraOverview.html

Amazon RDS Resources:

    https://aws.amazon.com/rds/developer-resources/

Best Practices for Amazon RDS:

    https://docs.aws.amazon.com/AmazonRDS/latest/UserGuide/
    CHAP_BestPractices.html

What Is a Document Database?

    https://aws.amazon.com/nosql/document/

What Is a Columnar Database?

    https://aws.amazon.com/nosql/columnar/

What Is NoSQL?

    https://aws.amazon.com/nosql/

Amazon DynamoDB:

    https://aws.amazon.com/dynamodb/

What Is Amazon DynamoDB?

    https://docs.aws.amazon.com/amazondynamodb/latest/developerguide/
    Introduction.html

Amazon DynamoDB Core Components:

    https://docs.aws.amazon.com/amazondynamodb/latest/developerguide/
    HowItWorks.CoreComponents.html

Amazon DynamoDB Developer Guide:

    http://docs.aws.amazon.com/amazondynamodb/latest/developerguide/

GSI Attribute Projections:

    https://docs.aws.amazon.com/amazondynamodb/latest/developerguide/
    GSI.html#GSI.Projections

Data Warehouse Concepts:

    https://aws.amazon.com/data-warehouse/

Getting Started with Amazon Redshift:

    http://docs.aws.amazon.com/redshift/latest/gsg/

Amazon Redshift Database Developer Guide:

    http://docs.aws.amazon.com/redshift/latest/dg/

Using Amazon Redshift Spectrum to Query External Data:

https://docs.aws.amazon.com/redshift/latest/dg/c-using-spectrum.html

What Is a Key-Value Database?

https://aws.amazon.com/nosql/key-value/

Amazon ElasticCache for Redis User Guide:

https://docs.aws.amazon.com/AmazonElastiCache/latest/red-ug/WhatIs.html

Amazon ElastiCache for Memcached User Guide:

https://docs.aws.amazon.com/AmazonElastiCache/latest/mem-ug/WhatIs.html

In-Memory Processing in the Cloud with Amazon ElastiCache (Whitepaper):

https://d1.awsstatic.com/elasticache/elasticache_in_memory_processing_intel.pdf

Performance at Scale with Amazon ElastiCache (Whitepaper):

https://d1.awsstatic.com/whitepapers/performance-at-scale-with-amazon-elasticache.pdf

Amazon DynamoDB Accelerator (DAX):

https://aws.amazon.com/dynamodb/dax/

Amazon DynamoDB Accelerator (DAX): A Read-Through/Write-Through Cache for DynamoDB:

https://aws.amazon.com/blogs/database/amazon-dynamodb-accelerator-dax-a-read-throughwrite-through-cache-for-dynamodb/

What Is a Graph Database?

https://aws.amazon.com/nosql/graph/

Amazon Neptune User Guide:

https://docs.aws.amazon.com/neptune/latest/userguide/intro.html

AWS Database Migration Service Documentation:

https://docs.aws.amazon.com/dms/index.html

Cloud Data Migration:

https://aws.amazon.com/cloud-data-migration/

AWS Database Migration Service User Guide:

http://docs.aws.amazon.com/dms/latest/userguide/

AWS Database Migration Service Step-by-Step Walkthroughs:

http://docs.aws.amazon.com/dms/latest/sbs/DMS-SBS-Welcome.html

AWS Schema Conversion Tool User Guide:

https://docs.aws.amazon.com/SchemaConversionTool/latest/userguide/CHAP_Welcome.html

Exercises

In the following exercises, you will launch two types of databases: the first database is an SQL database on Amazon RDS, and the second is Amazon DynamoDB (NoSQL). For these sets of exercises, you will use the Python 3 SDK. You can download the Python 3 SDK at https://aws.amazon.com/sdk-for-python/.

EXERCISE 4.1

Create a Security Group for the Database Tier on Amazon RDS

Before you can create your first Amazon RDS database, you must create a security group so that you can allow traffic from your development server to communicate with the database tier. To do this, you must use an Amazon EC2 client to create the security group. Security groups are a component of the Amazon EC2 service, even though you can use them as part of Amazon RDS to secure your database tier.

To create the security group, run the following script:

```
# Excercise 4.1
import boto3
import json
import datetime

# Let's create some variables we'll use throughout these Excercises in Chapter 4
# NOTE: Here we are using a CIDR range for incoming traffic. We have set it to
    0.0.0.0/0 which means
# ANYONE on the internet can access your database if they have the username and
    the password
# If possible, specify you're own CIDR range. You can figure out your CIDR range
    by visiting the following link
# https://www.google.com/search?q=what+is+my+ip
# In the variable don't forget to add /32!
# If you aren't sure, leave it open to the world

# Variables
sg_name = 'rds-sg-dev-demo'
sg_description = 'RDS Security Group for AWS Dev Study Guide'
my_ip_cidr = '0.0.0.0/0'

# Create the EC2 Client to create the Security Group for your Database
ec2_client = boto3.client('ec2')

# First we need to create a security group
```

```
response = ec2_client.create_security_group(
    Description=sg_description,
    GroupName=sg_name)
print(json.dumps(response, indent=2, sort_keys=True))
# Now add a rule for the security group
response = ec2_client.authorize_security_group_ingress(
    CidrIp=my_ip_cidr,
    FromPort=3306,
    GroupName=sg_name,
    ToPort=3306,
    IpProtocol='tcp'
    )
print("Security Group should be created! Verify this in the AWS Console.")
```

After running the Python code, verify that the security group was created successfully from the AWS Management Console. You can find this confirmation under the VPC or Amazon EC2 service.

EXERCISE 4.2

Spin Up the MariaDB Database Instance

Use the Python SDK to spin up your MariaDB database hosted on Amazon RDS.

To spin up the MariaDB database, run the following script and update the Variables section to meet your needs:

```
# Excercise 4.2
import boto3
import json
import datetime


# Just a quick helper function for date time conversions, in case you want to
    print the raw JSON
def date_time_converter(o):
    if isinstance(o, datetime.datetime):
        return o.__str__()

# Variables
sg_name = 'rds-sg-dev-demo'
rds_identifier = 'my-rds-db'
db_name = 'mytestdb'
```

(continued)

```python
user_name = 'masteruser'
user_password = 'mymasterpassw0rd1!'
admin_email = 'myemail@myemail.com'
sg_id_number = ''
rds_endpoint = ''


# We need to get the Security Group ID Number to use in the creation of the RDS
    Instance
ec2_client = boto3.client('ec2')
response = ec2_client.describe_security_groups(
    GroupNames=[
        sg_name
    ])

sg_id_number = json.dumps(response['SecurityGroups'][0]['GroupId'])
sg_id_number = sg_id_number.replace('"','')

#   Create the client for Amazon RDS
rds_client = boto3.client('rds')

# This will create our MariaDB Database
# NOTE: Here we are hardcoding passwords for simplicity and testing purposes
    only! In production
# you should never hardcode passwords in configuration files/code!
# NOTE: This will create an MariaDB Database. Be sure to remove it when you are
    done.
response = rds_client.create_db_instance(
    DBInstanceIdentifier=rds_identifier,
    DBName=db_name,
    DBInstanceClass='db.t2.micro',
    Engine='mariadb',
    MasterUsername='masteruser',
    MasterUserPassword='mymasterpassw0rd1!',
    VpcSecurityGroupIds=[
        sg_id_number
    ],
    AllocatedStorage=20,
    Tags=[
        {
```

```
            'Key': 'POC-Email',
            'Value': admin_email
        },
        {
            'Key': 'Purpose',
            'Value': 'AWS Developer Study Guide Demo'
        }
    ]
)

# We need to wait until the DB Cluster is up!
print('Creating the RDS instance. This may take several minutes...')
waiter = rds_client.get_waiter('db_instance_available')
waiter.wait(DBInstanceIdentifier=rds_identifier)

print('Okay! The Amazon RDS Database is up!')
```

After the script has executed, the following message is displayed:

```
Creating the RDS instance. This may take several minutes.
```

After the Amazon RDS database instance has been created successfully, the following confirmation is displayed:

```
Okay! The Amazon RDS Database is up!
```

You can also view these messages from the Amazon RDS console.

EXERCISE 4.3

Obtain the Endpoint Value for the Amazon RDS Instance

Before you can start using the Amazon RDS instance, you must first specify your end-point. In this exercise, you will use the Python SDK to obtain the value.

To obtain the Amazon RDS endpoint, run the following script:

```
# Exercise 4.3
import boto3
import json
import datetime

# Just a quick helper function for date time conversions, in case you want to
    print the raw JSON
```

(continued)

```
def date_time_converter(o):
    if isinstance(o, datetime.datetime):
        return o.__str__()

# Variables
rds_identifier = 'my-rds-db'

#  Create the client for Amazon RDS
rds_client = boto3.client('rds')

print("Fetching the RDS endpoint...")
response = rds_client.describe_db_instances(
    DBInstanceIdentifier=rds_identifier
)

rds_endpoint = json.dumps(response['DBInstances'][0]['Endpoint']['Address'])
rds_endpoint = rds_endpoint.replace('"','')
print('RDS Endpoint: ' + rds_endpoint)
```

After running the Python code, the following status is displayed:

```
Fetching the RDS endpoint.. RDS Endpoint:<endpoint_name>
```

If the endpoint is not returned, from the AWS Management Console, under the RDS service, verify that your Amazon RDS database instance was created.

Create a SQL Table and Add Records to It

You now have all the necessary information to create your first SQL table by using Amazon RDS. In this exercise, you will create a SQL table and add a couple of records. Remember to update the variables for your specific environment.

To update the variables, run the following script:

```
# Exercise 4.4
import boto3
import json
import datetime
import pymysql as mariadb

# Variables
rds_identifier = 'my-rds-db'
```

```
db_name = 'mytestdb'
user_name = 'masteruser'
user_password = 'mymasterpassw0rd1!'
rds_endpoint = 'my-rds-db.****.us-east-1.rds.amazonaws.com'

# Step 1 - Connect to the database to create the table
db_connection = mariadb.connect(host=rds_endpoint, user=user_name,
    password=user_password, database=db_name)
cursor = db_connection.cursor()
try:
    cursor.execute("CREATE TABLE Users (user_id INT NOT NULL AUTO_INCREMENT,
    user_fname VARCHAR(100) NOT NULL, user_lname VARCHAR(150) NOT NULL, user_
    email VARCHAR(175) NOT NULL, PRIMARY KEY (`user_id`))")
    print('Table Created!')
except mariadb.Error as e:
    print('Error: {}'.format(e))
finally:
    db_connection.close()

# Step 2 - Connect to the database to add users to the table
db_connection = mariadb.connect(host=rds_endpoint, user=user_name,
password=user_password, database=db_name)
cursor = db_connection.cursor()
try:
    sql = "INSERT INTO `Users` (`user_fname`, `user_lname`, `user_email`) VALUES
    (%s, %s, %s)"
    cursor.execute(sql, ('CJ', 'Smith', 'casey.smith@somewhere.com'))
    cursor.execute(sql, ('Casey', 'Smith', 'sam.smith@somewhere.com'))
    cursor.execute(sql, ('No', 'One', 'no.one@somewhere.com'))
# No data is saved unless we commit the transaction!
    db_connection.commit()
    print('Inserted Data to Database!')
except mariadb.Error as e:
    print('Error: {}'.format(e))
    print('Sorry, something has gone wrong!')
finally:
    db_connection.close()
```

After running the Python code, the following confirmation is displayed:

```
Table Created! Inserted Data to the Database!
```

Your Amazon RDS database now has some data stored in it.

(continued)

EXERCISE 4.4 *(continued)*

 In this exercise, you are hardcoding a password into your application code for demonstration purposes only. In a production environment, refrain from hard-coding application passwords. Instead, use services such as AWS Secrets Manager to keep your secrets secure.

EXERCISE 4.5

Query the Items in the SQL Table

After adding data to your SQL database, in this exercise you will be able to read or query the items in the *Users* table.

To read the items in the SQL table, run the following script:

```python
# Exercise 4.5
import boto3
import json
import datetime
import pymysql as mariadb

# Variables
rds_identifier = 'my-rds-db'
db_name = 'mytestdb'
user_name = 'masteruser'
user_password = 'mymasterpassw0rd1!'
rds_endpoint = 'my-rds-db.*****.us-east-1.rds.amazonaws.com'

db_connection = mariadb.connect(host=rds_endpoint, user=user_name,
password=user_password, database=db_name)
cursor = db_connection.cursor()
try:
    sql = "SELECT * FROM `Users`"
    cursor.execute(sql)
    query_result = cursor.fetchall()
    print('Querying the Users Table...')
    print(query_result)
except mariadb.Error as e:
    print('Error: {}'.format(e))
    print('Sorry, something has gone wrong!')
```

finally:
    db_connection.close()

After running the Python code, you will see the three records that you inserted in the previous exercise.

Remove Amazon RDS Database and Security Group

You've created an Amazon RDS DB instance and added data to it. In this exercise, you will remove a few resources from your account. Remove the Amazon RDS instance first.

To remove the Amazon RDS instance and the security group, run the following script:

```
# Exercise 4.6
import boto3
import json
import datetime

# Variables
rds_identifier = 'my-rds-db'
sg_name = 'rds-sg-dev-demo'
sg_id_number = ''

# Create the client for Amazon RDS
rds_client = boto3.client('rds')

# Delete the RDS Instance
response = rds_client.delete_db_instance(
    DBInstanceIdentifier=rds_identifier,
    SkipFinalSnapshot=True)

print('RDS Instance is being terminated...This may take several minutes.')

waiter = rds_client.get_waiter('db_instance_deleted')
waiter.wait(DBInstanceIdentifier=rds_identifier)

# We must wait to remove the security groups until the RDS database has been
    deleted, this is a dependency.
print('The Amazon RDS database has been deleted. Removing Security Groups')

# Create the client for Amazon EC2 SG
```

```
ec2_client = boto3.client('ec2')

# Get the Security Group ID Number
response = ec2_client.describe_security_groups(
    GroupNames=[
        sg_name
    ])
sg_id_number = json.dumps(response['SecurityGroups'][0]['GroupId'])
sg_id_number = sg_id_number.replace('"','')

# Delete the Security Group!
response = ec2_client.delete_security_group(
    GroupId=sg_id_number
    )

print('Cleanup is complete!')
```

After running the Python code, the following message is displayed:

```
Cleanup is complete!
```

The Amazon RDS database and the security group are removed. You can verify this from the AWS Management Console.

Create an Amazon DynamoDB Table

Amazon DynamoDB is a managed NoSQL database. One major difference between DynamoDB and Amazon RDS is that DynamoDB doesn't require a server that is running in your VPC, and you don't need to specify an instance type. Instead, create a table.

To create the table, run the following script:

```
# Exercise 4.7
import boto3
import json
import datetime
```

```python
dynamodb_resource = boto3.resource('dynamodb')

table = dynamodb_resource.create_table(
    TableName='Users',
    KeySchema=[
        {
            'AttributeName': 'user_id',
            'KeyType': 'HASH'
        },
        {
            'AttributeName': 'user_email',
            'KeyType': 'RANGE'
        }
    ],
    AttributeDefinitions=[
        {
            'AttributeName': 'user_id',
            'AttributeType': 'S'
        },
        {
            'AttributeName': 'user_email',
            'AttributeType': 'S'
        }
    ],
    ProvisionedThroughput={
        'ReadCapacityUnits': 5,
        'WriteCapacityUnits': 5
    }
)

print("The DynamoDB Table is being created, this may take a few minutes...")
table.meta.client.get_waiter('table_exists').wait(TableName='Users')
print("Table is ready!")
```

After running the Python code, the following message is displayed:

```
Table is ready!
```

From the AWS Management Console, under DynamoDB, verify that the table was created.

EXERCISE 4.8

Add Users to the Amazon DynamoDB Table

With DynamoDB, there are fewer components to set up than there are for Amazon RDS. In this exercise, you'll add users to your table. Experiment with updating and changing some of the code to add multiple items to the database.

To add users to the DynamoDB table, run the following script:

```
# Exercise 4.8
import boto3
import json
import datetime
# In this example we are not using uuid; however, you could use this to
autogenerate your user IDs.
# i.e. str(uuid.uuid4())
import uuid


# Create a DynamoDB Resource
dynamodb_resource = boto3.resource('dynamodb')
table = dynamodb_resource.Table('Users')


# Write a record to DynamoDB
response = table.put_item(
    Item={
        'user_id': '1234-5678',
        'user_email': 'someone@somewhere.com',
        'user_fname': 'Sam',
        'user_lname': 'Samuels'
    }
)

# Just printing the raw JSON response, you should see a 200 status code
print(json.dumps(response, indent=2, sort_keys=True))
```

After running the Python code, you receive a 200 HTTP Status Code from AWS. This means that the user record has been added.

From the AWS Management Console, under DynamoDB, review the table to verify that the user record was added.

EXERCISE 4.9

Look Up a User in the Amazon DynamoDB Table

In this exercise, you look up the one user you've added so far.

To look up users in the DynamoDB table, run the following script:

```
# Exercise 4.9
import boto3
from boto3.dynamodb.conditions import Key
import json
import datetime

# Create a DynamoDB Resource
dynamodb_resource = boto3.resource('dynamodb')
table = dynamodb_resource.Table('Users')

# Query a some data
response = table.query(
    KeyConditionExpression=Key('user_id').eq('1234-5678')
)

# Print the data out!
print(json.dumps(response['Items'], indent=2, sort_keys=True))
```

After running the Python code, the query results are returned in JSON format showing a single user.

EXERCISE 4.10

Write Data to the Table as a Batch Process

In this exercise, you will write data to the table through a batch process.

To write data using a batch process, run the following script:

```
# Exercise 4.10
import boto3
import json
import datetime
import uuid

# Create a DynamoDB Resource
```

(continued)

```
dynamodb_resource = boto3.resource('dynamodb')
table = dynamodb_resource.Table('Users')

# Generate some random data
with table.batch_writer() as user_data:
    for i in range(100):
        user_data.put_item(
            Item={
                'user_id': str(uuid.uuid4()),
                'user_email': 'someone' + str(i) + '@somewhere.com',
                'user_fname': 'User' + str(i),
                'user_lname': 'UserLast' + str(i)
            }
        )
        print('Writing record # ' + str(i+1) + ' to DynamoDB Users Table')
    print('Done!')
```

After running the Python code, the last few lines read as follows:

```
Writing record # 300 to DyanmoDB Users Table Done!
```

From the AWS Management Console, under DynamoDB Table, verify that the users were written to the table.

Scan the Amazon DynamoDB Table

In this exercise, you will scan the entire table.

To scan the table, run the following script:

```
# Exercise 4.11
import boto3
import json
import datetime
import uuid

# Create a DynamoDB Resource
dynamodb_resource = boto3.resource('dynamodb')
```

```
table = dynamodb_resource.Table('Users')

# Let's do a scan!
response = table.scan()

print('The total Count is: ' + json.dumps(response['Count']))
print(json.dumps(response['Items'], indent=2, sort_keys=True))
```

As you learned in this chapter, scans return the entire dataset located in the table. After running the script, all of the users are returned.

EXERCISE 4.12

Remove the Amazon DynamoDB Table

In this exercise, you will remove the DynamoDB table that you created in Exercise 4.7.

To remove the table, run the following script:

```
# Exercise 4.12
import boto3
import json
import datetime
import uuid

# Create a DynamoDB Resource
dynamodb_client = boto3.client('dynamodb')

# Delete the Table
response = dynamodb_client.delete_table(TableName='Users')
print(json.dumps(response, indent=2, sort_keys=True))
```

The DynamoDB table is deleted, or it is in the process of being deleted. Verify the deletion from the AWS Management Console, under the DynamoDB service.

Review Questions

1. Which of the following does Amazon Relational Database Service (Amazon RDS) manage on your behalf? (Select THREE.)

    A. Database settings

    B. Database software installation and patching

    C. Query optimization

    D. Hardware provisioning

    E. Backups

2. Which AWS database service is best suited for managing highly connected datasets?

    A. Amazon Aurora

    B. Amazon Neptune

    C. Amazon DynamoDB

    D. Amazon Redshift

3. You are designing an ecommerce web application that will scale to potentially hundreds of thousands of concurrent users. Which database technology is best suited to hold the session state for large numbers of concurrent users?

    A. Relational database by using Amazon Relational Database Service (Amazon RDS)

    B. NoSQL database table by using Amazon DynamoDB

    C. Data warehouse by using Amazon Redshift

    D. MySQL on Amazon EC2

4. How many read capacity units (RCUs) do you need to support 25 *strongly consistent* reads per seconds of 15 KB?

    A. 100 RCUs

    B. 25 RCUs

    C. 10 RCUs

    D. 15 RCUs

5. How many read capacity units (RCUs) do you need to support 25 *eventually consistent* reads per seconds of 15 KB?

    A. 10 RCUs

    B. 25 RCUs

    C. 50 RCUs

    D. 15 RCUs

6. How many write capacity units (WCUs) are needed to support 100 writers per second of 512 bytes?

   A. 129 WCUs

   B. 25 WCUs

   C. 10 WCUs

   D. 100 WCUs

7. Your company is using Amazon DynamoDB, and they would like to implement a write-through caching mechanism. They would like to get everything up and running in only a few short weeks. Additionally, your company would like to refrain from managing any additional servers. You are the lead developer on the project; what should you recommend?

   A. Build your own custom caching application.

   B. Implement Amazon DynamoDB Accelerator (DAX).

   C. Run Redis on Amazon EC2.

   D. Run Memcached on Amazon EC2.

8. Your company would like to implement a highly available caching solution for its SQL database running on Amazon RDS. Currently, all of its services are running in the AWS Cloud. As their lead developer, what should you recommend?

   A. Implement your own caching solution on-premises.

   B. Implement Amazon ElastiCache for Redis.

   C. Implement Amazon ElastiCache for Memcached.

   D. Implement Amazon DynamoDB Accelerator (DAX).

9. A company is looking to run analytical queries and would like to implement a data warehouse. It estimates that it has roughly 300 TB worth of data, which is expected to double in the next three years. Which AWS service should you recommend?

   A. Relational database by using Amazon Relational Database Service (Amazon RDS)

   B. NoSQL database table by using Amazon DynamoDB

   C. Data warehouse by using Amazon Redshift

   D. Amazon ElastiCache for Redis

10. A company is experiencing an issue with Amazon DynamoDB whereby the data is taking longer than expected to return from a query. You are tasked with investigating the problem. After looking at the application code, you realize that a Scan operation is being called for a large DynamoDB table. What should you do or recommend?

    A. Implement a query instead of a scan, if possible, as queries are more efficient than a scan.

    B. Do nothing; the problem should go away on its own.

    C. Implement a strongly consistent read.

    D. Increase the write capacity units (WCUs).

Chapter

5

Encryption on AWS

THE AWS CERTIFIED DEVELOPER – ASSOCIATE EXAM TOPICS COVERED IN THIS CHAPTER MAY INCLUDE, BUT ARE NOT LIMITED TO, THE FOLLOWING:

Domain 2: Security

✓ 2.2 Implement encryption using AWS services.

Domain 3: Development with AWS Services

✓ 3.4 Write code that interacts with AWS services by using APIs, SDKs, and AWS CLI.

Introduction to Encryption

AWS delivers a secure, scalable cloud computing platform with high availability, offering the flexibility for you to build a wide range of applications. If you require an additional layer of security for the data you store in the AWS Cloud, there are several options for encrypting data at rest. These options range from automated AWS encryption solutions to manual, client-side options. Choosing the right solutions depends on which AWS service you're using and your requirements for key management. This chapter provides an overview of various methods for encrypting data at rest in AWS. Specifically, it covers three options and compares and contrasts the advantages of each option.

Before exploring the different ways that you can use encryption in AWS, the following section describes two services that you can use for your encryption strategy: AWS Key Management Service and AWS CloudHSM.

AWS Key Management Service

AWS Key Management Service (AWS KMS) is a managed AWS service that makes it easy to create and manage encryption keys to encrypt your data across a wide range of AWS services and in your applications. As a secure, resilient service, AWS KMS uses FIPS 140-2 validated cryptographic modules, known as a hardware security module (HSM), to protect your master keys. The Federal Information Processing Standards (FIPS) are responsible for defining security requirements for cryptographic modules. For more information about FIPS 140-2 validation, see https://nvlpubs.nist.gov/nistpubs/FIPS/NIST.FIPS.140-2.pdf.

You can take advantage of a number of AWS KMS features and benefits when developing your applications. You can use AWS KMS to make the applications and data more secure while still enabling you to innovate quickly through an API.

AWS KMS offers the following features:

- Centralized key management
- Integration with other AWS services
- Audit capabilities and high availability
- Custom key store
- Compliance

Centralized Key Management

AWS KMS provides you with a centralized view of your encryption keys. You can create a *customer master key* (CMK) to control access to your data encryption keys (data keys) and to encrypt and decrypt your data. AWS KMS uses an Advanced Encryption Standard (AES) in 256-bit mode to encrypt and secure your data.

You can use AWS KMS to create keys in one of three ways: by using AWS KMS, by using AWS CloudHSM, or by importing your own key material. Regardless of the method you use to store your keys, you can manage them with AWS KMS through the AWS Management Console or by using the AWS SDK or the AWS CLI. AWS KMS also automatically rotates your keys once a year, without having to re-encrypt data that was previously encrypted.

Integration with Other AWS Services

AWS KMS provides seamless integration with other AWS services. This integration means that, as a developer, you can quickly create keys to encrypt data that is stored in other AWS services, such as Amazon Simple Storage Service (Amazon S3).

AWS KMS provides an AWS managed master key for a variety of AWS services that integrate with AWS KMS. You can track the AWS managed CMKs in your account, but the service itself manages the keys. For greater control over the encryption process, you can generate your own CMK.

At the time of this writing, AWS KMS supports 51 AWS services, as shown in Figure 5.1.

FIGURE 5.1 Supported AWS services

AWS Services Integrated with KMS

Alexa for Business*	Amazon EMR	Amazon SageMaker	AWS CodeDeploy
Amazon Athena	Amazon FSx for Windows File Server	Amazon Simple Email Service (Amazon SES)	AWS CodePipeline
Amazon Aurora	Amazon Simple Storage Service Glacier	Amazon Simple Notification Service (Amazon SNS)	AWS Database Migration Service
Amazon CloudWatch logs	Amazon Kinesis Data Streams	Amazon Simple Queue Service (Amazon SQS)	AWS Glue
Amazon Comprehend*	Amazon Kinesis Data Firehouse	Amazon Translate	AWS Lambda
Amazon Connect	Amazon Kinesis Video Streams	Amazon WorkMail	AWS Secrets Manager
Amazon DocumentDB	Amazon Lex	Amazon WorkSpaces	AWS Systems Manager
Amazon DynamoDB*	Amazon Lightsail*	AWS Backup	AWS Snowball
Amazon DynamoDB Accelerator (DAX)*	Amazon Managed Streaming for Kafka (MSK)	AWS Certificate Manager*	AWS Snowball Edge
Amazon Elastic Block Store (Amazon EBS)	Amazon Neptune	AWS Cloud9*	AWS Snowmobile
Amazon Elastic File System (Amazon EFS)	Amazon Redshift	AWS CloudTrail	AWS Storage Gateway
Amazon Elastic Transcoder	Amazon Relational Database Service (RDS)	AWS CodeBuild	AWS X-Ray
Amazon Elasticsearch Service	Amazon Simple Storage Service (Amazon S3)	AWS CodeCommit*	

Auditing Capabilities and High Availability

If AWS CloudTrail is enabled for your AWS account and Region, API requests and other activity in your AWS account are recorded to log files. With CloudTrail, you can see who has used a particular AWS KMS CMK, the API call that was sent, and when they attempted to use that particular key.

In addition to auditing capabilities, AWS KMS is a fully managed service, which means that as your encryption needs grow or change, AWS KMS can scale automatically to meet those needs. Additionally, because this is a managed service, AWS KMS stores encrypted copies or versions of your keys inside systems that are designed for 99.999999999 percent durability.

The AWS CMKs do not leave the CloudHSM instances. Your keys are stored securely within the AWS Region so that no one, including AWS employees, can retrieve your plaintext keys from AWS KMS. AWS KMS uses FIPS 140-2 validated HSMs to protect your keys and to help ensure the confidentiality and integrity of your data.

Custom Key Store

You can create your own custom key store in an CloudHSM cluster that you control, enabling you to store your AWS KMS keys in a single-tenant environment instead of the default multi-tenant environment of AWS KMS. The use of a custom key store incurs an additional cost for the CloudHSM cluster.

Compliance

Achieving compliance for your applications can be a lengthy and difficult process. The security and quality controls in AWS KMS have been validated and certified by a number of industry-specific compliance and regulatory standards. For a full list of compliance standards that have been met, see https://aws.amazon.com/compliance/services-in-scope/.

AWS CloudHSM

AWS CloudHSM offers third-party, validated FIPS 140-2, level-three hardware security modules in the AWS Cloud. The hardware security module is a computing device that provides a dedicated infrastructure to support cryptographic operations. You can use CloudHSM to support encryption for your application while running in your own Amazon Virtual Private Cloud (Amazon VPC). This means that your Amazon Elastic Compute Cloud (Amazon EC2) instances can access the CloudHSM device quickly while isolating them from other networks.

CloudHSM provides both asymmetric and symmetric encryption capabilities. Additionally, you can use the CloudHSM software libraries to integrate applications with HSMs in your cluster. The libraries include PKCS #11, Sun Java JCE (Java Cryptography Extension), and Cryptography API: Next Generation (CNG) providers for Microsoft. By using these libraries, you can perform cryptographic operations on the HSMs.

Controlling the Access Keys

Encryption on any system requires three components: data to encrypt, a method to encrypt the data using a cryptographic algorithm, and the use of encryption keys with the data and the algorithm. Most modern programming languages provide libraries with a wide range of available cryptographic algorithms, such as the Advanced Encryption Standard (AES). Choosing the right algorithm involves evaluating security, performance, and compliance requirements specific to your application. Although the selection of an encryption algorithm is important, protecting the keys from unauthorized access is critical. Managing the security of encryption keys is often performed using a *key management infrastructure* (KMI). A KMI is composed of two subcomponents: the storage layer that protects the plaintext keys and the management layer that authorizes key use. A common way to protect keys in a KMI is to use a hardware security module. An HSM is a dedicated storage and data processing device that performs cryptographic operations using keys on the device. An HSM typically provides tamper evidence, or resistance, to protect keys from unauthorized use. A software-based authorization layer controls who can administer the HSM and which users or applications can use which keys in the HSM.

As you deploy encryption for various data classifications in AWS, it is important to understand exactly who has access to your encryption keys or data and under what conditions. As shown in Figure 5.2, there are three different options for how you and AWS provide the encryption method and the KMI:

- You control the encryption method and the entire KMI.

- You control the encryption method, AWS provides the storage component of the KMI, and you provide the management layer of the KMI.

- AWS controls the encryption method and the entire KMI.

FIGURE 5.2   Encryption options in AWS

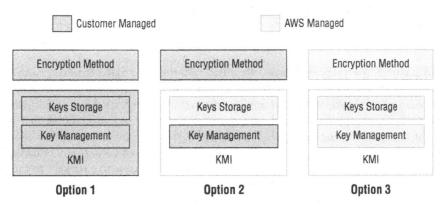

Option 1: You Control the Encryption Method and the Entire KMI

In this option, you use your own KMI to generate, store, and manage access to keys in addition to controlling all the encryption methods in your applications. This physical location of the KMI and the encryption method can be outside of AWS or in an Amazon EC2 instance that you own. The encryption method can be a combination of open source tools, AWS SDKs, or third-party software and hardware. The important security property of this option is that you have full control over the encryption keys and the execution environment that uses those keys in the encryption code. AWS has no access to your keys and cannot perform encryption or decryption on your behalf. You are responsible for the proper storage, management, and use of keys to ensure the confidentiality, integrity, and availability of your data. You can encrypt data in AWS services, as described in the following sections.

Amazon Simple Storage Service

You can encrypt data by using any encryption method you want and then upload the encrypted data using the Amazon Simple Storage Service (Amazon S3) API. Most common application languages include cryptographic libraries that enable you to perform encryption in your applications. There are many commonly available open source tools for data encryption; however, they go beyond the scope of this study guide. After you have encrypted an object and safely stored the key in your KMI, you can upload the encrypted object to Amazon S3 directly with a PUT request. To decrypt this data, issue the GET request in the Amazon S3 API and then pass the encrypted data to your local application for decryption.

AWS provides an alternative to these open source encryption tools with the *Amazon S3 encryption client*, which is an open source set of APIs embedded in the AWS SDKs. This client lets you supply a key from your KMI that can be used to encrypt or decrypt your data as part of the call to Amazon S3. The SDK leverages Java Cryptography Extensions (JCEs) in your application to take your symmetric or asymmetric key as input and encrypt the object before uploading it to Amazon S3. The process is reversed when the SDK is used to retrieve an object. The downloaded encrypted object from Amazon S3 is passed to the client along with the key from your KMI. The underlying JCE in your application decrypts the object.

The Amazon S3 encryption client is integrated into the AWS SDKs for Java, Ruby, and .NET. It provides a transparent drop-in replacement for any cryptographic code that you might have used previously with your application that interacts with Amazon S3. Although AWS provides the encryption method, you control the security of your data because you control the keys for that engine to use. If you're using the Amazon S3 encryption client on-premises, AWS does not have access to your keys or unencrypted data. If you're using the client in an application running in Amazon EC2, a best practice is to pass keys to the client by using secure transport (for example, Secure Sockets Layer [SSL] or Secure Shell [SSH]) from your KMI to help ensure confidentiality. Figure 5.3 shows an example of Amazon S3 client-side encryption from an on-premises system compared with encryption within an Amazon EC2 application.

FIGURE 5.3   Amazon S3 client-side encryption

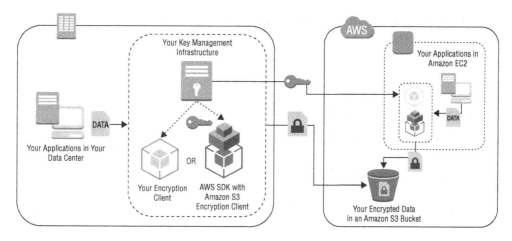

Amazon Elastic Block Store

Amazon Elastic Block Store (Amazon EBS) provides block-level storage volumes for use with Amazon EC2 instances. Amazon EBS volumes are network-attached and persist independently from the life of an instance.

System-level or block-level encryption   Because Amazon EBS volumes are presented to an instance as a block device, you can leverage most standard encryption tools for file system-level or block-level encryption. Some common block-level open source encryption solutions for Linux are *Loop-AES*, *dm-crypt* (with or without LUKS extension), and *TrueCrypt*. Each of these operates below the file system layer using kernel space device drivers to perform the encryption and decryption of data. These tools are useful when you want all data written to a volume to be encrypted regardless of what directory the data is stored in.

File-system encryption   You can use file system-level encryption, which works by stacking an encrypted file system on top of an existing file system. This method is typically used to encrypt a specific directory. *eCryptfs* and *EncFs* are two Linux-based open source examples of file system-level encryption tools.

These solutions require you to provide keys either manually or from your KMI. An important caveat with both block-level and file system-level encryption tools is that you can use them only to encrypt data volumes that are not Amazon EBS boot volumes. This is because these tools do not allow you to make a trusted key available automatically to the boot volume at startup.

AWS partner solutions help automate the process of encrypting Amazon EBS volumes in addition to supplying and protecting the necessary keys. Trend Micro SecureCloud and

SafeNet ProtectV are two such partner products that encrypt Amazon EBS volumes and include a KMI. Figure 5.4 shows how you can use the SafeNet and Trend Micro solutions to encrypt data stored on Amazon EBS using keys managed on-premises, via SaaS, or in applications running on Amazon EC2

FIGURE 5.4   Encryption in Amazon EBS using SafeNet ProtectV or Trend Micro SecureCloud

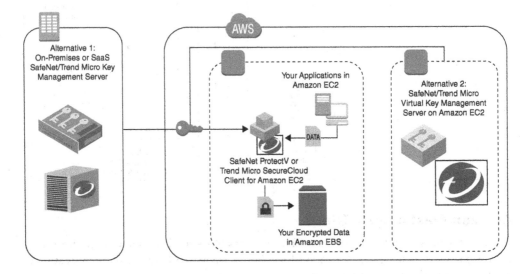

AWS Storage Gateway

AWS Storage Gateway is a service connecting an on-premises software appliance with Amazon S3. You can expose it to your network as an iSCSI disk to facilitate copying data from other sources. Data on disk volumes attached to the Storage Gateway are automatically uploaded to Amazon S3 based on policy. You can encrypt source data on the disk volumes by using any of the file encryption methods described previously, such as Bouncy Castle or OpenSSL, before it is written to the disk. To encrypt all the data on the disk volume, you can also use a block-level encryption tool, such as BitLocker or dm-crypt/LUKS, on the iSCSI endpoint exposed by Storage Gateway.

Amazon Relational Database Service

To encrypt data in *Amazon Relational Database Service* (Amazon RDS) using client-side technology, you must consider how you want data queries to work. Because Amazon RDS does not expose the attached disk it uses for data storage, transparent disk encryption using techniques described in the previous Amazon EBS section is not available. However, you can encrypt database fields in your application selectively by using any of the standard encryption libraries mentioned previously, such as Bouncy Castle and OpenSSL, before the data passes to your Amazon RDS instance.

Although this specific field data does not easily support range queries in the database, queries based on unencrypted fields can still return useful results. The encrypted fields of the returned results can be decrypted by your local application for presentation. To support more efficient querying of encrypted data, you can store a keyed-hash message authentication code (HMAC) of an encrypted field in your schema, and you can supply a key for the hash function. Subsequent queries of protected fields that contain the HMAC of the data being sought would not disclose the plaintext values in the query. This allows the database to perform a query against the encrypted data in your database without disclosing the plaintext values in the query. Any of the encryption methods you choose must be performed on your own application instance before data is sent to the Amazon RDS instance.

Amazon EMR

Amazon EMR provides an easy-to-use Hadoop implementation running on Amazon EC2. Performing encryption throughout the Hadoop operation involves encryption and key management at the following distinct phases:

- Source data

- Hadoop Distributed File System (HDFS)

- Shuffle phase

- Output data

If the source data is not encrypted, then this step can be skipped, and SSL can be used to help protect data in transit to the Amazon EMR cluster. If the source data is encrypted, then your Hadoop job must decrypt the data as it is ingested. If your job flow uses Java and the source data is in Amazon S3, you can use any of the client decryption methods described in the previous Amazon S3 sections.

The storage used for the HDFS mount point is the ephemeral storage of the cluster nodes. Depending on the instance type, there might be more than one mount. To encrypt these mount points, you must use an Amazon EMR bootstrap script that will do the following:

1. Stop the Hadoop service.

2. Install a file-system-encryption tool on the instance.

3. Create an encrypted directory to mount the encrypted file system on top of the existing mount points.

4. Restart the Hadoop service.

For example, you can perform these steps on each of the HDFS mounts by using the open source *eCryptfs* package and an ephemeral key generated in your code. You don't need to worry about persistent storage of this encryption key because the data it encrypts does not persist beyond the life of the HDFS instance.

The shuffle phase involves passing data between cluster nodes before the reduce step. To encrypt this data in transit, when you create your cluster, you can enable SSL with a configure Hadoop bootstrap option.

Finally, to enable encryption of the output data, your Hadoop job should encrypt the output using a key sourced from your KMI. This data can be sent to Amazon S3 for storage in encrypted form.

Option 2: You Control the Encryption Method, AWS Provides the KMI Storage Component, and You Provide the KMI Management Layer

This option is similar to option 1 in that you manage the encryption method, but it differs from option 1 in that the keys are stored in an AWS CloudHSM appliance rather than in a key storage system that you manage on-premises. While the keys are stored in the AWS environment, they are inaccessible to any employee at AWS because only you have access to the cryptographic partitions within the dedicated HSM to use the keys.

The CloudHSM appliance is a FIPS 140-2, level 3 HSM that has both physical and logical tamper detection and response mechanisms that trigger *zeroization* of the appliance. Zeroization erases the HSM's volatile memory where any decrypted keys were stored. Zeroization destroys the key that encrypts stored objects, effectively causing all keys on the HSM to be inaccessible and unrecoverable.

CloudHSM

To help you decide whether CloudHSM is appropriate for your deployment, it is important to understand the role that an HSM plays in encrypting data. You can use an HSM to generate and store key material and perform encryption and decryption operations. However, an HSM does not perform any key lifecycle management functions (such as access control policy, key rotation). This means you might need a compatible KMI, in addition to the CloudHSM appliance, before deploying your application. You can deploy the KMI either on-premises or within Amazon EC2. To help protect data and encryption keys, the KMI can communicate to the CloudHSM instance securely over SSL.

Amazon Virtual Private Cloud

Applications must be able to access your CloudHSM appliance in an Amazon Virtual Private Cloud (Amazon VPC). The CloudHSM client interacts with the CloudHSM appliance to encrypt data from your application. You can then send encrypted data to any AWS service for storage. CloudHSM and your custom application support database, disk volume, and file encryption applications. Figure 5.5 shows how the CloudHSM solution works with your applications running on Amazon EC2 in an Amazon VPC.

FIGURE 5.5   Deploying AWS CloudHSM in an Amazon VPC

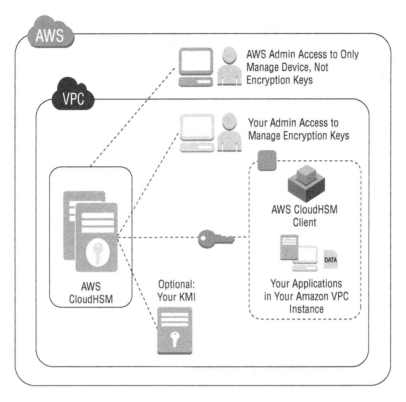

To achieve the highest availability and durability of keys in your CloudHSM appliance, AWS recommends deploying multiple CloudHSM applications across different Availability Zones or with an on-premises HSM appliance that you manage.

Option 3: AWS Controls the Encryption Method and the Entire KMI

AWS provides server-side encryption of your data, transparently managing the encryption method and keys.

AWS Key Management Service

AWS Key Management Service (AWS KMS) is a managed encryption service that lets you provision and use keys to encrypt your data in AWS services and your applications. Master keys in AWS KMS are used in a similar way to how master keys in an HSM are used. Master keys are designed never to be exported from the service. You can send data to the service to be encrypted or decrypted using a specific master key under your account. This design gives you centralized control over who can access your master keys to encrypt and decrypt data, and it gives you the ability to audit this access.

AWS KMS is natively integrated with other AWS services, including Amazon EBS, Amazon S3, and Amazon Redshift, to simplify encryption of your data within those services. AWS SDKs are integrated with AWS KMS to enable you to encrypt data in your custom applications. For applications that must encrypt data, AWS KMS provides global availability, low latency, and a high level of durability for your keys.

AWS KMS and other services that encrypt your data directly use a method called *envelope encryption* to balance performance and security. Figure 5.6 describes the flow of envelope encryption.

FIGURE 5.6   Flow of envelope encryption

1. A data key is generated by the AWS service at the time you request your data to be encrypted.

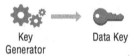

Key
Generator   Data Key

2. Data key is used to encrypt your data.

Plaintext   Data Key   Encrypted
Data   Data

3. The data key is then encrypted with a key-encrypting key unique to the service storing your data.

Data Key   Existing Key   Encrypted Data
                Encrypting Key   Key

4. The encrypted data key and the encrypted data are then stored by the AWS storage service on your behalf.

Encrypted Data   Encrypted   AWS Storage
Key   Data   Services

The key-encrypting keys that are used to encrypt data keys are stored and managed separately from the data and the data keys. Strict access controls are placed on the encryption keys designed to prevent unauthorized use by AWS employees. When you need access to your plaintext data, this process is reversed. The encrypted data key is decrypted using the key-encrypting key; the data key is used to decrypt your data.

The following AWS services offer a variety of encryption features from which you can choose.

Amazon S3

There are three ways to encrypt your data in Amazon S3 using server-side encryption.

Server-side encryption   You can set an API flag or use the AWS Management Console to encrypt data before it is written to disk in Amazon S3. Each object is encrypted with a unique data key. As an additional safeguard, this key is encrypted with a periodically rotated master key managed by Amazon S3. Amazon S3 server-side encryption uses 256-bit Advanced Encryption Standard (AES) keys for both object and master keys. This feature is offered at no additional cost beyond what you pay for using Amazon S3.

Server-side encryption using customer-provided keys   You can use your own encryption key while uploading an object to Amazon S3. Amazon S3 uses this encryption key to encrypt your data using AES-256. After the object is encrypted, the encryption key is deleted from the Amazon S3 system that used it to protect your data. When you retrieve this object from Amazon S3, you must provide the same encryption key in your request. Amazon S3 verifies that the encryption key matches, decrypts the object, and returns the object to you. This feature is offered at no additional cost beyond what you pay for using Amazon S3.

Server-side encryption using AWS KMS   You can encrypt your data in Amazon S3 by defining an AWS KMS master key within your account. This master key is used to encrypt the unique object key (referred to as a data key, as shown in Figure 5.6) that ultimately encrypts your object.

When you upload your object, a request is sent to AWS KMS to create an object key. AWS KMS generates this object key and encrypts it using the master key that you specified earlier; AWS KMS returns this encrypted object key along with the plaintext object key to Amazon S3. The Amazon S3 web server encrypts your object using the plaintext object key, stores the now encrypted object (with the encrypted object key), and deletes the plaintext object key from memory.

To retrieve this encrypted object, Amazon S3 sends the encrypted object key to AWS KMS. AWS KMS decrypts the object key using the correct master key and returns the decrypted (plaintext) object key to Amazon S3. With the plaintext object key, Amazon S3 decrypts the encrypted object and returns it to you.

Amazon S3 also enables you to define a default encryption policy. You can specify that all objects are encrypted when stored. You can also define a bucket policy that rejects uploads of unencrypted objects.

Amazon EBS

When creating a volume in Amazon EBS, you can choose to encrypt it using an AWS KMS master key within your account that encrypts the unique volume key that will ultimately encrypt your EBS volume. After you make your selection, the Amazon EC2 server sends an authenticated request to AWS KMS to create a volume key. AWS KMS generates this volume key, encrypts it using the master key, and returns the plaintext volume key and the encrypted volume key to the Amazon EC2 server. The plaintext volume key is stored in memory to encrypt and decrypt all data going to and from your attached EBS volume. When the encrypted volume (or any encrypted snapshots derived from that volume) needs to be re-attached to an instance, a call is made to AWS KMS to decrypt the encrypted volume key. AWS KMS decrypts this encrypted volume key with the correct master key and returns the decrypted volume key to Amazon EC2.

Amazon EMR

S3DistCp is an Amazon EMR feature that moves large amounts of data from Amazon S3 into HDFS, from HDFS to Amazon S3, and between Amazon S3 buckets. With S3DistCp, you can request Amazon S3 to use server-side encryption when it writes Amazon EMR data to an Amazon S3 bucket. This feature is offered at no additional cost beyond what you pay for using Amazon S3 to store your Amazon EMR data.

Amazon Redshift

When creating an Amazon Redshift cluster, you can choose to encrypt all data in user-created tables. For server-side encryption of an Amazon Redshift cluster, you can choose from the following options:

256-bit AES keys Data blocks (included backups) are encrypted using random 256-bit AES keys. These keys are themselves encrypted using a random 256-bit AES database key, which is encrypted by a 256-bit AES cluster master key that is unique to your cluster. The cluster master key is encrypted with a periodically rotated regional master key unique to the Amazon Redshift service that is stored in separate systems under AWS control. This feature is offered at no additional cost beyond what you pay for using Amazon Redshift.

CloudHSM cluster master key The 256-bit AES cluster master key used to encrypt your database keys is generated in your CloudHSM or by using HSM appliance on-premises. This cluster master key is then encrypted by a master key that never leaves your HSM.

When the Amazon Redshift cluster starts, the cluster master key is decrypted in your HSM and used to decrypt the database key. The database key is sent to the Amazon Redshift hosts and resides only in memory for the life of the cluster. If the cluster ever restarts, the cluster master key is again retrieved from your HSM—it is not stored on disk in plaintext. This option lets you more tightly control the hierarchy and lifecycle of the keys used to encrypt your data. This feature is offered at no additional cost beyond what you pay for using Amazon Redshift (and CloudHSM, if you choose this option for storing keys).

AWS KMS cluster master key The 256-bit AES cluster master key used to encrypt your database keys is generated in AWS KMS. This cluster master key is then encrypted by a master key within AWS KMS. When the Amazon Redshift cluster starts up, the cluster master key is decrypted in AWS KMS and used to decrypt the database key, which is sent to the Amazon Redshift hosts to reside only in memory for the life of the cluster. If the cluster ever restarts, the cluster master key is again retrieved from the hardened security appliance in AWS KMS—it is not stored on disk in plaintext. This option lets you define fine-grained controls over the access and use of your master keys and audit these controls through AWS CloudTrail. In addition to encrypting data generated within your Amazon Redshift cluster, you can also load encrypted data into Amazon Redshift from Amazon S3 that was previously encrypted using the Amazon S3 Encryption Client and keys that you provide. Amazon Redshift supports the decryption and re-encryption of data going between Amazon S3 and Amazon Redshift to protect the full lifecycle of your data.

These server-side encryption features across multiple services in AWS enable you to encrypt your data easily by setting the configuration in the AWS Management Console by making a CLI or API request for the given AWS service. AWS automatically and securely manages the authorized use of encryption keys. Because unauthorized access to those keys could lead to the disclosure of your data, AWS has built systems and processes with strong access controls that minimize the chance of unauthorized access. AWS had these systems verified by third-party audits to achieve security certifications, including SOC 1, 2, and 3; PCI-DSS; and FedRAMP.

Summary

If you take all responsibility for the encryption method and the KMI, you can have granular control over how your applications encrypt data. However, that granular control comes at a cost—both in terms of deployment effort and an inability to have AWS services tightly integrate with your applications' encryption methods. As an alternative, you can choose a managed service that enables easier deployment and tighter integration with AWS Cloud services. This option offers checkbox encryption for several services that store your data, control over your own keys, secured storage for your keys, and auditability on all data access attempts.

Exam Essentials

Know how to define key management infrastructure (KMI).   A KMI consists of two infrastructure components. The first component is a storage layer that protects plaintext keys. The second component is a management layer that authorizes use of stored keys.

Understand the available options for how you and AWS provide encryption using a KMI. With the first option, you control the encryption method in addition to the entire KMI. In the second option, you control the encryption method and the management layer of the KMI, and AWS provides the storage layer. In the third option, AWS controls the encryption method and both components of the KMI.

Understand the maintenance trade-offs of each key management option.   For any options that involve customers managing the components of the KMI or encryption method, maintenance increases significantly. The increased maintenance also reduces your ability to take advantage of built-in integrations between AWS KMS and other services. For options that involve using built-in AWS functionality, additional maintenance is required only when migrating legacy applications to take advantage of new features.

Understand the encryption options available in Amazon S3.   Regardless of the key management tools and process, you are able to encrypt any objects before uploading them to an Amazon S3 bucket. However, any custom encryption logic adds to processing overhead for the encryption and decryption of the data. AWS provides the Amazon S3 encryption client to help streamline this process (available in the Java, Ruby, and .NET AWS SDKs). When encrypting data on-premises, AWS has no visibility into the encryption keys or mechanisms used. For server-side encryption, Amazon S3 supports AWS-managed keys, customer-managed keys, and encryption using AWS KMS.

Understand the encryption options available in Amazon EBS.   Like any on-premises block storage, Amazon EBS supports both block-level and file-system encryption. However, an important caveat with block-level and file-system encryption tools, such as TrueCrypt and eCryptfs, is that you cannot use them to encrypt the boot volume of an Amazon EC2 instance. Amazon EBS supports encryption by using customer-managed keys and AWS KMS.

Understand the encryption options available in Amazon RDS.   Because Amazon RDS does not expose the underlying file system of databases, block-level and file-system encryption options are not available. However, standard libraries for encryption of database fields are fully supported. It is important to evaluate the types of queries that will be run against a database before selecting an encryption process, as this could affect the ability to run queries on encrypted data.

Resources to Review

AWS Key Management Service FAQs:

https://aws.amazon.com/kms/faqs/

AWS CloudHSM FAQs:

https://aws.amazon.com/cloudhsm/faqs/

Amazon S3: Protecting Data Using Encryption:

https://docs.aws.amazon.com/AmazonS3/latest/dev/UsingEncryption.html

Amazon S3 Default Encryption for S3 Buckets:

https://docs.aws.amazon.com/AmazonS3/latest/dev/bucket-encryption.html

AWS Security Blog:

https://aws.amazon.com/blogs/security/tag/encryption/

Encrypting Amazon RDS Resources:

https://docs.aws.amazon.com/AmazonRDS/latest/UserGuide/
Overview.Encryption.html

Amazon EBS Encryption:

https://docs.aws.amazon.com/AWSEC2/latest/UserGuide/EBSEncryption.html

Amazon Redshift Database Encryption:

https://docs.aws.amazon.com/redshift/latest/mgmt/working-with-db-
encryption.html

Exercises

EXERCISE 5.1

Configure an Amazon S3 Bucket to Deny Unencrypted Uploads

In this exercise, you will enforce object encryption for an Amazon S3 bucket by using a
bucket policy to reject PUT requests without encryption headers.

1. Sign in to the AWS Management Console, and open the Amazon S3 console at
    https://console.aws.amazon.com/s3/.

2. Create a new bucket with a name of your choice.

3. Apply the following policy to the bucket:

```
{
  "Version": "2012-10-17",
  "Statement": [
    {
      "Sid": "DenyIncorrectEncryption",
      "Effect": "Deny",
      "Principal": "*",
      "Action": "s3:PutObject",
      "Resource": "arn:aws:s3:::<bucket_name>/*",
      "Condition": {
        "StringNotEquals": {
          "s3:x-amz-server-side-encryption": "AES256"
        }
      }
    },
    {
      "Sid": "DenyMissingEncryption",
      "Effect": "Deny",
```

(continued)

EXERCISE 5.1 *(continued)*

```
        "Principal": "*",
        "Action": "s3:PutObject",
        "Resource": "arn:aws:s3:::<bucket_name>/*",
        "Condition": {
          "Null": {
            "s3:x-amz-server-side-encryption": true
          }
      }
    ]
  }
```

4. From the AWS Identity and Access Management (IAM) console, open the policy simulator.

5. Select an existing policy with access to the bucket that you created.

6. Test the PutObject Amazon S3 action with and without the x-amz-server-side-encryption header.

When you are uploading a new object or making a copy of an existing object, you can specify whether you want Amazon S3 to encrypt your data by adding the header to the API request.

EXERCISE 5.2

Create and Disable an AWS Key Management Service (AWS KMS) Key

In this exercise, you will create a customer master key (CMK) in the AWS Management Console and then disable it. You can disable and re-enable the AWS KMS CMKs that you manage.

1. Sign in to the AWS Management Console and open the AWS Key Management Service (AWS KMS) console at https://console.aws.amazon.com/kms.

2. Choose **Create key**.

3. Provide values for the key alias, description, and tag(s), and then choose **Next**.

   The alias name cannot begin with aws. The aws prefix is reserved by AWS to represent AWS managed CMKs in your account.

4. Select one or more IAM users who can administer the CMK and then choose **Next**. Make sure to select your IAM user.

5. Select one or more IAM users to use the CMK for cryptographic operations. Make sure to select your IAM user.

6.   Choose **Finish** to create the CMK.

7.   Locate the key in the AWS KMS console.

8.   Select the check box next to the alias of the CMK that you want to disable.

9.   Choose **Key actions ➢ Disable**.

If you disable a CMK, you cannot use it to encrypt or decrypt data until you re-enable it.

EXERCISE 5.3

Create an AWS KMS Customer Master Key with the Python SDK

In this exercise, you will create a new AWS KMS customer master key (CMK) using the AWS Command Line Interface (AWS CLI). You will use Python as one of the supported programming languages.

1.   To create the AWS KMS CMK, run the following Python script:

```
import boto3
import json

kms_client = boto3.client('kms', region_name='us-west-1')

response = kms_client.create_key(
    Description='My KMS Key',
    KeyUsage='ENCRYPT_DECRYPT',
    Origin='AWS_KMS',
    Tags=[
        {
            'TagKey': 'KeyPurpose',
            'TagValue': 'dev-on-aws-key'
        },
    ]
)

print(response)
```

2.   To list the CMKs and describe the available keys, run the following script:

```
import boto3
import json
# List the KMS Keys by ID
kms_client = boto3.client('kms', region_name='us-west-1')
try:
    response = kms_client.list_keys()
```

(continued)

EXERCISE 5.3 *(continued)*

```
except ClientError as e:
    logging.error(e)

print(json.dumps(response, indent=4, sort_keys=True))
```

3. To describe the keys inside AWS KMS, run the following script:

```
import boto3
import json
# List the KMS Keys by ID
kms_client = boto3.client('kms', region_name='us-west-1')

# Describe the Keys
for key in response['Keys']:
    try:
        key_info = kms_client.describe_key(KeyId=key['KeyArn'])
        key_id = key_info['KeyMetadata']['KeyId']
        key_arn = key_info['KeyMetadata']['Arn']
        key_state = key_info['KeyMetadata']['KeyState']
        key_description = key_info['KeyMetadata']['Description']
        print('Key ID: ' + key_id)
        print('Key ARN: ' + key_arn)
        print('Key State: ' + key_state)
        print('Key Description: ' + key_description)
        print('------------------------------------')
    except ClientError as e:
        logging.error(e)
```

4. To delete the AWS KMS key, run the following script:

```
import boto3

kms_client = boto3.client('kms', region_name='us-west-1')
response = kms_client.schedule_key_deletion(
    KeyId='fasdf1-2451b-151-bea2-easdfg8',
    PendingWindowInDays=7
)

print(response, indent=4, sort_keys=True)
```

Review Questions

1. Which components are required in an encryption system? (Select THREE.)

   A. A user to upload data

   B. Data to encrypt

   C. A database to store encryption keys

   D. A method to encrypt data

   E. A cryptographic algorithm

2. Which are the components of key management infrastructure (KMI)? (Select TWO.)

   A. Storage layer

   B. Data layer

   C. Management layer

   D. Encryption layer

3. Which of the following are methods for you and AWS to provide an encryption method and key management infrastructure (KMI)? (Select THREE.)

   A. You control the encryption method and key management, and AWS provides the storage component of the KMI.

   B. You control the storage component of the KMI, and AWS provides the encryption method and key management.

   C. You control the encryption method and KMI.

   D. AWS controls the encryption method and the entire KMI.

   E. None of the above.

4. Which option uses AWS Key Management Service (AWS KMS) to manage keys to provide server-side encryption to Amazon Simple Storage Service (Amazon S3)?

   A. Amazon S3 managed encryption keys (SSE-S3)

   B. Customer-provided encryption keys (SSE-C)

   C. Use client-side encryption

   D. None of the above

5. Which AWS encryption service provides asymmetric encryption capabilities?

   A. AWS Key Management Service (AWS KMS).

   B. AWS CloudHSM.

   C. AWS does not provide asymmetric encryption services.

   D. None of the above.

6. Which AWS encryption service provides symmetric encryption capabilities? (Select TWO.)

   A. AWS Key Management Service (AWS KMS).

   B. AWS CloudHSM.

   C. AWS does not provide symmetric encryption services.

   D. None of the above.

7. An organization is using Amazon Simple Storage Service (Amazon S3), and it would like to ensure that all objects that are stored in Amazon S3 are encrypted. However, it does not want to be responsible for managing any of the encryption keys. As their lead developer, which service and feature should you recommend?

   A. Server-side encryption with AWS Key Management Service (SSE-KMS).

   B. Customer-provided encryption keys (SSE-C).

   C. Amazon S3 managed encryption keys (SSE-S3).

   D. This is not possible in AWS.

8. Which feature of AWS Key Management Service (AWS KMS) enables you to use an AWS CloudHSM cluster for the storage of your encryption keys?

   A. Centralized key management

   B. AWS CloudHSM

   C. Custom key stores

   D. S3DistCp

9. An organization is using AWS Key Management Service (AWS KMS) to support encryption and would like to encrypt Amazon Elastic Block Store (Amazon EBS) volumes. It wants to encrypt its volumes quickly, with little development time. As their lead developer, what should you recommend?

   A. Implement AWS KMS to encrypt the Amazon EBS volumes.

   B. Use open source or third-party encryption tooling.

   C. Use AWS CloudHSM.

   D. AWS does not provide a mechanism to encrypt Amazon EBS volumes.

10. Which of the following AWS services does not integrate with AWS Key Management Service (AWS KMS)?

    A. Amazon Elastic Block Store (Amazon EBS)

    B. Amazon Simple Storage Service (Amazon S3)

    C. Amazon Redshift

    D. None of the above

Chapter

6

Deployment Strategies

**THE AWS CERTIFIED DEVELOPER –
ASSOCIATE EXAM TOPICS COVERED IN
THIS CHAPTER MAY INCLUDE, BUT ARE
NOT LIMITED TO, THE FOLLOWING:**

Domain 1: Deployment

✓ **1.1 Deploy written code in AWS using existing
CI/CD pipelines, processes, and patterns.**

✓ **1.2 Deploy applications using AWS Elastic Beanstalk.**

Content may include the following:

- Environments and architectures
- Environment variables
- Software Development Lifecycle (SDLC)
- AWS services for automating deployments
- AWS Cloud tiers: Web servers, worker applications, and databases
- Deployment strategies

Domain 2: Security

✓ **2.3 Implement application authentication and
authorization.**

Content may include the following:

- AWS Identity and Access Management (IAM) Roles in AWS Elastic Beanstalk

Domain 5: Monitoring and Troubleshooting

Content may include the following:

- Monitoring AWS Elastic Beanstalk
- Troubleshooting AWS Elastic Beanstalk

Deployments on the AWS Cloud

As a developer in the cloud, you will often create *three-tier architectures* that consist of a web tier, an application tier, and a database tier. To enable your customers to use your application immediately, you must rapidly deploy both your infrastructure and code. The AWS Cloud environment offers several deployment options and several ways to provision AWS services to set up highly available and reliable applications. Ideally, deployments are seamless streams of automated processes that create, build, deploy, monitor, and modify code throughout the entire *software development lifecycle* (SDLC). This stream of processes must be continuous and fully integrated with your AWS services.

In a traditional environment, deployments can require substantial time to push the code to multiple environments. AWS helps to speed up this process by automating the actions required to deploy code to your environments. When you need to upload and demonstrate a code project in the cloud, you can launch an application in minutes.

Phases of the Release Lifecycle

Each team's release lifecycle is different based on the needs of the team. Nearly all traditional release lifecycles are composed of five major phases, as shown in Figure 6.1: Source, Build, Test, Production, and Monitor. Each phase of the cycle provides increased confidence that the code will work in the intended way for customers. This also translates to a release lifecycle implemented in the AWS Cloud environment.

FIGURE 6.1   Major phases of the release lifecycle

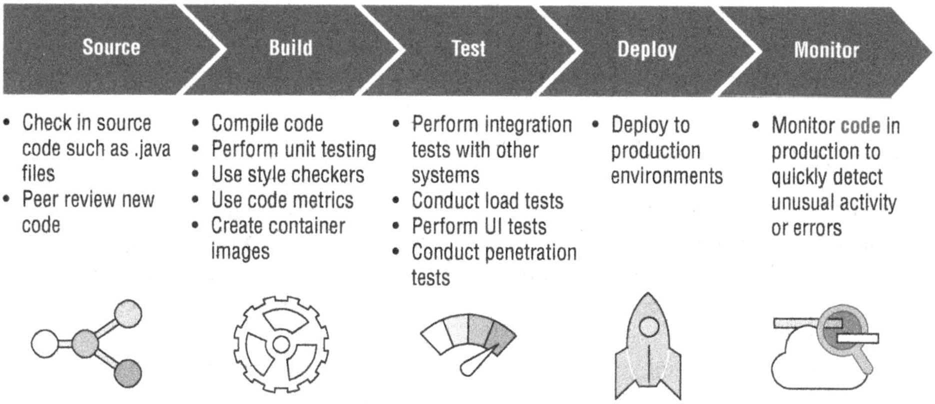

Source	Build	Test	Deploy	Monitor
• Check in source code such as .java files • Peer review new code	• Compile code • Perform unit testing • Use style checkers • Use code metrics • Create container images	• Perform integration tests with other systems • Conduct load tests • Perform UI tests • Conduct penetration tests	• Deploy to production environments	• Monitor code in production to quickly detect unusual activity or errors

Source Phase

During the *Source phase*, developers check changes into a source code repository. Many teams require peer feedback on code changes before delivering code to production or target environments. Teams may use several methods for code reviews, such as pair programming and tool-assisted options.

Build Phase

During the *Build phase*, an application's source code is built, and the quality of the code is tested on the build machine. The most common types of quality checks are automated tests that do not require a server to execute and can be initiated from a test harness. Some teams extend their quality tests to include code metrics and style checks. There is an opportunity for automation any time a human must decide on the code.

Test Phase

The goal of the *Test phase* is to perform tests that cannot be done during the Build phase and that require the software to be deployed to production-like stages. Often, these tests include testing integration with other live systems, load testing, user interface (UI) testing, and penetration testing. AWS has many different stages to which it deploys. Teams deploy to preproduction stages where their application interacts with other systems to ensure that the newly changed software works in an integrated environment.

Deployment Phase

In the Deployment phase, code is deployed to production. Different teams have different deployment strategies, though it is common to set goals to reduce risk when deploying new changes and minimize the impact when a bad change is rolled into production.

Monitor Phase

During the Monitor phase, you must check the application to detect unusual activities and errors quickly.

You can automate each of these phases without automating the entire release lifecycle.

Environment Variables

Before you deploy your infrastructure and code, first determine the environmental variables. The SDLC in a traditional infrastructure contains manual implementations to release, test, and deploy code, in addition to the corresponding required documentation. Most SDLC models would benefit from an efficient lifecycle with accurate execution and no administration.

In traditional deployments, operating system patching, updates, language versioning, and infrastructure changes frequently do not occur in synchronization and may not always match between environments. It is often difficult to replicate configurations between environments in a traditional infrastructure. Unit tests, user acceptance tests, and load tests can produce different results in test and production environments. These results differ because of differences in environment variables, such as unapplied patches or nonupdated configurations. An ideal test environment matches the production environment exactly, providing the capability to test an application as if it were running in production and to receive accurate results.

Additionally, the SDLC requires the maintenance of phases that you customize to meet business requirements. This includes configurations to audit and perform quality assurance. AWS Cloud solutions automatically align the phases and environments. You can choose an AWS service to automate deployments seamlessly, saving you hours that you would normally spend managing your infrastructure and code. Although certain environmental variables are clearly defined as business requirements, others evolve as you commit changes. Code modifications are also inherently environment-based and focused on the configuration of the modification itself.

AWS services enable you to deploy applications rapidly and manage environments and the multiple tiers of your infrastructure (web servers, worker applications, and databases) automatically. You can automatically provision and manage resources for the environments and configurations that you create. Your configurations can include Auto Scaling groups, security groups, Amazon Elastic Compute Cloud (Amazon EC2) instances, other AWS resources, and AWS Identity and Access Management (IAM) roles to manage resources from AWS deployment services.

Software Development Lifecycle with AWS Cloud

Determine how to manage the SDLC with AWS services based on environment variables, infrastructure tiers, and the type of applications or services you launch. Each of the AWS services you use in a deployment has its own configuration, or service-specific settings, which affect your deployment implementation. Consider the types of deployments that you will perform so that you can implement the most appropriate services into your seamless chain of events or a pipeline. This seamless or "continuous" chain of events on the AWS Cloud is the continuous integration/continuous deployment (CI/CD) pipeline.

Continuous Integration/Continuous Deployment

The CI/CD pipeline helps developers implement continuous builds, tests, and code deployments with multiple AWS resources and a continuous integration server. You can integrate AWS Elastic Beanstalk with the CI/CD pipeline as one of the deployment resources. You can also use AWS CodeCommit as a CI/CD resource paired with a Git repository, from which Elastic Beanstalk can extract and deploy code.

Continuous integration (CI) is the software development practice in which you continuously integrate (or check in) all code changes into a main branch of a central repository. This practice enables you to verify your code changes early and often with an automated build and test process. Whenever you check in code changes, engineers can automate various processes, such as building assets and testing code syntax. By implementing continuous integration practices, teams become more productive and develop new features more quickly. Teams also write scripts to validate the functionality and improve the quality of the software being released.

Continuous delivery (CD) is the software development practice in which all code changes are automatically prepared and always deployable (ready to go into production) at a single step.

Continuous delivery extends continuous integration to include testing production-like stages and running verification testing against those deployments. Although continuous delivery can extend to a production deployment, it requires manual intervention between a code check-in and when that code is available for customer use.

Practicing continuous delivery means that teams gain a greater level of certainty that their software will work in production.

Continuous deployment extends continuous delivery and is the automated release of software to customers, from check-in through production, without human intervention. Continuous deployment helps customers gain value quickly from the code base, with the development team getting faster feedback on the changes made.

An important distinction between continuous delivery and continuous deployment is that in continuous deployment, changes are automatically released to production after build/test stages; there is no manual approval step.

Figure 6.2 displays the CI/DI pipeline.

FIGURE 6.2   CI/DI pipeline

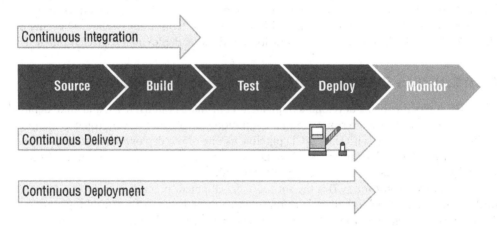

The CI/DI pipeline integrates with other AWS Code services, as illustrated in Figure 6.3.

FIGURE 6.3   AWS Code services

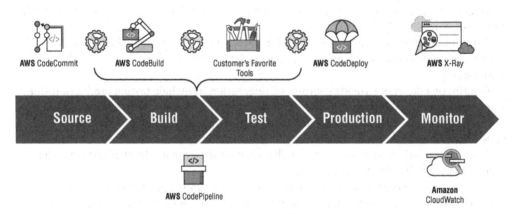

AWS CodePipeline   *AWS CodePipeline* is a service for fast and reliable application updates. You can model and visualize the software release process. To build, test, and deploy your code every time there is a code change, integrate this service with third-party tools and AWS.

AWS CodeCommit   *AWS CodeCommit* is a secure, highly scalable, managed source-control service that hosts private Git repositories. It enables you to store and manage assets (such as documents, source code, and binary files) privately in the AWS Cloud.

AWS CodeBuild   *AWS CodeBuild* compiles source code, runs tests, and produces ready-to-deploy software packages. There is no need to manage build servers.

AWS CodeDeploy   *AWS CodeDeploy* automates code deployments to any instance. It handles the complexity of updating your applications, which avoids downtime during application deployment. It deploys to Amazon EC2 or on-premises servers, in any language and on any operating system. It also integrates with third-party tools and AWS.

Deploying Highly Available and Scalable Applications

Load balancing is an integral part to directing and managing traffic among your instances. As you launch applications in your environments, you will want them to have high performance and high availability for your users. To enable both of these features, a load balancer will be necessary.

Elastic Load Balancing (ELB) supports three types of load balancers: Application Load Balancers, Network Load Balancers, and Classic Load Balancers. You select a load balancer based on your application needs.

- The *Application Load Balancer* provides advanced request routing targeted at delivery of modern application architectures, including microservices and container-based applications. It simplifies and improves the security of your application by ensuring that the latest Secure Sockets Layer (SSL)/Transport Layer Security (TLS) ciphers and protocols are used at all times. The Application Load Balancer operates at the request level (Layer 7) to route HTTP/HTTPS traffic to its targets: Amazon EC2 instances, containers, and IP addresses based on the content of the request. It is ideal for advanced load balancing of HTTP and HTTPS traffic.

- The *Network Load Balancer* operates at the connection level (Layer 4) to route TCP traffic to targets: Amazon EC2 instances, containers, and IP addresses based on IP protocol data. It is the best option for load balancing of TCP traffic because it's capable of handling millions of requests per second while maintaining ultra-low latencies. Network Load Balancer is optimized to handle sudden and volatile traffic patterns while using a single static IP address per Availability Zone. It is integrated with other popular AWS services, such as AWS Auto Scaling, Amazon Elastic Container Service (Amazon ECS), and AWS CloudFormation. Amazon ECS provides management for deployment, scheduling, and scaling, and management of containerized applications.

- The *Classic Load Balancer* provides basic load balancing across multiple Amazon EC2 instances and operates at both the request level and the connection level. The Classic Load Balancer is intended for applications that were built within the EC2-Classic network. When you're using Amazon Virtual Private Cloud (Amazon VPC), AWS recommends the Application Load Balancer for Layer 7 and Network Load Balancer for Layer 4).

Figure 6.4 displays the flow for deploying highly available and scalable applications.

FIGURE 6.4 Deploying highly available and scalable applications

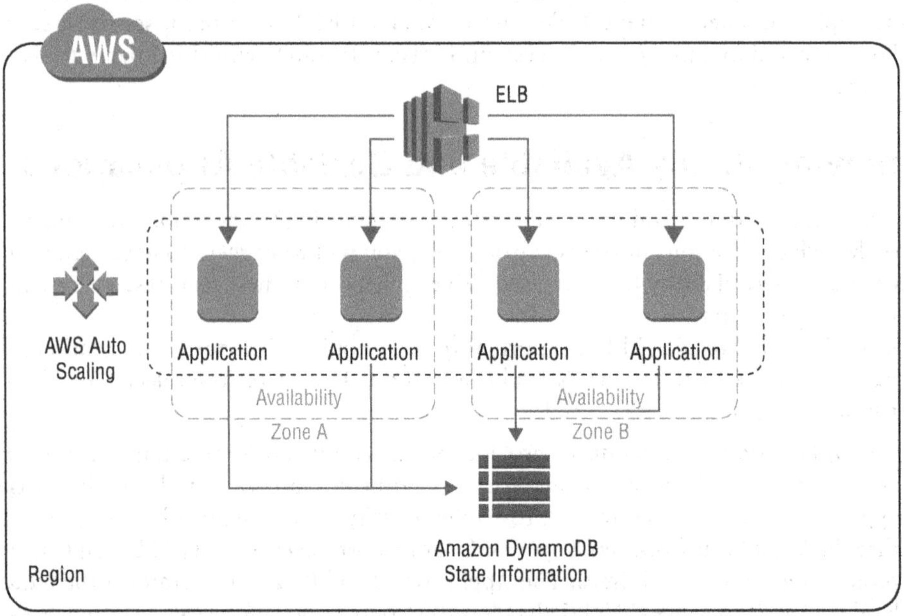

The flow for deploying highly available and scalable applications includes the following components:

- Multiple Availability Zones and AWS Regions.
- Health check and failover mechanism.
- Stateless application that stores the session state in a cache server or database.
- AWS services that help you to achieve your goal. For example, Auto Scaling helps you maintain high availability and scalability.

Elastic Load Balancing and Auto Scaling are designed to work together.

Deploying and Maintaining Applications

AWS provides several services to manage your application and resources, as shown in Figure 6.5.

FIGURE 6.5   Deployment and maintenance services

• Deploy Code in the Cloud   • Manage Infrastructure   • Define the Infrastructure

AWS Elastic Beanstalk   AWS OpsWorks   AWS CloudFormation

With AWS Elastic Beanstalk, you do not have to worry about managing the infrastructure for your application. You deploy your application, such as a Ruby application, in a Ruby container, and Elastic Beanstalk takes care of scaling and managing it.

AWS OpsWorks is a configuration and deployment management tool for your Chef or Puppet resource stacks. Specifically, *OpsWorks for Chef Automate* enables you to manage the lifecycle of your application in layers with Chef recipes. It provides custom Chef cookbooks for managing many different types of layers so that you can write custom Chef recipes to manage any layer that AWS does not support.

AWS CloudFormation is infrastructure as code. The service helps you model and set up AWS resources so that you can spend less time managing them. It is a template-based tool, with formatted text files in JSON or YAML. You can create templates to define what AWS infrastructure you want to build and any relationships that exist among the parts of your AWS infrastructure.

Use AWS CloudFormation templates to provision and configure your stack resources.

Automatically Adjust Capacity

Use AWS Auto Scaling to monitor the AWS resources that are part of your application. The service automatically adjusts capacity to maintain steady, predictable performance. You can build scaling plans to manage your resources, including Amazon EC2 instances and Spot Fleets, Amazon Elastic Container Registry (Amazon ECR) tasks, Amazon DynamoDB tables and indexes, and Amazon Aurora Replicas.

AWS Auto Scaling makes scaling simple, with recommendations that allow you to optimize performance, costs, or balance between them. If you are already using EC2 Auto Scaling to scale your Amazon EC2 instances dynamically, you can now combine it with AWS Auto Scaling to scale additional resources for other AWS services. With AWS Auto Scaling, your applications have the right resources at the right time.

Auto Scaling Groups

An Auto Scaling group contains a collection of Amazon EC2 instances that share similar characteristics. This collection is treated as a logical grouping to manage the scaling of instances. For example, if a single application operates across multiple instances, you might want to increase the number of instances in that group to improve the performance of the application or decrease the number of instances to reduce costs when demand is low.

You can use the Auto Scaling group to scale the number of instances automatically based on criteria that you specify or maintain a fixed number of instances even if an instance becomes unhealthy. This automatic scaling and maintaining the number of instances in an Auto Scaling group make up the core functionality of the EC2 Auto Scaling service.

An Auto Scaling group launches enough Amazon EC2 instances to meet its desired capacity. The Auto Scaling group maintains this number of instances by performing periodic health checks on the instances in the group. If an instance becomes unhealthy, the group terminates the unhealthy instance and launches another instance to replace it.

You can use scaling policies to increase or decrease the number of instances in your group dynamically to meet changing conditions. When the scaling policy is in effect, the Auto Scaling group adjusts the desired capacity of the group and launches or terminates the instances as needed. You can also manually scale or scale on a schedule.

AWS Elastic Beanstalk

AWS Elastic Beanstalk is an AWS service that you can use to deploy applications, services, and architecture. It provides provisioned scalability, load balancing, and high availability. It uses common languages, including Java, .NET, PHP, Node.js, Python, Ruby, Go, and Docker, on common-type web servers, such as Apache, NGINX, Passenger, and IIS.

 Elastic Beanstalk charges only for the resources you use to run your application.

Elastic Beanstalk is a solution that enables the automated deployments and management of applications on the AWS Cloud. Elastic Beanstalk can launch AWS resources automatically with Amazon Route 53, AWS Auto Scaling, Elastic Load Balancing, Amazon EC2, and Amazon Relational Database Service (Amazon RDS) instances, and it allows you to customize additional AWS resources.

Deploy applications without worrying about managing the underlying technologies, including the following:

Components

- Environments
- Application versions
- Environment configurations

Permission Model

- Service role
- Instance profile

Figure 6.6 displays the Elastic Beanstalk underlying technologies.

FIGURE 6.6   AWS Elastic Beanstalk underlying technologies

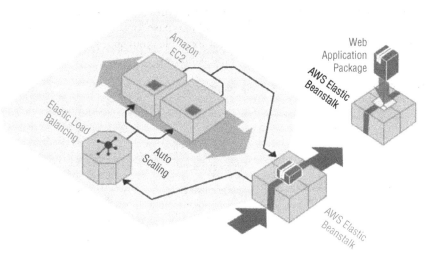

Elastic Beanstalk supports customization and N-tier architectures. It mitigates common manual configurations required in a traditional infrastructure deployment model. With Elastic Beanstalk, you can also create repeatable environments and reduce redundancy, thus rapidly updating environments and facilitating service-managed application stacks. You can deploy multiple environments in minutes and use various automated deployment strategies.

    AWS Elastic Beanstalk allows you to focus on building your application.

Implementation Responsibilities

AWS and our customers share responsibility for achieving a high level of software component security and compliance. This shared model reduces your operational burden. The service you select determines the level of your responsibility. For example, Elastic Beanstalk helps you perform your side of the shared responsibility model by providing a managed updates feature. This feature automatically applies patch and minor updates for an Elastic Beanstalk supported platform version.

Developer Teams

Using AWS Elastic Beanstalk, you build full-stack environments for web and worker tiers. The service provides a preconfigured infrastructure.

- Single-instance (development, low cost)
- Load balanced, AWS Auto Scaling (production)

Elastic Beanstalk Responsibilities

Elastic Beanstalk provisions the necessary infrastructure resources, such as the load balancer, Auto Scaling group, security groups, and database (optional). It also provides a unique domain name for your application (for example, yourapp.elasticbeanstalk.com).

Figure 6.7 displays Elastic Beanstalk responsibilities.

FIGURE 6.7   AWS Elastic Beanstalk responsibilities

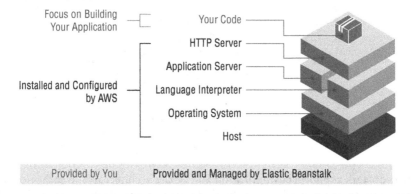

Working with Your Source Repository

Developer teams generally begin their SDLC processes by managing their source code in a source repository. Uploading and managing the multiple changes on application source code is a repeated process. With Elastic Beanstalk, you can create an application, upload a version of the application as a source bundle, and provide pertinent information about the application.

The first step is to integrate Elastic Beanstalk with your source code to create your source bundle. As your source repository, you can install Git for your applications or use an existing repository and map your current branch from a local repository in Git to retrieve the source code.

Alternatively, you can use AWS CodeCommit as a source control system to retrieve source code. By using Elastic Beanstalk with the AWS CodeCommit repository, you extract from a current branch on CodeCommit.

To deploy a new application or application version, Elastic Beanstalk works with source bundles or packaged code. Prepare the code package with all of the necessary code dependencies and components.

Elastic Beanstalk can either retrieve the source bundle from a source repository or download the bundle from an Amazon Simple Storage Service (Amazon S3) bucket. You can use the IAM role to grant Elastic Beanstalk access to all services. The service accesses the source bundle from the location you designate, extracts the components from the bundle, deploys new application versions by launching the code, creates and configures the infrastructure, and allocates the platform on Amazon EC2 instances to run the code.

The application runs on the resources and instances that the service generates. Your configuration for these resources and your application will become your environment settings, supporting the entire configuration of your deployment. Each deployment has an auto-incremented deployment identity (ID), so you are able to manage your multiple running deployments. Think of these as multiple running code releases in the AWS Cloud.

 You can also work with different hosting services, such as GitHub or Bitbucket, with your code source.

Concepts

AWS Elastic Beanstalk enables you to manage all the resources that run your application as environments. This section describes some key Elastic Beanstalk concepts.

Application

Elastic Beanstalk focuses on managing your applications as environments and all of the resources to run them. Each application that launches in the service is a logical collection of environment variables and components, application versions, and environment configurations.

Application Versions

Application versions are iterations of the application's deployable code. Application versions in Elastic Beanstalk point to an Amazon S3 object with the code source package. An application can have many versions, with each version being unique. You can deploy and access any application version at any time. For example, you may want to deploy different versions for different types of tests.

Environment

Each Elastic Beanstalk environment is a separate version of the application, and that version's AWS Cloud components deploy onto AWS resources to support that version. Each environment runs one application version at a time, but you can run multiple environments, with the same application on each, along with its own customizations and resources.

Environment Tier

To launch an environment, you must first choose an environment tier. Elastic Beanstalk provisions the required resources to support both the infrastructure and types of requests the application will support. The environment can launch and access other AWS resources. For example, it may pull tasks from Amazon Simple Queue Service (Amazon SQS) queues or store temporary configuration files in Amazon S3 buckets (according to your customizations). Each environment will then have an environment configuration—a collection of settings and parameters based on your customizations that define associated resources and how the environment will work.

Environment Configuration

You can change your environment to create, modify, delete, or deploy resources and change the settings for each. Your environment configuration saves to a configuration template exclusive to each environment and is accessible by either the Elastic Beanstalk application programming interface (API) calls or the service's command line interface (EB CLI).

In Elastic Beanstalk, you can run either a web server environment or a worker environment. Figure 6.8 displays an example of a web server environment running in Elastic Beanstalk with Amazon Route 53 as the domain name service (DNS) and ELB to route traffic to the web server instances.

FIGURE 6.8   Application running on AWS Elastic Beanstalk

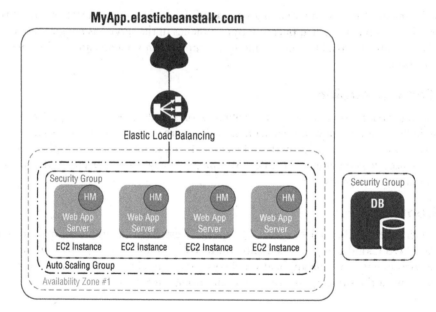

Figure 6.9 shows a worker environment architecture, where AWS resources create configurations, such as Auto Scaling groups, Amazon EC2 instances, and an IAM role, to manage resources for your worker applications.

FIGURE 6.9   Worker tier on AWS Elastic Beanstalk

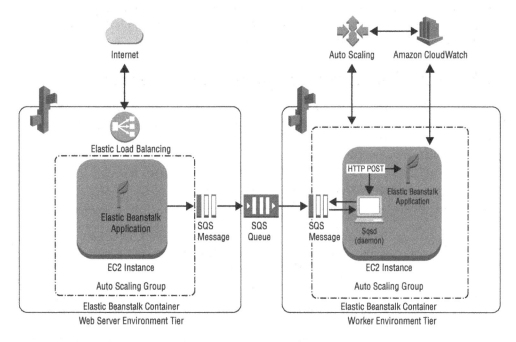

For the worker environment tier, Elastic Beanstalk creates and provisions additional resources and files to support the tier. This includes services like Amazon SQS queues operating between worker applications, AWS Auto Scaling groups, security groups, and EC2 instances.

The worker environment infrastructure uses all of your customization and provision resources to determine the types of requests it receives.

Docker Containers

You can also use Docker containers with Elastic Beanstalk to run your applications from a container. Install Docker, choose the software you require, and select the Docker images you want to launch. Define your runtime environment, platform, programming language, and application dependencies and tools. Docker containers are self-contained and include configurations and software that you specify for your application to run. Each Docker container restarts automatically if another container crashes. When you choose to deploy your applications with Docker containers, your infrastructure is provisioned with capacity provisioning, load balancing, scaling, and health monitoring, much like a noncontainer environment. You can continue to manage your application and the AWS resources you use.

Docker requires platform configurations that enable you to launch single or multicontainer deployments. A single container deployment launches a single Docker image, and your application uses a single container configuration for a single Amazon EC2 instance.

A multicontainer deployment uses the Amazon ECS to launch a cluster of containers with Docker images. A multicontainer configuration is applied to each instance. You can also run preconfigured Docker platform configurations with generic customization for popular software stacks that you want to use for your application.

AWS Elastic Beanstalk Command Line Interface

Elastic Beanstalk has its own command line interface separate from the AWS CLI tool. To create deployments from the command line, you download and install the AWS Elastic Beanstalk CLI (EB CLI).

Table 6.1 lists common EB CLI commands.

TABLE 6.1 Common AWS Elastic Beanstalk Commands

Command	Definition
eb init application-name	Sets default values for Elastic Beanstalk applications with the EB CLI configuration wizard
eb create	Creates a new environment and deploys an application version to it
eb deploy	Deploys the application source bundle from the initialized project directory to the running application
eb clone	Clones an environment to a new environment so that both have identical environment settings
eb codesource	Configures the EB CLI to deploy from an AWS CodeCommit repository, or disables AWS CodeCommit integration and uploads the source bundle from your local machine

Customizing Environment Configurations

You can use Elastic Beanstalk to customize the platforms used to support your application and your infrastructure. To do so, create a configuration file in the ebextensions directory (or .ebextensions) to include with your web application's source code. The configuration file allows for simple and advanced customizations of your environment and contains settings for your AWS resources. To deploy customized resources to support your application source bundle, use YAML to configure the file.

The configuration file has several sections. The option_settings section defines your configuration option values for your AWS resources. The resources section adds further customization in your application environment beyond the service functionality, which includes AWS CloudFormation–supported resources that Elastic Beanstalk can access and run. The remaining sections allow for fine-grained configurations to integrate packages, sources, files, and container commands.

> Launch environments from integrated development environment (IDE) tools to avoid poorly formatted configurations and source bundles that could cause unrecoverable failures.

You apply configuration files in the ebextensions directory to Elastic Beanstalk stacks. The stacks are the AWS resources that you allocate for your infrastructure and application. If you have any resource, such as Amazon VPC, Amazon EC2, or Amazon S3, that was updated or configured, these files deploy with your changes. You can zip your ebextension files, upload, and apply them to multiple application environments. You can view your environment variables in option_settings for future evaluation or changes. These are accessible from the AWS Management Console, command line, and API calls.

> You can view Elastic Beanstalk stacks in AWS CloudFormation, but always use the Elastic Beanstalk service and ebextensions to make modifications. This way, edits and modifications to the application stacks are simplified without introducing unrecoverable failures.

Elastic Beanstalk generates logs that you can view to troubleshoot your environments and resources. The logs display Amazon EC2 operational logs and logs that are specific to servers running for your applications.

Integrating with Other AWS Services

Elastic Beanstalk automatically integrates or manages other AWS services with application code to provision efficient working environments. However, you might find it necessary to add additional services, such as Amazon S3 for content storage or Amazon DynamoDB for data records, to work with an environment. To grant access between any integrated service and Elastic Beanstalk, you must configure permissions in IAM.

Amazon S3

You can use Amazon S3 to store static content you want to integrate with your application and point directly to objects you store in Amazon S3 from your application or from other resources. In addition to setting permissions in IAM policies, take advantage of presigned URLs for controlled Amazon S3 GET and PUT operations.

Amazon CloudFront

You can integrate your Elastic Beanstalk environment with Amazon CloudFront, which provides content delivery and distribution through the use of edge locations throughout the world. This can decrease the time in which your content is delivered to you, as the content is cached and routed through the closest edge location serving you. After you deploy your application on Elastic Beanstalk, use the Amazon CloudFront content delivery network (CDN) to cache static content from your application. To identify the source of your content in Amazon CloudFront, you can use URL path patterns to cache your content and then retrieve it from the cache. This approach serves your content more rapidly and offloads requests directly sourced from your application.

AWS Config

With *AWS Config*, you can visualize configuration history and how configurations evolve over time. Tracking changes helps you to fulfill compliance obligations and meet auditing requirements. You can integrate AWS Config directly with your application and its versions or your Elastic Beanstalk environment. *You can customize AWS Config to record changes per resource, per region, or globally.* In the AWS Config console, you can select Elastic Beanstalk resource types to record specific applications and environment resources. You can view the recorded information in the AWS Config dashboard under Resource Inventory.

Amazon RDS

Various options are available for creating databases for your environment, such as Amazon Relational Database Service (Amazon RDS) for SQL databases and Amazon DynamoDB for NoSQL databases. Elastic Beanstalk can create a database and store and retrieve data for any of your environments. Each service has its own features to handle scaling, capacity, performance, and availability.

To store, read, or write to your data records, you can set up an Amazon RDS database instance or an Amazon DynamoDB table by using the same configuration files for your other service option settings. You must create connections to the database, which require you to set up password management in Elastic Beanstalk. Your configurations are saved in the ebextensions directory. You can also create direct connections, within your application code or application configuration files, to both internal and external databases. When using Amazon RDS, avoid accidentally deleting and re-creating databases without a properly installed backup. To reduce the risk of losing data, take a manual snapshot of the master Amazon RDS database immediately before deleting.

 If you create periodic tasks with a worker environment, Elastic Beanstalk automatically creates an Amazon DynamoDB table to perform leader election and stores task information.

Amazon ElastiCache

For caching capabilities, you can integrate Amazon ElastiCache service clusters with the Elastic Beanstalk environment. If you use a nonlegacy container, you can set your configuration files to use the supported container and then offload requests to the cache cluster.

Doing so enables you to increase the performance of your application and databases running in your Elastic Beanstalk environment.

AWS Identity and Access Management Roles

Elastic Beanstalk integrates with AWS Identity and Access Management (IAM) roles to enable access to the services you require to run your architecture.

When you launch the service to create an environment, a default service role and instance profile are created for you through the service API. Managed policies for resources permissions are also attached, including policies for Elastic Beanstalk instance health monitoring within your infrastructure and platform updates that can be made on behalf of the service. These policies, called `AWSElasticBeanstalkEnhancedHealth` and `AWSElasticBeanstalkService`, attach to the default service role and enable the default service role to specify a trusted entity and trust policy.

When you use commands from the EB CLI, the role allows automatic management of the AWS Cloud that services you run. The service creates an environment, if you don't identify it specifically; creates a service-linked role; and uses it when you spin up a new environment. To create the environment successfully, the `CreateServiceLinkedRole` policy must be available in your IAM account.

You use IAM roles to automate the management of allocated services for your application through Elastic Beanstalk. With IAM, you can also launch code with inline policies. It is important to understand how the service creates and uses the roles to keep your application and data secure.

 For IAM to manage the policies for the account better, create policies at the account level.

Deployment Strategies

A *deployment* is the process of copying content and executing scripts on instances in your deployment group. To accomplish this, AWS CodeDeploy performs the tasks outlined in the AppSpec configuration file. For both Amazon EC2/on-premises instances and AWS Lambda functions, the deployment succeeds or fails based on whether individual AppSpec tasks complete successfully.

After you have created a deployment, you can update it as your application or service changes. You can update a deployment by adding or removing resources from a deployment, thus updating the properties of existing resources in a deployment.

 A serverless application is typically a combination of AWS Lambda and other AWS services.

To create seamless deployments, choose an effective deployment strategy. Each strategy has specific advantages relative to different use cases. Appropriate strategies help create deployments where you experience minimal or no downtime, and you can apply the strategy for different purposes within your environments. Each change needs a strategy that best fits your application deployments.

All-at-Once and In-Place Deployments

An *all-at-once deployment* applies updates to all your instances at once. When you execute this strategy, you experience downtime, as all instances receive the change at the same time.

This is an appropriate strategy for simple, immediate update requirements when it's not critical to have your application always available, and you're comfortable with the site being offline for a short duration. To enable all-at-once updates, set a deployment policy either in the AWS Management Console or in the command line (`DeploymentPolicy`).

When you perform an *in-place deployment*, AWS CodeDeploy stops currently running applications on the target instance, deploys the latest revision, restarts applications, and validates successful deployment. In-place deployments can support the automatic configuration of a load balancer. In this case, the instance is deregistered from the load balancer before deployment and registered again after the deployment processes successfully.

In-place updates are also available for your platform updates, such as a coding-language platform update for a web server. Select the new platform and then run the update from the AWS Management Console or command line directly as a platform update.

    AWS Lambda does not support in-place deployments.

Rolling Deployments

A *rolling deployment* applies changes to all of your instances by rolling the updates from one instance to another. Elastic Beanstalk can deploy configuration changes in batches. This approach reduces possible downtime during implementation of the change and allows available instances to run while you deploy.

As updates are applied in a batch, the batch will be out of service for a short period while the changes propagate and then relaunch with the new configuration. When the change is complete, the service moves on to the next batch of instances to apply the changes. With this strategy, you can implement both periodic changes and pauses between updates. For example, you might specify a time to wait between health-based updates so that instances must pass health checks before moving on to the next batch. If the rolling update fails, the service begins another rolling update for a rollback to the previous configuration.

Rolling updates include changes for Auto Scaling group configurations, Amazon EC2 instance configurations, and Amazon VPC settings. It is an effective method for updating an application version on fleets of instances through the Elastic Beanstalk service. To enable rolling updates, set a deployment policy either in the AWS Management Console or in the command line (`DeploymentPolicy`) and choose this strategy along with specific options. You can select *Rolling* or *Rolling with additional batch*. By using *Rolling with additional batch*, you can launch a new batch of instances before you begin to take instances out of service for your rolling updates. This option provides an available batch for rollback from a failed update. After the deployment is successfully executed, Elastic Beanstalk terminates the instances from the additional batch. This is helpful for a critical application that must continue running with less downtime than the standard rolling update.

Blue/Green Deployment

When high availability is critical for applications, you may want to choose a *blue/green deployment*, where your newer environment will be separate from your existing environment. The running production environment is considered the *blue environment*, and the newer environment with your update is considered the *green environment*. When your changes are ready and have gone through all tests in your green environment, you can swap the CNAMEs of the environments to redirect traffic to the newer running environment. This strategy provides an instantaneous update with typically zero downtime.

When you deploy to AWS Lambda functions, blue/green deployments publish new versions of each function. Traffic shifting then routes requests to the new functioning versions according to the deployment configuration you define.

If your infrastructure contains Amazon RDS database instances, the data does not automatically transfer to the new environment. Without performing backups, you will experience data loss when you use the blue/green strategy. If you have Amazon RDS instances in your infrastructure, implement a different deployment strategy or a series of steps to create snapshot backups outside of Elastic Beanstalk before you execute this type of deployment.

Immutable Deployment

An *immutable deployment* is best when an environment requires a total replacement of instances, rather than updates to an existing part of an infrastructure. This approach implements a safety feature for updates and rollbacks. Elastic Beanstalk creates a temporary Auto Scaling group behind your environment's load balancer to contain the new instances with the updates you apply. If the update fails, the rollback process terminates the Auto Scaling group. Immutable instances implement a number of health checks. If all instances pass these checks, Elastic Beanstalk transfers the new configurations to the original Auto Scaling group, providing an additional check before you apply your changes to other instances. Enhanced health reports evaluate instance health in the update. After the updates are made, Elastic Beanstalk deletes the temporary Auto Scaling group of the older instances.

During this type of deployment, your capacity doubles for a short duration between the updates and terminations of instances. Before you use this strategy, verify that your instances have a low on-demand limit and enough capacity to support immutable updates.

See Table 6.2 for feature comparisons between all deployment strategies. The check mark indicates options that the deployment strategy supports.

TABLE 6.2   Deployment Strategies

Method	Impact of Failed Deployment	Deploy Time	Zero Downtime	No DNS Change	Rollback Process	Code Deployed To
All-at-once	Downtime	🕐		✓	Redeploy	Existing instances
In-place	Downtime	🕐		✓	Redeploy	Existing instances
Rolling	Single batch out of service; any successful batches before failure running new application version	🕐🕐	✓	✓	Redeploy	Existing instances
Rolling with additional batch	Minimal if first batch fails; otherwise, similar to Rolling	🕐🕐🕐	✓	✓	Redeploy	New and existing instances
Blue/Green	Minimal	🕐🕐🕐 🕐	✓		Swap URL	New instances
Immutable	Minimal	🕐🕐🕐 🕐	✓	✓	Redeploy	New instances

Container Deployments

Elastic Beanstalk enables you to launch your applications with Docker containers. With a Docker container, you can create a runtime environment with all of the dependencies, packages, and tools that your application may require to run. Your container can have all of the configurations necessary for your application. By using Docker with Elastic Beanstalk, you have the infrastructure for capacity provisioning, scalability, load balancing, and health monitoring for the instances that run on containers. The containers integrate with your

Amazon VPC for network requirements and with IAM to enable resource management. You can launch different software engines with containers to provide various options and third-party tools to run containers.

You can choose from single container configurations and multicontainer configurations. A single container runs one container per instance. A multicontainer runs multiple applications or engines on one instance, with all of the software and settings you require. Preconfigured options are available with Docker, and you can integrate them with instances that run in your architecture through Elastic Beanstalk.

Monitoring and Troubleshooting

After you launch your code, check on its performance and availability. You can monitor statistics and view information about the health of your application, its environment, and specific services from the AWS Management Console. Elastic Beanstalk also creates alerts that trigger at established thresholds to monitor your environment's health. In the AWS Management Console, the AWS Elastic Beanstalk Monitoring page shows aggregated statistics and graphs for your applications and resources. Each environment is color-coded to indicate the environment's status. You can see at a glance whether your environment is available online at any point in time. Metrics gathered by the resources in your environment are published to Amazon CloudWatch in five-minute intervals. You can adjust the time range for the statistics and graphs and customize your views of the metrics.

Figure 6.10 shows an example of the statistics that you can view for your environment.

FIGURE 6.10   Health dashboard on AWS Elastic Beanstalk

Figure 6.11 shows an example of the graphs that you can view.

FIGURE 6.11 Metrics for monitoring on AWS Elastic Beanstalk

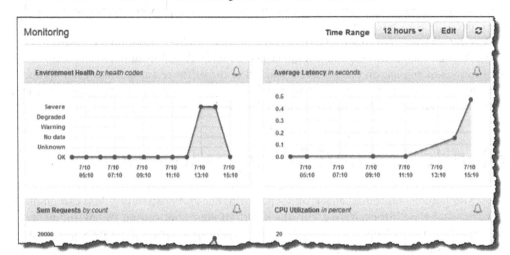

Table 6.3 defines the AWS Elastic Beanstalk Monitoring page colors.

TABLE 6.3 AWS Elastic Beanstalk Health Page Color Definitions

Color	Description
Gray	Your environment is being updated.
Green	Your environment has passed the most recent health check. At least one instance in your environment is available and taking requests.
Yellow	Your environment has failed one or more health checks. Requests to your environment are failing.
Red	Your environment has failed three or more health checks, or an environment resource has become unavailable. Requests are consistently failing.

By default, Elastic Beanstalk displays Amazon EC2, Auto Scaling, and Elastic Load Balancing metrics for your application environments. These metrics are available to you on your AWS Elastic Beanstalk Monitoring page as soon as you deploy your application environment. You can access the health status from the AWS Management Console or the EB CLI.

Basic Health Monitoring

To access the health status from the AWS Management Console, select the Elastic Beanstalk service and then select the tab for your specific application environment. An environment overview shows your architecture's instance status details, resource details, and filter capabilities. Health statuses are indicated in four distinct colors.

To access the health status from the EB CLI, enter the eb health command. The output shows the environment and the health of associated instances. Enhanced health reporting also provides the following seven health statuses, which are single-word descriptors that provide a better indication of the state of your environment:

ok   warning   degraded   severe   info   pending   unknown

You can also use the eb status command in the EB CLI or the DescribeEnvironments API call to retrieve the health status for an environment. You can check the health of the overall environment or the individual services of Amazon EC2 or an Elastic Load Balancing load balancer. Health checks on your Elastic Load Balancing port execute both for the default port 80 and a custom Elastic Load Balancing port/path.

For GET requests with the load balancer, 200 OK is the default success code and indicates a healthy status. The service can also return 400 level responses. You can also configure a health check URL for custom static page responses.

> Be sure to adjust the caching time to live for any health check static pages or URLs in Amazon CloudFront or for any caching mechanism you may use.

Elastic Beanstalk also reports missing configurations or other issues that could affect the health of the application environment.

Enhanced Health Monitoring

There are two types of reporting: the default health information about your resources and the enhanced health reporting that provides you more information for monitoring health.

You can use the enhanced health reporting feature to gather additional resource data and display graphs and statistics of environment health in greater detail. This is important when you deploy multiple versions of your application and when you need to analyze factors that could be degrading your application's availability or performance. You can view these details in the AWS Elastic Beanstalk Monitoring page from the AWS Management Console. These reports require the creation of two IAM roles: a *service role* to allow access between the services and Elastic Beanstalk and an *instance profile* to write logs into an Amazon S3 bucket.

> Running the enhanced health report requires a version 2 or newer platform configuration that supports all platforms except Windows Server with IIS. The enhanced health reports provide data directly to Elastic Beanstalk and do not run through Amazon CloudWatch.

By default, health monitoring on Elastic Beanstalk does not publish metrics to Amazon CloudWatch, so you are not charged for the metrics. There are also custom metrics that you can run and view, for which you are not charged a fee. You can enable custom metrics by using the PutMetricData operation in worker environments. For example, you might have an Amazon SQS daemon that publishes custom metrics for environment health under the same environment namespace. You can also enable custom metrics from Amazon CloudWatch, but AWS charges for these additional metrics you publish to your monthly Amazon CloudWatch. To save costs, use the available metrics on the Elastic Beanstalk service, or enable the custom metrics that you need, paying only for what you use.

Elastic Beanstalk runs a health agent to provide detailed health resource data for enhanced health monitoring. The health agent runs in the Amazon Machine Image (AMI) for each instance operating system on a platform configuration for your application. The agent analyzes system metrics and logs to communicate the health status to Elastic Beanstalk. You receive alerts, data, and actionable insights that you can use to monitor your applications and understand, prevent, and respond to performance issues.

You can monitor recent health events that you have enabled on Elastic Beanstalk in real time. There are several health event types that can change as an environment transitions from the create state to the run state. Figure 6.12 displays the health events available in the AWS Elastic Beanstalk Monitoring page and examples of the details that allow you to respond to issues identified.

FIGURE 6.12   Events on AWS Elastic Beanstalk

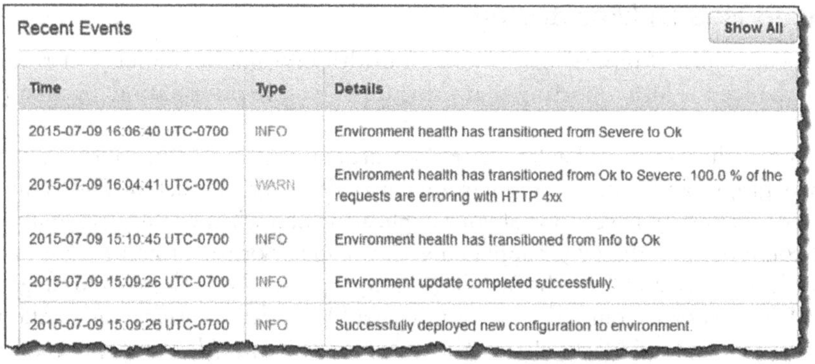

Recent Events			Show All
Time	**Type**	**Details**	
2015-07-09 16:06:40 UTC-0700	INFO	Environment health has transitioned from Severe to Ok	
2015-07-09 16:04:41 UTC-0700	WARN	Environment health has transitioned from Ok to Severe. 100.0 % of the requests are erroring with HTTP 4xx	
2015-07-09 15:10:45 UTC-0700	INFO	Environment health has transitioned from Info to Ok	
2015-07-09 15:09:26 UTC-0700	INFO	Environment update completed successfully.	
2015-07-09 15:09:26 UTC-0700	INFO	Successfully deployed new configuration to environment.	

Elastic Beanstalk integrates with AWS CloudTrail to capture Elastic Beanstalk API calls as log files that you can store in an Amazon S3 bucket. To view additional actions occurring with your running resources, you can also capture AWS API calls in your code using AWS CloudTrail.

Summary

In this chapter, you learned about the features of Elastic Beanstalk, how to automate deployments for your multi-tier architectures, and different deployment strategies. You also discovered options for configuring your environments and managing your resources with services such as IAM, Amazon VPC, Amazon EC2, and Amazon S3.

Exam Essentials

Know how to deploy AWS Elastic Beanstalk.   Know how to deploy an application AWS Elastic Beanstalk and what platforms it supports. To complete the exam successfully, you should also understand how the architectures and services interact with the web, application, and database tiers. Focus on foundational services and how you create and work with Elastic Beanstalk.

Know about ebextensions.   Understand ebextensions and the part they play in the service configuration. Be able to recognize the stacks you create and how to change them.

Know about Elastic Beanstalk resources.   Understand how to manage resources with Elastic Beanstalk, including IAM. Understand the definitions and differentiate between the functions of the default IAM service role and the instance profile, which are automatically created. Understand permissions for your AWS resources in your environment.

Know Elastic Beanstalk deployment strategies.   Understand what deployment strategies you can use, their differences, and which ones would be best for different use cases and other resources. Know which strategy offers less downtime and which is best suited for complex changes.

Know about Elastic Beanstalk components.   Understand all of the components of Elastic Beanstalk, including applications, environments, versions, configurations, and the AWS resources it launches and with which it integrates. Know how to retain or dispose of resources as needed.

Know about Elastic Beanstalk different environment tiers.   Know the differences between the single-instance tier and the web-server environment tier and when to choose one over the other. Understand the services and features used for both.

On the test itself, do not get sidetracked with small details about Elastic Beanstalk. Focus your understanding on how it works as a whole and interacts with other services.

Resources to Review

AWS Elastic Beanstalk Install:

> https://docs.aws.amazon.com/elasticbeanstalk/latest/dg/
> eb-cli3-install.html

AWS Elastic Beanstalk Developer Guide:

> https://docs.aws.amazon.com/elasticbeanstalk/latest/dg/
> Welcome.html

AWS Elastic Beanstalk Concepts:

> https://docs.aws.amazon.com/elasticbeanstalk/latest/dg/
> concepts.html

Using the EB CLI with AWS CodeCommit:

> https://docs.aws.amazon.com/elasticbeanstalk/latest/
> dg/eb-cli-codecommit.html

EB CLI Command Reference:

> https://docs.aws.amazon.com/elasticbeanstalk/latest/
> dg/eb3-cmd-commands.html

Deploying AWS Elastic Beanstalk Applications from Docker Containers:

> https://docs.aws.amazon.com/elasticbeanstalk/latest/dg/
> create_deploy_docker.html

Using AWS Elastic Beanstalk with Amazon Relational Database Service:

> https://docs.aws.amazon.com/elasticbeanstalk/latest/dg/
> AWSHowTo.RDS.html

Preconfigured Docker Containers:

> https://docs.aws.amazon.com/elasticbeanstalk/latest/dg/
> create_deploy_dockerpreconfig.html

AWS Elastic Beanstalk Supported Platforms:

> https://docs.aws.amazon.com/elasticbeanstalk/latest/dg/
> concepts.platforms.html

Enhanced Health Reporting and Monitoring:

> https://docs.aws.amazon.com/elasticbeanstalk/latest/dg/
> health-enhanced.html

Exercises

Deploy Your Application

In this exercise, you will sign up for an AWS account.

1. Verify that your source code is packaged as a .zip file and is ready to be retrieved from either your source repository directory or an Amazon S3 bucket.

   You can choose a sample application available from the AWS Management Console.

2. Launch the AWS Management Console.

3. To select a region in which to launch the application, select **AWS Elastic Beanstalk ≻ Region**.

4. Select **AWS Elastic Beanstalk Service**.

5. Select **Get Started** or **Create New Application**. The Get Started option takes you through a wizard of guided steps to launch your first application. After this initial start, the Create New Application dialog box will be displayed for future launches.

6. Select the type of application that you want to deploy.

7. Enter an application name.

8. Select the application platform for your code.

9. For your coding language, select the preconfigured platform.

10. Select **Upload your application**.

11. Locate the file directory where your .zip file of your code resides or choose the Amazon S3 bucket with the .zip file and select **Upload**.

12. Choose **Next**.

13. To use the architecture with high availability, select **High Availability**.

14. Modify the configurations for your architecture.

15. Select **Add databases**.

16. Select **RDS database**.

17. Choose **Create App (Application)**.

    You now have successfully deployed an application on Elastic Beanstalk.

EXERCISE 6.2

Deploy a Blue/Green Solution

In this exercise, you will deploy a blue/green solution.

1. Sign in to your AWS account.

2. Navigate to your existing AWS Elastic Beanstalk environment and application or upload the sample.

   You can launch a sample application from this location:

   https://docs.aws.amazon.com/elasticbeanstalk/latest/dg/tutorials.html

3. Clone your environment or launch a new environment with your new version.

4. Deploy the second application version to the new environment. Test that the new version is running.

5. From the new environment dashboard, select **Actions ➤ Swap Environment URLs**.

6. Under **Select an Environment to Swap**, select the current environment name.

7. Choose **Swap**.

   The Elastic Beanstalk service swaps the CNAME records between the two environments.

8. On the dashboard, under **Recent Events**, verify the swap.

You have successfully deployed a blue/green solution on AWS Elastic Beanstalk.

EXERCISE 6.3

Change Your Environment Configuration on AWS Elastic Beanstalk

In this exercise, you will change your environment configuration on AWS Elastic Beanstalk. Use an existing application that is running on Elastic Beanstalk.

1. Sign in to your AWS account.

2. Navigate to your existing AWS Elastic Beanstalk environment and application.

3. Choose Configuration.

4. On the **Capacity Configuration** tab, choose **Modify**.

5. Under **Auto Scaling Group**, select **Load balanced**.

6. In the Instances row, change Max to 4 and Min to 2.

7. On the **Modify capacity** page, choose **Save**.

8. On the **Configuration overview** page, choose **Apply**.

9. On the warning message, choose **Confirm**.

   The environment might take a few minutes to update. After your environment is updated, verify your changes.

10. Navigate to the Amazon EC2 service dashboard.

11. Choose **Load Balancers**.

12. Check for the instance-id value that matches your Elastic Beanstalk environment instance-id value and view the load balancers.

You have successfully changed an environment configuration on AWS Elastic Beanstalk.

EXERCISE 6.4

Update an Application Version on AWS Elastic Beanstalk

In this exercise, you will update an application version on AWS Elastic Beanstalk from the AWS Management Console.

1. Sign in to your AWS account.

2. Upload a second version your application that matches the configuration for your current running environment.

   If you are using a sample solution application, you can find other versions at the following address:

   https://docs.aws.amazon.com/elasticbeanstalk/latest/dg/GettingStarted
   .html#GettingStarted.Walkthrough.DeployApp

3. On the **AWS EB applications** page, select getting-started-app.

4. Select GettingStartedApp-env.

5. In **Overview**, choose **Upload and Deploy**.

6. Select **Choose File** and upload the next version of your source bundle that you created or downloaded.

   The console is automatically populated with the version label based on the name of the archive that you upload. For later deployments, if you use a source bundle with the same name, you must type a unique version label.

(continued)

7. Choose **Deploy**. Elastic Beanstalk deploys your application to your Amazon EC2 instances.

   You can view the status of the deployment on the environment's dashboard. The Environment Health status turns gray while the application version is being updated. When deployment is complete, Elastic Beanstalk executes an application health check. The status reverts to green when the application responds to the health check. The environment dashboard shows the new running version as the new version label. Your new application version is added to the table of application versions.

8. To view the table, select **Application Versions**.

   You have updated an application version on AWS Elastic Beanstalk.

Review Questions

1. Which of the following AWS services enables you to automate your build, test, deploy, and release process every time there is a code change?

   A. AWS CodeCommit

   B. AWS CodeDeploy

   C. AWS CodeBuild

   D. AWS CodePipeline

2. Which of the following resources can AWS Elastic Beanstalk use to create a web server environment? (Select FOUR.)

   A. Amazon Cognito User Pool

   B. AWS Serverless Application Model (AWS SAM) Local

   C. Auto Scaling group

   D. Amazon Elastic Compute Cloud (Amazon EC2)

   E. AWS Lambda

3. Which of the following languages is not supported by AWS Elastic Beanstalk?

   A. Java

   B. Node.js

   C. Objective C

   D. Go

4. What does the AWS Elastic Beanstalk service do?

   A. Deploys applications and architecture

   B. Stores static content

   C. Directs user traffic to Amazon Elastic Compute Cloud (Amazon EC2) instances

   D. Works with dynamic cloud changes as an IP address

5. Which operating systems does AWS Elastic Beanstalk support? (Select TWO.)

   A. Amazon Linux

   B. Ubuntu

   C. Windows Server

   D. Fedora

   E. Jetty

6. Which of the following components can AWS Elastic Beanstalk deploy? (Select TWO.)

   A. Amazon Elastic Compute Cloud (Amazon EC2) instances with write capabilities to an Amazon DynamoDB table

   B. A worker application using Amazon Simple Queue Service (Amazon SQS)

   C. An Amazon Elastic Container Service (Amazon ECS) cluster supporting multiple containers

   D. A mixed fleet of Spot and Reserved Instances with four applications running in each environment

   E. A mixed fleet of Reserved Instances scheduled between 9 a.m. to 5 p.m. and On-Demand Instances used for processing data workloads when needed randomly

7. Which of the following operations can AWS Elastic Beanstalk do? (Select TWO.)

   A. Access an Amazon Simple Storage Service (Amazon S3) bucket

   B. Connect to an Amazon Relational Database Service (Amazon RDS) database

   C. Install agents for Amazon GuardDuty service

   D. Create and manage Amazon WorkSpaces

8. Which service can be used to restrict access to AWS Elastic Beanstalk resources?

   A. AWS Config

   B. Amazon Relational Database Service (Amazon RDS)

   C. AWS Identity and Access Management (IAM)

   D. Amazon Simple Storage Service (Amazon S3)

9. Which AWS Identity and Access Management (IAM) entities are used when creating an environment? (Select TWO.)

   A. Federated role

   B. Service role

   C. Instance profile

   D. Profile role

   E. User name and access keys

10. Which of the following describes how customers are charged for AWS Elastic Beanstalk?

   A. A monthly fee based on an hourly rate for use.

   B. A one-time upfront cost for each environment running.

   C. No additional charges.

   D. A fee is charged only when scaling to support traffic changes.

11. Which account is billed for user-accessed AWS resources allocated by AWS Elastic Beanstalk?

    A. The account running the services

    B. The cross-account able to access the shared services

    C. The cross-account with the Amazon Simple Storage Service (Amazon S3) bucket holding a downloaded copy of the code artifact

    D. All accounts involved

12. What can you *not* do to an Amazon Relational Database Service (Amazon RDS) instance with AWS Elastic Beanstalk?

    A. Create a database connection.

    B. Create a supported Oracle edition.

    C. Retain a database instance despite the deletion of the environment's database.

    D. Create a snapshot of the existing database (before deletion).

Chapter

7

Deployment as Code

**THE AWS CERTIFIED DEVELOPER –
ASSOCIATE EXAM TOPICS COVERED IN
THIS CHAPTER MAY INCLUDE, BUT ARE
NOT LIMITED TO, THE FOLLOWING:**

Domain 1: Deployment

✓ **1.1** Deploy written code in AWS using existing CI/CD
pipelines, processes, and patterns.

✓ **1.3** Prepare the application deployment package to be
deployed to AWS.

✓ **1.4** Deploy serverless applications.

Domain 3: Development with AWS services

✓ **3.4** Write code that interacts with AWS services by using
Application Programming Interfaces (APIs),
Software Development Kits (SDKs), and AWS Command
Line Interface (CLI).

Introduction to AWS Code Services

In the previous chapter, you learned about deploying code packages to AWS Elastic Beanstalk. This is a great way to migrate existing applications to highly available, fault-tolerant infrastructure. As your experience with Amazon Web Services (AWS) deployment increases over time, you may find a need to customize your deployment workflow further than what is supported within a single service. AWS provides a number of deployment services designed for flexibility, empowering customers with complex infrastructure and application deployment requirements.

This chapter introduces the AWS "Code" services. These services are responsible for creating the foundation of a repeatable application, infrastructure, and configuration deployment process. As each service is explained, you will see how they fit into an "enterprise as code" philosophy. You use this approach with each aspect of an enterprise to deploy, configure, and maintain over time via versioned code. (This includes the process to deploy code.) The primary components of an enterprise as code are application, infrastructure, and configuration, though you can take advantage of many more, such as monitoring, compliance, and audit practices.

Continuous Delivery with AWS CodePipeline

The AWS "Code" services lay the foundation to deploy different parts of an enterprise starting from a source repository. You start with *AWS CodePipeline* to create a *continuous integration/continuous deployment pipeline* (CI/CD) that integrates various sources, tests, deployments, or other components. AWS CodePipeline implements *AWS CodeCommit* as a source in that it acts as the initialization point of your deployment process. *AWS CodeBuild* allows you to pull code and packages from various sources to create publishable build artifacts. Lastly, *AWS CodeDeploy* allows you to deploy compiled artifacts to infrastructure in your environment. AWS CodePipeline is not limited to deploying application code; it can also be used to provision, configure, and manage infrastructure.

In a fully realized enterprise as code, a single commit to a source repository can kick off processes, such as those shown in Figure 7.1.

FIGURE 7.1   Branch view

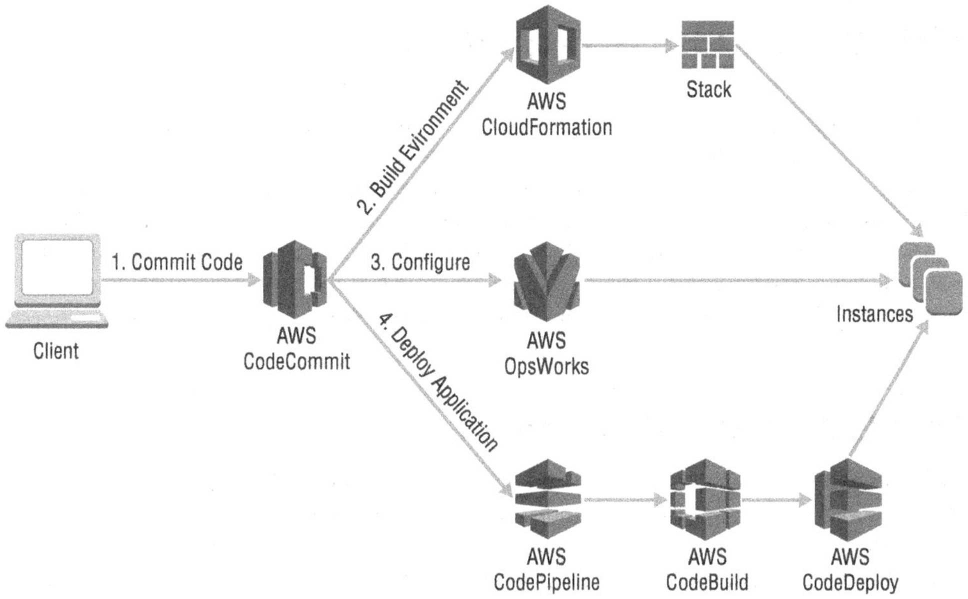

Benefits of Continuous Delivery

Organizations can realize a number of benefits from automating the process of testing and preparing software changes. First, there is reduced manual effort required to ensure code changes are tested prior to release. By automating tests, they are consistently run against every change made to a code repository.

Second, developers are no longer tasked with completing steps other than checking in code changes. After the change has been pushed to a source repository, initiation of the build/test process automatically begins. This allows the developers to focus on what they do best: develop software.

Third, the fact that changes are tested immediately after check-in ensures that more bugs are caught earlier in the development process. If bugs are not caught soon, the effort and cost to remediate the errors increases the further they make it in the release process.

Lastly, continuous delivery ensures that quality changes are delivered faster. This increases quality with decreased time to market. So, before you start considering storage options, take time to evaluate your data and decide which of these dimensions your data falls under. This will help you decide what type of storage is best for your data.

Using AWS CodePipeline to Automate Deployments

AWS CodePipeline is a continuous integration and continuous delivery service for fast and reliable application and infrastructure updates. AWS CodePipeline builds, tests, and deploys your code every time there is a code change, based on the release process models you define. This enables you to deliver features and updates rapidly and reliably. You can easily build an end-to-end solution with prebuilt plugins for popular third-party services like GitHub, or you can integrate your own custom plugins into any stage of your release process. With AWS CodePipeline, you pay only for what you use. There are no up-front fees or long-term commitments.

What Is AWS CodePipeline?

AWS CodePipeline is the underpinning of CI/CD processes in AWS. Because you define your delivery workflow as a set of stages and actions, multiple changes can be run simultaneously through the same set of processing steps every time. In Figure 7.2, the developer team is responsible for committing changes to a source repository. AWS CodePipeline automatically detects and moves into the source stage. The code change (revision) passes to the build stage, where changes are built into a package or product ready for deployment. A staging deployment is done where users can manually review the functionality that the changes introduce or modify. Before final production release, an authorized user provides a manual approval. After production release, further code changes can reliably pass through the same pipeline.

FIGURE 7.2   AWS CodePipeline workflow

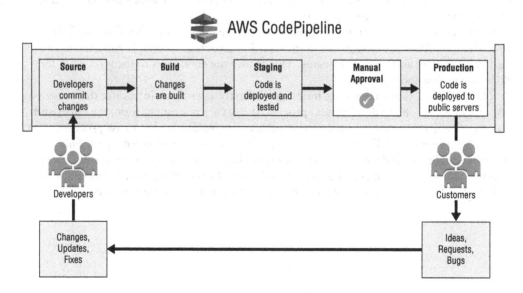

AWS CodePipeline provides a number of built-in integrations to other AWS services, such as AWS CloudFormation, AWS CodeBuild, AWS CodeCommit, AWS CodeDeploy, Amazon Elastic Container Service (ECS), Elastic Beanstalk, AWS Lambda, AWS OpsWorks Stacks, and Amazon Simple Storage Service (Amazon S3). Some partner tools include GitHub (https://github.com) and Jenkins (https://jenkins.io). Customers also have the ability to create their own integrations, which provides a great degree of flexibility.

You define workflow steps through a visual editor within the AWS Management Console or via a JavaScript Object Notation (JSON) structure for use in the AWS CLI or AWS SDKs. Access to create and manage release workflows is controlled by AWS Identity and Access Management (IAM). You can grant users fine-grained permissions, controlling what actions they can perform and on which workflows.

AWS CodePipeline provides a dashboard where you can review real-time progress of revisions, attempt to retry failed actions, and review version information about revisions that pass through the pipeline.

AWS CodePipeline Concepts

There are a number of different components that make up AWS CodePipeline and the workflows (*pipelines*) created by customers. Figure 7.3 displays the AWS CodePipeline concepts.

FIGURE 7.3   Pipeline structure

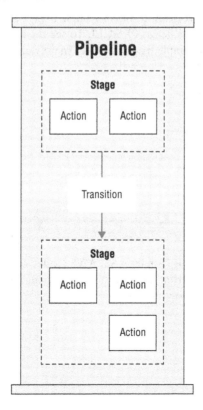

Pipeline

A *pipeline* is the overall workflow that defines what transformations software changes will undergo.

> You cannot change the name of a pipeline. If you would like to change the name, you must create a new pipeline.

Revision

A *revision* is the work item that passes through a pipeline. It can be a change to your source code or data stored in AWS CodeCommit or GitHub or a change to the version of an archive in Amazon S3. A pipeline can have multiple revisions flowing through it at the same time, but a single stage can process one revision at a time. A revision is immediately picked up by a source action when a change is detected in the source itself (such as a commit to an AWS CodeCommit repository).

> If you use Amazon S3 as a source action, you must enable versioning on the bucket.

Details of the most recent revision to pass through a stage are kept within the stage itself and are accessible from the console or AWS CLI. To see the last revision that was passed through a source stage, for example, you can select the revision details at the bottom of the stage, as shown in Figure 7.4.

FIGURE 7.4   Source stage

Depending on the source type (Amazon S3, AWS CodeCommit, or GitHub), additional information will be accessible from the revision details pane (such as a link to the commit on https://github.com), as shown in Figure 7.5.

FIGURE 7.5   Revision details

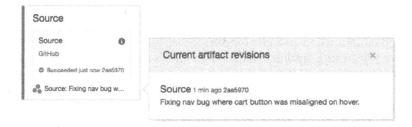

Stage

A *stage* is a group of one or more actions. Each stage must have a unique name. Should any one action in a stage fail, the entire stage fails for this revision.

Action

An *action* defines the work to perform on the revision. You can configure pipeline actions to run in series or in parallel. If all actions in a stage complete successfully for a revision, it passes to the next stage in the pipeline. However, if one action fails in the stage, the revision will not pass further through the pipeline. At this point, the stage that contains the failed action can be retried for the same revision. Otherwise, a new revision is able to pass through the stage.

> *A pipeline must have two or more stages.* The first stage includes one or more source actions only. Only the first stage may include source actions.

> Every action in the same stage must have a unique name.

Source

The *source* action defines the location where you store and update source files. Modifications to files in a source repository or archive trigger deployments to a pipeline. AWS CodePipeline supports these sources for your pipeline:

- Amazon S3
- AWS CodeCommit
- GitHub

A single pipeline can contain multiple source actions. If a change is detected in one of the sources, all source actions will be invoked.

To use GitHub as a source provider for AWS CodePipeline, you must authenticate to GitHub when you create a pipeline. You provide GitHub credentials to authorize AWS CodePipeline to connect to GitHub to list and view repositories accessible by the authenticating account. For this link, AWS recommends that you create a service account user so that the lifecycle of personal accounts is not tied to the link between AWS CodePipeline and GitHub.

After you authenticate GitHub, a link is created between AWS CodePipeline for this AWS region and GitHub. This allows IAM users to list repositories and branches accessible by the authenticated GitHub user.

Build

You use a *build* action to define tasks such as compiling source code, running unit tests, and performing other tasks that produce output artifacts for later use in your pipeline. For example, you can use a build stage to import large assets that are not part of a source bundle into the artifact to deploy it to Amazon Elastic Compute Cloud (Amazon EC2) instances. AWS CodePipeline supports the integrations for the following build actions:

- AWS CodeBuild
- CloudBees
- Jenkins
- Solano CI
- TeamCity

Test

You can use *test* actions to run various tests against source and compiled code, such as lint or syntax tests on source code, and unit tests on compiled, running applications. AWS CodePipeline supports the following test integrations:

- AWS CodeBuild
- BlazeMeter
- Ghost Inspector
- Hewlett Packard Enterprise (HPE) StormRunner Load
- Nouvola
- Runscope

Deploy

The *deploy* action is responsible for taking compiled or prepared assets and installing them on instances, on-premises servers, serverless functions, or deploying and updating infrastructure using AWS CloudFormation templates. The following services are supported as deploy actions:

- AWS CloudFormation
- AWS CodeDeploy
- Amazon Elastic Container Service
- AWS Elastic Beanstalk
- OpsWorks Stacks
- Xebia Labs

Approval

An *approval* action is a manual gate that controls whether a revision can proceed to the next stage in a pipeline. Further progress by a revision is halted until a manual approval by an IAM user or IAM role occurs.

> Specifically, the `codepipeline:PutApprovalResult` action must be included in the IAM policy.

Upon approval, AWS CodePipeline approves the revision to proceed to the next stage in the pipeline. However, if the revision is not approved (rejected or the approval expires), the change halts and will stop progress through the pipeline. The purpose of this action is to allow manual review of the code or other quality assurance tasks prior to moving further down the pipeline.

> Approval actions cannot occur within source stages.

You must approve actions manually within seven days; otherwise, AWS CodePipeline rejects the code. When an approval action rejects, the outcome is equivalent to when the stage fails. You can retire the action, which initiates the approval process again. Approval actions provide several options that you can use to provide additional information about what you choose to approve.

Publish approval notifications   Amazon Simple Notification Service (Amazon SNS) sends notices to one or more targets that approval is pending.

Specify a Universal Resource Locator (URL) for review   You can include a URL in the approval action notification, for example, to review a website published to a fleet of test instances.

Enter comments for approvers   You can add additional comments in the notifications for the reviewer's reference.

Invoke

You can customize the *invoke* action within AWS CodePipeline if you leverage the power and flexibility of AWS Lambda. Invoke actions execute AWS Lambda functions, which allows arbitrary code to be run as part of the pipeline execution. Uses for custom actions in your pipeline can include the following:

- Backing up data volumes, Amazon S3 buckets, or databases

- Interacting with third-party products, such as posting messages to Slack channels

- Running through test interactions with deployed web applications, such as executing a test transaction on a shopping site

- Updating IAM Roles to allow permissions to newly created resources

When you deploy changes to multiple AWS Elastic Beanstalk environments, for example, you can use AWS Lambda to invoke a stage to swap the environment CNAMEs (SwapEnvironmentCNAMEs). This effectively implements blue/green deployments via AWS CodePipeline.

Artifact

Artifacts are actions that act on a file or set of files. Artifacts can pass between actions and stages in a pipeline to provide a final result or version of the files. For example, an artifact that passes from a build action would deploy to Amazon EC2 during a deploy action.

Multiple actions in a single pipeline cannot output artifacts with the same name.

Every stage makes use of the Amazon S3 artifact bucket that you define when you create the pipeline. Depending on the type of action(s) in the stage, AWS CodePipeline will package the output artifact. For example, the output artifact of a source action would be an archive (.zip) containing the repository contents, which would then act as the input artifact to a build action.

For an artifact to transition between stages successfully, you must provide unique input and output artifact names. In Figure 7.6, the output artifact name for the source action must match the input artifact for the corresponding build action.

FIGURE 7.6   Artifact transition

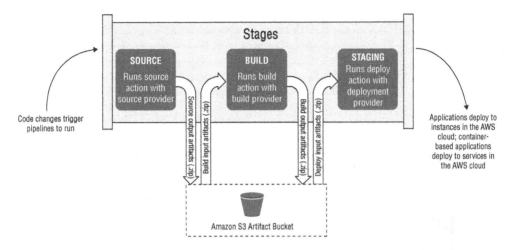

Transition

Transitions connect stages in a pipeline and define which stages should transition to one another. When all actions in a stage complete successfully, the revision passes to the next stage(s) in the pipeline.

You can manually disable transitions, which stops all revisions in the pipeline once they complete the preceding stage (successfully or unsuccessfully). Once you enable the transition again, the most recent successful revision resumes. Other previous successful revisions will not resume through the pipeline at this time. This concept also applies to stages that are not yet available by the time the next revision completes. If more than one revision completes while the next stage is unavailable, they will be batched. This means that the most current revision will continue through the pipeline once the next stage becomes available.

Managing Approval Actions

Approval actions halt further progress through a pipeline until an authorized IAM user or IAM rule approves the transition. You can use approvals to review changes manually before final release into production, or as a code review step.

Figure 7.7 shows a pipeline with three stages: Source, Staging, and LambdaStage. The Source stage contains a source action referencing an Amazon S3 bucket. The source action has already completed and passed the source artifact to Staging. In Staging, the deploy action deploys the source artifact to Amazon EC2 with AWS CodeDeploy. If this action completes successfully, the LambdaStage stage begins, which also deploys to Amazon EC2 via AWS CodeDeploy.

FIGURE 7.7 Full pipeline

AWS CodePipeline Service Limits

Table 7.1 lists the AWS CodePipeline service limits.

TABLE 7.1 AWS CodePipeline Service Limits

Limit	Value
Pipelines per region	US East (N. Virginia) (us-east-1): 40 US West (Oregon) (us-west-2): 60 EU (Ireland) (eu-west-1): 60 Other supported regions: 20
Stages per pipeline	Minimum: 2 Maximum: 10
Actions per stage	Minimum: 1 Maximum: 20
Parallel actions per stage	Maximum: 10
Sequential actions per stage	Maximum: 10
Maximum artifact size	Amazon S3 source: 2 GB AWS CodeCommit source: 1 GB GitHub source: 1 GB

When you deploy to AWS CloudFormation, the maximum artifact size is 256 MB.

AWS CodePipeline Tasks

The remainder of this section will focus on the tasks you need to build and execute a simple pipeline and how to outline the requirements to build cross-account pipelines. This concept is particularly important for organizations that have multiple AWS accounts, especially when you separate environments across accounts (such as Account A for development, Account B for Quality Assurance [QA], and Account C for production), as AWS CodePipeline will need access to resources in each account to automate deployments successfully.

Before you start the next steps, make sure that you have an IAM user with an access key and secret access key and that the user has sufficient AWS CodePipeline permissions.

Create an AWS CodePipeline

It is best to name your pipeline something meaningful, such as Dev_S3_Bucket. After you select a source provider (Amazon S3, AWS CodeCommit, or GitHub), you must enter a full object path. This corresponds to the .zip archive that will be tracked for changes.

When you select Amazon S3, AWS CodePipeline creates an Amazon CloudWatch Events rule, IAM role, and AWS CloudTrail trail. These are the default methods that notify AWS CodePipeline of changes to the source archive. You can also use AWS CodePipeline to check regularly for changes. This, however, will provide a slower update experience.

You select AWS CodeBuild, Jenkins, or Solano CI for a build provider.

> The Jenkins build provider requires you to install the AWS CodePipeline plugin for Jenkins on the server.
>
> The Solano CI build provider requires authentication to GitHub with a valid user. After authenticating to GitHub, you must authenticate to Solano CI.

If you do not select a build provider, you must select a deployment provider (if you select a build provider, the deployment step is optional). This option is useful if you desire the pipeline execution to be a finished build artifact, such as the case with custom media transcoding with AWS CodeBuild. The available providers for the deployment stage are Amazon ECS, AWS CloudFormation, AWS CodeDeploy, AWS Elastic Beanstalk, and AWS OpsWorks Stacks.

AWS Elastic Beanstalk allows customers to automate deployment of application archives to one or more Amazon EC2 instances. It also handles health checks, load balancing, log gathering, and other important tasks automatically. Since it requires a bundled application archive to upload to instances for deployment, it is a natural fit for AWS CodePipeline, which provides artifacts as archives. To deploy to AWS Elastic Beanstalk from AWS CodePipeline, simply provide the application and environment name.

> For deployment to AWS Elastic Beanstalk, the maximum application archive size is 512 MB. The deployment artifact must not exceed this size, or the deployment will fail.

You select a service role for AWS CodePipeline to access AWS resources within your account. You can select an existing IAM role or create a new role.

> You can only select IAM roles with a trust policy that allows AWS CodePipeline to assume them.

Start a Pipeline

After you create a pipeline, the first stage updates the source repository or archive, and then the pipeline will automatically begin execution. To rerun the pipeline for the most recent revision, select Release Change in the AWS CodePipeline console, or invoke the aws codepipeline `start-pipeline-execution` AWS CLI command.

```
aws codepipeline start-pipeline-execution --name SamplePipeline
```

Retry a Failed Action

If a pipeline action fails for any reason, you can retry that action on the same revision in the console or use the aws `codepipeline retry-stage-execution` AWS CLI command. However, there are certain situations where a failed action may become ineligible for retries.

- The pipeline itself has changed after the action failed.
- Other actions in the same stage have not completed.
- The retry attempt is already in progress.

Create a Cross-Account Pipeline

In some architectures, environments may be spread across two or more AWS accounts. You can implement a single CI/CD workflow with AWS CodePipeline that interacts with resources in multiple AWS accounts.

If an organization has separate accounts for development, test, and production workloads, you can leverage one pipeline to deploy to resources in all three. To do so, you must create and shard several components between accounts.

A source action of Amazon S3 cannot reference buckets in accounts other than the pipeline account.

Pipeline Account Steps

In the following steps, the account that contains the pipeline will be the *pipeline account*. The account to deploy resources will be the *target account*.

1. Create an AWS Key Management Service (AWS KMS) key in the pipeline account, and apply it to the pipeline. This key encrypts artifacts that pass between stages, and you configure it to allow access to the target account in a later step. After you create the AWS KMS key, you apply a key policy that allows access to the key by both the AWS CodePipeline service role in the pipeline account and the Amazon Resource Name (ARN) of the target account.

2. Apply a bucket policy to the Amazon S3 bucket for the pipeline. This policy must grant access to the bucket by the target account.

3. Create a policy that allows the pipeline account to assume a role in the target account. You attach this policy to the AWS CodePipeline service role.

Target Account Steps

 If you deploy revisions to Amazon EC2 instances (as with AWS CodeDeploy), you apply a policy to the instance role that allows access to the Amazon S3 bucket that the AWS CodePipeline uses in the pipeline account. Additionally, the instance role must also have a policy that allows access to the AWS KMS key.

1. Create an IAM role that contains a trust relationship policy that allows the pipeline account to assume the role.

2. Create an IAM policy that allows access to deploy to the pipeline's resources. Attach this policy to the IAM role.

3. Create an IAM policy that allows access to the Amazon S3 bucket in the pipeline account, and attach it to the IAM role. After completing the previous steps, revisions that pass through the pipeline account will be accessible by the target account.

Using AWS CodeCommit as a Source Repository

AWS CodeCommit is a fully managed source control service that makes it easy for companies to host secure and highly scalable private Git repositories. AWS CodeCommit eliminates the need to operate your own source control system or worry about scaling its infrastructure. You can use AWS CodeCommit to store anything securely, from source code to binaries, and it works seamlessly with your existing Git tools.

What Is AWS CodeCommit?

Before any activities can occur to deploy applications, you must first have a location where you can store and version application code in a reliable fashion. AWS CodeCommit is a cloud-based, highly available, and redundant version control service. AWS CodeCommit leverages the Git framework, and it is fully compatible with existing tooling. There are a number of benefits to this service, such as the following:

- Automatic encryption in-transit and at rest.
- Scaling to handle rapid release cycles and large repositories.
- Access control to the repository using IAM users, IAM roles, and IAM policies.
- Hypertext Transfer Protocol Secure (HTTPS) and Secure Shell (SSH) connectivity.

However, the biggest benefit of AWS CodeCommit is built-in integration with multiple other AWS services, like AWS CodePipeline. With these integrations, AWS CodeCommit acts as the initial step to automate application code releases.

AWS CodeCommit Concepts

This section details the concepts behind AWS CodeCommit.

Credentials

When you interact with AWS, you specify your AWS security credentials to verify who you are and whether you have permission to access the resources that you request. AWS uses the security credentials to authenticate and authorize your requests.

HTTPS

HTTPS connectivity to a Git-based repository requires a username and password, which pass to the repository as part of a request. To use AWS CodeCommit with HTTPS credentials, you must first add them to an IAM user with sufficient permissions to interact with the repository. To create Git credentials for your IAM user, you open the IAM console, and select the user who will need to authenticate to the AWS CodeCommit repository via HTTPS.

AWS generates security credentials for the usernames and passwords, and they cannot be set to custom values.

> Make sure to download or copy the credentials because the password will be lost after you close the success window.

After you configure your Git CLI/application to use the repository's HTTPS endpoint and the username/password, you will have access to the AWS CodeCommit repository.

SSH

With SSH authentication, there is no need to install the AWS CLI to connect to your repository. However, you perform some additional configuration tasks.

- Your IAM user must have the ability to manage their own SSH keys. To accomplish this, you add the IAMUserSSHKeys managed policy to the account.
- Scaling to handle rapid release cycles and large repositories.
- For Windows users, install a bash emulator, such as Git Bash.

To configure SSH authentication to AWS CodeCommit repositories, follow these steps:

1. In the IAM console, select the user account you want to modify.
2. Upload the public SSH key on the Security Credentials tab.
3. Copy the SSH key identity (ID). This follows the form APKAEIGHANK3EXAMPLE.

4. Update the ~/.ssh/config file on your workstation to include these contents:

```
Host git-codecommit.*.amazonaws.com
User YOUR_SSH_KEY_ID
IdentityFile YOUR_PRIVATE_KEY_FILE
```

5. To verify the configuration, test a simple SSH connection to the AWS CodeCommit endpoint, as shown here:

```
# Format: ssh git-codecommit.[REGION_CODE].amazonaws.com
ssh git-codecommit.us-east-1.amazonaws.com
```

Use the Credential Helper

The previous HTTPS and SSH authentication methods both rely on additional credentials aside from IAM access/secret keys. It is also possible to authenticate to AWS CodeCommit with IAM credentials and the *AWS CodeCommit credential helper*. The credential helper translates IAM credentials to those that AWS CodeCommit can use to perform Git actions, such as to clone a repository or merge a pull request. To configure the credential helper on your workstation, do the following:

1. Install and configure the AWS CLI.

2. Install Git.

3. Configure Git to leverage the credential helper from the AWS CLI with these commands:

```
git config --global \
credential.helper '!aws codecommit credential-helper $@'

git config --global credential.UseHttpPath true
```

Once complete, HTTPS interactions with the AWS CodeCommit repository should work as expected.

 The credential helper authentication method is the only one available for root and federated IAM Users.

Development Tools and Integrated Development Environment

AWS CodeCommit integrates automatically with any development tools that support IAM credentials. Additionally, after you set up HTTPS Git credentials, you are able to use any tools that support this authentication mechanism instead. Examples of supported integrated development environment (IDE) include the following:

▪ AWS Cloud9

▪ Eclipse

▪ IntelliJ

▪ Visual Studio

Repository

A *repository* (repo) is the foundation of AWS CodeCommit. This is the location where you store source code files, track revisions, and merge contributions (commits). When you create a repository, it will contain an empty master branch by default. To configure additional branches and commit code changes, you connect the repository to a local workstation where changes can be made before you upload or push them.

> Repository names must be unique within an individual AWS account; however, you can change them without re-creating the repository. When you change a repository name, you need to update any local copies of the repository to have their remote point to the new HTTPS or SSH URL with the git remote add command.

Repository Notifications

AWS CodeCommit supports triggers via Amazon SNS, which you can use to leverage other AWS services for post-commit actions, such as firing a webhook with AWS Lambda after a commit is pushed to a development branch. To implement this, AWS CodeCommit uses AWS CloudWatch Events. You create event rules that trigger for each of the event types that you select in AWS CodeCommit. Event types that will fire notifications include the following:

- Pull Request Update Events
- Create a Pull Request
- Close a Pull Request
- Update Code in a Pull Request
- Title or Description Changes
- Pull Request Comment Events
- Commit Comment Events
- Comments on Code Changes
- Comments on Files in a Commit
- Comments on the Commit Itself

> If you change the name of the repository through the AWS CLI or SDK, the notifications cease to function. (This behavior is not present when you change names in the AWS Management Console.) To restore lost notifications, delete the settings and configure them a second time.

Repository Triggers

Repository triggers are not the same as notifications, as the events that fire each differ greatly. Use *repository triggers* to send notifications to Amazon SNS or AWS Lambda during these events:

- Push to Existing Branch
- Create a Branch or Tag
- Delete a Branch or Tag

Triggers are similar in functionality to webhooks used by other Git providers, like GitHub. You can use triggers to perform automated tasks such as to start external builds, to notify administrators of code pushes, or to perform unit tests. There are some restrictions on how to configure triggers.

- The trigger destination, Amazon SNS or AWS Lambda, must exist in the same AWS region as the repository.
- If the destination is Amazon SNS in another AWS account, the Amazon SNS topic must have a policy that allows notifications from the account that contains the repository.

Cross-Account Access to a Different Account

In some situations, the repository that contains the application source code may be located in a separate AWS account from the IAM user/role attempting to access it. In these situations, there are several steps that you must perform in the *repository account* and the *user account*.

Repository Account Actions

1. Create a policy for access to the repository. This policy should allow users in the user account to access one or more specific repositories, as well as (optionally) to view a list of all repositories.
2. Attach this policy to a role in the same account, and allow users in the user account to assume this role.

User Account Actions

1. Create an IAM user or IAM group. This user or group will be able to access the repository after the next step.
2. Assign a policy to the user or group that allows them to assume the role created in the repository account as part of the previous steps.

Once these steps are complete, the IAM user will first need to assume the cross-account role before you attempt to clone or otherwise access the repository. You adjust the AWS credentials file ~/.aws/config (Linux/macOS) or drive:\Users\username\.aws\config (Windows). A profile will be added to this config file that specifies the cross-account role to assume.

```
[profile MyCrossAccountProfile]
region = US East (Ohio)
role_arn=arn:aws:iam:111122223333:role/MyCrossAccountContributorRole
source_profile=default
```

Lastly, you need to modify the AWS CLI credential helper so that you use MyCrossAccountProfile.

```
git config --global credential.helper \
  '!aws codecommit credential-helper --profile MyCrossAccountProfile $@'
```

From this point, the IAM user in the user account will be able to clone and interact with the repository in the repository account.

Files

A *file* is a piece of data that is subject to version control by AWS CodeCommit. AWS CodeCommit tracks any modifications made to this file on a per-line level. You use the Git client to push changes in a file to the repository, where it tracks against other changes in previous commits.

Pull Requests

Pull requests are the primary vehicle on which you review and merge code changes between branches. Unlike branch merging, pull requests allow multiple users to comment on changes before they merge with the destination branch. The typical workflow of a pull request is as follows:

1. Create a new branch off the default branch for the feature or bug fix.

2. Make changes to the branch files, commit, and push to the remote repository.

3. Create a pull request for the changes to integrate them with the default branch, as shown in Figure 7.8.

4. Other users can review the changes in the pull request and provide comments, as shown in Figure 7.9.

5. You can push any additional changes from user feedback to the same branch to include them in the pull request.

6. Once all reviewers provide approval, the pull request merges into the default branch and closes. You can close pull requests when you merge the branches locally or when you close the request via the AWS CodeCommit console or the AWS CLI.

FIGURE 7.8 Creating a pull request

FIGURE 7.9 Reviewing changes

Commits

Commits are point-in-time changes to contents of files in a repository. A commit is not a new copy of the file, but it is instead a way to track changes in the line(s) in a file, by whom, and when. When you push a commit to the repository, AWS CodeCommit tracks the following file changes:

- Author Name
- Author Email
- Commit Message

Commits to a repository in AWS CodeCommit can be made in one of two ways. The most common workflow is to use the Git CLI and update the repository using `git push`. The AWS CLI supports the `aws codecommit put-file` action, which allows you to update a file on the repository with a local copy and specify a branch, parent commit, and message.

```
aws codecommit put-file --repository-name MyDemoRepo \
  --branch-name feature-branch \
  --file-content file://MyDirectory/ExampleFile.txt \
  --file-path /solutions/ExampleFile.txt \
  --parent-commit-id 11112222EXAMPLE \
  --name "Developer" \
  --email developer@myexamplesite.com \
  --commit-message "Fixed a bug"
```

The AWS CodeCommit console supports viewing differences between commits. To view differences between a commit and its parent, open the Commits pane on the repository dashboard and then select the commit ID, as shown in Figure 7.10.

FIGURE 7.10   Selecting the commit ID

After doing so, you can view changes in this commit either side by side (*Split view*) or in the same pane (*Unified view*), as shown in Figure 7.11.

FIGURE 7.11 Split view

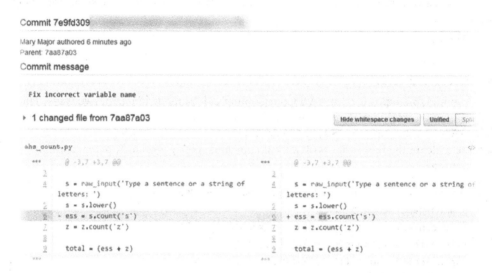

You can also view differences between arbitrary commit IDs in the same repository. In the Compare window of the repository dashboard, you can choose two commit IDs for comparison, as shown in Figure 7.12.

FIGURE 7.12 Select and compare

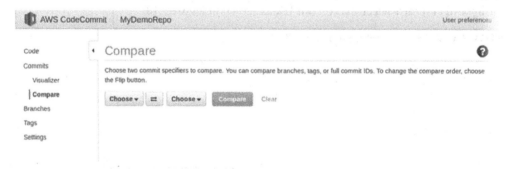

After you select two commit IDs, click the Compare button. This will provide a similar split or unified view of changes.

Branches

Branches are ways to separate and organize groups of commits. This allows developers to organize work in a meaningful fashion, separating changes into logical groups based on the feature or bug-fix being developed. For example, as you can see in Figure 7.13, a single repository may have branches for each environment: dev, test, and prod. Or, individual features and bug fixes can have separate branches.

FIGURE 7.13   Branch view

A *default branch* is the base when you clone the repository. When you clone a repository to your local machine, the default branch (such as "master" or "prod") clones. You cannot delete the default branch until a new branch is set as default, or you will delete the entire repository.

> You can change the default branch for a repository, but first the new default branch must exist in the remote repository.

Migrate to AWS CodeCommit

This section details how to migrate a Git repository, unversioned files, or another repository type, and it is important when you migrate a high volume of or large files.

Migrate a Git Repository

You use an AWS CodeCommit to migrate from a Git repository, as shown in Figure 7.14.

FIGURE 7.14 Migrating from a Git repository

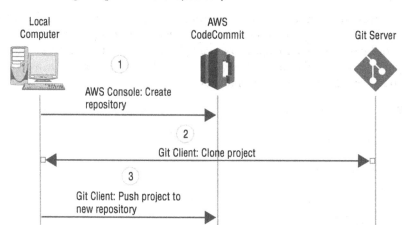

The first step is to create the AWS CodeCommit repository (via either the AWS Management Console or the AWS CLI or AWS SDK). After you create the repository, clone the project to a local workstation. To push this repository to AWS CodeCommit, set the repository's remote to the AWS CodeCommit repository's HTTPS or SSH URL.

```
git push \
  https://git-codecommit.us-east-2.amazonaws.com/v1/repos/MyClonedRepository \
  --all
```

If you need to push any tags to the new repository, run the following code:

```
git push \
  https://git-codecommit.us-east-2.amazonaws.com/v1/repos/MyClonedRepository \
  --tags
```

Migrate Unversioned Content

You can migrate any local or unversioned content to AWS CodeCommit in a similar manner, as if the content exists in another Git-based repository service. The primary difference is that you set up a new repository instead of cloning an existing one to migrate. Refer to Figure 7.15.

First create the AWS CodeCommit repository (either via the AWS Management Console or via the AWS CLI or AWS SDK). Next, create a local directory with the files to migrate, and run `git init` from the command line or terminal in that directory. This will initialize the directory to work with Git so that any file changes are tracked. After the directory initializes, run `git add .` to add all current files to Git. Run `git commit -m 'Initial Commit'` to generate a commit. Lastly, push the commit to AWS CodeCommit with `git push https://git-codecommit.us-east-2.amazonaws.com/v1/repos/MyFirstRepo --all`.

FIGURE 7.15 Migrating unversioned content

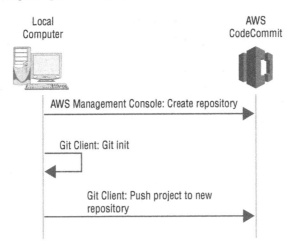

Migrate Incrementally

For large repositories, you can migrate in incremental steps and push many smaller files. This prevents any network issues that may cause the entire push to fail. If any smaller commit fails, it is a trivial matter to restart it when you compare it to a single, monolithic commit.

Additionally, when you push large repositories, AWS recommends that you use SSH over HTTPS, as there is a chance that the HTTPS connection may terminate because of various network or firewall issues.

AWS CodeCommit Service Limits

AWS CodeCommit enforces the service limits in Table 7.2. An asterisk (*) indicates limits that require you to submit a request to AWS Support to increase the limits.

TABLE 7.2 AWS CodeCommit Service Limits

Limit	Value
Repositories per account*	1,000
References per push	4,000
Triggers per repository	10
Git blob size	2 GB

Using AWS CodeCommit with AWS CodePipeline

You can use AWS CodeCommit as a source action in your pipeline. This allows you to utilize a highly available, redundant version control system as the initialization point of your CI/CD pipeline.

When you select AWS CodeCommit as the source provider, you must provide a repository name and branch. If you use AWS CodeCommit, it creates an Amazon CloudWatch Events rule and an IAM role to monitor the repository and branch for changes, as shown in Figure 7.16.

FIGURE 7.16 Source location

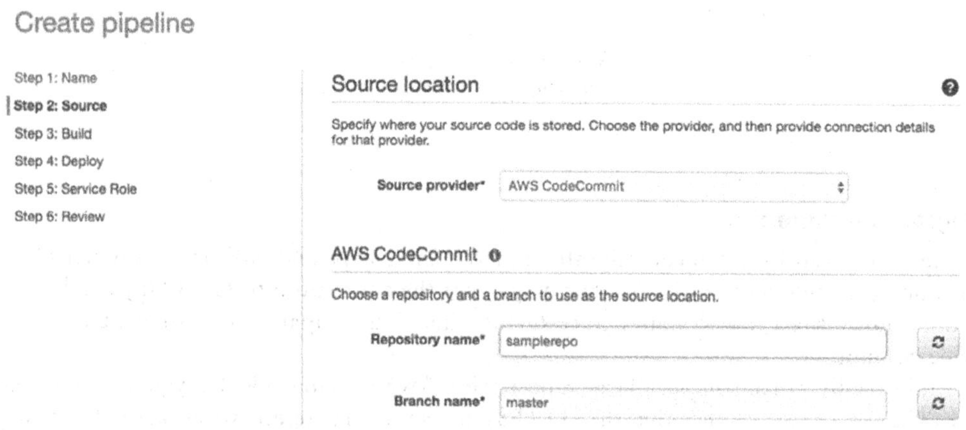

One issue that can arise is if you store large binary files. Because of the system Git uses to track file changes, Git creates a new copy of every modification to a binary file within the repository. Over time, this can cause repositories to grow rapidly in size. Instead of storing binary files in AWS CodeCommit, add an additional Amazon S3 source action to the pipeline. If you store large binary files in Amazon S3, you can reduce the overall cost and development time because of the reduction of time it takes to push/pull commits. Since Amazon S3 already supports versioning (and requires it for use with AWS CodePipeline), changes to binary objects will still be tracked so that rollbacks are straightforward.

Using AWS CodeBuild to Create Build Artifacts

AWS CodeBuild is a fully managed build service that compiles source code, runs tests, and produces software packages that are ready to deploy. With AWS CodeBuild, you do not need to provision, manage, and scale your own build servers. AWS CodeBuild scales continuously and processes multiple builds concurrently, so your builds do not wait in a queue. AWS

CodeBuild has prepackaged build environments, or you can create custom build environments that use your own build tools. With AWS CodeBuild, AWS charges by the minute for the compute resources you use.

What Is AWS CodeBuild?

AWS CodeBuild enables you to define the build environment to perform build tasks and the actual tasks that it will perform. AWS CodeBuild comes with prepackaged build environments for most common workloads and build tools (Apache Maven, Grade, and others), and it allows you to create custom environments for any custom tools or processes.

AWS CodePipeline includes built-in integration with AWS CodeBuild, which can act as a provider for any build or test actions in your pipeline, as shown in Figure 7.17.

FIGURE 7.17 Using AWS CodeBuild in AWS CodePipeline

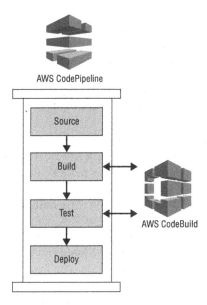

AWS CodeBuild Concepts

AWS CodeBuild initiates build tasks inside a build project, which defines the environmental settings, build steps to perform, and any output artifacts. The build container's operating system, runtime, and build tools make up the build environment.

Build Projects

Build projects define all aspects of a build. This includes the environment in which to perform builds, any tools to include in the environment, the actual build steps to perform, and outputs to save.

Create a Build Project

When you create a build project, you first select a source provider. AWS CodeBuild supports AWS CodeCommit, Amazon S3, GitHub, and BitBucket as source providers. When you use GitHub or BitBucket, a separate authentication flow will be invoked. This allows access to the source repository from AWS CodeBuild. GitHub source repositories also support webhooks to trigger builds automatically any time you push a commit to a specific repository and branch.

After AWS CodeBuild successfully connects to the source repository or location, you select a *build environment*. AWS CodeBuild provides preconfigured build environments for some operating systems, runtimes, and runtime versions, such as Ubuntu with Java 9.

Next, you will configure the *build specification*. This can be done in one of two ways. You can insert build commands in the console or specify a buildspec.yml file in your source code. Both options are valid, but if you use a buildspec.yml file, you will see additional configuration options.

If your build creates artifacts you would like to use in later steps of your pipeline/process, you can specify *output artifacts* to save to Amazon S3. Otherwise, you can choose not to save any artifacts. You will need to specify individual filename(s) for AWS CodeBuild to save on your behalf.

AWS CodeBuild supports caching, which you can configure in the next step. Caching saves some components of the build environment to reduce the time to create environments when you submit build jobs.

Every build project requires an IAM service role that is accessible by AWS CodeBuild. When you create new projects, you can automatically create a service role that you restrict to this project only. You can update service roles to work with up to 10 build projects at a time.

Lastly, you can configure AWS CodeBuild to create build environments with connectivity to an Amazon Virtual Private Cloud (Amazon VPC) in your account. To do so, specify the Amazon VPC ID, subnets, and security groups to assign to the build environment. You can configure other settings when you create the build, such as to run the Docker daemon in privileged mode to build Docker images.

After you set the build project properties, you can select the compute type (memory and vCPU settings), any environment variables to pass to the build container, and tags to apply to the project.

When you set environment variables, they will be visible in plain text in the AWS CodeBuild console and AWS CLI or SDK. If there is sensitive information that you would like to pass to build jobs, consider using the *AWS Systems Manager Parameter Store*. This will require the build project's IAM role to have permissions to access the parameter store.

Build Specification (buildspec.yml)

The `buildspec.yml` file can provide the build specification to your build projects in the AWS CodeBuild console, the AWS CLI, or the AWS SDK when you create the build project, or as part of your source repository in a YAML-formatted `buildspec.yml` file. You can supply only one build specification to a build project. A build specification's format is as follows:

```
version: 0.2

env:
  variables:
    key: "value"
  parameter-store:
    key: "value"

phases:
  install:
    commands:
      - command
  pre_build:
    commands:
      - command
  build:
    commands:
      - command
  post_build:
    commands:
      - command
artifacts:
  files:
    - location
  discard-paths: yes
  base-directory: location
cache:
  paths:
    - path
```

Version

AWS supports multiple build specification versions; however, AWS recommends you use the latest version whenever possible.

Environment Variables (env)

You can add optional environment variables to build jobs. Any key/value pairs that you provide in the variables section are available as environment variables in plain text.

 Any environment variables that you define here will overwrite those you define elsewhere in the build project, such as those in the container itself or by Docker.

The parameter-store mapping specifies parameters to query in AWS Systems Manager Parameter Store.

Phases

The phases mapping specifies commands to run at each stage of the build job. When you specify build settings in the AWS CodeBuild console, AWS CLI, or AWS SDK, you are not able to separate commands into phases. With a build specifications file, you can separate commands into phases.

install   Commands to execute during installation of the build environment.

pre_build   Commands to be run before the build begins.

build   Commands to be run during the build.

post_build   Commands to be run after the build completes.

 If a command fails in any stage, subsequent stages will not run.

Artifacts

The artifacts mapping specifies where AWS CodeBuild will place output artifacts, if any. This is required only if your build job produces actual outputs. For example, unit tests would not produce output artifacts for later use in a pipeline. The files list specifies individual files in the build environment that will act as output artifacts. You can specify individual files, directories, or recursive directories. You can use discard-paths and base-directory to specify a different directory structure to package output artifacts.

Cache

If you configure caching for the build project, the cache map specifies which files to upload to Amazon S3 for use in subsequent builds.

Build Project Cache

This example sets the JAVA_HOME and LOGIN_PASSWORD environment variables (the latter is retrieved from AWS Systems Manager Parameter Store), installs updates in the build environment, runs a Maven installation, and saves the .jar output to Amazon S3 as a build artifact. For future builds, the content of the /root/.m2 directory (and any subdirectories) is cached to Amazon S3.

```
version: 0.2

env:
  variables:
    JAVA_HOME: "/usr/lib/jvm/java-8-openjdk-amd64"
  parameter-store:
    LOGIN_PASSWORD: "dockerLoginPassword"

phases:
  install:
    commands:
      - echo Entered the install phase...
      - apt-get update -y
      - apt-get install -y maven
  pre_build:
    commands:
      - echo Entered the pre_build phase...
      - docker login -u User -p $LOGIN_PASSWORD
  build:
    commands:
      - echo Entered the build phase...
      - echo Build started on 'date'
      - mvn install
  post_build:
    commands:
      - echo Entered the post_build phase...
      - echo Build completed on 'date'
artifacts:
  files:
    - target/messageUtil-1.0.jar
  discard-paths: yes
cache:
  paths:
    - '/root/.m2/**/*'
```

Build Environments

A *build environment* is a Docker image with a preconfigured operating system, programming language runtime, and any other tools that AWS CodeBuild uses to perform build tasks and communicate with the service, along with other metadata for the environment, such as the compute settings. AWS CodeBuild maintains its own repository of preconfigured build environments. If these environments do not meet your requirements, you can use public Docker Hub images. Alternatively, you can use container images in Amazon Elastic Container Registry (Amazon ECR).

AWS CodeBuild Environments

AWS CodeBuild provides build environments for Ubuntu and Amazon Linux operating systems, and it supports the following:

- Android
- Docker
- Golang
- Java
- Node.js
- PHP
- Python
- Ruby
- .NET Core

> Not all programming languages support both Ubuntu and Amazon Linux build environments.

Compute Types

Table 7.3 lists the memory, virtual central processing unit (vCPU), and disk space configurations for build environments.

TABLE 7.3 Compute Configurations for Build Environments

Compute Type	Memory	vCPUs	Disk Space
BUILD_GENERAL1_SMALL	3 GB	2	64 GB
BUILD_GENERAL1_MEDIUM	7 GB	4	128 GB
BUILD_GENERAL1_LARGE	15 GB	8	128 GB

Environment Variables

AWS CodeBuild provides several environment variables by default, such as AWS_REGION, CODEBUILD_BUILD_ID, and HOME.

> When you create your own environment variables, AWS CodeBuild reserves the CODEBUILD_ prefix.

Builds

When you initiate a build, AWS CodeBuild copies the input artifact(s) into the build environment. AWS CodeBuild uses the build specification to run the build process, which includes any steps to perform and outputs to provide after the build completes. Build logs are made available to Amazon CloudWatch Logs for real-time monitoring.

When you run builds manually in the AWS CodeBuild console, AWS CLI, or AWS SDK, you have the option to change several properties before you run a build job.

- Source version (Amazon S3)
- Source branch, version, and Git clone depth (AWS CodeCommit, GitHub, and Bitbucket)
- Output artifact type, name, or location
- Build timeout
- Environment variables

AWS CodeBuild Service Limits

AWS CodeBuild enforces service limits in Table 7.4. An asterisk (*) indicates that you can increase limits if you submit a request to AWS Support.

TABLE 7.4 AWS CodeBuild Service Limits

Limit	Value
Build projects per region per account*	1,000
Build timeout	8 hours
Concurrently running builds*	20

Using AWS CodeBuild with AWS CodePipeline

AWS CodePipeline enables you to build jobs for both build and test actions. Both action types require exactly one input artifact and may return zero or one output artifacts. When you create a build or test actions in your pipeline with your build projects, the only input that you require is the build project name. The AWS CodePipeline console also has the option to create new build projects when you create the action, as shown in Figure 7.18.

FIGURE 7.18   Build provider

Using AWS CodeDeploy to Deploy Applications

AWS CodeDeploy is a service that automates software deployments to a variety of compute services, such as Amazon EC2, AWS Lambda, and instances running on-premises. AWS CodeDeploy makes it easier for you to release new features rapidly, helps you avoid downtime through application deployment, and handles the complexity to update your applications. You can use AWS CodeDeploy to automate software deployments and eliminate the need for error-prone manual operations. The service scales to match your deployment needs, from a single AWS Lambda function to thousands of Amazon EC2 instances.

What Is AWS CodeDeploy?

AWS CodeDeploy standardizes and automates deployments of any types of content or configuration to Amazon EC2 instances, on-premises servers, or AWS Lambda functions. Because of its flexibility, it is not restricted to deploy only application code, and it can perform various administrative tasks that are part of your deployment process. Additionally, you can create custom deployment configurations tailored to your specific infrastructure needs.

AWS CodeDeploy and NGINX

You can install and enable NGINX as part of a deployment of configuration files to reverse proxy instances. The service itself does not involve any changes to your current source code, and it only requires you to install a lightweight agent on any managed instances or on-premises servers.

Should deployments fail in your environment, you can configure AWS CodeDeploy with a predetermined failure tolerance. Once this tolerance is breached, deployment will automatically roll back to the last version that works.

You can automate deployment of AWS CodeDeploy with AWS Lambda functions through traffic switching. When updates to functions deploy, AWS CodeDeploy will create new versions of each updated function and gradually route requests from the previous version to the updated function. AWS Lambda functions also support custom deployment configurations, which can specify the rate and percentage of traffic to switch.

AWS CodeDeploy Concepts

When you deploy to Amazon EC2/on-premises instances, a revision occurs.

Revision

A *revision* is an artifact that contains both application files to deploy and an AppSpec configuration file. Application files can include compiled libraries, configuration files, installation packages, static media, and other content. The AppSpec file specifies what steps AWS CodeDeploy will follow when it performs deployments of an individual revision.

A revision must contain any source files and scripts to execute on the target instance inside a root directory. Within this root directory, the appspec.yml file must exist at the topmost level and *not* in any subfolders.

```
/tmp/ or c:\temp (root folder)
  |--content (subfolder)
  |    |--myTextFile.txt
  |    |--mySourceFile.rb
  |    |--myExecutableFile.exe
  |    |--myInstallerFile.msi
```

```
|    |--myPackage.rpm
|    |--myImageFile.png
|--scripts (subfolder)
|    |--myShellScript.sh
|    |--myBatchScript.bat
|    |--myPowerShellScript.ps1
|--appspec.yml
```

When you deploy to AWS Lambda, a revision contains only the AppSpec file. It contains information about the functions to deploy, as well as the steps to validate that the deployment was successful.

In either case, when a code revision is ready to deploy, you package it into an archive file and store it in one of these three repositories:

- Amazon S3

- GitHub

- Bitbucket

When you use GitHub or Bitbucket, the source code does not need to be a .zip archive, as AWS CodeDeploy will package the repository contents on your behalf. Amazon S3, however, requires a .zip archive file.

AWS Lambda deployments support only Amazon S3 buckets as a source repository.

Deployments

A *deployment* is the process of copying content and executing scripts on instances in your deployment group. To accomplish this, AWS CodeDeploy performs the tasks outlined in the AppSpec configuration file. For both Amazon EC2/on-premises instances and AWS Lambda functions, the deployment succeeds or fails based on whether individual AppSpec tasks complete successfully. *There are two types of deployments supported by AWS CodeDeploy: in-place and blue/green.*

In-Place Deployments

In *in-place deployments*, revisions deploy to new infrastructure instead of an existing one. After deployment completes successfully, the new infrastructure gradually replaces old code in a phased rollout. After all traffic routes to the new infrastructure, you can keep the old code for review or discard it.

On-premises instances do not support blue/green deployments.

Blue/Green Deployments

When you deploy to AWS Lambda functions, *blue/green deployments* publish new versions of each function, after which traffic shifting routes requests to the new function versions according to the deployment configuration that you define.

Stop Deployments

You can stop deployments via the AWS CodeDeploy console or AWS CLI. If you stop deployments to Amazon EC2/on-premises instances, this can result in some deployment groups being left in an undesired deployment state. For example, when you deploy to instances in an Auto Scaling group, if you stop the deployment, it may result in some instances having different application versions. In situations where this occurs, you can configure the application to roll back to the last valid deployment automatically. To do this, you submit a new deployment to the instances with the previous revision, and they appear as a new deployment in the console.

> Some instances that fail the most recent deployment may still have scripts run or files placed that are part of the failed deployment. If you configure automatic rollbacks, AWS CodeDeploy will attempt to remove any successfully created files.

Rollbacks

AWS CodeDeploy achieves automatic rollbacks by redeploying the last working revision to any instances in the deployment group (this will generate a new deployment ID). If you do not configure automatic rollbacks for the application, you can perform a manual rollback by redeploying a previous revision as a new deployment. This will accomplish the same result as an automatic rollback.

During the rollback process, AWS CodeDeploy will attempt to remove any file(s) that were created on the instance during the failed deployment. A record of the created files is kept in the location on your instances.

Linux: `/opt/codedeploy-agent/deployment-root/deployment-instructions/` `[deployment-group-id]-cleanup`

Windows: `C:\ProgramData\Amazon\CodeDeploy\deployment-instructions\` `[deployment-group-id]-cleanup`

The *AWS CodeDeploy agent* that runs on the instance will reference this cleanup file as a record of what files were created during the last deployment.

> By default, AWS CodeDeploy will not overwrite any files that were not created as part of a deployment. You can override this setting for new deployments.

AWS CodeDeploy tracks cleanup files; however, script executions are not tracked. Any configuration or modification to the instance that is done by scripts run on your instance cannot be rolled back automatically by AWS CodeDeploy. As an administrator, you will be responsible for implementing logic in your deployment scripts to ensure that the desired state is reached during deployments and rollbacks.

Test Deployments Locally

If you would like to test whether a revision will successfully deploy to an instance you are able to access, you can use the codedeploy-local command in the AWS CodeDeploy agent. This command will search the execution path for an AppSpec file and any content to deploy. If this is found, the agent will attempt a deployment on the instance and provide feedback on the results. This provides a useful alternative to executing the full workflow when you want simply to validate the deployment package.

The following example command attempts to perform a local deployment of an archive file located in Amazon S3:

```
codedeploy-local --bundle-location s3://mybucket/bundle.tgz --type tgz
```

The codedeploy-local command requires the AWS CodeDeploy agent that you install on the instance or on-premises server where you execute the command.

Deployment Group

A *deployment group* designates the Amazon EC2/on-premises instances that a revision deploys. When you deploy to AWS Lambda functions, this specifies what functions will deploy new versions. Deployment groups also specify alarms that trigger automatic rollbacks after a specified number or percentage of instances, or functions fail their deployment.

For Amazon EC2 on-premises deployments, you can add instances to a deployment group based on tag name/value pairs or Amazon EC2 Auto Scaling group names. An individual application can have one or more deployment groups defined. This allows you to separate groups of instances into environments so that changes can be progressively rolled out and tested before going to production. You can identify instances by individual tags or tag groups. If an instance matches one or more tags in a tag group, it is associated with the deployment group. If you would like to require that an instance match multiple tags, each tag must be in a separate tag group. A single deployment group supports up to 10 tags in up to three tag groups.

In Figure 7.19, if tags Environment, Region, and Type are present in tag groups 1, 2, and 3 respectively, then instances must have at least one tag in each tag group to identify with the deployment group.

FIGURE 7.19   Selecting instances with multiple tags

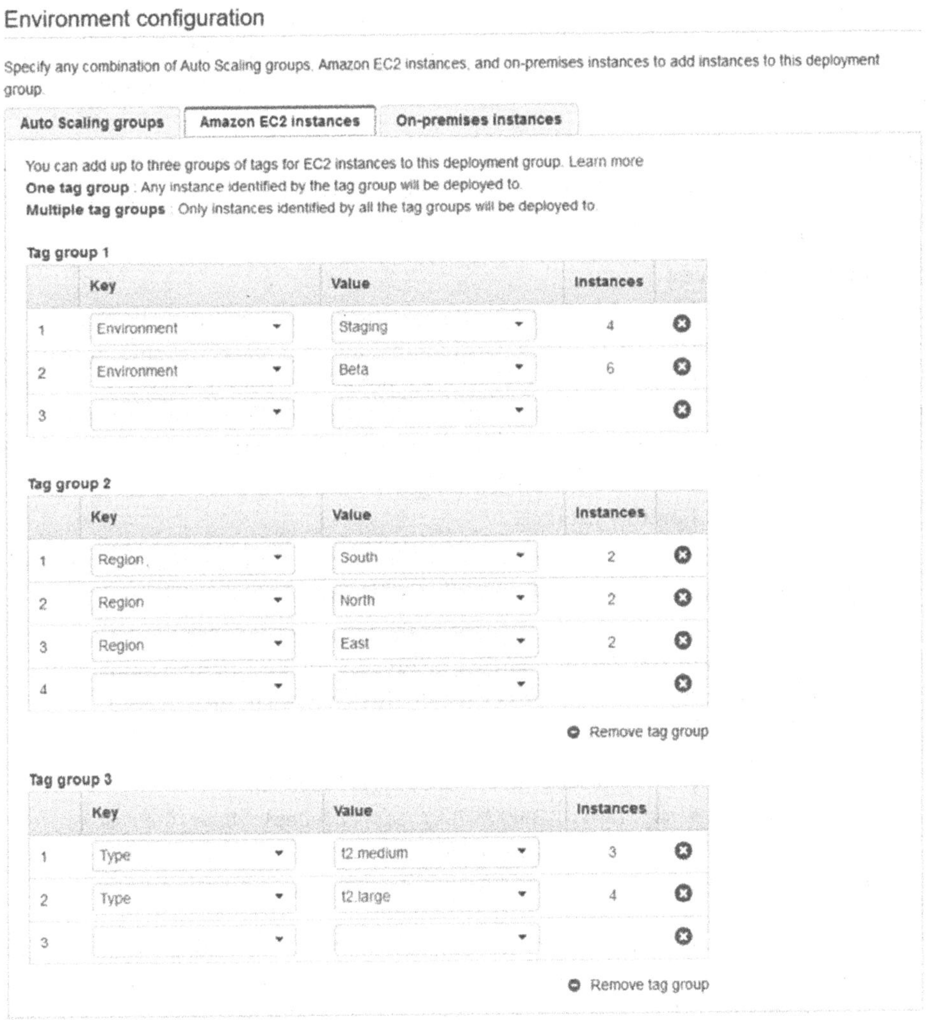

Environment configuration

Specify any combination of Auto Scaling groups, Amazon EC2 instances, and on-premises instances to add instances to this deployment group.

Auto Scaling groups	**Amazon EC2 instances**	On-premises instances

You can add up to three groups of tags for EC2 instances to this deployment group. Learn more
One tag group : Any instance identified by the tag group will be deployed to.
Multiple tag groups : Only instances identified by all the tag groups will be deployed to.

Tag group 1

	Key	Value	Instances	
1	Environment ▼	Staging ▼	4	✕
2	Environment ▼	Beta ▼	6	✕
3	▼	▼		✕

Tag group 2

	Key	Value	Instances	
1	Region ▼	South ▼	2	✕
2	Region ▼	North ▼	2	✕
3	Region ▼	East ▼	2	✕
4	▼	▼		✕

⊖ Remove tag group

Tag group 3

	Key	Value	Instances	
1	Type ▼	t2.medium ▼	3	✕
2	Type ▼	t2.large ▼	4	✕
3	▼	▼		✕

⊖ Remove tag group

When you create deployment groups, you can also configure the following:

Amazon SNS notifications   Any recipients that subscribe to the topic will receive notifications when deployment events occur. You must create the topic before you configure this notification, and the AWS CodeDeploy service role must have permission to publish messages to the topic.

Amazon CloudWatch alarms   You can configure alarms to trigger cancellation and roll-back of deployments whenever the metric has passed a certain threshold. For example, you could configure an alarm to trigger when CPU utilization exceeds a certain percentage for instances in an AWS Auto Scaling group. If this alarm triggers, the deployment automatically rolls back. For AWS Lambda deployments, you can configure alarms to monitor function invocation errors.

Automatic rollbacks   You can configure rollbacks to initiate automatically when a deploy-ment fails or based on Amazon CloudWatch alarms. To test deployments, you can disable automatic rollbacks when you create a new deployment.

On-Premises Instances

You can host instances for an Amazon EC2 on-premises deployment group in either an AWS account or your own data center. To configure an on-premises instance to work with AWS CodeDeploy, you must complete several tasks. Before you begin, you need to ensure that the instance has the ability to communicate with AWS CodeDeploy service endpoints over HTTPS (port 443). You will also need to create an IAM user that the instance assumes and has permissions to interact with AWS CodeDeploy.

1. Install the AWS CLI on the instance.

2. Configure the AWS CLI with an IAM user. Call the `aws configure` command, and specify the secret key ID and secret access key of the IAM user.

3. Register the instance with AWS CodeDeploy. Call the `aws codedeploy register` AWS CLI command from the on-premises instance. Provide a unique name with the `--instance-name` property. When you execute this command, include an IAM user to associate with the instance and tags to apply.

    ```
    aws deploy register --instance-name AssetTag12010298EX \
    --iam-user-arn arn:aws:iam::8039EXAMPLE:user/CodeDeployUser-OnPrem \
    --tags Key=Name,Value=CodeDeloyDemo-OnPrem \
    --region us-west-2
    ```

4. Register the instance with AWS CodeDeploy. Install the AWS CodeDeploy agent. Run the `aws codedeploy install` AWS CLI command. By default, it will install a basic configuration file with preconfigured settings. If you would like to override this, you can provide your own configuration file with the `--config-file` parameter. If you specify the `--override-config` parameter, this will override the current configuration file on the instance.

    ```
    aws deploy install --override-config \
    --config-file /tmp/codedeploy.onpremises.yml \
    --region us-west-2
    ```

After you complete the previous steps, the instance will be available for deployments to the deployment group(s).

Deploy to Amazon EC2 Auto Scaling Groups

When you deploy to Amazon EC2 Auto Scaling groups, AWS CodeDeploy will automatically run the latest successful deployment on any new instances created when the group scales out. If the deployment fails on an instance, it updates to maintain the count of healthy instances. For this reason, AWS does not recommend that you associate the same Auto Scaling group with multiple deployment groups (for example, you want to deploy multiple applications to the same Auto Scaling group). If both deployment groups perform a deployment at roughly the same time and the first deployment fails on the new instance, it terminates by AWS CodeDeploy. The second deployment, unaware that the instance terminated, will not fail until the deployment times out (*the default timeout value is 1 hour*). Instead, you should combine your application deployments into one or consider the use of multiple Auto Scaling groups with smaller instance types.

Deployment Configuration

You use *deployment configurations* to drive how quickly Amazon EC2/on-premises instances update by AWS CodeDeploy. You can configure deployments to deploy to all instances in a deployment group at once or subgroups of instances at a time, or you can create an entire new group of instances (*blue/green deployment*). A deployment configuration also specifies the fault tolerance of deployments, so you can roll back changes if a specified number or percentage of instances or functions in your deployment group fail to complete their deployments and signal success back to AWS CodeDeploy.

Amazon EC2 On-Premises Deployment Configurations

When you deploy to Amazon EC2/on-premises instances, you can configure either in-place or blue/green deployments.

In-Place deployments   These deployments recycle currently running instances and deploy revisions on existing instances.

Blue/Green deployments   These deployments replace currently running instances with sets of newly created instances.

In both scenarios, you can specify wait times between groups of deployed instances (batches). Additionally, if you register the deployment group with an *elastic load balancer*, newly deployed instances also register with the load balancer and are subject to its health checks.

The deployment configuration specifies success criteria for deployments, such as the minimum number of healthy instances that must pass health checks during the deployment process. This is done to maintain required availability during application updates. AWS CodeDeploy provides three built-in deployment configurations.

CodeDeployDefault.AllAtOnce

For in-place deployments, AWS CodeDeploy will attempt to deploy to all instances in the deployment group at the same time. The success criteria for this deployment configuration requires that at least once instance succeed for the deployment to be successful. If all instances fail the deployment, then the deployment itself fails.

For blue/green deployments, AWS CodeDeploy will attempt to deploy to the entire set of replacement instances at the same time and follows the same success criteria as in-place deployments. Once deployment to the replacement instances succeeds (at least one instance deploys successfully), traffic routes to all replacement instances at the same time. The deployment fails only if all traffic routing to replacement instances fails.

CodeDeployDefault.HalfAtATime

For in-place deployments, up to half of the instances in the deployment group deploy at the same time (rounded down). Success criteria for this deployment configuration requires that at least half of the instances (rounded up) deploy successfully.

Blue/green deployments use the same rules for the replacement environment, with the exception that the deployment will fail if less than half of the instances in the replacement environment successfully handle rerouted traffic.

CodeDeployDefault.OneAtATime

For in-place and blue/green deployments, this is the most stringent of the built-in deployment configurations, as it requires all instances to deploy the new application revision successfully, with the exception of the final instance in the deployment. For deployment groups with only one instance, the instance must complete successfully for the deployment to complete.

For blue/green deployments, the same rule applies for traffic routing. If all but the last instance registers successfully, the deployment is successful (with the exception of single-instance environments, where it must register without error).

AWS Lambda Deployment Configurations

AWS CodeDeploy handles updates to AWS Lambda functions differently than to Amazon EC2 or on-premises instances. When you deploy to AWS Lambda, the deployment configuration specifies the traffic switching policy to follow, which stipulates how quickly to route requests from the original function versions to the new versions. You can configure AWS CodeDeploy to deploy instances only in a blue/green fashion. AWS Lambda does not support in-place deployments. This is because AWS CodeDeploy will deploy updates to new functions.

AWS CodeDeploy supports three methods for handling traffic switching in an AWS Lambda environment.

Canary

Traffic shifts in two percentage-based increments. The first increment routes to the new function version, and it is monitored for the number of minutes you define. After this time period, the remainder of traffic routes to the new version if the initial increment of request executes.

AWS CodeDeploy provides a number of built-in canary-based deployment configurations, such as `CodeDeployDefault.LambdaCanary10Percent15Minutes`. If you use this deployment configuration, 10 percent of traffic shifts in the first increment and is monitored for 15 minutes. After this time period, the 90 percent of traffic that remains shifts to the new function version. You can create additional configurations as needed.

Linear

Traffic can be shifted in a number of percentage-based increments, with a set number of minutes between each increment. During the waiting period between each increment, the requests routed to the new function versions must complete successfully for the deployment to continue.

AWS CodeDeploy provides a number of built-in linear deployment configurations, such as `CodeDeployDefault.LambdaLinear10PercentEvery1Minute`. With this configuration, 10 percent of traffic is routed to the new function version every minute, until all traffic is routed after 10 minutes.

All-at-Once

All traffic is shifted at once to the new function versions.

Application

An *application* is a logical grouping of a deployment group, revision, and deployment configuration. This serves as a reference to the entire set of objects needed to complete a deployment to your instances or functions.

AppSpec File

The AppSpec configuration file is a JSON or YAML file that manages deployments on instances or functions in your environment. The actual format and purpose of an AppSpec file differs between Amazon EC2/on-premises and AWS Lambda deployments.

Amazon EC2 On-Premises AppSpec

For Amazon EC2 on-premises deployments, the AppSpec file must be YAML formatted and follow the YAML specifications for spacing and indentation. You place the AppSpec file (`appspec.yml`) in the root of the revision's source code directory structure (it cannot be in a subfolder).

When you deploy to Amazon EC2/on-premises instances, the AppSpec file defines the following:

- A mapping of files from the revision and location on the instance
- The permissions of files to deploy
- Scripts to execute throughout the lifecycle of the deployment

The AppSpec file specifies scripts to execute at each stage of the deployment lifecycle. These scripts must exist in the revision for AWS CodeDeploy to call them successfully; however, they can call any other scripts, commands, or tools present on the instance. The AWS CodeDeploy agent uses the hooks section of the AppSpec file to reference which scripts must execute at specific times in the deployment lifecycle. When the deployment is at the specified stage (such as ApplicationStop), the AWS CodeDeploy agent will execute any scripts in that stage in the hooks section of the AppSpec file. *All scripts must return an exit code of 0 to be successful.*

For any files to place on the instance, the AWS CodeDeploy agent refers to the files section of the AppSpec file, where a mapping of files and directories in the revision dictates where on the instance these files reside and with what permissions. Here's an example of an appspec.yml file:

```
version: 0.0
os: linux
files:
  - source: /
    destination: /var/www/html/WordPress
hooks:
  BeforeInstall:
    - location: scripts/install_dependencies.sh
      timeout: 300
      runas: root
  AfterInstall:
    - location: scripts/change_permissions.sh
      timeout: 300
      runas: root
  ApplicationStart:
    - location: scripts/start_server.sh
    - location: scripts/create_test_db.sh
      timeout: 300
      runas: root
  ApplicationStop:
    - location: scripts/stop_server.sh
      timeout: 300
      runas: root
```

In the previous example, the following events occur during deployment:

- During the install phase of the deployment, all files from the revision (source: /) are placed on the instance in the /var/www/html/WordPress directory.

- The `install_dependencies.sh` script (located in the `scripts` directory of the revision) executes during the `BeforeInstall` phase.

- The `change_permissions.sh` script executes in the `AfterInstall` phase.

- The `start_server.sh` and `create_test_db.sh` scripts execute in the `ApplicationStart` phase.

- The `stop_server.sh` script executes in the `ApplicationStop` phase.

The high-level structure of an Amazon EC2 on-premises AppSpec file is as follows:

```
version: 0.0
os: operating-system-name
files:
  source-destination-files-mappings
permissions:
  permissions-specifications
hooks:
  deployment-lifecycle-event-mappings
```

version Currently the only supported version number is 0.0.

os The os section defines the target operating system of the deployment group. Either `windows` or `linux` (Amazon Linux, Ubuntu, or Red Hat Enterprise Linux) is supported.

files The `files` section defines the mapping of revision files and their location to deploy on-instance during the install lifecycle event. This section is not required if no files are being copied from the revision to your instance. The `files` section supports a list of source/destination pairs.

```
files:
  - source: source-file-location
    destination: destination-file-location
```

The source key refers to a file or a directory's local path within the revision (use / for all files in the revision). If source refers to a file, the file copies to `destination`, specified as the fully qualified path on the instance. If source refers to a directory, the directory contents copy to the instance.

permissions For any deployed files or directories, the `permissions` section specifies the permissions to apply to files and directories on the target instance. You can also apply permissions to files on the instance by AWS CodeDeploy using the `files` directive of the AppSpec configuration.

```
permissions:
  - object: object-specification
    pattern: pattern-specification
    except: exception-specification
    owner: owner-account-name
    group: group-name
    mode: mode-specification
    acls:
      - acls-specification
    context:
      user: user-specification
      type: type-specification
      range: range-specification
    type:
      - object-type
```

Each object specification includes a set of files or directories to which the permissions will apply. You can select files based on a pattern expression and ignore them with a comma-delimited list in the except property. The owner, group, and mode properties correspond to their Linux equivalents. You can apply access control lists with the acls property, providing a list of user/group permissions assignments (such as u:ec2-user:rw). The context property is reserved for SELinux-enabled instances. This property corresponds to a set of context labels to apply to objects. Lastly, you use the type property to specify to which types of objects (file or directory) the specified permissions will apply.

NOTE   Windows instances do not support permissions.

hooks   The hooks section specifies the scripts to run at each lifecycle event and under what user context to execute them.

One or more scripts can execute for each *lifecycle hook*.

ApplicationStop   Before the application revision downloads to the instance, this lifecycle event can stop any running services on the instance that would be affected by the update. It is important to note that, since the revision has not yet been downloaded, the scripts execute from the previous revision. Because of this, the ApplicationStop hook does not run on the first deployment to an instance.

DownloadBundle   The AWS CodeDeploy agent uses this lifecycle event to copy application revision files to a temporary location on the instance.

Linux `/opt/codedeploy-agent/deployment-root/[deployment-group-id]/`
`[deployment-id]/deployment-archive`

Windows `C:\ProgramData\Amazon\CodeDeploy\[deployment-group-id]\`
`[deployment-id]\deployment-archive`

This event cannot run custom scripts, as it is reserved for the AWS CodeDeploy agent.

BeforeInstall Use this event for any pre-installation tasks, such as to clear log files or to create backups.

Install This event is reserved for the AWS CodeDeploy agent.

AfterInstall Use this event for any post-installation tasks, such as to modify the application configuration.

ApplicationStart Use this event to start any services that were stopped during the ApplicationStop event.

ValidateService Use this event to verify deployment completed successfully.

If your deployment group is registered with a load balancer, additional lifecycle events become available. These can be used to control certain behaviors as the instance is registered or deregistered from the load balancer.

BeforeBlockTraffic Use this event to run tasks before the instance is deregistered from the load balancer.

BlockTraffic This event is reserved for the AWS CodeDeploy agent.

AfterBlockTraffic Use this event to run tasks after the instance is deregistered from the load balancer.

BeforeAllowTraffic Similar in concept to BeforeBlockTraffic, this event occurs before instances register with the load balancer.

AllowTraffic This event is reserved for the AWS CodeDeploy agent.

AfterAllowTraffic Similar in concept to AfterBlockTraffic, this event occurs after instances register with the load balancer.

```
hooks:
  deployment-lifecycle-event-name:
    - location: script-location
      timeout: timeout-in-seconds
      runas: user-name
```

In the hooks section, the lifecycle name must match one of the previous event names, which are not reserved for the AWS CodeDeploy agent. The location property refers to the relative path in the revision archive where the script is located. You can configure an optional `timeout` to limit how long a script can run before it is considered failed. (Note that this does not stop the script's execution.) *The maximum script duration is 1 hour (3,600 seconds) for each lifecycle event.* Lastly, the runas property can specify the user to execute the script. This user must exist on the instance and cannot require a password.

Figure 7.20 displays lifecycle hooks and their availability for in-place deployments with and without a load balancer.

FIGURE 7.20   Lifecycle hook availability with load balancer

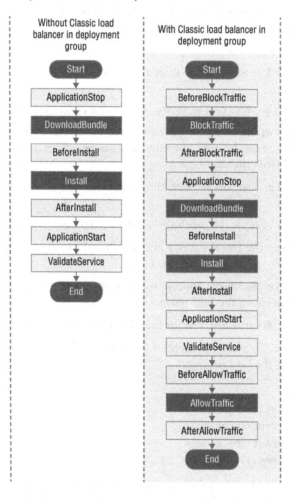

Figure 7.21 displays lifecycle hooks and their availability for blue/green deployments.

FIGURE 7.21 Lifecycle hook availability with blue/green deployments

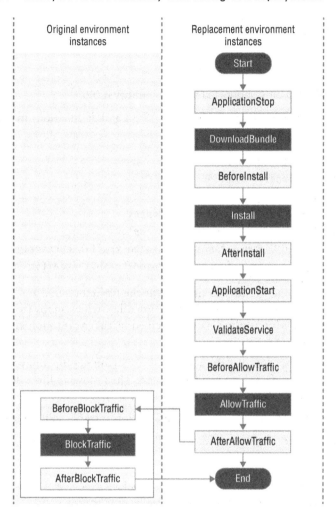

AWS Lambda AppSpec

When you deploy to AWS Lambda functions, the AppSpec file can be in JSON or YAML format, and it specifies the function versions to deploy as well as other functions to execute for validation testing.

AWS Lambda deployments do not use the AWS CodeDeploy agent.

The high-level structure of an AWS Lambda deployment AppSpec file is as follows:

```
version: 0.0
resources:
  lambda-function-specifications
hooks:
  deployment-lifecycle-event-mappings
```

version   Currently the only supported version number is 0.0.

resources   The resources section defines the AWS Lambda functions to deploy.

```
resources:
  - name-of-function-to-deploy:
      type: "AWS::Lambda::Function"
      properties:
        name: name-of-lambda-function-to-deploy
        alias: alias-of-lambda-function-to-deploy
        currentversion: lambda-function-version-traffic-currently-points-to
        targetversion: lambda-function-version-to-shift-traffic-to
```

Name each function in the resources list both as the list item name and in the name property. The alias property specifies the function alias, which maps from the version specified in currentversion to the version specified in targetversion after the update deploys.

hooks   The hooks section specifies the additional AWS Lambda functions to run at specific stages of the deployment lifecycle to validate success. The following lifecycle events support hooks in AWS Lambda deployments:

BeforeAllowTraffic   For running any tasks prior to traffic shifting taking place

AfterAllowTraffic   For any tasks after all traffic shifting has completed

```
hooks:
  - BeforeAllowTraffic: BeforeAllowTrafficHookFunctionName
  - AfterAllowTraffic: AfterAllowTrafficHookFunctionName
```

Figure 7.22 displays the lifecycle hook availability for AWS Lambda deployments.

NOTE   AWS CodeDeploy reserves the Start, AllowTraffic, and End lifecycle events.

FIGURE 7.22   Lifecycle hook availability for AWS Lambda deployments

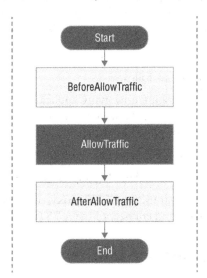

For any functions in the hooks section, the function is responsible for notifying AWS CodeDeploy of success or failure with the `PutLifecycleEventHookExecutionStatus` call API from within your validation function. Here's an example for Node.js:

```
CodeDeploy the prepared validation test results.
codedeploy.putLifecycleEventHookExecutionStatus(params, function(err, data) {
    if (err) {
        // Validation failed.
        callback('Validation test failed');
    } else {
        // Validation succeeded.
        callback(null, 'Validation test succeeded');
    }
});
```

AWS CodeDeploy Agent

The *AWS CodeDeploy agent* is responsible for driving and validating deployments on Amazon EC2/on-premises instances. The agent currently supports Amazon Linux (Amazon EC2 only), Ubuntu Server, Microsoft Windows Server, and Red Hat Enterprise Linux, and it is available as an open source repository on GitHub (`https://github.com/aws/aws-codedeploy-agent`).

When the agent installs, a codedeployagent.yml configuration file copies to the instances. You can use this file to adjust the behavior of the AWS CodeDeploy agent on instances throughout various deployments. This configuration file is stored in /etc/codedeploy-agent/conf on Linux instances and C:\ProgramData\Amazon\AWS CodeDeploy on Windows Server instances.

The most common settings are as follows:

max_revisions Use this to configure how many application revisions to archive on an instance. If you are experiencing storage limitations on your instances, turn this value down and release some storage space consumed by the agent.

root_dir Use this to change the default storage location for revisions, scripts, and archives.

verbose Set this to true to enable verbose logging output for debugging purposes.

proxy_url For environments that use an HTTP proxy, this specifies the URL and credentials to authenticate to the proxy and connect to the AWS CodeDeploy service.

AWS CodeDeploy Service Limits

AWS CodeDeploy enforces the service limits, as shown in Table 7.5. An asterisk (*) indicates limits that you can increase with a request to AWS Support.

TABLE 7.5 AWS CodeDeploy Service Limits

Limit	Value
Applications per account per region	100
Allowed revision file types	.zip, .tar, .tar, and.gz
Concurrent deployments per deployment group	1
Concurrent deployments per account	100
Maximum deployment lifecycle event duration	3600 seconds
Custom deployment configurations per account	25
Deployment groups per application*	100
Tags per deployment group	10
Auto Scaling groups per deployment group	10
Instances per deployment	500

Using AWS CodeDeploy with AWS CodePipeline

AWS CodeDeploy can integrate automatically with AWS CodePipeline as a deployment action to deploy changes to Amazon EC2/on-premises instances or AWS Lambda functions. You can configure applications, deployment groups, and deployments directly in the AWS CodePipeline console when you create or edit a pipeline, or you can do this ahead of time with the AWS CodeDeploy console or the AWS CLI or AWS SDK.

After you define the deployment provider, application name, and deployment group in the AWS CodePipeline console, the pipeline will automatically configure to pass a pipeline artifact to AWS CodeDeploy for deployment to the specified application/group, as shown in Figure 7.23.

FIGURE 7.23   Deployment provider

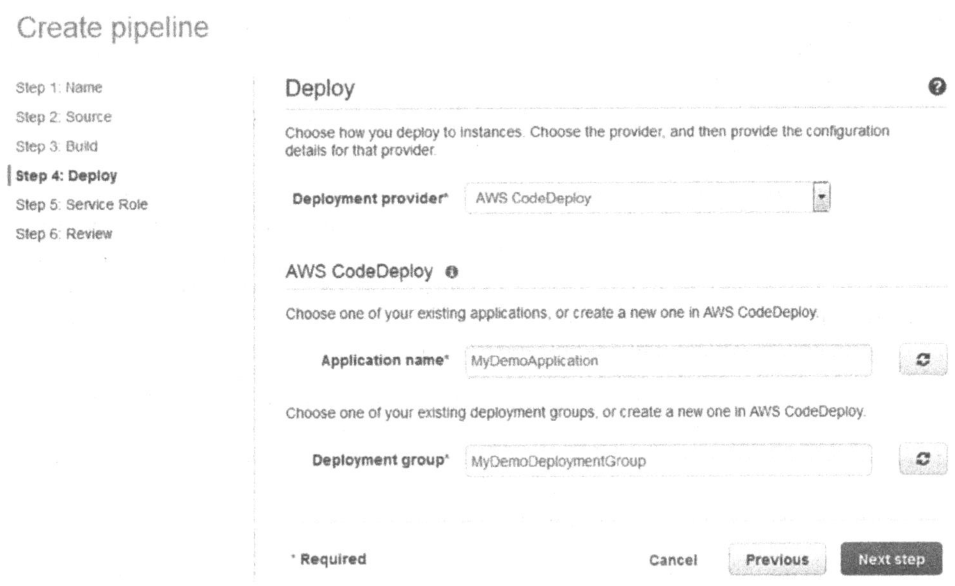

AWS CodeDeploy monitors the progress of any revisions to deploy and report success or failure to AWS CodePipeline.

Summary

In this chapter, you learned about these deployment services:

- AWS CodePipeline
- AWS CodeCommit
- AWS CodeBuild
- AWS CodeDeploy

AWS CodePipeline drives application deployments starting with a source repository (AWS CodeCommit), performing builds with AWS CodeBuild, and finally deploying to Amazon EC2 instance or AWS Lambda functions using AWS CodeDeploy. You can use AWS CloudFormation to provision and manage infrastructure in your environment. By integrating this with AWS CodePipeline, you can automate the entire process of creating development, testing, and production environments into a fully hands-off process. In a fully realized enterprise as code, a single commit to a source repository can kick off processes such as those shown in Figure 7.1.

Exam Essentials

Know the difference between continuous integration, continuous delivery, and continuous deployment.   *Continuous integration* is the practice where all code changes merge into a repository. *Continuous delivery* is the practice where all code changes are prepared for release. *Continuous deployment* is the practice where all code is prepared for release and automatically released to production environments.

Know the basics of AWS CodePipeline.   AWS CodePipeline contains the steps in the *continuous integration and deployment pipeline* (CI/CD) workflow, driving automation between different tasks after assets have been committed to a repository or saved in a bucket. AWS CodePipeline uses stages, which correspond to different steps in a workflow. Within each stage, different actions can perform tasks in series or in parallel. Transitions between stages can be automatic or require manual approval by an authorized user.

Understand how revisions can move through a pipeline.   Revisions move automatically between stages in a pipeline, provided that all actions in the preceding stage complete. If a manual approval is required, the revision will not proceed until an authorized user allows it to do so. When two changes are pushed to a source repository in a short time span, the latest of the two changes will proceed through the pipeline.

Know the different pipeline actions that are available.   A pipeline stage can include one or more actions: build, test, deploy, and invoke. You can also create custom actions.

Know how to deploy a cross-account pipeline.   The account containing the pipeline must create a KMS key that can be used by both AWS CodePipeline and the other account. The pipeline account must also specify a bucket policy on the assets bucket that the pipeline uses, which allows the second account to access assets. The AWS CodePipeline service IAM role must include a policy that allows it to assume a role in the second account. The second account must have a role that can be assumed by the pipeline account, which allows the pipeline account to deploy resources and access the assets bucket.

Know the basic concepts of AWS CodeCommit.   AWS CodeCommit is a Git-based repository service. It is fully compatible with existing Git tooling. AWS CodeCommit provides various benefits, such as encryption in transit and at rest; automatic scaling to handle increases in activity; access control using IAM users, roles, and policies; and HTTPS/SSH connectivity. AWS CodeCommit supports normal Git workflows, such as pull requests.

Know how to use the credential helper to connect to repositories. It is possible to connect to AWS CodeCommit repositories using IAM credentials. The AWS CodeCommit credential helper translates an IAM access key and secret access key into valid Git credentials. This requires the AWS CLI and a Git configuration file that specifies the credential helper.

Understand the different strategies for migrating to AWS CodeCommit. You can migrate an existing Git repository by cloning to your local workstation and adding a new remote, pointing to the AWS CodeCommit repository you create. You can push the repository contents to the new remote. You can migrate unversioned content in a similar manner; however, you must create a new local Git repository (instead of cloning an existing one). Large repositories can be migrated incrementally because large pushes may fail because of network issues.

Know the basics of AWS CodeBuild. AWS CodeBuild allows you to perform long-running build tasks repeatedly and reliably without having to manage the underlying infrastructure. You are responsible only for specifying the build environment settings and the actual tasks to perform.

Know the basics of AWS CodeDeploy. AWS CodeDeploy standardizes and automates deployments to Amazon EC2 instances, on-premises servers, and AWS Lambda functions. Deployments can include application/static files, configuration tasks, or arbitrary scripts to execute. For Amazon EC2 on-premises deployments, a lightweight agent is required.

Understand how AWS CodeDeploy works with Amazon EC2 Auto Scaling groups. When you deploy to Amazon EC2 Auto Scaling groups, AWS CodeDeploy will automatically run the last successful deployment on any new instances that you add to the group. If the deployment fails on the instance, it will be terminated and replaced (to maintain the desired count of healthy instances). If two deployment groups for separate AWS CodeDeploy applications specify the same Auto Scaling group, issues can occur. If both applications deploy at roughly the same time and one fails, the instance will be terminated before success/failure can be reported for the second application deployment. This will result in AWS CodeDeploy waiting until the timeout period expires before taking any further action.

Resources to Review

What is DevOps?

https://aws.amazon.com/devops/what-is-devops/

AWS DevOps Blog:

https://aws.amazon.com/blogs/devops/

Introduction to DevOps on AWS:

https://d1.awsstatic.com/whitepapers/AWS_DevOps.pdf

Practicing Continuous Integration and Continuous Delivery on AWS:

https://d1.awsstatic.com/whitepapers/DevOps/practicing-continuous-integration-continuous-delivery-on-AWS.pdf

AWS CodePipeline User Guide:

https://docs.aws.amazon.com/codepipeline/latest/userguide/welcome.html

Set Up a CI/CD Pipeline on AWS:

https://aws.amazon.com/getting-started/projects/set-up-ci-cd-pipeline/

AWS CodePipeline:

https://aws.amazon.com/codepipeline/

AWS CodeCommit:

https://aws.amazon.com/codecommit/

AWS CodeBuild:

https://aws.amazon.com/codebuild/

AWS CodeDeploy:

https://aws.amazon.com/codedeploy/

Exercises

EXERCISE 7.1

Create an AWS CodeCommit Repository and Submit a Pull Request

This exercise demonstrates how to use AWS CodeCommit to submit and merge pull requests to a repository.

1. Create an AWS CodeCommit repository with a name and description. You do not need to configure email notifications for repository events.

2. In the AWS CodeCommit console, select **Create File** to add a simple markdown file to test the repository.

3. Clone the repository to your local machine with HTTPS or SSH authentication.

4. Create a file locally, commit it to the repository, and push it to test the AWS CodeCommit.

5. Create a feature branch from the master branch in the repository.

6. Edit the file and commit the changes to the feature branch.

7. Use the AWS CodeCommit console to create a pull request. Use the master branch of the repository as the destination and the feature branch as the source.

8. After the pull request successfully creates, merge the changes from the feature branch with the master branch.

The pull request has been merged with the master branch, which can be confirmed by viewing the source code of the markdown file in the master branch.

EXERCISE 7.2

Create an Application in AWS CodeDeploy

This exercise demonstrates how to use AWS CodeDeploy to perform an in-place deployment to Amazon EC2 instances in your account.

1. Create a new application in the AWS CodeDeploy console.

    For the compute platform type, select **EC2 On-premises**.

2. Create a new deployment group for your application. Specify the following values:

    Deployment type   In-place

    Environment configuration   Amazon EC2 instances

    Tag group   Create a tag group that is easy to identify, such as a "Name" for the key, and "CodeDeployInstance" as the value.

    Load balancer   Clear the **Enable load balancing** check box.

3. Launch new **Amazon EC2 instance**.

    Make sure to specify the tag value chosen in the previous step.

4. Download the **sample application bundle** to your local machine for future updates.

    Sample application bundles for each operating system can be found using the following links:

    Windows Server https://docs.aws.amazon.com/codedeploy/latest/userguide/tutorials-windows.html

    Amazon Linux or Red Hat Enterprise Linux (RHEL) https://docs.aws.amazon.com/codedeploy/latest/userguide/tutorials-wordpress.html

5. Create a deployment group, and verify that the sample application **deploys**.

6. **Update** the application code, and **submit** a new deployment to the deployment group.

7. Verify your changes after the deployment completes.

EXERCISE 7.3

Create an AWS CodeBuild Project

This exercise demonstrates how to use AWS CodeBuild to perform builds and the compilation of artifacts prior to deployment to Amazon EC2 instances.

1. Create an Amazon S3 bucket to hold artifacts.

2. Upload two or more arbitrary files to the bucket.

(continued)

3. Use the AWS CodeBuild console to create a build project with the following settings:

Project name   Provide a name of your choice.

Source   Use Amazon S3.

Bucket   Provide the name of the bucket you created.

S3 object key   Provide the name of one of the objects you uploaded.

Environment image   Select the **Managed Image** type.

Operating system   Use **Ubuntu**.

Runtime   Use **Python**.

Runtime version   Select a version of your choice.

Service role   Select **New Service Role**.

Role name   Provide a name for your service role.

Build specifications   Select **Insert Build Commands**.

Build commands   Select **Switch To Editor** and enter the following. Replace the Amazon S3 object paths with paths to the objects you uploaded to your bucket.

```
version: 0.2

phases:
  build:
    commands:
      - aws s3 cp s3://yourbucket/file1 /tmp/file1
      - aws s3 cp s3://yourbucket/file2 /tmp/file2
artifacts:
  files:
    - /tmp/file1
    - /tmp/file2
```

Artifact Type   Use **Amazon S3**.

Bucket name   Select your Amazon S3 bucket.

Artifacts packaging   Select **Zip**.

4. Save your build project.

5. Run your build project, and observe the output archive file created in your Amazon S3 bucket.

Review Questions

1. You have two AWS CodeDeploy applications that deploy to the same Amazon EC2 Auto Scaling group. The first deploys an e-commerce app, while the second deploys custom administration software. You are attempting to deploy an update to one application but cannot do so because another deployment is already in progress. You do not see any instances undergoing deployment at this time. What could be the cause of this?

   A. If both deployment groups reference the same Auto Scaling group, a failure of the first group's deployment can block the second until the deployment times out. Since the instance that failed deployment has been terminated from the Auto Scaling group, the AWS CodeDeploy agent is unable to provide results to the service.

   B. The AWS CodeDeploy agent is not installed on the instances as part of the launch configuration user data script.

   C. If both deployment groups reference the same Auto Scaling group, a failure of the first group's deployment can block the second until the deployment times out. Since the instance that failed deployment has been terminated from the Auto Scaling group, the AWS CodeDeploy service is unable to request status updates from the Amazon EC2 API.

   D. The AWS CodeDeploy agent is not installed in the Amazon Machine Image (AMI) being used.

2. If you specify a hook script in the `ApplicationStop` lifecycle event of an AWS CodeDeploy `appspec.yml`, will it run on the first deployment to your instance(s)?

   A. Yes

   B. No

   C. The `ApplicationStop` lifecycle event does not exist.

   D. It will run only if your application is running.

3. If a single pipeline contains multiple sources, such as an AWS CodeCommit repository and an Amazon S3 archive, under what circumstances will the pipeline be triggered?

   A. When either a commit is pushed to the repository or the archive is updated, regardless of timing.

   B. When a commit is pushed to the repository and the archive is updated at the same time.

   C. When either a commit is pushed to the repository or the archive is updated, but not when both are updated at the same time.

   D. AWS CodePipeline does not support multiple sources in the same pipeline.

4. If you want to implement a deployment pipeline that deploys both source files and large binary objects to instance(s), how would you best achieve this while taking cost into consideration?

   A. Store both the source files and binary objects in AWS CodeCommit.

   B. Build the binary objects into the AMI of the instance(s) being deployed. Store the source files in AWS CodeCommit.

   C. Store the source files in AWS CodeCommit. Store the binary objects in an Amazon S3 archive.

D. Store the source files in AWS CodeCommit. Store the binary objects on an Amazon Elastic Block Store (Amazon EBS) volume, taking snapshots of the volume whenever a new one needs to be created.

E. Store the source files in AWS CodeCommit. Store the binary objects in Amazon S3 and access them from an Amazon CloudFront distribution.

5. Your team is building a deployment pipeline to a sensitive application in your environment using AWS CodeDeploy. The application consists of an Amazon EC2 Auto Scaling group of instances behind an Elastic Load Balancing load balancer. The nature of the application requires 100 percent availability for both successful and failed deployments. The development team want to deploy changes multiple times per day.

How would this be achieved at the lowest cost and with the fastest deployments?

A. Rolling deployments with an additional batch

B. Rolling deployments without an additional batch

C. Blue/green deployments

D. Immutable updates

6. What would cause an access denied error when attempting to download an archive file from Amazon S3 during a pipeline execution?

A. Insufficient user permissions for the user initiating the pipeline

B. Insufficient user permissions for the user uploading the Amazon S3 archive

C. Insufficient role permissions for the Amazon S3 service role

D. Insufficient role permissions for the AWS CodePipeline service role

7. How do you output build artifacts from AWS CodeBuild to AWS CodePipeline?

A. Write the outputs to STDOUT from the build container.

B. Specify artifact files in the buildspec.yml configuration file.

C. Upload the files to Amazon S3 from the build environment.

D. Output artifacts are not supported with AWS CodeBuild.

8. What would be the most secure means of providing secrets to an AWS CodeBuild environment?

A. Create a custom build environment with the secrets included in configuration files.

B. Upload the secrets to Amazon S3 and download the object when the build job runs. Protect the bucket and object with an appropriate bucket policy.

C. Save the secrets in AWS Systems Manager Parameter Store and query them as needed. Encrypt the secrets with an AWS Key Management Service (AWS KMS) key. Include appropriate AWS KMS permissions to your build environment's IAM role.

D. Include the secrets in the source repository or archive.

9. In which of the pipeline actions can you execute AWS Lambda functions?

A. Invoke

B. Deploy

    C. Build

    D. Approval

    E. Test

10. In what ways can pipeline actions be ordered in a stage? (Select TWO.)

    A. Series

    B. Parallel

    C. Stages support only one action each

    D. First-in-first-out (FIFO)

    E. Last-in-first-out (LIFO)

11. If you would like to delete an AWS CloudFormation stack before you deploy a new one in your pipeline, what would be the correct set of actions?

    A. One action that specifies "Create or update a stack."

    B. Two actions: the first specifies "Create or update a stack," and the second specifies "Delete a stack."

    C. Three actions: the first specifies "Delete a stack," the second specifies "Create or update a stack," and the third specifies "Replace a failed stack."

    D. Two actions: the first specifies "Delete a stack," and the second specifies "Create or update a stack."

12. How can you connect to an AWS CodeCommit repository without Git credentials?

    A. It is not possible.

    B. HTTPS

    C. SSH

    D. AWS CodeCommit credential helper

13. Of the following, which event cannot be used to generate notifications to an Amazon Simple Notification Service (SNS) topic from AWS CodeCommit without using a trigger?

    A. Pull Request Creation

    B. Commit Comments

    C. Commit Creation

    D. Pull Request Comments

14. Which pipeline actions support AWS CodeBuild projects? (Select TWO.)

    A. Invoke

    B. Deploy

    C. Build

    D. Approval

    E. Test

15. Can data passed to build projects using environment variables be encrypted or protected?

   A. Yes, this is supported natively by AWS CodeBuild.

   B. No, it is not supported.

   C. No, but this can be enabled in the console.

   D. No, but this can be supported using other AWS products and services.

16. What is the only deployment type supported by on-premises instances?

   A. In-place

   B. Blue/green

   C. Immutable

   D. Progressive

17. If your AWS CodeDeploy configuration includes creation of a file, `nginx.conf`, but the file already exists on the server (prior to the use of AWS CodeDeploy), what is the default behavior that will occur during deployment?

   A. The file will be replaced.

   B. The file will be renamed `nginx.conf.bak`, and the new file will be created.

   C. The deployment will fail.

   D. The deployment will continue, but the file will not be modified.

18. How does AWS Lambda support in-place deployments?

   A. Function versions are overwritten during the deployment.

   B. New function versions are created, and then version numbers are switched.

   C. AWS Lambda does not support in-place deployments.

   D. Function aliases are overwritten during the deployment.

19. What is the minimum number of stages required by a pipeline in AWS CodePipeline?

   A. 0

   B. 1

   C. 2

   D. 3

20. If an instance is running low on storage, and you find that there are a large number of deployment revisions stored by AWS CodeDeploy, what can be done to free up this space permanently?

   A. Delete the old revisions.

   B. Add an additional Amazon EBS volume.

   C. Configure the AWS CodeDeploy agent to store fewer revisions.

   D. Delete all of the revisions, and push all new code.

Chapter 8

Infrastructure as Code

THE AWS CERTIFIED DEVELOPER – ASSOCIATE EXAM TOPICS COVERED IN THIS CHAPTER MAY INCLUDE, BUT ARE NOT LIMITED TO, THE FOLLOWING:

Domain 1: Deployment

✓ 1.1   Infrastructure as Code (IaC).

✓ 1.2   Use AWS CloudFormation to Deploy Infrastructure.

Domain 5: Monitoring and Troubleshooting

✓ 5.1   Custom Resource Success/Failure.

Introduction to Infrastructure as Code

Chapter 7 covered deployment tools, processes, and methodologies in AWS services. These services can leverage and be read by *AWS CloudFormation* to provision and manage AWS infrastructure from Amazon Elastic Compute Cloud (Amazon EC2) instances to Amazon API Gateway REST APIs. For all intents and purposes, if you provision and update code with an AWS API, you can use AWS CloudFormation to move this process entirely to template code updates.

 If you create an AWS Auto Scaling group of instances with the AWS Management Console, you must perform a number of steps. You can launch and test multiple instances of the user data script with Amazon EC2 launch configurations, you can use Amazon CloudWatch alarms to scale your application, and finally you can implement the AWS Auto Scaling group itself. A better solution is to use AWS CloudFormation to create and manage all of the aforementioned resources over time with a simple, declarative template syntax.

Infrastructure as Code

Using an *infrastructure as code* (IaC) model, instead of manually provisioning or using scripting languages, helps remove the dependency on human intervention when you create and manage infrastructure over time. You can use tools such as AWS CloudFormation to deploy infrastructure from a declarative template syntax. For example, a typical provisioning script that uses the *AWS Command Line Interface* (AWS CLI) includes many procedural steps that are prone to error because of invalid inputs, incorrect command syntax, and resource dependency conflicts. AWS CloudFormation templates provide the ability to validate inputs and automatically detect dependencies between resources.

Provisioning infrastructure with AWS CloudFormation templates provides some built-in benefits, such as the ability to track changes with a "source of truth," such as a Git-based repository. Since repositories track changes over time, you can roll back an undesired change by resubmitting the last working version of the template(s). This can significantly reduce the time needed to roll back undesired changes.

You can view users' resources with appropriate permissions within an AWS account. An issue can arise where, as your infrastructure grows over time, it can be difficult to determine what resources belong to what functional group, application, team, and so on. Use of tags can alleviate this somewhat, but this is not possible for resources that do not yet support tags. AWS CloudFormation organizes resources into stacks, which you describe in the AWS Management Console, the AWS CLI, or AWS software development kits (AWS SDKs). AWS CloudFormation stacks provide a comprehensive list of any infrastructures in a functional group.

Using AWS CloudFormation to Deploy Infrastructure

> *AWS CloudFormation provides a common language for you to describe and provision all of the infrastructure resources in your cloud environment.*

AWS CloudFormation allows you to use a simple text file to model and provision, in an automated and secure manner, all of the resources for your applications across all regions and accounts. This file serves as the single source of truth for your cloud environment.

AWS CloudFormation is available at no additional charge, and you pay only for the AWS resources required to run your applications.

What Is AWS CloudFormation?

Before you deploy any application code, the first requirement is that infrastructure exists where you will deploy the code. AWS CloudFormation aims to alleviate previous deployment issues with the use of a service that allows you to describe your infrastructure with standardized JSON or YAML template syntax. The template contains the infrastructure that AWS will deploy and all the related configuration properties. When you submit this template to the AWS CloudFormation service, it creates a stack, which is a logical group of resources that the template describes.

When you manually create resources with the AWS Management Console or AWS CLI or AWS SDK, you cannot easily define relationships between resources.

 If you manually create an AWS Auto Scaling Group (ASG) and attach this to an Elastic Load Balancing (ELB) load balancer, it requires several API calls or console actions—one for each resource and one to attach the ASG to the ELB. With AWS CloudFormation, you define the resources and any relationships in one location for easy deployment and updates over time.

Two key benefits of AWS CloudFormation over procedural scripting or manual console actions are that your infrastructure is now *repeatable* and that it is *versionable*.

Any template that you deploy one time in an account you can deploy again (either in the same account and/or region or in others). This offers you an opportunity for dynamically provisioning short-lived environments to test or roll over to a new production environment (blue/green deployment). Since templates describe your infrastructure, you check the templates themselves into a source code repository. With this, you can track changes over time, and updates roll back when they revert commits and redeploy the previous template(s). Over time, this creates self-documenting infrastructure that shows changes over the lifecycle of an environment.

AWS CloudFormation Concepts

This section details AWS CloudFormation concepts, such as stacks, change sets, permissions, templates, and instinct functions.

Stacks

A *stack* represents a collection of resources to deploy and manage by AWS CloudFormation. When you submit a template, the resources you configure are provisioned and then make up the stack itself. Any modifications to the stack affect underlying resources. For example, if you remove an AWS::EC2::Instance resource from the template and update the stack, AWS CloudFormation causes the referred instance to terminate.

AWS CloudFormation manages all of the resources you declare in a stack when the stack updates. If you manually update the resource outside of AWS CloudFormation, the result will be inconsistencies between the state AWS CloudFormation expects and the actual resource state. This can cause future stack operations to fail.

Change Sets

There may be times where you would like to see what changes will occur to resources when you update a template, before the update occurs. Instead of submitting the update directly, you can generate a change set. A *change set* is a description of the changes that will occur to a stack, should you submit the template. If the changes are acceptable, the change set itself can execute on the stack and implement the proposed modifications. This is especially important in situations where there is a potential for data loss.

Amazon Relational Database Service Instances

There are several properties in Amazon Relational Database Service (Amazon RDS) instances that AWS CloudFormation modifies and requires replacement in the underlying database instance resource. If backups are not being taken, data loss will occur. You use a change set to preview the replacement event, make the necessary backups, and take the required precautions before you update the resources.

Permissions

AWS CloudFormation, unless otherwise specified, functions within the context of the IAM user or AWS role to invoke a stack action. This means that if you submit a template that creates an Amazon EC2 instance (or instances), AWS CloudFormation will fail unless your IAM user or AWS role has permissions to create instances. Any action that AWS CloudFormation performs is done on your behalf, with your authorizations. With this, you can control what stack actions perform (create, update, or delete) and what actions are performed on the underlying resources.

If there is a need to restrict what permissions a single IAM user or AWS role can have, you can provide a service role the stack uses for the create, update, or delete actions. When the role passes to AWS CloudFormation, it will use the role's credentials to determine what operations it performs. To create an AWS CloudFormation service role, make sure that the role as a trust policy allows cloudformation.amazonaws.com to assume the role.

As a user, your IAM credentials will need to include the ability to pass the role to AWS CloudFormation, using the iam:PassRole permission. An additional benefit when you use a service role is that it will extend the default timeout for stack create, update, and delete actions. This is especially important when you work with resources that take a longer time because of their size or distribution. Certain services can time out in AWS CloudFormation, returning a Resource failed to stabilize error.

- AWS::AutoScaling::AutoScalingGroup
- AWS::CertificateManager::Certificate
- AWS::CloudFormation::Stack
- AWS::ElasticSearch::Domain
- AWS::RDS::DBCluster
- AWS::RDS::DBInstance
- AWS::Redshift::Cluster

 After a service role passes to AWS CloudFormation, other users with the ability to perform updates will be able to do so with the same role, regardless of whether they have the ability to pass it. Make sure that the service role follows least-privilege practices.

When you assign permissions for IAM users or AWS roles, you have the ability to specify conditions to control whether policies are in effect. For example, you can allow your users to create stacks only with certain names. However, do not use the aws:SourceIp condition. This is because AWS CloudFormation actions originate from AWS IP addresses, not the IP address of the request.

When you create a stack, you can submit a template from a local file or via a URL that points to an object in Amazon S3. If you submit the template as a local file, it uploads to Amazon S3 on your behalf. Because of this, you must add these permissions to create a stack:

- cloudformation:CreateUploadBucket

- s3:PutObject

- s3:ListBucket

- s3:GetObject

- s3:CreateBucket

Template Structure

AWS CloudFormation uses specific template syntax in JSON or YAML. (The primary difference is YAML's support of comments using the # symbol.) The high-level structure of a template is as follows:

```
{
  "AWSTemplateFormatVersion": "2010-09-09",
  "Description": "String Description",
  "Metadata": { },
  "Parameters": { },
  "Mappings": { },
  "Conditions": { },
  "Transform": { },
  "Resources": { },
  "Outputs": { }
}
```

Of the previous properties, *AWS CloudFormation requires only the Resources section.* Each property can be in any order, with the exception that Description must follow the AWSTemplateFormatVersion command.

AWSTemplateFormatVersion

AWSTemplateFormatVersion corresponds to the template version to which this template adheres. Do not confuse this with an API version or the version of the developer's template draft. Currently, AWS CloudFormation only supports the value "2010-09-09", which you must provide as a literal string.

Description

The *Description* section allows you to provide a text explanation of the template's purpose or other arbitrary information. The maximum length of the Description field is 1,024 bytes. Similar to the AWSTemplateFormatVersion section, Description supports only literal text.

Metadata

The *Metadata* section of a template allows you to provide structured details about the template. For example, you can provide Metadata about the overall infrastructure to deploy and which sections correspond to certain environments, functional groups, and so on. The Metadata you provide is made available to AWS CloudFormation for reference in other sections of a template or on Amazon EC2 instances being provisioned by AWS CloudFormation.

Updating the Metadata Section of a Template

You cannot update template metadata by itself; you must perform an update to one or more resources when you update the Metadata section of a template.

```
"Metadata": {
  "ApplicationLayer": {
    "Description": "Information about resources in the app layer."
  },
  "DatabaseLayer": {
    "Description": "Information about resources in the DB layer."
  }
}
```

In the Metadata section of the template, you have the ability to specify properties that affect the behavior of different components of the AWS CloudFormation service, such as how template parameters display in the AWS CloudFormation console.

Parameters

You can use *Parameters* to provide inputs into your template, which allows for more flexibility in how this template behaves when you deploy it. Parameter values can be set either when you create the stack or when you perform updates.

The Parameters section must include a unique logical ID (in the next example, InstanceTypeParameter). A parameter must include a value, either a default or one that you provide. Lastly, you cannot reference parameters outside a single template.

AllowedValues Error

This example defines a String parameter named InstanceTypeParameter with a default value of t2.micro. The parameter allows t2.micro, m1.small, or m1.large. The Allowed-Values section specifies what options you can select for this parameter in the AWS CloudFormation console. AWS CloudFormation will throw an error if you add a value not in AllowedValues.

```
"Parameters": {
  "InstanceTypeParam": {
    "Type": "String",
```
(continued)

(continued)

```
    "Default": "t2.micro",
    "AllowedValues": [ "t2.micro", "m1.small", "m1.large" ],
    "Description": "Enter t2.micro, m1.small, or m1.large. Default is t2.micro."
  }
}
```

Once you specify a parameter, you can use it within the template using the Ref intrinsic function. When AWS CloudFormation evaluates it, the Ref statement converts it to the value of the parameter.

```
"EC2Instance": {
  "Type": "AWS::EC2::Instance",
  "Properties": {
    "InstanceType": { "Ref": "InstanceTypeParam" },
    "ImageId": "ami-12345678"
  }
}
```

AWS CloudFormation supports the following parameter types:

- String
- Number
- List of numbers
- Comma-delimited list
- AWS parameter types
- AWS Systems Manager Parameter Store (Systems Manager) parameter types

If a parameter value is sensitive, you can add the NoEcho property. When this is set, the parameter value displays as asterisks (***) for any cloudformation:Describe* calls. Within the template itself, the value will resolve to the actual input when making Ref calls.

AWS parameter types When you use *AWS parameter types*, AWS CloudFormation automatically queries existing properties and values within your AWS account. This can include information such as Amazon EC2 key pair names, IDs of resources, AWS regions/availability zones, or other properties of your account. These input values must exist in your account and are validated to ensure that they are correct. For example, you can use the AWS::EC2::KeyPair::KeyName parameter type to require a valid Amazon EC2 key pair. This way, there is reduced risk that a user will input an incorrect value that results in improper stack behavior.

AWS System Manager parameter types *AWS Systems Manager parameter types* can reference parameters that exist in the AWS Systems Manager Parameter Store. If you specify a parameter key, AWS CloudFormation will search your Systems Manager Parameter Store for the correct value and input this into the stack. When you perform stack updates, AWS CloudFormation queries the same key again and could result in a new value for the AWS CloudFormation parameter.

Mappings

You can use the *Mappings* section of a template to create a rudimentary lookup tables that you can reference in other sections of your template when you create the stack.

A common example of mappings usage is to look up Amazon EC2 instance AMI IDs based on the region and architecture type. Note in the following example that mappings entries may contain only string values. (Mappings does not support parameters, conditions, or intrinsic functions.)

```
"Mappings" : {
  "RegionMap" : {
    "us-east-1"       : { "32" : "ami-6411e20d", "64" : "ami-7a11e213" },
    "us-west-1"       : { "32" : "ami-c9c7978c", "64" : "ami-cfc7978a" },
    "eu-west-1"       : { "32" : "ami-37c2f643", "64" : "ami-31c2f645" },
    "ap-southeast-1" : { "32" : "ami-66f28c34", "64" : "ami-60f28c32" },
    "ap-northeast-1" : { "32" : "ami-9c03a89d", "64" : "ami-a003a8a1" }
  }
}
```

After you declare the Mappings section, you can query the values within the mapping with the Fn::FindInMap intrinsic function. The example shows an Fn::FindInMap call that queries the AMI ID based on region and architecture type (32- or 64-bit). If the region was us-east-1, for example, the previous template snippet would resolve to ami-6411e20d.

Pseudo Parameter: AWS::Region

The AWS::Region reference is a pseudoparameter; that is, it's a parameter that AWS defines automatically on your behalf. The AWS::Region parameter, for example, resolves to the region code where the stack is being deployed (such as us-east-1).

```
"Resources" : {
  "myEC2Instance" : {
    "Type" : "AWS::EC2::Instance",
    "Properties" : {
      "ImageId" : { "Fn::FindInMap" : [ "RegionMap", { "Ref" : "AWS::Region" },
"32"]},
      "InstanceType" : "m1.small"
    }
  }
}
```

Conditions

You can use Conditions in AWS CloudFormation templates to determine when to create a resource or when a property of a resource is defined (either in the Resources or Outputs section of the stack). Conditional statements make use of intrinsic functions to evaluate multiple inputs against one other.

A common use case for this would be to conditionally set an Amazon EC2 instance to use a larger instance type if the environment to which you deploy is prod versus dev. The environment type is input as a template parameter, EnvType, which the conditional statement, CreateProdResources, uses. The conditional statement decides whether to create an additional Amazon Elastic Block Store (Amazon EBS) volume and mount it to the instance with the Condition property of the resource.

 A single condition can reference input parameters, mappings, or other conditions to determine whether the final value is true or false.

```
{
  "AWSTemplateFormatVersion" : "2010-09-09",
  "Mappings" : {
    "RegionMap" : {
      "us-east-1"     : { "AMI" : "ami-7f418316", "TestAz" : "us-east-1a" },
      "us-west-1"     : { "AMI" : "ami-951945d0", "TestAz" : "us-west-1a" },
      "us-west-2"     : { "AMI" : "ami-16fd7026", "TestAz" : "us-west-2a" }
    }
  },
  "Parameters" : {
    "EnvType" : {
      "Description" : "Environment type.",
      "Default" : "test",
      "Type" : "String",
      "AllowedValues" : ["prod", "test"]
    }
  },
  "Conditions" : {
    "CreateProdResources" : {"Fn::Equals" : [{"Ref" : "EnvType"}, "prod"]}
  },
  "Resources" : {
    "EC2Instance" : {
      "Type" : "AWS::EC2::Instance",
      "Properties" : {
        "ImageId" : { "Fn::FindInMap" : [ "RegionMap", { "Ref" : "AWS::Region" }, "AMI" ]}
      }
    },
    "MountPoint" : {
      "Type" : "AWS::EC2::VolumeAttachment",
      "Condition" : "CreateProdResources",
```

```
      "Properties" : {
        "InstanceId" : { "Ref" : "EC2Instance" },
        "VolumeId"   : { "Ref" : "NewVolume" },
        "Device" : "/dev/sdh"
      }
    },
    "NewVolume" : {
      "Type" : "AWS::EC2::Volume",
      "Condition" : "CreateProdResources",
      "Properties" : {
        "Size" : "100",
        "AvailabilityZone" : { "Fn::GetAtt" : [ "EC2Instance",
"AvailabilityZone" ]}
      }
    }
  }
}
```

You can also use `Conditions` to declare different resource properties based on whether the condition evaluates to true with the `Fn::If` intrinsic function. The following example uses the `UseDBSnapshot` condition to determine whether to pass a value to the `DBSnapshotIdentifier` property of an `AWS::RDS::DBInstance` resource. You use the `AWS::NoValue` pseudoparameter in place of a `null` value in AWS CloudFormation templates. When you provide it as a value to a resource property, `AWS::NoValue` removes that property declaration.

```
"MyDB" : {
  "Type" : "AWS::RDS::DBInstance",
  "Properties" : {
    "AllocatedStorage" : "5",
    "DBInstanceClass" : "db.m1.small",
    "Engine" : "MySQL",
    "EngineVersion" : "5.5",
    "MasterUsername" : { "Ref" : "DBUser" },
    "MasterUserPassword" : { "Ref" : "DBPassword" },
    "DBParameterGroupName" : { "Ref" : "MyRDSParamGroup" },
    "DBSnapshotIdentifier" : {
      "Fn::If" : [
        "UseDBSnapshot",
        {"Ref" : "DBSnapshotName"},
        {"Ref" : "AWS::NoValue"}
      ]
    }
  }
}
```

Transforms

As templates grow in size and complexity, there may be situations where you use certain components repeatedly across multiple templates, such as common resources or mappings. Transforms allow you to simplify the template authoring process through a powerful set of macros you use to reduce the amount of time spent in the authoring process. AWS CloudFormation transforms first create a change set for the stack. Transforms are applied to the template during the change set creation process.

 Once a change set is complete, the template updates with output of the executed macros. The finalized template deploys to AWS CloudFormation, not the original with the transform declarations. This can cause confusion, as the original template will not be available via the console or AWS CLI or AWS SDK actions.

There are two types of supported transforms.

AWS::Include Transform   AWS::Include Transform acts as a tool to import template snippets from Amazon S3 buckets into the template being developed. When the template is evaluated, a change set is created, and the template snippet is copied from its location and is added to the overall template structure. You can use this transform anywhere in a template, except the Parameters and AWSTemplateFormatVersion sections.

When you use the AWS::Include Transform at the top level of a template, the syntax must match the example. (Note that the transform is declared as Transform.) This is especially useful if there is a set of common mappings that you use across multiple teams or template authors, as they can share this set and update it in one location.

```
{
  "Transform" : {
    "Name" : "AWS::Include",
    "Parameters" : {
      "Location" : "s3://MyAmazonS3BucketName/MyFileName.json"
    }
  }
}
```

When you use a transform in nested sections of a template, such as the Properties section of an AWS::EC2::Instance resource, use the following syntax. (Note that this is now an intrinsic function call.)

```
{
  "Fn::Transform" : {
    "Name" : "AWS::Include",
    "Parameters" : {
      "Location" : "s3://MyAmazonS3BucketName/MyFileName.json"
    }
  }
}
```

When you process stack updates, the template snippets you reference in any transforms pull from their Amazon S3 locations. This means that if a snippet updates without your knowledge, the updated snippet will import into the template. We recommend that you create change sets first so that any accidental updates can be caught before you deploy.

AWS CloudFormation does not support nested transforms. If the snippet being imported into a template includes an additional transform declaration, the stack creation or update will fail.

AWS::Serverless Transform   You can use the AWS::Serverless Transform to convert AWS Serverless Application Model (AWS SAM) templates to valid AWS CloudFormation templates for deployment. AWS SAM uses an abbreviated template syntax to deploy serverless applications with AWS Lambda, Amazon API Gateway, and Amazon DynamoDB.

The following example creates a function that uses the serverless transform. When AWS CloudFormation evaluates the transform, the transform expands the template to include an AWS Lambda function and its IAM execution role.

```
Transform: AWS::Serverless-2016-10-31
Resources:
  MyServerlessFunctionLogicalID:
    Type: AWS::Serverless::Function
    Properties:
      Handler: index.handler
      Runtime: nodejs4.3
      CodeUri: 's3://testBucket/mySourceCode.zip'
```

Resources

The *Resources* section of an AWS CloudFormation template declares the actual AWS resources to be provisioned and their properties. *AWS CloudFormation requires this template section when you create stacks.* The Resources section follows a standard syntax, where a logical ID acts as the resource key and type/properties subkeys define the actual type of resource to deploy and what properties it should have.

The *logical ID* of the resource allows it to be referenced in other parts of a template. You can refer to Resources in other sections of a template, build relationships between interdependent resources, output property values of the resources, perform other useful functions. The Resource Type defines the actual type of resource being managed. For example, an Amazon S3 bucket type is AWS::S3::Bucket. There are too many resource types available to list in this book, and they are updated regularly. Check the AWS CloudFormation documentation for available resource types.

```
https://docs.aws.amazon.com/AWSCloudFormation/latest/UserGuide/aws-template-
resource-type-ref.html
```

The resource properties section defines what configuration a resource should have. In the same example, the AWS::S3::Bucket resource has an optional property called BucketName, which defines the name of the bucket to create.

```
{
  "Resources": {
    "MyBucket": {
      "Type": "AWS::S3::Bucket",
      "Properties": {
        "BucketName": "MyBucketName1234"
      }
    }
  }
}
```

Resource properties are either optional or required and may be any of the following types:

- String
- List of strings
- Boolean
- References to parameters or pseudoparameters
- Intrinsic functions

Outputs

Outputs are values that can be made available to use outside a single stack. You can reference these values in a number of different ways, such as cross-stack references, nested stacks, describe-stack API calls, or in the AWS CloudFormation console. Outputs are useful in providing meaningful information after a stack has been created or updated successfully. For example, it would be helpful to output an Elastic Load Balancing load balancer URL to the user when a web application stack deploys successfully.

The basic structure for AWS CloudFormation outputs follows. Similar to resources, outputs must have a logical ID so that AWS CloudFormation can reference them. The Description field provides a friendly explanation of the purpose of the output, which can be useful to users of your template. The value being returned can be produced using intrinsic functions, or it can be a static string value. Lastly, the Export key (optional) creates cross-stack references.

Here is an example of outputting the ELB load balancer URL:

```
"Outputs" : {
  "BackupLoadBalancerDNSName" : {
    "Description": "The DNSName of the backup load balancer",
    "Value" : { "Fn::GetAtt" : [ "BackupLoadBalancer", "DNSName" ]}
  }
}
```

Intrinsic Functions

Situations can occur where values input into a template cannot be determined until the stack or change set actually is created. If you create an Amazon RDS instance, which is referenced in a configuration file added to an Amazon EC2 instance in the same template, the actual database connection string cannot be determined until the database instance is created. Other attributes, settings, or values may need to be calculated from several inputs at once.

Intrinsic functions aim to resolve this issue by adding dynamic functionality into AWS CloudFormation templates. Multiple intrinsic functions are available to add significant power and flexibility to your templates.

Fn::Base64

The *Fn::Base64* intrinsic function converts an input string into its Base64 equivalent. The primary purpose of this function is to pass instructions written in string format to an Amazon EC2 instance's UserData property.

```
{ "Fn::Base64": valueToEncode }
```

Fn::Cidr

When you create Amazon VPCs and subnets, you must provide Classless Inter-Domain Routing (CIDR) blocks to map a group of IP addresses to the resource being created. The *Fn::Cidr* intrinsic function allows you to convert an IP address block, subnet count, and size mask (optional) into valid CIDR notation.

```
{ "Fn::Cidr": [ ipBlock, count, sizeMask ] }
```

Fn::FindInMap

After you create mappings in AWS CloudFormation, you use the *Fn::FindInMap* intrinsic function to query information stored within the mapping table. Note that mappings have two key levels, and thus top-level and second-level keys must be supplied as inputs, along with the mapping name itself.

```
{ "Fn::FindInMap": [ "MapName", "TopLevelKey", "SecondLevelKey" ] }
```

Consider the following Mappings section. The Fn::FindInMap call would return ami-c9c7978c.

```
"Mappings" : {
  "RegionMap" : {
    "us-east-1" : { "32" : "ami-6411e20d", "64" : "ami-7a11e213" },
    "us-west-1" : { "32" : "ami-c9c7978c", "64" : "ami-cfc7978a" },
    "eu-west-1" : { "32" : "ami-37c2f643", "64" : "ami-31c2f645" }
  }
}

. . .

{ "Fn::FindInMap" : [ "RegionMap", { "Ref" : "AWS::Region" }, "32" ] }
```

Fn::GetAtt

Resources you create in AWS CloudFormation contain information that you can query in other parts of the same template. For example, if you create an IAM role to use when log in to AWS CloudTrail events to Amazon CloudWatch Logs, you must provide the Amazon Resource Name (ARN) of the AWS role to the trail configuration. Since the ARN is not returned when you use the Ref intrinsic function (this returns the role name), you can use *Fn::GetAtt* to query additional resource properties. In this case, you would be able to use this intrinsic function to determine the ARN of the role.

```
{ "Fn::GetAtt" : [ "logicalIDOfResource", "attributeName" ] }
```

Fn::GetAZs

For each AWS region, different availability zones (with different names) are available. The specific availability zones will not always match between different accounts (in fact, two accounts with the same availability zone by name may not use the same physical location). Because of this, it is not easy to determine which availability zones are usable when you create a stack. The *Fn::GetAZs* intrinsic function returns a list of availability zones for the account in which the stack is being created.

```
{ "Fn::GetAZs" : "region" }
```

 Only availability zones where a default subnet exists will be returned by Fn::GetAZ.

To increase flexibility further and remove the need to hard-code a region in the template, you can use the AWS::Region pseudoparameter to return the list of availability zones for the region in which the stack is being created.

```
{ "Fn::GetAZs" : { "Ref": "AWS::Region" } }
```

Fn::Join

In some situations, string values must be concatenated from multiple input strings, as is the case when building Java Database Connectivity (JDBC) connection strings. AWS CloudFormation supports string concatenation with the *Fn::Join* intrinsic function. You can join string values with a predefined delimiter, which you supply to the function along with a list of strings to join.

When you define the UserData for an AWS::EC2::Instance resource, it may be required that you add various parameters to commands being run on the instance.

Fn::Join Appending Data Dynamically

This example shows how you can use Fn::Join to append various data dynamically to create complex commands.

```
"Resources" : {
    "Ec2Instance" : {
      "Type" : "AWS::EC2::Instance",
```

```
    "Properties" : {
      "ImageId" : "ami-12345678",
      "Tags" : [ {"Key" : "Role", "Value" : "Test Instance"}],
      "UserData" : { "Fn::Base64" : { "Fn::Join" : [ "", [
        "#!/bin/bash -ex", "\n",
        "echo deploying into region: ", { "Ref": "AWS::Region" }, "\n",
        "\n", "yum install ec2-net-utils -y", "\n",
        "ec2ifup eth1", "\n",
        "service httpd start" ] ] }
    }
  }
 }
}
```

Fn::Select

If you pass a list of values into your template, there needs to be a way to select an item from the list based on what position (index) it is in the list. *Fn::Select* allows you to choose an item in a list based on the zero-based index.

 The Fn::Select intrinsic function does not check for issues such as whether an index is out of bounds or whether the values in a list equal null. You need to verify that the input list does not contain null values and has a known length.

```
{ "Fn::Select" : [ index, listOfObjects ] }
```

Fn::Split

Counter to the Fn::Join intrinsic function, you use *Fn::Split* to create a list of strings by separating a single string by a known delimiter. You can use Fn::Select to access the output list of strings and pass them to an index to select from different substrings.

```
{ "Fn::Split" : [ "delimiter", "source string" ] }
```

Fn::Sub

If you need to build an input string with multiple variables determined at runtime, use the *Fn::Sub* function to populate a template string with input variables from a variable map.

This intrinsic function can also use parameters, resources, and resource attributes already present in your template. Note in the following example that two template values are present in the string, but only one mapping value is provided. This is because the

AWS::AccountId pseudoparameter will automatically resolve to the account ID where the stack is being created, and AWS::Region automatically resolves to the region ID.

```
{
  "Fn::Sub": [ "arn:aws:ec2:${AWS::Region}:${AWS::AccountId}:vpc/${vpc}", {
    "vpc": { "Ref": "MyVPC" }
  }
}
```

Ref

You will use the *Ref* intrinsic function a lot within your template, especially when multiple resources have dependencies and relationships between one another (such as if you create an AWS::EC2::VPC resource with two AWS::EC2::Subnet resources). The behavior of the Ref function can differ slightly depending on the resource type being referenced. In some cases, such as with AWS::S3::Bucket or AWS::AutoScaling::AutoScalingGroup resources, you use Ref to return the resource name (in this situation, either the bucket or AWS Auto Scaling group name). In other cases, different properties such as the resource ARN or physical ID returns. Make sure to check the documentation for the resource type being referenced to verify what data returns.

```
{ "Ref" : "logicalName" }
```

Condition Functions

Condition functions are special intrinsic functions for which you can optionally create resources or set resource properties, depending on whether the condition evaluates to true or false. Other than Fn::If, you must use all other condition functions within the Conditions section of a template. The Fn::If intrinsic function allows you to pass different data to resource properties depending on the state of the referenced condition.

FN::AND

Returns true only if all contained conditions evaluate to true; otherwise, false returns.

```
"Fn::And": [{condition}, {...}]
```

FN::EQUALS

Returns true if both compared values are equal; otherwise, false returns.

```
"Fn::Equals" : ["value_1", "value_2"]
```

FN::IF

Returns one of two values, depending on whether the specified condition evaluates to true or false. If you would like to return a null value, pass a reference the AWS::NoValue pseudoparameter with the Ref intrinsic function.

```
"Fn::If": [condition_name, value_if_true, value_if_false]
```

FN::NOT

Acts as a negation, returning the opposite of the evaluated condition.

```
"Fn::Not": [{condition}]
```

FN::OR

Returns true if any of the provided conditions are true. Otherwise, false returns.

```
"Fn::Or": [{condition}, {...}]
```

Built-in Metadata Keys

This section details built-in metadata keys for AWS::CloudFormation:Init, AWS::CloudFormation::Interface, and AWS::CloudFormation::Designer.

AWS::CloudFormation::Init

This section defines what operations the cfn-init helper script performs on Amazon EC2 instances being provisioned by AWS CloudFormation (either as stand-alone instances or in AWS Auto Scaling groups). This metadata key allows you to develop a more declarative infrastructure configuration, instead of having to procedurally script every individual action (such as installing packages, which can vary based on the instance's operating system).

This Metadata section is organized by config keys, which contain a list of configurations to apply.

AWS::CloudFormation::Init: Resource Metadata

Unless otherwise specified, AWS CloudFormation will look for config wherever the AWS::CloudFormation::Init Metadata section appears.

```
"Resources": {
  "MyInstance": {
    "Type": "AWS::EC2::Instance",
    "Metadata" : {
      "AWS::CloudFormation::Init" : {
        "config" : {
          "packages" : { },
          "groups" :   { },
          "users" :    { },
          "sources" :  { },
          "files" :    { },
          "commands" : { },
          "services" : { }
        }
      }
    },
    "Properties": { }
  }
}
```

PACKAGES

The packages key allows installation of arbitrary packages on the system. Packages must be available to one of the supported package managers (yum, apt, python, and others). Packages nest under the supported package manager and include a package name followed by an optional version string (or list of versions). If you do not provide a version, the version installs. If the package is not available in the package manager repository, you must include a download URL.

```
"packages": {
  "rpm" : {
    "epel" : "http://download.fedoraproject.org/pub/epel/5/i386/
epel-release-5-4.noarch.rpm"

  },
  "yum" : {
    "httpd" : [],
    "php" : [],
    "wordpress" : []
  }
}
```

    On Windows systems, the packages key only supports MSI installers.

GROUPS

Use the groups key to generate Linux/UNIX groups on the target system. The name of the group is derived from the key name, and you can provide an optional group ID. For example, you create two groups with the following syntax. The first group, groupOne, randomly generates the gid value. The second group, groupTwo, will be assigned a gid of 45.

```
"groups" : {
    "groupOne" : {},
    "groupTwo" : { "gid" : "45" }
}
```

    Windows systems do not support the groups key.

USERS

The users key allows you to create Linux/UNIX users on your instance. By default, users you create with this key are noninteractive system users, and their default shell is set to /sbin/nologon. If you want to modify this behavior, you will have to issue a separate command on the system after the user generates.

```
"users" : {
    "myUser" : {
        "groups" : ["groupOne", "groupTwo"],
        "uid" : "50",
        "homeDir" : "/tmp"
    }
}
```

     Windows systems do not support the users key.

SOURCES

Similar in operation to the files key, you use the sources key to download files from remote locations. However, the sources key supports unpacking archives into target directories on the instance. For example, to download and unpack an archive hosted in a public Amazon S3 bucket, use this snippet:

```
"sources" : {
  "/etc/myapp" : "https://s3.amazonaws.com/mybucket/myapp.tar.gz"
}
```

FILES

The files key creates files based on either inline content in the template or content from a remote location (URL). An example of inline file content written to /tmp/setup.mysql is as follows:

```
"files" : {
  "/tmp/setup.mysql" : {
    "content" : { "Fn::Join" : [ "", [
      "CREATE DATABASE ", { "Ref" : "DBName" }, ";\n",
      "CREATE USER '", { "Ref" : "DBUsername" }, "'@'localhost' IDENTIFIED BY
'",
      { "Ref" : "DBPassword" }, "';\n",
      "GRANT ALL ON ", { "Ref" : "DBName" }, ".* TO '", { "Ref" : "DBUsername"
},
      "'@'localhost';\n",
      "FLUSH PRIVILEGES;\n"
    ]]},
    "mode"  : "000644",
    "owner" : "root",
    "group" : "root"
  }
}
```

Additional file options, such as symlinks and mustache templates, are also supported.

COMMANDS

The commands key allows the execution of arbitrary commands on an Amazon EC2 instance, such as calling a custom application or script file.

Command Order of Execution

The commands section processes commands in alphabetical order based on the command name key. In this snippet, the command test would be called before test2.

```
"commands" : {
  "test" : {
    "command" : "echo \"$MAGIC\" > test.txt",
    "env" : { "MAGIC" : "I come from the environment!" },
    "cwd" : "~",
    "test" : "test ! -e ~/test.txt",
    "ignoreErrors" : "false"
  },
  "test2" : {
    "command" : "echo \"$MAGIC2\" > test2.txt",
    "env" : { "MAGIC2" : "I come from the environment!" },
    "cwd" : "~",
    "test" : "test ! -e ~/test2.txt",
    "ignoreErrors" : "false"
  }
}
```

SERVICES

The services key defines which services are enabled or disabled on the instance being configured. Linux systems utilize sysvinit to support the services key, while Windows systems use Windows Service Manager. Additionally, you can configure services to restart when dependencies update, such as files and packages. The following example enables nginx, configures it to run when the instance starts, and restarts whenever /var/www/html updates on the instance.

```
"services" : {
  "sysvinit" : {
    "nginx" : {
      "enabled" : "true",
      "ensureRunning" : "true",
      "files" : ["/etc/nginx/nginx.conf"],
      "sources" : ["/var/www/html"]
    }
  }
}
```

CONFIGSETS

You can organize config keys into *configSets*, which allow you to call groups of configurations at different times during an instance's setup process and change the order in which configurations are applied. The following example shows two configSets, which reverse the order in which configurations execute.

```
"AWS::CloudFormation::Init" : {
    "configSets" : {
        "ascending" : [ "config1" , "config2" ],
        "descending" : [ "config2" , "config1" ]
    },
    "config1" : {
        "commands" : {
            "test" : {
                "command" : "echo \"$CFNTEST\" > test.txt",
                "env" : { "CFNTEST" : "I come from config1." },
                "cwd" : "~"
            }
        }
    },
    "config2" : {
        "commands" : {
            "test" : {
                "command" : "echo \"$CFNTEST\" > test.txt",
                "env" : { "CFNTEST" : "I come from config2" },
                "cwd" : "~"
            }
        }
    }
}
```

ENFORCING AWS::CLOUDFORMATION::INIT METADATA

To enforce the AWS::CloudFormation::Init metadata, instances being provisioned in your template must call the cfn-init helper script as part of UserData execution (either in the AWS::EC2::Instance UserData property or in the same property of an AWS::AutoScaling::LaunchConfiguration resource). When doing so, you must provide the stack name and resource logical ID. Optionally, you can execute a configSet or list of configSets in the call.

You must pass UserData to instances in Base64 format. Thus, you call the Fn::Base64 function to convert the text-based script to a Base64 encoding.

```
"UserData" : { "Fn::Base64" :
  { "Fn::Join" : ["", [
    "#!/bin/bash -xe\n",
```

```
     "# Install the files and packages from the metadata\n",
     "/opt/aws/bin/cfn-init -v ",
     "           --stack ", { "Ref" : "AWS::StackName" },
     "           --resource WebServerInstance ",
     "           --configsets InstallAndRun ",
     "           --region ", { "Ref" : "AWS::Region" }, "\n"
  ]]}
}
```

AWS::CloudFormation::Interface

This section details how to modify the ordering and presentation of parameters in the AWS CloudFormation console. Without this section, parameters display alphabetically without any additional clarification. This is especially useful when providing templates to other groups who are not familiar with the purpose of each input parameter.

> **NOTE** This Metadata section is only for the visual appearance of parameters in the AWS CloudFormation console. metadata does not have change templates that you submit via the AWS CLI or AWS SDK.

The AWS::CloudFormation::Interface metadata key uses two child keys, ParameterGroups and ParameterLabels.

```
"Metadata" : {
  "AWS::CloudFormation::Interface" : {
    "ParameterGroups" : [ ParameterGroup, ... ],
    "ParameterLabels" : ParameterLabel
  }
}
```

PARAMETERGROUPS

You use the ParameterGroups section to organize sets of parameters into logical groupings, which are then separated by horizontal lines in the console. Each entry in ParameterGroups is defined as an object with a Label key and Parameters key. The Label key contains a friendly text name for each grouping of parameters. The Parameters key contains a list of logical IDs for each parameter in the group.

```
"ParameterGroups" : [
    {
        "Label" : { "default" : "Network Configuration" },
        "Parameters" : [ "VPCID", "SubnetId", "SecurityGroupID" ]
    },
    {
```

```
        "Label" : { "default":"Amazon EC2 Configuration" },
        "Parameters" : [ "InstanceType", "KeyName" ]
    }
]
```

PARAMETERLABELS

The `ParameterLabels` section lets you define friendly names for parameters in the console. A logical ID such as `BastionSecurityGroupName` may be confusing to consumers of your template, especially if the template is shared outside your organization or team. By providing a more human-readable name, template portability is increased. The `ParameterLabels` key takes a list of parameter logical IDs, each of which has a friendly description as a subkey.

```
"ParameterLabels" : {
    "VPCID" : { "default" : "Which VPC should this be deployed to?" }
}
```

The inclusion of the `AWS::CloudFormation::Interface` definition results in an easy-to-understand list of parameters that you can complete, as shown in Figure 8.1.

FIGURE 8.1   AWS CloudFormation parameters

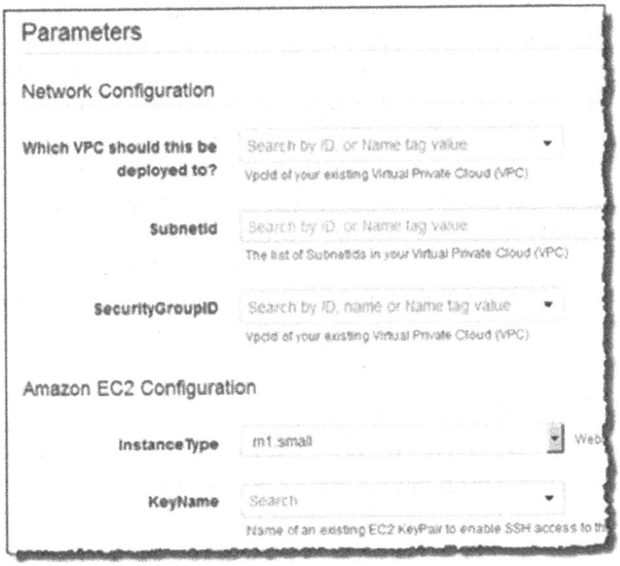

AWS::CloudFormation::Designer

This `Metadata` section specifies the visual layout and representation of resources when you design templates in the AWS CloudFormation Designer. Since it is used by Designer, we do not recommend that you manually modify this section.

AWS CloudFormation Designer

AWS CloudFormation Designer is a web-based graphical interface used to design and deploy AWS CloudFormation templates. You can design templates with a drag-and-drop interface of resource objects. You can create connections to make relationships between resources, which automatically update dependencies between them. When you are ready to deploy, you can submit the template directly to AWS CloudFormation or download it in JSON or YAML format.

AWS CloudFormation Designer keeps track of resource positions and relationships with metadata information in AWS::CloudFormation::Designer. Since no other service or component uses this information, it is safe to leave as is within your template.

Custom Resources

Sometimes custom provisioning logic is required when creating resources in AWS. Common examples of this include managing resources not currently supported by AWS CloudFormation, interacting with third-party tools, or other situations where more complexity is involved in the provisioning process.

AWS CloudFormation uses *custom resource providers* to handle the provisioning and configuration of custom resources. Custom resource providers may be AWS Lambda functions or Amazon Simple Notification Service (Amazon SNS) topics. When you create, update, or delete a custom resource, either the AWS Lambda function is invoked or a message is sent to the Amazon SNS topic you configure in the resource declaration.

In the custom resource declaration, you must provide a service token along with any optional input parameters. The *service token* acts as a reference to where custom resource requests are sent. This can be either an AWS Lambda function or Amazon SNS topic. Any input parameters you include are sent with the request body. After the resource provider processes the request, a SUCCESS or FAILED result is sent to the presigned Amazon S3 URL you included in the request body. AWS CloudFormation monitors this bucket location for a response, which it processes once it is sent by the provider. Custom resources can provide outputs back to AWS CloudFormation, which are made accessible as properties of the custom resource. You can access these properties with the Fn::GetAtt intrinsic function to pass the logical ID of the resource and the attribute you desire to query.

AWS Lambda Backed Custom Resources

Custom resources that are backed by AWS Lambda invoke functions whenever create, update, or delete actions are sent to the resource provider. This resource type is incredibly useful to reference other AWS services and resources that may not support AWS CloudFormation. Also, you can use them to look up data from other resources, such as Amazon EC2 instance IDs or entries in an Amazon DynamoDB table.

You can include the AWS Lambda function, which acts as a resource provider in the same AWS CloudFormation template that creates the custom resource and adds additional flexibility for stack update events. In this case, you can define the code for the

AWS Lambda function itself inline in the template or store it in a separate location such as Amazon S3. The following example demonstrates a custom resource, AMIInfo, which makes use of an AWS Lambda function, AMIInfoFunction, as the resource provider. Two additional properties, Region and OSName, provide inputs to the resource provider.

```
"AMIInfo": {
  "Type": "Custom::AMIInfo",
  "Properties": {
    "ServiceToken": { "Fn::GetAtt" : ["AMIInfoFunction", "Arn"] },
    "Region": { "Ref": "AWS::Region" },
    "OSName": { "Ref": "WindowsVersion" }
  }
}
```

For the AWS Lambda function to execute successfully, you must supply it with an IAM role. If the function will interact with other AWS services, you need the following permissions at minimum:

- logs:CreateLogGroup
- logs:CreateLogStream
- logs:PutLogEvents

Custom Resources Associated with Amazon SNS

Although AWS Lambda functions are incredibly powerful and versatile, they have a limit of 5 minutes of execution time, at which point the function will exit prematurely. This may not be desirable, especially when custom resources take a long time to provision or update. In these situations, use *custom resources associated with Amazon SNS*.

With this resource type, notifications are sent to an Amazon SNS topic any time the custom resource triggers. As the developer you are responsible for managing the system that receives notifications and performs processing. For instance, transcoding of long video files may take a longer time than AWS Lambda allows. In these situations, you subscribe an Amazon EC2 instance to the Amazon SNS topic to listen for requests, consume the input request object, perform the transcoding work, and place an appropriate response.

Custom Resource Success/Failure

For a custom resource to be successful in AWS CloudFormation, the resource provider must return a success response to the presigned Amazon S3 URL that you provide in the request. If you do not provide a response, the custom resource will eventually time out. This is especially important with regard to update and delete actions. The custom resource provider will need to respond appropriately to every action type (create, update, and delete) for both successful and unsuccessful attempts. If you do not provide a response to an update action, for example, the entire stack update will fail after the custom resource times out, and this results in a stack rollback.

Resource Relationships

By default, AWS CloudFormation will track most dependencies between resources. There are, however, some exceptions to this process. For example, an application server may not function properly until the backend database is up and running. In this case, you can add a DependsOn attribute to your template to specify the order of creation. The *DependsOn* attribute specifies that creation of a resource should not begin until another completes. A resource can have a dependency on one or more other resources in a stack. The following code demonstrates that the resource EC2Instance has a dependency on MyDB, which means the instance resource will not begin creation until the database resource is in a CREATE_COMPLETE state.

```
{
    "Resources" : {
        "Ec2Instance" : {
            "Type" : "AWS::EC2::Instance",
            "Properties" : {
                "ImageId" : {
                    "Fn::FindInMap" : [ "RegionMap", { "Ref" : "AWS::Region" }, "AMI" ]
                }
            },
            "DependsOn" : "myDB"
        },
        "myDB" : {
            "Type" : "AWS::RDS::DBInstance",
            "Properties" : {
                "AllocatedStorage" : "5",
                "DBInstanceClass" : "db.m1.small",
                "Engine" : "MySQL",
                "EngineVersion" : "5.5",
                "MasterUsername" : "MyName",
                "MasterUserPassword" : "MyPassword"
            }
        }
    }
}
```

Creation Policies

There may be situations where a dependency is not enough, such as when you install and configure applications on an instance before you attach it to an elastic load balancer. In this case, you can use a CreationPolicy. A *CreationPolicy* instructs AWS CloudFormation not to mark a resource as CREATE_COMPLETE until the resource itself signals back to the service.

You can configure the creation policy to require a specific number of signals in a certain amount of time; otherwise, the resource will show CREATE_FAILED. Signals sent to a resource are visible events in the AWS CloudFormation stack logs.

You can define creation policies with this syntax. When you configure creation policies for AWS Auto Scaling groups, you must specify the MinSuccessfulInstancesPercent property so that a certain percentage of instances in the group setup successfully complete before the group itself shows CREATE_COMPLETE. You can also configure creation policies to require a certain number of signals (Count) in a certain amount of time (Timeout). The following code example displays an AWS Auto Scaling group resource with a creation policy. This policy specifies that at least three signals must be received in 15 minutes for the group to create successfully.

```
"AutoScalingGroup": {
  "Type": "AWS::AutoScaling::AutoScalingGroup",
  "Properties": {
    "AvailabilityZones": { "Fn::GetAZs": "" },
    "LaunchConfigurationName": { "Ref": "LaunchConfig" },
    "DesiredCapacity": "3",
    "MinSize": "1",
    "MaxSize": "4"
  },
  "CreationPolicy": {
    "ResourceSignal": {
      "Count": "3",
      "Timeout": "PT15M"
    }
  }
}
```

Wait Conditions

You can use the *WaitCondition* property to insert arbitrary pauses until resources complete. If you require additional tracking of stack creation, you can use the WaitCondition property to add pauses to wait for external configuration tasks. An example of this would be if you create an Amazon DynamoDB table with a custom resource associated with AWS Lambda to load data into the table and then install software on an Amazon EC2 instance that reads data from the table. You can insert a WaitCondition into this template to prevent the creation of the instance until the custom resource function signals that data has been successfully loaded.

For Amazon EC2 instances and AWS Auto Scaling groups, we recommend that you use creation policies instead of wait conditions.

Wait conditions consist of two resources in a template, an AWS::CloudFormation::WaitCondition (wait condition) and an AWS::CloudFormation::WaitConditionHandle (wait condition handle).

The first resource, the wait condition, is similar to a creation policy. It requires a signal count and timeout value. However, it also requires a reference to a wait condition handle. The wait condition handle acts as a reference to a presigned URL where signals are sent to AWS CloudFormation, which it monitors.

WARNING   Wait condition handles should never be reused between stack creation and subsequent updates, as it may result in signals from previous stack actions being evaluated. Instead, create new wait conditions for each stack action.

In the following example, the WebServerGroup resource creates an AWS Auto Scaling group with a count equal to the WebServerCapacity parameter. The example also creates a wait condition and wait condition handle, where the wait condition handle expects a number of signals equal to the WebServerCapacity parameter.

```
"WebServerGroup" : {
   "Type" : "AWS::AutoScaling::AutoScalingGroup",
   "Properties" : {
      "AvailabilityZones" : { "Fn::GetAZs" : "" },
      "LaunchConfigurationName" : { "Ref" : "LaunchConfig" },
      "MinSize" : "1",
      "MaxSize" : "5",
      "DesiredCapacity" : { "Ref" : "WebServerCapacity" },
      "LoadBalancerNames" : [ { "Ref" : "ElasticLoadBalancer" } ]
   }
},
"WaitHandle" : {
   "Type" : "AWS::CloudFormation::WaitConditionHandle"
},
"WaitCondition" : {
   "Type" : "AWS::CloudFormation::WaitCondition",
   "DependsOn" : "WebServerGroup",
   "Properties" : {
      "Handle"  : { "Ref" : "WaitHandle" },
      "Timeout" : "300",
      "Count"   : { "Ref" : "WebServerCapacity" }
   }
}
```

With this approach, you need to ensure that the signal is sent to the wait condition handle. This is done in the Amazon EC2 instance's user data, which you define in the launch configuration for AWS Auto Scaling groups. In this case, the LaunchConfig resource must include a signal to the wait condition handle. To do this, you reference the wait condition handle within the launch configuration's UserData script.

```
"UserData" : {
   "Fn::Base64" : {
       "Fn::Join" : [ "", ["SignalURL=", { "Ref" : "myWaitHandle" } ] ]
   }
}
```

Within UserData, you can use a curl command to send the success signal back to AWS CloudFormation.

```
curl -T /tmp/a "WAIT_CONDITION_HANDLE_URL"
```

The file /tmp/a must be in the following format:

```
{
   "Status" : "SUCCESS",
   "Reason" : "Configuration Complete",
   "UniqueId" : "ID1234",
   "Data" : "Application has completed configuration."
}
```

The Data section of the JSON response can include arbitrary data about the signal. You can make it accessible in the AWS CloudFormation template with the Fn::GetAtt intrinsic function.

```
"Outputs": {
   "WaitConditionData" : {
       "Value" : { "Fn::GetAtt" : [ "mywaitcondition", "Data" ]},
       "Description" : "The data passed back as part of signalling the
WaitCondition"
   }
}
```

Stack Create, Update, and Delete Statuses

Whenever you perform an action on an AWS CloudFormation stack, the end result will bring the stack into one of three possible statuses: Create, Update, and Delete. These statuses are visible in the AWS CloudFormation console, or if you use the DescribeStacks action.

CREATE_COMPLETE

The stack has created successfully.

CREATE_IN_PROGRESS

The stack is currently undergoing creation. No error has been detected.

CREATE_FAILED

One or more resources has failed to create successfully, causing the entire stack creation to fail. Review the stack failure messages to determine which resource(s) failed to create.

DELETE_COMPLETE

The stack has deleted successfully and will remain visible for 90 days.

DELETE_IN_PROGRESS

The stack is currently deleting.

DELETE_FAILED

The stack delete action has failed because of one or more underlying resources failing to delete. Review the stack output events to determine which resource(s) failed to delete. There you can manually delete the resource to prevent the stack delete from failing again.

ROLLBACK_COMPLETE

If a stack creation action fails to complete, AWS CloudFormation will automatically attempt to roll the stack back and delete any created resources. This status is achieved when the resources have been removed.

ROLLBACK_IN_PROGRESS

The stack has failed to create and is currently rolling back.

ROLLBACK_FAILED

If AWS CloudFormation is not able to delete resources that were provisioned during a failed stack create action, the stack will enter ROLLBACK_FAILED. The remaining resources will not be deleted until the error condition is corrected. Other than attempting to continue deleting the stack, no other actions can be performed on the stack itself. To resolve this, review the stack events to determine which resource(s) failed to delete.

UPDATE_COMPLETE

The stack has updated successfully.

UPDATE_IN_PROGRESS

The stack is currently performing an update.

UPDATE_COMPLETE_CLEANUP_IN_PROGRESS

When AWS CloudFormation updates certain resources, the type of update may require a replacement of the original physical resource. In these situations, AWS CloudFormation will first create the replacement resource and verify that the provision was successful. After all resources update, the stack will enter this phase and remove any previous resources. For example, when you update the Name property of an AWS::S3::Bucket resource, AWS CloudFormation will create a bucket with the new name value and then delete the previous bucket during the cleanup phase.

UPDATE_ROLLBACK_COMPLETE

If a stack update fails, AWS CloudFormation will attempt to roll the stack back to the last working state. Once complete, the stack will enter the UPDATE_ROLLBACK_COMPLETE state.

UPDATE_ROLLBACK_IN_PROGRESS

After a stack update fails, AWS CloudFormation begins to roll back any changes to bring the stack back to the last working state.

UPDATE_ROLLBACK_COMPLETE_CLEANUP_IN_PROGRESS

A failed rollback will require a cleanup of any newly created resources that would have originally replaced existing ones. During this phase, replacement resources are deleted in place of the originals.

UPDATE_ROLLBACK_FAILED

If the stack update fails and the rollback is unable to return it to a working state, it will enter UPDATE_ROLLBACK_FAILED. You can delete the entire stack. Otherwise, you can review to determine what failed to roll back and continue the update rollback again.

Stack Updates

You do not need to re-create stacks any time you need to update an underlying resource. You can modify and resubmit the same template, and AWS CloudFormation will parse it for changes and apply the modifications to the resources. This can include the ability to add new resources or modify and delete existing ones. You can perform stack updates when you create a new template or parameters directly, or you can create a change set with the updates.

> Some template sections, such as Metadata, require you to modify one or more resources when the stack updates, as you cannot change them on their own. You can change parameters without modifying the stack's template.

When performing a stack action, such as an update, one or more stack events are created. The event contains information such as the resource being modified, the action being performed, and resource IDs. One critical piece of information in the stack event is the ClientRequestToken.

All events triggered by a single stack action are assigned the same token value. For example, if a stack update modifies an Amazon S3 bucket and Amazon EC2 instance, the corresponding Amazon S3 and Amazon EC2 API calls will contain the same request token. This lets you easily track what API activity corresponds to particular stack actions. This API activity can be tracked in AWS CloudTrail and stored in Amazon S3 for later review.

When you update a stack, underlying resources can exhibit one of several behaviors. This depends on the update to the resource property or properties. Resource property changes can cause one of update types to occur, as shown in Table 8.1.

TABLE 8.1 AWS CloudFormation Update Types

Update Type	Resource Downtime	Resource Replacement
Update with No Interruption	No	No
Update with Some Interruption	Yes	No
Replacing Update	Yes	Yes

For resource properties that require replacement, the resource's physical ID will change.

Some resource properties do not support updates. In these cases, you must create new resources first. After this, you can remove the original resource from the stack.

Update Policies

You use the AWS CloudFormation *UpdatePolicy* to determine how to respond to changes to AWS::AutoScaling::AutoScalingGroup and AWS::Lambda::Alias resources.

For AWS Auto Scaling group update policies, there are policies that you can enforce. These depend on the type of change you make and whether you configure the AWS Auto Scaling scheduled actions. Table 8.2 displays the types of policies that take effect under each scenario.

TABLE 8.2 AWS Auto Scaling Update Types in AWS CloudFormation

AWS Auto Scaling Update Type	Change AWS Auto Scaling group Launch Configuration	Change AWS Auto Scaling group VPCZoneIdentifier Property	AWS Auto Scaling group Has a Scheduled Action
AutoScalingReplacingUpdate	X	X	
AutoScalingRollingUpdate	X	X	
AutoScalingScheduledAction			X

You can configure the WillReplace property for an UpdatePolicy to true and give precedence to the AutoScalingReplacingUpdate settings.

The AutoScalingReplacingUpdate policy defines how to replace updates. You can replace the entire AWS Auto Scaling group or only instances inside.

```
"UpdatePolicy" : {
  "AutoScalingReplacingUpdate" : {
    "WillReplace" : Boolean
  }
}
```

The AutoScalingRollingUpdate policy allows you to define the update process for instances in an AWS Auto Scaling group. This lets you configure the group to update instances all at once, in batches, or with an additional batch.

SuspendProcesses Attribute

The SuspendProcesses attribute can define whether to suspend AWS Auto Scaling scheduled actions or those you invoke by alarms, which can otherwise cause the update to fail.

```
"UpdatePolicy" : {
  "AutoScalingRollingUpdate" : {
    "MaxBatchSize" : Integer,
    "MinInstancesInService" : Integer,
    "MinSuccessfulInstancesPercent" : Integer
    "PauseTime" : String,
    "SuspendProcesses" : [ List of processes ],
    "WaitOnResourceSignals" : Boolean
  }
}
```

Lastly, for AWS Auto Scaling groups, the AutoScalingScheduledAction property defines whether to adhere to the group sizes (minimum, maximum, and desired counts) you define in your template. If your AWS Auto Scaling group has enabled scheduled actions, there is a possibility that the actual group sizes no longer reflect those in the template. If you run an update without this policy set, it can cause the group to be reverted to its original size. If you configure the IgnoreUnmodifiedGroupSizeProperties property to true, it will cause

AWS CloudFormation to ignore different group sizes when it compares the template to the actual AWS Auto Scaling group.

```
"UpdatePolicy" : {
  "AutoScalingScheduledAction" : {
    "IgnoreUnmodifiedGroupSizeProperties" : Boolean
  }
}
```

For changes to an AWS::Lambda::Alias resource, you can define the CodeDeployLambdaAliasUpdate policy. This controls whether a deployment is made with AWS CodeDeploy whenever it detects version changes.

```
"UpdatePolicy" : {
  "CodeDeployLambdaAliasUpdate" : {
    "AfterAllowTrafficHook" : String,
    "ApplicationName" : String,
    "BeforeAllowTrafficHook" : String,
    "DeploymentGroupName" : String
  }
}
```

In the previous examples, you only require the ApplicationName and DeploymentGroupName properties. These refer to the AWS CodeDeploy application and deployment group, which should update when the alias changes.

Deletion Policies

When you delete a stack, by default all underlying stack resources are also deleted. If this behavior is not desirable, apply the *DeletionPolicy* to resources in the stack to modify their behavior when the stack is deleted. You use deletion policies to preserve resources when you delete a stack (set DeletionPolicy to Retain). Some resources can instead have a snapshot or backup taken before you delete the resource (set DeletionPolicy to Snapshot). The following resource types support snapshots:

- AWS::EC2::Volume
- AWS::ElastiCache::CacheCluster
- AWS::ElastiCache::ReplicationGroup
- AWS::RDS::DBInstance
- AWS::RDS::DBCluster
- AWS::Redshift::Cluster

The following template example creates an Amazon S3 bucket with a deletion policy set to retain the bucket when you delete the stack.

```
{
  "AWSTemplateFormatVersion" : "2010-09-09",
  "Resources" : {
    "myS3Bucket" : {
      "Type" : "AWS::S3::Bucket",
      "DeletionPolicy" : "Retain"
    }
  }
}
```

Exports and Nested Stacks

Since AWS CloudFormation enforces limits on how large templates can grow and how many resources, outputs, and parameters you can declare in one template, situations can arise where you will need to manage more infrastructure than a single stack will allow. There are two approaches to manage relationships between multiple stacks. You use *stack exports* to share information between separate stacks or manage AWS CloudFormation stacks themselves as resources in a "parent" or "master" stack (a *nested stack* relationship).

Export and Import Stack Outputs

You can export stack output values to import them into other stacks in the same account and region. This allows you to share data that generates in one stack out to other stacks in your account. If, for example, you create a networking infrastructure such as an Amazon VPC in one stack, you can export the IDs of such resources from this stack and import them into others at a later date.

To export a stack value, update the Outputs section to include an Export declaration for every output you want to share.

```
"Outputs" : {
  "Logical ID" : {
    "Description" : "Information about the value",
    "Value" : "Value to return",
    "Export" : {
      "Name" : "Value to export"
    }
  }
}
```

 Export values must have a unique name within the AWS account and AWS region.

After you declare the export and the stack creates or updates, it displays in the AWS CloudFormation console on the Exports tab, as shown in Figure 8.2.

FIGURE 8.2   AWS CloudFormation Exports tab

To import this value into another stack, you use the *Fn::ImportValue* intrinsic function. This intrinsic function requires only the export name as an input parameter (the name present in the AWS CloudFormation console).

You cannot change export values after you import them into another stack. You must first modify the import stack so that it no longer uses the export. To list stacks that import an exported output, use the ListImports API action.

```
https://cloudformation.us-east-1.amazonaws.com/
 ?Action=ListImports
 &ExportName=SampleStack-MyExportedValue
 &Version=2010-05-15
 &X-Amz-Algorithm=AWS4-HMAC-SHA256
 &X-Amz-Credential=[Access key ID and scope]
 &X-Amz-Date=20160316T233349Z
 &X-Amz-SignedHeaders=content-type;host
 &X-Amz-Signature=[Signature]
```

Nesting with the AWS::CloudFormation::Stack Resource

You can manage stacks as resources within the service in AWS CloudFormation. A single parent stack can create one or more AWS::CloudFormation::Stack resources, which act as child stacks that the parent manages. The direct benefits of this are as follows:

▪ You can work around template limits that AWS CloudFormation imposes.

▪ It provides the ability to separate resources into logical groups, such as network, database, and web application.

▪ It lets you separate duties. (Each team is responsible only for maintaining their respective child stack.)

You can increase the nesting levels, as shown in Figure 8.3, with the AWS::CloudFormation::Stack resources.

FIGURE 8.3   Nested stack structure

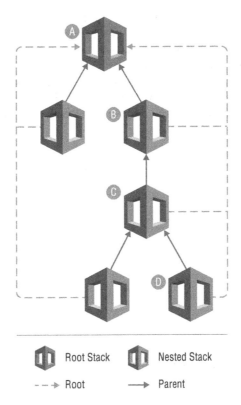

	Root Stack		Nested Stack
- - - ►	Root	──────►	Parent

> From a workflow perspective, the "topmost" parent stack should manage all updates to child stacks. In Figure 8.3, if you need to update stack D, you perform the update on stack A, the topmost parent, to accomplish this.

You can share data from each nested stack if you use a combination of stack outputs and the Fn::GetAtt function calls. If there is an output value from a nested stack that you would like to access from its parent, the following syntax will let you access stack outputs.

```
{ "Fn::GetAtt" : [ "logicalNameOfChildStack", "Outputs.attributeName" ] }
```

> Outputs from stacks created by a nested stack (such as to access outputs in stack C from stack A, as shown in Figure 8.3) can be accessed from the parent stack(s). First, you will need to output the value in the originating stack and then its parent and finally access the output from the parent. To clarify, the output would originate in stack C and be added as an output to stack B, and then stack A references it.

Stack Policies

Though you can assign resources to create, update, and delete policies to stacks directly, there may be situations where you will want to prevent certain types of updates to stacks themselves. By default, anyone with permissions to modify stacks can perform updates to all underlying stack resources (if they have permissions to modify the resources themselves, or the AWS CloudFormation service role attached to the stack has these permissions). You can assign a *stack policy* to a stack to allow or deny access to modify certain stack resources, which you can filter by the type of update. Stack policies apply to all users, regardless of their IAM permissions.

```
{
  "Statement" : [
    {
      "Effect" : "Allow",
      "Action" : "Update:*",
      "Principal": "*",
      "Resource" : "*"
    },
    {
      "Effect" : "Deny",
      "Action" : "Update:*",
      "Principal": "*",
      "Resource" : "LogicalResourceId/ProductionDatabase"
    }
  ]
}
```

> **NOTE** Stack policies are not a replacement for appropriate access control from an IAM policy. Stack policies are an additional fail-safe to prevent accidental updates to critical resources.

Stack policies protect all resources by default with an implicit deny. To allow access to actions on stack resources, you must apply explicit allow statements to the policy. In the previous example, an explicit allow specifies that you can perform all updates on all resources in the stack. However, the explicit deny for the ProductionDatabase resource prevents update actions to this specific resource. You can specify allow and deny actions for either resource logical IDs or generic resource types. To specify policies for generic resource types, use a condition statement as follows:

```
{
  "Statement" : [
    {
      "Effect" : "Deny",
      "Principal" : "*",
      "Action" : "Update:*",
      "Resource" : "*",
      "Condition" : {
        "StringEquals" : {
          "ResourceType" : ["AWS::EC2::Instance", "AWS::RDS::DBInstance"]
        }
      }
    }
  ]
}
```

Once you apply a stack policy, you cannot remove it. During future updates, the policy must be temporarily replaced.

You can allow or deny specific types of updates for resources in your stack. Action types include the following:

Update:Modify Update actions where resources will experience some or no interruption

Update:Replace Update actions where replacement resources create (the physical ID of the resource changes)

Update:Delete Update actions where resources delete from the stack

Update:* All update actions

Once a stack policy has been set, it will need to be overridden during updates to protected resources. To do so, you supply a new, temporary stack policy. You add this stack policy in the console under the Stack policy property, as shown in Figure 8.4.

FIGURE 8.4   AWS CloudFormation Stack Policy field

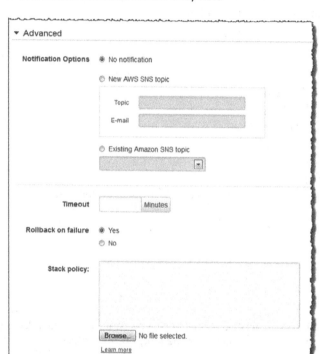

 When you supply a stack policy during an update, it only modifies the policy for the duration of the update after which the original policy reinstates.

AWS CloudFormation Command Line Interface

AWS CloudFormation provides several utility functions apart from the standard API-based component of the AWS CloudFormation CLI.

Packaging Local Dependencies

When you develop templates locally, you may require additional files for your infrastructure that you do not want to define inline as part of the template syntax. For example, you may need to place configuration files on Amazon EC2 instances or AWS Lambda function code. You can use the aws cloudformation package command to upload local files and convert local references in your template to Amazon S3 URIs. Consider the following example:

```
AWSTemplateFormatVersion: '2010-09-09'
Transform: 'AWS::Serverless-2016-10-31'
```

```
Resources:
  MyFunction:
    Type: 'AWS::Serverless::Function'
    Properties:
      Handler: index.handler
      Runtime: nodejs4.3
      CodeUri: /home/user/code/lambdafunction
```

The CodeUri property refers to a local path on the user's workstation (/home/user/code/lambdafunction). To prepare this for deployment, you can run the following command:

```
aws cloudformation package --template /path_to_template/template.json --s3-bucket
mybucket --output json > packaged-template.json
```

When you execute this command, the AWS CLI will package the contents of /home/user/code/lambdafunction into a .zip archive and upload it to the Amazon S3 bucket you specify in the --s3-bucket parameter. After doing so, the template updates to refer to the Amazon S3 URI for the archive file and generates the following:

```
AWSTemplateFormatVersion: '2010-09-09'
Transform: 'AWS::Serverless-2016-10-31'
Resources:
  MyFunction:
    Type: 'AWS::Serverless::Function'
    Properties:
      Handler: index.handler
      Runtime: nodejs4.3
      CodeUri: s3://mybucket/lambdafunction.zip
```

Deploy Templates with Transforms

Any time that you want to deploy an AWS CloudFormation template that contains transforms, you must first create a change set. The *change set* is responsible for executing the transform to generate a final template that you can deploy. If you would like to reduce this to a one-step process, the aws cloudformation deploy command will generate and execute the change set on your behalf. This is especially useful for rapid testing, as it eliminates the need to approve change sets manually.

When you use this command, you can override default parameters with the --parameter-overrides property.

```
aws cloudformation deploy --template /path_to_template/my-template.json --stack-
name my-new-stack --parameter-overrides Key1=Value1 Key2=Value2
```

AWS CloudFormation Helper Scripts

When you execute custom scripts on Amazon EC2 instances as part of your UserData, AWS CloudFormation provides several important helper scripts. You can use these to interact with the stack to query metadata, notify a CreationPolicy or WaitCondition, and process scripts when AWS CloudFormation detects metadata updates.

cfn-init

You use this helper script to read AWS::CloudFormation::Init metadata from the AWS::EC2::LaunchConfiguration or AWS::EC2::Instance resource being declared. It is responsible for installing packages, adding files, creating users and groups, and any other configuration you specify in your AWS::CloudFormation::Init metadata.

AWS::CloudFormation::Init metadata is not enforced automatically. You must call the cfn-init helper script in your instances' UserData. The following example demonstrates a cfn-init call on an instance in an AWS CloudFormation stack. In this case, the InstallAndRun configuration set executes on the instance.

```
"UserData" : { "Fn::Base64" :
  { "Fn::Join" : ["", [
    "#!/bin/bash -xe\n",
    "# Install the files and packages from the metadata\n",
    "/opt/aws/bin/cfn-init -v ",
    "         --stack ", { "Ref" : "AWS::StackName" },
    "         --resource WebServerInstance ",
    "         --configsets InstallAndRun ",
    "         --region ", { "Ref" : "AWS::Region" }, "\n"
  ]]}
}
```

cfn-signal

After cfn-init has been called and the AWS::CloudFormation::Init metadata has been enforced successfully (or unsuccessfully), you can use *cfn-signal* to notify AWS CloudFormation that the instance has completed its configuration. For example, if your template contains a CreationPolicy or WaitCondition to prevent the setup of an AWS::ElasticLoadBalancing:: LoadBalancer resource until instances in your AWS::AutoScaling::AutoScalingGroup have configured a custom application, cfn-signal performs the notification. The following UserData example demonstrates how to pass the result of cfn-init to cfn-signal:

```
"UserData": {
  "Fn::Base64": {
    "Fn::Join": [
      "",
      [
        "#!/bin/bash -x\n",
        "# Install the files and packages from the metadata\n",
```

```
        "/opt/aws/bin/cfn-init -v ",
        "          --stack ", { "Ref": "AWS::StackName" },
        "          --resource MyInstance ",
        "          --region ", { "Ref": "AWS::Region" },
        "\n",
        "# Signal the status from cfn-init\n",
        "/opt/aws/bin/cfn-signal -e $? ",
        "          --stack ", { "Ref": "AWS::StackName" },
        "          --resource MyInstance ",
        "          --region ", { "Ref": "AWS::Region" },
        "\n"
      ]
    ]
  }
}
```

cfn-get-metadata

If your template contains arbitrary metadata, use `cfn-get-metadata` to fetch this information for use on your instance(s). You can use this helper script to query either an entire metadata block or a subtree. AWS CloudFormation supports only top-level keys.

cfn-hup

Since AWS CloudFormation executes `UserData` only on resource creation, instances will not detect changes to `AWS::CloudFormation::Init` metadata automatically. Unlike other helper scripts, you can configure *cfn-hup* to run as a daemon on instances. This script checks for changes to resource metadata, can execute custom scripts whenever they are detected, and allows you to perform configuration updates on instances in a stack.

The `cfn-hup` helper script requires you to perform several configuration steps before it detects updates.

DAEMON CONFIGURATION FILE

You must create the `cfn-hup.conf` configuration file on the instance, and it needs to contain the stack name. You can also use `cfn-hup.conf` to contain AWS credentials the daemon requires, though it can also leverage IAM instance profiles. Here's an example:

```
[main]
stack=<stack-name-or-id>
```

HOOKS CONFIGURATION FILE

Whenever AWS CloudFormation detects changes to instance metadata, user-defined actions are called based on settings in the `hooks.conf` configuration file. You can configure hooks to run on one or more resource actions (add, update, or remove) and can execute arbitrary commands. If there are scripts you want to call, you must add the scripts to the instance before you execute the hook. If you require more than one configuration file, you can add /etc/cfn/hooks.d/ on Linux instances. The hooks.conf file structure is as follows:

```
[hookname]
triggers=post.add or post.update or post.remove
path=Resources.<logicalResourceId> (.Metadata or
.PhysicalResourceId) (.<optionalMetadatapath>)
action=<arbitrary shell command>
runas=<runas user>
```

This template snippet demonstrates how to add a cfn-hup hook file to instances in an AWS::AutoScaling::LaunchConfiguration resource. This hook file will detect updates to the LaunchConfig resource and execute the wordpress_install config set you specify in the AWS::CloudFormation::Init metadata.

```
[hookname]
triggers=post.add or post.update or post.remove
path=Resources.<logicalResourceId> (.Metadata or
.PhysicalResourceId) (.<optionalMetadatapath>)
action=<arbitrary shell command>
runas=<runas user>
"LaunchConfig": {
  "Type" : "AWS::AutoScaling::LaunchConfiguration",
  "Metadata" : {
    "AWS::CloudFormation::Init" : {
      ...
      "/etc/cfn/hooks.d/cfn-auto-reloader.conf": {
        "content": { "Fn::Join": [ "", [
          "[cfn-auto-reloader-hook]\n",
            "triggers=post.update\n",
            "path=Resources.LaunchConfig.Metadata.AWS::CloudFormation::Init\n",
            "action=/opt/aws/bin/cfn-init -v ",
            "          --stack ", { "Ref" : "AWS::StackName" },
            "          --resource LaunchConfig ",
            "          --configsets wordpress_install ",
            "          --region ", { "Ref" : "AWS::Region" }, "\n",
            "runas=root\n"
        ]]},
        "mode"  : "000400",
        "owner" : "root",
        "group" : "root"
}
```

AWS CloudFormation StackSets

AWS CloudFormation *StackSets* gives users the ability to control, provision, and manage stacks across multiple accounts, as shown in Figure 8.5. From a centralized administrator account, you can develop a template as the basis for provisioning similar stacks across a fleet of accounts.

FIGURE 8.5 AWS CloudFormation StackSets structure

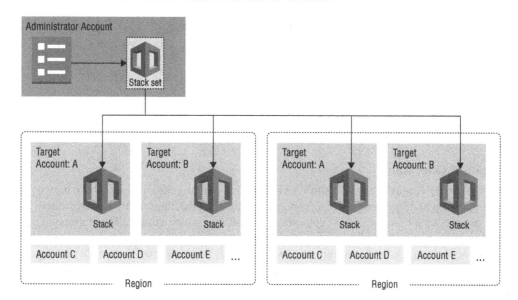

Stack Set

A *stack set* acts as a logical container for stack information in an administrator account. Each stack set will contain information about the stacks you deploy to a single target account in one or more regions. You can configure stack sets to deploy to regions in a specific order and how many unsuccessful deployments are required to fail the entire deployment.

 Though a stack set allows you to deploy stacks to multiple regions, the stack set itself exists in one region, and you must manage it there.

Stack Instance

Stack instances allow you to manage stacks in a target account, as shown in Figure 8.6. For example, if a stack set deploys to four regions in a target account, you create four stack instances. An update to a stack set propagates to all stack instances in all accounts and regions.

FIGURE 8.6   AWS CloudFormation StackSet actions

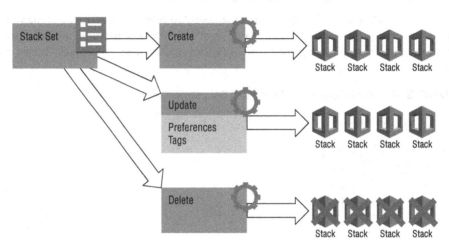

Stack Set Operations

When you perform operations on stack sets, you can configure how to control the flow of updates across accounts and regions. You can specify a maximum number or percentage of target accounts for concurrent deployment. Additionally, you can specify a maximum number of percentage of failures (per region). Lastly, you can configure delete operations to remove only the stack instances and stack set and leave the stack itself present in the target account. This option is useful when removing control from an administrator account for resources that need to remain operational in the target account.

 If you specify a maximum number of failures per region, stack updates will not progress to the next region when this threshold is breached. The stack set operation will stop completely.

Stack Set Permissions

For an administrator account to deploy to any target accounts, you must create a trust relationship between the accounts. To do this, you create an IAM role in each account.

The administrator account requires an IAM service role with permissions to execute stack set operations and assume an execution role in any target accounts. This service role must have a trust policy that allows `cloudformation.amazonaws.com`.

Any target accounts will require an execution role that you create in the administrator account, which the service role can assume. This execution role will require AWS CloudFormation permissions and permissions to manage any resources you define in the template being deployed by the stack set, as shown in Figure 8.7.

FIGURE 8.7   AWS CloudFormation StackSets permissions

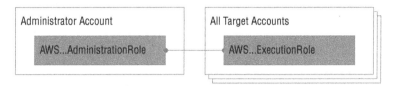

Target Account Gate

Before you create or update a stack set, evaluate potential blockers in target accounts. If a certain resource type is not available in different regions, for example, this can cause the stack set operation to fail. You can use a *target account gate* to perform evaluation tasks with AWS Lambda functions in the target account. Depending on the return value of the function, the stack set operation will either continue or stop. You can configure this so that account gate failures count toward the stack set's configured tolerance settings.

AWS CloudFormation Service Limits

Important service limits for AWS CloudFormation are listed in Table 8.3. *You cannot raise template-specific limits through a support request.* You can raise some limits such as the number of stacks per account.

TABLE 8.3   AWS CloudFormation Service Limits

Limit	Value
Mappings per template	100
Outputs per template	60
Parameters per template	60
Resources per template	200
Stacks per account	200
Template body size	51,200 B (local file) 460,800 B (S3)

Using AWS CloudFormation with AWS CodePipeline

AWS CloudFormation has built-in integrations with AWS CodePipeline as a deployment provider. Refer to Figure 8.8. When a template revision passes through a pipeline, AWS CloudFormation can reference input parameters, stack policies, and other configuration data in the AWS CodePipeline deployment.

FIGURE 8.8   CloudFormation as a deployment provider

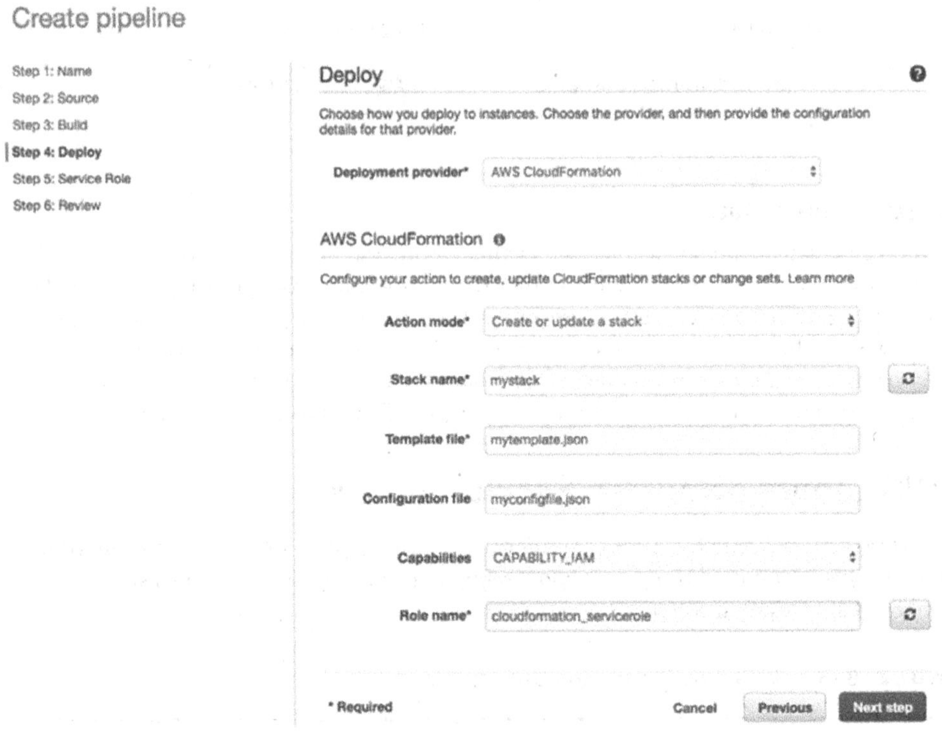

Create pipeline

Step 1: Name
Step 2: Source
Step 3: Build
Step 4: Deploy
Step 5: Service Role
Step 6: Review

Deploy   ❷

Choose how you deploy to instances. Choose the provider, and then provide the configuration
details for that provider.

Deployment provider*   AWS CloudFormation   ⬍

AWS CloudFormation ❶

Configure your action to create, update CloudFormation stacks or change sets. Learn more

Action mode*   Create or update a stack   ⬍

Stack name*   mystack   ⟳

Template file*   mytemplate.json

Configuration file   myconfigfile.json

Capabilities   CAPABILITY_IAM   ⬍

Role name*   cloudformation_servicerole   ⟳

* Required   Cancel   Previous   Next step

Deployment Configuration Properties

This section details deployment configuration properties including the following: Action Mode, Stack or Change Set Name, Templates, Template Configurations, Capabilities, Role Names, Output File Names, and Parameter Overrides.

Action Mode

You can use change sets in a pipeline to include a manual review step to ensure that the changes you deploy are valid and desired before they actually execute. AWS CodePipeline supports the following AWS CloudFormation actions:

- Create or replace a change set
- Create or update a stack
- Delete a stack
- Execute a change set
- Replace a failed stack

Stack or Change Set Name

These refer to the new or existing stack or change set to be created, updated, or deleted.

Template

This is the location of the template file to submit. Since AWS CodePipeline uses artifacts to pass files between stages, you must define this file within the artifact with the following:

```
ArtifactName::TemplateFileName
```

Template Configuration

The template configuration is where you specify properties such as template parameters and the stack policy.

> Do not commit sensitive information to your repository. If this file contains information such as passwords, restrict access and pull it into the artifact from another source, such as Amazon S3.

Capabilities

You must specify any templates which create, update, or delete IAM resources with either the CAPABILITY_IAM or CAPABILITY_NAMED_IAM within this property.

Role Name

Unlike manually provisioned stacks, AWS CodePipeline requires a service role to assume when you perform actions in AWS CloudFormation.

Output File Name

This is an optional output that you can add to the output artifact after the deploy action completes. This will add any stack outputs to the pipeline output artifact.

Parameter Overrides

Though you can define parameters in the template configuration file, the parameter overrides section lets you specify a JSON input file to override any already-specified parameters. You can retrieve data from pipeline artifacts with the Fn::GetParam intrinsic function. The following example demonstrates how to specify a parameter override for ParameterName.

```
{
  "ParameterName" : {
    "Fn::GetParam" : ["ArtifactName", "config-file-name.json", "ParamName"]
  }
}
```

> All parameters you specify in the parameter overrides or template configuration file must already exist in the Parameters section of the template you want to deploy.

Parameter overrides can leverage two intrinsic functions specific to AWS CodePipeline. These functions allow you to specify dynamic pipeline values and data from artifacts being passed through the pipeline.

FN::GETARTIFACTATT

You use *Fn::GetArtifactAtt* to query values of an input artifact attribute, such as the Amazon S3 bucket name where the artifact is stored. This function enables you to gather information about the artifact itself, not data within the artifact.

When you run a pipeline, AWS CodePipeline copies and writes files to the pipeline's artifact store (Amazon S3 bucket). AWS CodePipeline generates the filenames in the artifact store. These filenames are unknown before you run the pipeline. This attribute requires the Amazon S3 bucket name (BucketName), artifact object key (ObjectKey), and artifact URL (URL).

Use the following syntax to retrieve an attribute value of an artifact:

```
{ "Fn::GetArtifactAtt" : [ "artifactName", "attributeName" ] }
```

FN::GETPARAM

Complimentary to Fn::GetArtifactAtt, the *Fn::GetParam* function allows you to query information within an artifact. Any files in the artifact that you query must be in valid JSON format. For example, you can add outputs from a stack as a JSON file to the pipeline artifact, which you use Fn::GetParam to query.

```
{ "Fn::GetParam" : [ "artifactName", "JSONFileName", "keyName" ] }
```

Summary

In this chapter, you became familiar with provisioning and managing AWS infrastructure using AWS CloudFormation. AWS CloudFormation allows you to describe an entire enterprise's infrastructure as one or more template files, achieving infrastructure as code (IaC) in an environment.

By leveraging AWS CloudFormation in a deployment pipeline, you can dynamically provision and update infrastructure over time by simply committing code to a Git-based repository (AWS CodeCommit). *You can use AWS CodePipeline to reliably automate complex deployment processes.*

AWS CloudFormation uses a declarative language (JSON or YAML template) to describe, model, and provision all infrastructure resources for your applications across all regions and accounts in your cloud environment in an automated and secure manner. This file serves as the single source of truth for your cloud environment. You pay only for the AWS resources you require to run your applications.

The template contains the infrastructure to where AWS will deploy and configuration properties. After you deploy a template in an account, you can redeploy it again in the same or different account and/or region.

A stack is a collection of resources that will be deployed and managed by AWS CloudFormation. When you submit a template, the resources you configure are provisioned and then make up the stack itself. Any modifications to the stack affect underlying resources. Stacks use the IAM user or AWS role authorizations to invoke an action. The template only requires the Resources section.

When you create a stack, you can submit a template from a local file or via a URL that points to an object in Amazon S3. If you submit the template as a local file, it uploads to Amazon S3 on your behalf.

Two key benefits of AWS CloudFormation are that your infrastructure is repeatable and that it is versionable.

A change set is a description of the changes that will occur to a stack should you submit the template and/or parameter updates. When you process stack updates, the template snippets you reference in any transforms pull from their Amazon S3 locations. If a snippet updates without your knowledge, the updated snippet will import into the template. Use a change set where there is a potential for data loss.

If values input into a template cannot be determined until the stack or change set is actually created, intrinsic functions resolve this by adding dynamic functionality into AWS CloudFormation templates. Condition functions are intrinsic functions to create resources or set resource properties that evaluate true or false conditions.

AWS CloudFormation Designer is a web-based graphical interface to design and deploy AWS CloudFormation templates. You can create connections to make relationships between resources that automatically update dependencies between them.

AWS CloudFormation uses custom resource providers to handle the provisioning and configuration of custom resources with AWS Lambda functions or Amazon SNS topics. You must provide a service token along with any optional input parameters. *The service token acts as a reference to where custom resource requests are sent.* This can be an AWS Lambda function or Amazon SNS topic. Custom resources can provide outputs back to AWS CloudFormation, which are made accessible as properties of the custom resource.

Custom resources associated with AWS Lambda invoke functions whenever create, update, or delete actions are sent to the resource provider. This resource type is incredibly useful to reference other AWS services and resources that may not support AWS CloudFormation.

You can use custom resources associated with Amazon SNS for any long-running custom resource tasks, such as transcoding a large video file.

By default, AWS CloudFormation will track most dependencies between resources. *A resource can have a dependency on one or more other resources in a stack, in which case you create a resource relationship to control the order of resource creation, updates, and deletion.*

Whenever you perform an action on an AWS CloudFormation stack, the end result will bring the stack into one of several possible statuses. These actions can complete or fail. In the case of a failed event, you can roll back the release based on your update or deletion policies.

To update stacks, you can modify and resubmit the same template or create a change set; AWS CloudFormation will parse it for changes (add, modify, or delete) and apply the modifications to the resources. You use the AWS CloudFormation UpdatePolicy to determine how to respond to changes. When you delete a stack, by default all underlying stack resources also delete. *You use deletion policies to preserve resources when you delete a stack.*

AWS Auto Scaling group update policies enforce the behavior that will occur when an update is performed on an AWS Auto Scaling group. This depends on the type of change you make and whether you configure the AWS Auto Scaling scheduled actions. You can replace the entire AWS Auto Scaling group or only instances inside it. When you delete a stack, all underlying stack resources are deleted. You can apply the DeletionPolicy to resources in the stack to modify their behavior when the stack deletes.

You use stack exports to share information between separate stacks. Or, you can manage AWS CloudFormation stacks themselves as resources in a nested stack relationship. *You can export stack output values to import them into other stacks in the same account and region.* This allows you to share data that generates in one stack out to other stacks in your account.

You can assign a stack policy to a stack to allow or deny access to modify certain stack resources, which you can filter by the type of update. Stack policies protect all resources by default with an *implicit deny*. To allow access to actions on stack resources, you must apply *explicit allow* statements to the policy.

When you execute custom scripts on Amazon EC2 instances as part of your UserData, AWS CloudFormation provides several important helper scripts. You can use these to interact with the stack to query metadata, notify a CreationPolicy or WaitCondition, and process scripts when AWS CloudFormation detects metadata updates.

AWS CloudFormation *StackSets* give users the ability to control, provision, and manage stacks across multiple accounts and regions. A stack set as a logical container for stack information in an administrator account. Each stack set will contain information about stacks that you deploy to a single target account in one or more regions. Stack instances allow you to manage stacks in a target account. An update to a stack set propagates to all stack instances in all accounts and regions. When you perform operations on stack sets, you can configure how to control the flow of updates across accounts and regions. The administrator account requires an IAM service role with permissions to execute stack set operations and assume an execution role in any target account(s).

You can use a target account gate to perform evaluation tasks with AWS Lambda functions in the target account.

You cannot raise AWS CloudFormation template-specific limits through a support request. You can raise some limits, such as the number of stacks per account.

AWS CloudFormation has built-in integrations with AWS CodePipeline as a deployment provider. When a template revision passes through a pipeline, AWS CloudFormation can reference input parameters, stack policies, and other configuration data in the AWS CodePipeline deployment.

You can use change sets in a pipeline to include a manual review step to ensure that the changes you deploy are valid and desired before they actually execute with the use of the Action Mode.

Exam Essentials

Understand Infrastructure as Code (IaC).   You model infrastructure as code to automate the provisioning, maintenance, and retirement of complex infrastructure across an organization. The declarative syntax allows you to describe the resource state you desire, instead of the steps to create it. You can version and maintain IaC with the same development workflow as application and configuration code.

Understand the purpose of change sets.   Change sets allow administrators to preview the changes that will take place when a given template deploys to the AWS CloudFormation.

This includes a description of resources that you will update or replace entirely. You create change sets to help prevent stack updates that could accidentally result in the replacement of critical resources, such as databases.

Know the AWS CloudFormation permissions model. When you create, update, or delete stacks, AWS CloudFormation will operate with the same permissions as the IAM user or IAM role that performs the stack action. For example, a user who deletes a stack that contains an Amazon EC2 instance must also have the ability to terminate instances; otherwise, the stack delete fails. AWS CloudFormation also supports service roles, which you can pass to the service when you perform stack actions. This requires that the user or role have permissions to pass the service role to perform the stack action.

Know the AWS CloudFormation template structure. You can use these AWS CloudFormation template properties: AWSTemplateFormatVersion, Description, Metadata, Parameters, Mappings, Conditions, Transform, Resources, and Outputs. Templates only require the Resources property, and you must define at least one resource in every template.

Know how to use the intrinsic functions. It is important to understand the AWS CloudFormation templates intrinsic functions.

- Fn::FindInMap
- Fn::GetAtt
- Fn::Join
- Fn::Split
- Ref

Understand the purpose of AWS::CloudFormation::Init. This template section defines the configuration tasks the cfn-init helper script will perform on instances that you create individually or as part of AWS Auto Scaling launch configurations. This metadata key allows you to define a more declarative syntax for configuration tasks compared to using procedural steps in the UserData property.

Know the use cases for both custom resource types. You can implement custom resources with AWS Lambda functions or Amazon SNS topics. The primary difference between each type is that AWS Lambda-backed custom resources have a maximum execution duration of 5 minutes. This may not work for custom resources that take a long time to provision or update. In those cases, Amazon SNS topics backed by Amazon EC2 instances would allow for long running tasks.

Understand how AWS CloudFormation manages resource relationships. AWS CloudFormation will automatically reorder resource provisioning and update steps based on known dependencies. For example, if a template declares an Amazon VPC and a subnet, the subnet will not create before the Amazon VPC (a subnet requires an Amazon VPC ID during creation). However, AWS CloudFormation is not aware of all possible relationships, so you must manually declare them with the DependsOn property. If a template declares an Amazon EC2 instance and AWS DynamoDB table, and the table is referenced inside the instance's UserData property, you must declare a DependsOn property that states the instance depends on the table.

Understand wait conditions and creation policies.   In some cases, resources in a template should wait for other resources to provision and configure before starting their tasks. For example, you may want to prevent creation of a load balancer resource until instances in an AWS Auto Scaling group have installed a web application. In those cases, you can use either wait conditions or creation policies. Wait conditions require you to add two separate resources to the template (`AWS::CloudFormation::WaitCondition` and `AWS::CloudFormation::WaitConditionHandle`). The instance's `UserData` property references the wait condition handle, where a success or failure signal will be sent. A creation policy does not require the additional resources, and it allows for additional options such as timeouts and signal counts.

Understand how stack updates affect resources.   When you update a stack, resources may behave differently when properties update. If an Amazon S3 bucket is created as part of a stack and later the bucket policy is updated, the resource will update with no interruption. However, if the bucket name later updates, you must replace the bucket. Resources can undergo one of three types of updates: update with no interruption, update with some interruption, and replace update.

Know how to use exports and nested stacks to share stacks.   Stack exports allow you to access stack outputs in other stacks in the same region. Exports, however, come with some limitations. For example, you cannot delete stacks that export values until all other stacks that import the exported value have been modified to no longer include the import. Nested stacks make use for the `AWS::CloudFormation::Stack` resource type. This way, a single stack can create multiple "child" stacks, which can declare their own resources (including other stacks). This is a useful mechanism to work around some service limits such as the number of resources per template (200).

Understand stack policies.   To prevent updates to critical stack resources, you implement stack policies. A stack policy declares what resources you can and cannot update and under what circumstances. A stack containing an Amazon RDS instance, for example, can include a stack policy that prevents updates that require replacement of the database instance.

Resources to Review

AWS CloudFormation:

> https://docs.aws.amazon.com/AWSCloudFormation/latest/UserGuide/Welcome
> .html

Infrastructure as Code:

> https://d1.awsstatic.com/whitepapers/DevOps/infrastructure-as-code.pdf

AWS Quick Starts:

> https://aws.amazon.com/quickstart/

Quick Start Builder's Guide:

`https://aws-quickstart.github.io/templates-examples.html`

Bootstrapping Applications via AWS CloudFormation:

`https://s3.amazonaws.com/cloudformation-examples/`
`BoostrappingApplicationsWithAWSCloudFormation.pdf`

AWS CloudFormation Templates:

`https://aws.amazon.com/cloudformation/templates/`

AWS Resource Types Reference:

`https://docs.aws.amazon.com/AWSCloudFormation/latest/UserGuide/`
`aws-template-resource-type-ref.html`

Exercises

EXERCISE 8.1

Write Your Own AWS CloudFormation Template

1. Create an Amazon S3 bucket with a static website configuration that includes references to index and error documents, such as `index.html` and `error.html`, respectively.

2. Create an output to the bucket's website URL.

3. Create an output that displays the bucket name.

4. Upload the code as `index.html` to the root of the bucket for the index document.

```
<html>
    <body>
        <h1>Hello, World!</h1>
    </body>
</html>
```

5. Upload the code as `error.html` to the root of the bucket for the error document.

```
<html>
    <body>
        <h1>Oops! Something went wrong.</h1>
    </body>
</html>
```

6. Access the URL the output provides from your AWS CloudFormation stack to verify the static website works.

EXERCISE 8.2

Troubleshoot a Failed Stack Deletion

1. Deploy the AWS CloudFormation code template, which provisions an Amazon S3 bucket in your account.

```
{
    "Resources" : {
        "ExampleBucket" : {
            "Type": "AWS::S3::Bucket"
        }
    },
    "Outputs" : {
        "BucketName" : {
            "Value": { "Ref": "ExampleBucket" }
        }
    }
}
```

2. Upload several files and objects to the Amazon S3 bucket that the template creates.

3. Delete the stack and monitor progress until it fails.

    Note the error output by AWS CloudFormation when the stack reaches the DELETE_ FAILED state.

4. Delete all files from the Amazon S3 bucket.

5. Attempt to delete the stack again, but do not enable the option to retain the bucket.

EXERCISE 8.3

Monitor Stack Update Activity

1. Deploy the AWS CloudFormation code template, which provisions an Amazon S3 bucket in your account.

```
{
    "Resources" : {
        "ExampleBucket" : {
            "Type": "AWS::S3::Bucket"
        }
    },
     "Outputs" : {
```

```
            "BucketName" : {
                "Value": { "Ref": "ExampleBucket" }
            }
        }
    }
```

2. After the stack is created, make note of the output value. This is the name of your Amazon S3 bucket.

3. Use the template code to update the stack, and replace BUCKET_NAME with a name of your choice.

```
{
    "Resources" : {
        "ExampleBucket" : {
            "Type": "AWS::S3::Bucket",
            "Properties": {
                "BucketName": "BUCKET_NAME"
            }
        }
    },
    "Outputs" : {
        "BucketName" : {
            "Value": { "Ref": "ExampleBucket" }
        }
    }
}
```

Note that a new bucket is created, and the original bucket is deleted. This is because you cannot change bucket names after initial creation, so a replacement must be provisioned.

Review Questions

1. Which of the AWS CloudFormation template sections is/are required?

   A. AWSTemplateFormatVersion

   B. Parameters

   C. Metadata

   D. Resources

   E. All of the above

2. You are writing an AWS CloudFormation template and would like to create an output value corresponding to your application's website URL. The application is composed of two application servers in a private subnet behind an Elastic Load Balancing load balancer. The application servers read from the Amazon Relational Database Service (Amazon RDS) database instance. The logical IDs of the instances are AppServerA and AppServerB. The logical IDs of the load balancer and database are AppLB and AppDB, respectively.

   ```
   "Outputs" : {
       "AppEndpoint" : {
           "Description" : "URL to access the application",
           "Value" : "Value to return"
       }
   }
   ```

   Which code correctly completes the previous output declaration?

   A. { "Fn::Join": ["", [https://, { "Ref": "AppLB" }, "/login.php"]] }

   B. { "Fn::Join": ["", [https://, { "Fn::GetAtt": ["AppServerA", "PublicDNSName"] }, "/login.php"]] }

   C. { "Fn::Join": ["", [https://, { "Ref": ["AppLB", "DNSName"] }, "/login.php"]] }

   D. { "Fn::Join": ["", [https://, { "Fn::GetAtt": ["AppDB", "Endpoint .Address"] }, "/login.php"]] }

   E. { "Fn::Join": ["", [https://, { "Fn::GetAtt": ["AppLB", "DNSName"] }, "/login.php"]] }

3. An AWS CloudFormation template you have written uses a CreationPolicy to ensure that video transcoding instances launch and configure before the application server instances so that they are available before users are able to access the website. However, you are finding that the stack always reaches the creation policy's timeout value before the transcoding instances complete setup.

   Why could this be? (Select THREE.)

   A. The user data script does not include a call to cfn-signal.

   B. The instance could not be launched because of account limits.

C. The user data script fails before reaching the `cfn-signal` step.

D. The instance cannot connect to the AWS CloudFormation endpoint when calling `cfn-signal`.

4. When you attempt to update an Amazon Relational Database Service (Amazon RDS) instance in your AWS CloudFormation stack, you experience a `Resource failed to stabilize` error, which causes the stack to roll back any changes you attempted.

   What might be the cause of this error, and how could it be resolved?

   A. The database is corrupted and cannot be updated. Take a snapshot of the database, and use it to create a replacement.

   B. The database took too long to update. Remove the database from the AWS CloudFormation stack by applying a `DeletionPolicy` of `Retain`, and manage the stack using the Amazon RDS console or AWS CLI.

   C. The database took too long to update, and the session credentials used by AWS CloudFormation timed out. Use a service role to perform the update.

   D. You have attempted to perform an update that is not supported by Amazon RDS. Review the specification documentation and attempt a valid update.

   E. I/O has not been halted on the database before performing the update, and AWS CloudFormation timed out waiting for database transactions to halt. Temporarily block I/O and attempt the update again.

5. A custom resource associated with AWS Lambda in your stack creates successfully; however, it attempts to update the resource result in the failure message `Custom Resource failed to stabilize in the expected time`. After you add a service role to extend the timeout duration, the issue still persists.

   What may also be the cause of this error?

   A. The custom resource defined a function for handling the `CREATE` action but did not do the same for the `UPDATE` action; thus, a success or failure signal was not sent to AWS CloudFormation.

   B. The service role does not have appropriate permissions to invoke the custom resource function.

   C. The custom resource function no longer exists.

   D. All of the above.

6. After you deploy an AWS Serverless Application Model (AWS SAM) template to AWS CloudFormation, can you view the original template? Why or why not?

   A. No, after the template is submitted and the `AWS::Serverless` transform is executed, an AWS CloudFormation-supported template is generated.

   B. Yes, the original template is saved and accessible using the `get-stack-template` AWS CLI command.

   C. Yes, it is saved in the Amazon Simple Storage Service (Amazon S3) bucket created by AWS CloudFormation for AWS SAM templates.

   D. No, AWS CloudFormation does not retain processed templates.

7. When defining an AWS Serverless Application Model (AWS SAM) template, how can you create an Amazon API Gateway as part of the stack?

    A. By defining an `AWS::ApiGateway::RestApi` resource and any associated `AWS::ApiGateway::Method` resources

    B. One will be created automatically for you whenever `AWS::Serverless::Function` resources are declared with one or more `Events`.

    C. By defining an `AWS::Serverless::Api` and providing an inline or external Swagger definition

    D. `AWS::ApiGateway::RestApi` resources are not supported in AWS SAM templates.

    E. A, B, and C

8. Which of these helper scripts performs updates to OS configuration when an AWS CloudFormation stack updates?

    A. `cfn-hup`

    B. `cfn-init`

    C. `cfn-signal`

    D. `cfn-update`

9. Which of these options allows you to specify a required number of signals to mark the resource as `CREATE_COMPLETE`?

    A. Wait Condition

    B. Wait Condition Handler

    C. `CreationPolicy`

    D. `WaitCount`

10. How would you preview the changes a stack update will make without affecting any resources in your account?

    A. Create a change set.

    B. Perform the stack update, and then manually roll back.

    C. Perform the stack update on a test stack.

    D. Do a manual diff of both templates.

11. How would you access a property of a resource created in a nested stack?

    A. This cannot be done.

    B. In the child stack, declare the resource property as a stack output. In the parent stack, use `Fn::GetAtt` and pass in two parameters, the child stack logical ID and `Outputs.`*`NestedStackOutputName`*.

    C. In the child stack, export the resource property. In the parent stack, import the exported value.

    D. Use the cross-stack references.

12. By default, with what permissions will AWS CloudFormation stack operations perform?

  A. Full administrator

  B. The permissions of the user performing the operation

  C. The AWS CloudFormation service role

  D. The AWS CloudFormation does not use permissions

13. An AWS CloudFormation template declares two resources: an AWS Lambda function and an Amazon DynamoDB table. The function code is declared inline as part of the template and references the table. In what order will AWS CloudFormation provision the two resources?

  A. Amazon DynamoDB table, AWS Lambda function

  B. AWS Lambda function, Amazon DynamoDB table

  C. This cannot be determined ahead of time.

  D. This depends on the template.

14. Which occurs during a replacing update?

  A. The resource becomes unavailable.

  B. The resource physical ID changes.

  C. A new resource is created.

  D. The original resource is deleted during the cleanup phase.

  E. All of the above

15. Which of the update types results in resource downtime? (Select TWO.)

  A. Update with No Interruption

  B. Update with Some Interruption

  C. Replacing Update

  D. Update with No Data

  E. Static Update

16. What must occur before a stack that exports an output can be deleted?

  A. Any stacks importing the exported value must remove the import.

  B. The export must be removed from the stack.

  C. Nothing is required.

  D. The stack must be deleted.

17. If an AWS CloudFormation stack is in `UPDATE_IN_PROGRESS` state, which of the states are possible transitions? (Select THREE.)

  A. `UPDATE_ROLLBACK_COMPLETE`

  B. `UPDATE_FAILED`

  C. `UPDATE_ROLLBACK_FAILED`

  D. `UPDATE_COMPLETE`

  E. `UPDATE_COMPLETE_CLEANUP_IN_PROGRESS`

18. What does it mean when an AWS CloudFormation stack is in UPDATE_COMPLETE_CLEANUP_IN_PROGRESS state?

    A. The stack has failed to update, and it is removing newly created resources.

    B. The stack has successfully updated, and it is removing old resources.

    C. The stack has successfully updated, and it is removing new resources.

    D. The stack has failed to update, and it is removing old resources.

19. Which of the formats are valid for an AWS CloudFormation template? (Select TWO.)

    A. YAML

    B. XML

    C. JSON

    D. Markdown

    E. LaTeX

20. What are some challenges to consider when using the AWS Command Line Interface (AWS CLI) or AWS software development kits (AWS SDKs) to provision and manage infrastructure compared to AWS CloudFormation?

    A. Reduction of human error

    B. Repeatable infrastructure

    C. Reduced IAM permissions requirements

    D. Versionable infrastructure

    E. All of the above

21. What does a service token represent in a custom resource declaration?

    A. The AWS service that receives the request

    B. The Amazon Simple Notification Service (Amazon SNS) or AWS Lambda resource Amazon Resource Name (ARN) that receives the request

    C. The on-premises server IP address that receives the request

    D. The type of action to take

    E. The commands to execute for the custom resource

22. You are creating a custom resource associated with AWS Lambda that will execute several database functions in an Amazon Relational Database Service (Amazon RDS) database instance. As part of this, the functions will return data you would like to use in other resources declared in your AWS CloudFormation template.

    How would you best pass this data to the other resources declared in the template?

    A. Store the data in a JSON file in an Amazon Simple Storage Service (Amazon S3) bucket, and use the AWS Command Line Interface (AWS CLI) to download the object.

    B. Store the output data in AWS Systems Manager Parameter Store, and query the parameter store using the AWS CLI.

    C. Use custom resource outputs to declare the returned data as resource properties. Then, query the properties using the Fn::GetAtt intrinsic function.

    D. This cannot be accomplished.

Chapter

9

Configuration as Code

THE AWS CERTIFIED DEVELOPER – ASSOCIATE EXAM TOPICS COVERED IN THIS CHAPTER MAY INCLUDE, BUT ARE NOT LIMITED TO, THE FOLLOWING:

Domain 1: Deployment

✓ 1.1 Deploy Serverless Applications.

✓ 1.2 Use AWS OpsWorks Stacks to Deploy Applications.

✓ 1.3 Use Amazon Elastic Container Service (Amazon ECS) to Deploy Containers.

Domain 3: Development with AWS Services

✓ 3.1 Write code for serverless applications.

✓ 3.2 Write code that interacts with AWS services by using APIs, SDKs, and AWS CLI.

Introduction to Configuration as Code

To expand on the theme of automation, you can add configuration to AWS enterprise as code.

AWS CloudFormation leverages standard AWS APIs to provision and update infrastructure in your account. Though AWS CloudFormation is highly effective at this task, there are some configuration tasks that are either inaccessible from the AWS API or more easily done with standard configuration management tools, such as Chef and Puppet. *AWS OpsWorks Stacks* provides a serverless Chef infrastructure to configure servers with Chef code, known as *recipes*. Much like AWS CloudFormation templates, Chef recipe code is declarative in nature. This means you do not have to rely on the accuracy of procedural steps, as you would with a userdata script you apply to Amazon Elastic Compute Cloud (Amazon EC2) instances or launch configurations. If you separate infrastructure from configuration, you also gain the ability to update each on separate cadences.

If a security vulnerability is found that requires a configuration update, use a recipe update. When you do the same in AWS CloudFormation, this requires a combination of userdata updates and cfn-hup configuration. A specific configuration management tool, however, requires only a new configuration code to submit to the instance, which will digest and apply the changes automatically.

In containerized environments, configuration of the container itself must also be done. *Amazon Elastic Container Service* (Amazon ECS) allows you to define the requirements of, schedule, and configure Docker containers to deploy to a cluster of Amazon EC2 instances. The cluster itself can be easy to provision with AWS CloudFormation, along with configuration of container requirements such as CPU and memory needs. By combining this with configuration management tools, both the cluster and any active containers can be configured dynamically.

Using AWS OpsWorks Stacks to Deploy Applications

AWS OpsWorks Stacks lets you manage applications and servers on AWS and on-premises. With AWS OpsWorks Stacks, you can model your application as a stack that contains different layers, such as load balancing, database, and application server. You can deploy and configure Amazon EC2 instances in each layer or connect other resources such as Amazon Relational Database Service (Amazon RDS) databases. AWS OpsWorks Stacks lets you set automatic scaling for your servers on preset schedules or in response to a constant change of traffic levels, and it uses lifecycle hooks to orchestrate changes as your environment scales. You run Chef recipes with *Chef Solo*, which allows you to automate tasks such as install packages and program languages or frameworks, configure software, and more.

What Is AWS OpsWorks Stacks?

AWS OpsWorks Stacks is the only service that performs configuration management tasks. *Configuration management* is the process designed to ensure that infrastructure in a given system adheres to a specific set of standards, settings, or attributes (its configuration). Popular configuration management tools include Chef and Puppet. AWS OpsWorks Stacks allows you to manage the configuration of both on-premises and cloud infrastructures. To accomplish this, you organize units of infrastructure into stacks and layers. AWS OpsWorks Stacks can also perform application deployments by the configuration of apps. You can implement configuration changes at specific times in the lifecycle of your infrastructure through the use of lifecycle events, such as when an instance is first brought online or offline. Unlike traditional Chef Server installations, AWS OpsWorks Stacks uses Chef Zero, Chef Solo, or local mode Chef Client. You do not need to involve an actual Chef Server in the configuration management process.

There are two additional AWS OpsWorks services, *AWS OpsWorks for Chef Automate* and *AWS OpsWorks for Puppet Enterprise*. Unlike AWS OpsWorks Stacks, both services provision an Amazon EC2 instance in your AWS account with either Chef Automate or Puppet Enterprise software. Table 9.1 lists key differences between each service.

TABLE 9.1 AWS OpsWorks Services

	AWS OpsWorks Stacks	AWS OpsWorks for Chef Automate	AWS OpsWorks for Puppet Enterprise
Manage infrastructure	X		
Chef	X	X	

TABLE 9.1   AWS OpsWorks Services *(continued)*

	AWS OpsWorks Stacks	AWS OpsWorks for Chef Automate	AWS OpsWorks for Puppet Enterprise
Puppet			X
Code repository		X	X
Built-in automatic scaling	X		
Amazon EC2 Auto Scaling	X	X	X
Compliance		X	

Code repository   Unlike AWS OpsWorks Stacks, the other two AWS OpsWorks services create an Amazon EC2 instance in your account. This instance will store any Chef or Puppet code for access by any cloud or on-premises instances (nodes) in your environment. AWS OpsWorks Stacks, however, requires you to store Chef code in an external location such as an Amazon Simple Storage Service (Amazon S3) bucket.

Amazon EC2 Auto scaling   AWS OpsWorks includes the ability to have instances automatically come online in response to changes in demand. All three AWS OpsWorks services also support "traditional" automatic scaling.

Chef compliance   You can use Chef Compliance to track, alert, report on, and remediate compliance violations in your infrastructure. For example, if your organization has strict requirements on SSH access to Linux systems, you can use InSpec (https://www.inspec.io) policies in Chef Compliance to scan nodes in your environment periodically for violations of the current SSH policy.

AWS OpsWorks Stacks supports these Chef versions:

- Chef 11.10 (Linux)
- Chef 12.0 (Linux)
- Chef 12.2 (Windows)

AWS OpsWorks Stack Concepts

This section details AWS OpsWorks Stack concepts including cookbooks, recipes, packaging, stacks, layers, instances, apps, users, permissions, lifecycle events, resources, data bags, Chef, and monitoring your configuration.

Cookbooks and Recipes

 AWS OpsWorks Stacks leverages Chef to implement configuration. Chef itself is not in scope for the AWS Certified Developer – Associate exam. For more information, refer to the Chef training material (https://learn.chef.io).

Chef is a Ruby-based configuration management language that AWS OpsWorks Stacks uses to enforce configuration on Amazon EC2 on-premises instance nodes. Chef uses a declarative syntax to describe how to configure a node without detailing the actual steps to achieve the desired configuration. Chef organizes these declarative statements into *recipes*, which act as a collection of resources to configure on nodes.

```
template '/tmp/somefile' do
  mode '0755'
  source 'somefile.erb'
  not_if { File.exist?('/etc/passwd') }
end
```

In the previous example, the file /tmp/*somefile* is created from the *somefile*.erb template. This template file is in a *cookbook*, which acts as a container for recipes and any files, templates, attributes, or other components to enforce configuration on a node. *Attribute files* provide data to recipes, and AWS OpsWorks Stacks can modify them with custom JSON at the stack, layer, and deployment levels. You can copy files from cookbooks to nodes to create static files and use templates to provide dynamic data to files before you create them on the node.

Cookbooks normally belong to a cookbook repository, or *chef-repo*, which is a versioned directory that contains cookbooks and their recipes. A single cookbook repository can contain one or more cookbooks. When you set the cookbook repository for a stack, all cookbooks in the repository copy to each instance in the stack. The directory structure of a chef-repo must match Figure 9.1.

FIGURE 9.1 Cookbook repository structure

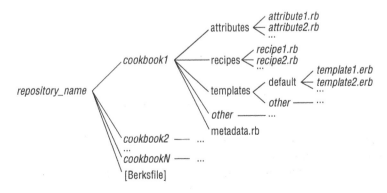

Recipes use nodes to execute in their "run list." Recipes that you assign to a node's run list execute in the order in which they appear. You can assign recipes to roles, which you assign to a node's run list.

Assigning Recipes to Roles

If a role named `database-server` contains two recipes, `postgresql::default` and `monitoring::default`, the following two run lists are the same:

    RUN_LIST="recipe['postgresql::default'],recipe['monitoring::default']"

    RUN_LIST="role['database-server']"

In a typical Chef installation, one or more Chef Servers manage multiple nodes across an enterprise. The Chef Server is responsible for distributing cookbooks, managing node information, and providing data to nodes as the Chef runs (an execution of `chef-client` on a node that enforces any assigned recipes).

 In AWS OpsWorks Stacks, there is no Chef Server to manage nodes. Chef is run with `chef-client` in local mode on the instance. Local mode creates an in-memory Chef Server to duplicate needed functionality.

Managing Cookbooks

To install custom cookbooks in your stack, you first have to enable the Use Custom Chef Cookbooks field in the stack properties. Once you enable this field, you can then provide the details of the cookbook repository, such as the Git Repository URL, as shown in Figure 9.2.

FIGURE 9.2   Enabling custom cookbooks

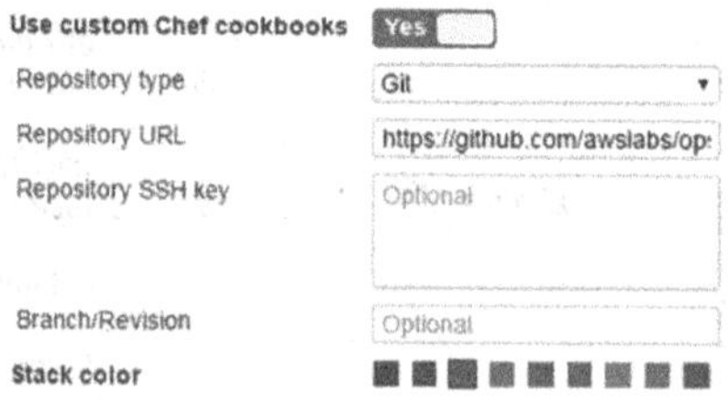

Use custom Chef cookbooks	Yes
Repository type	Git
Repository URL	https://github.com/awslabs/op:
Repository SSH key	Optional
Branch/Revision	Optional
Stack color	■ ■ ■ ■ ■ ■ ■ ■

When instances first create and start in a stack, they will download custom cookbooks from the repository you select. However, running instances will not download new cookbooks automatically. You must manually set the Run Command's Command option to Update Custom Cookbooks, as shown in Figure 9.3.

FIGURE 9.3 Running a command

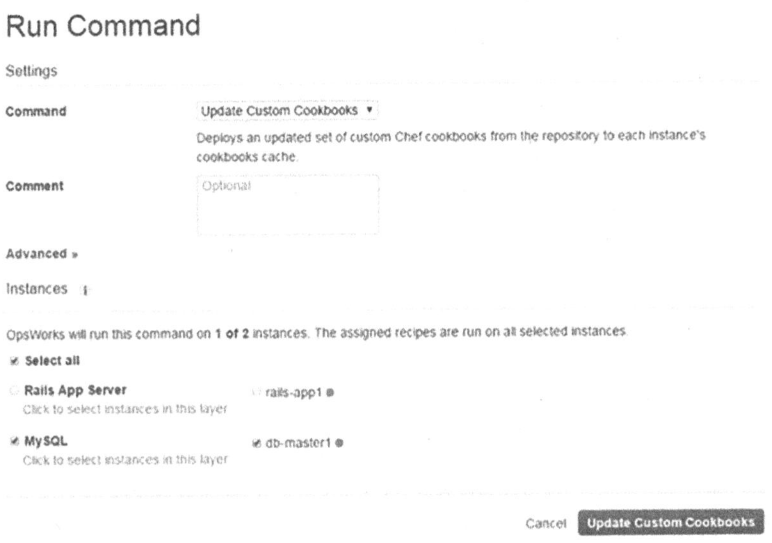

Run Command

Settings

Command   Update Custom Cookbooks ▾

Deploys an updated set of custom Chef cookbooks from the repository to each instance's
cookbooks cache.

Comment   Optional

Advanced »

Instances ℹ

OpsWorks will run this command on **1 of 2** instances. The assigned recipes are run on all selected instances.

☑ Select all

  Rails App Server   ☐ rails-app1 ●
   Click to select instances in this layer

☑ **MySQL**   ☑ db-master1 ●
   Click to select instances in this layer

                                                    Cancel   **Update Custom Cookbooks**

You cannot manually start stopped Amazon EBS backed load-based and time-based instances, and thus you must replace the instance to update custom cookbooks.

Package Cookbook Dependencies

Chef provides a utility called *Berkshelf* (https://docs.chef.io/berkshelf.html) to manage dependencies of cookbooks throughout the development and deployment process. In Chef 11.10 stacks, you can install Berkshelf automatically on any instances in your stack. For a production environment, AWS recommends that you do not use Berkshelf to import dependencies during Chef runs. This process introduces a dependency on the external Chef Supermarket API (https://supermarket.chef.io). If the supermarket is unavailable when instances create in your stack, the initial Chef run may fail.

Instead, package the custom cookbooks you develop and their dependencies into a single .zip archive with the berks package Berkshelf command. When you execute this command in a cookbook directory, it will automatically scan any Berksfile and metadata.rb to list any dependencies, download them from their external location, and package them into a compressed .tar archive. You can upload this archive to Amazon S3 and configure it as the custom cookbook repository location for your stack.

```
berks package cookbooks.tar.gz
Cookbook(s) packaged to /Users/username/tmp/berks/cookbooks.tar.gz
```

When you package dependencies for multiple cookbooks in the parent directory of the cookbooks, create a `Berksfile` such as this:

```
source "https://supermarket.chef.io"
cookbook "server-app", path: "./server-app"
cookbook "server-utils", path: "./server-utils"
```

After you package the dependencies, run the berks package command from this directory to download and dependencies for your cookbooks.

```
berks package cookbooks.tar.gz
```

Stack

A typical workload in AWS will include systems for various purposes, such as load balancers, application servers, proxy servers, databases, and more. The set of Amazon EC2/on-premises instances, Amazon RDS, Elastic Load Balancing, and other systems make up a stack. You can organize stacks across an enterprise.

Suppose you have a single application with dev, test, and production environments. Each of these environments has a stack that enables you to separate resources to ensure stability of changes. You group resources into stacks by logical or functional purposes. The example stack in Figure 9.4 includes three layers, a cookbook repository, an application repository, and one app to deploy to the application server instances. This stack manages a full application available to users over the Internet.

FIGURE 9.4 Example stack structure

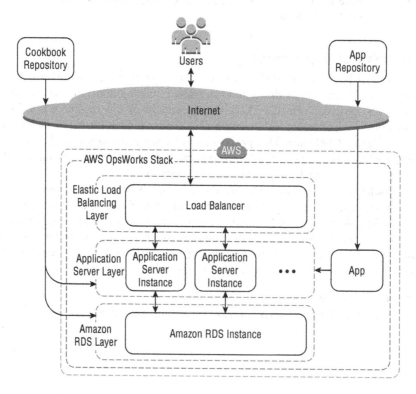

When you create a new stack, you will have the option to set the stack's properties.

Stack Name

Stack Name identifies stacks in the AWS OpsWorks Stacks console. Since this name is not unique, AWS OpsWorks assigns a Globally Unique Identifier (GUID) to the stack after you create it.

API Endpoint Region

AWS OpsWorks associates a stack with either a global endpoint or one of multiple regional endpoints. When you create a resource in the stack, such as an instance, it is available only from the endpoint you specify when you create the stack. For example, if a stack is created with the global "classic" endpoint, any instances will be accessible only by AWS OpsWorks Stacks that use the global API endpoint in the US East (N. Virginia) region. Resources are not available across regional endpoints.

Amazon Virtual Private Cloud

Stacks can create and manage instances in Amazon EC2 Classic or an Amazon Virtual Private Cloud (Amazon VPC). When you select an Amazon VPC, you will be able to specify in what subnets to deploy instances when they are created.

Default Operating System

AWS OpsWorks Stacks supports many built-in Linux operating systems and Windows Server (only in Chef 12.2 stacks). If there is a custom Amazon Machine Images (AMI) you want to use, you must configure other tasks on the AMI to make it compatible with AWS OpsWorks Stacks. You must base the custom AMI off an AMI that AWS OpsWorks supports.

- The AMI must support `cloud-init`.
- The AMI must support the instance types you plan to launch.
- The AMI must utilize a 64-bit operating system.

Layer

A *layer* acts as a subset of instances or resources in a stack. Layers act as groups of instances or resources based on a common function. This is especially important, as the Chef recipe code applies to a layer and all instances in a layer. A layer is the point where any configuration of nodes will be set, such as what Chef recipes to execute at each life-cycle hook. A layer can contain any one or more nodes, and a node must be a member of one or more layers. When a node is a member of multiple layers, it will run any recipes you configure for each lifecycle event for both layers in the layer and recipe order you specify.

From the point of view of a Chef Server installation, a layer is synonymous with a Chef Role. In the node object, the layer and role data are equivalent. This is primarily to ensure compatibility with open-source cookbooks that are not written specifically for AWS OpsWorks Stacks.

Elastic Load Balancing

After a layer is created, any elastic load balancers in the same region associate with the layer. Any instances that come online in the layer will automatically register with the load balancer. The instances will also deregister from the load balancer when they go offline.

Elastic IP Addresses

You can configure layers to assign public or elastic IP addresses to instances when they come online. For Amazon Elastic Block Store (Amazon EBS) backed instances, the IP address will remain assigned after the instance stops and starts again. For instance-store backed instances, the IP address may not be the same as the original AWS OpsWorks instance.

Amazon EBS Volumes

Linux stacks include the option to assign one or more Amazon EBS volumes to a layer. In the process, you configure the mount point, size, Redundant Array of Independent Disks (RAID) configuration, volume type, Input/Output Operations Per Second (IOPS), and encryption settings. When new instances start in the layer, AWS OpsWorks Stacks will attempt to create an Amazon EBS volume with the configuration and attach it to the instance. Through the instance's setup lifecycle event, AWS OpsWorks Stacks runs a Chef cookbook to mount the volume to the instance. When the volumes add or remove volumes to or from a layer, only new instances will receive the configuration updates. Existing instances' volumes do not change.

    Only Chef 11.10 stacks support RAID configurations.

Amazon RDS Layer

Amazon RDS layers pass connection information to an existing Amazon RDS instance. When you associate an Amazon RDS instance to a stack, it is assigned to an app. This passes the connection information to the instances via the app's `deploy` attributes, and you can access the data within your Chef recipes with `node[:deploy][:app_name][:database]` hash.

You can associate a single Amazon RDS instance with multiple apps in the same stack. However, you cannot associate multiple Amazon RDS instances with the same app. If your application needs to connect to multiple databases, use custom JSON to include the connection information for the other database(s).

Amazon ECS Cluster Layer

Amazon ECS cluster layers provide configuration management capabilities to Linux instances in your Amazon ECS cluster. You can associate a single cluster with a single stack at a time. To create this layer, you must register the cluster with the stack. After this, it will appear in the Layer type drop-down list of available clusters from which to create a layer, as shown in Figure 9.5.

FIGURE 9.5   Creating a layer

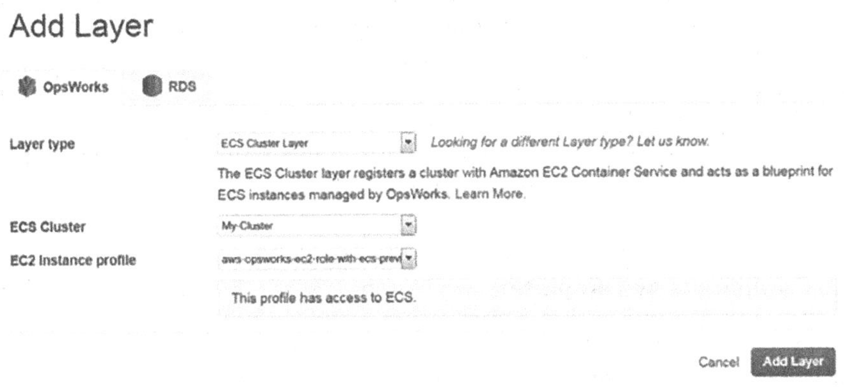

Add Layer

OpsWorks   RDS

Layer type	ECS Cluster Layer ▾ *Looking for a different Layer type? Let us know.*
	The ECS Cluster layer registers a cluster with Amazon EC2 Container Service and acts as a blueprint for ECS instances managed by OpsWorks. Learn More.
ECS Cluster	My-Cluster ▾
EC2 Instance profile	aws-opsworks-ec2-role-with-ecs-prev ▾
	This profile has access to ECS.

Cancel   **Add Layer**

Use the console or AWS CLI/SDK commands to create the cluster.

After the layer is created, any existing cluster instances will not import into the stack. Instead, the instances need to register with the stack as on-premises instances, or you need to create a new instance in the layer with the AWS OpsWorks Stacks console or CLI and replace them with new instances. When you create new instances, AWS OpsWorks Stacks will automatically install Docker and the Amazon ECS agent before it registers the instance with the cluster.

An instance *cannot* belong to both an Amazon ECS cluster layer and a Chef 11.10 built-in layer. However, the instance can belong to an Amazon ECS cluster layer and other custom layer(s).

Chef 11.10 Built-in Layers

AWS OpsWorks Stacks provides several types of built-in layers for Chef 11.10 stacks.

- HAProxy layer
- MySQL layer
- AWS Flow (Ruby) layer
- Java app server layer
- Node.js app server layer
- PHP app server layer
- Rails layer
- Static web server layer
- Amazon ECS cluster layer

Each of the built-in layers provides a number of preconfigured recipes that speed up the process to deploy applications and manage underlying infrastructure. For example, the Node.js app server layer requires you to specify only one or more apps in the stack and associate it with the layer. When you use the built-in recipes, the app (or apps) automatically deploys to any instances in the layer.

Much like wrapper cookbooks in Chef, you can override built-in layers if you specify a custom attribute or template files. To do so, you can create a cookbook with the same name as the cookbook you want to override and include only the files you want to replace.

Custom Cookbooks or Templates

The built-in apache2 recipe includes an apache2.conf.erb template file that you can override if you create a directory structure as a custom cookbook in your repository.

```
apache2
|- templates
|-- default
|--- apache2.conf.erb
```

When your instance updates its cookbooks, it will merge both the built-in layer's cookbooks with your custom ones and override the template file with your changes.

Instances

An *instance* represents either an Amazon EC2 or on-premises instance, and the configuration AWS OpsWorks Stacks enforces upon it. You can associate instances with one or more layers, which will define the configuration to apply to the instance. AWS OpsWorks Stacks can create instances. For existing instances or on-premises servers, they can register with a stack, and you can manage them in the same manner as if you created them as AWS OpsWorks Stacks.

   Some Linux distributions can register instances.

Instance Type

AWS OpsWorks Stacks supports three instance types.

24/7 instances   This instance type runs until you manually stop it.

Time-based instances   Instances of this type run on a daily and weekly schedule that you configure and are useful for handling predictable changes in a load on your stack.

Load-based instances   Load-based instances start and stop automatically based on metrics such as NetworkOut or CPUUtilization.

You can use time-based and load-based instances to implement automatic scaling in response to predictable or sudden changes in demand. However, unlike Amazon EC2 Auto Scaling groups, you must create time-based and load-based instances ahead of time with the AWS OpsWorks console or AWS CLI. The underlying Amazon EC2 instance will not be created until the time you specify, or the load threshold occurs, but the AWS OpsWorks instance object must exist ahead of time.

If your stack contains more than several instances, a mix of the previous instance types will provide adequate scalability in response to predictable and sudden changes in demand.

For example, if the lowest demand throughout the day in your environment requires three running instances, then it would make sense to include at least three 24/7 instances in the stack. If demand has a predictable pattern throughout the rest of the day, you can use a number of time-based instances to scale out to meet known increases in demand. To accommodate any potential changes outside the norm, you can configure additional load-based instances as well. Figure 9.6 demonstrates the use of each instance type to react dynamically to changes in request volume.

FIGURE 9.6   Instance usage over time

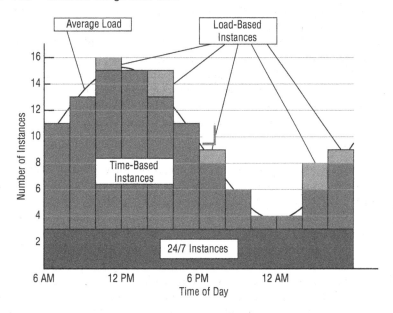

Root Device Type

When you create an Amazon EC2 instance, you have the option to choose either the instance-store or Amazon EBS backed instance types. There are several advantages and disadvantages to each type, as shown in Table 9.2.

TABLE 9.2 Instance-Store–Backed vs. Amazon EBS Backed

Type	Advantages	Disadvantages
Instance-store–backed	Lower cost	Slower boot after initial No data persistence
Amazon EBS backed	Faster boot after initial Retain disk contents	Higher cost

You can apply more configuration settings at the layer, such as Amazon EBS volumes and elastic IP addresses.

Instance Updates

When an instance first boots, AWS OpsWorks Stacks will automatically install any new security and package updates. However, after the initial boot, this will not occur again. This is to ensure that future updates do not affect the performance of your applications. For Linux stacks, you can initiate updates with the Update Dependencies command. Windows stacks do not provide any built-in means to perform updates.

As an alternative to updating instances directly, you can instead regularly launch new instances to replace old ones. As the new instances are created, they will be patched with the latest available security and operating system updates. If you would like to prevent updates entirely and manage this through a separate process, instances can be set to not install updates on startup when you create them. Additionally, this can be set at the layer level to propagate to any new instances that you add to the layer.

Register Instances

If there are instances running in your own data center or other Amazon EC2 instances in your account (or even other accounts), you can register those instances with your stack. You can perform tasks such as user management, package updates, operating system upgrades, and application deployments on registered instances in the same manner as "native" instances.

To register an instance with a stack, you use the aws opsworks register AWS CLI command. The command itself will install the AWS OpsWorks agent on the instance, which is responsible for communicating with the AWS OpsWorks Stacks service endpoint to receive commands and publish information. When you register with other Amazon EC2 instances, they will need both an AWS Identity and Access Management (IAM) instance profile or IAM user credentials with access to register instances with the AWS CLI via the AWS-managed policy, AWSOpsWorksRegisterWithCLI.

When you register instances, you must provide a valid SSH user and private key or valid username and password. These must correspond to a Linux user on the target system (unless you call the register command from the target system itself). After the instance registers, it will display in the AWS OpsWorks Stacks console for assignment to one or more layers in your stack.

You can also deregister an instance from a stack if you no longer want to manage it as part of that stack. This frees it up for you to register it with a different stack or management process.

AWS OpsWorks Agent

The *AWS OpsWorks Agent* installs on any instances that the stack registers or creates. The agent is responsible for querying the AWS OpsWorks Stacks endpoint for commands to execute on the instance, provide instance metrics to the service, provide health checks for auto healing, and update itself (if configured to do so). You can configure the stack to use a specific agent version or automatically update to the latest available version.

Auto-Healing Instances

If you enable auto healing for a layer, instances that fail to communicate with the AWS OpsWorks service endpoint for more than 5 minutes restart automatically. You can view this in the Amazon CloudWatch Events console where initiated_by is set to auto-healing. Auto healing is enabled by default on all layers in a stack, but you can disable them at any time.

When instances are auto-healed, the exact behavior depends on the type of instance.

- For instance-store backed instances, the underlying instance terminates, and a new one is created in its place.

- Amazon EBS backed instances stop and start with the appropriate Amazon EC2 API command.

Apps

An *app* refers to the location where you store application code and other files. This can be an Amazon S3 bucket, a Git repository, or an HTTP bundle. If you require credentials to connect to the repository, the app configuration provides them as well. The Deploy lifecycle event includes any apps that you configure for an instance at the layer or layers to which it corresponds.

 AWS OpsWorks Stacks automatically downloads and deploys applications in built-in layers. For custom layers, you must include this functionality in your recipe code.

After you configure one or more apps for a layer, running a deployment on instances in that layer will copy the application code from the configured repository and perform any needed deployment steps. In Chef 11.10 built-in layers, this occurs automatically. For custom layers in any Chef version, the deployment process is not automatic, and you must use custom cookbooks.

To perform app updates, you first modify the app itself to point to a new version. Either the current location (Amazon S3 file, Git branch, or HTTP archive) must have the update of the new application code or the app must point to a new revision. Currently running instances will not automatically update. Instances that create after the app updates will deploy the latest version. Any instances that stop at the time of the update will update when the instance starts again.

Users and Permissions Management

AWS OpsWorks Stacks provides the ability to manage users at the stack level, independent of IAM permissions. This is incredibly useful to provide access to instances in a stack without giving a user actual permission to your account. Since most large organizations have strict access policies for third-party contractors, AWS OpsWorks Stacks allows you to give access to perform some stack management tasks, as well as Secure Socket Shell (SSH) or Remote Desktop Protocol (RDP) access to stack instances, and not allow nonemployees access to perform tasks within your account.

AWS OpsWorks Stacks users associate with regional endpoints and cannot be given access to stacks not in the same region. In this case, you need to import the user into the other region(s).

Managing Permissions

There are four permission types you can apply to a user to provide stack-level permission.

Deny   No action is allowed on the stack.

Show   The user can view stack configuration but cannot interact with it in any way.

Deploy   The user can view stack configuration and deploy apps.

Manage   The user can view stack configuration, deploy apps, and manage stack configuration.

AWS OpsWorks Stacks permissions do not allow certain actions, such as to create or clone stacks. IAM permissions restrict these actions, and you must assign them to an IAM user or IAM role. If the user in question is also an IAM user, you can fine-tune the permissions levels.

You can give an IAM user the Manage permission at the stack level but deny the ability to delete layers (opsworks:DeleteLayer) at the IAM level. Like IAM, explicit deny will always take precedence over explicit allow.

Along with stack-level permissions, you can give AWS OpsWorks users SSH or RDP access into instances with or without administrative access. You can also configure users to manage their own SSH keys so that they can set their key once they provide access and do not require shared key files through other means. This is also more secure than Amazon EC2 key pairs, as the keys are unique to individual users.

User permissions are set at the stack level in the AWS OpsWorks console, as shown in Figure 9.7. Here you can assign stack and instance permissions to individual user accounts.

FIGURE 9.7   AWS OpsWorks Stacks user permissions

Permissions

User Name	Deny	IAM Policies Only	Show	Deploy	Manage	SSH / RDP	sudo / admin
			Permission level			Instance access	
admin_user	⦿	⦿	⦿	⦿	⦿	☑	☑
cli-user-test	⦿	⦿	⦿	⦿	⦿	☐	☐
development	⦿	⦿	⦿	⦿	⦿	☐	☐

Managing Users

For existing IAM users for whom you would like to configure stack-level access, you can import them into AWS OpsWorks Stacks on the Users page of the AWS OpsWorks console. Once you import them, you can assign stack-level permissions. These permissions combine with current IAM policies before AWS OpsWorks evaluates them. For example, if you would like to deny access to a specific stack for an IAM user, you can import the user into AWS OpsWorks Stacks and then assign the Deny permission for that stack.

If you import an IAM user into AWS OpsWorks Stacks and then later delete that user, you must manually delete the AWS OpsWorks Stacks user as well to revoke any SSH or RDP access.

Lifecycle Events

At each layer of a stack, you will set which Chef recipes you would like to execute at each stage of a node's lifecycle, such as when it comes online or goes offline. These stages are *lifecycle events*. The recipes at each lifecycle event execute in the order you specify in the *AWS OpsWorks Agent*.

Outside of the lifecycle events, you can execute recipes manually with the Execute Recipes command in the AWS OpsWorks console (see Figure 9.8) or AWS CLI. When invoking the command, you can provide a list of recipes to execute in order.

FIGURE 9.8   Running command recipes to execute

Run Command

Settings

Command	Execute Recipes ⬍
	Executes a specified set of recipes.
Recipes to execute	apache2, apache2::mod_ssl
Comment	Install Apache2 with mod_ssl

You can add more custom recipes to each lifecycle event in the layer's configuration. Recipes execute in the order they appear in the Custom Chef recipes lifecycle event, as shown in Figure 9.9.

FIGURE 9.9   Custom Chef recipes for lifecycle events

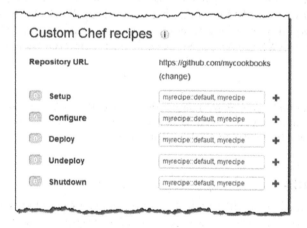

Custom Chef recipes ⓘ

Repository URL	https://github.com/mycookbooks (change)
🔲 Setup	myrecipe::default, myrecipe ➕
🔲 Configure	myrecipe::default, myrecipe ➕
🔲 Deploy	myrecipe::default, myrecipe ➕
🔲 Undeploy	myrecipe::default, myrecipe ➕
🔲 Shutdown	myrecipe::default, myrecipe ➕

Setup

This event occurs once the instance has come online after initial creation or when the instance stops and starts. Setup automatically invokes the Deploy command after it completes successfully.

Configure

Any time an instance in a stack comes online or goes offline, all instances in the same stack will undergo a Configure lifecycle event. This ensures that all instances in a stack are "aware" of each other. For example, if a layer in your stack installs and configures haproxy for load balancing, any instances in the same layer will need to update to include the new node in /etc/hosts (or remove the node that went offline).

Deploy

After an instance has come online and completes the initial Setup and Configure events, a Deploy event deploys any apps that you configure for the layer. This step can copy application code from a repository, start or refresh services, and perform other tasks to bring your application(s) online.

After an instance has run Deploy for the first time, it will never do so again automatically. This prevents untested changes from reaching production instances. After you test a feature change or bug fix, you must manually run the Deploy event with the AWS OpsWorks Stacks console or AWS CLI.

Undeploy

The Undeploy lifecycle event runs when you delete or remove an app from a layer. You use this to perform tasks such as when you want to remove an application's configuration or other cleanup tasks when you remove an app.

Shutdown

Before the actual shutdown command issues to an instance, the Shutdown lifecycle event gives you the opportunity to perform tasks such as taking snapshots and copying log files to Amazon S3 for later use. If the instance's layer also includes a load balancer, the instance deregisters after the configured connection draining time.

Resource Management

AWS OpsWorks Stacks allows for management of other resources in your account as part of your stack, and it includes elastic IP addresses, Amazon EBS volumes, and Amazon RDS instances. You register the resources with the stack to make them available to assign them to instances or layers. If you attach resources to instances in the stack and you delete the instance, the resource remains registered with the stack until it is manually deregistered. Deregistering resources does not automatically delete them. You must delete the resource itself with the respective service console or AWS CLI command.

Amazon EBS Volumes

Amazon EBS volumes that are not currently attached to any instances can register with a stack, and you can assign them to instances if the volume uses XFS formatting. You cannot attach volumes to running instances. To attach a volume to a running instance, you must stop it. You can move a volume between instances that are both offline.

 You cannot attach Amazon EBS volumes to Windows stacks.

Elastic IP Addresses

As with Amazon EBS volumes, elastic IP addresses that are not associated with resources in your account may be registered with the stack. You can assign an elastic IP address to an instance regardless of whether it is running or not. After an Elastic IP address is disassociated from an instance, a configure lifecycle event updates instances in the stack with the instance's new IP address.

Amazon RDS Instances

You can register Amazon EBS instances to only one stack at a time. However, you can register a single Amazon RDS instance with multiple apps in the same stack.

Chef 11 and Chef 12

Both Chef 11 and Chef 12 provide unique functionality differences that are important to note before you use AWS OpsWorks Stacks. Each of the major differences is outlined in this section.

The differences in this section are with respect to AWS OpsWorks Stacks as a service, and they do not include differences between Chef versions 11.10 and 12.0. Since version 11.10 has been deprecated by Chef, community support will not be as strong as for later versions.

Separate Chef Runs

In Chef 11.10 stacks, AWS-provided cookbooks were run in the same Chef run as any custom cookbooks. The AWS cookbooks performed various tasks such as mounting Amazon EBS volumes that had been attached to the instance in the AWS OpsWorks console. However, this could result in situations where custom cookbooks had naming conflicts with those provided by AWS. You had to split this into two separate Chef runs on the instance to eliminate any potential namespace conflicts.

Community Support

Since the deprecation of Chef 11.10, community support has gradually decreased. Any open source cookbooks on the Chef Supermarket, for example, will likely make use of Chef 12.0 functionality, removing backward compatibility for Chef 11.10 stacks.

Built-in Layers

Chef 12.0 stacks no longer include the built-in layers as in Chef 11.10 stacks, such as the Rails layer. To implement these layers in Chef 12.0 stacks, you can still copy the built-in cookbooks from a Chef 11.10 stack and update them to be compatible with Chef 12.0. Chef 12.0 stacks still support built-in layer types from Chef 11.10 stacks.

- Amazon RDS instance layers
- Amazon ECS cluster layers

Berkshelf

Berkshelf is no longer available for the automatic installation on Chef 12.0 instances. Instead, install Berkshelf with a custom cookbook.

Data Bags

In lieu of custom JSON, Chef 12.0 stacks support data bags to provide better compatibility with community cookbooks. You can declare data bags in the custom JSON field of the stack, layer, and deployment configurations to provide instances in your stack for any additional data that you would like to provide. The attributes set in the data bags will no longer be available in the node object, as with Chef 11.10 stacks, but instead are available with Chef search.

Example: Searching Data Bag Content

Here's an example of searching a data bag for a value:

```
app = search("aws_opsworks_app").first
Chef::Log.info("********** The app's short name is '#{app['shortname']}' **********")
Chef::Log.info("********** The app's URL is '#{app['app_source']['url']}' **********")
```

Data Bags and Custom JSON

In Chef 11.10 stacks, you provide data to instances with custom JSON, which populates in the node object when Chef runs. You can access this information in your recipe code to specify configuration based on the value of custom JSON. You can specify custom JSON at the stack, layer, and deployment levels. Any data that you define at the deployment level overrides the data set at the layer or stack levels. Any data set at the layer level overrides the data set at the stack level.

Example: Stack-Level Settings in Custom JSON

Here's a JSON example at the stack level:

```
{
  "state": "visible",
  "colors": {
    "foreground": "light-blue",
    "background": "dark-gray"
  }
}
```

Now set the custom JSON for the layer to override the stack-level settings.

```
{
  "state": "hidden",
  "colors": {
    "foreground": "light-blue",
    "background": "dark-gray"
  }
}
```

(continued)

(continued)

Next, execute the recipe on an instance; the value of node['state'] will be hidden.

```
Chef::Log.info("********** The app's initial state is '#{node['state']}' **********")
Chef::Log.info("********** The app's initial foreground color is '#{node['colors']['foreground']}' **********")
Chef::Log.info("********** The app's initial background color is '#{node['colors']['background']}' **********")
```

Custom JSON is limited to 80 KB in size. If you need to provide larger data, consider the use of Amazon S3 and retrieve files with a custom cookbook.

Chef 12.0 and 12.2 stacks use *data bags* instead of custom JSON. This provides better integration with community cookbooks that rely on data bags as the latest Chef standard to provide structured data to cookbooks. Data bags are also written in JSON at the stack, layer, and deployment levels. Any stack data originally provided in the node object on Chef 11.10 stacks is instead made available through one of several data bags during Chef runs.

App Data Bag (aws_opsworks_app)

Suppose the aws_opsworks_app data bag provides information about any apps associated with the layer. In Chef 11.10 stacks, you can access app information in the node object.

```
Chef::Log.info ("********** The app's short name is '#{node['opsworks']['applications'].first['slug_name']}' **********")
Chef::Log.info("********** The app's URL is '#{node['deploy']['simplephpapp']['scm']['repository']}' **********")
```

Moving to data bags in Chef 12.0 and 12.2 stacks, Chef search is used to query data bag contents. The above example would instead look like:

```
app = search("aws_opsworks_app").first

Chef::Log.info("********** The app's short name is '#{app['shortname']}' **********")
Chef::Log.info("********** The app's URL is '#{app['app_source']['url']}' **********")
```

To add custom data bags to your stack, specify them in either the stack, layer, or deployment custom JSON field. To create data bags to call users with a single item, you can do the following:

```
{
  "opsworks": {
    "data_bags": {
      "users": {
        {
          "id": "nick",
          "comment": "Nick Alteen",
          "home": "/opt/alteen",
```

```
        "ssh_keys": ["123…", "456…"]
      }
    }
  }
 }
}
```

Monitor Instance Metrics

AWS OpsWorks Stacks provides a custom dashboard to monitor up to 13 custom metrics for each instance in the stack. The agent that runs on each instance will publish the information to the AWS OpsWorks Stacks service. If you enable the layer, system, application, and custom logs, they automatically publish to Amazon CloudWatch Logs for review without access the instance itself. You can monitor details at the stack, layer, and instance levels. The metrics that the AWS OpsWorks Agent publishes include cpu_idle, memory_free, procs, and others. Since these metrics are provided by the AWS OpsWorks Agent running on the instance itself, information not available to the underlying host of the instance is provided.

Windows instance monitoring provides only the standard Amazon EC2 metrics.

For each stack in your account, a dashboard displays these metrics over time. The metrics divide by layer and display over time periods that vary, as shown in Figure 9.10.

FIGURE 9.10   Monitoring all layers in a stack

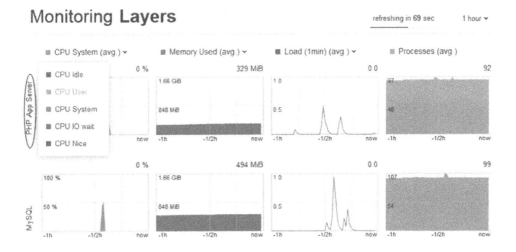

If you select a layer name in the monitoring dashboard, you can review each individual layer. In the layer's dashboard, metrics divide by individual instances. For example, if you select PHP App Server, as shown in Figure 9.10, the screen in Figure 9.11 displays.

FIGURE 9.11   Monitoring a single layer

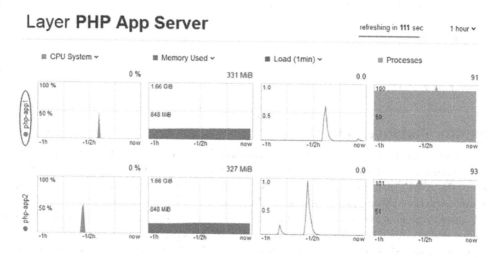

From the layer dashboard, you can review individual instance metrics if you select the instance name. For example, if you select php-app1, as shown in Figure 9.11, the screen in Figure 9.12 displays.

FIGURE 9.12   Monitoring an instance

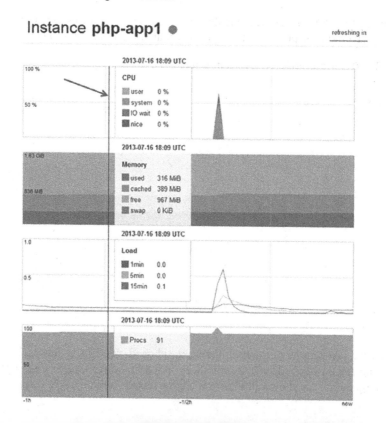

If you enable Amazon CloudWatch Logs on Linux stacks, you can configure the AWS OpsWorks Agent to send system, application, and custom logs to Amazon CloudWatch Logs. With this, alerts can be set when the logs detect specific string patterns, such as HTTP 500 responses in web servers. To publish logs, the instance profile for any instances in the layer must contain permission to push logs. To do this, you assign the AWSOpsWorksCloudWatchLogs managed policy to the corresponding role. Since this integration requires a later agent version, enabling it for your layer will result in all instances being upgraded to a compatible agent version (if they do not already have one).

When you stream logs to Amazon CloudWatch Logs, the log groups use the following naming convention:

`stack_name\layer_name\chef_log_name`

Custom logs, which you define by the file path in the layer settings, add to log groups with the naming convention.

`/stack_name/layer_short_name/file_path_name`

Along with CloudWatch Logs, CloudWatch Events support stacks. Any time the following types of events occur, you can invoke custom actions in response.

- Instance state change
- Command state change
- Deployment state change
- Alerts

AWS OpsWorks Stacks Service Limits

AWS OpsWorks Stacks enforces the service limits shown in Table 9.3. These limits can be increased by submitting a request to AWS Support.

TABLE 9.3   AWS OpsWorks Stacks Service Limits

Limit	Value
Stacks per region per account	40
Layers per stack	40
Instances per stack	40
Apps per stack	40

Using AWS OpsWorks Stacks with AWS CodePipeline

Inside a stack, you specify a value for App to refer to a repository or archive that contains application code to deploy to one or more layers. You can use AWS CodePipeline to update an AWS OpsWorks app, which then deploys to any instances in layers you associate with this app.

To configure AWS CodePipeline to deploy to a stack, select the appropriate stack, layer, and app to update with the input artifact, as shown in Figure 9.13.

FIGURE 9.13   Using AWS OpsWorks Stacks with AWS CodePipeline

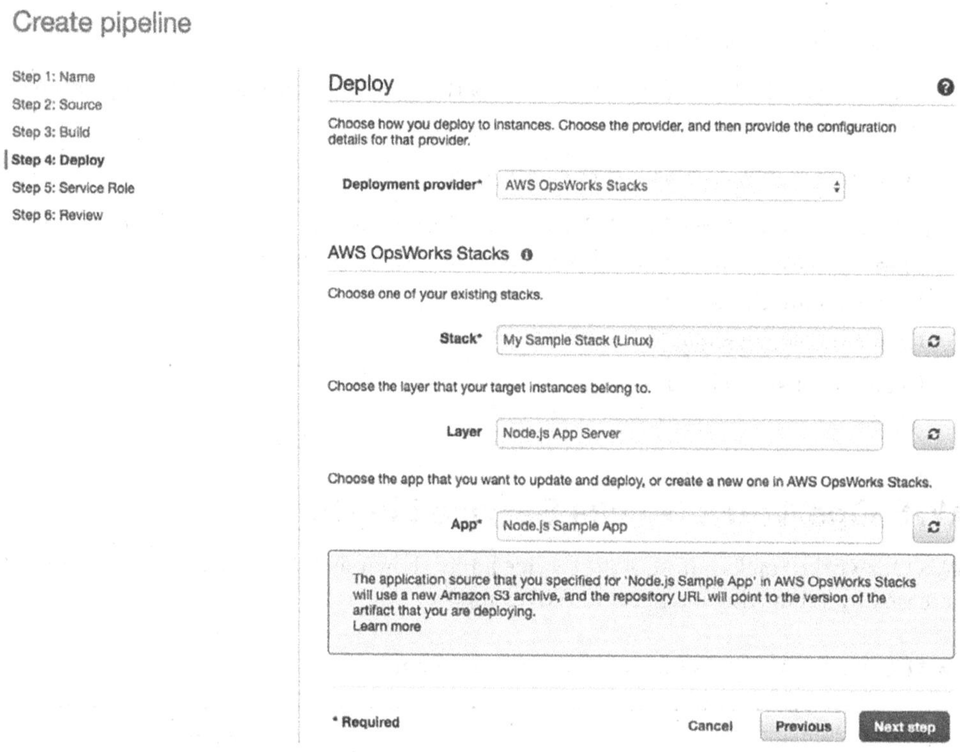

Deployment Best Practices

Since app or cookbook updates do not deploy automatically to running instances, you need a robust deployment strategy to ensure that changes complete successfully (or do not cause outages if they fail). This section details the deployment best practices recommended by AWS.

Rolling Deployments

You can issue commands to subsets of instances in a stack or layer at a time. If you split the deployment into multiple phases, the blast radius of failures will be minimized to only a few instances that you can replace, roll back, or repair.

Blue/Green Deployments (Separate Stacks)

Much like you use separate stacks for different environments of the same application, you can also use separate stacks for different deployments. This ensures that all features and updates to an application can be thoroughly tested before routing requests to the new environment. Additionally, you can leave the previous environment running for some time to perform backups, investigate logs, or perform other tasks.

When you use Elastic Load Balancing layers and Amazon Route 53, you can route traffic to the new environment with built-in weighted routing policies. You can progressively increase traffic to the new stack as health checks and other monitoring indicate the new application version has deployed without error.

Manage Databases Between Deployments

In either deployment strategy, there will likely be a backend database with which instances running either version will need to communicate. Currently, Amazon RDS layers support registering a database with only one stack at a time.

If you do not want to create a new database and migrate data as part of the deployment process, you can configure both application version instances to connect to the same database (if there are no schema changes that would prevent this). Whichever stack does not have the Amazon RDS instance registered will need to obtain credentials via another means, such as custom JSON or a configuration file in a secure Amazon S3 bucket.

If there are schema changes that are not backward compatible, create a new database to provide the most seamless transition. However, it will be important to ensure that data is not lost or corrupted during the transition process. You should heavily test this before you attempt it in a production deployment.

Using Amazon Elastic Container Service to Deploy Containers

Amazon ECS is a highly scalable, high-performance container orchestration service that supports Docker containers and allows you to easily run and scale containerized applications on AWS. Amazon ECS eliminates the need for you to install and operate your own container orchestration software, manage and scale a cluster of virtual machines, or schedule containers on those virtual machines.

With simple API calls, you can launch and stop Docker-enabled applications, query the complete state of your application, and access many familiar features such as IAM roles, security groups, load balancers, Amazon CloudWatch Events, AWS CloudFormation templates, and AWS CloudTrail logs.

What Is Amazon ECS?

Amazon ECS streamlines the process for managing and scheduling containers across fleets of Amazon EC2 instances, without the need to include separate management tools for container orchestration or cluster scaling. *AWS Fargate* reduces management further as it deploys containers to serverless architecture and removes cluster management requirements entirely. To create a cluster and deploy services, you need only configure the resource requirements of containers and availability requirements. Amazon ECS manages the rest with the use of an agent that runs on cluster instances. AWS Fargate requires no agent management.

To react to changes in demands for your service or application, Amazon ECS supports Amazon EC2 Auto Scaling groups of cluster instances that allow your service to increase running container counts across multiple instances as demand increases. You can define container isolation and dependencies as part of the service definition. You can use the service definition to enforce requirements without user interaction, such as "only one container of type A may run on a cluster instance at a time."

Amazon ECS Concepts

This section details Amazon ECS concepts.

Amazon ECS Cluster

Amazon ECS clusters are the foundational infrastructure components on which containers run. Clusters consist of one or more Amazon EC2 instances in your Amazon VPC. Each instance in a cluster (cluster instance) has an agent installed. The agent is responsible for receiving container scheduling/shutdown commands from the Amazon ECS service and to report the current health status of containers (restart or replace). Figure 9.14 demonstrates an Amazon EC2 launch type, where instances make up the Amazon ECS cluster.

FIGURE 9.14   Amazon ECS architecture

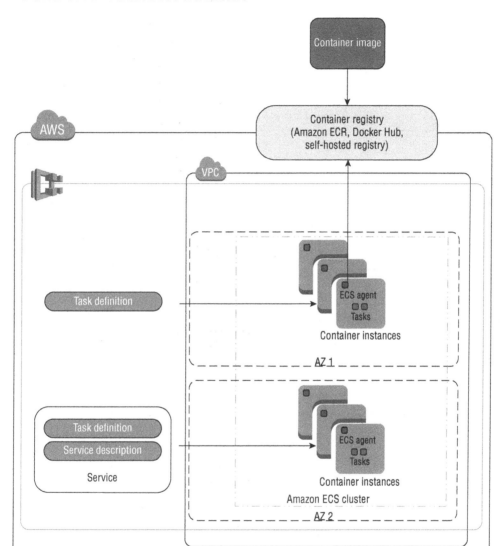

In an AWS Fargate launch type, Amazon ECS clusters are no longer made up of Amazon EC2 instances. Since the tasks themselves launch on the AWS infrastructure, AWS assigns each one an elastic network interface with an Amazon VPC. This provides network connectivity for the container without the need to manage the infrastructure on which it runs. Figure 9.15 demonstrates an AWS Fargate cluster that runs in multiple availability zones (AZs).

FIGURE 9.15   AWS Fargate architecture

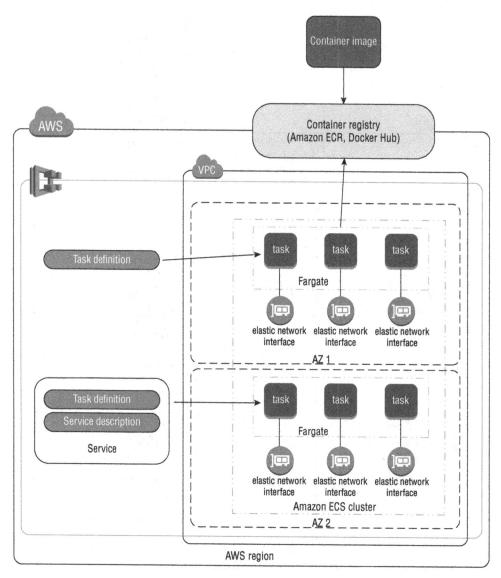

An individual cluster can support both Amazon EC2 and AWS Fargate launch types. However, a single cluster instance can belong to only one cluster at a time. Amazon EC2 launch types support both on-demand and spot instances, and they allow you to reduce cost for noncritical workloads.

To enable network connectivity for containers that run on your instance, the corresponding task definition must outline port mappings from the container to the host instance. When you create a container instance, you can select the instance type to use. The compute resources available to this instance type will determine how many containers can be run on the instance. For example, if a t2.micro instance has one vCPU and 1 GB of RAM, it will not be able to run containers that require two vCPUs.

After you add a container instance to a cluster and you place containers on it, there may be situations where you would need to remove the container from the cluster temporarily—for a regular patch, for example. However, if critical tasks run on a container instance, you may want to wait for the containers to terminate gracefully. Container instance draining can be used to drain running containers from an instance and prevent new ones from being started. Depending on the service's configuration, replacement tasks start before or after the original tasks terminate.

- If the value of minimumHealthyPercent is less than 100 percent, the service will terminate the task and launch a replacement.
- If the value is greater than 100 percent, the service will attempt to launch a replacement task before it terminates the original.

To make room for launching additional tasks, you can scale out a cluster with Amazon EC2 Auto Scaling groups. For an EC2 Auto Scaling group to work with an Amazon ECS cluster, you must install the Amazon ECS agent either as part of the AMI or via instance userdata. To change the number container instances that run, you can adjust the size of the corresponding EC2 Auto Scaling group. If you need to terminate instances, any tasks that run on them will also halt.

Scaling out a cluster does not also increase the running task count. You use service automatic scaling for this process.

AWS Fargate

AWS Fargate simplifies the process of managing containers in your environment and removes the need to manage underlying cluster instances. Instead, you only need to specify the compute requirements of your containers in your task definition. AWS Fargate automatically launches containers without your interaction.

With AWS Fargate, there are several restrictions on the types of tasks that you can launch. For example, when you specify a task definition, containers cannot be run in privileged mode. To verify that a given task definition is acceptable by AWS Fargate, use the **Requires** capabilities field of the Amazon ECS console or the --requires-capabilities command option of the AWS CLI.

AWS Fargate requires that containers launch with the network mode set to awsvpc. In other words, you can launch only AWS Fargate containers into Amazon VPCs.

AWS Fargate requires the `awslogs` driver to enable log configuration.

Containers and Images

    Amazon ECS launches and manages Docker containers. However, Docker is not in scope for the AWS Certified Developer – Associate Exam.

Any workloads that run on Amazon ECS must reside in Docker containers. In a virtual server environment, multiple virtual machines share physical hardware, each of which acts as its own operating system. In a containerized environment, you package components of the operating system itself into containers. This removes the need to run any nonessential aspects of a full-fledged virtual machine to increase portability. In other words, virtual machines share the same physical hardware, while containers share the same operating system.

Container images are similar in concept to AMIs. Images provision a Docker container. You store images in registries, such as a Docker Hub or an Amazon Elastic Container Repository (ECR).

    You can create your own private image repository; however, AWS Fargate does not support this launch type.

Docker provides mobility and flexibility of your workload to allow containers to be run on any system that supports Docker. Compute resources can be better utilized when you run multiple containers on the same cluster, which makes the best possible use of resources and reduces idle compute capacity. Since you separate service components into containers, you can update individual components more frequently and at reduced risk.

Task Definition

Though you can package entire applications into a single container, it may be more efficient to run multiple smaller containers, each of which contains a subset of functionality of your full application. This is referred to as *service-oriented architecture* (SOA). In SOA, each unit of functionality for an overall system is contained separately from the rest. Individual services work with one another to perform a larger task. For example, an e-commerce website that uses SOA could have sets of containers for load balancing, credit card processing, order fulfillment, or any other tasks that users require. You design each component of the system as a black box so that other components do not need to be aware of inner workings to interact with them.

A *task definition* is a JSON document that describes what containers launch for your application or system. A single task definition can describe between one and 10 containers and their requirements. Task definitions can also specify compute, networking, and storage requirements, such as which ports to expose to which containers and which volumes to mount.

You should add containers to the same task definition under the following circumstances:

- The containers all share a common lifecycle.

- The containers need to run on the same common host or container instance.

- The containers need to share local resources or volumes.

An entire application does not need to deploy with a single task definition. Instead, you should separate larger application segments into separate task definitions. This will reduce the impact of breaking changes in your environment. If you allocate the right-sized container instances, you can also better control scaling and resource consumption of the containers.

After a task definition creates and uploads to Amazon ECS, it can launch one or more *tasks*. When a task is created, the containers in the task definition are scheduled to launch into the target cluster via the task scheduler.

Task Definition with Two Containers

The following example demonstrates a task definition with two containers. The first container runs a WordPress installation and binds the container instance's port 80 to the same port on the container. The second container installs MySQL to act as the backend data store of the WordPress container. The task definition also specifies a link between the containers, which allows them to communicate without port mappings if the network setting for the task definition is set to bridge.

```
{
  "containerDefinitions": [
    {
      "name": "wordpress",
      "links": [
        "mysql"
      ],
      "image": "wordpress",
      "essential": true,
      "portMappings": [
        {
          "containerPort": 80,
          "hostPort": 80
        }
      ],
```

(continued)

```
(continued)
     "memory": 500,
     "cpu": 10
  },
  {
    "environment": [
      {
        "name": "MYSQL_ROOT_PASSWORD",
        "value": "password"
      }
    ],
    "name": "mysql",
    "image": "mysql",
    "cpu": 10,
    "memory": 500,
    "essential": true
  }
  ],
  "family": "hello_world"
}
```

Services

When creating a *service*, you can specify the task definition and number of tasks to maintain at any point in time. After the service creates, it will launch the desired number of tasks; thus, it launches each of the containers in the task definition. If any containers in the task become unhealthy, the service is responsible and launches replacement tasks.

Deployment Strategies

When you define a service, you can also configure deployment strategies to ensure a minimum number of healthy tasks are available to serve requests while other tasks in the service update. The maximumPercent parameter defines the maximum percentage of tasks that can be in RUNNING or PENDING state. The minimumHealthyPercent parameter specifies the minimum percentage of tasks that must be in a healthy (RUNNING) state during deployments.

Suppose you configure one task for your service, and you would like to ensure that the application is available during deployments. If you set the maximumPercent to 200 percent and minimumHealthyPercent to 100 percent, it will ensure that the new task launches before the old task terminates. If you configure two tasks for your service and some loss of availability is acceptable, you can set maximumPercent to 100 percent and minimumHealthyPercent to 50 percent. This will cause the service scheduler to terminate one task, launch its replacement, and then do the same with the other task. The difference is that the first approach requires double the normal cluster capacity to accommodate the additional tasks.

Balance Loads

You can configure services to run behind a load balancer to distribute traffic automatically to tasks in the service. Amazon ECS supports classic load balancers, application load balancers, and network load balancers to distribute requests. Of the three load balancer types, application load balancers provide several unique features.

Application Load Balancing (ALB) load balancers route traffic at layer 7 (HTTP/HTTPS). Because of this, they can take advantage of dynamic host port mapping when you use them in front of Amazon ECS clusters. ALBs also support path-based routing so that multiple services can listen on the same port. This means that requests will be to different tasks based on the path specified in the request.

Classic load balancers, because they register and deregister instances, require that any tasks being run behind the load balancer all exist on the same container instance. This may not be desirable in some cases, and it would be better to use an ALB.

Schedule Tasks

If you increase the number of instances in an Amazon ECS cluster, it does not automatically increase the number of running tasks as well. When you configure a service, the service scheduler determines how many tasks run on one or more clusters and automatically starts replacement tasks should any fail. This is especially ideal for long-running tasks such as web servers. If you configure it to do so, the service scheduler will ensure that tasks register with an elastic load balancer.

You can also run a task manually with the RunTask action, or you can run tasks on a cron-like schedule (such as every N minutes on Tuesdays and Thursdays). This works well for tasks such as log rotation, batch jobs, or other data aggregation tasks.

To dynamically adjust the run task count dynamically, you use Amazon CloudWatch Alarms in conjunction with Application Auto Scaling to increase or decrease the task count based on alarm status. You can use two approaches for automatically scaling Amazon ECS services and tasks: Target Tracking Policies and Step Scaling Policies.

Target Tracking Policies

Target tracking policies determine when to scale the number of tasks based on a target metric. If the metric is above the target, such as CPU utilization being above 75 percent, Amazon ECS can automatically launch more tasks to bring the metric below the desired value. You can specify multiple target tracking policies for the same service. In the case of a conflict, the policy that would result in the highest task count wins.

Step Scaling Policies

Unlike target tracking policies, *step scaling policies* can continue to scale in or out as metrics increase or decrease. For example, you can configure a step scaling policy to scale out when CPU utilization reaches 75 percent, again at 80 percent, and one final time at 90 percent. With this approach, a single policy can result in multiple scaling activities as metrics increase or decrease.

Task Placement Strategies

Regardless of the method you use, *task placement strategies* determine on which instances tasks launch or which tasks terminate during scaling actions. For example, the spread task placement strategy distributes tasks across multiple AZs as much as possible. Task placement strategies perform on a best-effort basis. If the strategy cannot be honored, such as when there are insufficient compute resources in the AZ you select, Amazon ECS will still try to launch the task(s) on other cluster instances. Other strategies include binpack (uses CPU and memory on each instance at a time) and random.

Task placement strategies associate with specific attributes, which are evaluated during task placement. For example, to spread tasks across availability zones, the placement strategy to use is as follows:

```
"placementStrategy": [
    {
        "field": "attribute:ecs.availability-zone",
        "type": "spread"
    }
]
```

Task Placement Constraints

Task placement constraints enforce specific requirements on the container instances on which tasks launch, such as to specify the instance type as t2.micro.

```
"placementConstraints": [
    {
        "expression": "attribute:ecs.instance-type == t2.micro",
        "type": "memberOf"
    }
]
```

Amazon ECS Service Discovery

Amazon ECS Service Discovery allows you to assign Amazon Route 53 DNS entries automatically for tasks your service manages. To do so, you create a private service namespace for each Amazon ECS cluster. As tasks launch or terminate, the private service namespace updates to include DNS entries for each task. A service directory maps DNS entries to available service endpoints. Amazon ECS Service Discovery maintains health checks of containers, and it removes them from the service directory should they become unavailable.

To use public namespaces, you must purchase or register the public hosted zone with Amazon Route 53.

Private Image Repositories

Amazon ECS can connect to private image repositories with basic authentication. This is useful to connect to Docker Hub or other private registries with a username and password. To do so, the ECS_ENGINE_AUTH_TYPE and ECS_ENGINE_AUTH_DATA environment variables must be set with the authorization type and actual credentials to connect. However, you should not set these properties directly. Instead, store your container instance configuration file in an Amazon S3 bucket and copy it to the instance with userdata.

Amazon Elastic Container Repository

Amazon Elastic Container Repository (Amazon ECR) is a Docker registry service that is fully compatible with existing Docker CLI tools. Amazon ECR supports resource-level permissions for private repositories and allows you to preserve a secure registry without the need to maintain an additional application. Since it integrates with IAM users and Amazon ECS cluster instances, it can take advantage of IAM users or instance profiles to access and maintain images securely without the need to provide a username and password.

Amazon ECS Container Agent

The *Amazon ECS container agent* is responsible for monitoring the status of tasks that run on cluster instances. If a new task needs to launch, the container agent will download the container images and start or stop containers. If any containers fail health checks, the container agent will replace them. Since the AWS Fargate launch type uses AWS-managed compute resources, you do not need to configure the agent.

To register an instance with an Amazon ECS cluster, you must first install the Amazon ECS Agent. This agent installs automatically on Amazon ECS optimized AMIs. If you would like to use a custom AMI, it must adhere to the following requirements:

- Linux kernel 3.10 or greater
- Docker version 1.9.0 or greater and any corresponding dependencies

The Amazon ECS container agent updates regularly and can update on your instance(s) without any service interruptions. To perform updates to the agent, replace the container instance entirely or use the Update Container Agent command on Amazon ECS optimized AMIs.

You cannot perform agent updates on Windows instances using these methods. Instead, terminate the instance and create a new server in its absence.

To configure the Amazon ECS container agent, update /etc/ecs/config on the container instance and then restart the agent. You can configure properties such as the cluster to register with, reserved ports, proxy settings, and how much system memory to reserve for the agent.

Amazon ECS Service Limits

Table 9.4 displays the limits that AWS enforces for Amazon ECS. You can change limits with an asterisk (*) by making a request to AWS Support.

TABLE 9.4 Amazon ECS Service Limits

Limit	Value
Clusters per region per account*	1,000
Container instances per cluster*	1,000
Services per cluster*	500
Tasks that use Amazon EC2 launch type per service*	1,000
Tasks that use AWS Fargate launch type per region per account*	20
Public IP addresses for tasks that use AWS Fargate launch type*	20
Load balancers per service	1
Task definition size	32 KiB
Task definition containers	10
Layer size of image that use AWS Fargate task	4 GB
Shared volume that use AWS Fargate tasks	10 GB
Container storage that use AWS Fargate tasks	10 GB

Using Amazon ECS with AWS CodePipeline

When you select Amazon ECS as a deployment provider, there is no option to create the cluster and service as part of the pipeline creation process. This must be done ahead of time. After the cluster is created, select the appropriate cluster and service names in the AWS CodePipeline console, as shown in Figure 9.16.

FIGURE 9.16   Amazon ECS as a deployment provider

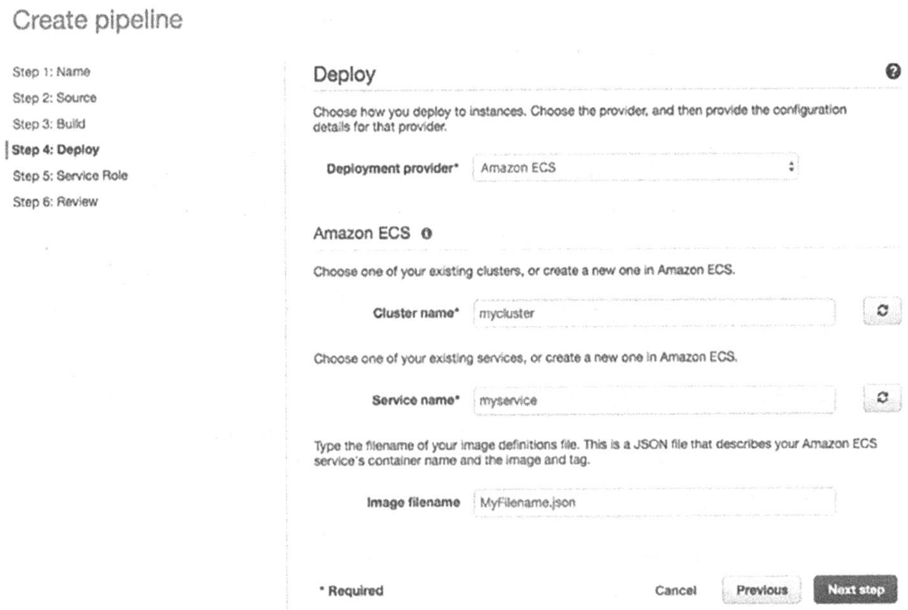

You must provide an image filename as part of this configuration. This is a JSON-formatted document inside your code repository or archive or as an output build artifact, which specifies the service's container name and image tag. We recommend that the cluster contain at least two Amazon EC2 instances so that one can act as primary while the other handles deployment of new containers.

Summary

This chapter includes infrastructure, configuration, and deployment services that you use to deploy configuration as code.

AWS CloudFormation leverages standard AWS APIs to provision and update infrastructure in your account. AWS CloudFormation uses standard configuration management tools such as Chef and Puppet.

Configuration management of infrastructure over an extended period of time is best served with the use of a dedicated tool such as AWS OpsWorks Stacks. You define the configuration in one or more Chef recipes to achieve configuration as code on top of your infrastructure. AWS OpsWorks Stacks can be used to provide a serverless Chef infrastructure to configure servers with Chef code (recipes).

Chef recipe code is declarative in nature, and you do not have to rely on the accuracy of procedural steps, as you would with a userdata script you apply to Amazon ECS instances or launch configurations. You can use Amazon ECS instead of instances or serverless functions to use a containerization method to manage applications. If you separate infrastructure from configuration, you also gain the ability to update each on separate cadences.

Amazon ECS supports Docker containers, and it allows you to run and scale containerized applications on AWS. Amazon ECS eliminates the need to install and operate your own container orchestration software, manage and scale a cluster of virtual machines, or schedule containers on those virtual machines.

AWS Fargate reduces management further as it deploys containers to serverless architecture and removes cluster management requirements. To create a cluster and deploy services, you configure the resource requirements of containers and availability requirements. Amazon ECS manages the rest through an agent that runs on cluster instances. AWS Fargate requires no agent management.

Amazon ECS clusters are the foundational infrastructure components on which containers run. Clusters consist of Amazon EC2 instances in your Amazon VPC. Each cluster instance has an agent installed that is responsible for receiving scheduling/shutdown commands from the Amazon ECS service and reporting the current health status of containers (restart or replace).

In lieu of custom JSON, Chef 12.0 stacks support data bags to provide better compatibility with community cookbooks. You can declare data bags in the custom JSON field of the stack, layer, and deployment configurations to provide instances in your stack for any additional data that you would like to provide.

AWS OpsWorks Stacks lets you manage applications and servers on AWS and on-premises. You can model your application as a stack that contains different layers, such as load balancing, database, and application server. You can deploy and configure Amazon EC2 instances in each layer or connect other resources such as Amazon RDS databases. AWS OpsWorks Stacks lets you set automatic scaling for your servers on preset schedules or in response to a constant change of traffic levels, and it uses lifecycle hooks to orchestrate changes as your environment scales. You run Chef recipes with Chef Solo, which allows you to automate tasks such as installing packages and program languages or frameworks, configuring software, and more.

An app is the location where you store application code and other files, such as an Amazon S3 bucket, a Git repository, or an HTTP bundle, and it includes sign-in credentials. The Deploy lifecycle event includes any apps that you configure for an instance at the layer or layers to which it corresponds.

At each layer of a stack, you set which Chef recipes to execute at each stage of a node's lifecycle, such as when it comes online or goes offline (lifecycle events). The recipes at each lifecycle event are executed by the AWS OpsWorks Agent in the order you specify.

AWS OpsWorks Stacks allows for management of other resources in your account as part of your stack and include elastic IP addresses, Amazon EBS volumes, and Amazon RDS instances.

The AWS OpsWorks Stacks dashboard monitors up to 13 custom metrics for each instance in the stack. The agent that runs on each instance will publish the information to the AWS OpsWorks Stacks service. If you enable the layer, system, application, and custom logs, they automatically publish to Amazon CloudWatch Logs for review without accessing the instance itself.

When you define a consistent deployment pattern for infrastructure, configuration, and application code, you can convert entire enterprises to code. You can remove manual management of most common processes and replace them with seamless management of entire application stacks through a simple commit action.

Exam Essentials

Understand configuration management and Chef.   Configuration management is the process designed to ensure the infrastructure in a given system adheres to a specific set of standards, settings, or attributes. Chef is a Ruby-based configuration management language that AWS OpsWorks Stacks uses to enforce configuration on Amazon EC2/on-premises instances, or *nodes*. Chef uses a declarative syntax to describe the desired state of a node, abstracting the actual steps needed to achieve the desired configuration. This code is organized into *recipes*, which are organized into collections called *cookbooks*.

Know how AWS OpsWorks Stacks organizes configuration code into cookbooks.   In traditional Chef implementations, cookbooks belong to a chef-repo, which is a versioned directory that contains cookbooks and their underlying recipes and files. A single cookbook repository can contain one or more cookbooks. When you define the custom cookbook location for a stack, all cookbooks copy to instances in the stack.

Know how to update custom cookbooks on a node.   When instances first launch in a stack, they will download cookbooks from the custom cookbook repository. You must manually issue an Update Custom Cookbooks command to instances in your stack to update the instance.

Understand the different AWS OpsWorks Stacks components.   The topmost object in AWS OpsWorks Stacks is a stack, which contains all elements of a given environment or system. Within a stack, one or more layers contain instances you group by common purpose. A single instance references either an Amazon EC2 or on-premises instance and contains additional configuration data. A stack can contain one or more apps, which refer to repositories where application code copies to for deployment. Users are regional resources that you can configure to access one or more stacks in an account.

Know the different AWS OpsWorks Stacks instance types and their purpose.   AWS OpsWorks Stacks has three different instance types: 24/7, time-based, and load-based. The 24/7 instances run continuously unless an authorized user manually stops it, and they are useful for handling the minimum expected load of a system. Time-based instances start and stop on a given 24-hour schedule and are recommended for predicable increases in load at different times of the day. Load-based instances start and stop in response to metrics, such as CPU utilization for a layer, and you use them to respond to sudden increases in traffic.

Understand how AWS OpsWorks Stacks implements auto healing.   The AWS OpsWorks Stacks agent that runs on an instance performs a health check every minute and sends the response to AWS. If the AWS OpsWorks Stacks agent does not receive the health check for five continuous minutes, the instance restarts automatically. You can disable this feature. Auto healing events publish to Amazon CloudWatch for reference.

Understand the AWS OpsWorks Stacks permissions model.   AWS OpsWorks Stacks provides the ability to manage users at the stack level, independent of IAM permissions. This is useful for providing access to instances in a stack but not to the AWS Management Console or API. You can assign AWS OpsWorks Stacks users to one of four permission levels: Deny, Show, Deploy, and Manage. Additionally, you can give users SSH/RDP access to instances in a stack (with or without sudo/administrator permission). AWS OpsWorks Stacks users are regional resources. If you would like to give a user in one region access to a stack in another region, you need to copy the user to the second region. Some AWS OpsWorks Stacks activities are available only through IAM permissions, such as to delete and create stacks.

Know the different AWS OpsWorks Stacks lifecycle events.   Instances in a stack are provisioned, configured, and retired using lifecycle events. The AWS OpsWorks Stacks supports the lifecycle events: Setup, Configure, Deploy, Undeploy, and Shutdown. The Configure event runs on all instances in a stack any time one instance comes online or goes offline.

Know the components of an Amazon ECS cluster.   A cluster is the foundational infrastructure component on which containers are run. Clusters are made up of one or more Amazon EC2 instances, or they can be run on AWS-managed infrastructure using AWS Fargate. A task definition is a JSON file that describes which containers to launch on a cluster. Task definitions can be defined by grouping containers that are used for a common purpose, such as for compute, networking, and storage requirements. A service launches on a cluster and specifies the task definition and number of tasks to maintain. If any containers become unhealthy, the service is responsible for launching replacements.

Know the difference between Amazon ECS and AWS Fargate launch types.   The AWS Fargate launch type uses AWS-managed infrastructure to launch tasks. As a customer, you are no longer required to provision and manage cluster instances. With AWS Fargate, each cluster instance is assigned a network interface in your VPC. Amazon ECS launch types require a cluster in your account, which you must manage over time.

Know how to scale running tasks in a cluster.   Changing the number of instances in a cluster does not automatically cause the number of running tasks to scale in or out. You can use target tracking policies and step scaling policies to scale tasks automatically based on target metrics. A target tracking policy determines when to scale based on metrics such as CPU utilization or network traffic. Target tracking policies keep metrics within a certain boundary. For example, you can launch additional tasks if CPU utilization is above 75 percent. Step scaling policies can continuously scale as metrics increase or decrease. You can configure a step scaling policy to scale tasks out when CPU utilization reaches 75 percent and again at 80 percent and 90 percent. A single step scaling policy can result in multiple scaling activities.

Know how images are stored in Amazon Elastic Container Repository (Amazon ECR). Amazon ECR is a Docker registry service that is fully compatible with existing Docker tools. Amazon ECR supports resource-level permissions for private repositories, and it allows you to maintain a secure registry without the need to maintain additional instances/applications.

Resources to Review

Continuous Deployment to Amazon ECS with AWS CodePipeline, AWS CodeBuild, Amazon ECR, and AWS CloudFormation:

> `https://aws.amazon.com/blogs/compute/continuous-deployment-to-amazon-ecs-using-aws-codepipeline-aws-codebuild-amazon-ecr-and-aws-cloudformation/`

How to set up AWS OpsWorks Stacks auto healing notifications in Amazon CloudWatch Events:

> `https://aws.amazon.com/blogs/mt/how-to-set-up-aws-opsworks-stacks-auto-healing-notifications-in-amazon-cloudwatch-events/`

Managing Multi-Tiered Applications with AWS OpsWorks:

> `https://d0.awsstatic.com/whitepapers/managing-multi-tiered-web-applications-with-opsworks.pdf`

AWS OpsWorks Stacks:

> `https://aws.amazon.com/opsworks/stacks/`

How do I implement a configuration management solution on AWS?:

> `https://aws.amazon.com/answers/configuration-management/aws-infrastructure-configuration-management/`

Docker on AWS:

> `https://d1.awsstatic.com/whitepapers/docker-on-aws.pdf`

What are Containers?

> `https://aws.amazon.com/containers/`

Amazon Elastic Container Service (ECS):

> `https://aws.amazon.com/ecs/`

Exercises

Launch a Sample AWS OpsWorks Stacks Environment

1. Launch the **AWS Management Console**.

2. Select **Services** ➢ **AWS OpsWorks**.

3. Select **Add Stack**, and select **Sample stack**.

4. Select your preferred operating system (**Linux** or **Windows**).

5. Select **Add Instance**, and monitor the stack's progress until it enters the online state. This deploys the app to the stack.

6. Copy the public IP Address, and paste it into a web browser to display the sample app.

7. Open the instance in the **AWS OpsWorks Stacks** console, and view the log entries.

8. Verify that the Chef run was a success and which resources deploy to the instance in the log entries.

9. Update the recipes of the automatically created layer.

10. Remove the deploy recipe.

11. Add a new instance to the stack and monitor its progress.

12. Once the instance is in the online state, view the run logs to verify that the sample website is not deployed to the instance.

Launch an Amazon ECS Cluster and Containers

1. Launch the Amazon ECS console.

2. Create a new cluster with an Amazon EC2 container instances.

3. Create a new task definition that launches a WordPress and MySQL container.

4. Use the official images from **Docker Hub**:

    a. https://registry.hub.docker.com/wordpress/

    b. https://registry.hub.docker.com/mysql/

5. Create a new service that launches this task definition on the cluster.

6. Copy the public IP address, and paste it into a web browser to access WordPress on the cluster instance.

7. Modify the service to launch two tasks.

   As the second task attempts to launch, note that this will fail because of the ports configured in the task definition already being registered with the running containers.

8. Launch an additional cluster instance in your cluster.

9. Monitor the service status to verify that the second task deploys to the new cluster instance.

Migrate an Amazon RDS Database

1. Launch the **Amazon RDS console**.

2. Create a new database instance.

3. Connect to your database and create a user with a password. For example, to create a user with full privileges on MySQL, use the following command:

   GRANT ALL PRIVILEGES ON *.* TO 'username'@'localhost' IDENTIFIED BY 'password';

4. Launch the **AWS OpsWorks console**.

5. Create two stacks (one "A" stack and one "B" stack). For ease of use, try the sample Linux stack with a Node.js app.

6. Register the RDS database instance that you created with stack A, providing the database username and password you created.

7. Edit the stack's app to include **Amazon RDS** as a data source. Select the database you registered and provide the database name.

8. Verify that you can connect to your database by creating a simple recipe to output the credentials. Specifically, try to output to the database field of the deploy attributes.

9. Run this recipe to verify that the connection information passes to your nodes.

10. Pass the same connection information into stack A using custom JSON.

11. **Deregister** the database from stack A and **register** it with stack B.

12. Perform the same tasks to verify that connection details pass to the instances in stack B.

13. Remove the custom JSON from stack A to complete the migration.

EXERCISE 9.4

Configure Auto Healing Event Notifications in AWS OpsWorks Stacks

1. Launch the **Amazon SNS console**.

2. Create a new notification topic with your email address as a recipient.

3. Launch the **Amazon CloudWatch console**.

4. Create an Amazon CloudWatch Rule.

   a. Edit the JSON version of the rule pattern to use:

   ```
   {
     "source": [ "aws.opsworks" ],
     "detail": {
       "initiated_by": [
         "auto-healing"
       ]
     }
   }
   ```

5. Add the Amazon SNS topic that you created as a target.

6. Add permissions to the Amazon SNS topic so that it can be invoked by Amazon CloudWatch Events. An example policy statement is shown here. Replace the value of the Resource block with your topic Amazon Resource Name (ARN).

   ```
   {
     "Version": "2008-10-17",
     "Id": "AutoHealingNotificationPolicy",
     "Statement": [{
       "Effect": "Allow",
       "Principal": {
         "Service": "events.amazonaws.com"
       },
       "Action": "sns:Publish",
       "Resource": "arn:aws:sns:REGION:ACCOUNT:MyTopic"
     }]
   }
   ```

7. Create a stack and add an instance. Make sure that Auto Healing is enabled on the stack.

8. Launch the instance.

9. SSH or RDP into the instance.

10. Uninstall the **AWS OpsWorks Stacks Agent**.

11. Wait until the instance is stopped and started by AWS OpsWorks Stacks. You will receive a notification shortly after this occurs.

Review Questions

1.   Which of the following AWS OpsWorks Stacks limits cannot be raised?

   A.   Maximum stacks per account, per region

   B.   Maximum layers per stack

   C.   Maximum instances per layer

   D.   Maximum apps per stack

   E.   None of the above

2.   After submitting changes to your cookbook repository, you notice that executing cookbooks on your AWS OpsWorks instances does not result in any changes taking place, even though the logs show successful Chef runs.

   What could be the cause of this?

   A.   The instances are unable to connect to the cookbook repository or archive location because of networking or permissions errors.

   B.   The AWS OpsWorks Stacks agent running on the instance is enforcing cookbook caching, resulting in cached copies being used instead of the new versions.

   C.   The version of the cookbook specified in the recipe list for the lifecycle event is incorrect.

   D.   The custom cookbooks have not yet been downloaded to the instances.

3.   When will an AWS OpsWorks Stacks instance register and deregister from an Elastic Load Balancing load balancer associated with the layer?

   A.   Instances are registered or deregistered manually only.

   B.   Instances will be registered when they enter an online state and are deregistered when they leave an online state.

   C.   As an administrator, you are responsible for including the registration and deregistration within your Chef recipes and assigning the recipes to the appropriate lifecycle event.

   D.   Instances are registered when they are created and not deregistered until they are terminated.

4.   You have an Amazon ECS cluster that runs on a single service with one task. The cluster currently contains enough instances to support the containers you define in your task, with no additional compute resources to spare (other than those needed by the underlying OS and Docker). Currently the service is configured with a maximum in-service percentage of 100 percent and a minimum of 100 percent. When you attempt to update the service, nothing happens for an extended period of time, as the replacement task appears to be stuck as it launches.

   How would you resolve this? (Select TWO.)

   A.   The current configuration prevents new tasks from starting because of insufficient resources. Add enough instances to the cluster to support the additional task temporarily.

   B.   The current configuration prevents new tasks from starting because of insufficient resources. Modify the configuration to have a maximum in-service percentage of 200 percent and a minimum of 0 percent.

C. Configure the cluster to leverage an AWS Auto Scaling group and scale out additional cluster instances when CPU Utilization is over 90 percent.

D. Submit a new update to replace the one that appears to be failing.

5. Which party is responsible for patching and maintaining underlying clusters when you use the AWS Fargate launch type?

    A. The customer

    B. Amazon Web Services (AWS)

    C. Docker

    D. Independent software vendors

6. Why should instances in a single AWS OpsWorks Stacks layer have the same functionality and purpose?

    A. Because all instances in a layer run the same recipes

    B. To keep the console clean

    C. To stop and start at the same time

    D. To all run configure lifecycle events at the same time

7. Where do instances in an AWS OpsWorks Stacks stack download custom cookbooks?

    A. The Chef Server

    B. They are included in the Amazon Machine Image (AMI).

    C. The custom cookbook repository

    D. Amazon Elastic Container Service (Amazon ECS)

8. How would you migrate an Amazon Relational Database Service (Amazon RDS) layer between two stacks in the same region?

    A. Supply the connection information to the second stack as custom JSON to ensure that the instances can connect. Remove the Amazon RDS layer from the first stack. Add the Amazon RDS layer to the second stack. Remove the connection custom JSON.

    B. Add the Amazon RDS layer to the second stack and remove it from the first.

    C. Create a new database instance, migrate data to the new instance, and associate it with the second stack using an Amazon RDS layer.

    D. This is not possible.

9. Which AWS OpsWorks Stacks instance type would you use for predictable increases in traffic or workload for a stack?

    A. 24/7

    B. Load-based

    C. Time-based

    D. On demand

10. Which AWS OpsWorks Stacks instance type would you use for random, unpredictable increases in traffic or workload for a stack?

    A. 24/7

    B. Load-based

    C. Time-based

    D. Spot

11. What component is responsible for stopping and starting containers on an Amazon Elastic Container Service (Amazon ECS) cluster instance?

    A. The Amazon ECS agent running on the instance

    B. The Amazon ECS service role

    C. AWS Systems Manager

    D. The customer

12. What is Service-Oriented Architecture (SOA)?

    A. The use of multiple AWS services to decouple infrastructure components and achieve high availability

    B. A software design practice where applications divide into discrete components (services) that communicate with each other in such a way that individual services do not rely on one another for their successful operation

    C. Involves multiple teams to develop application components with no knowledge of other teams and their components

    D. Leasing services from different vendors instead of doing internal development

13. How many containers can a single task definition describe?

    A. 1

    B. Up to 3

    C. Up to 5

    D. Up to 10

14. You have a web proxy application that you would like to deploy in containers with the use of Amazon Elastic Container Service (Amazon ECS). Typically, your application binds to port 80 on the instance on which it runs. How can you use an application load balancer to run more than one proxy container on each instance in your cluster?

    A. Do not configure the container to bind to port 80. Instead, configure Application Load Balancing (ALB) with dynamic host port mapping so that a random port is bound. The ALB will route traffic coming in on port 80 to the port on which the container is listening.

    B. Configure a Port Address Translation (PAT) instance in Amazon Virtual Private Cloud (Amazon VPC).

    C. If the container binds to a specific port, only one copy can launch per instance.

    D. Configure a classic load balancer to use dynamic host port mapping.

15. Which Amazon Elastic Container Service (Amazon ECS) task placement policy ensures that tasks are distributed as much as possible in a single cluster?

   A. Spread

   B. Binpack

   C. Random

   D. Least Cost

Chapter

10

Authentication and Authorization

**THE AWS CERTIFIED DEVELOPER –
ASSOCIATE EXAM TOPICS COVERED IN
THIS CHAPTER MAY INCLUDE, BUT ARE
NOT LIMITED TO, THE FOLLOWING:**

Domain 2: Security

✓ 2.1 Make authenticated calls to AWS services.

✓ 2.3 Implement application authentication and
authorization.

Introduction to Authentication and Authorization

Authentication is the process or action that verifies the identity of a user or process. *Authorization* is a security mechanism that determines access levels or permissions related to system resources including files, services, computer programs, data, and application features. The authentication and authorization process grants or denies user access to network resources based on the identity.

AWS Identity and Access Management (IAM) allows you to create identities (users, groups, or roles) and control access to various AWS services through the use of policies. IAM serves as an *identity provider* (IdP).

The following are the benefits of integrating an *existing IdP*:

- Users are no longer required to manage multiple sets of credentials.

- There are fewer credentials to administer.

- Credentials are centrally managed.

- It is easier to establish and enforce compliance standards.

As an IdP, AWS is responsible for storing identities and providing the mechanism for authentication. You can use AWS as an IdP for the following:

- AWS services

- Applications running on AWS infrastructure

- Applications running on non-AWS infrastructure, such as web or mobile applications

There are multiple benefits for using AWS as the IdP. AWS provides a managed service, eliminates single points of failure, is highly available, and can scale as needed. AWS also provides a number of tools, such as Amazon CloudWatch and AWS CloudTrail, to manage, control, and audit this service.

Using a third party to provide identity services is known as *federation*.

In this chapter, you learn the various ways to integrate existing identity providers into AWS and how to use AWS as an identity provider to control access to applications, both inside and outside the AWS infrastructure.

Different Planes of Control

There are two different planes of access used to manage and access AWS services: a control plane and a data plane.

The *control plane* permits access to perform operations on a particular AWS instance. AWS can control access to this plane through various AWS application programming interface (AWS API) operations. The *data plane* permits access to the application running on AWS. The data plane permits access to sign in to the compute instance using *Secure Shell* (SSH) or *Remote Desktop Protocol* (RDP) and to make changes to the guest operating system or to the application itself.

The control and data planes use different paths, different protocols, and different credentials; however, for several AWS services, the control and data planes are identical. Amazon DynamoDB allows you to stop and start the compute instances (control plane) and stop and start the database (data plane) using an AWS API.

Identity and Authorization

A discussion of federation requires a review of the concept's identity and authorization. Each of these concepts asks and answers two different questions. Identity asks and answers "Who are you?"; and authorization asks and answers "What can you do?"

AWS establishes identity in several different ways, as shown in Table 10.1.

TABLE 10.1 AWS Identity

Name	Identifier	Credential
Root user	Email	Password
User	Email	Password
User, group, or role	Access key ID	Secret access key
API	Access	Secret access key

AWS establishes authorization by user-executed APIs. AWS controls operations and tasks through APIs. Policies are JavaScript Object Notation (JSON) documents that show attribute-value pairs. Every policy document requires a minimum of three attribute-value pairs: effect, action, and resource.

Effect has the API value of either ALLOW or DENY. The entity (whether a user, group, or role) is either granted the permission to execute that API or denied the permission to execute that API.

Action determines whether the API is allowed or denied. Actions can be determined by an individual API, a grouping of APIs for the same service using a wildcard (for example, S3:* includes all Amazon Simple Storage Service (Amazon S3 APIs), or APIs for different services.

Resource determines where the API is being allowed or denied. For example, with Amazon S3, you can allow the execution of an API in a particular bucket, object, or particular group of objects (using the wildcard *).

> Though the order of the three attribute-value pairs has no impact on their execution, use the acronym EAR to remember the three attribute-value pairs: effect, action, and resource (EAR).

Federation Defined

A federation consists of two components: identity provider and identity consumer.

Each component plays a different role in the process of federation. An *identity provider* stores identities, provides a mechanism for authentication, and provides a course level of authorization. An *identity consumer* stores a reference to the identity, providing authorization at a greater granularity than the identity provider.

An identity provider and an identity consumer work together to create a federation. The identity provider and the identity consumer establish a trust relationship between each other. They agree on the type of information to exchange, what information to exchange, in what format, and what security methods and measures they will use.

An identity provider answers the question "Who are you?" Because a prior trust relationship has been established between the identity provider and the identity consumer, the identity consumer trusts the answer supplied by the identity provider and grants access.

There is no expectation that there will be either a synchronization or replication of data between an identity provider and an identity consumer or that an identity provider and an identity consumer are operated by the same organization or entity.

Federation with AWS

Federation with AWS allows for two things. First, it allows you to use AWS as an IdP to gain access to both AWS and non-AWS resources. *Amazon Cognito* is an AWS service that acts as an IdP. Second, you can use non-AWS resources like Security Assertion Markup Language (SAML) 2.0, OpenID Connect (OIDC), or Microsoft Active Directory as the IdP to facilitate single sign-on (SSO).

Federation enables you to manage access to your AWS resources centrally. With federation, you can use SSO to access your AWS accounts with credentials from your corporate directory. Federation uses open standards, such as SAML or OIDC, to exchange identity and security information between an IdP and an application.

The five mechanisms that the AWS federation can facilitate are as follows:

- Custom-built IdP
- Cross-account access
- SAML
- OIDC
- Microsoft Active Directory

Custom Build an Identity Provider

Custom builds were the original method of federation within AWS, but they have since been supplanted by SAML, OIDC, and Microsoft Active Directory. With SAML, you can build a custom IdP that verifies users and their identities. Though building a custom IdP offers a high degree of customization, it is a complex process, and most customers now use standard solutions.

Cross-Account Access

When you need to access resources across multiple AWS accounts, *cross-account access* enables you to do so by using only one set of credentials. You can grant users access to resources in company accounts without having to maintain multiple user entities, and your users do not have to remember multiple passwords. Users can access the resources they need in AWS accounts by switching AWS roles. Access is permitted by the policies attached to each role. There are two accounts in cross-account access: the account in which the user resides, or *source account*, and the account with the resources to which the user wants access, or *target account.*

The target account has an IAM role that includes two components: a permissions policy and a trust policy. The *permissions policy* controls access to AWS services and resources, while the *trust policy* specifies who can assume the role and their external ID.

The source account is given an IAM role (`AssumeRole`) with a permissions policy that allows you to assume this role. The target account issues short-term credentials to the `AssumeRole`, which allows access to AWS services and the resources you specify in this credential.

Use cross-account access when you own either the target account or the source account and require no more than coordination between the owners of the source account and the target account. Cross-account access allows users to access the AWS Management Console, AWS APIs (control plane APIs and data plane APIs), and the AWS CLI.

Security Assertion Markup Language

Security Assertion Markup Language (SAML) provides federation between an IdP and a service provider (SP) when you are in an AWS account and a trust relationship has been established between the IdP and the SP. The IdP and the SP exchange metadata in an .xml file that contains both the certificates and attributes that form the basis of the trust relationship between the IdP and the SP.

You interact only with the IdP, and all authentication and authorization occurs between you and the IdP. Based on a successful authentication and authorization, the IdP makes an assertion to the service provider. Based on the previously established trust relationship, the service provider accepts this assertion and provides access.

Use SAML to provide access to the AWS Management Console, AWS APIs (control plane APIs and data plane APIs), and the AWS CLI. SAML can also access Amazon Cognito to control access to cloud services that exist outside AWS, such as software as a solution (SaaS) applications.

OpenID Connect

OpenID Connect (OIDC) is the successor to SAML. OIDC is easier to configure than SAML and uses tokens rather than assertions to provide access. Most use cases for OIDC involve external versus internal users.

With OIDC, *OpenID provider* (OP) uses a *relying party* (RP) trust to track the service provider. OP and RP exchange metadata by focusing on the OP providing information to the RP about the location of its endpoints. The RP must register with the OP and then receive a client ID and a client secret. This exchange establishes a trust relationship between the OP and the RP.

Because you interact solitarily with the OP, all authentication and authorization occur only between you and the OP. The OP issues a token to the service provider, which accepts this token and provides access. OIDC includes three different types of tokens.

- *ID token* establishes a user's identity.

- *Access token* provides access to APIs.

- *Refresh token* allows you to acquire a new access token when the previous one expires.

Companies such as Google, Twitter, Facebook, and Amazon can also establish their own OpenID provider.

After authentication and authorization occur, you can access numerous services, including the AWS Management Console, AWS APIs, and AWS CLIs. You can use OIDC to grant access to AWS services, including Amazon Cognito, Amazon AppStream 2.0, and Amazon Redshift. You can also use OIDC to grant access to SaaS applications outside of AWS.

Microsoft Active Directory

Microsoft Active Directory is the identity provider for a majority of corporations. You use the *Active Directory forest trusts* to establish trust between an Active Directory domain controller and AWS Directory Service for Microsoft Active Directory (AWS Managed Microsoft AD). For Microsoft Active Directory, the domain controller is on-premises or in the AWS Cloud.

In the Microsoft Active Directory setup, the Active Directory domain controller defines the user. However, you add users to the groups that you define in the AWS Managed Microsoft AD. Access to services depends on membership within these groups.

Use Microsoft Active Directory to provide data plane access to Amazon Elastic Compute Cloud (Amazon EC2) instances running Windows, Amazon Relational Database Service (Amazon RDS) instances running SQL Server, Amazon WorkSpaces, Amazon WorkDocs, Amazon WorkMail, and, with limitations, the AWS Management Console.

AWS Single Sign-On

AWS Single Sign-On (AWS SSO) is an AWS service that manages SSO access. AWS SSO allows users to sign in to a user portal with their existing corporate credentials and access both AWS accounts and business accounts. You can have multiple permission sets, allowing for greater granularity and control over access.

Setting Up AWS Single Sign-On

To set up AWS SSO, do the following:

1. Enable AWS SSO.

2. Connect your directory.

3. Configure SSO to your AWS accounts.

4. Configure SSO to your cloud applications (if applicable).

Prerequisites for AWS SSO

There are several prerequisites for using AWS SSO:

- Configure and enable all AWS Organizations features.

- Use Organizations master account credentials for the initial configuration.

- Configure a Microsoft Active Directory in the AWS Directory Service.

- Ensure that the Active Directory resides in the US-East-1 Region.

AWS CLI Access

You can sign in to the AWS SSO user portal with your existing corporate credentials and receive all AWS CLI credentials for your AWS accounts from a central location. These AWS CLI credentials automatically expire after 60 minutes to prevent unauthorized access to AWS accounts.

Management with AWS Organizations

AWS SSO enables management of SSO access and user permissions for your AWS accounts managed through AWS Organizations. Additional setup in the individual accounts is not required. AWS SSO automatically configures and maintains the necessary permissions in your accounts. You can assign user permissions based on common job functions and customize these permissions to meet your specific security requirements.

AWS SSO records all user portal sign-in activities in AWS CloudTrail, providing visibility into data, such as which users accessed specific accounts and applications from the user portal. AWS SSO records details, including IP address, user name, date, and time of the sign-in request. Changes made by administrators in the AWS SSO console are also recorded in CloudTrail.

Integration with Microsoft Active Directory

AWS SSO integrates with Microsoft Active Directory through the Directory Service, enabling you to sign in to the user portal using your Active Directory credentials. With the Active Directory integration, you can manage SSO access to your accounts and applications for users and groups in your corporate directory. For instance, when you add DevOps

Active Directory users to your production AWS group, you are granted access to your production AWS accounts automatically. This makes it easier to onboard new users and gives existing users SSO access so that they can quickly access new accounts and applications.

Figure 10.1 shows the various AWS SSO options.

FIGURE 10.1   AWS SSO use cases model

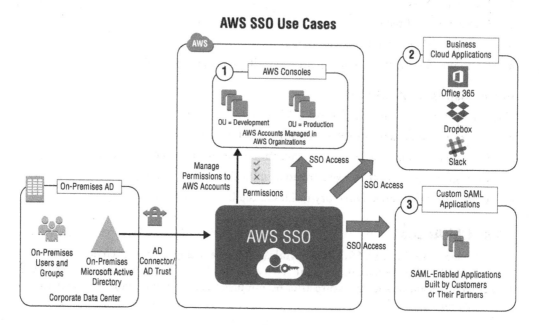

AWS Security Token Service

AWS Security Token Service (AWS STS) creates temporary security credentials and provides trusted users with those temporary security credentials. The trusted users then access AWS resources with those credentials. Temporary security credentials work similarly to long-term access key credentials, but with the following differences:

- Temporary security credentials consist of an *access key ID*, a *secret access key*, and a *security token*.

- Temporary security credentials are short-term, and you configure them to remain valid for a duration between a few minutes to several hours. After the credentials expire, AWS no longer recognizes them or allows any kind of access from API requests made with them.

- Temporary security credentials are not stored with you; they are generated dynamically and provided to you upon request. You can request new credentials before or after the temporary security credentials expire, if you still have permission to do so.

Because of these differences, temporary credentials offer the following advantages:

- You do not have to distribute or embed long-term AWS security credentials with an application.

- You can provide users access to your AWS resources without defining an AWS identity for them. Temporary credentials are the basis for AWS roles and identity federation.

- The temporary security credentials have a limited lifetime. You do not have to rotate or explicitly revoke them when the user no longer requires them.

- After temporary security credentials expire, they cannot be reused. You can specify how long the credentials are valid, up to a maximum limit.

AWS STS IdPs come from different sources, including the following:

- IAM users from another account

- Microsoft Active Directory

- Users of IdPs that are SAML 2.0–based

- Web IdPs

- Customer identity brokers

 Use Amazon Cognito to authenticate for mobile applications. Amazon Cognito supports the same IdPs as AWS STS. However, it also supports unauthenticated (or guest) access and provides a means for synchronizing user data between multiple devices owned by the same user.

AWS STS supports the following APIs:

- AssumeRole

- AssumeRoleWithSAML

- AssumeRoleWithWebIdentity

- DecodeAuthorizationMessage

- GetCallerIdentity

- GetFederationToken

- GetSessionToken

AssumeRole This API provides a set of temporary security credentials to access AWS resources. Use AssumeRole to grant access to existing IAM users who have identities in other AWS accounts. Use this API if you need to support multi-factor authentication (MFA). By default, the maximum duration of the credentials that this API issues is 60 minutes.

 The default maximum duration for AssumeRole APIs is 60 minutes. However, you can change the maximum duration to 12 hours (720 minutes) for a specific role.

AssumeRoleWithSAML AssumeRoleWithSAML provides a set of temporary security credentials (consisting of an *access key ID*, a *secret access key*, and a *security token*) to access AWS resources. Use this API when you are using an identity store or directory that is SAML-based, rather than having an identity from an IAM user in another AWS account. This API does not support MFA.

AssumeRoleWithWebIdentity AssumeRoleWithWebIdentity provides a set of temporary security credentials that you use to access AWS resources. Use this API when users have been authenticated in a mobile or web application with a web IdP, such as Amazon Cognito, Login with Amazon, Facebook, Google, or any OIDC-compatible identity provider. This API does not support MFA.

DecodeAuthorizationMessage DecodeAuthorizationMessage decodes additional information about the authorization status of a request from an encoded message returned in response to an AWS request. The message is encoded to prevent the requesting user from seeing details of the authorization status, which can contain privileged information.

The decoded message includes the following:

- Whether the request was denied because of an explicit deny or because of the absence of an explicit allow
- Principal who made the request
- Requested action
- Requested resource
- Values of condition keys in the context of the user's request

GetCallerIdentity The GetCallerIdentity API returns details about the IAM identity whose credentials call the API.

GetFederationToken The GetFederationToken API provides a set of temporary security credentials to access AWS resources. For example, a typical use is within a proxy application that retrieves temporary security credentials on behalf of distributed applications inside a corporate network.

The permissions for the temporary security credentials returned by GetFederationToken are a combination of the policy or policies that are attached to the IAM user, whose credentials call the GetFederationToken, and the policy passes as a parameter in the call.

Because the call for the GetFederationToken action uses the long-term security credentials of an IAM user, this call is appropriate in contexts where credentials can be safely stored. The API credentials can have a duration of up to 36 hours. This API does not support MFA.

Remember that the most restrictive policy is the one enforced. So, if you have a user who has a policy that ALLOWS access to an API, but a policy is passed as a parameter that DENIES access to that API, the result is a DENY.

GetSessionToken   GetSessionsToken provides a set of temporary security credentials to access AWS resources. You normally use GetSessionToken to enable MFA to protect programmatic calls to specific AWS APIs like Amazon EC2 StopInstances.

MFA-enabled IAM users call GetSessionToken and submit an MFA code that is associated with their MFA device. Using the temporary security credentials that return from the call, IAM users can then make programmatic calls to APIs that require MFA authentication.

Amazon Cognito

Amazon Cognito is a service that allows you to manage sign-in and permissions for mobile and web applications through two services: Amazon Cognito Sync store and Amazon Cognito Sync.

With *Amazon Cognito Sync store*, you can authenticate users using third-party social identity providers or create your own identity store. With *Amazon Cognito Sync*, you can synchronize identities across multiple devices and the web.

By using Amazon Cognito, you can grant users access to AWS resources without having to embed AWS credentials into the web or mobile application. Amazon Cognito integrates with AWS STS to identify the user and give the user a consistent identity throughout the lifetime of an application, even if the device is offline or the user is accessing the application on a different device. Amazon Cognito is a managed service, providing scaling, redundancy, and high availability. You provide authentication with Amazon Cognito in one of three ways:

- Your own identity store
- Social identity providers such as Amazon or Facebook
- SAML-based identity solutions

Amazon Cognito provides a variety of mechanisms to secure the application. You can configure guest access, multi-factor authentication, and confirmation of account with Short Message Service (SMS) or email, among other mechanisms. Amazon Cognito integrates with AWS CloudTrail to track creations, deletions, and configuration changes. You can also use Amazon CloudWatch alarms to monitor for a specific activity and receive Amazon Simple Notification Service (Amazon SNS) or email notifications, if that activity occurs.

Amazon Cognito uses identity for user pools and identity pools. You use Amazon Cognito to access the AWS Management Console, AWS CLI, and AWS SDKs.

Microsoft Active Directory as Identity Provider

Many enterprises already use Microsoft Active Directory as their identity store. Integrating Active Directory, rather than configuring a new identity store, simplifies administrative overhead. *AWS Managed Microsoft AD* provides multiple ways to use Amazon Cloud Directory and Microsoft Active Directory with other AWS services.

Directories store information about users, groups, and devices, which administrators use to manage access to information and resources. AWS Directory Service provides multiple directory choices for customers who want to use an existing Microsoft Active Directory or *Lightweight Directory Access Protocol* (LDAP)–aware applications in the cloud. It also offers those same choices to developers who need a directory to manage users, groups, devices, and access.

There are four different ways to implement Microsoft Active Directory in an AWS infrastructure.

- Run Microsoft Active Directory on Amazon EC2 with an AWS account.

- Use *Active Directory Connector* (AD Connector) to connect AWS services with an on-premises Microsoft Active Directory.

- Create a *Simple Active Directory* (Simple AD) that provides basic Active Directory compatibility.

- Deploy AWS Managed Microsoft AD.

AWS publishes a number of Quick Start reference deployment guides, including a deployment guide for Active Directory Domain Services. For more information, see https://docs.aws.amazon.com/quickstart/latest/active-directory-ds/youlcome.html.

Microsoft Active Directory on Amazon EC2 with AWS Account

AWS provides a comprehensive set of services and tools for deploying Microsoft Windows-based workloads in its secure cloud infrastructure. *Active Directory Domain Services* (AD DS) and *Domain Name System* (DNS) are core Windows services that provide the foundation for many enterprise-class Microsoft-based solutions, including Microsoft SharePoint, Microsoft Exchange, and .NET applications.

When deploying AD DS on Amazon EC2, you are responsible for deploying in a highly available configuration. You are also responsible for verifying that AD DS is backed up and configured in a fault-tolerant mode. Microsoft Active Directory deploys either as a primary or secondary domain controller, and you can choose to use Amazon Machine Images (AMI) or import your own virtual machine images.

Active Directory Connector

Active Directory Connector (AD Connector) connects your existing on-premises Microsoft Active Directory with compatible AWS applications. AWS-compatible applications include Amazon WorkSpaces, Amazon QuickSight, Amazon WorkMail, and Amazon EC2 for Windows Server instances, among others. With AD Connector acting as a proxy service, you can add a service account to your Active Directory, and AD Connector eliminates the need for directory synchronization or the cost and complexity of hosting a federation infrastructure.

When you add users to AWS applications, AD Connector reads your existing Active Directory to create lists of users and groups from which to select. When users sign in to the AWS applications, AD Connector forwards sign-in requests to your on-premises Active Directory domain controllers for authentication.

 NOTE AD Connector is not compatible with Amazon Relational Database Service (Amazon RDS) SQL Server.

Management of your Active Directory does not change; you add new users and groups and update passwords using the standard Active Directory administration tools in your on-premises Active Directory. This helps you to consistently enforce your security policies, such as password expiration, password history, and account lockouts, regardless of whether users are accessing resources on-premises or on the AWS Cloud.

AD Connector enables you to access the AWS Management Console and manage AWS resources by signing in with your existing Active Directory credentials. AD Connector is not compatible with Amazon RDS for SQL Server.

You can use the AD Connector to enable MFA for your AWS application users by connecting it to your existing RADIUS-based MFA infrastructure. This provides an additional layer of security when users access AWS applications.

Simple Active Directory

Simple Active Directory (Simple AD) is a Microsoft Active Directory that is compatible with AWS Directory Service and is powered by Samba 4. Simple AD is a standalone directory in the cloud, where you create and manage identities and manage access to applications. You can use many familiar Active Directory–aware applications and tools that require basic Active Directory features.

Simple AD supports basic Active Directory features such as user accounts, group memberships, memberships for a Linux domain or Windows-based Amazon EC2 instances, Kerberos-based SSO, and group policies. However, Simple AD does not support trust relationships, DNS dynamic update, schema extensions, MFA, communication over LDAPs, PowerShell Active Directory cmdlets, or Flexible Single Master Operation (FSMO) role transfer. In addition, Simple AD is not compatible with RDS SQL Server.

Simple AD is compatible with the following AWS applications: Amazon WorkSpaces, WorkDocs, Amazon QuickSight, and WorkMail. You can sign in to the AWS Management Console and manage AWS resources with Simple AD user accounts.

AWS Managed Microsoft AD

AWS Managed Microsoft AD is an actual Microsoft Windows Server Active Directory, managed by AWS in the AWS Cloud. It enables you to migrate a broad range of Active Directory–aware applications to the AWS Cloud. AWS Managed Microsoft AD works with Microsoft SharePoint, Microsoft SQL Server Always-On Availability Groups, and many .NET applications.

Figure 10.2 illustrates Directory Service and its relation to AWS applications and services: Amazon EC2, Active Directory–aware workloads, cloud applications, and on-premises Active Directory.

FIGURE 10.2   AWS Directory Service chart

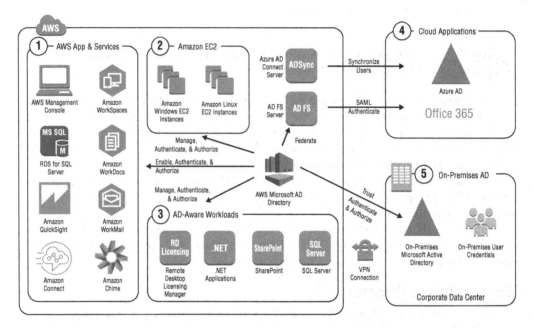

Directory Service includes key features that enable you to extend your schema, manage password policies, and enable secure LDAP communications through Secure Socket Layer (SSL)/Transport Layer Security (TLS). The service is approved for applications in the AWS Cloud that are subject to the United States *Health Insurance Portability and Accountability Act* (HIPAA) or *Payment Card Industry Data Security Standard* (PCI DSS) compliance when you enable compliance for your directory.

You can add users and groups to AWS Managed Microsoft AD and administration to group policies using familiar Active Directory tools. You scale the directory by deploying additional domain controllers and improve performance by distributing requests across a larger number of domain controllers.

AWS provides monitoring, daily snapshots, and recovery as part of the service. You can connect AWS Managed Microsoft AD with a trust and use credentials to an Active Directory running on-premises. Trust relationship support includes one-way (both in and out) and two-way.

AWS Managed Microsoft AD can support AWS managed applications and services, including Amazon WorkSpaces, WorkDocs, Amazon QuickSight, Amazon Chime, Amazon Connect, and Amazon RDS for SQL Server.

Summary

This chapter discussed the concepts of identity and authorization and how you can use AWS services to provide them. You learned that identity and authorization can operate at different planes of access—the control plane and the data plane. You also learned that these planes differ in terms of paths used, protocols configured, services managed, and credentials deployed.

In addition, you learned about the various AWS services and where you use identity and authorization, including the following:

- AWS SSO
- AWS STS
- Amazon Cognito
- AWS Managed Microsoft AD

Exam Essentials

Understand what federation is.   Know the difference between federation and SSO. Understand when you would use federation and when you would use SSO.

Understand the role of an identity provider (IdP).   Know what an IdP does, how it operates, and how it interacts with an identity consumer.

Know the different federation services that AWS offers.   Understand which services act as IdPs, which act as identity consumers, and which act as SSO.

Understand AWS Directory Service options.   Know the use cases for Microsoft Active Directory, Cloud Directory, and Amazon Cognito.

Understand how policies work.   Know the structure of policies and how to apply them.

Recognize the role of policies in controlling access to AWS resources.   Know how to use AWS services to control access to non-AWS resources and how to use non-AWS services to control access to AWS resources.

Understand the difference between the data plane and control plane with regard to protocols and commands.   Know how AWS STS and AWS SSO work and how to implement these services.

Resources to Review

AWS Security Token Service (AWS STS):

    https://docs.aws.amazon.com/STS/latest/APIReference/Welcome.html

Identity Federation in the AWS Cloud:

    https://aws.amazon.com/identity/federation/

AWS Identity and Access Management (IAM):

    https://docs.aws.amazon.com/iam/

AWS Directory Service:

    https://aws.amazon.com/directoryservice

Amazon Cognito:

https://aws.amazon.com/cognito

AWS Single Sign-On:

https://docs.aws.amazon.com/singlesignon

Exercises

Setting Up a Simple Active Directory

In this exercise, you will set up an AWS Simple Active Directory (Simple AD). Simple AD is a standalone directory that is powered by a Samba 4 Active Directory Compatible Server. Because it's a standalone managed directory, you do not have to manage user accounts and group memberships. This is achieved through the Microsoft Active Directory.

Step 1: Create a Virtual Private Cloud

In this step, you will use the Amazon Virtual Private Cloud (Amazon VPC) wizard in the Amazon VPC console to create a virtual private cloud. The wizard steps create a VPC with a /16 IPv4 CIDR block and attach an internet gateway to the VPC.

1. In the AWS Management Console navigation pane, choose **VPC** and then choose **Launch VPC Wizard**.

2. On the left, select **VPC with a Single Public Subnet**, and then choose **Select**.

   To communicate with an Active Directory outside of AWS, you must create the Simple AD directory in a public subnet.

3. On the next page, enter the following settings:

   a. Enter a valid, unused IP CIDER block (for example **10.40.0.0/16**).

   b. Choose a valid name (for example, **simple-ad-demo**).

   c. Choose a valid subnet (for example, **10.40.1.0/24**)

   d. Choose an Availability Zone in which to create the subnet. (Record your selection; you will need this information for the next step.)

4. Choose **Create VPC**.

   You have launched a VPC that has a public subnet, an internet gateway attached to it, and the necessary route table and security group configurations to allow traffic to flow between the subnet and the internet gateway. However, because Simple AD is a highly available service, you must create a second public subnet on this VPC.

5. Navigate to the VPC dashboard and choose **Subnets**.

6. Choose **Create Subnet**.

7. On the next page, enter the following settings:

    a. Choose a name tag.

    b. Choose the VPC that you created in the previous steps.

    c. Choose an Availability Zone that is different from the one selected in the previous steps.

    d. Choose a valid subnet.

8. Choose **Create VPC**.

    You have created a VPC that has two public subnets. When you create a Simple AD directory, each node is located in a different Availability Zone.

Step 2: Create Your Simple AD Instance in AWS

Create your AWS Managed Microsoft AD directory using the AWS Management Console.

1. In the AWS Directory Service console navigation pane, choose **Directories** and then choose **Set up directory**.

2. On the **Select directory type** page, select **AWS Simple AD** and then choose **Next**.

3. On the **Enter directory information** page, provide the following and then choose **Next**.

    a. Directory size (Small or Large).

    b. Directory DNS name.

    c. (Optional) Directory NetBIOS name (CORP, for example). If one is not provided, a name is created by default.

    d. An administrator password, which must be 8–24 characters in length. It must also contain at least one character from three of the following four categories: uppercase letters, lowercase letters, numbers, or nonalphanumeric characters.

    e. (Optional) Description of the directory. This is useful in tracking your services within AWS.

4. On the **VPC and subnets** page, provide the following information, and then choose **Next**.

    a. For **VPC**, choose the VPC you created earlier (simple-ad-demo).

    b. Under **Subnets**, choose the two subnets you created for the domain controllers.

5. Review your settings and choose **Create directory**.

    It takes 5–10 minutes to create your directory. You may need to refresh the page. When the directory creation is complete, the Status value changes to *Active*.

(continued)

Step 3: Management and Maintenance of Simple AD Directory in AWS

When the status changes to *Active*, the AWS Managed Microsoft AD directory is ready to do the following:

- Manage the AWS applications and services available to users

- Perform various maintenance activities, such as creating Amazon Simple Notification Service (Amazon SNS) email or text messages to inform you of changes in status to your directory, performing a point-in time backup (snapshot) of your directory, and modifying the schema of your AWS Managed AD directory

Setting Up an AWS Managed Microsoft AD

In this exercise, you will set up an AWS Managed Microsoft AD. Because this is an Active Directory managed by AWS, you do not have to consider the size or type of compute instances that will be running on this Active Directory. You will, however, have to choose the Amazon VPC that this service will run on.

This service is designed for high availability, so two domain controllers are created. Therefore, two corresponding subnets are used.

To simplify the installation, you will first create the necessary VPC, and then you will create the AWS Managed Microsoft AD.

Step 1: Create a Virtual Private Cloud

Create your Amazon VPC by using the AWS Management Console.

1. In the AWS Services console navigation pane, choose **VPC** and then choose **Your VPCs**.

2. Note the VPCs used (to avoid address conflict), and choose **Create VPC**.

3. In **VPC name**, enter, **My Directory Service** and specify an IPv4 CIDR block.

   Choose a CIDR block that is not currently used (for example, 10.30.0.0/16).

4. For **Hardware tenancy**, select **Default**, and choose **Create**.

5. After the VPC is created, return to the VPC dashboard and select **Subnets**.

6. Choose **Create subnet**.

7. In the **Create Subnet** dialog box, enter a name tag, choose the VPC you just created, select an Availability Zone, and specify an IPv4 CIDR block within that VPC (for example, 10.30.1.0/24).

8. Choose **Create**.

9. Repeat steps 6–8 to create a second subnet, making sure to choose a different Availability Zone and a different subnet other than the ones specified in step 7.

Step 2: Create Your AWS Managed Microsoft AD Directory in AWS

Create your AWS Managed Microsoft AD directory by using the AWS Management Console.

1. In the AWS Directory Service console navigation pane, choose **Directories** and then choose **Set up directory**.

2. On the **Select directory type** page, choose **AWS Managed Microsoft AD** and choose **Next**.

3. On the **Enter directory information** page, provide the following information and then choose **Next**.

4. For **Edition**, you can select either **Standard Edition** or **Enterprise Edition**. For this exercise, select **Standard Edition**.

   For more information about editions, see AWS Directory Service for Microsoft Active Directory at https://docs.aws.amazon.com/directoryservice/latest/admin-guide/what_is.html#microsoftad.

5. For **Directory DNS name**, enter `corp.example.com`.

6. For **Directory NetBIOS name**, enter `corp`.

7. For **Directory description**, enter `AWS DS Managed`.

8. For **Admin password**, enter the password that you want to use for this account.

   This admin account is automatically created during the directory creation process. The password cannot include the word *admin*. The directory administrator password is case-sensitive, and it must be 8–64 characters in length. It must also contain at least one character from three of the following four categories:

   ■ Lowercase letters (a–z)

   ■ Uppercase letters (A–Z)

   ■ Numbers (0–9)

   ■ Nonalphanumeric characters (~!@#$%^&*_-+=`|\(){}[]:;"'<>,.?/)

9. In **Confirm Password**, enter the password again.

(continued)

10. On the **Choose VPC and subnets** page, provide the following information and then choose **Next**.

    a. For **VPC**, choose the option that begins with AWS-DS-VPC and ends with (10.0.0.0/16).

    b. For **Subnets**, choose the 10.0.128.0/20 and 10.0.144.0/20 public subnets.

    c. On the **Review & create** page, review the directory information and make any necessary changes. When the information is correct, choose **Create directory**.

Creating the directory takes 20–40 minutes. After the directory is created, the Status value changes to *Active*.

Step 3: Management and Maintenance of AWS Managed Microsoft AD

After AWS Managed Microsoft AD is set up, you are able to perform the following maintenance and management operations:

- Manage the AWS applications and services available to users.

- Share directories, see the Availability Zone and subnet of existing controllers, and add additional controllers.

- Create trust relationships, establish IP routing, enable log forwarding, and use multi-factor authentication.

- Create Amazon SNS email or text messages to inform you of changes in status to your directory, perform a point-in time backup (snapshot) of your directory, and modify the schema of your AWS Managed AD directory.

Setting Up an Amazon Cloud Directory

In this exercise, you will set up an Amazon Cloud Directory. Cloud Directory is a highly available multitenant directory-based store where AWS is responsible for scaling. AWS manages the directory infrastructure, while the administrators focus on building the directories and the applications that use those directories.

Step 1: Create a Schema

You'll first create a schema (which defines objects in a directory) and then assign that schema to a directory. A single schema can be assigned to multiple directories, and a directory can have multiple schemas assigned to it (though typically it does not).

1. In the AWS Services console navigation pane, under **Security, Identity & Compliance**, choose **Directory Service ➤ Schemas**.

2. To create a custom schema based on an existing one, in the table listing the schemas, select the schema named **person**.

3. Choose **Actions**.

4. Choose **Download schema**.

5. In the location where you downloaded the schema, rename the file to **test-person**.

6. On the **Schemas** page, choose **Upload new schema**.

7. Select test-person and choose **Upload**.

8. To prevent modifications to the schema, choose **schema test-person**.

9. Choose **Actions**.

10. In **Major Version**, enter the identifier **1**, and choose **Publish**.

    You are returned to the Schemas page. You have two versions of the test-person schema: one schema version shows versions and is listed under State as Published; the other schema version does not show versions and is listed under State as Development.

    You have successfully created a schema that you will use to create a directory.

Step 2: Create a Directory

Before you can create a directory in Cloud Directory, Directory Service requires that you first apply a schema to it. A directory cannot be created without a schema and typically has one schema applied to it.

Create a directory that uses the schema you created in step 1.

1. In the AWS Directory Service console navigation pane, under **Security, Identity & Compliance**, choose **Directory Service ➤ Directories**.

2. Choose **Set up Cloud Directory**.

3. Under **Choose a schema to apply to your new directory**, in **Cloud Directory name**, enter **test-cloud-directory**.

4. Choose **Custom schema**.

5. Select the custom schema named test-person with the Status of Published, and then choose **Next**.

6. Review the directory information and make the necessary changes. When the information is correct, choose **Create**.

You have successfully created a Cloud Directory. You can modify and delete the directory, including the schema associated with the directory.

EXERCISE 10.4

Setting Up Amazon Cognito

In this exercise, you will set up Amazon Cognito, which is the service that provides authentication, authorization, and user management for web and mobile applications.

The two main components of Amazon Cognito are user pools and identity pools. User pools is a user directory that provides sign-up and sign-in services. Identity pools are used to provide access to other AWS services.

You can use identity pools and user pools separately or together. In this exercise, you will set up a user pool.

1. In the AWS Directory Services console navigation pane, under Security, Identity & Compliance, choose **Cognito** and then choose **Manage User Pools**.

2. Provide a name for your user pool. Enter **admin-group**.

3. Specify how a user signs in. In this example, select **user name**, and then choose **Next step**.

4. Retain the default settings and choose **Next step**.

   You can set MFA as optional or required. After a user pool is configured, you cannot change the MFA setting. Amazon Cognito uses Amazon SNS to send SMS messages. If MFA is enabled, you must assign a role with the correct policy to send SMS messages.

5. Retain the default settings and choose **Next step**.

6. On the **Attributes** page, retain the default settings for email customization, and choose **Next step**.

7. To manage the AWS infrastructure, apply tags. Enter the following information, and then choose **Next step**:

   a. In **Tag Key**, enter **user**

   b. In **Tag Value**, enter **admin-user**.

8. Select **No** and choose **Next step**.

   Amazon Cognito can detect and retain your user's device. This step enables you to configure that capability. In this example, however, you will select **No**. Choose **Next step**.

9. Retain the default settings and choose **Next step**.

   You can configure how client applications gain access to the user pool. In this exercise, no access is granted.

10. Retain the default settings and choose **Next step**.

    You can configure AWS Lambda functions that can be triggered during the Amazon Cognito operation. For this exercise, you will not configure any Lambda functions.

11. On the **Review** page, review your configurations, and choose **Create pool**.

    You have successfully created a user pool in Amazon Cognito.

Review Questions

1. You need to grant a user, who is outside your AWS account, access to an object in an Amazon Simple Storage Service (Amazon S3) bucket. Which is the best way to provide access?

    A. Create a role and assign that role to the user.

    B. Create a user ID within Identity and Access Management (IAM) and assign the user ID a policy that allows access.

    C. Create a new AWS account, assign that user to the account, and then give the account cross-account access.

    D. Have the user create a user ID using a third-party identity provider (IdP), and based on that user ID, assign a policy that permits access.

2. Which of the following is the purpose of an identity provider (IdP)?

    A. To control access to applications

    B. To control access to the AWS infrastructure

    C. To minimize the opportunity to assign the incorrect policy

    D. To answer the question "Who are you?"

3. Which of the following is the best way to minimize misuse of AWS credentials?

    A. Set up multi-factor authentication (MFA).

    B. Embed the credentials in the bastion host and control access to the bastion host.

    C. Put a condition on all of your policies that allows execution only from your corporate IP range.

    D. Make sure that you have a limited number of credentials and limit the number of people that can use them.

4. Which of the following is not a valid identity provider (IdP) for Amazon Cognito?

    A. Google

    B. Microsoft Active Directory

    C. Your own identity store

    D. A Security Assertion Markup Language (SAML) 1.0–based IdP

5. Which of the following is one benefit of using AWS as an identity provider (IdP) to access non-AWS resources?

    A. AWS cannot be used as an IdP for non-AWS services.

    B. Using AWS as an IdP allows you to use Amazon CloudWatch to monitor activity.

    C. Using AWS as an IdP allows you to use AWS CloudTrail to audit who is using the service.

    D. Using AWS as an IdP allows you to assign policies to non-AWS resources.

6. Which of the following are benefits from using the Active Directory Connector (AD Connector)? (Select TWO.)

   A. Easy setup

   B. Ability to connect to multiple Active Directory domains with a single connection

   C. Ability to configure changes to Active Directory on your existing Active Directory console

   D. Ability to support authentication to non-AWS services

7. Which of the following is a prerequisite for using AWS Single Sign-On (AWS SSO)?

   A. Set up AWS Organizations and enable all features.

   B. Make sure that your identity provider (IdP) is Security Assertion Markup Language (SAML) 2.0 compatible.

   C. Deploy AWS Simple Active Directory (Simple AD).

   D. Deploy Amazon Cognito.

8. AWS Security Token Service (AWS STS) supports a number of different tokens.

   Which token would you use to establish a longer-term session?

   A. AssumeRole

   B. GetUserToken

   C. GetFederationToken

   D. GetSessionToken

9. Which of the following is not a service that AWS Managed Microsoft AD provides?

   A. Daily snapshots

   B. Ability to manage the Amazon Elastic Compute Cloud (Amazon EC2) instances that AWS Managed Microsoft AD is running on

   C. Monitoring

   D. Ability to sync with on-premises Active Directory

10. You are using an existing RADIUS-based multi-factor authentication (MFA) infrastructure.

    Which AWS service is your best choice?

    A. Active Directory Connector (AD Connector)

    B. AWS Managed Microsoft AD

    C. Simple Active Directory (Simple AD)

    D. No AWS service would be suitable.

Chapter 11

Refactor to Microservices

THE AWS CERTIFIED DEVELOPER – ASSOCIATE EXAM TOPICS COVERED IN THIS CHAPTER MAY INCLUDE, BUT ARE NOT LIMITED TO, THE FOLLOWING:

Domain 4: Refactoring

✓ **4.1 Optimize application to best use AWS services and features.**

Content may include the following:

- Amazon Simple Queue Service (Amazon SQS) message queue service
- Amazon Simple Notification Service (Amazon SNS) producer/consumer (publisher/subscriber) messaging and mobile notifications web
- Amazon Kinesis Data Streams real-time ingestion and real-time analytics
- Replacement of Amazon Kinesis Data Firehose with the CoDA service for data ingestion
- Process and analysis of Amazon Kinesis Data Analytics data with standard structured query language (SQL)
- Process and detection of content patterns in Amazon Kinesis Video Streams
- Publishing messages when Amazon DynamoDB tables change
- Using AWS IoT Device Management to manage IoT devices throughout their lifecycle

- Amazon MQ message broker service for Apache ActiveMQ
- Using AWS Step Functions to develop, launch, and monitor the progress of workflows

Domain 5: Monitoring and Troubleshooting

Content may include the following:

- Troubleshooting dead-letter queue

Introduction to Refactor to Microservices

As applications grow, they become harder to manage and maintain. Application components are tightly coupled with each other, and the failure of one component can cause the failure of the whole application.

Microservices architecture is a method to design and build software applications as a suite of modular services, each performing a specific functional task, which deploy and access application components via well-defined standard application programming interfaces (APIs). Where possible, you automate the provisioning, termination, and configuration of resources. A best-practice scenario is shown in Figure 11.1. In this case, if an application fails, Amazon CloudWatch automatically detects the unhealthy instance and alerts AWS Auto Scaling to launch and configure an identical server, notifies the administrator, and logs the action to your change management solution.

FIGURE 11.1 Microservices in action

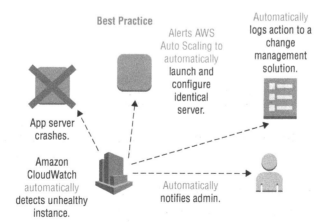

Containers are software-defined execution environments that you can rapidly provision and independently deploy in server and serverless environments. Microservices that run in containers take portability and interoperability to a new level because the services function the same on-premises as they do in any cloud that supports containers. Independence and modularity also provide opportunities to design for elastic scalability and operational resilience.

To *refactor to microservices* is to separate the application components into separate microservices so that each microservice has its own data store, scales independently, and deploys on its own infrastructure. Refactoring includes rewriting and decoupling applications, re-architecting a solution, and determining whether you will perform a complete refactor (lift and shift—all in) or only a partial refactor (lift and shift—hybrid).

To refactor to microservices requires a *message infrastructure* so that the microservices can communicate with each other. Message queues communicate between applications. AWS provides the message infrastructure that enables you to build microservice architectures without the need to spend the time and effort for a connective infrastructure.

A serverless solution is provisioned at the time of need. You can store static web assets externally, such as in an Amazon S3 bucket, and user authentication and user state storage are handled by managed AWS offerings and services.

You can further safeguard your application against latency because of failure if you avoid a single point of failure, as shown in Figure 11.2.

FIGURE 11.2   Avoiding single points of failure

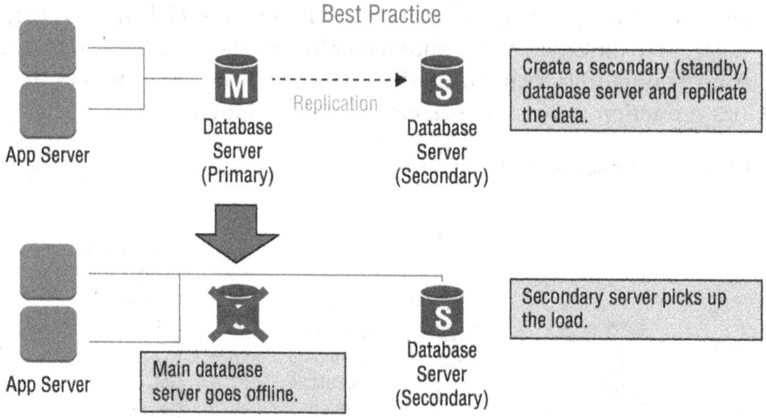

This section describes the different services AWS provides to enable the building of microservice architectures. The certification exam objectives for refactoring to microservices include the following:

- Optimizing an application to best use AWS offerings, services, and features
- Migrating existing application code to run on AWS

Amazon Simple Queue Service

Message-oriented middleware (MoM) supports messaging types in which the messages that are produced (producers) can broadcast and publish to multiple message consumers, also known as *message subscribers*.

Amazon Simple Queue Service (Amazon SQS) is a fully managed message queuing service that makes it easy to decouple and scale microservices, distributed systems, and serverless applications to assist in event-driven solutions. Amazon SQS both moves data between distributed application components and helps you to decouple these components. Amazon SQS is the best option for cloud-designed applications that need unlimited scalability, capacity, throughput, and high availability. *Amazon SQS temporarily stores messages from a message producer while they wait for a message consumer to process the message.*

With the use of Amazon SQS, application components send messages to each other and do not have to wait for a response, as shown in Figure 11.3.

FIGURE 11.3   Amazon Simple Queue Service (Amazon SQS) flow

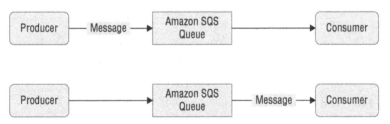

The *producer* is the component that *sends* the message. The *consumer* is the component that *pulls* the message off the queue. The queue passively stores messages and does not notify you of new messages. When you poll the *Amazon SQS queue*, the queue *responds* with messages that it includes, as shown in Figure 11.4.

FIGURE 11.4   Amazon SQS queue

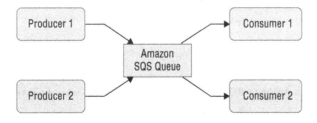

With Amazon SQS, multiple producers can write messages, and multiple consumers can process the messages. One of the consumers processes each message, and when a consumer processes a message, they remove it from the queue. That message is no longer available for other consumers. If the amount of work on the queue exceeds the capacity for a single consumer, you can add more consumers to help the process.

Figure 11.5 illustrates the way that the Amazon SQS queue interacts with both Amazon EC2 and the process servers.

FIGURE 11.5 Amazon Simple Queue Service

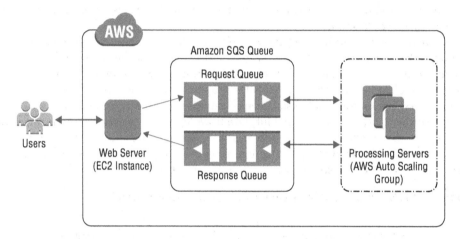

As shown in Figure 11.6, a sign-in service run on a single *log server* is dependent on the reliability of the log server to send and receive messages. If the log server experiences any issues, the sign-in service can go offline.

FIGURE 11.6 Log server

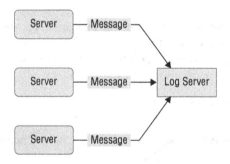

Use Amazon SQS Queue to Alleviate Log Server Failures

If you replace the log server with an Amazon SQS queue with multiple log servers, you can remove this point of failure.

As the other servers in your application send their sign-in messages to the queue, the sign-in server can pull messages off the queue and process them, as shown in Figure 11.7.

FIGURE 11.7 Amazon SQS queue

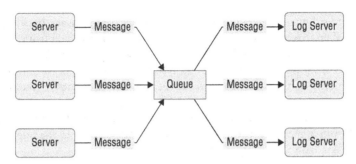

There are several benefits to using the Amazon SQS queue:

- If you need to take a sign-in server offline for maintenance, the service does not interrupt. The messages remain in the queue until the sign-in server comes back online.
- If the number of messages grows, you can *scale* your sign-in service and add more servers.
- Amazon SQS automatically scales to handle an increase in incoming messages.
- Messages remain in order and deliver only one message.
- Messages can be sent to the dead-letter queue.
- Messages have a visibility timeout, a message retention period, and a receive-message wait time.
- Messages can have a long polling interval or a short polling interval (default).

The Amazon SQS is a *distributed cluster of servers*. There is no limit on the number of producers that can write to the queue, and there is no limit on the number of messages that the queue can store.

 Amazon SQS is a Payment Card Industry Data Security Standard (PCI DSS) service.

Amazon SQS Parameters

An Amazon SQS message has three basic states:

1. Sent to a queue by a producer
2. Received from the queue by a consumer
3. Deleted from the queue

A message is *stored* after it is sent to a queue by a producer but not yet received from the queue by a consumer (that is, between states 1 and 2). There is no limit to the number of stored messages. A message is considered to be *in-flight* after it is received from a queue by a consumer but not yet deleted from the queue (that is, between states 2 and 3). There is a limit to the number of in-flight messages.

Limits that apply to in-flight messages are unrelated to the unlimited number of stored messages.

For most *standard queues* (depending on queue traffic and message backlog), there can be a maximum of approximately 120,000 in-flight messages (received from a queue by a consumer but not yet deleted from the queue). If you reach this limit, Amazon SQS returns the OverLimit error message. To avoid reaching the limit, delete messages from the queue after they are processed. You can also increase the number of queues if you file an AWS Support request.

For *first-in, first-out* (FIFO) queues, there can be a maximum of 20,000 in-flight messages (received from a queue by a consumer but not yet deleted from the queue). If you reach this limit, Amazon SQS returns no error messages.

ReceiveMessage

The ReceiveMessage action waits for a message to arrive. Valid values are integers from 0 to 20 seconds, with the default value of 0.

Long Polling

Long polling helps reduce the cost of Amazon SQS by eliminating the number of empty responses (when there are no messages available for a ReceiveMessage request) and false empty responses (when messages are available but are not included in a response).

To ensure optimal message processing, do the following:

- *Set the ReceiveMessage wait time to 20 seconds, which is the default and the maximum value. If 20 seconds is too long for your application, set a shorter ReceiveMessage wait time (1 second minimum).* You might have to modify your Amazon SQS client either to enable longer requests or to use a shorter wait time for long polling.

- If you implement long polling for multiple queues, use one thread for each queue instead of a single thread for all queues. This enables your application to process the messages in each of the queues as they become available.

VisibilityTimeout

The VisibilityTimeout action is the duration (in seconds) that the received messages are hidden from subsequent retrieve requests after being retrieved by a ReceiveMessage request. *The default VisibilityTimeout for a message is 30 seconds. The minimum is 0 seconds. The maximum is 12 hours.*

How you set the VisibilityTimeout depends on how long it takes your application to process and delete a message. To ensure that there is sufficient time to process messages, use one of the following strategies:

- If you know (reasonably estimate) how long it takes to process a message, extend the message's VisibilityTimeout to the maximum time it takes to process and delete the message.

- If you do not know how long it takes to process a message, create a heartbeat for your consumer process: specify the initial VisibilityTimeout (for example, 2 minutes) and then—as long as your consumer still works on the message—keep extending the VisibilityTimeout by 2 minutes every minute.

To extend the `VisibilityTimeout` action for longer than 12 hours, consider using AWS Step Functions.

For example, if your application requires 10 seconds to process a message and you set `VisibilityTimeout` to 15 minutes, you must wait for a relatively long time to attempt to process the message again if the previous processing attempt fails. Alternatively, if your application requires 10 seconds to process a message but you set `VisibilityTimeout` to only 2 seconds, a duplicate message is received by another consumer while the original consumer is still working on the original message.

WaitTimeSeconds

`WaitTimeSeconds` is the duration (in seconds) for which the call waits for a message to arrive in the queue before returning. If a message is available, the call returns sooner than `WaitTimeSeconds`. If no messages are available and the wait time expires, the call returns successfully with an empty list of messages.

ReceiveMessageWaitTimeSeconds

`ReceiveMessageWaitTimeSeconds` is the length of time, in seconds, for which a `ReceiveMessage` action waits for a message to arrive. Valid values are integers from 0 to 20 (seconds), with the default value equal to 0.

ChangeMessageVisibility

`ChangeMessageVisibility` changes the visibility timeout of a message in a queue to a new value. The default `VisibilityTimeout` setting for a message is 30 seconds. The minimum is 0 seconds. The maximum is 12 hours.

If you attempt to set `VisibilityTimeout` to a value greater than the maximum time left, Amazon SQS returns an error. Amazon SQS doesn't automatically recalculate and increase the timeout to the maximum remaining time.

Unlike with a queue, when you change the `VisibilityTimeout` value for a specific message, the `TimeoutValue` action applies immediately but is not saved in memory for that message. If you do not delete a message after it is received, the next time the message is received, the `VisibilityTimeout` setting for the message reverts to the original `TimeoutValue` setting and not to the value of the `ChangeMessageVisibility` action.

For example, suppose that you have a message with a `VisibilityTimeout` setting of 5 minutes. After 3 minutes, you call ChangeMessageVisibility with a timeout of 10 minutes. You can continue to call ChangeMessageVisibility to extend the `VisibilityTimeout` to the maximum allowed time. If you try to extend the `VisibilityTimeout` beyond the maximum, your request is rejected.

DelaySeconds

DelaySeconds is the length of time, in seconds, that a specific message will be delayed. Valid values are 0–900, with a maximum of 15 minutes. Messages with a positive DelaySeconds value become available for processing after the delay period is finished. If you do not specify a value, the default value for the queue applies.

> When you set FifoQueue, you cannot set DelaySeconds per message. You can set this parameter only on a queue level.

MessageRetentionPeriod

MessageRetentionPeriod is the length of time, in seconds, that Amazon SQS retains a message. It is an integer representing seconds, from 60 (1 minute) to 1,209,600 (14 days). Changes made to the MessageRetentionPeriod attribute can take up to 15 minutes to take effect.

DeleteMessage

DeleteMessage deletes the specified message from the specified queue. To select the message to delete, use the ReceiptHandle value of the message (not the MessageId that you receive when you send the message). Amazon SQS can delete a message from a queue even if a VisibilityTimeout setting causes the message to be locked by another consumer. Amazon SQS automatically deletes messages kept in a queue longer than the retention period configured for the queue.

> Refer to Table 11.5 to view the differences between the Amazon Simple Notification Service (Amazon SNS) and Amazon SQS event-driven solutions.

Dead-Letter Queue

Amazon SQS supports *dead-letter queues*, which other queues (*source queues*) can target for messages that cannot process (be consumed) successfully. Dead-letter queues are useful when you debug your application or message system because the queues let you isolate problematic messages to determine why their process did not succeed.

Sometimes messages do not process because of a variety of possible issues, such as erroneous conditions within the producer or consumer application or an unexpected state change that causes an issue with your application code. For example, if a user places a web order with a particular product ID but the product ID is deleted, the web store's code fails and displays an error, and the message with the order request is sent to a dead-letter queue.

Occasionally, producers and consumers might fail to interpret aspects of the protocol that they use to communicate, causing message corruption or loss. Also, the consumer's hardware errors might corrupt message payload.

If the consumer of the source queue fails to process a message in the number of times you specify, the *redrive policy* (RedrivePolicy) specifies the source queue, the dead-letter queue, and the conditions under which Amazon SQS moves messages from the former to the latter. When the ReceiveCount value for a message exceeds the maxReceiveCount value for a queue, Amazon SQS moves the message to a dead-letter queue. For example, if the source queue has a redrive policy with maxReceiveCount set to 5 and the consumer of the source queue receives a message five times and it does not delete, Amazon SQS moves the message to the dead-letter queue.

To specify a dead-letter queue, you can use the AWS Management Console or the AWS SDK for Java for each queue that sends messages to a dead-letter queue. Multiple queues can target a single dead-letter queue. The dead-letter queue uses the CreateQueue or SetQueueAttributes action.

Use the same AWS account to create the dead-letter queue and the other queues that send messages to the dead-letter queue. Also, dead-letter queues must reside in the same region as the other queues that use the dead-letter queue. For example, if you create a queue in the US East (Ohio) Region, and you want to use a dead-letter queue with that queue, the second queue must also be in the US East (Ohio) Region.

The expiration of a message is based on its original enqueue timestamp. When a message moves to a dead-letter queue, the enqueue timestamp does not change. For example, if a message spends one day in the original queue before it moves to a dead-letter queue and the retention period of the dead-letter queue is set to 5 days, the message is deleted from the dead-letter queue after 3 days. *Thus, AWS recommends that you set the retention period of a dead-letter queue to be longer than the retention period of the original queue.*

Benefits of Dead-Letter Queues

The main task of a dead-letter queue is to handle message failure. Use a dead-letter queue to set aside and isolate messages that cannot be processed correctly to determine why their processes failed. The dead-letter queue enables you to do the following:

- Configure an alarm for any messages delivered to a dead-letter queue.

- Examine logs for exceptions that might have caused messages to be delivered to a dead-letter queue.

- Analyze the contents of messages delivered to a dead-letter queue to diagnose software or the producer's or consumer's hardware issues.

- Determine whether you have given your consumer sufficient time to process messages.

Standard Queue Message Failures

Standard queues continue to process messages until the expiration of the retention period. This ensures continuous processing of messages, which minimizes the chances of your queue being blocked by messages that cannot process. It also ensures fast recovery for your queue.

Amazon SQS standard queues work by using *scalability* and *throughput*. To achieve this, they trade off two qualities:

▪ Order is not guaranteed.

▪ Messages can appear twice.

In a system that processes thousands of messages and in which you have a large number of messages that the consumer repeatedly fails to acknowledge and delete, standard queues may increase costs and place an extra load on the hardware. Instead of trying to process messages that fail until they expire, move them to a dead-letter queue after a few process attempts.

 Standard queues support a high number of in-flight messages. If the majority of your messages cannot be consumed and are not sent to a dead-letter queue, your rate of processing valid messages can slow down. Thus, to maintain the efficiency of your queue, you must ensure that your application handles message processing correctly.

Dead-Letter Queue First-In, First-Out Message Queues

Amazon SQS uses FIFO message queues that place the messages in the queue in the order that you receive them. The first messages that you receive display first in the queue. *Message groups* also follow this order so that when you publish messages to different message groups, each message group preserves the messages' internal order.

FIFO queues support 3,000 operations (`read`, `write`, and `delete`) per second with batching and support 300 operations per second without batching.

Amazon SQS standard queues use scalability and throughput, unlike Amazon SQS FIFO queues. To achieve this, they trade off two qualities:

▪ Order is not guaranteed.

▪ Messages can appear twice.

If the removal of either or both of these two constraints is important, use Amazon SQS FIFO queues. *Amazon SQS FIFO queues provide order within message groups, and they delete any duplicate messages that occur within 5-minute intervals.*

FIFO queues ensure single processing by consuming messages in sequence from a message group. Thus, although the consumer can continue to retrieve ordered messages from another message group, the first message group remains unavailable until the message that is blocking the queue processes successfully.

 FIFO queues support a lower number of in-flight messages. To ensure that your FIFO queue does not get blocked by a message, you must make sure that your application handles message processing correctly.

When to Use a Dead-Letter Queue

Use dead-letter queues with Amazon SQS standard queues when your application does not depend on the order of messages. Dead-letter queues help you troubleshoot incorrect message transmission operations.

The dead-letter queue of a *FIFO queue* must also be a FIFO queue. Similarly, the dead-letter queue of a *standard queue* must also be a standard queue.

Even when you use dead-letter queues, continue to monitor your queues, and retry to send messages that fail for transient reasons.

Do use dead-letter queues to decrease the number of messages and to reduce the possibility that you expose your system to messages that you can receive but cannot process.

Do not use a dead-letter queue with standard queues when you want to retry the transmission of a message indefinitely. For example, do not use a dead-letter queue if your program must wait for a dependent process to become active or available.

Do not use a dead-letter queue with a FIFO queue if you do not want to break the exact order of messages or operations.

Troubleshooting Dead-Letter Queues

In some cases, Amazon SQS dead-letter queues might not behave as you expect. This section gives an overview of common issues and shows how to resolve them.

Viewing Messages Using the AWS Management Console Causes Messages to Be Moved to a Dead-Letter Queue

Amazon SQS counts a message you view in the AWS Management Console against the queue's redrive policy. As a result, if you view a message in the console the number of times you specify in the queue's redrive policy, the message moves to the queue's dead-letter queue.

To adjust this behavior, do the following:

- Increase the *Maximum Receives* setting for the corresponding queue's redrive policy.
- Avoid viewing the corresponding queue's messages in the AWS Management Console.

The Number of Messages Sent and Number of Messages Received for a Dead-Letter Queue Do Not Match

If you send a message to a dead-letter queue manually, the NumberOfMessagesSent metric counts it. However, if a message is sent to a dead-letter queue because of a failed process attempt, the metric does not count it. Thus, the values of NumberOfMessagesSent and NumberOfMessagesReceived can be different.

Amazon SQS Attributes, Dead-Letter Queue Settings, and Server-Side Encryption Settings

Table 11.1, Table 11.2, and Table 11.3 provide all the details of the Amazon SQS message attributes, DLQ settings, and server-side encryption (SSE) settings.

TABLE 11.1   Amazon SQS Message Attributes

Attribute	Default	Meaning
Default Visibility Timeout	30 seconds	How long a message is hidden while it is processed. Maximum limit is 12 hours.
Message Retention Period	4 days	How long a queue retains a message before deleting it.
Maximum Message Size	256-KB text	Maximum size of a message with 10 items maximum.
Delivery Delay	0 seconds	How long to delay before publishing the message to the queue.
Receive Message Wait Time	0 seconds	Maximum time consumer receives call waits for new messages.

Large Messages

To send a message larger than 256 KB, use Amazon SQS to save the file in Amazon Simple Storage Service (Amazon S3) and then send a link to the file on Amazon SQS.

TABLE 11.2   Dead-Letter Queue Settings

Setting	Meaning
Use Redrive Policy	Send messages to the dead-letter queue if consumers keep failing to process it.
Dead-Letter Queue	Name of dead-letter queue.
Maximum Receives	Maximum number of times a message is received before it is sent to the dead-letter queue.

TABLE 11.3   Server-Side Encryption (SSE) Settings

Setting	Meaning
Use SSE	Amazon SQS encrypts all messages sent to this queue.
AWS Key Management Service (AWS KMS) Customer Master Key	The AWS KMS master key that generates the data keys.
Data Key Reuse Period	Length of time to reuse a data key before a new one regenerates.

Monitoring Amazon SQS Queues Using Amazon CloudWatch

Amazon CloudWatch monitors your AWS resources and the applications you run on AWS in real time. You can use CloudWatch to collect and track metrics, which are variables that you can measure for your resources and applications.

CloudWatch alarms send notifications or automatically make changes to the resources you monitor based on rules that you define, for example, when a message is sent to the dead-letter queue.

If you must pass messages to other users, create an Amazon SQS queue, subscribe all the administrators to this queue, and then configure *Amazon CloudWatch Events* to send a message on a daily cron schedule into the Amazon SQS queue.

CloudWatch provides a reliable, scalable, and flexible monitoring solution with no need to set up, manage, and scale your own monitoring systems and infrastructure. You may also use Amazon CloudWatch Logs to monitor, store, and access your log files from Amazon EC2 instances, AWS CloudTrail, or other sources.

The AWS/Events namespace includes the DeadLetterInvocations metric, as shown in Table 11.4. The DeadLetterInvocations metric uses Count as the unit, so Sum and SampleCount are the most useful statistics.

TABLE 11.4   Amazon CloudWatch Dead-Letter Queue

Metric	Description
DeadLetterInvocations	Measures the number of times a rule's target is not invoked in response to an event. This includes invocations that would result in triggering the same rule again, causing an infinite loop. Valid Dimensions: RuleName Units: Count

Amazon Simple Notification Service

Amazon Simple Notification Service (Amazon SNS) is a flexible, fully managed *producer/consumer* (publisher/subscriber) messaging and mobile notifications web service that coordinates the delivery of messages to subscribing endpoints and clients. Amazon SNS coordinates and manages the delivery or sending of messages to subscriber endpoints or clients to assist in event-driven solutions.

Amazon SNS is based on the publish-subscribe model, and it allows the message producer to send a message to a *topic* that has multiple subscribers that choose to receive the same message. The message is delivered to multiple subscribers, which can then consume the message to trigger subsequent processes. A *topic* allows multiple receivers of the message to subscribe dynamically for identical copies of the same notification.

With Amazon SNS, you can easily set up, operate, and reliably send notifications to all your endpoints at any scale. You can also send messages to a large number of subscribers, including distributed systems and services and mobile devices. *By default, Amazon SNS offers 10 million subscriptions per topic and 100,000 topics per account.* To request a higher limit, contact AWS Support.

Amazon SNS enables you to send notifications from the cloud, and it allows applications to publish messages that are immediately delivered to a subscriber, as shown in Figure 11.8.

FIGURE 11.8   Amazon SNS

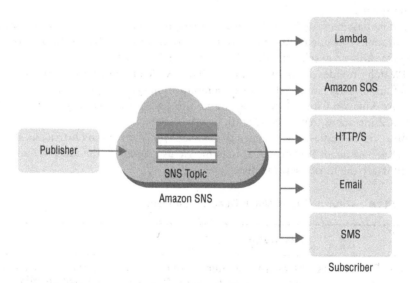

There are two types of *clients* in Amazon SNS: *producers* (publishers) and *consumers* (subscribers).

Producers communicate asynchronously with subscribers by producing and sending a message to a topic, which, in the context of Amazon SNS, is a logical access point and communication channel. Subscribers, such as web servers, email addresses, Amazon SQS queues, and AWS Lambda functions, consume or receive the message or notification over one of the supported protocols, such as Amazon SQS, HTTPS, email, Short Message Service (SMS), and AWS Lambda, when the consumer subscribes to the topic.

The sequence of operations in Amazon SNS includes the following:

1. The administrator creates a topic.
2. Users subscribe to the topic by using email addresses, SMS numbers, Amazon SQS queues, and other endpoints.
3. The administrator publishes a message on the topic.
4. The subscribers to the topic receive the message that was published.

If a user subscribes to the topic after a message was published, the user will *not* receive the message. A subscriber receives messages that are published only after they have subscribed to the topic. The topics do not buffer messages.

You can use Amazon SNS to produce a single message to multiple subscribers, as shown in Figure 11.9.

FIGURE 11.9   Amazon SNS workflow

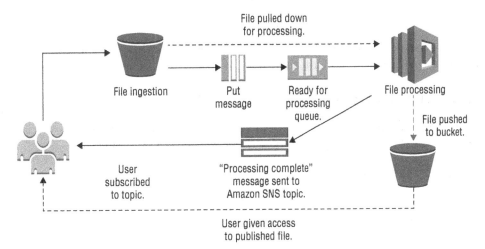

For example, when a cryptocurrency price fluctuates, you must update the *dashboard* to indicate the new price and update the *value* of the portfolio to reflect the new price. All users who subscribed to your cryptocurrency topic then receive a notification on the new prices.

Amazon SNS supports the following *endpoints*:

- AWS Lambda
- Amazon SQS
- HTTP and HTTPS
- Email
- SMS
- Mobile PushRecords

Amazon SNS retries sending messages for HTTPS endpoints as a REST call to these endpoints. You can configure the number of retries and the delay between them.

Features and Functionality

Amazon SNS topic names have a limit of 256 characters. Topic names must be unique within an AWS account and can include alphanumeric characters plus hyphens (-) and underscores (_). After you delete a topic, you can reuse the topic name. When a topic is created, Amazon SNS assigns a unique Amazon Resource Name (ARN) to the topic, which includes the service name (SNS), AWS Region, AWS ID of the user, and topic name. *The ARN returns as part of the API call to create the topic. Whenever a producer or consumer needs to perform any action on the topic, you reference the unique topic ARN.*

For example, Amazon SNS clients use the ARN address to identify the right topic.

```
aws sns publish --topic-arn topic-arn --message "message" --message-attributes
'{"store":{"DataType":"String","StringValue":"example_corp"}}'
```

This is the ARN for a topic named `mytopic` that you create with the account ID 123456789012 and host in the US East Region:

```
arn:aws:sns:us-east-1:1234567890123456:mytopic
```

Do *not* attempt to build the topic ARN from its separate components—topics should use the name the API calls to create the topic returns.

Amazon SNS APIs

Amazon SNS provides a set of simple APIs to enable event notifications for topic owners, consumers, and producers.

Owner Operations

These are the owner operations:

CreateTopic: Creates a new topic.

DeleteTopic: Deletes a previously created topic.

ListTopics: Lists topics owned by a particular user (AWS account ID).

ListSubscriptionsByTopic: Lists subscriptions for a particular topic. It allows a topic owner to see the list of all subscribers actively registered to a topic.

ListSubscriptions: Allows a user to get a list of all of their active subscriptions (to one or more topics).

SetTopicAttributes: Sets/modifies topic attributes, including setting and modifying producer/consumer permissions, transports supported, and so on.

GetTopicAttributes: Gets/views existing attributes of a topic.

AddPermission: Grants access to selected users for the specified actions.

RemovePermission: Removes permissions for selected users for the specified actions.

Subscriber Operations

These are the subscriber operations:

- **Subscribe**: Registers a new subscription on a particular topic, which will generate a confirmation message from Amazon SNS.

- **ConfirmSubscription**: Responds to a subscription confirmation message, confirming the subscription request to receive notifications from the subscribed topic.

- **UnSubscribe**: Cancels a previously registered subscription.

- **ListSubscriptions**: Lists subscriptions owned by a particular user (AWS account ID).

Clean Up

After you create a topic, subscribe to it, and publish a message to the topic. You unsubscribe from the topics and delete them to clean up your environment from the Amazon SNS console.

The subscription is deleted unless it is a pending subscription, meaning that it has not yet been confirmed. *You cannot delete a pending subscription, but if it remains pending for 3 days, Amazon SNS automatically deletes it.*

Transport Protocols

Amazon SNS supports notifications over multiple transport protocols. You can select transports as part of the subscription requests.

- **HTTP, HTTPS:** Subscribers specify a URL as part of the subscription registration; notifications are delivered through an HTTP POST to the specified URL.

- **Email, Email-JSON:** Messages are sent to registered addresses as email. Email-JSON sends notifications as a JSON object, while Email sends text-based email.

- **Amazon SQS:** Users specify an Amazon SQS standard queue as the endpoint. Amazon SNS enqueues a notification message to the specified queue (which subscribers can then process with Amazon SQS APIs, such as ReceiveMessage and DeleteMessage). Amazon SQS does not support FIFO queues.

- **SMS:** Messages are sent to registered phone numbers as AWS SMS text messages.

Amazon SNS Mobile Push Notifications

With Amazon SNS, you can send push notification messages directly to apps on mobile devices. Push notification messages sent to a mobile endpoint can appear in the mobile app as message alerts, badge updates, or even sound alerts.

You send push notification messages to both mobile devices and desktops with the following push notification services:

- Amazon Device Messaging (ADM)

- Apple Push Notification Service (APNS) for both iOS and macOS

- Baidu Cloud Push (Baidu)

- Google Cloud Messaging for Android (GCM)
- Microsoft Push Notification Service for Windows Phone (MPNS)
- Windows Push Notification Services (WNS)

Push notification services, such as APNS and GCM, maintain a connection with each app and mobile device registered to use their service. When an app and mobile device are registered, the push notification service returns a device token. Amazon SNS uses the device token to create a mobile endpoint to which it can send direct push notification messages. For Amazon SNS to communicate with the different push notification services, you submit your push notification service credentials to Amazon SNS.

You can also use Amazon SNS to send messages to mobile endpoints subscribed to a topic. The concept is the same as subscribing other endpoint types. The difference is that Amazon SNS communicates with the push notification services for the subscribed mobile endpoints to receive push notification messages sent to the topic. Figure 11.10 shows a mobile endpoint as a subscriber to an Amazon SNS topic. The mobile endpoint communicates with push notification services, whereas the other endpoints do not.

FIGURE 11.10   Amazon SNS mobile endpoint subscriber

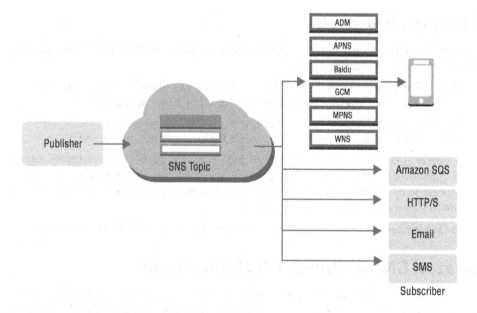

Add Device Tokens or Registration IDs

When you first register an app and mobile device with a notification service, such as Apple Push Notification Service (APNS) and Google Cloud Messaging for Android (GCM), device tokens or registration IDs return from the notification service. When you add the device tokens or registration IDs to Amazon SNS, they use the PlatformApplicationArn

API to create an endpoint for the app and device. When Amazon SNS creates the endpoint, an EndpointArn returns, and this is how Amazon SNS knows to which app and mobile device to send the notification message.

You can add device tokens and registration IDs to Amazon SNS by using these methods:

- Manually add a single token to AWS from the AWS Management Console.
- Migrate existing tokens from a CSV file to AWS from the AWS Management Console.
- Upload several tokens by using the CreatePlatformEndpoint API.
- Register tokens from devices that will install your apps in the future.

Create Amazon SNS Endpoints

You can use one of two options to create Amazon SNS endpoints for device tokens or registration IDs.

Amazon Cognito   Your mobile app requires credentials to create and associate endpoints with your Amazon SNS platform application. AWS recommends that you use temporary security credentials that expire after a period of time. You can use Amazon SNS to receive an event with the new endpoint ARN, or you can use the ListEndpointByPlatformApplication API to view the full list of endpoints registered with Amazon SNS.

Proxy Server   If your application infrastructure is already set up for your mobile apps to call in and register on each installation, you can use your server to act as a proxy and pass the device token to Amazon SNS mobile push notifications. This includes any user data that you would like to store. The proxy server connects to Amazon SNS with your AWS credentials and uses the CreatePlatformEndpoint API call to upload the token information. The newly created endpoint ARN is returned, which your server can store to make subsequent publish calls to Amazon SNS.

Billing, Limits, and Restrictions

Amazon SNS includes a Free Tier, which allows you to use Amazon SNS free of charge for the first 1 million Amazon SNS requests, and with no charges for the first 100,000 notifications over HTTP, no charges for the first 100 notifications over SMS, and no charges for the first 1,000 notifications over email.

With Amazon SNS, there is no minimum fee, and you pay only for what you use. You pay $0.50 per 1 million Amazon SNS requests, $0.06 per 100,000 notification deliveries over HTTP, and $2 per 100,000 notification deliveries over email. *For SMS messaging, users can send 100 free notification deliveries, and for subsequent messages, charges vary by destination country.*

By default, Amazon SNS offers 10 million subscriptions per topic and 100,000 topics per account. To request a higher limit, contact AWS Support.

   Amazon SNS supports the same attributes and parameters as Amazon SQS. For more information, refer to Table 11.2, Table 11.3, and Table 11.4.

When compared with Amazon SQS, which is a queue with a pull mechanism, Amazon SNS is a fanout with a push mechanism to send messages to subscribers. This means that the Amazon SNS message is sent to a topic and then replicated and pushed to multiple Amazon SQS queues, HTTP endpoints, or email addresses. This operation eliminates the need for the message consumers to poll for any new messages. There several differences between the Amazon SNS and Amazon SQS event-driven solutions, as listed in Table 11.5.

TABLE 11.5   Amazon SNS and Amazon SQS Feature Comparison

Features	Amazon SNS	Amazon SQS
Message persistence	Not persisted	Persisted
Delivery mechanism	Push (passive)	Pull (active)
Producer/consumer	Publish/subscribe (1 to N)	Send/receive (1 to 1)

Amazon Kinesis Data Streams

Amazon Kinesis Data Streams is a service that ingests large amounts of data in real time and performs real-time analytics on the data. Producers write data into Amazon Kinesis Data Streams, and consumers read data from it.

Figure 11.11 illustrates the high-level architecture of Amazon Kinesis Data Streams. The producers continually push (PushRecords) data to Amazon Kinesis Data Streams, and the consumers process the data in *real time*. Consumers (such as a custom application running on Amazon EC2, or an Amazon Kinesis Data Firehose delivery stream) can store their results by using an AWS service, such as Amazon DynamoDB, Amazon Redshift, or Amazon Simple Storage Service (Amazon S3).

FIGURE 11.11   Amazon Kinesis Data Streams

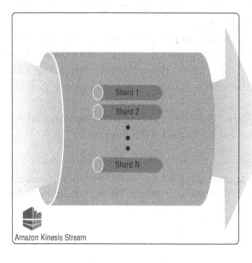
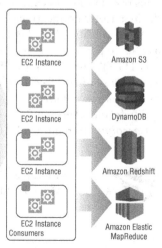

Multiple types of consumers can consume from the same Amazon Kinesis Data stream. *The messages are not deleted when they are consumed.* The consumers save a reference to the last message they view, and messages iterate based on sequence IDs to fetch the latest messages.

To place (PutRecords) data into the stream, specify the *name* of the stream, a *partition key*, and the *data blob* to add to the stream. The partition key determines the shard in the stream to which to add the data record.

All data in the shard is sent to the same worker that processes the shard. The partition key determines how to map a data record to a particular shard, so which partition key you use depends on your application logic. The number of partition keys should typically be much greater than the number of shards, and if you have enough partition keys, the data can be evenly distributed across the shards in a stream.

For example, you use the two-letter abbreviation of the state for each partition key, such as WA for Washington and WY for Wyoming. In this example, all records with a partition key of WA reside in the Washington stream, and all records with a partition key of WY reside in the Wyoming stream.

Multiple Applications

There are several differences between Amazon Kinesis Data Streams and Amazon SQS.

In Amazon SQS, when a consumer receives a message off the queue and then processes and deletes it, the message is no longer available for any other consumer.

In Amazon Kinesis Data Streams, you can process the same message by multiple applications. Each application tracks which records it last processed. Then it requests the records that came after it. It is the application's responsibility to track its checkpoint within the data stream.

Amazon Kinesis Data Streams do not delete records after they process them, as it is possible that another application will request the message. *Records automatically delete after their retention interval expires, which you configure.* The default retention interval is 1 day, but you can extend it up to 7 days. Before the record's interval expires, multiple applications can consume the message.

High Throughput

Amazon Kinesis uses shards to configure and support high throughput. When you create an Amazon Kinesis data stream, specify the number of shards in your stream. You can increase or decrease the number of shards through the API.

On the producer side, the shard supports 1 MB per second of ingest, or 1,000 transactions per second. Producers can write up to 1 MB per second of data, or 1000 writes.

On the consumer side, each shard supports 2 MB per second of reads, or five transactions per second. Amazon Kinesis Data Streams support twice as much data for reads as they do for writes (2 MB per second of read versus 1 MB per second of write) per shard. This allows multiple applications to read from a stream to enable more reads. Because the same records might be read by multiple applications, you require more throughput on the read side.

Amazon Kinesis Data Streams support 5,000 transactions per second for writes, but only five transactions per second for reads per shard. Reads frequently acquire many records at once. When a read request asks for all the records that came in after the last read, it acquires a large number of records. Because of this, five transactions per second per shard is sufficient to handle reads.

To increase your throughput capacity, reshard the stream to adjust the number of shards.

Real-Time Analytics

Unlike Amazon SQS, *Amazon Kinesis Data Streams enable real-time analytics, which produces metrics from incoming data as it arrives.* The alternative is batch analytics in which the data accumulates for a period, such as 24 hours, and then is analyzed as a batch job. Real-time analytics allow you to detect patterns in the data immediately as it arrives, with a delay of only a few seconds to a few minutes.

After you define your monitoring goals and create your monitoring plan, the next step is to establish a baseline for normal *Kinesis Video Streams* performance in your environment. Measure Kinesis Video Streams performance at various times and under different load conditions. As you monitor Kinesis Video Streams, you should store a history of the monitored data that you collect. You can compare current Kinesis Video Streams performance to this historical data to help you identify normal performance patterns and performance anomalies and devise methods to address issues that may arise.

Open Source Tools

Open source tools, such as Fluentd and Flume, support Amazon Kinesis Data Streams as a destination, and you can use them to publish messages into an Amazon Kinesis data stream.

Your custom applications, real-time or batch-oriented, can run on Amazon EC2 instances. These applications might process data with open source deep-learning algorithms or use third-party applications that integrate with Kinesis Video Streams.

Producer Options

After you create the stream in Amazon Kinesis data stream, you need two applications to build your pipeline: a collection of *producers* that write data into the stream and *consumers* to read the data from the stream.

Here are options for you to build producers that can write into Amazon Kinesis Data Streams:

Amazon Kinesis Agent   This is an application that reads data, appends to a log file, and writes to the stream. The benefit of the Amazon Kinesis Agent is that it does not require you to write application code.

Amazon Kinesis Data Steams API   You write an application to use the Amazon Kinesis Data Streams API to put data on the stream.

Amazon Kinesis Producer Library (KPL)   The KPL gives you a higher-level interface over the low-level Amazon Kinesis Data Streams API. It has the logic to retry failures and to buffer and batch-send multiple messages together. The KPL makes it easier to write messages into a stream than if you use the low-level API.

Consumer Options

Consumers have the following options for the Amazon Kinesis Data Streams:

Amazon Kinesis Data Streams API   You can write an application with the Amazon Kinesis Data Streams API to read data from a stream. To scale this to process large volumes of data, create a shard for each consumer. With multiple consumers that run independently, there is a risk that one of them might fail. To handle failure, coordinate between the consumers. Use the Amazon Kinesis Client Library (KCL) to track your consumers and shards.

Amazon Kinesis Client Library   The Amazon Kinesis Client Library handles the complexity of coordinating between different consumers that read from different shards in a stream. It ensures that *no shard is ignored*, and *no shard is processed by two consumers*. The library creates a table in Amazon DynamoDB with the same name as the application name and uses this table to coordinate between the different consumers.

AWS Lambda   AWS Lambda is another option that you can use to build Amazon Kinesis Data Streams for consumers. AWS Lambda can scale and handle fault tolerance automatically. It does not require the use of the KCL.

Amazon Kinesis Data Firehose

Amazon Kinesis Data Firehose can replace the CoDA service to ingest data. In many business applications, you require a real-time pipeline, but you do not require latency of a few seconds. You can afford to have latency that can run anywhere from 1–15 minutes.

Amazon Kinesis Data Firehose is easier to use than Amazon Kinesis Data Streams, as it does not require you to write a consumer application. Data that arrives at the Amazon Kinesis Data Firehose is automatically delivered to both Amazon S3 and the other destinations. From Amazon S3, you can deliver the data to Amazon Redshift, Amazon Elasticsearch Service, and Splunk.

Amazon Kinesis Data Firehose also handles dynamically scaling the underlying shards of the stream based on the amount of traffic.

Amazon Kinesis Data Firehose buffers the data before it writes it to Amazon S3, with a delayed reaction to real-time data based on the length of the buffer, as detailed in Table 11.6.

TABLE 11.6 Amazon Kinesis Data Firehose Buffers

Parameter	Min	Max	Description
Buffer size	1 MB	128 MB	How much data Kinesis Data Firehose buffers
Buffer interval	60 seconds	900 seconds	How long to buffer data

With Amazon Kinesis Data Firehose, you do not need to write consumer applications or manage resources. Configure data producers to send data to Amazon Kinesis Data Firehose, and it will automatically deliver the data to the destination you specify. You can also configure Amazon Kinesis Data Firehose to transform your data before you deliver it. For example, you run a news site, and you analyze the stream of clicks from users who read the articles on your site. You want to use this analysis to move the most popular articles to the top of the page to capture news stories that are going viral. It is simple to verify that a story acquires a large number of hits, with a lag of only a few minutes.

Amazon Kinesis Data Analytics

Amazon Kinesis Data Analytics enables you to process and analyze streaming data with standard structured query language (SQL). It also enables you to run SQL code against streaming sources to perform time-series analytics, feed real-time dashboards, and create real-time metrics. Amazon Kinesis Data Analytics supports ingesting from either Amazon Kinesis Data Streams or Amazon Kinesis Data Firehose, and it continuously reads and processes streaming data. You can configure destinations where Amazon Kinesis Data Analytics sends the results, as shown in Figure 11.12. Amazon Kinesis Data Analytics supports the following destinations:

- Amazon Kinesis Data Firehose
- Amazon S3
- Amazon Redshift
- Amazon ES
- Splunk
- AWS Lambda
- Amazon Kinesis Data Streams

FIGURE 11.12 Amazon Kinesis Data Analytics flow

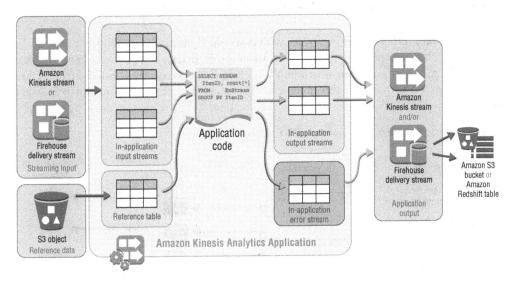

Use cases for Amazon Kinesis Data Analytics include the following:

Generate time series analytics   You can calculate metrics over time windows and stream values to Amazon S3 or Amazon Redshift through a Firehose delivery stream.

Feed real-time dashboards   You can send aggregated and processed streaming data results downstream to feed real-time dashboards.

Create real-time metrics   You can create custom metrics and triggers for use in real-time monitoring, notifications, and alarms.

Amazon Kinesis Video Streams

Use the *Amazon Kinesis Video Streams* service to push device video content into AWS and then onto the cloud to process that content and detect patterns in it.

You can use Amazon Kinesis Video Streams to build computer vision and machine learning applications.

A single stream can support one producer connection and three consumer connections at a time.

Amazon DynamoDB Streams

Amazon DynamoDB Streams integrates with Amazon DynamoDB to publish a message every time a change is made in a table. When you insert, delete, or update an item, Amazon DynamoDB produces an *event*, which publishes it to the Amazon DynamoDB Streams, as shown in Figure 11.13. To use this table-level feature, enable Amazon DynamoDB Streams on the table.

FIGURE 11.13   Amazon DynamoDB Stream

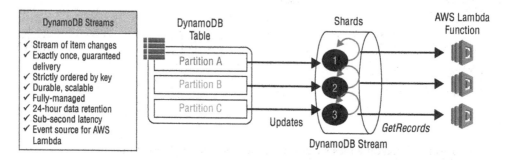

Amazon DynamoDB Streams Use Case

Amazon DynamoDB Streams is a database trigger for Amazon DynamoDB tables that you can use in any situation in which you continuously poll the database to indicate if a variable changes. An example would be a customer who publishes a vote in an Amazon DynamDB table called votes in an online application. With Amazon DynamoDB Streams, you can automatically track that change in both the votes table and in the consumer table to update the aggregate votes counted.

Amazon DynamoDB Streams Consumers

Amazon DynamoDB integrates with AWS Lambda so that you can create *triggers*, which are pieces of code that automatically respond to events in DynamoDB Streams. With triggers, you can build applications that react to data modifications in DynamoDB tables.

An AWS Lambda function or application that accesses the Amazon DynamoDB Streams API consumes the event when it publishes in the stream.

If you enable DynamoDB Streams on a table, you can associate the stream ARN with a Lambda function that you write. Immediately after you modify an item in the table, a new record appears in the table's stream. AWS Lambda polls the stream and invokes your AWS Lambda function synchronously when it detects new stream records.

The AWS Lambda function can perform any actions you specify, such as to send a notification or initiate a workflow. For example, you can write a Lambda function simply to copy each stream record to persistent storage, such as Amazon S3, to create a permanent audit trail of write activity in your table. Or, suppose that you have a mobile gaming app that writes to a GameScores table. Whenever the TopScore attribute of the GameScores table updates, a stream record writes to the table's stream. This event could then trigger an AWS Lambda function that posts a congratulatory message on a social media network. The function would ignore any stream records that are not updates to GameScores or that do not modify the TopScore attribute.

Amazon DynamoDB Streams Concurrency and Shards

When you run an Amazon DynamoDB as a database backend, a large number of changes can occur at the same time. Amazon DynamoDB Streams publishes the changes in your table into multiple *shards*.

If you create a consumer application using AWS Lambda, each AWS Lambda instance processes the messages in a particular shard. This enables *concurrent* processing and allows Amazon DynamoDB Streams to scale to handle a high volume of concurrent changes. At any given time, each partition in an Amazon DynamoDB table maps to a single shard. The single shard captures all updates to that partition.

AWS IoT Device Management

AWS IoT Device Management is a cloud-based service that makes it easy for customers to manage IoT devices securely throughout their lifecycle. Customers can use *AWS IoT Device Management* to onboard device information and configuration, organize their device inventory, monitor their fleet of devices, and remotely manage devices deployed across many locations. This remote management includes *over-the-air* (OTA) updates to device software.

AWS IoT is a service that manages devices associated with the Internet of Things, collects data from them, and sends out commands with updates to their state. The devices can communicate to the service with Message Queuing Telemetry Transport (MQTT) or HTTP. MQTT is a fire-and-forget asynchronous communication protocol that uses binary encoding. To view the AWS flow for IoT, refer to Figure 11.14.

FIGURE 11.14 AWS IoT Device Management

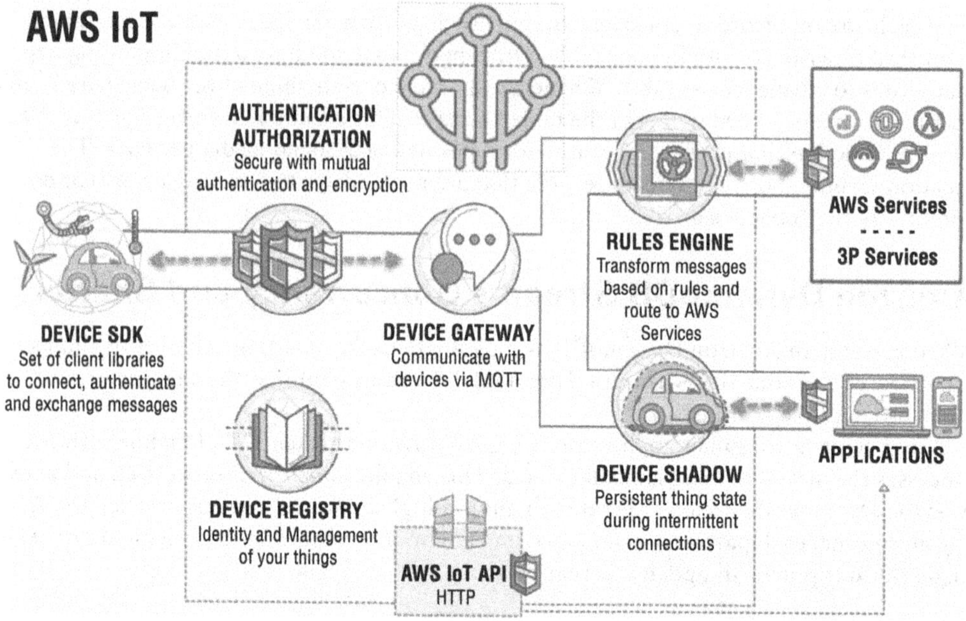

Rules Engine

When messages enter the AWS IoT Device Management service, the service dispatches them to different AWS endpoints. AWS IoT rule actions specify what to do when a rule is triggered. AWS IoT can dispatch the messages to AWS Lambda, an Amazon Kinesis data stream, a DynamoDB database, and other services. This dispatch is done through the *AWS IoT rules engine*. Rules give your devices the ability to interact with AWS products and services. Rules are analyzed, and actions occur based on the MQTT topic stream.

The IoT rules engine supports the following actions:

CloudWatch alarm action Use this to change the Amazon CloudWatch alarm state. Specify the state change reason and value in this call.

Amazon CloudWatch metric action The CloudWatch metric action allows you to capture an Amazon CloudWatch metric. Specify the metric namespace, name, value, unit, and timestamp.

DynamoDB action The dynamoDB action allows you to write all or part of an MQTT message to an Amazon DynamoDB table.

DynamoDBv2 action The dynamoDBv2 action allows you to write all or part of an MQTT message to an Amazon DynamoDB table. Each attribute in the payload is written to a separate column in the Amazon DynamoDB database.

Elasticsearch action The elasticsearch action allows you to write data from MQTT messages to an Amazon ES domain. You can query and visualize data in Amazon ES with tools such as Kibana.

Firehose action   A firehose action sends data from an MQTT message that triggers the rule to a Kinesis Data Firehose stream.

IoT Analytics action   An iotAnalytics action sends data from the MQTT message that triggers the rule to an AWS IoT Analytics channel.

Kinesis action   The kinesis action allows you to write data from MQTT messages into a Kinesis stream.

Lambda action   A lambda action calls an AWS Lambda function to pass it to a MQTT message that triggers the rule.

Republish action   The republish action allows you to republish the message that triggers the role to another MQTT topic.

S3 action   An s3 action writes the data from the MQTT message that triggers the rule to an Amazon S3 bucket.

Salesforce action   A salesforce action sends data from the MQTT message that triggers the rule to a Salesforce IoT Input Stream.

SNS action   An sns action sends the data from the MQTT message that triggers the rule as an Amazon SNS push notification.

Amazon SQS action   An sqs action sends data from the MQTT message that triggers the rule to an Amazon SQS queue.

Step Functions action   A stepFunctions action starts execution of an AWS Step Functions state machine.

The AWS IoT rules engine does not currently retry delivery for messages that fail to publish to another service.

Message Broker

The *AWS IoT message broker* is a publish/subscribe broker service that enables you to send messages to and receive messages from IoT. When you communicate with AWS IoT, a client sends a message to a topic address such as Sensor/temp/room1. The message broker then sends the message to all clients that have registered to receive messages for that topic. The act of sending the message is referred to as *publishing*. The act of registering to receive messages for a topic filter is referred to as *subscribing*.

The topic namespace is isolated for each account and region pair. For example, the Sensor/temp/room1 topic for an account is independent from the Sensor/temp/room1 topic for another account. This is true of regions, too. The Sensor/temp/room1 topic in the same account in us-east-1 is independent from the same topic in us-east-2.

AWS IoT does not send and receive messages across AWS accounts and regions.

The message broker maintains a list of all client sessions and the subscriptions for each session. When a message publishes on a topic, the broker checks for sessions with subscriptions that map to the topic. The broker then forwards the message to all sessions that have a currently connected client.

Device Shadow

The *AWS IoT device shadow* is an always-available representation of the device, which allows communications back from cloud applications to the IoT devices. Cloud applications can update the device shadow even when the underlying IoT device is offline. Then when the device is brought back online, it synchronizes its final state with a query to the AWS IoT service for the current state of the instances.

A device's shadow is a JavaScript Object Notation (JSON) document that stores and retrieves current state information for a device. The device shadow service maintains a shadow for each device that you connect to AWS IoT. You can use the shadow to get and set the state of a device over MQTT or HTTP, regardless of whether the device is connected to the internet. Each device's shadow is uniquely identified by the name of the corresponding thing. The device shadow service acts as an intermediary that allows devices and applications to retrieve and update a device's shadow.

Amazon MQ

Amazon MQ is a managed message broker service for Apache ActiveMQ that makes it easy to migrate to a message broker on the cloud. Amazon MQ is a managed Apache Active MQ that runs on Amazon EC2 instances that you select. AWS manages the instances, the operating system, and the Apache Active MQ software stack. You place these instances in your Amazon Virtual Private Cloud (Amazon VPC) and control access to them through security groups.

Amazon MQ makes it easy to migrate to a message broker on the cloud. A message broker allows software applications and components to communicate with the use of various programming languages, operating systems, and formal messaging protocols.

A broker is a message broker environment that runs on Amazon MQ. It is the basic building block of Amazon MQ. The combined description of the broker instance class (m5, t2) and size (large, micro) is a broker instance type (for example, mq.m5.large).

A *single-instance broker* is composed of one broker in one Availability Zone. The broker communicates with your application and with an AWS storage location.

An *active/standby broker for high availability* consists of two brokers in two different Availability Zones, which you configure in a redundant pair. These brokers communicate synchronously with your application and with a shared storage location.

You can enable automatic minor version upgrades to new versions of the broker engine, as Apache releases new versions. Automatic upgrades occur during the 2-hour maintenance window that you define by the day of the week, the time of day (in the 24-hour format), and the time zone (UTC, by default).

Amazon MQ works with your existing applications and services without the need to manage, operate, or maintain your own messaging system.

Amazon MQ is a managed message broker service that provides compatibility with many popular message brokers. AWS recommends Amazon MQ to migrate applications from current message brokers that rely on compatibility with APIs, such as JMS, or protocols like Advanced Message Queuing Protocol (AMQP), MQTT, OpenWire, and STOMP.

Amazon SQS and Amazon SNS are queue and topic services that are highly scalable, simple to use, and do not require you to set up message brokers. AWS recommends these services for new applications that can benefit from nearly unlimited scalability and simple APIs.

AWS Step Functions

The *AWS Step Functions* service enables you to launch and develop workflows that can run for up to several months, and it allows you to monitor the progress of these workflows. You can coordinate the components of distributed applications and microservices by using visual workflows to build applications quickly, scale and recover reliably, and evolve application easily. Figure 11.15 displays the AWS Step Functions service.

FIGURE 11.15 AWS Step Functions

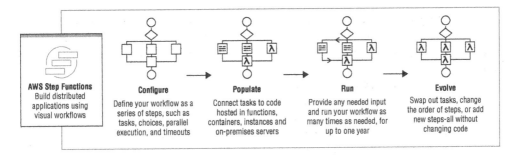

State Machine

The *state machine* is the workflow template that is made up of a collection of states. Each time you launch a workflow, you provide it with an input. Each state that is part of the state machine receives the input, modifies it, and passes it to the next state.

These workflow templates are called *state machines*. You can use AWS Step Functions as event sources to trigger AWS Lambda. Figure 11.16 is an example of using the AWS Step Functions service.

FIGURE 11.16   State machine code and visual workflow

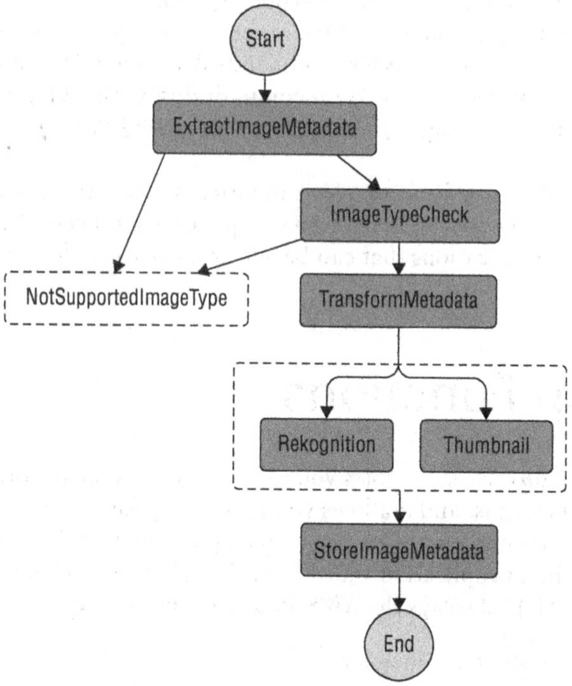

Use AWS Step Functions to build visual workflows that enable fast translation of business requirements into technical requirements. You can build applications in a matter of minutes. When your needs change, you can swap or reorganize components without customizing any code.

AWS Step Functions manages state, checkpoints, and restarts for you to make sure that your application executes in order and as you would expect. Built-in try/catch, retry, and rollback capabilities deal with errors and exceptions automatically.

AWS Step Functions manages the logic of your application for you, and it implements basic primitives such as branching, parallel execution, and timeouts. This removes extra code that may be repeated in your microservices and functions.

A finite state machine can express an algorithm as a number of states, their relationships, and their input and output. AWS Step Functions allows you to coordinate individual tasks by expressing your workflow as a finite state machine, written in the *Amazon States Language*. Individual states can decide based on their input, perform actions, and pass output to other states. In Step Functions, you can express your workflows in the Amazon States Language, and the *Step Functions console* provides a graphical representation of that state machine to help visualize your application logic.

Names identify states, which can be any string, but must be unique within the state machine specification. Otherwise, it can be any valid string in JSON text format.

 An instance of a state exists until the end of its execution.

States can perform the following functions in your state machine:

Task state: Performs work in your state machine

Choice state: Makes a choice between branches of execution

Fail or Succeed state: Stops an execution with a failure or success

Pass state: Passes inputs to outputs or inject corrected data

Wait state: Provides a delay for a certain amount of time or until a specified time/date

Parallel state: Begins parallel branches of execution

Here is an example state named HelloWorld, which performs an AWS Lambda function:

```
"HelloWorld": {
  "Type": "Task",
  "Resource": "arn:aws:lambda:us-east-1:123456789012:function:HelloFunction",
  "Next": "AfterHelloWorldState",
  "Comment": "Run the HelloWorld Lambda function"
}
```

States share the following common features:

- Each state must have a Type field to indicate what type of state it is.
- Each state can have an optional Comment field to hold a human-readable comment about, or description of, the state.
- Each state (except a Succeed or Fail state) requires a Next field or, alternatively, can become a terminal state if you specify an End field.

These fields are common within each state:

- **Type** (Required): The state's type.
- **Next:** The name of the next state that runs when the current state finishes. Some state types, such as Choice, allow multiple transition states.
- **End:** Designates this state as a terminal state (it ends the execution) if set to true. There can be any number of terminal states per state machine. State supports only one Next or End statement. Some state types, such as Choice, do not support or use the End field.

- **Comment** (Optional): Holds a human-readable description of the state.

- **InputPath** (Optional): A path that selects a portion of the state's input to pass to the state's task process. If omitted, it has the value $, which designates the entire input.

- **OutputPath** (Optional): A path that selects a portion of the state's input to pass to the state's output. If omitted, it has the value $, which designates the entire input.

To see the Amazon Function State Language, refer to Figure 11.17.

FIGURE 11.17   Amazon Function State Language

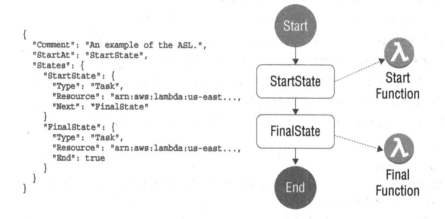

```
{
    "Comment": "An example of the ASL.",
    "StartAt": "StartState",
    "States": {
      "StartState": {
        "Type": "Task",
        "Resource": "arn:aws:lambda:us-east...",
        "Next": "FinalState"
      }
      "FinalState": {
        "Type": "Task",
        "Resource": "arn:aws:lambda:us-east...",
        "End": true
      }
    }
}
```

Task State

A *task state* involves a form of compute. A task executes on an AWS Lambda function or on an Amazon EC2 instance. An *activity* is a task that executes on an Amazon EC2 instance.

A task state ("Type": "Task") represents a single unit of work that a state machine performs.

In addition to the common state fields, task state fields include the following:

Resource (Required): Amazon Resource Name (ARN) that uniquely identifies the specific task to execute.

ResultPath (Optional): Specifies where in the input to place the results from the task Resource. The input is filtered as prescribed by the OutputPath field (if present) before being used as the state's output.

Retry (Optional): An array of objects, called *Retriers*, that define a retry policy if the state encounters runtime errors.

Catch (Optional): An array of objects, called *Catchers*, that define a fallback state. This state is executed if the state encounters runtime errors and the retry policy has been exhausted or is not defined.

TimeoutSeconds (Optional): If the task runs longer than the specified number of seconds, this state fails with a States.Timeout error name. This must be a positive, nonzero integer. If not provided, the default value is 99999999.

HeartbeatSeconds (Optional): If more time than the specified seconds elapses between heartbeats from the task, then this state fails with a States.Timeout error name. This must be a positive, nonzero integer less than the number of seconds specified in the TimeoutSeconds field. If not provided, the default value is 99999999.

A Task state either must set the End field to true if the state ends the execution or must provide a state in the Next field that runs upon completion of the Task state. Here's an example:

```
"ActivityState": {
  "Type": "Task",
  "Resource": "arn:aws:states:us-east-1:123456789012:activity:HelloWorld",
  "TimeoutSeconds": 300,
  "HeartbeatSeconds": 60,
  "Next": "NextState"
}
```

The ActivityState schedules the HelloWorld activity for execution in the us-east-1 region on the caller's account. When HelloWorld completes, the Next state (NextState) runs.

If this task fails to complete within 300 seconds or it does not send heartbeat notifications in intervals of 60 seconds, then the task is marked as failed. Set a Timeout value and a HeartbeatSeconds interval for long-running activities.

Specify Resource Amazon Resource Names in Tasks

To specify the Resource field's Amazon Resource Name (ARN), use the syntax:

```
arn:partition:service:region:account:task_type:name
```

where:

- partition is the AWS Step Functions partition to use, most commonly aws.
- service indicates the AWS service that you use to execute the task, which is one of the following values:
  - states for an activity
  - lambda for an AWS Lambda function
- region is the AWS region in which the Step Functions activity/state machine type or AWS Lambda function has been created.
- account is your Account ID.
- task_type is the type of task to run. It is one of the following:
  - activity: An activity
  - function: An AWS Lambda function
- name is the registered resource name (activity name or AWS Lambda function name).

Step Functions Referencing ARNs

You cannot reference ARNs across partitions with Step Functions. For example, aws-cn cannot invoke tasks in the aws partition, and vice versa.

Task Types

Task types support activity and AWS Lambda functions.

Activity   Activities represent workers (processes or threads) that you implement and host, which perform a specific task.

Activity resource ARNs use the following syntax:

```
arn:partition:states:region:account:activity:name
```

Create activities with Step Functions (using a CreateActivity API action or the Step Functions console) before their first use.

AWS Lambda Functions   Lambda tasks execute a function using AWS Lambda. To specify an AWS Lambda function, use the ARN of the AWS Lambda function in the Resource field. AWS Lambda function Resource ARNs use the following syntax:

```
arn:partition:lambda:region:account:function:function_name
```
Here's an example:
```
"LambdaState": {
  "Type": "Task",
  "Resource": "arn:aws:lambda:us-east-1:123456789012:function:HelloWorld",
  "Next": "NextState"
}
```

When the AWS Lambda function you specify in the Resource field completes, its output is sent to the state you identify in the Next field (NextState).

Choice State

The *Choice state* enables control flow between several different paths based on the input you select. In a choice state, you place a *condition* on the input. The state machine evaluates the condition, and it follows the path of the first condition that is true about the input.

A Choice state may have more than one Next, but only one within each Choice Rule. A Choice state cannot use End.

A Choice state ("Type": "Choice") adds branch logic to a state machine.

Other Choice state fields include the following:

Choices (Required) An array of Choice Rules that determines which state the state machine transitions to next

Default (Optional, Recommended) The name of the state to transition to if none of the transitions in Choices is taken

Choice states do not support the End field. They also use Next only inside their Choices field.

You must specify the $.type field. If the state input does not contain the $.type field, the execution fails, and an error displays in the execution history.

This is an example of a Choice state and other states to which it transitions:

```
"ChoiceStateX": {
  "Type": "Choice",
  "Choices": [
    {
        "Not": {
          "Variable": "$.type",
          "StringEquals": "Private"
        },
        "Next": "Public"
    },
    {
      "Variable": "$.value",
      "NumericEquals": 0,
      "Next": "ValueIsZero"
    },
    {
      "And": [
        {
          "Variable": "$.value",
          "NumericGreaterThanEquals": 20
        },
        {
          "Variable": "$.value",
          "NumericLessThan": 30
```

```
        }
      ],
        "Next": "ValueInTwenties"
      }
    ],
    "Default": "DefaultState"
},

"Public": {
  "Type" : "Task",
  "Resource": "arn:aws:lambda:us-east-1:123456789012:function:Foo",
  "Next": "NextState"
},

"ValueIsZero": {
  "Type" : "Task",
  "Resource": "arn:aws:lambda:us-east-1:123456789012:function:Zero",
  "Next": "NextState"
},

"ValueInTwenties": {
  "Type" : "Task",
  "Resource": "arn:aws:lambda:us-east-1:123456789012:function:Bar",
  "Next": "NextState"
},

"DefaultState": {
  "Type": "Fail",
  "Cause": "No Matches!"
}
```

In this example, the state machine starts with the input value:

```
{
  "type": "Private",
  "value": 22
}
```

Step Functions transitions to the ValueInTwenties state, based on the value field.

If there are no matches for the Choice state's Choices, the state in the Default field runs instead. If there is no value in the Default state, the execution fails with an error.

Choice Rules

A Choice state must have a `Choices` field whose value is a nonempty array and whose every element is an object called a Choice Rule. A Choice Rule contains the following:

Comparison   Two fields that specify an input variable to compare, the type of comparison, and the value to which to compare the variable.

Next field   The value of this field must match a `state` name in the state machine.

This example checks whether the numerical value is equal to 1:

```
{
  "Variable": "$.foo",
  "NumericEquals": 1,
  "Next": "FirstMatchState"
}
```

This example checks whether the string is equal to `MyString`:

```
{
  "Variable": "$.foo",
  "StringEquals": "MyString",
  "Next": "FirstMatchState"
}
```

This example checks whether the string is greater than `MyStringABC`:

```
{
  "Variable": "$.foo",
  "StringGreaterThan": "MyStringABC",
  "Next": "FirstMatchState"
}
```

This example checks whether the timestamp is equal to `2018-01-01T12:00:00Z`:

```
{
  "Variable": "$.foo",
  "TimestampEquals": "2018-01-01T12:00:00Z",
  "Next": "FirstMatchState"
}
```

Step Functions examines each of the Choice Rules in the order that they appear in the `Choices` field and transitions to the state you specify in the `Next` field of the first Choice Rule in which the variable matches the value equal to the comparison operator.

The comparison supports the following operators:

- And
- BooleanEquals

- Not
- NumericEquals
- NumericGreaterThan
- NumericGreaterThanEquals
- NumericLessThan
- NumericLessThanEquals
- Or
- StringEquals
- StringGreaterThan
- StringGreaterThanEquals
- StringLessThan
- StringLessThanEquals
- TimestampEquals
- TimestampGreaterThan
- TimestampGreaterThanEquals
- TimestampLessThan
- TimestampLessThanEquals

For each of these operators, the value corresponds to the appropriate type: string, number, Boolean, or timestamp. Step Functions do not attempt to match a numeric field to a string value. However, because timestamp fields are logically strings, you can match a timestamp field by a StringEquals comparator.

 For interoperability, do not assume that numeric comparisons work with values outside the magnitude or precision that the IEEE 754-2008 binary64 data type represents. In particular, integers outside of the range [-253+1, 253-1] might fail to compare in the way that you would expect.

Timestamps (for example, 2016-08-18T17:33:00Z) must conform to RFC3339 profile ISO 8601, with the following further restrictions:

- An uppercase T must separate the date and time portions.
- An uppercase Z must denote that a numeric time zone offset is not present.

To understand the behavior of string comparisons, see the Java compareTo documentation here:

```
https://docs.oracle.com/javase/8/docs/api/java/lang/
String.html#compareTo-java.lang.String-
```

The values of the And and Or operators must be nonempty arrays of Choice Rules that do not themselves contain Next fields. Likewise, the value of a Not operator must be a single Choice Rule with no Next fields.

You can create complex, nested Choice Rules using And, Not, and Or. However, the Next field can appear only in a top-level Choice Rule.

Parallel State

The *Parallel state* enables control flow to execute several different execution paths at the same time in parallel. This is useful if you have activities or tasks that do not depend on each other, can execute in parallel, and can help your workflow complete faster.

You can use the Parallel state ("Type": "Parallel") to create parallel branches of execution in your state machine.

In addition to the common state fields, Parallel states introduce these additional fields:

Branches (Required) An array of objects that specify state machines to execute in parallel. Each such state machine object must have the fields States and StartAt and mean the same as those in the top level of a state machine.

ResultPath (Optional) Specifies where in the input to place the output of the branches. The OutputPath field (if present) filters the input before it becomes the state's output.

Retry (Optional) An array of objects, called *Retriers*, which define a retry policy in case the state encounters runtime errors.

Catch (Optional) An array of objects, called *Catchers*, which define a fallback state that executes in case the state encounters runtime errors and you do not define the retry policy or it has been exhausted.

A Parallel state causes AWS Step Functions to execute each branch. The state starts with the name of the state in that branch's StartAt field, as concurrently as possible, and waits until all branches terminate (reach a terminal state) before it processes the Parallel state's Next field. Here's an example:

```
{
  "Comment": "Parallel Example.",
  "StartAt": "LookupCustomerInfo",
  "States": {
    "LookupCustomerInfo": {
      "Type": "Parallel",
      "End": true,
      "Branches": [
        {
          "StartAt": "LookupAddress",
          "States": {
            "LookupAddress": {
              "Type": "Task",
              "Resource":
                "arn:aws:lambda:us-east-1:123456789012:function:AddressFinder",
              "End": true
```

```
          }
        }
      },
      {
        "StartAt": "LookupPhone",
        "States": {
          "LookupPhone": {
            "Type": "Task",
            "Resource":
              "arn:aws:lambda:us-east-1:123456789012:function:PhoneFinder",
            "End": true
          }
        }
      }
    ]
  }
}
}
```

In this example, the LookupAddress and LookupPhone branches execute in parallel. Figure 11.18 displays the workflow in the Step Functions console.

FIGURE 11.18 Parallel state visual workflow

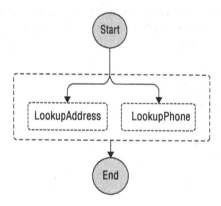

Each branch must be self-contained. A state in one branch of a Parallel state must not have a Next field that targets a field outside of that branch, nor can any other state outside the branch transition into that branch.

Parallel State Output

A Parallel state provides each branch with a copy of its own input data (InputPath). It generates output, which is an array with one element for each branch that contains the output from that branch. There is no requirement that all elements be of the same type. You can insert the output array into the input data (and the whole sent as the Parallel state's output) with a ResultPath field. Here's an example:

```
{
  "Comment": "Parallel Example.",
  "StartAt": "FunWithMath",
  "States": {
    "FunWithMath": {
    "Type": "Parallel",
    "End": true,
    "Branches": [
      {
        "StartAt": "Add",
        "States": {
          "Add": {
            "Type": "Task",
            "Resource": "arn:aws:swf:us-east-1:123456789012:task:Add",
            "End": true
          }
        }
      },
      {
        "StartAt": "Subtract",
        "States": {
          "Subtract": {
            "Type": "Task",
            "Resource": "arn:aws:swf:us-east-1:123456789012:task:Subtract",
            "End": true
          }
        }
      }
    ]
  }
 }
}
```

If the FunWithMath state was given the array [3, 2] as input, then both the Add and Subtract states receive that array as input. The output of Add would be 5, that of Subtract would be 1, and the output of the Parallel state would be an array.

[5, 1]

Error Handling

If any branch fails, because of an unhandled error or by a transition to a Fail state, the entire Parallel state fails, and all of its branches stop. If the error is not handled by the Parallel state itself, Step Functions stops the execution with an error.

 When a Parallel state fails, invoked AWS Lambda functions continue to run, and activity workers that process a task token do not stop.

To stop long-running activities, use heartbeats to detect whether Step Functions has stopped its branch, and stop workers that are processing tasks. If the state has failed, calling SendTaskHeartbeat, SendTaskSuccess, or SendTaskFailure generates an error.

You cannot stop AWS Lambda functions that are running. If you have implemented a fallback, use a Wait state so that cleanup work happens after the AWS Lambda function finishes.

End State

A state machine completes its execution when it reaches an *end state*. Each state defines either a next state or an end state, and the end state terminates the execution of the step function.

Input and Output

Each execution of the state machine requires an input as a JSON object and passes that input to the first state in the workflow. The state machine receives the initial input by the process initiating the execution. Each state modifies the input JSON object that it receives and injects its output into this object. The final state produces the output of the state machine.

Individual states receive JSON as the input and usually pass JSON as the output to the next state. *Understand how this information flows from state to state and learn how to filter and manipulate this data to design and implement workflows in AWS Step Functions effectively.*

In the Amazon States Language, three components filter and control the flow of JSON from state to state: InputPath, OutputPath, and ResultPath.

Figure 11.19 shows how JSON information moves through a task state. InputPath selects which components from the input to pass to the task of the Task state, for example, an AWS Lambda function. ResultPath then selects what combination of the state input and the task result to pass to the output. OutputPath can filter the JSON output to limit further the information that passes to the output.

FIGURE 11.19   Input and output processing

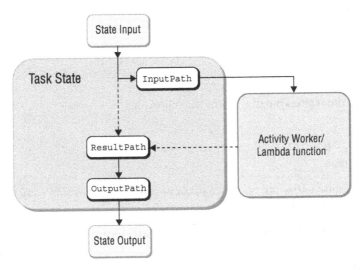

InputPath, OutputPath, and ResultPath each use paths to manipulate JSON as it moves through each state in your workflow.

> ResultPath uses reference paths, which limit scope so that it can identify only a single node in JSON.

Paths and Reference Paths

In this section, you will learn how to use paths and reference paths to process inputs and outputs.

Paths   In Amazon States Language, a *path* is a string that begins with $ that you can use to identify components within JSON text. Paths follow the JsonPath syntax.

Reference paths   A *reference path* is a path whose syntax can identify only a single node in a JSON structure.

You can access object fields with only a dot (.) and square brackets ([ ]) notation.

> Paths and reference paths do not support the operators @ .. , : ? * and functions such as length().

For example, state input data contains the following values:

```
{
    "foo": 123,
    "bar": ["a", "b", "c"],
    "car": {
        "cdr": true
    }
}
```

In this case, the reference paths return the following:

```
$.foo => 123
$.bar => ["a", "b", "c"]
$.car.cdr => true
```

Certain states use paths and reference paths to control the flow of a state machine or configure a state's options.

Paths in InputPath, ResultPath, and OutputPath Fields

To specify how to use part of the state's input and what to send as output to the next state, you can use InputPath, OutputPath, and ResultPath.

For InputPath and OutputPath, you must use a path that follows the JsonPath syntax.
For ResultPath, you must use a reference path.

InputPath The InputPath field selects a portion of the state's input to pass to the state's task to process. If you omit the field, it receives the $ value, which represents the entire input. If you use null, the input is not sent to the state's task, and the task receives JSON text representing an empty object {}.

A path can yield a selection of values. Here's an example:

```
{ "a": [1, 2, 3, 4] }
```

If you apply the path $.a[0:2], the result is as follows:

```
[ 1, 2 ]
```

ResultPath If a state executes a task, the task results are sent along as the state's output, which becomes the input for the next task.

If a state does not execute a task, the state's own input is sent, unmodified, as its output. However, when you specify a path in the value of a state's ResultPath and OutputPath fields, different scenarios become possible.

The ResultPath field takes the results of the state's task that executes and places them in the input. Next, the OutputPath field selects a portion of the input to send as the state's output. The ResultPath field might add the results of the state's task that executes to the input, overwrites an existing part, or overwrites the entire input.

- If the ResultPath matches an item in the state's input, only that input item is overwritten with the results of executing the state's task. The entire modified input becomes available to the state's output.

- If the ResultPath does not match an item in the state's input, an item adds to the input. The item contains the results of executing the state's task. The expanded input becomes available to the state's output.

- If the ResultPath has the default value of $, it matches the entire input. In this case, the results of the state execution overwrite the input entirely, and the input becomes available to pass along.

- If the ResultPath is null, the results of executing the state are discarded, and the input remains the same.

 ResultPath field values must be reference paths.

OutputPath If the OutputPath matches an item in the state's input, only that input item is selected. This input item becomes the state's output.

- If the OutputPath does not match an item in the state's input, an exception specifies an invalid path.

- If the OutputPath has the default value of $, this matches the entire input completely. In this case, the entire input passes to the next state.

- If the OutputPath is null, JSON text represents an empty object, {}, and is sent to the next state.

The following example demonstrates how InputPath, ResultPath, and OutputPath fields work in practice. Consider this input for the current state:

```
{
  "title": "Numbers to add",
  "numbers": { "val1": 3, "val2": 4 }
}
```

In addition, the state has the following InputPath, ResultPath, and OutputPath fields:

```
"InputPath": "$.numbers",
"ResultPath": "$.sum",
"OutputPath": "$"
```

The state's task receives only the numbers object from the input. In turn, if this task returns 7, the output of this state equals the following:

```
{
  "title": "Numbers to add",
  "numbers": { "val1": 3, "val2": 4 }
  "sum": 7
}
```

You can modify the OutputPath as follows:

```
"InputPath": "$.numbers",
"ResultPath": "$.sum",
"OutputPath": "$.sum"
```

As before, you use the following state input data:

```
{
  "numbers": { "val1": 3, "val2": 4 }
}
```

However, now the state output data is 7.

AWS Step Functions Use Case

You can use state machines to process long-running workflows. For example, if a customer orders a book and it requires several different events, use the state machine to run all the events. When the customer orders the book, the state machine creates a credit card transaction, generates a tracking number for the book, notifies the warehouse to ship the order, and then emails the tracking number to the customer. The AWS Step Functions service runs all these steps.

The benefit of AWS Step Functions is that it enables the compute to be stateless. The AWS Lambda functions and the Amazon EC2 instances provide compute to the state machine to execute in a stateless way. AWS Lambda functions and Amazon EC2 do not have to remember the information about the state of the current execution. The AWS Step Functions service remembers the information about the state of the current execution.

Summary

This chapter covered the different services to refactor larger systems into smaller components that can communicate with each other through infrastructure services. To be successful, the refactoring infrastructure must exist, which enables the different components to communicate with each other. You also now know about the different infrastructure communication services that AWS provides for different use cases.

Exam Essentials

Know how refactoring to microservices is beneficial and what services it includes.   This includes the use of the Amazon Simple Queue Service (Amazon SQS), Amazon Simple Notification Service (Amazon SNS), Amazon Kinesis Data Streams, Amazon Kinesis services, Amazon DynamoDB Streams, AWS Internet of Things (IoT), Amazon Message Query (Amazon MQ), and AWS Step Functions.

Know about the Amazon Simple Queue Service.   Know that the Amazon Simple Queue Service (Amazon SQS) is a fully managed message queuing service that makes it easy to decouple and scale microservices, distributed systems, and serverless applications. *There will be questions about the dead-letter queue and how to pass messages with Amazon CloudWatch.*

Know about the Amazon Simple Notification Service.   Familiarize yourself with the Amazon Simple Notification Service (Amazon SNS) and how it is a flexible, fully managed producer/consumer (publisher/subscriber) messaging and mobile notifications web service for coordinating the delivery of messages to subscribing to endpoints and clients. Amazon SNS coordinates and manages the delivery or sending of messages to subscriber endpoints or clients.

Know about Amazon Kinesis Data Streams.   Study how Amazon Kinesis Data Streams is a service for ingesting large amounts of data in real time and for performing real-time analytics on the data. Producers write data into Amazon Kinesis Data Streams, and consumers read data from it. Be familiar with the use of multiple applications, high throughput, real-time analytics, and open source tools that Kinesis supports. *There will be questions about producer and consumer options on the exam.*

Know about Amazon Kinesis Data Firehose.   Familiarize yourself with Amazon Kinesis Data Firehose latency. Amazon Kinesis Data Firehose also handles automatic scaling of the underlying shards of the stream based on the amount of traffic.

Know about Amazon Kinesis Data Analytics.   *There will also be questions about how Amazon Kinesis Data Analytics enables you to process and analyze streaming data with standard SQL.* Make sure that you know which destinations it supports.

Know about Amazon Kinesis Video Streams.   Know that the Amazon Kinesis Video Streams service allows you to push device video content into AWS and then onto the cloud to process that content and detect patterns in it. You can also use Amazon Kinesis Video Streams to build computer vision and machine learning applications.

Know about Amazon DynamoDB Streams.   Remember that Amazon DynamoDB Streams allows Amazon DynamoDB to publish a message every time a change is made in a table. When you insert, update, or delete an item, Amazon DynamoDB produces an event that publishes it to the Amazon DynamoDB Streams. Familiarize yourself with tables, consumers, concurrency, and streams.

Know about AWS Internet of Things (AWS IoT).   Make sure that you know that AWS IoT Device Management is a cloud-based device management service that makes it easy for customers to manage IoT devices securely throughout their lifecycle. Memorize information on the rules engine, message, broker, and device shadow.

Know about Amazon MQ.   Know that the primary use for Amazon MQ is to enable customers who use Apache Active MQ to migrate to the cloud. A message broker allows software applications and components to communicate with various programming languages, operating systems, and formal messaging protocols. Know how the Amazon SQS and Amazon SNS differ from Amazon MQ.

Know about AWS Step Functions.   The exam includes questions that require a thorough understanding of AWS Step Functions. Ensure that you know each step in the state machine, task state, Choice state, Parallel state, and end state. Remember the inputs and outputs in the step functions.

Know how state information flows and how to filter it.   Understand how this information flows from state to state and learn how to filter and manipulate this data to design and implement workflows effectively in AWS Step Functions.

Resources to Review

Amazon Simple Notification Service (Amazon SNS):

> `https://aws.amazon.com/sns/`

Amazon SNS Documentation:

> `https://docs.aws.amazon.com/sns/latest/dg/welcome.html`

Amazon SNS FAQs:

> `https://aws.amazon.com/sns/faqs/`

Amazon SNS Message Filtering:

> `https://docs.aws.amazon.com/sns/latest/dg/message-filtering.html`

Amazon SNS Mobile Push Notifications:

> `https://docs.aws.amazon.com/sns/latest/dg/SNSMobilePush.html`

Amazon SNS Mobile Push High-Level Steps:

> `https://docs.aws.amazon.com/sns/latest/dg/mobile-push-pseudo.html`

Add Amazon SNS Device Tokens or Registration IDs:

> `https://docs.aws.amazon.com/sns/latest/dg/`
> `mobile-push-send-devicetoken.html`

Amazon Simple Queue Service (Amazon SQS) Documentation:

> `https://aws.amazon.com/documentation/sqs/?id=docs_gateway`

Amazon SQS Dead-Letter Queues:

> https://docs.aws.amazon.com/AWSSimpleQueueService/latest/
> SQSDeveloperGuide/sqs-dead-letter-queues.html

Amazon SQS FAQs:

> https://aws.amazon.com/sqs/faqs/

Amazon SQS Features:

> https://aws.amazon.com/sqs/features/

Amazon SQS Resources:

> https://aws.amazon.com/sqs/resources/

Amazon SQS Visibility Timeout:

> https://docs.aws.amazon.com/AWSSimpleQueueService/latest/
> SQSDeveloperGuide/sqs-visibility-timeout.html

Amazon SQS FIFO Queues:

> https://docs.aws.amazon.com/AWSSimpleQueueService/latest/
> SQSDeveloperGuide/FIFO-queues.html

Amazon CloudWatch Documentation:

> https://aws.amazon.com/documentation/cloudwatch/

What is Amazon CloudWatch?

> https://docs.aws.amazon.com/AmazonCloudWatch/latest/monitoring/
> WhatIsCloudWatch.html

Pass Messages via Amazon CloudWatch:

> https://docs.aws.amazon.com/AmazonCloudWatch/latest/monitoring/
> US_SetupSNS.html

Amazon Kinesis:

> https://aws.amazon.com/kinesis/

Amazon Kinesis Data Streams Data Streams:

> https://aws.amazon.com/kinesis/data-streams/

Amazon Kinesis Data Streams Resources:

> https://aws.amazon.com/kinesis/data-streams/resources/

Resharding Amazon Kinesis Data Streams:

> https://docs.aws.amazon.com/streams/latest/dev/
> kinesis-using-sdk-java-resharding.html

Splitting Amazon Kinesis Data Streams Shards:

> https://docs.aws.amazon.com/streams/latest/dev/
> kinesis-using-sdk-java-resharding-split.html

Amazon Kinesis Data Firehose Data Delivery:

> https://docs.aws.amazon.com/firehose/latest/dev/basic-deliver.html

Amazon Kinesis Data Firehose FAQs:

> https://aws.amazon.com/kinesis/data-firehose/faqs/

Amazon Kinesis Data Firehose Streaming:

> https://aws.amazon.com/kinesis/data-firehose/

Amazon Kinesis Video Streams and How It Works:

> https://docs.aws.amazon.com/kinesisvideostreams/latest/dg/
> how-it-works.html

Amazon Kinesis Video Streams and What It is:

> https://docs.aws.amazon.com/kinesisvideostreams/latest/dg/
> what-is-kinesis-video.html

Amazon Kinesis Analytics RecordFormat:

> https://docs.aws.amazon.com/kinesisanalytics/latest/dev/
> API_RecordFormat.html

Amazon Kinesis Analytics API CSV Mapping Parameters:

> https://docs.aws.amazon.com/kinesisanalytics/latest/dev/
> API_CSVMappingParameters.html

Amazon Kinesis Analytics API Mapping Parameters:

> https://docs.aws.amazon.com/kinesisanalytics/latest/dev/
> API_MappingParameters.html

Amazon Kinesis Analytics Source Reference:

> https://docs.aws.amazon.com/kinesisanalytics/latest/dev/
> how-it-works-input.html#source-reference

Amazon DynamoDB Streams KCL Adapter:

> https://docs.aws.amazon.com/amazondynamodb/latest/developerguide/
> Streams.KCLAdapter.html

Amazon DynamoDB Streams:

> https://docs.aws.amazon.com/amazondynamodb/latest/developerguide/
> Streams.html

AWS IoT Analytics User Guide

> https://aws.amazon.com/documentation/iotanalytics/?id=docs_gateway

AWS Internet of Things (IoT):

> https://docs.aws.amazon.com/iotanalytics/latest/userguide/welcome.html

AWS IoT Analytics Rule Actions:

> https://docs.aws.amazon.com/iot/latest/developerguide/
> iot-rule-actions.html

Amazon MQ:

> https://aws.amazon.com/amazon-mq/

AWS Step Functions:

https://aws.amazon.com/step-functions/

AWS Step Functions Documentation:

https://aws.amazon.com/documentation/step-functions/

AWS Step Functions Input/Output Filters:

https://docs.aws.amazon.com/step-functions/latest/dg/
concepts-input-output-filtering.html

AWS Step Functions State Languages:

https://docs.aws.amazon.com/step-functions/latest/dg/
amazon-states-language-states.html

Amazon States Languages:

https://docs.aws.amazon.com/step-functions/latest/dg/
concepts-amazon-states-language.html

Download the code files from the book page at https://www.wiley.com/
en-us/AWS+Certified+Developer+Official+Study+Guide%3A+Associate
+%28DVA+C01%29+Exam-p-9781119508199. Click Downloads to access the
Online Materials for Chapter 11.

Exercises

EXERCISE 11.1

Create an Amazon SQS Queue, Add Messages, and Receive Messages

In this exercise, you will use the AWS SDK for Python (Boto) to create an Amazon SQS
queue, and then you will put messages in the queue. Finally, you will receive messages
from this queue and delete them.

1.   Make sure that you have AWS administrator credentials set up in your account.

2.   Install the AWS SDK for Python (Boto).

Refer to https://aws.amazon.com/sdk-for-python/.

3.   Enter the following code into your development environment for Python or the
IPython shell.

This is the code that you downloaded at the beginning of the exercises.

```
# Test SQS.
import boto3

# Pretty print.
import pprint
```

(continued)

```
pp = pprint.PrettyPrinter(indent=2)

# Create queue.
sqs = boto3.resource('sqs')
queue = sqs.create_queue(QueueName='test1')
print(queue.url)

# Get existing queue.
queue = sqs.get_queue_by_name(QueueName='test1')
print(queue.url)

# Get all queues.
for queue in sqs.queues.all(): print queue

# Send message.
response = queue.send_message(MessageBody='world')
pp.pprint(response)

# Send batch.
response = queue.send_messages(Entries=[
    { 'Id': '1', 'MessageBody': 'world' },
    { 'Id': '2', 'MessageBody': 'hello' } ])
pp.pprint(response)

# Receive and delete all messages.
for message in queue.receive_messages():
    pp.pprint(message)
    message.delete()

# Delete queue.
queue.delete()
```

4. Run the code.

   This creates a queue, sends messages to it, receives messages from it, deletes the messages, and then deletes the queue.

5. To experiment with the queue further, remove the comment //queue.delete() from the last line, which deletes the queue.

6. After you are satisfied with your changes, delete the code.

EXERCISE 11.2

Send an SMS Text Message to Your Mobile Phone with Amazon SNS

In this exercise, you will use Amazon SNS to publish an SMS message to your mobile phone. This solution can be useful when you run a job that will take several hours to complete, and you do not want to wait for it to finish. Instead, you can have your app send you an SMS text message when it is done.

1. Enter the following code into your development environment for Python or the IPython shell.

    This is the code that you downloaded at the beginning of the exercises.

    ```
    import boto3

    # Create SNS client.
    sns_client = boto3.client('sns')

    # Send message to your mobile number.
    # (Replace dummy mobile number with your number.)
    sns_client.publish(
      PhoneNumber='1-222-333-3333',
      Message='Hello from your app')
    ```

2. Replace the PhoneNumber value with your own number.

    The 1 at the beginning is the U.S. country code, 222 is the area code, and 333-3333 is the mobile phone number.

3. Run the code.

    Check your phone to view the message.

EXERCISE 11.3

Create an Amazon Kinesis Data Stream and Write/Read Data

In this exercise, you will create an Amazon Kinesis data stream, put records on it (write to the stream), and then get those records back (read from the stream). At the end, you will delete the stream.

1. Enter this code into your development environment for Python or the IPython shell.

    This is the code that you downloaded at the beginning of the exercises.

    ```
    import boto3
    import random
    ```

(continued)

```python
import json

# Create the client.
kinesis_client = boto3.client('kinesis')

# Create the stream.
kinesis_client.create_stream(
  StreamName='donut-sales',
  ShardCount=2)

# Wait for stream to be created.
waiter = kinesis_client.get_waiter('stream_exists')
waiter.wait(StreamName='donut-sales')

# Store each donut sale using location as partition key.
location = 'california'
data = b'{"flavor":"chocolate","quantity":12}'
kinesis_client.put_record(
    StreamName='donut-sales',
    PartitionKey=location, Data=data)
print("put_record: " + location + " -> " + data)

# Next lets put some random records.

# List of location, flavors, quantities.
locations = ['california', 'oregon', 'washington', 'alaska']
flavors = ['chocolate', 'glazed', 'apple', 'birthday']
quantities = [1, 6, 12, 20, 40]

# Generate some random records.
for i in xrange(20):

    # Generate random record.
    flavor = random.choice(flavors)
    location = random.choice(locations)
    quantity = random.choice(quantities)
    data = json.dumps({"flavor": flavor, "quantity": quantity})

    # Put record onto the stream.
    kinesis_client.put_record(
        StreamName='donut-sales',
        PartitionKey=location, Data=data)
```

```
        print("put_record: " + location + " -> " + data)

    # Get the records.

    # Get shard_ids.
    response = kinesis_client.list_shards(StreamName='donut-sales')
    shard_ids = [shard['ShardId'] for shard in response['Shards']]
    print("list_shards: " + str(shard_ids))

    # For each shard_id print out the records.
    for shard_id in shard_ids:

        # Print current shard_id.
        print("shard_id=" + shard_id)

        # Get a shard iterator from this shard.
        # TRIM_HORIZON means start from earliest record.
        response = kinesis_client.get_shard_iterator(
            StreamName='donut-sales',
            ShardId=shard_id,
            ShardIteratorType='TRIM_HORIZON')
        shard_iterator = response['ShardIterator']

        # Get records on shard and print them out.
        response = kinesis_client.get_records(ShardIterator=shard_iterator)
        records = response['Records']
        for record in records:
            location = record['PartitionKey']
            data = record['Data']
            print("get_records: " + location + " -> " + data)

    # Delete the stream.
    kinesis_client.delete_stream(
      StreamName='donut-sales')

    # Wait for stream to be deleted.
    waiter = kinesis_client.get_waiter('stream_not_exists')

    waiter.wait(StreamName='donut-sales')
```

2. Run the code.

Observe the output and how all the records for a specific location occur in the same shard. This is because they have the same partition keys. All records with the same partition key are sent to the same shard.

EXERCISE 11.4

Create an AWS Step Functions State Machine 1

In this exercise, you will create an AWS Step Functions state machine. The state machine will extract price and quantity from the input and inject the billing amount into the output.

This state machine will calculate how much to bill a customer based on the price and quantity of an item they purchased.

1. Sign in to the AWS Management Console and open the Step Functions console at `https://console.aws.amazon.com/step-functions/`.

2. Select **Get Started**.

3. On the **Define state machine** page, select **Author from scratch**.

4. In **Name type**, enter `order-machine`.

5. Enter the code for the state machine definition.

    This is the code that you downloaded at the beginning of the exercises.

    ```
    {
      "StartAt": "CreateOrder",
      "States": {
        "CreateOrder": {
          "Type": "Pass",
          "Result": {
            "Order" : {
              "Customer" : "Alice",
              "Product" : "Coffee",
              "Billing" : { "Price": 10.0, "Quantity": 4.0 }
            }
          },
          "Next": "CalculateAmount"
        },
        "CalculateAmount": {
          "Type": "Pass",
          "Result": 40.0,
          "ResultPath": "$.Order.Billing.Amount",
          "OutputPath": "$.Order.Billing",
          "End": true
        }
      }
    }
    ```

6. On the **State machine definition** page, select **Reload**.

   This updates the visual representation of the state machine. The state machine consists of two states: CreateOrder and CalculateAmount. They are both Pass types and pass hardcoded values.

   This is useful for build the outline of your final state machine. You can also use this to debug ResultPath and OutputPath. ResultPath determines where in the input to inject the result. OutputPath determines what data passes to the next state.

7. Select **Create state machine**.

8. Select **Start execution**.

9. In **Input type**, enter {}.

10. Select **Start execution**.

11. Expand **Output**, and it should look like the following:

    ```
    {
      "Price": 10,
      "Quantity": 4,
      "Amount": 40
    }
    ```

    In CalculateAmount, "ResultPath": "$.Order.Billing.Amount" injected Amount under Billing under Order. Then in the same element, "OutputPath": "$.Order.Billing" threw away the rest of the input and passed only the contents of the Billing element forward. This is why the output contains only Price, Quantity, and Amount.

12. (Optional) Experiment with different values of ResultPath to understand how it affects where the result of a state inserts into the input.

13. (Optional) Experiment with different values of OutputPath to understand how it affects what part of the data passes to the next state.

EXERCISE 11.5

Create an AWS Step Functions State Machine 2

In this exercise, you will create an AWS Step Functions state machine. The state machine will contain a conditional branch. It will use the Choice state to choose which state to transition to next.

(continued)

The state machine inspects the input and based on it decides whether the user ordered green tea, ordered black tea, or entered invalid input.

1. Sign in to the AWS Management Console and open the Step Functions console at: https://console.aws.amazon.com/step-functions/.

2. Select **Get Started**.

3. On the **Define state machine** page, select **Author from scratch**.

4. In **Name type**, enter **tea-machine**.

5. Enter the state machine definition.

   This is the code that you downloaded at the beginning of the exercises.

```
{
  "Comment" :
    "Input should look like {'tea':'green'} with double quotes instead of
single.",
  "StartAt": "MakeTea",
  "States" : {
    "MakeTea": {
      "Type": "Choice",
      "Choices": [
        {"Variable":"$.tea","StringEquals":"green","Next":"Green"},
        {"Variable":"$.tea","StringEquals":"black","Next":"Black"}
      ],
      "Default": "Error"
    },
    "Green": { "Type": "Pass", "End": true, "Result": "Green tea" },
    "Black": { "Type": "Pass", "End": true, "Result": "Black tea" },
    "Error": { "Type": "Pass", "End": true, "Result": "Bad input" }
  }
}
```

6. On the **State machine definition** page, select **Reload**.

   This updates the visual representation of the state machine. The MakeTea state is a Choice state. Based on the input it receives, it will branch out to Green, Black, or Error.

7. Select **Create state machine**.

8. Select **Start execution**.

9. In **Input type**, enter this value:

   `{ "tea" : "green" }`

10. Select **Start execution**.

11. Select **Expand Output**, and it should look like this:

    `"Green tea"`

12. (Optional) Experiment with different inputs to the state machine.

    For example, try the following inputs:

    For **Input type**, enter **black tea**. This input works.

    `{ "tea" : "black" }`

    For **Input type**, enter **orange tea**. This produces an error.

    `{ "tea" : "orange" }`

13. Change the state machine so that orange tea also works.

Review Questions

1. When a user submits a build into the build system, you want to send an email to the user, acknowledging that you have received the build request, and start the build. To perform these actions at the same time, what type of a state should you use?

   A. Choice

   B. Parallel

   C. Task

   D. Wait

2. Suppose that a queue has no consumers. The queue has a maximum message retention period of 14 days. After 14 days, what happens?

   A. After 14 days, the messages are deleted and move to the dead-letter queue.

   B. After 14 days, the messages are deleted and do not move to the dead-letter queue.

   C. After 14 days, the messages are not deleted.

   D. After 14 days, the messages become invisible.

3. What is size of an Amazon Simple Queue Service (Amazon SQS) message?

   A. 256 KB

   B. 128 KB

   C. 1 MB

   D. 5 MB

4. You want to send a 1 GB file through Amazon Simple Queue Service (Amazon SQS). How can you do this?

   A. This is not possible.

   B. Save the file in Amazon Simple Storage Service (Amazon S3) and then send a link to the file on Amazon SQS.

   C. Use AWS Lambda to push the file.

   D. Bypass the log server so that it does not get overloaded.

5. You want to design an application that sends a status email every morning to the system administrators. Which option will work?

   A. Create an Amazon SQS queue. Subscribe all the administrators to this queue. Set up an Amazon CloudWatch event to send a message on a daily cron schedule into the Amazon SQS queue.

   B. Create an Amazon SNS topic. Subscribe all the administrators to this topic. Set up an Amazon CloudWatch event to send a message on a daily cron schedule to this topic.

C. Create an Amazon SNS topic. Subscribe all the administrators to this topic. Set up an Amazon CloudWatch event to send a message on a daily cron schedule to an AWS Lambda function that generates a summary and publishes it to this topic.

D. Create an AWS Lambda function that sends out an email to the administrators every day directly with SMTP.

6. What is the size of an Amazon Simple Notification Service (Amazon SNS) message?

   A. 256 KB

   B. 128 KB

   C. 1 MB

   D. 5 MB

7. You have an Amazon Kinesis data stream with one shard and one producer. How many consumer applications can you consume from the stream?

   A. One consumer

   B. Two consumers

   C. Limitless number of consumers

   D. Limitless number of consumers as long as all consumers consume fewer than 2 MB and five transactions per second

8. A company has a website that sells books. It wants to find out which book is selling the most in real time. Every time a book is purchased, it produces an event. What service can you use to provide real-time analytics on the sales with a latency of 30 seconds?

   A. Amazon Simple Queue Service (Amazon SQS)

   B. Amazon Simple Notification Service (Amazon SNS)

   C. Amazon Kinesis Data Streams

   D. Amazon Kinesis Data Firehose

9. A company sells books in the 50 states of the United States. It publishes each sale into an Amazon Kinesis data stream with two shards. For the partition key, it uses the two-letter abbreviation of the state, such as WA for Washington, WY for Wyoming, and so on. Which of the following statements is true?

   A. The records for Washington are all on the same shard.

   B. The records for both Washington and Wyoming are on the same shard.

   C. The records for Washington are on a different shard than the records for Wyoming.

   D. The records for Washington are evenly distributed between the two shards.

10. What are the options for Amazon Kinesis Data Streams producers?

    A. Amazon Kinesis Agent

    B. Amazon Kinesis Data Steams API

    C. Amazon Kinesis Producer Library (KPL)

    D. Open-Source Tools

    E. All of these are valid options.

Chapter

12

Serverless Compute

**THE AWS CERTIFIED DEVELOPER –
ASSOCIATE EXAM TOPICS COVERED IN
THIS CHAPTER MAY INCLUDE, BUT ARE
NOT LIMITED TO, THE FOLLOWING:**

Domain 1: Deployment

✓ **1.3 Prepare the application deployment package to be
deployed to AWS.**

✓ **1.4 Deploy serverless applications.**

Domain 2: Security

✓ **2.1 Make authenticated calls to AWS Services.**

Domain 3: Development with AWS Services

✓ **3.1 Write code for serverless applications.**

✓ **3.4 Write code that interacts with AWS services by using
APIs, SDKs, and AWS CLI.**

Domain 5: Monitoring and Troubleshooting

✓ **5.1 Write code that can be monitored.**

✓ **5.2 Perform root cause analysis on faults found in
testing or production.**

Introduction to Serverless Compute

Serverless compute is a cloud computing execution model in which the AWS Cloud acts as the server and dynamically manages the allocation of machine resources. AWS bases the price on the amount of resources the application consumes rather than on prepurchased units of capacity.

For decades, people used local computers to interpret, process, and execute code, and they have encountered relatively few serious issues when they ran powerful web and data processing applications on their servers. However, this model has its problems.

The first issue with running servers is that you have to purchase them; a costly endeavor depending on the number of servers that you require for your project. Servers also depreciate and become obsolete, which facilitates the need to replace them.

Second, you must patch servers on a frequent and consistent manner to prevent security exploits. They require time-consuming maintenance to prolong their longevity. Servers may also experience hardware failures, which you must diagnose and repair. All of this consumes both time and money, which could be spent on other efforts such as improving applications.

Third, the needs of the users change over time. When an application first releases, it is not frequently accessed, and infrastructure needs are minimal. Over time, the application grows, and the infrastructure must also grow to accommodate it. This requires more servers, more maintenance, and more hardware costs. It also requires more time, as to add new servers to your data center can take several weeks or months.

AWS Lambda

AWS Lambda is the *AWS serverless compute* platform that enables you to run code without provisioning or managing servers. With AWS Lambda, you can run code for nearly any type of application or backend service—with zero administration. Only upload your code, and AWS Lambda performs all the tasks you require to run and scale your code with high availability. You can configure code to trigger automatically from other AWS services, or call it directly from any web or mobile app. AWS Lambda is sometimes referred to as a *function-as-a-service* (FaaS). AWS Lambda executes code whenever the function is triggered, and no *Amazon Elastic Compute Cloud* (Amazon EC2) instances need to be spun up in your infrastructure.

AWS Lambda offers several key benefits over Amazon EC2. First, there are no servers to manage. You are no longer responsible for provisioning or managing servers, patching servers, or worrying about high availability.

Second, you do not have to concern yourself with scaling. AWS Lambda automatically scales your application by running code in response to each trigger. Your code runs in parallel and processes each trigger individually, scaling precisely with the size of the workload.

Third, when you run Amazon EC2 instances, you are responsible for costs associated with the instance runtime. It does not matter whether your site receives little to no traffic— if the server is running, there are costs. With AWS Lambda, if no one executes the function or if the function is not triggered, no charges are incurred.

With the use of AWS Lambda and other AWS services, you can begin to decouple the application, which allows you to improve your ability to both scale horizontally and create asynchronous systems.

Where Did the Servers Go?

Serverless computing still requires servers, but the server management and capacity planning decisions are hidden from the developer or operator. You can use serverless code with code you deploy in traditional styles, such as microservices. Alternatively, you can write applications to be purely serverless with no provisioned servers.

AWS Lambda uses containerization to run your code. When your function is triggered, it creates a *container*. Then your code executes and returns your application or services the result. If a container is created on the first invocation, AWS refers to this as a *cold start*. Once the container starts to run, it remains active for several minutes before it terminates. If an invocation runs on a container that is already available, that invocation runs on a *warm container*.

By default, AWS Lambda runs containers inside the AWS environment, and not within your personal AWS account. However, you can also run AWS Lambda inside your *Amazon Virtual Private Cloud* (Amazon VPC). Figure 12.1 shows the execution flow process.

FIGURE 12.1 AWS Lambda execution flow

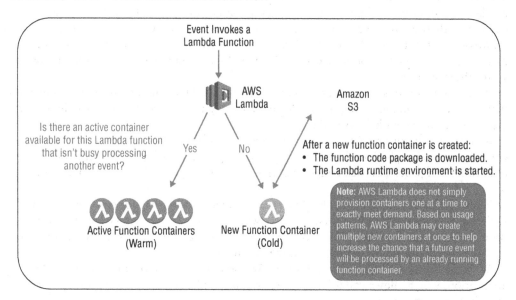

Monolithic vs. Microservices Architecture

Microservices are an architectural and organizational approach to software development whereby software is composed of small independent services that communicate over well-defined application programming interfaces (APIs). Small, self-contained teams own these services.

Historically, applications have been developed as *monolithic* architectures. With monolithic architectures, all processes are tightly coupled and run as a single service. If one process of the application experiences a spike in demand, you have to scale the entire architecture. To add or improve a monolithic application's features, it becomes more complicated as the code base grows. This complexity limits experimentation and makes it difficult to implement new ideas. Monolithic architectures increase the risk for application availability, as many dependent and tightly coupled processes increase the impact of a single process failure.

Microservices are more agile, and scaling is more flexible than with monolithic applications. You can deploy new portions of your code faster and more easily. With AWS Lambda and other services, you can begin to create microservices for your application.

AWS Lambda Functions

This section discusses how to use AWS Lambda to execute functions, such as how to create, secure, trigger, debug, monitor, improve, and test AWS Lambda functions.

Languages AWS Lambda Supports

AWS Lambda functions currently support the following languages:

- C# (.NET Core 1.0)
- C# (.NET Core 2.0)
- Go 1.*x*
- Java 8
- Node.js 4.3
- Node.js 6.10
- Node.js 8.10
- Python 2.7
- Python 3.6

Creating an AWS Lambda Function

You can use any of the following methods to access AWS services and create an AWS Lambda function that will call an AWS service:

- AWS Management Console—graphical user interface (GUI)
- AWS command line interface (AWS CLI)—Linux Shell and Windows PowerShell
- AWS Software Development Kit (AWS SDK)—Java, .NET, Node.js, PHP, Python, Ruby, Go, Browser, and C++
- AWS application programming interface (API)—send HTTP/HTTPS requests manually using API endpoints

In this chapter, you will create an AWS Lambda function and properties with the AWS Management Console. In the "Exercises" section, you will use AWS CLI and the Python SDK for the AWS Lambda function.

Launch the AWS Management Console, and select the AWS Lambda service under the Compute section (see Figure 12.2).

FIGURE 12.2   AWS Management Console

When you create an AWS Lambda function, there are three options:

Author from scratch   Manually create all settings and options.

Blueprints   Select a preconfigured template that you can modify.

Serverless application repository   Deploy a publicly shared application with the AWS Serverless Application Model (AWS SAM).

   There is no charge for this repository, as it is where you deploy a prebuilt application and then modify it.

When authoring from scratch, you must provide three details to create an AWS Lambda function:

- Name—name of the AWS Lambda function
- Runtime—language in which the AWS Lambda function is written
- Role—permissions of your functions

After you name the function and select a runtime language, you define an *AWS Identity and Access Management (IAM) role.*

Execution Methods/Invocation Models

There are two invocation models for AWS Lambda.

- Nonstreaming Event Source (Push Model)—Amazon Echo, Amazon Simple Storage Service (Amazon S3), Amazon Simple Notification Service (Amazon SNS), and Amazon Cognito
- Streaming Event Source (Pull Model)—Amazon Kinesis or Amazon DynamoDB stream

Additionally, you can execute an AWS Lambda function synchronously or asynchronously. The `InvocationType` parameter determines when to invoke an AWS Lambda function. This parameter has three possible values:

- **RequestReponse**—Execute synchronously.
- **Event**—Execute asynchronously.
- **DryRun**—Test that the caller permits the invocation but does not execute the function.

With an event source (*push model*), a service such as Amazon S3 invokes the AWS Lambda function each time an event occurs with the bucket you specify.

Figure 12.3 illustrates the push model flow.

1. You create an object in a bucket.
2. Amazon S3 detects the object-created event.
3. Amazon S3 invokes your AWS Lambda function according to the event source mapping in the bucket notification configuration.
4. AWS Lambda verifies the permissions policy attached to the AWS Lambda function to ensure that Amazon S3 has the necessary permissions.
5. AWS Lambda executes the AWS Lambda function, and the AWS Lambda function receives the event as a parameter.

FIGURE 12.3   Amazon S3 push model

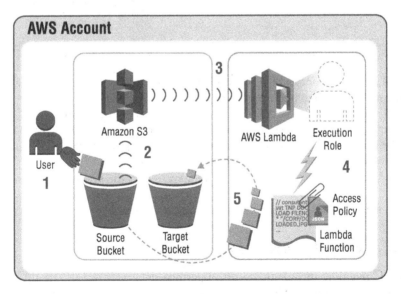

With a *pull model* invocation, AWS Lambda polls a stream and invokes the function upon detection of a new record on the stream. Amazon Kinesis uses the pull model.

Figure 12.4 illustrates the sequence for a pull model.

1. A custom application writes records to an Amazon Kinesis stream.

2. AWS Lambda continuously polls the stream and invokes the AWS Lambda function when the service detects new records on the stream. AWS Lambda knows which stream to poll and which AWS Lambda function to invoke based on the event source mapping you create in AWS Lambda.

3. Assuming that the attached permissions policy, which allows AWS Lambda to poll the stream, is verified, then AWS Lambda executes the function.

FIGURE 12.4   Amazon Kinesis pull model

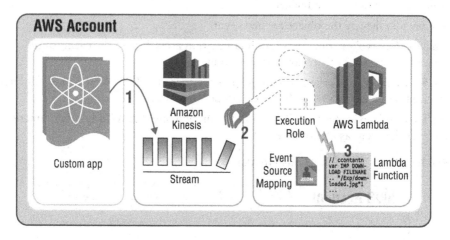

Figure 12.4 uses an Amazon Kinesis stream, but the same principle applies when you work with an Amazon DynamoDB stream.

The final way to invocate an AWS Lambda function applies to custom applications with the RequestReponse invocation type. Using this invocation method, AWS Lambda executes the function synchronously, returns the response immediately to the calling application, and alerts you to whether the invocation occurs.

Your application creates an HTTP POST request to pass the necessary parameters and invoke the function. To use this type of invocation model, you must set the RequestResponse in the X-Amz-Invocation-Type HTTP header.

Securing AWS Lambda Functions

AWS Lambda functions include two types of permissions.

Execution permissions enable the AWS Lambda function to access other AWS resources in your account. For example, if the AWS Lambda function needs access to Amazon S3 objects, you grant permissions through an AWS IAM role that AWS Lambda refers to as an *execution role*.

Invocation permissions are the permissions that an event source needs to communicate with your AWS Lambda function. Depending on the invocation model (push or pull), you can either update the access policy you associate with your AWS Lambda function (push) or update the execution role (pull).

AWS Lambda provides the following AWS permissions policies:

LambdaBasicExecutionRole   Grants permissions only for the Amazon CloudWatch logactions to write logs. Use this policy if your AWS Lambda function does not access any other AWS resources except writing logs.

LambdaKinesisExecutionRole   Grants permissions for Amazon Kinesis data stream and Amazon CloudWatch log actions. If you are writing an AWS Lambda function to process Amazon Kinesis stream events, attach this permissions policy.

LambdaDynamoDBExecutionRole   Grants permissions for Amazon DynamoDB stream and Amazon CloudWatch log actions. If you are writing an AWS Lambda function to process Amazon DynamoDB stream events, attach this permissions policy.

LambdaVPCAccessExecutionRole   Grants permissions for Amazon EC2 actions to manage elastic network interfaces. If you are writing an AWS Lambda function to access resources inside the Amazon VPC service, attach this permissions policy. The policy also grants permissions for Amazon CloudWatch log actions to write logs.

Inside the AWS Lambda Function

The primary purpose of AWS Lambda is to execute your code. You can use any libraries, artifacts, or compiled native binaries that execute on top of the runtime environment as part of your function code package. Because the runtime environment is a Linux-based *Amazon Machine Image* (AMI), always compile and test your components within the matching environment. To accomplish this, use AWS Serverless Application Model (AWS SAM) CLI to test AWS Lambda functions locally, which is also referred to as AWS SAM CLI (`https://github.com/awslabs/aws-sam-cli`).

Function Package

Two parts of the AWS Lambda function are considered critical: the *function package* and the *function handler.* The function code package contains everything you need to be available locally when your function is executed. At minimum, it contains your code for the function itself, but it may also contain other assets or files that your code references upon execution. This includes binaries, imports, or configuration files that your code/function needs. The maximum size of a function code package is 50 MB compressed and 250 MB extracted/decompressed.

You can create the AWS Lambda function by using the AWS Management Console, SDK, API, or with the `CreateFunction` API.

Use the AWS CLI to create a function with the commands, as shown here:

```
aws lambda create-function \
--region us-east-2 \
--function-name MyCLITestFunction \
--role arn:aws:iam:account-id:role/role_name \
--runtime python3.6 \
--handler MyCLITestFunction.my_handler \
--zip-file fileb://path/to/function/file.zip
```

Function Handler

When the AWS Lambda function is invoked, the code execution begins at the handler. The handler is a method inside the AWS Lambda function that you create and include in your package. The handler syntax depends on the language you use for the AWS Lambda function.

For *Python*, the handler is written as follows:

```
def aws lambda_handler(event, context):
        return "My First AWS Lambda Function"
```

For *Java*, it is written as follows:

```
MyOutput output handlerName(MyEvent event, Context context) {
        return "My First AWS Lambda Function"
    }
```

For *Node.js*, it is written as follows:

```
exports.handlerName = function(event, context, callback) {
        return "My First AWS Lambda Function"
    }
```

And for *C#*, it is written as follows:

```
myOutput HandlerName(MyEvent event, ILambdaContext context) {
        return "My First AWS Lambda Function"
    }
```

When the handler is specified and invoked, the code inside the handler executes. Your code can call other methods and functions within other files and classes that you store in the ZIP archive. The handler function can interact with other AWS services and make third-party API requests to web services that it might need to interact with.

Event Object

You can pass event objects that you pass into the handler function. For example, the Python function is written as follows:

```
def aws lambda_handler(event, context):
        return "My First AWS Lambda Function"
```

This first object you pass is the event object. The event includes all the data and metadata that your AWS Lambda function needs to implement the logic.

If you use the Amazon API Gateway service with the AWS Lambda function, it contains details of the HTTPS request that was made by the API client. Values, such as the path, query string, and the request body, are within the event object. The event object has different data depending on the event that it creates. For example, Amazon S3 has different values inside the event object than the Amazon API Gateway service.

Context Object

The second object that you pass to the handler is the context object. The context object contains data about the AWS Lambda function invocation itself. The context and structure of the object vary based on the AWS Lambda function language. There are three primary data points that the context object contains.

AWS Requestid   Tracks specific invocations of an AWS Lambda function, and it is important for error reports or when you need to contact AWS Support.

Remaining time   Amount of time in milliseconds that remain before your function timeout occurs. AWS Lambda functions can run a maximum of 300 seconds (5 minutes) as of this writing, but you can configure a shorter timeout.

Logging   Each language runtime provides the ability to stream log statements to Amazon CloudWatch Logs. The context object contains information about which Amazon CloudWatch Log stream your log statements are sent to.

Configuring the AWS Lambda Function

This section details how to configure the AWS Lambda functions.

Descriptions and Tags

An AWS best practice is to tag and give descriptions of your resources. As you start to scale services and create more resources on the AWS Cloud, identifying resources becomes a challenge if you do not implement a tagging strategy.

Memory

After you write your AWS Lambda function code, configure the function options. The first parameter is function memory. For each AWS Lambda function, increase or decrease the function resources (amount of random access memory). You can allocate 128 MB of RAM up to 3008 MB of RAM in 64-MB increments. This dictates the amount of memory available to your function when it executes and influences the central processing unit (CPU) and network resources available to your function.

Timeout

When you write your code, you must also configure how long your function executes for before a timeout is returned. The default timeout value is 3 seconds; however, you can specify a maximum of 300 seconds (5 minutes), the longest timeout value. You should not automatically set this function for the maximum value for your AWS Lambda function, as AWS charges based on execution time in 100-ms increments. If you have a function that fails quickly, you spend less money, because you do not wait a full 5 minutes to fail. If you wait on an external dependency that fails or you have programmed code incorrectly in your function, AWS Lambda processes the error for 5 minutes, or you can set it to fail within a fraction of that time to save time, cost, and resources.

After the execution of an AWS Lambda function completes or a timeout occurs, the response returns and all execution ceases. This includes any processes, subprocesses, or asynchronous process that your AWS Lambda function may have spawned during its execution.

Network Configuration

There are two ways to integrate your AWS Lambda functions with external dependencies (other AWS services, publicly hosted web services, and such) with an outbound network connection: default network configuration and Amazon VPC.

With the default network configuration, your AWS Lambda function communicates from inside an Amazon VPC that AWS Lambda manages. The AWS Lambda function can connect to the internet, but not to any privately deployed resources that run within your own VPCs, such as Amazon EC2 servers.

Your AWS Lambda function uses an Amazon VPC network configuration to communicate through an elastic network interface (NIC). This interface is provisioned within the Amazon VPC and subnets, which you choose within your own account. You can assign NIC to security groups, and traffic routes based on the route tables of the subnets where you place the NIC with the Amazon EC2 service.

If your AWS Lambda function does not need to connect to any privately deployed resources, such as an Amazon EC2, select the default networking option, as the VPC option requires you to manage more details when implementing an AWS Lambda function. These details include the following:

- Select an appropriate number of subnets, while you keep in mind the principles of high availability and Availability Zones.

- Allocate enough IP addresses for each subnet.

- Implement an Amazon VPC network design that permits your AWS Lambda function to have the correct connectivity and security to meet your requirements.

- Increase the AWS Lambda cold start times if your invocation pattern requires a new NIC to create just in time.

- Configure a network address translation (NAT) (instance or gateway) to enable outbound internet access.

If you deploy an AWS Lambda function with access to your Amazon VPC, use the following formula to estimate the NIC capacity:

```
Projected peak concurrent executions * (Memory in GB / 3GB)
```

If you had a peak of 400 concurrent executions, use 512 MB of memory. This results in about 68 network interfaces. You therefore need an Amazon VPC with at least 68 IP addresses available. This provides a /25 network that includes 128 IP addresses, minus the five that AWS uses. Next, you subtract the AWS addresses from the /25 network, which gives you 123 IP addresses.

AWS Lambda easily integrates with *AWS CloudTrail*, which records and delivers log files to your Amazon S3 bucket to monitor API usage inside your account.

Concurrency

Though AWS allows you to scale infinitely, AWS recommends that you fine-tune your concurrency options. By default, the account-level concurrency within a given region is set with 1,000 functions as a maximum to provide you 1,000 concurrent functions to execute. You can request a limit increase for concurrent executions from the AWS Support Center.

To view the account-level setting, use the GetAccountSettings API and view the AccountLimit object and the ConcurrentExecutions element.

For example, run this command in the AWS CLI:

```
aws lambda get-account-settings
```

This returns the following:

```
{
    "AccountLimit": {
        "CodeSizeUnzipped": number,
        "CodeSizeZipped": number,
        "ConcurrentExecutions": number,
        "TotalCodeSize": number,
        "UnreservedConcurrentExecutions": number
    },
    "AccountUsage": {
        "FunctionCount": number,
        "TotalCodeSize": number
    }
}
```

Concurrency Limits

Set a function-level concurrent execution limit. By default, the concurrent execution limit is enforced against the sum of the concurrent executions of all functions. The shared concurrent execution pool is referred to as the *unreserved concurrency allocation*. If you have not set up any function-level concurrency limit, the unreserved concurrency limit is the same as the *account level concurrency limit*. Any increases to the account-level limit will have a corresponding increase in the unreserved concurrency limit.

You can optionally set the *concurrent execution limit* for a function. Here are some examples:

- The default behavior is described as a surge of concurrent executions in one function, preventing the function you have isolated with an execution limit from being throttled. By setting a concurrent execution limit on a function, you reserve the specified concurrent execution value for that function.

- Functions scale automatically based on the incoming request rate, but not all resources in your architecture may be able to do so. For example, relational databases have limits on how many concurrent connections they can handle. You can set the concurrent execution limit for a function to align with the values of its downstream resources support.

- If your function connects to an Amazon VPC based resource, each concurrent execution consumes one IP within the assigned subnet. You can set the concurrent execution limit for a function to match the subnet size limits.

- If you need a function to stop processing any invocations, set the *concurrency* to 0 and then throttle all incoming executions.

By setting a concurrency limit on a function, AWS Lambda ensures that the allocation applies individually to that function, regardless of the number of traffic-processing remaining functions. If that limit is exceeded, the function is throttled. How that function behaves when throttled depends on the event source.

Dead Letter Queues

All applications and services experience failure. Reasons that an AWS Lambda function can fail include (but are not limited to) the following:

- Function times out while trying to reach an endpoint
- Function fails to parse input data successfully
- Function experiences resource constraints, such as out-of-memory errors or other timeouts

If any of these failures occur, your function generates an exception, which you handle with a dead letter queue (DLQ). A DLQ is either an Amazon Simple Notification Service (Amazon SNS) topic or an Amazon Simple Queue Service (Amazon SQS) queue, which you configure as the destination for all failed invocation events. If a failure event occurs, the DLQ retains the message that failed, analyzes it further, and reprocesses it if necessary.

For asynchronous event sources (InvocationType is a declared event), after two retries with automatic back-off between the retries, the event enters the DLQ, and you configure it as either an Amazon SNS topic or Amazon SQS queue.

After you enable DLQ on an AWS Lambda function, an Amazon CloudWatch metric (DeadLetterErrors) is available. The metric increments whenever the dead letter message payload cannot be sent to the DLQ at any time.

Environment Variables

AWS recommends that you separate code and configuration settings. Use *environment variables* for configuration settings. Environment variables are key-value pairs that you create and modify as part of your function configuration. These key-value pairs pass variables to your AWS Lambda function at execution time.

By default, environment variables are encrypted at rest, using a default KMS key of *aws/lambda*. Examples of environment variables that you can store include database (DB) connection strings and the type of environment (PROD, DEV, TEST, and such).

Versioning

You can publish one or more *versions* and *aliases* for your AWS Lambda functions. Versioning is an important feature to develop serverless compute architectures, as it allows you to create multiple versions without affecting what is currently deployed in the production environment. Each AWS Lambda function version has a unique *Amazon Resource Name* (ARN). After you publish a version, it is immutable, and you cannot change it.

After you create an AWS Lambda function, you can publish a version of that function. Here's an example with the AWS CLI:

```
aws lambda publish-version \
--region region \
--function-name myCoolFunction \
--profile devuser
```

This returns the version number along with other details after the command executes.

```
{
    "TracingConfig": {
        "Mode": "PassThrough"
    },
    "CodeSha256": "Sha265Hash",
    "FunctionName": "myCoolFunction",
    "CodeSize": 218,
    "MemorySize": 128,
    "FunctionArn": "arn:aws:lambda:region:account:function:myCoolFunction:1",
    "Version": "1",
    "Role": "arn:aws:iam::account:role/service-role/lambda-basic",
    "Timeout": 3,
    "LastModified": "2018-05-11T14:59:47.753+0000",
    "Handler":lambda_function.lambda_handler",
    "Runtime": "python3.6",
    "Description": ""
}
```

Creating an Alias

After you create a version of an AWS Lambda function, you *could* use that version number in the ARN to reference that exact version of the function. However, if you release an update to the AWS Lambda function, you must then locate all the places where you call that ARN inside the application and change the ARN to the new version number. Instead, assign an alias to a particular version and use that alias in the application.

Assign an alias of PROD to the newly created version 1, and use the alias version of the ARN in the application. This way, you change the AWS Lambda function without affecting the production environment. When you are ready to move the function to production for the next version, reassign the alias to a different version, as you can reassign the alias while the version numbers remain static. To create an alias with the AWS CLI, use this:

```
aws lambda create-alias \
--region region \
--function-name myCoolFunction \
--description "My Alias for Production" \
--function-version "1" \
--name PROD \
--profile devuser
```

Now point applications to the PROD alias for the AWS Lambda function. This allows you to modify the function and improve code without affecting production. To migrate the PROD alias to the next version, run the command where 4 is the example version.

```
aws lambda update-alias \
--region region \
--function-name myCoolFunction \
--function-version 4 \
--name PROD \
--profile devuser
```

The production system points to version 4 of the AWS Lambda function. As you can see with versioning and aliases, you can continue to innovate your service without affecting the current production systems.

Invoking AWS Lambda Functions

There are many ways to invoke an AWS Lambda function. You can use the push or pull method, use a custom application, or use a schedule and event to run an AWS Lambda trigger. AWS Lambda supports the following AWS services as event sources:

- Amazon S3
- Amazon DynamoDB
- Amazon Kinesis Data Streams
- Amazon SNS
- Amazon Simple Email Service
- Amazon Cognito
- AWS CloudFormation
- Amazon CloudWatch Logs
- Amazon CloudWatch Events

- AWS CodeCommit
- Scheduled events (powered by Amazon CloudWatch Events)
- AWS Config
- Amazon Alexa
- Amazon Lex
- Amazon API Gateway
- AWS IoT Button
- Amazon CloudFront
- Amazon Kinesis Data Firehose
- Manually invoking a Lambda function on demand

Monitoring AWS Lambda Functions

As with all AWS services and all applications, it is critical to monitor your environment and application. With AWS Lambda, there are two primary tools to monitor functions to ensure that they are running correctly and efficiently: *Amazon CloudWatch* and *AWS X-Ray*.

Using Amazon CloudWatch

Amazon CloudWatch monitors AWS Lambda functions. By default, AWS Lambda enables these metrics: invocation count, invocation duration, invocation errors, throttled invocations, iterator age, and DLQ errors.

You can leverage the reported metrics to set CloudWatch custom alarms. You can create a CloudWatch alarm that watches a single CloudWatch metric. The alarm performs one or more actions based on the value of the metric. The action can be an Amazon EC2 action, an Amazon EC2 Auto Scaling action, or a notification sent to an Amazon SNS topic.

The AWS Lambda namespace includes the metrics shown in Table 12.1.

TABLE 12.1   AWS Lambda Amazon CloudWatch Metrics

Metric	Description
Invocations	Measures the number of times a function is invoked in response to an event or invocation API call.
	Replaces the deprecated RequestCount metric.
	Includes successful and failed invocations but does not include throttled attempts. This equals the billed requests for the function.
	AWS Lambda sends these metrics to CloudWatch only if they have a nonzero value.
	Units: Count

Metric	Description
Errors	Measures the number of invocations that failed as the result of errors in the function (response code 4XX). Replaces the deprecated ErrorCount metric. Failed invocations may trigger a retry attempt that succeeds. This includes the following: • Handled exceptions (for example, context.fail(error)) • Unhandled exceptions causing the code to exit • Out-of-memory exceptions • Timeouts • Permissions errors This does not include invocations that fail because invocation rates exceeded default concurrent limits (error code 429) or failures resulting from internal service errors (error code 500). Units: Count
DeadLetterErrors	Incremented when AWS Lambda is unable to write the failed event payload to DLQs that you configure. This could be because of the following: • Permissions errors • Throttles from downstream services • Misconfigured resources • Timeouts Units: Count

Using AWS X-Ray

AWS X-Ray is a service that collects data about requests that your application serves, and it provides tools to view, filter, and gain insights into that data to identify issues and opportunities for optimization. For any traced request to the application, information displays about the request and response, but also about calls that the application makes to downstream AWS resources, microservices, databases, and HTTP web APIs.

There are three main parts to the X-Ray service:

• Application code runs and uses the *AWS X-Ray SDK* (Node.js, Java, and .NET, Ruby, Python, and Go).

• *AWS X-Ray daemon* is an application that listens for traffic on User Datagram Protocol (UDP) port 2000, gathers raw segment data, and relays it to the AWS X-Ray API.

• AWS X-Ray displays in the AWS Management Console.

With the AWS SDK, you integrate X-Ray into the application code. The AWS SDK records data about incoming and outgoing requests and sends it to the X-Ray daemon, which relays the data in batches to X-Ray. For example, when your application calls Amazon DynamoDB to retrieve user information from an Amazon DynamoDB table, the X-Ray SDK records data from both the client request and the downstream call to Amazon DynamoDB.

When the SDK sends data to the X-Ray daemon, the SDK sends JSON segment documents to a daemon process listening for UDP traffic. The X-Ray daemon buffers segments in a queue and uploads them to X-Ray in batches. The X-Ray daemon is available for Linux, Windows, and macOS, and it is included on both AWS Elastic Beanstalk and AWS Lambda platforms.

When the daemon sends the data to X-Ray, X-Ray uses trace data from the AWS resources that power the cloud applications to generate a detailed service graph. The *service graph* shows the client, your frontend service, and backend services that your frontend service calls to process requests and persist data. Use the service graph to identify bottlenecks, latency spikes, and other issues to improve the performance of your applications.

With X-Ray and the service map, as shown in Figure 12.5, you can visualize how your application is running and troubleshoot any errors.

FIGURE 12.5   AWS X-Ray service map

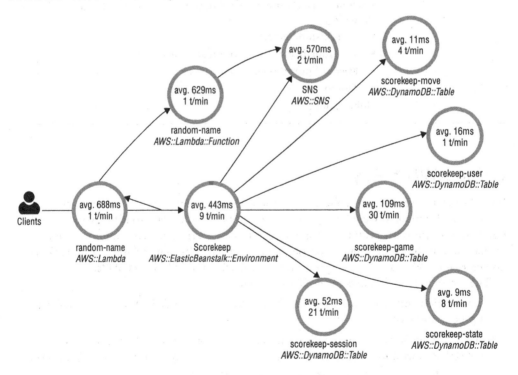

Summary

In this chapter, you learned about serverless compute, explored what it means to use a serverless service, and took an in-depth look at AWS Lambda. With AWS Lambda, you learned how to create a Lambda function with the AWS Management Console and AWS CLI and how to scale Lambda functions by specifying appropriate memory allocation settings and properly defining timeout values. Additionally, you took a closer look at the Lambda function handler, the event object, and the context object to use data from an event source with AWS Lambda. Finally, you looked at how to invoke Lambda functions by using both the push and pull models and monitor functions. We wrapped up the chapter with a brief look at Amazon CloudWatch and AWS X-Ray.

Exam Essentials

Know how to use execution context for reuse.   Take advantage of execution context reuse to improve the performance of your AWS Lambda function. Verify that any externalized configuration or dependencies that your code retrieves are stored and referenced locally after initial execution. Limit the re-initialization of variables or objects on every invocation. Instead, use static initialization/constructor, global/static variables, and singletons. Keep connections (HTTP or database) active, and reuse any that were established during a previous invocation.

Know how to use environmental variables.   Use environment variables to pass operational parameters to your AWS Lambda function. For example, if you are writing to an Amazon S3 bucket, instead of hardcoding the bucket name to which you are writing, configure the bucket name as an environment variable.

Know how to control the dependencies in your function's deployment package.   The AWS Lambda execution environment contains libraries, such as the AWS SDK, for the Node.js and Python runtimes. To enable the latest set of features and security updates, AWS Lambda periodically updates these libraries. These updates may introduce subtle changes to the behavior of your AWS Lambda function. Package all your dependencies with your deployment package to have full control of the dependencies that your function uses.

Know how to minimize your deployment package size to its runtime necessities.
Minimizing your deployment package size reduces the amount of time that it takes for your deployment package to download and unpack ahead of invocation. For functions authored in Java or .NET Core, it is best to not upload the entire AWS SDK library as part of your deployment package. Instead, select only the modules that include components of the SDK you need, such as Amazon DynamoDB, Amazon S3 SDK modules, and AWS Lambda core libraries.

Know how memory works.   Performing AWS Lambda function tests is a crucial step to ensure that you choose the optimum memory size configuration. Any increase in memory size triggers an equivalent increase in CPU that is available to your function. The memory usage for your function is determined per invocation, and it displays in the Amazon CloudWatch Logs.

Know how to load test your AWS Lambda function to determine an optimum timeout value. It is essential to analyze how long your function runs to determine any problems with a dependency service. Dependency services may increase the concurrency of the function beyond what you expect. This is especially important when your AWS Lambda function makes network calls to resources that may not handle AWS Lambda's scaling.

Know how permissions for IAM policies work.   Use the most-restrictive permissions when you set AWS IAM policies. Understand the resources and operations that your AWS Lambda function needs, and limit the execution role to these permissions.

Know how to use AWS Lambda metrics and Amazon CloudWatch alarms.   Use AWS Lambda metrics and Amazon CloudWatch alarms (instead of creating or updating a metric from within your AWS Lambda function code). This is a much more efficient way to track the health of your AWS Lambda functions, and it allows you to catch issues early in the development process. For instance, you can configure an alarm based on the expected duration of your AWS Lambda function execution time to address any bottlenecks or latencies attributable to your function code.

Know how to capture application errors.   Leverage your log library and AWS Lambda metrics and dimensions to catch application errors, such as ERR, ERROR, and WARNING.

Know how to create and use dead letter queues (DLQs).   Create and use DLQs to address and replay asynchronous function errors.

Resources to Review

AWS Lambda Documentation:

>   https://aws.amazon.com/documentation/lambda/

AWS Lambda Developer Guide

>   https://docs.aws.amazon.com/lambda/latest/dg/welcome.html

Invoke AWS Lambda Functions:

>   https://docs.aws.amazon.com/lambda/latest/dg/invoking-lambda-functions.html

Invoke AWS API:

>   https://docs.aws.amazon.com/lambda/latest/dg/API_Invoke.html

CreateFunction API:

>   https://docs.aws.amazon.com/lambda/latest/dg/API_CreateFunction.html

Function Handler Syntax:

https://docs.aws.amazon.com/lambda/latest/dg/programming-model-v2.html

AWS Lambda Pricing:

https://aws.amazon.com/lambda/pricing/

AWS Lambda with Amazon CloudWatch Metrics:

https://docs.aws.amazon.com/lambda/latest/dg/monitoring-functions-access-metrics.html

AWS Lambda Execution Environment and Libraries:

https://docs.aws.amazon.com/lambda/latest/dg/current-supported-versions.html

Python SDK Reference:

https://boto3.readthedocs.io/en/latest/reference/services/index.html

Invoke AWS Lambda Functions:

https://docs.aws.amazon.com/lambda/latest/dg/invoking-lambda-function.html#supported-event-source-dynamo-db

AWS Lambda Deployment Package:

https://docs.aws.amazon.com/lambda/latest/dg/deployment-package-v2.html

AWS Lambda Limits:

https://docs.aws.amazon.com/lambda/latest/dg/limits.html

AWS Serverless Application Model (SAM) Local (AWS SAM Local):

https://github.com/awslabs/aws-sam-cli

Exercises

Download the code files from the book page at https://www.wiley.com/en-us/AWS+Certified+Developer+Official+Study+Guide%3A+Associate+%28DVA+C01%29+Exam-p-9781119508199. Click Downloads to access the Online Materials for Chapter 12.

For these exercises, you are a developer for a shoe company. The shoe company has a third-party check processor who sends checks, pay stubs, and direct deposits to the shoe company's employees. The third-party service requires a JSON document with the employee's name, the number of hours they worked for the current week, and the employee's hourly rate. Unfortunately, the shoe company's payroll system exports this data only in CSV format. Devise a serverless method to convert the exported CSV file to JSON.

Create an Amazon S3 Bucket for CSV Ingestion

To solve this, create two Amazon S3 buckets (CSV ingestion and JSON output) and an AWS Lambda function to process the file.

After you export the CSV file, upload the file to Amazon S3. First, create an Amazon S3 bucket with the following Python code:

```python
import boto3
# Variables for the bucket name and the region we will be using.
# Important Note: s3 Buckets are globally unique, as such you need to change the
name of the bucket to something else.
# Important Note: If you would like to use us-east-1 as the region, when making
the s3.create_bucket call, then do not specify any region.
bucketName = "shoe-company-2018-ingestion-csv-demo"
bucketRegion = "us-west-1"

# Creates an s3 Resource; this is a higher level API type service for s3.
s3 = boto3.resource('s3')

# Creates a bucket
bucket = s3.create_bucket(ACL='private',Bucket=bucketName,CreateBucketConfiguration
={'LocationConstraint': bucketRegion})
```

This Python code creates a resource for interacting with the Amazon S3 service. After the resource is created, you can call the function .create_bucket to create a bucket.

After executing this Python code, verify that the bucket has been successfully created inside the Amazon S3 console. If it is not successfully created, the most likely cause is that the bucket name is not unique; therefore, renaming the bucket should solve the issue.

Create an Amazon S3 Bucket for Final Output JSON

To create the second bucket for final output, run the following:

```python
import boto3
# Variables for the bucket name and the region we will be using.
# Important Note: s3 Buckets are globally unique, as such you need to change the
name of the bucket to something else.
```

```
    # Important Note: If you would like to use us-east-1 as the region, when
    making the s3.create_bucket call, then do not specify any region.
bucketName = "shoe-company-2018-final-json-demo"
bucketRegion = "us-west-1"

# Creates an s3 Resource; this is a higher level API type service for s3.
s3 = boto3.resource('s3')

# Creates a bucket
bucket = s3.create_bucket(ACL='private',Bucket=bucketName,CreateBucketConfiguratio
n={'LocationConstraint': bucketRegion})
```

In the first exercise, you created the initial bucket for ingestion of the .csv file. This bucket
will be used for the final JSON output. Again, if you see any errors here, look at the error
logs. Verify that the bucket exists inside the Amazon S3 console. You will verify the
buckets programmatically in the next exercise.

EXERCISE 12.3

Verify List Buckets

To verify the two buckets, use the Python 3 SDK and run the following:

```
    import boto3
# Variables for the bucket name and the region we will be using.
# Important Note: Be sure to use the same bucket names you used in the previous
two exercises.
bucketInputName = "shoe-company-2018-ingestion-csv-demo"
bucketOutputName = "shoe-company-2018-final-json-demo"
bucketRegion = "us-west-1"

# Creates an s3 Resource; this is a higher level API type service for s3.
s3 = boto3.resource('s3')

# Get all of the buckets
bucket_iterator = s3.buckets.all()

# Loop through the buckets

for bucket in bucket_iterator:
    if bucket.name == bucketInputName:
        print("Found the input bucket\t:\t", bucket.name)
    if bucket.name == bucketOutputName:
        print("Found the output bucket\t:\t", bucket.name)
```

(continued)

Here, you are looping through the buckets, and if the two that you created are found, they are displayed. If everything is successful, then you should see output similar to the following:

```
Found the output bucket : shoe-company-2018-final-json-demo
Found the input bucket  : shoe-company-2018-ingestion-csv-demo
```

Prepare the AWS Lambda Function

To perform the conversion using the AWS CLI and the Python SDK, create the AWS Lambda function. The AWS CLI creates the AWS Lambda function. The Python SDK processes the files inside the AWS Lambda service.

In the following code, change the bucket names to bucket names you defined. The lambda_handler function passes the event parameter. This allows you to acquire the Amazon S3 bucket name.

Save this code to a file called lambda_function.py, and then compress the file.

 You can use a descriptive file name; however, remember to update the handler code in Exercise 12.6.

```python
import boto3
import csv
import json
import time
# The csv and json modules provide functionality for parsing
# and writing csv/json files. We can use these modules to
# quickly perform a data transformation
# You can read about the csv module here:
# https://docs.python.org/2/library/csv.html
# and JSON here:
# https://docs.python.org/2/library/json.html

# Create an s3 Resource: https://boto3.readthedocs.io/en/latest/guide/resources.html
s3 = boto3.resource('s3')
csv_local_file = '/tmp/input-payroll-data.csv'
json_local_file = '/tmp/output-payroll-data.json'

# Change this value to whatever you named the output s3 bucket in the previous
exercise
```

```
output_s3_bucket = 'shoe-company-2018-final-json-demo'

def lambda_handler(event, context):

    # Need to get the bucket name
    bucket_name = event['Records'][0]['s3']['bucket']['name']
    key = event['Records'][0]['s3']['object']['key']

    # Download the file to our AWS Lambda container environment
    try:
        s3.Bucket(bucket_name).download_file(key, csv_local_file)
    except Exception as e:
        print(e)
        print('Error getting object {} from bucket {}. Make sure they exist and your
        bucket is in the same region as this function.'.format(key, bucket_name))
        raise e

    # Open the csv and json files
    csv_file = open(csv_local_file, 'r')
    json_file = open(json_local_file, 'w')

    # Get a csv DictReader object to convert file to json
    dict_reader = csv.DictReader( csv_file )

    # Create an Employees array for JSON, use json.dumps to pass in the string
    json_conversion = json.dumps({'Employees': [row for row in dict_reader]})

    # Write to our json file
    json_file.write(json_conversion)

        # Close out the files
    csv_file.close()
    json_file.close()

    # Upload finished file to s3 bucket
    try:
        s3.Bucket(output_s3_bucket).upload_file(json_local_file, 'final-output-
        payroll.json')
    except Exception as e:
        print(e)
        print('Error uploading object {} to bucket {}. Make sure the file paths
        are correct.'.format(key, bucket_name))
        raise e

    print('Payroll processing completed at: ', time.asctime( time.localtime(time.
    time()) ) )
    return 'Payroll conversion from CSV to JSON complete.'
```

(continued)

After you create the code for the function, upload this file to Amazon S3 with the AWS CLI. This saves the code locally on your desktop and runs the following command. Be sure to compress the file.

```
aws s3 cp lambda_function.zip s3://shoe-company-2018-ingestion-csv-demo
```

If the following command successfully executed, you should see something similar to the following printed to the console:

```
upload: .\lambda_function.zip to s3://shoe-company-2018-ingestion-csv-demo/lambda_
function.zip
```

You may also verify that the file has been uploaded by using the AWS Management Console inside the Amazon S3 service.

Create AWS IAM Roles

In this exercise, create an AWS IAM role so that the AWS Lambda function has the correct permissions to execute the function with the AWS CLI. Create a JSON file of the trust relationship, which allows the AWS Lambda service to assume this particular IAM role with the Security Token Service.

Also create a policy document. A predefined policy document was distributed in the code example that you downloaded in Exercise 12.1. However, if you prefer to create the file manually, you can do so. The following is required for the exercise to work correctly:

```
lambda-trust-policy.json
{
    "Version": "2012-10-17",
    "Statement": [
        {
            "Effect": "Allow",
            "Principal": {
                "Service": "lambda.amazonaws.com"
            },
            "Action": "sts:AssumeRole"
        }
    ]
}
```

After the `lambda-trust-policy.json` document has been created, run the following command to create the IAM role:

```
aws iam create-role --role-name PayrollProcessingLambdaRole --description
"Provides AWS Lambda with access to s3 and cloudwatch to execute the
PayrollProcessing function" --assume-role-policy-document file://lambda-trust-
policy.json
```

A JSON object returns. Copy the RoleName and ARN roles for the next steps.

```
{
    "Role": {
        "AssumeRolePolicyDocument": {
            "Version": "2012-10-17",
            "Statement": [
                {
                    "Action": "sts:AssumeRole",
                    "Effect": "Allow",
                    "Principal": {
                        "Service": "lambda.amazonaws.com"
                    }
                }
            ]
        },
        "RoleId": "roleidnumber",
        "CreateDate": "2018-05-19T17:30:05.020Z",
        "RoleName": "PayrollProcessingLambdaRole",
        "Path": "/",
        "Arn": "arn:aws:iam::accountnumber:role/PayrollProcessingLambdaRole"
    }
}
```

After you create an AWS role, attach a policy to the role. There are two types of AWS policies: AWS managed and customer managed. AWS creates predefined policies that you can use called *AWS managed policies*. You may create *customer managed policies* specific to your requirements.

For this example, you will use an AWS managed policy built for AWS Lambda called AWSLambdaExecute. This provides AWS Lambda access to Amazon CloudWatch Logs and Amazon S3 GetObject and PutObject API calls.

```
aws iam attach-role-policy --role-name PayrollProcessingLambdaRole --policy-arn
arn:aws:iam::aws:policy/AWSLambdaExecute
```

(continued)

If this command successfully executes, it does not return results. To verify that the IAM role has been properly configured, from the AWS Management Console, go to the IAM service. Click Roles, and search for PayrollProcessingLambdaRole. On the **Permissions** tab, verify that the AWSLambdaExecute policy has been attached. On the **Trust relationships** tab, verify that the trusted entities states the following: "The identify provider(s) lambda.amazonaws.com."

You have successfully uploaded the Python code that has been compressed to Amazon S3, and you created an IAM role. In the next exercise, you will create the AWS Lambda function.

Create the AWS Lambda Function

In this exercise, create the AWS Lambda function. You can view the AWS Lambda API reference here:

https://docs.aws.amazon.com/cli/latest/reference/lambda/index.html

 For the --handler parameter, make sure that you specify the name of the .py file you created in Exercise 12.4. Also, make sure that for the S3Key parameter, you specify the name of the compressed file inside the Amazon S3 bucket.

Run this AWS CLI command:

```
aws lambda create-function --function-name PayrollProcessing --runtime python3.7
--role arn:aws:iam::accountnumber:role/PayrollProcessingLambdaRole --handler
lambda_function.lambda_handler --description "Converts Payroll CSVs to JSON
and puts the results in an s3 bucket." --timeout 3 --memory-size 128 --code
S3Bucket=shoe-company-2018-ingestion-csv-demo,S3Key=lambda_function.zip --tags
Environment="Production",Application="Payroll" --region us-west-1
```

If the command was successful, you receive a JSON response similar to the following:

```
{
    "FunctionName": "PayrollProcessing",
    "FunctionArn": "arn:aws:lambda:us-east-2:accountnumber:function:
    PayrollProcessing",
    "Runtime": "python3.7",
    "Role": "arn:aws:iam::accountnumber:role/PayrollProcessingLambdaRole",
    "Handler": "payroll.lambda_handler",
    "CodeSize": 1123,
    "Description": "Converts Payroll CSVs to JSON and puts the results in an s3
    bucket.",
```

```
    "Timeout": 3,
    "MemorySize": 128,
    "LastModified": "2018-12-10T06:36:27.990+0000",
    "CodeSha256": "NUKm2kp/fLzVr58t8XCTw6YGBmxR2E1Q9MHuW11QXfw=",
    "Version": "$LATEST",
    "TracingConfig": {
        "Mode": "PassThrough"
    },
    "RevisionId": "ae30524f-26a9-426a-b43a-efa522cb1545"
}
```

You have successfully created the AWS Lambda function. You can verify this from the AWS Management Console and opening the AWS Lambda console.

EXERCISE 12.7

Give Amazon S3 Permission to Invoke an AWS Lambda Function

In this exercise, use the AWS Lambda CLI add-permission command to invoke the AWS Lambda function.

```
aws lambda add-permission --function-name PayrollProcessing --statement-id
lambdas3permission --action lambda:InvokeFunction --principal s3.amazonaws.com
--source-arn arn:aws:s3:::shoe-company-2018-ingestion-csv-demo --source-account
yourawsaccountnumber --region us-west-1
```

After you run this command and it is successful, you should receive a JSON response that looks similar to the following:

```
{
    "Statement": {
        "Sid": "lambdas3permission",
        "Effect": "Allow",
        "Principal": {
            "Service": "s3.amazonaws.com"
        },
        "Action": "lambda:InvokeFunction",
        "Resource": "arn:aws:lambda:us-east-2:accountnumber:function:PayrollProce
        ssing",
        "Condition": {
            "StringEquals": {
                "AWS:SourceAccount": "accountnumber"
            },
```

(continued)

```
        "ArnLike": {
            "AWS:SourceArn": "arn:aws:s3:::shoe-company-2018-ingestion-csv-demo"
        }
      }
    }
}
```

This provides a function policy to the AWS Lambda function that allows the S3 bucket that you created to call the action `lambda:InvokeFunction`. You can verify this by navigating to the AWS Lambda service inside the AWS Management Console. In the **Designer** section, click the key icon to view permissions, and under **Function policy,** you will see the policy you just created.

Add the Amazon S3 Event Trigger

In this exercise, add the trigger for Amazon S3 using AWS CLI for the s3api commands. The `notification-config.json` file was provided in the exercise files. Its contents are as follows:

```
{
    "LambdaFunctionConfigurations": [
        {
            "Id": "s3PayrollFunctionObjectCreation",
            "LambdaFunctionArn": "arn:aws:lambda:us-west-1:accountnumber:function:
            PayrollProcessing",
            "Events": [
                "s3:ObjectCreated:*"
            ],
            "Filter": {
                "Key": {
                    "FilterRules": [
                        {
                            "Name": "suffix",
                            "Value": ".csv"
                        }
                    ]
                }
```

```
        }
      }
    ]
}
```

```
aws s3api put-bucket-notification-configuration --bucket shoe-company-2018-
ingestion-csv-demo --notification-configuration file://notification-config.json
```

If the execution is successful, no response is sent. To verify that the trigger has been added to the AWS Lambda function, navigate to the AWS Lambda console inside the AWS Management Console, and verify that there is now an Amazon S3 trigger.

EXERCISE 12.9

Test the AWS Lambda Function

To test the AWS Lambda function, use the AWS CLI to upload the CSV file to the Amazon S3 bucket; then check whether the function transforms the data and puts the result file in the output bucket.

```
aws s3 cp input-payroll-data.csv s3://shoe-company-2018-ingestion-csv-demo
```

If everything executes successfully, in the output bucket that you created, you should see the transformed JSON file. You accepted input into one Amazon S3 bucket as a .csv, transformed it to serverless by using AWS Lambda, and then stored the resulting .json file in a separate Amazon S3 bucket. If you do not see the file, retrace your steps through the exercises. It is a good idea to view the Amazon CloudWatch Logs, which can be found on the **Monitoring** tab in the AWS Lambda console. This way, you can determine whether there are any errors.

Review Questions

1. A company currently uses a serverless web application stack, which consists of Amazon API Gateway, Amazon Simple Storage Service (Amazon S3), Amazon DynamoDB, and AWS Lambda. They would like to make improvements to their AWS Lambda functions but do not want to impact their production functions.

    How can they accomplish this?

    A. Create new AWS Lambda functions with a different name, and update resources to point to the new functions when they are ready to test.

    B. Copy their AWS Lambda function to a new region where they can update their resources to the new region when ready.

    C. Create a new AWS account, and re-create all their serverless infrastructure for their application testing.

    D. Publish the current version of their AWS Lambda function, and create an alias as PROD. Then, assign PROD to the current version number, update resources with the PROD alias ARN, and create a new version of the updated AWS Lambda function and assign an alias of $DEV.

2. What is the maximum amount of memory that you can assign an AWS Lambda function?

    A. AWS runs the AWS Lambda function; it is a managed service, so you do not need to configure memory settings.

    B. 3008 MB

    C. 1000 MB

    D. 9008 MB

3. What is the default timeout value for an AWS Lambda function?

    A. 3 seconds

    B. 10 seconds

    C. 15 seconds

    D. 25 seconds

4. A company uses a third-party service to send checks to its employees for payroll. The company is required to send the third-party service a JSON file with the person's name and the check amount. The company's internal payroll application supports exporting only to CSVs, and it currently has *cron* jobs set up on their internal network to process these files. The server that is processing the data is aging, and the company is concerned that it might fail in the future. It is also looking to have the AWS services perform the payroll function.

    What would be the best serverless option to accomplish this goal?

    A. Create an Amazon Elastic Compute Cloud (Amazon EC2) and the necessary *cron* job to process the file from CSV to JSON.

    B. Use AWS Import/Export to create a virtual machine (VM) image of the on-premises server and upload the Amazon Machine Images (AMI) to AWS.

C. Use AWS Lambda to process the file with Amazon Simple Storage Service (Amazon S3).

D. There is no way to process this file with AWS.

5. What is the maximum execution time allowed for an AWS Lambda function?

A. 60 seconds

B. 120 seconds

C. 230 seconds

D. 300 seconds

6. Which language is *not* supported for AWS Lambda functions?

A. Ruby

B. Python 3.6

C. Node.js

D. C# (.NET Core)

7. How can you increase the limit of AWS Lambda concurrent executions?

A. Use the Support Center page in the AWS Management Console to open a case and send a Server Limit Increase request.

B. AWS Lambda does not have any limits for concurrent executions.

C. Send an email to limits@amazon.com with the subject "AWS Lambda Increase."

D. You cannot increase concurrent executions for AWS Lambda.

8. A company is receiving *permission denied* after its AWS Lambda function is invoked and executes and has a valid trust policy. After investigating, the company realizes that its AWS Lambda function does not have access to download objects from Amazon Simple Storage Service (Amazon S3).

Which type of policy do you need to correct to give access to the AWS Lambda function?

A. Function policy

B. Trust policy

C. Execution policy

D. None of the above

9. A company wants to be able to send event payloads to an Amazon Simple Queue Service (Amazon SQS) queue if the AWS Lambda function fails.

Which of the following configuration options does the company need to be able to do this in AWS Lambda?

A. Enable a dead-letter queue.

B. Define an Amazon Virtual Private Cloud (Amazon VPC) network.

C. Enable concurrency.

D. AWS Lambda does not support such a feature.

10. A company wants to be able to pass configuration settings as variables to their AWS Lambda function at execution time.

Which feature should the company use?

A. Dead-letter queues

B. AWS Lambda does not support such a feature.

C. Environment variables

D. None of the above

Chapter

13

Serverless Applications

**THE AWS CERTIFIED DEVELOPER –
ASSOCIATE EXAM TOPICS COVERED IN
THIS CHAPTER MAY INCLUDE, BUT ARE
NOT LIMITED TO, THE FOLLOWING:**

Domain 1: Deployment

✓ 1.4 Deploy serverless applications.

Domain 2: Security

✓ 2.1 Make authenticated calls to AWS Services.

✓ 2.3 Implement application authentication and
authorization.

Domain 3: Development with AWS Services

✓ 3.1 Write code for serverless applications.

✓ 3.2 Translate functional requirements into application
design.

✓ 3.3 Implement application design into application code.

✓ 3.3 Write code that interacts with AWS Services by
using APIs, SDKs, and AWS CLI.

Domain 5: Monitoring and Troubleshooting

✓ 5.1 Write code that you can monitor.

Introduction to Serverless Applications

In the previous chapter, you learned about AWS Lambda and how you can write functions that run in a serverless manner. A serverless application is typically a combination of AWS Lambda and other Amazon services. You build serverless applications to allow developers to focus on their core product instead of the need to manage and operate servers or runtimes in the cloud or on-premises. This reduces overhead and lets developers reclaim time and energy that can be better spent developing reliable, scalable products and new features for applications.

Serverless applications have the following three main benefits:

- No server management
- Flexible scaling
- Automated high availability

Without server management, you no longer have to provision or maintain servers. With AWS Lambda, you upload your code, run it, and focus on your application updates.

With flexible scaling, you no longer have to disable Amazon Elastic Compute Cloud (Amazon EC2) instances to scale them vertically, groups do not need to be auto-scaled, and you do not need to create Amazon CloudWatch alarms to add them to load balancers. With AWS Lambda, you adjust the units of consumption (memory and execution time) and AWS adjusts the rest of the instance appropriately.

Finally, serverless applications have built-in availability and fault tolerance. You do not need to architect for these capabilities, as the services that run the application provide them by default. Additionally, when periods of low traffic occur in the web application, you do not spend money on Amazon EC2 instances that do not run at their full capacity.

Web Server with Amazon Simple Storage Service (Presentation Tier)

Amazon Simple Storage Service (Amazon S3) can store HTML, CSS, images, and JavaScript files within an Amazon S3 bucket, and can host the website like a traditional web server. Though Amazon S3 hosts static websites, today many websites are dynamic applications, where you can use JavaScript to create HTTP requests. These HTTP requests are sent to a Representational State Transfer (REST) endpoint service called *Amazon API Gateway*, which allows the application to save and retrieve data dynamically.

Amazon API Gateway opens up a variety of application tier possibilities. An internet-accessible HTTPS API can be consumed by any client capable of HTTPS communication. Some common presentation tier examples that you could use for your application's include the following:

Mobile app   Not only can you integrate with custom business logic via Amazon API Gateway and AWS Lambda, you can use Amazon Cognito to create and manage user identities.

Static website content hosted in Amazon S3   You can enable your Amazon API Gateway APIs to be cross-origin resource sharing–compliant. This allows web browsers to invoke your APIs directly from within the static web pages.

Any other HTTPS-enabled client device   Many devices can connect and communicate via HTTPS. There is nothing unique or proprietary about how clients communicate with the APIs that you create with the Amazon API Gateway service; it is pure HTTPS. No specific client software or licenses are required.

Additionally, there are several JavaScript frameworks that are widely available today, such as Angular and React, which allow you to benefit from a *Model-View-Controller* (MVC) architecture.

Amazon S3 Static Website

For the remainder of this chapter, the example bucket's name is examplebucket. This is for illustration purposes only, as Amazon S3 bucket names must be globally unique.

To create an Amazon S3 static website, you first need to create a bucket. Name the bucket something meaningful, such as examplebucket. When you use virtual hosted-style buckets with Secure Sockets Layer (SSL), the SSL wildcard certificate only matches buckets that do *not* contain periods. To work around this, use HTTP or write your own certificate verification logic. AWS recommends that you do not use periods (.) in bucket names when using virtual hosted-style buckets with SSL.

After you create your Amazon S3 bucket, you must enable and configure it to use static website hosting, index document, error document, and redirection rules (optional) in the AWS Management Console ➤ Amazon S3 Service. Use this examplebucket bucket to host a website.

The Amazon S3 bucket includes the region based on latency, cost, and regulatory requirements. Each object has a unique key. You grant permissions at the object or bucket level.

For the index document, enter the name of your home page's HTML file (typically index.html). Additionally, you may load a custom error page such as error.html. As with many of the Amazon services, you can make these changes with the AWS Command Line Interface (AWS CLI) or in an AWS software development kit (AWS SDK). To enable this option with the AWS CLI, run the following command:

```
aws S3 website s3://examplebucket/ --index-document index.html --error-document
error.html
```

After you enable the Amazon S3 static website hosting feature, enter an endpoint that reflects your AWS Region: examplebucket.s3-website.region.amazonaws.com.

Configuring Web Traffic Logs

Amazon S3 allows you to log and capture information such as the number of visitors who access your website. To enable logs, create a new Amazon S3 bucket to store your logs. This excludes your log files from the website-hosting bucket. You can create a logs-examplebucket-com bucket, and inside of that bucket, you can create a folder you call logs/ (or any name you choose). Use this folder to store all of your logs.

 The term *folder* is used to describe logs; however, the Amazon S3 data model is a flat structure that allows you to create a bucket, and the bucket stores objects. There is no hierarchy of sub-buckets or subfolders; nevertheless, you can infer a logical hierarchy using key name prefixes and delimiters as the Amazon S3 console does. In other words, you should know that, as a developer, there is technically no such thing as an Amazon S3 folder—it is simply a key.

Now you use Amazon S3 to enable the static website–hosted bucket called examplebucket to log files. You can configure the target bucket for the log files at logs-examplebucket-com, and you can create a target prefix to send log files to a particular prefix key only.

To enable this feature with the AWS CLI, create an access control list that provides access to the log files that you want to create and then apply the logging policy. Here's an example:

```
aws s3api put-bucket-acl --bucket examplebucket --grant-write
'URI="http://acs.amazonaws.com.cn/groups/s3/LogDelivery"' --grant-read-acp
'URI="http://acs.amazonaws.com.cn/groups/s3/LogDelivery"'


aws s3api put-bucket-logging --bucket examplebucket --bucket-logging-status
file://logging.json
```

Here's the file logging.json:

```
{
  "LoggingEnabled": {
    "TargetBucket": "examplebucket",
```

```
      "TargetPrefix": "examplebucket/",
      "TargetGrants": [
        {
          "Grantee": {
            "Type": "AmazonCustomerByEmail",
            "EmailAddress": "user@example.com"
          },
          "Permission": "FULL_CONTROL"
        },
        {
          "Grantee": {
            "Type": "Group",
            "URI": "http://acs.amazonaws.com/groups/global/AllUsers"
          },
          "Permission": "READ"
        }
      ]
    }
}
```

Creating Custom Domain Name with Amazon Route 53

Amazon Route 53 is a highly available and scalable cloud Domain Name System (DNS) web service. It is designed to give developers and businesses an extremely reliable and cost-effective way to route end users to internet applications by translating names like www.example.com into the numeric IP addresses like 192.0.2.1 that computers use to connect to each other. Amazon Route 53 is fully compliant with IPv6 as well.

You may not want to use the Amazon S3 endpoint such as bucket-name.s3-website-region.amazonaws.com. Instead, you may want a more user-friendly URL such as myexamplewebsite.com. To accomplish this, purchase a domain name with Amazon Route 53.

 You can purchase your domain from another provider and then update the name servers to use Amazon Route 53.

Amazon Route 53 effectively connects user requests to infrastructure running in AWS—such as Amazon EC2 instances, Elastic Load Balancing (ELB) load balancers, or Amazon S3 buckets—and can route users to infrastructure outside of AWS. You can use Amazon

Route 53 to configure DNS health checks to route traffic to healthy endpoints or to monitor independently the health of your application and its endpoints. Amazon Route 53 Traffic Flow makes it easy for you to manage traffic globally through a variety of routing types, including latency-based routing, geolocation, geoproximity, and weighted round-robin, all of which can be combined with DNS failover to enable a variety of low-latency, fault-tolerant architectures.

Using Amazon Route 53 Traffic Flow's simple visual editor, you can easily manage how your end users are routed to your application's endpoints—whether in a single AWS Region or distributed around the globe. Amazon Route 53 also offers domain name registration. You can purchase and manage domain names such as example.com, and Amazon Route 53 will automatically configure DNS settings for your domains.

Speeding Up Content Delivery with Amazon CloudFront

Latency is an increasingly important aspect when you deliver web applications to the end user, as you always want your end user to have an efficient, low-latency experience on your website. Increased latency can result in both decreased customer satisfaction and decreased sales. One way to decrease latency is to use *Amazon CloudFront* to move your content closer to your end users. Amazon CloudFront has two delivery methods to deliver content. The first is a web distribution, and this is for storing of .html, .css, and graphic files. Amazon CloudFront also provides the ability to have an RTMP distribution, which speeds up distribution of your streaming media files using Adoble Flash Media Server's RTMP protocol. An RTMP distribution allows an end user to begin playing a media file before the file has finished downloading from a CloudFront edge location.

To use Amazon CloudFront with your Amazon S3 static website, perform these tasks:

1. Choose a delivery method.

   In the example, Amazon S3 is used to store a static web page; thus, you will be using the Web delivery method. However, as mentioned previously, you could also use RTMP for streaming media files.

2. Specify the cache behavior. A cache behavior lets you configure a variety of CloudFront functionality for a given URL path pattern for files on your website.

3. Choose the distribution settings and network that you want to use. For example, you can use all edge locations or only U.S., Canada, and Europe locations.

Amazon CloudFront enables you to cache your data to minimize redundant data-retrieval operations. Amazon CloudFront reduces the number of requests to which your origin server must respond directly. This reduces the load on your origin server and reduces latency because more objects are served from Amazon CloudFront edge locations, which are closer to your users.

The Amazon S3 bucket pushes the first request to Amazon CloudFront's cache. The second, third, and n^{th} requests pull from the Amazon CloudFront's cache at a lower latency and cost, as shown in Figure 13.1.

FIGURE 13.1 Amazon CloudFront cache

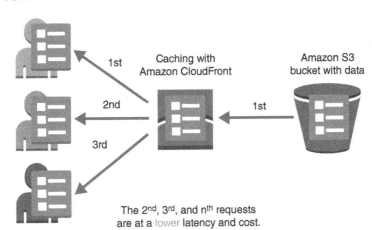

The more requests that Amazon CloudFront is able to serve from edge caches as a proportion of all requests (that is, the greater the cache hit ratio), the fewer viewer requests that Amazon CloudFront needs to forward to your origin to get the latest version or a unique version of an object. You can view the percentage of viewer requests that are hits, misses, and errors in the Amazon CloudFront console.

A number of factors affect the cache hit ratio. You can adjust your Amazon CloudFront distribution configuration to improve the cache hit ratio.

Use Amazon CloudFront with Amazon S3 to improve your performance, decrease your application's latency and costs, and provide a better user experience. Amazon CloudFront is also a serverless service, and it fits well with serverless stack services, especially when you use it in conjunction with Amazon S3.

Dynamic Data with Amazon API Gateway (Logic or App Tier)

This section details how to use dynamic data with the Amazon API Gateway service in a logic tier or app tier.

Amazon API Gateway is a fully managed, serverless AWS service, with no server that runs inside your environment to define, deploy, monitor, maintain, and secure APIs at any scale. Clients integrate with the APIs that use standard HTTPS requests. Amazon API Gateway can integrate with a service-oriented multitier architecture with Amazon services, such as AWS Lambda and Amazon EC2. It also has specific features and qualities that make it a powerful edge for your logic tier. You can use these features and qualities to enhance and build your dynamic web application.

The Amazon API Gateway integration strategy that provides access to your code includes the following:

Control service Uses REST to provide access to Amazon services, such as AWS Lambda, Amazon Kinesis, Amazon S3, and Amazon DynamoDB. The access methods include the following:

- Consoles
- CLI
- SDKs
- REST API requests and responses

Execution service Uses standard HTTP protocols or language-specific SDKs to deploy API access to backend functionality.

WARNING Do not directly expose resources or the API—always use AWS edge services and the Amazon API Gateway service to safeguard your resources and APIs.

Endpoints

There are three types of *endpoints* for Amazon API Gateway.

Regional endpoints Live inside the AWS Region, such as us-west-2.

Edge optimized endpoints Use Amazon CloudFront, a content delivery web service with the AWS global network of edge locations as connection points for clients, and integrate with your API.

Private endpoints Can live only inside of a *virtual private cloud* (VPC).

You use Amazon API Gateway to help drive down the total response time latency of your API. You can improve the performance of specific API requests with Amazon API Gateway to store responses in an optional in-memory cache. This not only provides performance benefits for API requests that repeat, but it also reduces backend executions, which helps to reduce overall costs.

The API endpoint can be a default host name or a custom domain name. The default host name is as follows:

```
{api-id}.execute-api.{region}.amazonaws.com
```

Resources

Amazon API Gateway consists of resources and methods. A *resource* is an object that provides operations you use to interact with HTTP commands such as GET, POST, or DELETE. If you combine a resource path with a specific operation on a resource, you create a *method*. Users can call API methods to obtain controlled access to resources and to receive a response. You define *mappings* between the method and the backend to maintain control. If the frontend payload does not match the corresponding backend payload, you can create mapping templates to enable them to communicate and return a response.

Before you can interact with a resource, you use a *model* to describe the data format for the request or response. You use the model with the AWS SDK for an API to validate data and generate a mapping template. Models save time and money, as they reduce the likelihood that your API will experience security and reliability issues.

In the Amazon API Gateway service, you expose addressable *resources* as a tree of *API Resources* entities, with the root resource (/) at the top of the hierarchy. The root resource is relative to the API's base URL, which consists of the API endpoint and a *stage name*. In the Amazon API Gateway console, this base URL is referred to as the *Invoke URL*, and it displays in the API's stage editor after the API deploys.

If you own a pizza restaurant and run a website to display your menu options, you can create a *root resource* called menu (for production) that results in /menu with a GET method and returns the JSON values for your entire menu. When individuals visit your website and navigate to the menu, you can return all of this data.

For example, the following:

```
{api-id}.execute-api.region.amazonaws.com/menu
```

will return the dataset through the Amazon API Gateway service:

```
[
  {
    "id": 1,
    "menu-item": "cheese pizza",
    "price": "14.99"
  },
  {
    "id": 2,
    "menu-item": "pepperoni pizza",
    "price": "17.99"
  }
]
```

With resources, you create paths such as /menu, /specials, and /orders to pull different datasets with HTTP methods.

HTTP Methods

The *Internet Engineering Task Force* (IETF) is responsible for developing and documenting the HTTP protocol and how it operates. Amazon API Gateway uses the HTTP protocol to process these HTTP methods. Amazon API Gateway supports the following methods:

- GET
- HEAD
- POST
- PUT
- PATCH
- OPTIONS
- DELETE

These methods send and receive data to and from the backend. Serverless data can be sent to AWS Lambda to process.

Stages

A *stage* is a named reference to a deployment, which is a snapshot of the API. Use a stage to manage and optimize a particular deployment. For example, stage settings enable caching, customize request throttling, configure logging, define stage variables, or attach a canary release to test. A *canary release* is a software deployment strategy in which a new version of an API is deployed at the same time that the original base version remains deployed as a production release. This means that in a canary deployment, you will have the majority of your traffic route to the current production environment and will have a small portion of your traffic route to the canary environment for testing purposes.

When you create a stage, your API is considered deployed and accessible to whomever you grant access. An advisable API strategy is to create stages for each of your environments such as DEV, TEST, and PROD, so that you can continue to develop and update your API and applications without affecting production.

Authorizers

Use Amazon API Gateway to set up *authorizers* with *Amazon Cognito user pools* on an AWS Lambda function. This enables you to secure your APIs and only allow users to whom you have granted specific access to your API.

 You have a customer relationship management application, and you only want certain users to be able to modify customer data. With authorizers, you create an API and restrict who can call that API with an authorizer in conjunction with AWS Lambda or Amazon Cognito.

API Keys

With the Amazon API Gateway service, you can generate *API keys* to provide access to your API for external users, use them to sell to your customer base, and use the API call apikey:create to create an API key.

Cross-Origin Resource Sharing

Cross-origin resource sharing (CORS) remedies the inability of a client-side web application that runs on one server to be retrieved from another service. This remedy is called a *same-origin policy*, and primarily it prevents malicious actors from calling your APIs from different servers and creates a *denial of service* for your endpoint. While you implement CORS, you still need servers to exchange data for valid reasons, such as to deliver APIs to different users, clients, or customers. You can read the specification at https://www.w3.org/TR/cors/.

CORS allows you to set certain HTTP headers to enable cross-origin access to call APIs or services to which you need access. The HTTP headers include the following:

- Access-Control-Allow-Origin
- Access-Control-Allow-Credentials
- Access-Control-Allow-Headers
- Access-Control-Allow-Methods
- Access-Control-Expose-Headers
- Access-Control-Max-Age
- Access-Control-Request-Headers
- Access-Control-Request-Method
- Origin

To use Amazon API Gateway, you must enable the CORS *resource* inside of the Amazon API Gateway console so that your web application makes calls to the Amazon API Gateway service successfully. Without CORS, any calls made to the Amazon API Gateway service will fail.

Integrating with AWS Lambda

With Amazon API Gateway, you can build *RESTful APIs* without the need to manage a server. Amazon API Gateway gives your application a simple way (HTTPS requests) to leverage the innovation of AWS Lambda directly. Amazon API Gateway forms the bridge that connects your presentation tier and the functions you write in AWS Lambda. After defining the client/server relationship with your API, the contents of the client's HTTPS request can be passed to AWS Lambda for execution, where you can write a function to talk to your database tier. For example, once someone accesses the API endpoint, contents of the request—which includes the request metadata, request headers, and the request body—can be passed to AWS Lambda. This then allows AWS Lambda to request dynamic data from your database tier—for example, Amazon DynamoDB.

Monitoring Amazon API Gateway with Amazon CloudWatch

Amazon API Gateway also integrates with *Amazon CloudWatch*. Amazon CloudWatch provides preconfigured metrics to help you monitor your APIs and build both dashboards and alarms. At the time of this writing, there are nine metrics available by default with Amazon CloudWatch, as shown in Table 13.1.

TABLE 13.1 Amazon CloudWatch Metrics

Metric	Description
4XXError	The number of client-side errors captured in a specified period. The Sum statistic represents this metric, namely, the total count of the 4XXError errors in the given period. The Average statistic represents the 4XXError error rate, namely, the total count of the 4XXError errors divided by the total number of requests during the period. The denominator corresponds to the Count metric. Unit: Count
5XXError	The number of server-side errors captured in a given period. The Sum statistic represents this metric, namely, the total count of the 5XXError errors in the given period. The Average statistic represents the 5XXError error rate, namely, the total count of the 5XXError errors divided by the total number of requests during the period. The denominator corresponds to the Count metric. Unit: Count
CacheHitCount	The number of requests served from the API cache in a given period. The Sum statistic represents this metric, namely, the total count of the cache hits in the specified period. The Average statistic represents the cache hit rate, namely, the total count of the cache hits divided by the total number of requests during the period. The denominator corresponds to the Count metric. Unit: Count
CacheMissCount	The number of requests served from the backend in a given period, when API caching is enabled. The Sum statistic represents this metric, namely, the total count of the cache misses in the specified period. The Average statistic represents the cache miss rate, namely, the total count of the cache hits divided by the total number of requests during the period. The denominator corresponds to the Count metric. Unit: Count

Metric	Description
Count	The total number API requests in a given period. The Sample-Count statistic represents this metric. Unit: Count
IntegrationLatency	The time between when Amazon API Gateway relays a request to the backend and when it receives a response from the backend. Unit: Millisecond
Latency	The time between when Amazon API Gateway receives a request from a client and when it returns a response to the client. The latency includes the integration latency and other Amazon API Gateway overhead. Unit: Millisecond

See Figure 13.2 for a sample dashboard.

FIGURE 13.2   Sample dashboard for Amazon API Gateway using Amazon CloudWatch

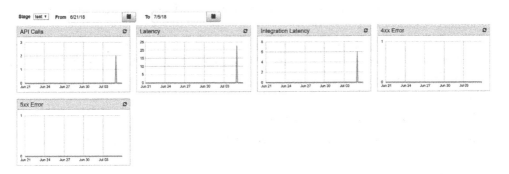

If you use Amazon CloudWatch with Amazon API Gateway, you can monitor your application from an API standpoint to see whether any issues occur as the application is being used. Particularly, you can view metrics such as CacheMissCount and Latency.

Other Notable Features

Amazon API Gateway has several notable features.

Security   Amazon API Gateway exposes HTTPS endpoints only. AWS recommends that you use IAM roles and policies to secure access to the backend, but you can use Lambda authorizers too. The adminstrator-managed policy is AmazonAPIGatewayAdministrator.

Definition support   The OpenAPI Specification, formerly known as Swagger Specification, is used to define a RESTful interface. If you create a document that conforms to the OpenAPI Specification, you can upload it to Amazon API Gateway to have it create your desired API endpoint. For more information on the OpenAPI Specification you can visit https://swagger.io/specification.

Free tier   Amazon API Gateway has a free tier, and it allows one million API receive calls per month, for free, for the first 12 months.

User Authentication with Amazon Cognito

A crucial aspect of building web applications is *user authentication*. Nearly every web application today has a user authentication *system*. From banking websites to social media websites, user authentication is a critical component to secure your web and mobile applications. *Amazon Cognito* allows for simple and secure user sign-up, sign-in, and access control mechanisms designed to handle web application authentication.

Amazon Cognito includes the following features:

- Amazon Cognito user pools, which are secure and scalable user directories
- Amazon Cognito identity pools (federated identities), which offer social and enterprise identity federation
- Standards-based Web Identity Federation Authentication through Open Authorization (OAuth) 2.0, Security Assertion Markup Language (SAML) 2.0, and OpenID Connect (OIDC) support
- Multi-factor authentication
- Encryption for data at rest and data in transit
- Access control with AWS Identity and Access Management (IAM) integration
- Easy application integration (prebuilt user interface)
- iOS Object C, Android, iOS Swift, and JavaScript
- Adherence to compliance requirements such as Payment Card Industry Data Security Standard (PCI DSS)

Amazon Cognito User Pools

A *user pool* is a user directory in Amazon Cognito. With a user pool, your users can sign in to your web or mobile app through Amazon Cognito. Users can also sign in through social identity providers, such as Facebook or Amazon, and through *Security Assertion Markup Language* (SAML) identity providers. Whether your users sign in directly or through a third party, all members of the user pool have a directory profile that you can access through an SDK.

User pools provide the following:

- Sign-up and sign-in services
- A built-in, customizable web user interface (UI) to sign in users
- Social sign-in with Facebook, Google, and Amazon, and sign-in with Security Assertion Markup Language (SAML) identity providers from your user pool
- User directory management and user profiles
- Security features, such as *multi-factor authentication* (MFA), check for compromised credentials, account takeover protection, and phone and email verification
- Customized workflows and user migration through AWS Lambda triggers

After successfully authenticating a user, Amazon Cognito issues *JSON Web Tokens* (JWT) that you can use to secure and authorize access to your own APIs or exchange them for AWS credentials.

With Amazon Cognito, you can choose how you want your users to sign in: with a username, an email address, and/or a phone number. Additionally, user pools allow you to select *attributes*. Attributes are properties that you want to store about your end users, with standard attributes that are created for you, if you enable the option. You can also develop custom attributes.

The standard attributes are as follows:

- address
- birthdate
- email
- family name
- gender
- given name
- locale
- middle name
- name
- nickname
- phone number
- picture
- preferred username
- profile
- zoneinfo
- updated at
- website

Password Policies

In addition to attributes, you can configure *password policies*. You can set the minimum password length and require specific character types, including uppercase letters and lowercase letters. Furthermore, you can either allow users to sign up and enroll themselves or allow only administrators to create users. If administrators create the account, you can also set the account to expire if it remains unused for a specified period of time.

Multi-factor Authentication

Multi-factor authentication (MFA) prevents anyone from signing in to a system without authenticating through two different sources, such as a password and a mobile-device generated token. With Amazon Cognito, you can enable multi-factor authentication to secure your application further. To enable this option with Amazon Cognito, create a role that enables Amazon Cognito to send Short Message Service (SMS) messages to users.

Besides MFA, you can customize your SMS verification messages, email verification messages, and user invitation messages. For example, you could send your end users a welcome message when they verify their account.

Device Tracking and Remembering

If you enable multi-factor authentication, this increases the security of an application to require a second authentication challenge from the user. However, this does require a new two-factor sign-in after a prolonged absence of activity, even when the user device has not been signed out or shut off.

With device tracking and remembering, you can save that user's device and remember it so that they do not have to provide a token again, as the application has already seen this specific device. Figure 13.3 shows how to enable this feature.

FIGURE 13.3   Device tracking

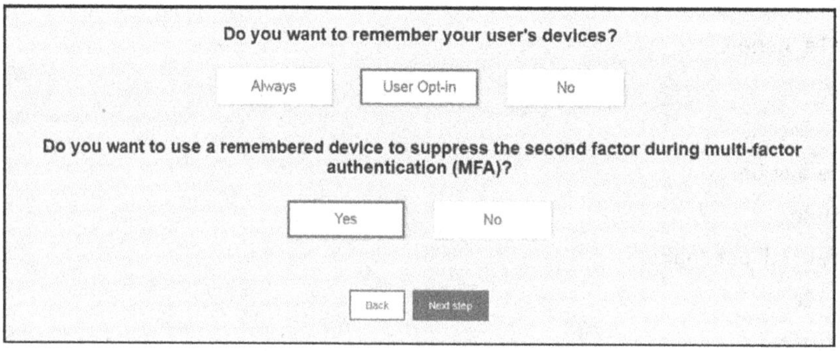

The specifics of the configuration terminology include the following:

Tracked   A *tracked device* is assigned a set of device credentials and consists of a *key* and *secret key pair*. You can view all tracked devices for a specific user on the Users screen of the Amazon Cognito console. In addition, you can view the devices metadata (whether it is remembered, the time it began being tracked, the last authenticated time, and such) and the devices usage.

Remembered   A *remembered device* is also tracked. During user authentication, the key and secret pair assigned to a remembered device authenticates the device to verify that it is the same device that the user previously used to sign in to the application. You can view remembered devices in the Amazon Cognito console.

Not remembered   A *not-remembered device*, while still tracked, is treated as if it was never used during the user authentication flow. The device credentials are not used to authenticate the device. The new APIs in the *AWS Mobile SDK* do not expose these devices, but you can see them in the Amazon Cognito console.

The first configuration setting reads "Do you want to remember devices?" and has the following options:

No (the default)   Devices are neither remembered nor tracked.

Always   Every device used with your application is remembered.

User opt-in   The user's device is remembered only if that user opts to remember the device. This enables your users to decide whether your application should remember the devices they use to sign in, though all devices are tracked regardless of which setting they choose. This is a useful option when you require a higher security level, but the user may sign in from a shared device. For example, if a user signs in to a banking application from a public computer at a library, the user requires the option to decide whether their device is to be remembered.

The second configuration option is "Do you want to use a remembered device to suppress the second factor during multi-factor authentication (MFA)?" It appears when you select either Always or User Opt-In for the first configuration option. The second factor suppression option enables your application to use a remembered device as a second factor of authentication, and it suppresses the SMS-based challenge in the MFA flow. This feature works together with MFA, and it requires MFA to be enabled for the user pool. The device must first be remembered before it can be used to suppress the SMS-based challenge. Upon the initial sign-in with a new device, the user must complete the SMS challenge. Afterward, the user no longer has to complete the SMS challenge.

User Interface Customization

An Amazon Cognito user pool includes a prebuilt *user interface* (UI) that you can use inside of your application to build a user authentication flow quickly, as shown in Figure 13.4.

FIGURE 13.4 Amazon Cognito prebuilt UI

You can modify the UI with the AWS Management Console, the AWS CLI, or the API. You can also upload your own custom logo with a maximum file size of 100 KB. The *CSS classes* you can customize in the prebuilt UI are as follows:

- background-customizable
- banner-customizable
- errorMessage-customizable
- idpButton-customizable
- idpButton-customizable:hover
- inputField-customizable
- inputField-customizable:focus
- label-customizable
- legalText-customizable
- logo-customizable
- submitButton-customizable
- submitButton-customizable:hover
- textDescription-customizable

You can customize the UI and CLI with two commands: `get-ui-customization` to retrieve the customization settings and `set-ui-customization` to set the UI customization, as shown in the following example code:

```
aws cognito-idp get-ui-customization
aws cognito-idp set-ui-customization --user-pool-id <your-user-pool-id>
--client-id <your-app-client-id> --image-file <path-to-logo-image-file>
--css ".label-customizable{ color: <color>;}"
```

Amazon Cognito Identity Pools

Amazon Cognito identity pools allow you to create unique identities and assign permissions for your users. Inside the *identity pool*, you can include the following:

- Users in an Amazon Cognito user pool
- Users who authenticate with external identity providers such as Facebook, Google, or a SAML-based identity provider
- Users authenticated via your own existing authentication process

An identity pool allows you to obtain temporary AWS credentials with permissions that you define either to access other Amazon services directly or to access resources through Amazon API Gateway. Amazon Cognito identity pools help you integrate several authentication providers, such as the following:

- Amazon Cognito user pools
- Amazon.com users
- Facebook
- Google
- Twitter
- OpenID
- SAML
- Custom—supports your own identities such as *(login).(mycompany).(myapp)*

Once you enable the third-party resources that you want to allow to sign in to your apps, you can assign permissions to these users. With the combination of *user pools* and *identity pools*, you can create a serverless user authentication system.

Use this command to create an Amazon Cognito user pool with the CLI:

```
aws cognito-idp create-user-pool --pool-name <value>
```

Amazon Cognito SDK

You can start developing for Amazon Cognito using the *AWS Mobile SDK*. Amazon Cognito currently supports the following SDKs through the AWS Mobile SDK:

- JavaScript SDK
- iOS SDK
- Android SDK

In addition to using the higher-level mobile and JavaScript SDKs, you can also use the lower-level APIs available via the following AWS SDKs to integrate all Amazon Cognito functionality in your applications:

- Java SDK
- .NET SDK
- Node.js SDK
- Python SDK
- PHP SDK
- Ruby SDK

Standard Three-Tier vs. the Serverless Stack

This chapter has introduced serverless services and their benefits. Now that you know about some of the serverless services that are available in AWS, let's compare a traditional three-tier application against a serverless application architecture. Figure 13.5 shows a typical three-tier web application.

FIGURE 13.5   Standard three-tier web infrastructure architecture

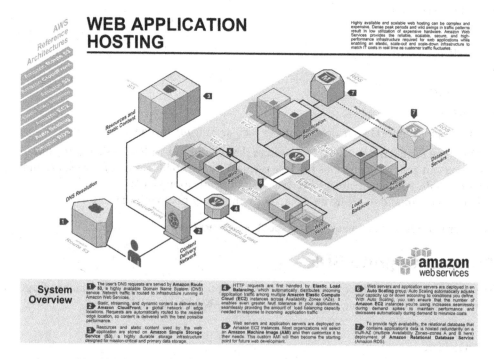

Source: https://media.amazonwebservices.com/architecturecenter/AWS_ac_ra_web_01.pdf

This architecture uses the following components and services:

Routing: Amazon Route 53

Content distribution network (CDN): Amazon CloudFront

Static data: Amazon S3

High availability/decoupling: Application load balancers

Web servers: Amazon EC2 with Auto Scaling

App servers: Amazon EC2 with Auto Scaling

Database: Amazon RDS in a multi-AZ configuration

Amazon Route 53 provides a DNS service that allows you to take domain names such as examplecompany.com and translate them to an IP address that points to running servers.

The CDN shown in Figure 13.6 is the Amazon CloudFront service, which improves your site performance with the use of its global content delivery network.

FIGURE 13.6   Serverless web application architecture

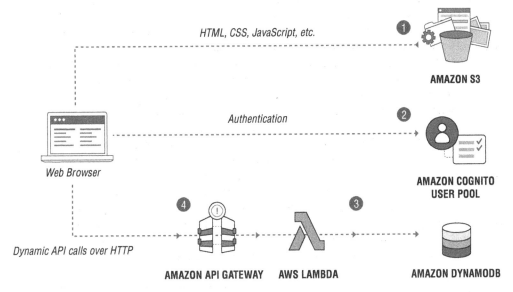

Source: https://aws.amazon.com/getting-started/projects/build-serverless-web-app-lambda-apigateway-s3-dynamodb-cognito/

Amazon S3 stores your static files such as photos or movie files.

Application load balancers are responsible for distributing load across Availability Zones to your Amazon EC2 servers, which run your web application with a service such as Apache or NGINX.

Application servers are responsible for performing business logic prior to storing the data in your database servers that are run by Amazon RDS.

Amazon RDS is the managed database server, and it can run an Amazon Aurora, Microsoft SQL Server, Oracle SQL Server, MySQL, PostgreSQL, or MariaDB database server.

While this architecture is a robust and highly available service, there are several downsides, including the fact that you have to manage servers. You are responsible for patching those servers, preventing downtime associated with those patches, and proper server scaling.

In a typical serverless web application architecture, you also run a web application, but you have zero servers that run inside your AWS account, as shown in Figure 13.6.

Serverless web application architecture services include the following:

Routing: Amazon Route 53

Web servers/static data: Amazon S3

User authentication: Amazon Cognito user pools

App servers: Amazon API Gateway and AWS Lambda

Database: Amazon DynamoDB

Amazon Route 53 is your DNS, and you can use Amazon CloudFront for your CDN.

You can also use Amazon S3 for your web servers. In this architecture, you use Amazon S3 to host your entire static website. You use JavaScript to make API calls to the Amazon API Gateway service.

For your business or application servers, you use Amazon API Gateway in conjunction with AWS Lambda. This allows you to retrieve and save data dynamically.

You use Amazon DynamoDB as a serverless database service, and you do not provision any Amazon EC2s inside of your Amazon VPC account. Amazon DynamoDB is also a great database service for storing session state for stateful applications. You can use Amazon RDS instead if you need a relational database. However, it would not then be a fully serverless stack. There is a new service released called *Amazon Aurora Serverless*, which is a full RDS MySQL 5.6–compatible service that is completely serverless. This would allow you to run a traditional SQL database, but one that has the benefit of being serverless. Amazon Aurora Serverless is discussed in the next section.

You use Amazon Cognito user pools for user authentication, which provides a secure user directory that can scale to hundreds of millions of users. Amazon Cognito User Pools is a fully managed service with no servers for you to manage. While user authentication was not shown in Figure 13.6, you can use your web server tier to talk to a user directory, such as *Lightweight Directory Access Protocol* (LDAP), for user authentication.

As you can see, while some of the components are the same, you may use them in slightly different ways. By taking advantage of the AWS global network, you can develop fully scalable, highly available web applications—all without having to worry about maintaining or patching servers.

Amazon Aurora Serverless

Amazon Aurora Serverless is an on-demand, auto-scaling configuration for the Aurora MySQL-compatible edition, where the database automatically starts, shuts down, and scales up or down as needed by your application. This allows you to run a traditional SQL database in the cloud without needing to manage any infrastructure or instances.

With Amazon Aurora Serverless, you also get the same high availability as traditional Amazon Aurora, which means that you get six-way replication across three Availability Zones inside of a region in order to prevent against data loss.

Amazon Aurora Serverless is great for infrequently used applications, new applications, variable workloads, unpredictable workloads, development and test databases, and multitenant applications. This is because you can scale automatically when you need to and scale down when application demand is not high. This can help cut costs and save you the heartache of managing your own database infrastructure.

Amazon Aurora Serverless is easy to set up, either through the console or directly with the CLI. To create an Amazon Aurora Serverless cluster with the CLI, you can run the following command:

```
aws rds create-db-cluster --db-cluster-identifier sample-cluster --engine aurora
--engine-version 5.6.10a \
--engine-mode serverless --scaling-configuration
MinCapacity=4,MaxCapacity=32,SecondsUntilAutoPause=1000,AutoPause=true \
--master-username user-name --master-user-password password \
--db-subnet-group-name mysubnetgroup --vpc-security-group-ids sg-c7e5b0d2
-region us-east-1
```

Amazon Aurora Serverless gives you many of the similar benefits as other serverless technologies, such as AWS Lambda, but from a database perspective. Managing databases is hard work, and with Amazon Aurora Serverless, you can utilize a database that automatically scales and you don't have to manage any of the underlying infrastructure.

AWS Serverless Application Model

The *AWS Serverless Application Model* (AWS SAM) allows you to create and manage resources in your serverless application with *AWS CloudFormation* to define your serverless application infrastructure as a SAM template. A *SAM template* is a JSON or YAML configuration file that describes the AWS Lambda functions, API endpoints, tables, and other resources in your application. With simple commands, you upload this template to AWS CloudFormation, which creates the individual resources and groups them into an *AWS CloudFormation stack* for ease of management. When you update your AWS SAM template, you re-deploy the changes to this stack. AWS CloudFormation updates the individual resources for you.

AWS SAM is an extension of AWS CloudFormation. You can define resources by using the AWS CloudFormation in your AWS SAM template. This is a powerful feature, as you can use AWS SAM to create a template of your serverless infrastructure, which you can then build into a DevOps pipeline. For example, examine the following:

```
AWSTemplateFormatVersion: '2010-09-09'
Transform: 'AWS::Serverless-2016-10-31'
Description: 'Example of Multiple-Origin CORS using API Gateway and Lambda'
```

```
Resources:
  ExampleRoot:
    Type: 'AWS::Serverless::Function'
    Properties:
      CodeUri: '.'
      Handler: 'routes/root.handler'
      Runtime: 'nodejs8.10'
      Events:
        Get:
          Type: 'Api'
          Properties:
            Path: '/'
            Method: 'get'
  ExampleTest:
    Type: 'AWS::Serverless::Function'
    Properties:
      CodeUri: '.'
      Handler: 'routes/test.handler'
      Runtime: 'nodejs8.10'
      Events:
        Delete:
          Type: 'Api'
          Properties:
            Path: '/test'
            Method: 'delete'
        Options:
          Type: 'Api'
          Properties:
            Path: '/test'
            Method: 'options'

Outputs:
  ExampleApi:
    Description: "API Gateway endpoint URL for Prod stage for API Gateway
Multi-Origin CORS Function"
    Value: !Sub "https://${ServerlessRestApi}.execute-api.${AWS::Region}
.amazonaws.com/Prod/"
  ExampleRoot:
    Description: "API Gateway Multi-Origin CORS Lambda Function (Root) ARN"
    Value: !GetAtt ExampleRoot.Arn
  ExampleRootIamRole:
```

```
    Description: "Implicit IAM Role created for API Gateway Multi-Origin CORS
Function (Root)"
      Value: !GetAtt ExampleRootRole.Arn
    ExampleTest:
      Description: "API Gateway Multi-Origin CORS Lambda Function (Test) ARN"
      Value: !GetAtt ExampleTest.Arn
    ExampleTestIamRole:
      Description: "Implicit IAM Role created for API Gateway Multi-Origin CORS
Function (Test)"
      Value: !GetAtt ExampleTestRole.Arn
```

In the previous code example, you create two AWS Lambda functions and then associate *three* different Amazon API Gateway endpoints to trigger those functions. To deploy this AWS SAM template, download the template and all of the necessary dependencies from here:

https://github.com/awslabs/serverless-application-model/tree/develop/
examples/apps/api-gateway-multiple-origin-cors

AWS SAM is similar to AWS CloudFormation, with a few key differences, as shown in the second line:

Transform: 'AWS::Serverless-2016-10-31'

This important line of code transforms the AWS SAM template into an AWS CloudFormation template. Without it, the AWS SAM template will not work.

Similar to the AWS CloudFormation, you also have a Resources property where you define infrastructure to provision. The difference is that you provision serverless services with a new Type called AWS::Serverless::Function. This provisions an AWS Lambda function to define all properties from an AWS Lambda point of view. AWS Lambda includes Properties, such as MemorySize, Timeout, Role, Runtime, Handler, and others.

While you can create an AWS Lambda function with AWS CloudFormation using AWS::Lambda::Function, the benefit of AWS SAM lies in a property called Event, where you can tie in a trigger to an AWS Lambda function, all from within the AWS::Serverless::Function resource. This Event property makes it simple to provision an AWS Lambda function and configure it with an Amazon API Gateway trigger. If you use AWS CloudFormation, you would have to declare an Amazon API Gateway separately with AWS::ApiGateway::Resource.

To summarize, AWS SAM allows you to provision serverless resources more rapidly with less code by extending AWS CloudFormation.

AWS SAM CLI

Now that we've addressed AWS SAM, let's take a closer look at the AWS SAM CLI. With AWS SAM, you can define templates, in JSON or YAML, which are designed for provisioning serverless applications through AWS CloudFormation.

AWS SAM CLI is a command line interface tool that creates an environment in which you can develop, test, and analyze your serverless-based application, all locally. This allows you to test your AWS Lambda functions before uploading them to the AWS service. AWS SAM CLI also allows you to develop and test your code quickly, and this gives you the ability to test it locally, which allows you to develop it faster. Previously, you would have had to upload your code each time you wanted to test an AWS Lambda function. Now, with the AWS SAM CLI, you can develop faster and get your application out the door more quickly.

To use AWS SAM CLI, you must meet a few prerequisites. You must install Docker, have Python 2.7 or 3.6 installed, have pip installed, install the AWS CLI, and finally install the AWS SAM CLI. You can read more about how to install AWS SAM CLI at `https://github.com/awslabs/aws-sam-cli`.

With AWS SAM CLI, you must define three key things.

- You must have a valid AWS SAM template, which defines a serverless application.

- You must have the AWS Lambda function defined. This can be in any valid language that Lambda currently supports, such as Node.js, Java 8, Python, and so on.

- You must have an event source. An *event source* is simply an event.json file that contains all the data that the Lambda function expects to receive. Valid event sources are as follows:

  - Amazon Alexa

  - Amazon API Gateway

  - AWS Batch

  - AWS CloudFormation

  - Amazon CloudFront

  - AWS CodeCommit

  - AWS CodePipeline

  - Amazon Cognito

  - AWS Config

  - Amazon DynamoDB

  - Amazon Kinesis

  - Amazon Lex

  - Amazon Rekognition

  - Amazon Simple Storage Service (Amazon S3)

  - Amazon Simple Email Service (Amazon SES)

  - Amazon Simple Notification Service (Amazon SNS)

  - Amazon Simple Queue Service (Amazon SQS)

  - AWS Step Functions

To generate this JSON event source, you can simply run this command in the AWS SAM CLI:

```
sam local generate-event <service> <event>
```

AWS SAM CLI is a great tool that allows developers to iterate quickly on their serverless applications. You will learn how to create and test an AWS Lambda function locally in the "Exercises" section of this chapter.

AWS Serverless Application Repository

The *AWS Serverless Application Repository* enables you to deploy code samples, components, and complete applications quickly for common use cases, such as web and mobile backends, event and data processing, logging, monitoring, Internet of Things (IoT), and more. Each application is packaged with an AWS SAM template that defines the AWS resources. Publicly shared applications also include a link to the application's source code. There is no additional charge to use the serverless application repository. You pay only for the AWS resources you use in the applications you deploy.

You can also use the serverless application repository to publish your own applications and share them within your team, across your organization, or with the community at large. This allows you to see what other people and organizations are developing.

Serverless Application Use Cases

Case studies on running serverless applications are located at the following URLs:

The Coca-Cola Company:

```
https://aws.amazon.com/blogs/aws/things-go-better-with-step-functions/
```

FINRA:

```
https://aws.amazon.com/solutions/case-studies/finra-data-validation/
```

iRobot:

```
https://aws.amazon.com/solutions/case-studies/irobot/
```

Localytics:

```
https://aws.amazon.com/solutions/case-studies/localytics/
```

Summary

This chapter covered the AWS serverless core services, how to store your static files inside of Amazon S3, how to use Amazon CloudFront in conjunction with Amazon S3, how to integrate your application with user authentication flows using Amazon Cognito, and how to deploy and scale your API quickly and automatically with Amazon API Gateway.

Serverless applications have three main benefits: no server management, flexible scaling, and automated high availability. Without server management, you no longer have to provision or maintain servers. With AWS Lambda, you upload your code, run it, and focus on your application updates. With flexible scaling, you no longer have to disable Amazon EC2 instances to scale them vertically, groups do not need to be auto-scaled, and you do not need to create Amazon CloudWatch alarms to add them to load balancers. With AWS Lambda, you adjust the units of consumption (memory and execution time), and AWS adjusts the rest of the instance appropriately. Finally, serverless applications have built-in availability and fault tolerance. When periods of low traffic occur, you do not spend money on Amazon EC2 instances that do not run at their full capacity.

You can use an Amazon S3 web server to create your presentation tier. Within an Amazon S3 bucket, you can store HTML, CSS, and JavaScript files. JavaScript can create HTTP requests. These HTTP requests are sent to a REST endpoint service called Amazon API Gateway, which allows the application to save and retrieve data dynamically by triggering a Lambda function.

After you create your Amazon S3 bucket, you configure it to use static website hosting in the AWS Management Console and enter an endpoint that reflects your AWS Region.

Amazon S3 allows you to configure web traffic logs to capture information, such as the number of visitors who access your website in the Amazon S3 bucket.

One way to decrease latency and improve your performance is to use Amazon CloudFront with Amazon S3 to move your content closer to your end users. Amazon CloudFront is a serverless service.

The Amazon API Gateway is a fully managed service designed to define, deploy, and maintain APIs. Clients integrate with the APIs using standard HTTPS requests. Amazon API Gateway can integrate with a service-oriented multitier architecture. The Amazon API Gateway provides dynamic data in the logic or app tier.

There are three types of endpoints for Amazon API Gateway: regional endpoints, edge-optimized endpoints, and private endpoints.

In the Amazon API Gateway service, you expose addressable resources as a tree of API Resources entities, with the root resource (/) at the top of the hierarchy. The root resource is relative to the API's base URL, which consists of the API endpoint and a stage name.

You use Amazon API Gateways to help drive down the total response-time latency of your API. Amazon API Gateway uses the HTTP protocol to process these HTTP methods and send/receive data to and from the backend. Serverless data is sent to AWS Lambda to process.

You can use Amazon Route 53 to create a more user-friendly domain name instead of using the default host name (Amazon S3 endpoint). To support two subdomains, you create two Amazon S3 buckets that match your domain name and subdomain.

A stage is a named reference to a deployment, which is a snapshot of the API. Use a stage to manage and optimize a particular deployment. You create stages for each of your environments such as DEV, TEST, and PROD, so you can develop and update your API and applications without affecting production. Use Amazon API Gateway to set up authorizers with Amazon Cognito user pools on an AWS Lambda function. This enables you to secure your APIs.

An Amazon Cognito user pool includes a prebuilt user interface (UI) that you can use inside your application to build a user authentication flow quickly. A user pool is a user directory in Amazon Cognito. With a user pool, your users can sign in to your web or mobile app through Amazon Cognito. Users can also sign in through social identity providers such as Facebook or Amazon and through Security Assertion Markup Language (SAML) identity providers.

Amazon Cognito identity pools allow you to create unique identities and assign permissions for your users to help you integrate with authentication providers. With the combination of user pools and identity pools, you can create a serverless user authentication system.

You can choose how users sign in with a username, an email address, and/or a phone number and to select attributes. Attributes are properties that you want to store about your end users. You can also configure password policies. Multi-factor authentication (MFA) prevents anyone from signing in to a system without authenticating through two different sources, such as a password and a mobile device–generated token. You create an Amazon Cognito role to send Short Message Service (SMS) messages to users.

The AWS Serverless Application Model (AWS SAM) allows you to create and manage resources in your serverless application with AWS CloudFormation as a SAM template. A SAM template is a JSON or YAML file that describes the AWS Lambda function, API endpoints, and other resources. You upload the template to AWS CloudFormation to create a stack. When you update your AWS SAM template, you redeploy the changes to this stack, and AWS CloudFormation updates the resources. You can use AWS SAM to create a template of your serverless infrastructure, which you can then build into a DevOps pipeline.

The `Transform: 'AWS::Serverless-2016-10-31'` code converts the AWS SAM template into an AWS CloudFormation template.

The AWS Serverless Application Repository enables you to deploy code samples, components, and complete applications for common use cases. Each application is packaged with an AWS SAM template that defines the AWS resources.

Additionally, you learned the differences between the standard three-tier web applications and the AWS serverless stack. You learned how to build your infrastructure quickly with AWS SAM and AWS SAM CLI for testing and development purposes.

Exam Essentials

Know serverless applications' three main benefits. The benefits are as follows:

- No server management
- Flexible scaling
- Automated high availability

Know what no server management means. Without server management, you no longer have to provision or maintain servers. With AWS Lambda, you upload your code, run it, and focus on your application updates.

Know what flexible scaling means.   With flexible scaling, you no longer have to disable Amazon Elastic Compute Cloud (Amazon EC2) instances to scale them vertically, groups do not need to be auto-scaled, and you do not need to create Amazon Cloud-Watch alarms to add them to load balancers. With AWS Lambda, you adjust the units of consumption (memory and execution time), and AWS adjusts the rest of the instances appropriately.

Know what serverless applications mean.   Serverless applications have built-in availability and fault tolerance. You do not need to architect for these capabilities, as the services that run the application provide them by default. Additionally, when periods of low traffic occur on the web application, you do not spend money on Amazon EC2 instances that do not run at their full capacity.

Know what services are serverless.   On the exam, it is important to understand which Amazon services are serverless and which ones are not. The following services are serverless:

- Amazon API Gateway
- AWS Lambda
- Amazon SQS
- Amazon SNS
- Amazon Kinesis
- Amazon Cognito
- Amazon Aurora Serverless
- Amazon S3

Know how to host a serverless web application.   Hosting a serverless application means that you need Amazon S3 to host your static website, which comprises your HTML, JavaScript, and CSS files. For your database infrastructure, you can use Amazon DynamoDB or Amazon Aurora Serverless. For your business logic tier, you can use AWS Lambda. For DNS services, you can utilize Amazon Route 53. If you need the ability to host an API, you can use Amazon API Gateway. Finally, if you need to decrease latency to portions of your application, you can utilize services like Amazon CloudFront, which allows you to host your content at the edge.

Resources to Review

Serverless Computing and Applications:

    https://aws.amazon.com/serverless/

Amazon S3 Website Endpoints:

> https://docs.aws.amazon.com/general/latest/gr/rande.html#s3_website_
> region_endpoints

Amazon Cognito FAQs:

> https://aws.amazon.com/cognito/faqs/

Amazon API Gateway FAQ:

> https://aws.amazon.com/api-gateway/faqs/

AWS Well-Architected Framework—Serverless Applications Lens:

> https://d1.awsstatic.com/whitepapers/architecture/AWS-Serverless-
> Applications-Lens.pdf

Serverless Architectures with AWS Lambda:

> https://d1.awsstatic.com/whitepapers/serverless-architectures-with-aws-
> lambda.pdf

AWS Serverless Multi-Tier Architectures (Amazon API Gateway and AWS Lambda):

> https://d1.awsstatic.com/whitepapers/AWS_Serverless_Multi-Tier_
> Architectures.pdf

Serverless Streaming Architectures and Best Practices:

> https://d1.awsstatic.com/whitepapers/Serverless_Streaming_Architecture_
> Best_Practices.pdf

Optimizing Enterprise Economics with Serverless Architectures:

> https://d1.awsstatic.com/whitepapers/optimizing-enterprise-economics-
> serverless-architectures.pdf

Common Serverless Architectures discussed at re:Invent 2017 (Video):

> https://www.youtube.com/watch?v=xJcm9V2jagc

AWS Serverless Application Model (AWS SAM) FAQs:

> https://aws.amazon.com/serverless/sam/faqs/

Exercises

For this "Exercises" section, expand the OpenPets API Template that comes with Amazon API Gateway and build a frontend with HTML and JavaScript. You use AWS Lambda for some compute processing to save data to an Amazon DynamoDB database.

Create an Amazon S3 Bucket for the Swagger Template

In this exercise, you use an AWS SAM template and a Swagger template to deploy your infrastructure. You will need to create an Amazon S3 bucket for the Swagger file.

1. Create an Amazon S3 bucket.

```
aws s3 mb s3://my-bucket-name --region us-east-1
```

If the command was successful, you should see output similar to the following, which means the bucket has been created:

```
make_bucket: my-bucket-name
```

2. Upload the **Swagger template**.

```
aws s3 cp petstore-api-swagger.yaml s3://my-bucket-name/petstore-api-swagger
.yaml
```

If the file was successfully uploaded, you should be able to navigate to the Amazon S3 bucket and see it. This file is for the Swagger template, and it is used to create the REST API inside the Amazon API Gateway. You have not yet deployed the API.

3. Use AWS SAM to deploy your serverless infrastructure. To package your SAM template, run the following command:

```
aws cloudformation package \
    --template-file ./petStoreSAM.yaml \
    --s3-bucket my-bucket-name \
    --output-template-file petStoreSAM-output.yaml \
    --region us-east-1
```

If the command was successful, you should see that the file has been uploaded, and a new file called petStoreSAM-output.yaml has been created locally. You have packaged the AWS SAM template and converted it to a full AWS CloudFormation template. You will use this template in the next step to deploy the package to the Amazon API Gateway.

4. Deploy the package.

```
aws cloudformation deploy \
    --template-file ./petStoreSAM-output.yaml \
    --stack-name petStoreStack \
    --capabilities CAPABILITY_IAM \
    --parameter-overrides S3BucketName=s3://my-bucket-name/
petstore-api-swagger.yaml \
    --region us-east-1
```

If the command was successful, you should see that the cloudformation stack has been deployed. While it is in the process of deploying the resources, you will see something similar to the following:

```
Waiting for stack create/update to complete
```

This make take a few minutes. When it is finished deploying, the console displays the following message:

```
Successfully created/updated stack - petStoreStack
```

You have now successfully deployed the cloudformation stack and can view the resources it created inside the AWS Management Console under the **AWS CloudFormation** service.

5. After the stack is created, run the command and write the results down for subsequent steps:

```
aws cloudformation describe-stacks --stack-name petStoreStack --region
us-east-1 --query 'Stacks[0].Outputs[0].{PetStoreAPI:OutputValue}'
```

After running this command, the URL for the API is returned. Navigate to this URL to view the default page returned by the PetStore API. You will be changing this in the next exercise.

You have successfully completed the first exercise, created your AWS SAM template, and deployed it using AWS CloudFormation. Now your Amazon API Gateway is active, and you have the URL for accessing it.

EXERCISE 13.2

Edit the HTML Files

In steps 1 through 5, you are going to update the URL inside your .html files to point to the Amazon API Gateway stage that you have created. You do this so that your web application (.html files) knows the endpoint where to send your pet data.

1. Open index.html in the project folder and locate line 68 to find the variable named api_gw_endpoint. Input the value you retrieved from the previous command in Exercise 13.1.

```
var api_gw_endpoint = "https://cdvhqasdfnk444fe.execute-api.us-east-1
.amazonaws.com/PetStoreProd/"
```

2. Open pets.html.

(continued)

3. Input the value you received from the last command on line 96, and add /pets to the end of the string:

   ```
   var api_gw_endpoint = "https://cdvhqasdfnk444fe.execute-api.us-east-1.
   amazonaws.com/PetStoreProd/pets"
   ```

4. Open add-pet.html.

5. Input the value you received from the last command on line 87, and add /pets to the end.

   ```
   var api_gw_endpoint = "https://cdvhqasdfnk444fe.execute-api.us-east-1
   .amazonaws.com/PetStoreProd/pets"
   ```

6. Create a new Amazon S3 bucket for your website.

   ```
   aws s3 mb s3://my-bucket-name --region us-east-1
   ```

7. Copy the project files to the website.

   ```
   aws s3 cp . s3://my-bucket-name --recursive
   aws s3 rm s3://my-bucket-name/sam –recursive
   ```

   Here you are uploading all the files from your project folder to Amazon S3 and then removing the SAM template from the bucket. You do not want others to have access to your template files and AWS Lambda functions. You want others to have access only to the end application.

8. Change the Amazon S3 bucket name inside of the policy.json to your bucket name. This will be on line 12.

9. Enable public read access for the bucket:

   ```
   aws s3api put-bucket-policy --bucket my-bucket-name --policy file://policy.json
   ```

   If successful, this command will not return any information. You are enabling the Amazon S3 bucket to be publicly accessible, meaning that everyone can access your website.

10. Enable the static website.

    ```
    aws s3 website s3://my-bucket-name/ --index-document index.html --error-
    document index.html
    ```

    The Amazon S3 bucket now acts as a web server and is running your pet store application.

11. Navigate to the website.

    ```
    url: http://my-bucket-name.s3-website-us-east-1.amazonaws.com/index.html
    ```

12. Navigate Amazon API Gateway, AWS Lambda, Amazon DynamoDB, and the AWS SAM template to view the configuration.

Now that the application has been deployed, you can view all the individual components inside the AWS Management Console.

Inside Amazon API Gateway, you should see the `PetStoreAPIGW`. If you review the resources, you will see the various HTTP methods that you are allowing for your API.

In AWS Lambda, two functions were created: `savePet` for saving pets to Amazon DynamoDB and `getPets` for retrieving pets stored in Amazon DynamoDB.

In Amazon DynamoDB, you should have a table called `PetStore`. You can view the items in this table, though by default there should be none. After you create your first pet, however, you will be able to see some items in the table.

You can view the AWS SAM template and the AWS CloudFormation stack to see exactly how each of these resources were created.

With YAML, tab indentations are extremely important. Make sure that you have a valid YAML template. There are a variety of tools that you can use to validate YAML syntax. You can use the following websites to validate the YAML:

`https://codebeautify.org/yaml-validator`

`http://www.yamllint.com/`

If you want to perform client-side validation and not use a website, a number of IDEs support YAML validation. Refer to your IDE documentation to check for YAML support.

EXERCISE 13.3

Define an AWS SAM Template

In this exercise, you will develop an AWS Lambda function locally and then test that Lambda function using the AWS SAM CLI. To perform this exercise successfully, you must have AWS SAM CLI installed. For information on how to install the AWS SAM CLI, review the following documentation: `https://github.com/awslabs/aws-sam-cli`. The following steps assume that you have a working AWS SAM CLI installation.

1. Once you have installed AWS SAM CLI, open your favorite integrated development environment (IDE) and define an AWS SAM template.

(continued)

EXERCISE 13.3 *(continued)*

---

2. Enter the following in your template file:

```
AWSTemplateFormatVersion: '2010-09-09'
Transform: AWS::Serverless-2016-10-31

Description: Welcome to the Pet Store Demo

Resources:
  PetStore:
    Type: AWS::Serverless::Function
    Properties:
      Runtime: nodejs8.10
      Handler: index.handler
```

3. Save the file as template.yaml.

You have created the SAM template and saved the file locally. In subsequent exercises, you will use this information to execute an AWS Lambda function.

EXERCISE 13.4

Define an AWS Lambda Function Locally

Now that you have a valid SAM template, you can define your AWS Lambda function locally. In this example, use Nodejs 8.10, but you can use any AWS Lambda supported language.

1. Open your favorite IDE, and type the following Nodejs code:

```
'use strict';

//A simple Lambda function
exports.handler = (event, context, callback) => {

    console.log('This is our local lambda function');
    console.log('Creating a PetStore service');
    callback(null, "Hello " + event.Records[0].dynamodb.NewImage.Message.S + "!
What kind of pet are you interested in?");
}
```

2. Save the file as index.js.

You have two files: an index.js and the SAM template. In the next exercise, you will generate an event source that will be used as the trigger for the AWS Lambda function.

EXERCISE 13.5

Generate an Event Source

Now that you have a valid SAM template and a valid AWS Lambda Nodejs 8.10 function, you can generate an event source.

1. Inside your terminal, type the following to generate an event source:

    `sam local generate-event dynamodb update > event.json`

    This will generate an Amazon DynamoDB update event. For a list of all of the event sources, type the following:

    `sam local generate-event -help`

2. Modify the event source JSON file (event.json). On line 17, change New Item! to your first and last names.

    `"S": "John Smith"`

You have now configured the three pieces that you need: the AWS SAM template, the AWS Lambda function, and the event source. In the next exercise, you will be able to run the AWS Lambda function locally.

EXERCISE 13.6

Run the AWS Lambda Function

Trigger and execute the AWS Lambda function.

1. In your terminal, type the following to execute the AWS Lambda function:

    `sam local invoke "PetStore" -e event.json`

    You will see the following message:

    Hello Casey Gerena! What kind of pet are you interested in?

    The AWS Lambda Docker image is downloaded to your local environment, and the event.json serves as all of the data that will be received as an event source to the AWS Lambda function. Inside the AWS SAM template, you will have given this function the name PetStore; however, you can define as many functions as you need to in order to build your application.

EXERCISE 13.7

Modify the AWS SAM template to Include an API Locally

To make your pet store into an API, modify the template.yaml.

1. Open the template.yaml file, and modify it to look like the following:

```
AWSTemplateFormatVersion: '2010-09-09'
Transform: AWS::Serverless-2016-10-31


Description: Welcome to the Pet Store Demo


Resources:
  PetStore:
    Type: AWS::Serverless::Function
    Properties:
      Runtime: nodejs8.10
      Handler: index.handler
      Events:
        PetStore:
          Type: Api
          Properties:
            Path: /
            Method: any
```

2. Save the template.yaml file.

You have modified the AWS SAM template to connect an Amazon API Gateway event for any method (GET, POST, and so on) to the AWS Lambda function. In the next exercise, you will modify the AWS Lambda function to work with the API.

EXERCISE 13.8

Modify Your AWS Lambda Function for the API

After you have defined an API, modify your AWS Lambda function.

1. Open the index.js file, and make the following changes:

```
'use strict';


//A simple Lambda function
exports.handler = (event, context, callback) => {

    console.log('DEBUG: This is our local lambda function');
```

```
        console.log('DEBUG: Creating a PetStore service');

        callback(null, {
            statusCode: 200,
            headers: { "x-petstore-custom-header": "custom header from petstore
service" },
            body: '{"message": "Hello! Welcome to the PetStore. What kind of Pet
are you interested in?"}'
        })


    }
```

2. Save the index.js file.

You have modified the AWS Lambda function to respond to an API REST request. However, you have not actually executed anything—you will do that in the next exercise.

EXERCISE 13.9

Run Amazon API Gateway Locally

Now that you have everything defined, run Amazon API Gateway locally.

1. Open a terminal and type the following:

    `sam local start-api`

    You will see output that looks like the following. Take note of the URL.

    ```
    2018-10-11 23:05:25 Mounting PetStore at http://127.0.0.1:3000/hello [GET]
    2018-10-11 23:05:25 You can now browse to the above endpoints to invoke your
    functions. You do not need to restart/reload SAM CLI while working on your
    functions changes will be reflected instantly/automatically. You only need to
    restart SAM CLI if you update your AWS SAM template
    2018-10-11 23:05:25  * Running on http://127.0.0.1:3000/ (Press CTRL+C to quit)
    ```

2. Open a web browser, and navigate to the previous URL.

    You will see the following message:

    `Message: "Hello! Welcome to the Pet Store. What kind of Pet are you interested in?"`

    When you navigate to the URL, the local API Gateway forwards the request to AWS Lambda, which is also running locally, provided by index.js. You can now build serverless applications locally. When you are ready to deploy to a development or production environment, deploy the serverless applications to the AWS Cloud with AWS SAM. This allows developers to iterate through their code quickly and make improvements locally.

Review Questions

1. Which templating engine can you use to deploy infrastructure inside of AWS that is built for serverless technologies?

   A. AWS CloudFormation

   B. Ansible

   C. AWS OpsWorks for Automate Operations

   D. AWS Serverless Application Model (AWS SAM)

2. What option do you need to enable to call Amazon API Gateway from another server or service?

   A. You do not need to enable any options. Amazon API Gateway is ready to use as soon as it's deployed.

   B. Enable cross-origin resource sharing (CORS).

   C. Deploy a stage.

   D. Deploy a resource.

3. A company is considering moving to the AWS serverless stack. What are two benefits of serverless stacks? (Select TWO.)

   A. No server management

   B. It costs less than Amazon Elastic Compute Cloud (Amazon EC2).

   C. Flexible scaling

   D. There are no benefits to serverless stacks.

4. Can you create HTTP endpoints with Amazon API Gateway?

   A. Yes. You can create HTTP endpoints with Amazon API Gateway.

   B. No. API Gateway creates FTP endpoints.

   C. No. API Gateway only supports SSH endpoints.

   D. No. API Gateway is a secure service that only supports HTTPS.

5. A company is moving to a serverless application, using Amazon Simple Storage Service (Amazon S3), AWS Lambda, and Amazon DynamoDB. They are currently using Amazon CloudFront for their content delivery network (CDN) network. They are concerned that they can no longer use Amazon CloudFront because they will have no Amazon Elastic Compute Cloud (Amazon EC2) instances running. Is their concern valid?

   A. Their concerns are valid: Amazon CloudFront only supports Amazon EC2.

   B. Their concerns are valid because all serverless applications are fully dynamic and contain no static information; thus, Amazon CloudFront does not support serverless applications.

   C. Their concerns are not valid. Amazon CloudFront supports serverless applications

   D. Their concerns are valid. Amazon CloudFront does support serverless applications; however, it does not support Amazon S3.

6. Amazon Cognito Mobile SDK does *not* support which language/platform?

    A. iOS

    B. Android

    C. JavaScript

    D. All of these languages/platform are supported.

7. Does Amazon Cognito support Short Message Service (SMS)–based multi-factor authentication (MFA)?

    A. No. Amazon Cognito does not support SMS-based MFA.

    B. No. Amazon Cognito does not support SMS-based MFA; however, it does support MFA.

    C. Yes. Amazon Cognito does support SMS-based MFA.

    D. None of the above.

8. Does Amazon Cognito support device tracking and remembering?

    A. Amazon Cognito does not support device tracking and remembering.

    B. Amazon Cognito supports device tracking but not remembering.

    C. Amazon Cognito supports device remembering but not tracking.

    D. Amazon Cognito supports device remembering and tracking.

9. What is the property name that you use to connect an AWS Lambda function to the Amazon API Gateway inside of an AWS Serverless Application Model (AWS SAM) template?

    A. events

    B. handler

    C. context

    D. runtime

10. A company wants to use a serverless application to run its dynamic website that is currently running on Amazon Elastic Compute Cloud (Amazon EC2) and Elastic Load Balancing (ELB). Currently, the application uses HTML, CSS, and React, and the database is a NoSQL flavor. You are the advisor—is this possible?

    A. No. This is not possible, because there is no way to run React in AWS. React is a Facebook technology.

    B. No. This is not possible, because you need an Amazon EC2 to run the web server.

    C. No. This is not possible, because there is no way to load balance a serverless application.

    D. Yes. This is possible; however, some refactoring will be required.

Chapter

14

Stateless Application Patterns

THE AWS CERTIFIED DEVELOPER – ASSOCIATE EXAM TOPICS COVERED IN THIS CHAPTER INCLUDE, BUT ARE NOT LIMITED TO, THE FOLLOWING:

Domain 1: Deployment

✓ 1.4 Deploy serverless applications.

Domain 2: Security

✓ 2.1 Make authenticated calls to AWS services.

✓ 2.2 Implement encryption using AWS services.

✓ 2.3 Implement application authentication and authorization.

Domain 3: Development with AWS Services

✓ 3.2 Translate functional requirements into application design.

✓ 3.3 Implement application design into application code.

✓ 3.4 Write code that interacts with AWS services by using APIs, SDKs, and AWS CLI.

Introduction to the Stateless Application Pattern

In previous chapters, you were introduced to compute, networking, databases, and storage on the AWS Cloud. This chapter covers the fully managed services that you use to build stateless applications on AWS. Scalability is an important consideration when you create and deploy applications that are highly available, and stateless applications are easier to scale.

When users or services interact with an application, they often perform a sequence of interactions that form a session. A *stateless application* is one that requires no knowledge of previous interactions and stores no session information. Given the same input, an application can provide the same response to any user.

A stateless application can scale horizontally because requests can be serviced by any of the available compute resources, such as Amazon Elastic Compute Cloud (Amazon EC2) instances or AWS Lambda functions. With no session data sharing, you can add more compute resources as necessary. When that compute capacity is no longer needed, you can safely terminate any individual resource. Those resources do not need to be aware of the presence of their peers, and they only need a way to share the workload among them.

This chapter discusses the AWS services that provide a mechanism for persisting state outside of the application: Amazon DynamoDB, Amazon Simple Storage Service (Amazon S3), Amazon ElastiCache, and Amazon Elastic File System (Amazon EFS).

Amazon DynamoDB

Amazon DynamoDB is a fast and flexible NoSQL database service that applications use that require consistent, single-digit millisecond latency at any scale. A fully managed NoSQL database supports both document and key-value store models. DynamoDB is ideal for mobile, web, gaming, ad tech, and Internet of Things (IoT) applications. DynamoDB provides an effective solution for sharing session states across web servers, Amazon EC2 instances, or computing nodes.

Using Amazon DynamoDB to Store State

DynamoDB provides fast and predictable performance with seamless scalability. It enables you to offload the administrative burdens of operating and scaling a distributed database, including hardware provisioning, setup and configuration, replication, software patching, or cluster scaling. Also, DynamoDB offers encryption at rest, which reduces the operational tasks and complexity involved in protecting sensitive data.

With DynamoDB, you can create database *tables* that can store and retrieve any amount of data (*collection*) and serve any level of request traffic. You can scale up or scale down the throughput capacity of your tables without downtime or performance degradation and use the *AWS Management Console* to monitor resource utilization and performance metrics. DynamoDB provides on-demand backup capability to create full backups of tables for long-term retention and archives for regulatory compliance. Use DynamoDB to delete expired items from tables automatically to reduce both storage usage and the cost to store irrelevant data.

DynamoDB automatically spreads data and traffic for tables over a sufficient number of servers to handle throughput and storage requirements while maintaining consistent and fast performance. All of your data is stored on solid-state drive (SSDs) and automatically replicates across multiple Availability Zones in an AWS Region, providing built-in high availability and data durability. You can use global tables to keep DynamoDB tables synchronized across AWS Regions, and you can access this service using the DynamoDB console, the AWS Command Line Interface (AWS CLI), a generic web services Application Programming Interface (API), or any programming language that the AWS software development kit (AWS SDK) supports.

Tables, items, and attributes are core components of DynamoDB. A *table* is a collection of items, and each item is a collection of attributes. For example, you could have a table called *Cars*, which stores information about vehicles. DynamoDB uses *primary keys* to identify each item in a table (e.g., Ford) uniquely and *secondary indexes* to provide more querying flexibility (e.g., Mustang). You can use *Amazon DynamoDB Streams* to capture data modification events in DynamoDB tables.

Primary Key, Partition Key, and Sort Key

When you create a table, you must configure both the *table name* and the *primary key* of the table. The *primary key* uniquely identifies each item in the table so that no two items have the same key. DynamoDB supports two different kinds of primary keys: a partition key and sort key.

A *partition key* is a simple *primary key*, composed of only a *partition key attribute*. The partition key of an item is also known as its *hash attribute*. The term *hash attribute* derives from the use of an internal hash function in DynamoDB that evenly distributes data items across partitions based on their partition key values. DynamoDB uses the partition key's value as input to an internal hash function. The output from the hash function determines the partition (physical storage internal to DynamoDB) in which the item will be stored.

In a table that has only a partition key, no two items can have the same partition key value.

You can also create a *primary key* as a *composite primary key*, consisting of a partition key (first attribute) and a sort key (second attribute).

The *sort key* of an item is also known as its *range attribute*. The term *range attribute* derives from the way that DynamoDB stores items with the same partition key physically close together, in sorted order, by the sort key value.

Each primary key attribute must be a *scalar*, meaning that it can hold only a single value. The only data types allowed for primary key attributes are string, number, or binary. There are no such restrictions for other, nonkey attributes.

Best Practices for Designing and Using Partition Keys

When DynamoDB stores data, it divides table items into multiple physical partitions primarily based on the partition key values, and it distributes the table data accordingly. The primary key that uniquely identifies each item in a DynamoDB table can be either *simple* (partition key only) or *composite* (partition key combined with a sort key). *Partition key values* determine the logical partitions in which a table's data is stored, which affects the table's underlying physical partitions. Efficient partition key design keeps your workload spread evenly across these partitions.

A single physical DynamoDB partition supports a maximum of 3,000 read-capacity units (RCUs) or 1,000 write-capacity units (WCUs). Provisioned I/O capacity for the table is divided evenly among all physical partitions. Therefore, design your partition keys to spread I/O requests as evenly as possible across the table's partitions to prevent "hot spots" that use provisioned I/O capacity inefficiently.

Example 1: Hotspot

If a table has a small number of heavily accessed partition key values (possibly even one heavily used partition key value), request traffic is concentrated on a small number of partitions, or only one partition. If the workload is heavily unbalanced, meaning that it is disproportionately focused on one or a few partitions, the requests do not achieve the overall provisioned throughput level.

To achieve the maximum DynamoDB throughput, create tables where the partition key has a large number of distinct values, and values are requested fairly uniformly, as randomly as possible.

Designing Partition Keys to Distribute Even Workloads

The partition key portion of a table's primary key determines the logical partitions in which a table's data is stored, and it affects the underlying physical partitions. *Provisioned I/O* capacity for the table is divided evenly among these physical partitions, but a partition key design that does not distribute I/O requests evenly can create "hot" partitions that use your provisioned I/O capacity inefficiently and result in throttling.

The optimal usage of a table's provisioned throughput depends on both the workload patterns of individual items and the partition key design. This does not mean that you must access all partition key values to achieve an efficient throughput level or even that the percentage of accessed partition key values must be high. It does mean that the more distinct partition key values that your workload accesses, the more those requests are spread across the partitioned space. You will use your provisioned throughput more efficiently as the ratio of partition key values accessed to the total number of partition key values increases.

Table 14.1 provides a comparison of the provisioned throughput efficiency of some common partition key schemas.

TABLE 14.1   Partition Key Schemas

Partition Key Value	Uniformity
User Identification (ID) where the application has many users	Good
Status Code where there are only a few possible status codes	Bad
Item Creation Date rounded to the nearest period (day, hour, or minute)	Bad
Device ID where each device accesses data at relatively similar intervals	Good
Device ID where even if there are many devices being tracked, one is by far more popular than all the others	Bad

If a single table has only a small number of partition key values, consider distributing your write operations across more distinct partition key values, and structure the primary key elements to avoid one "hot" (heavily requested) partition key value that slows overall performance.

Consider a table with a composite primary key. The partition key represents the item's creation date, rounded to the nearest day. The sort key is an item identifier. On a given day, all new items are written to that single partition key value and corresponding physical partition.

If the table fits entirely into a single partition (considering the growth of your data over time), and if your application's read and write throughput requirements do not exceed the read and write capabilities of a single partition, your application does not encounter any unexpected throttling because of partitioning.

However, if you anticipate your table scaling beyond a single partition, architect your application so that it can use more of the table's full provisioned throughput.

Using Write Shards to Distribute Workloads Evenly

A *shard* is a uniquely identified group of stream records within a stream. To distribute writes better across a partition key space in DynamoDB, expand the space. You can add a random number to the partition key values to distribute the items among partitions, or you can use a number that is calculated based on what you want to query.

Random Suffixes in Shards

To distribute loads more evenly across a partition key space, add a random number to the end of the partition key values and then randomize the writes across the larger space. For example, if a partition key represents today's date, choose a random number from 1 through 200, and add it as a suffix to the date. This yields partition key values such as 2018-07-09.1, 2014-07-09.2, and so on, through 2018-07-09.200. Because you are randomizing the partition key, the writes to the table on each day are spread evenly across multiple partitions. This results in better parallelism and higher overall throughput.

To read all of the items for a given day, you would have to query the items for all of the suffixes and then merge the results. For example, first issue a Query request for the partition key value 2018-07-09.1, then another Query for 2018-07-09.2, and so on, through 2018-07-09.200. When complete, your application then merges the results from all Query requests.

Calculated Suffixes in Shards

A *random strategy* can improve write throughput, but it is difficult to read a specific item because you do not know which suffix value was written to the item. To make it easier to read individual items, instead of using a random number to distribute the items among partitions, use a number that you can calculate based on what you want to query.

Consider the previous example, where a table uses today's date in the partition key. Now suppose that each item has an accessible OrderId attribute and that you most often need to find items by OrderId in addition to date. Before your application writes the item to the table, it can calculate a hash suffix based on the OrderId, append it to the partition key date, and generate numbers from 1 through 200 that evenly distribute, similar to what the random strategy produces. You can use a simple calculation, such as the product of the UTF-8 code point values, for the characters in the OrderId, modulo 200, + 1. The partition key value would then be the date concatenated with the calculation result.

With this strategy, the writes are spread evenly across the partition key values and across the physical partitions. You can easily perform a GetItem operation for a particular item and date because you can calculate the partition key value for a specific OrderId value.

To read all of the items for a given day, you must query each of the 2018-07-09.N keys (where N is 1 through 200), and your application then merges the results. With this strategy, you avoid a single "hot" partition key value taking the entire workload.

Items

Each table contains zero or more items. An *item* is a group of attributes that is uniquely identifiable among all other entities in the table. For example, in a *People* table, each item represents a person, and in a *Cars* table, each item represents one vehicle. Items in DynamoDB are similar to rows, records, or tables in other database systems. However, in DynamoDB, there is no limit to the number of items that you can store in a table.

Attributes

Each item in a table is composed of one or more attributes. An *attribute* is a fundamental data element, something that does not need to be broken down any further. For example, an item in a *People* table contains attributes called `PersonID`, `LastName`, `FirstName`, and so on. For a *Department* table, an item may have attributes such as `DepartmentID`, `Name`, `Manager`, and so on. Attributes in DynamoDB are similar in many ways to fields or columns in other database systems.

The naming rules for DynamoDB tables are as follows:

- All names must be encoded using UTF-8 and be case-sensitive.
- Table names must be between 3 and 255 characters long and can contain only the following characters:
  - a–z
  - A–Z
  - 0–9
  - _ (underscore)
  - – (dash)
  - . (period)
- Attribute names must be between 1 and 255 characters long.
- Each item in the table has a unique identifier, or primary key, which distinguishes the item from all others in the table. In a *People* table, the primary key consists of one attribute, `PersonID`.
- Other than the primary key, the *People* table is *schema-less*, meaning that you are not required to define the attributes or their data types beforehand. Each item can have its own distinct attributes.
- Most of the attributes are *scalar*, meaning that they can have only one value. Strings and numbers are common scalars.
- Some of the items have a nested attribute. For example, in a *People* table, the `Address` attribute may have nested attributes such as `Street`, `City`, and `PostalCode`. DynamoDB supports nested attributes up to 32 levels deep.

Data Types

DynamoDB supports several *data types* for attributes within a table.

Scalar

A *scalar type* can represent exactly one value. The scalar types are number, string, binary, Boolean, and null.

Number   *Numbers* can be positive, negative, or zero and can have up to 38 digits of precision. Exceeding this limit results in an exception. Numbers are presented as variable length. Leading and trailing zeros are trimmed. All numbers are sent as strings to maximize compatibility across languages and libraries. DynamoDB treats them as number-type attributes for mathematical operations. You can use the number data type to represent a date or a timestamp. One way to do this is with the epoch time, the number of seconds since 00:00:00 Coordinated Universal Time (UTC) on January 1, 1970.

String   *Strings* are Unicode with UTF-8 binary encoding. The length of a string must be greater than zero, and it is constrained by the maximum DynamoDB item size limit of 400 KB. If a primary key attribute is a string type, the following additional constraints apply:

- For a *simple primary key*, the maximum length of the first attribute value (partition key) is 2,048 bytes.

- For a *composite primary key*, the maximum length of the second attribute value (sort key) is 1,024 bytes.

- DynamoDB collates and compares strings using the bytes of the underlying UTF-8 string encoding. For instance, "a" (0x61) is greater than "A" (0x41).

You can use the string data type to represent a date or a timestamp. One way to do this is to use ISO 8601 strings as follows:

- `2018-04-19T12:34:56Z`

- `2018-02-31T10:22:18Z`

- `2017-05-08T12:22:46Z`

Binary   *Binary type attributes* can store any binary data, such as compressed text, encrypted data, or images. Whenever DynamoDB compares binary values, it treats each byte of the binary data as unsigned. The length of a binary attribute must be greater than zero, and it is constrained by the maximum DynamoDB item size limit of 400 KB. If a primary key attribute is a binary type, the following additional constraints apply:

- For a simple primary key, the maximum length of the first attribute value (partition key) is 2,048 bytes.

- For a composite primary key, the maximum length of the second attribute value (sort key) is 1,024 bytes.

Applications must encode binary values in base64-encoded format before sending them to DynamoDB. Upon receipt, DynamoDB decodes the data into an unsigned byte array and uses it as the length of the binary attribute.

Boolean   A *Boolean type attribute* can store one of two values: `true` or `false`.

Null   A *null attribute* is one with an unknown or undefined state.

Document

There are two document types, list and map, which you can nest within each other to represent complex data structures up to 32 levels deep. There is no limit on the number of values in a list or a map, as long as the item containing the values fits within the DynamoDB item size limit of 400 KB.

> An attribute value cannot be an empty string or an empty set; however, empty lists and maps are allowed.

List A *list type attribute* can store an ordered collection of values. Lists are enclosed in square brackets [...] and are similar to a JavaScript Object Notation (JSON) array. There are no restrictions on the data types that can be stored in a list element, and the elements in a list element can be of different types. Here is an example of a list with strings and numbers:

```
MyFavoriteThings: ["Thriller", "Purple Rain", 1983, 2]
```

Map A *map type attribute* can store an unordered collection of name/value pairs. Maps are enclosed in curly braces { ... } and are similar to a JSON object. There are no restrictions on the data types that you can store in a map element, and elements in a map do not have to be the same type. Maps are ideal for storing JSON documents in DynamoDB. The following example shows a map that contains a string, a number, and a nested list that contains another map:

```
{
  Location: "Labrynth",
  MagicStaff: 1,
  MagicRings: [
   "The One Ring",
   {
      "ElevenKings: { Quantity : 3},
      "DwarfLords: { Quantity  : 7},
      "MortalMen:  {  Quantity  : 9}
   }
  ]
}
```

> DynamoDB enables you to work with individual elements within maps—even if those elements are deeply nested.

Set DynamoDB supports types that represent *sets* of number, string, or binary values. There is no limit on the number of values in a set, as long as the item containing the value fits within the DynamoDB 400 KB item size limit. Each value within a set must be unique. The order of the values within a set is not preserved. Applications must not rely on the order of elements within the set. DynamoDB does not support empty sets.

All of the elements within a set must be of the same type.

Amazon DynamoDB Tables

DynamoDB global tables provide a fully managed solution for deploying a multiregion, multi-master database, without having to build and maintain your own replication solution. When you create a global table, you configure the AWS Regions where you want the table to be available. DynamoDB performs all of the necessary tasks to create identical tables in these regions and propagate ongoing data changes to all of the regions.

DynamoDB global tables are ideal for massively scaled applications, with globally dispersed users. In such an environment, you can expect fast application performance. Global tables provide automatic multi-master replication to AWS Regions worldwide, so you can deliver low-latency data access to your users no matter where they are located.

There is no practical limit on a table's size. Tables are unconstrained in terms of the number of items or the number of bytes. For any AWS account, there is an initial limit of 256 tables per region.

Provisioned Throughput

With DynamoDB, you can create *database tables* that store and retrieve any amount of data and serve any level of request traffic. You can scale your table's throughput capacity up or down without downtime or performance degradation, and you can use the AWS Management Console to monitor resource utilization and performance metrics.

For any table or global secondary index, the minimum settings for provisioned throughput are one read capacity unit and one write capacity unit.

AWS places some default limits on the throughput that you can provision. These are the limits unless you request a higher amount.

You can apply all of the available throughput of an account to a single table or across multiple tables.

Throughput Capacity for Reads and Writes in Tables and Indexes

When you create a *table* or *index* in DynamoDB, you must configure your capacity requirements for read and write activity. If you define the throughput capacity in advance,

DynamoDB can reserve the necessary resources to meet the read and write activity that your application requires, while it ensures consistent, low-latency performance.

Throughput capacity is specified in terms of read capacity units or write capacity units:

- One read capacity unit represents one strongly consistent read per second, or two eventually consistent reads per second, for an item up to 4 KB in size. If you need to read an item larger than 4 KB, DynamoDB must consume additional read capacity units. The total number of read capacity units required depends on both the item size and whether you want an eventually consistent read or strongly consistent read.

- One write capacity unit represents one write per second for an item up to 1 KB in size. If you need to write an item larger than 1 KB, DynamoDB must consume additional write capacity units. The total number of write capacity units required depends on the item size.

  For example, if you create a table with five read capacity units and five write capacity units, your application could do the following:

  - Perform strongly consistent reads of up to 20 KB per second (4 KB × 5 read capacity units)
  - Perform eventually consistent reads of up to 40 KB per second (twice as much read throughput)
  - Write up to 5 KB per second (1 KB × 5 write capacity units)

If your application reads or writes larger items (up to the DynamoDB maximum item size of 400 KB), it will consume more capacity units.

If your read or write requests exceed the throughput settings for a table, DynamoDB can throttle that request. DynamoDB can also throttle read requests exceeds for an index. Throttling prevents your application from consuming too many capacity units. When a request is throttled, it fails with HTTP 400 code (Bad Request) and a ProvisionedThroughputExceededException. The AWS SDKs have built-in support for retrying throttled requests, so you do not need to write this logic yourself.

You can use the AWS Management Console to monitor your provisioned and actual throughput and modify your throughput settings if necessary.

DynamoDB provides the following mechanisms for managing throughput:

- DynamoDB automatic scaling
- Provisioned throughput
- Reserved capacity
- AWS Lambda triggers in DynamoDB streams

Setting Initial Throughput Settings

Every application has different requirements for reading and writing from a database. When you determine the initial throughput settings for a DynamoDB table, take the following attributes into consideration:

Item sizes   Some items are small enough that they can be read or written by using a single capacity unit. Larger items require multiple capacity units. By estimating the sizes of the items that will be in your table, you can configure accurate settings for your table's provisioned throughput.

Expected read and write request rates   In addition to item size, estimate the number of reads and writes to perform per second.

Read consistency requirements   Read capacity units are based on strongly consistent read operations, which consume twice as many database resources as eventually consistent reads. Determine whether your application requires strongly consistent reads, or whether it can relax this requirement and perform eventually consistent reads instead.

 Read operations in DynamoDB are by default eventually consistent, but you can request strongly consistent reads for these operations if necessary.

Item Sizes and Capacity Unit Consumption

Before you choose read and write capacity settings for your table, understand your data and how your application will access it. These inputs help you determine your table's overall storage and throughput needs and how much throughput capacity your application will require. Except for the primary key, DynamoDB tables are *schemaless*, so the items in a table can all have different attributes, sizes, and data types. The *total size of an item is the sum of the lengths of its attribute names and values.* You can use the following guidelines to estimate attribute sizes:

- Strings are Unicode with UTF-8 binary encoding. The size of a string is as follows:

    (length of attribute name) + (number of UTF-8-encoded bytes)

- Numbers are variable length, with up to 38 significant digits. Leading and trailing zeroes are trimmed.

- The size of a number is approximately as follows:

    (length of attribute name) + (1 byte per two significant digits) + (1 byte)

- A binary value must be encoded in base64 format before it can be sent to DynamoDB, but the value's raw byte length is used for calculating size. The size of a binary attribute is as follows:

    (length of attribute name) + (number of raw bytes)

- The size of a null attribute or a Boolean attribute is as follows:

  (length of attribute name) + (1 byte)

- An attribute of type List or Map requires 3 bytes of overhead, regardless of its contents. The size of a List or Map is as follows:

  (length of attribute name) + sum (size of nested elements) + (3 bytes).

- The size of an empty List or Map is as follows:

  (length of attribute name) + (3 bytes)

 Choose short attribute names rather than long ones. This helps to optimize capacity unit consumption and reduce the amount of storage required for your data.

Capacity Unit Consumption for Reads

The following describes how read operations for DynamoDB consume read capacity units:

GetItem Reads a single item from a table. To determine the number of capacity units GetItem will consume, take the item size and round it up to the next 4 KB boundary. If you specified a strongly consistent read, this is the number of capacity units required. For an eventually consistent read (the default), take this number and divide it by 2.

For example, if you read an item that is 3.5 KB, DynamoDB rounds the item size to 4 KB. If you read an item of 10 KB, DynamoDB rounds the item size to 12 KB.

BatchGetItem Reads up to 100 items, from one or more tables. DynamoDB processes each item in the batch as an individual GetItem request, so DynamoDB first rounds up the size of each item to the next 4-KB boundary and then calculates the total size. The result is not necessarily the same as the total size of all the items.

For example, if BatchGetItem reads a 1.5-KB item and a 6.5-KB item, DynamoDB calculates the size as 12 KB (4 KB + 8 KB), not 8 KB (1.5 KB + 6.5 KB).

Query Reads multiple items that have the same partition key value. All of the items returned are treated as a single read operation, whereby DynamoDB computes the total size of all items and then rounds up to the next 4-KB boundary.

For example, suppose that your query returns 10 items whose combined size is 40.8 KB. Amazon DynamoDB rounds the item size for the operation to 44 KB. If a query returns 1,500 items of 64 bytes each, the cumulative size is 96 KB.

Scan Reads all items in a table. DynamoDB considers the size of the items that are evaluated, not the size of the items returned by the scan.

If you perform a read operation on an item that does not exist, DynamoDB will still consume provisioned read throughput. A request for a strongly consistent read consumes one read capacity unit, whereas a request for an eventually consistent read consumes 0.5 of a read capacity unit.

For any operation that returns items, request a subset of attributes to retrieve. However, doing so has no impact on the item size calculations. In addition, Query and Scan can return item counts instead of attribute values. Getting the count of items uses the same quantity of read capacity units and is subject to the same item size calculations, because DynamoDB has to read each item to increment the count:

Read operations and read consistency   The preceding calculations assumed requests for strongly consistent reads. For a request for eventually consistent reads, the operation consumes only half of the capacity units. For example, of an eventually consistent read, if the total item size is 80 KB, the operation consumes only 10 capacity units.

Read consistency for Scan   A Scan operation performs eventually consistent reads, by default. This means that the Scan results might not reflect changes as the result of recently completed PutItem or UpdateItem operations. If you require strongly consistent reads, when the Scan begins, set the ConsistentRead parameter to true in the Scan request. This ensures that all of the write operations that completed before the Scan began are included in the Scan response. Setting ConsistentRead to true can be useful in table backup or replication scenarios. With DynamoDB streams, to obtain a consistent copy of the data in the table, first use Scan with ConsistentRead set to true. During the Scan, DynamoDB streams record any additional write activity that occurs on the table. After the Scan completes, apply the write activity from the stream to the table.

A Scan operation with ConsistentRead set to true consumes twice as many read capacity units as compared to keeping ConsistentRead at the default value (false).

Capacity Unit Consumption for Writes

The following describes how DynamoDB write operations consume write capacity units:

PutItem   Writes a single item to a table. If an item with the same primary key exists in the table, the operation replaces the item. For calculating provisioned throughput consumption, the item size that matters is the larger of the two.

UpdateItem   Modifies a single item in the table. DynamoDB considers the size of the item as it appears before and after the update. The provisioned throughput consumed reflects the larger of these item sizes. Even if you update only a subset of the item's attributes, UpdateItem will consume the full amount of provisioned throughput (the larger of the "before" and "after" item sizes).

DeleteItem   Removes a single item from a table. The provisioned throughput consumption is based on the size of the deleted item.

BatchWriteItem   Writes up to 25 items to one or more tables. DynamoDB processes each item in the batch as an individual PutItem or DeleteItem request (updates are not supported). DynamoDB first rounds up the size of each item to the next 1-KB boundary and then calculates the total size. The result is not necessarily the same as the total size of all the items. For example, if BatchWriteItem writes a 500-byte item and a 3.5-KB item, DynamoDB calculates the size as 5 KB (1 KB + 4 KB), not 4 KB (500 bytes + 3.5 KB).

For PutItem, UpdateItem, and DeleteItem operations, DynamoDB rounds the item size up to the next 1 KB. If you put or delete an item of 1.6 KB, DynamoDB rounds the item size up to 2 KB.

PutItem, UpdateItem, and DeleteItem allow *conditional writes*, whereby you configure an expression that must evaluate to true for the operation to succeed. If the expression evaluates to false, DynamoDB consumes write capacity units from the table.

For an existing item, the number of write capacity units consumed depends on the size of the new item. For example, a failed conditional write of a 1-KB item would consume one write capacity unit. If the new item were twice that size, the failed conditional write would consume two write capacity units.

> For a new item, DynamoDB consumes one write capacity unit.

If a ConditionExpression evaluates to false during a conditional write, DynamoDB will consume write capacity from the table based on the following conditions:

- If the item does not currently exist in the table, DynamoDB consumes one write capacity unit.
- If the item does exist, then the number of write capacity units consumed depends on the size of the item. For example, a failed conditional write of a 1-KB item would consume one write capacity unit. If the item were twice that size, the failed conditional write would consume two write capacity units.

> Write operations consume write capacity units only. Write operations do not consume read capacity units.

A failed conditional write returns a ConditionalCheckFailedException. When this occurs, you do not receive any information in the response about the write capacity that was consumed. However, you can view the ConsumedWriteCapacityUnits metric for the table in Amazon CloudWatch.

To return the number of write capacity units consumed during a conditional write, use the ReturnConsumedCapacity parameter with any of the following attributes:

Total   Returns the total number of write capacity units consumed.

Indexes   Returns the total number of write capacity units consumed with subtotals for the table and any secondary indexes that were affected by the operation.

None   No write capacity details are returned (default).

> Unlike a global secondary index, a local secondary index shares its provisioned throughput capacity with its table. Read and write activity on a local secondary index consumes provisioned throughput capacity from the table.

Capacity Unit Sizes

One *read* capacity unit = one strongly consistent read per second, or two eventually consistent reads per second, for items up to 4 KB in size.

One *write* capacity unit = one write per second, for items up to 1 KB in size.

Creating Tables to Store the State

Before you store state in DynamoDB, you must create a table. To work with DynamoDB, your application must use several API operations and be organized by category.

Control Plane

Control plane operations let you create and manage DynamoDB tables and work with indexes, streams, and other objects that are dependent on tables.

CreateTable   Creates a new table. You can create one or more secondary indexes and enable DynamoDB Streams for the table.

DescribeTable   Returns information about a table, such as its primary key schema, throughput settings, and index information.

ListTables   Returns the names of all of the tables in a list.

UpdateTable   Modifies the settings of a table or its indexes, creates or remove new indexes on a table, or modifies settings for a table in DynamoDB Streams.

DeleteTable   Removes a table and its dependent objects from DynamoDB.

Data Plane

Data plane operations let you perform *create/read/update/delete (CRUD)* actions on data in a table. Some data plane operations also enable you to read data from a secondary index.

Creating Data

The following data plane operations enable you to perform create actions on data in a table:

PutItem   Writes a single item to a table. You must configure the primary key attributes, but you do not have to configure other attributes.

BatchWriteItem   Writes up to 25 items to a table. This is more efficient than multiple PutItem commands because your application needs only a single network round trip to write the items. You can also use BatchWriteItem to delete multiple items from one or more tables.

Performing Batch Operations

DynamoDB provides the BatchGetItem and BatchWriteItem operations for applications that need to read or write multiple items. Use these operations to reduce the number of network round trips from your application to DynamoDB. In addition, DynamoDB performs the individual read or write operations in *parallel*. Your applications benefit from this parallelism without having to manage concurrency or threading.

The batch operations are wrappers around multiple read or write requests. If a BatchGetItem request contains five items, DynamoDB performs five GetItem operations on your behalf. Similarly, if a BatchWriteItem request contains two put requests and four delete requests, DynamoDB performs two PutItem and four DeleteItem requests.

In general, a batch operation does not fail unless *all* requests in that batch fail. If you perform a BatchGetItem operation, but one of the individual GetItem requests in the batch fails, the BatchGetItem returns the keys and data from the GetItem request that failed. The other GetItem requests in the batch are not affected.

BatchGetItem   A single BatchGetItem operation can contain up to 100 individual GetItem requests and can retrieve up to 16 MB of data. In addition, a BatchGetItem operation can retrieve items from multiple tables.

BatchWriteItem   The BatchWriteItem operation can contain up to 25 individual PutItem and DeleteItem requests and can write up to 16 MB of data. The maximum size of an individual item is 400 KB. In addition, a BatchWriteItem operation can put or delete items in multiple tables.

   BatchWriteItem does not support UpdateItem requests.

Reading Data

The following data plane operations enable you to perform read actions on data in a table:

GetItem   Retrieves a single item from a table. You must configure the primary key for the item that you want. You can retrieve the entire item or only a subset of its attributes.

BatchGetItem   Retrieves up to 100 items from one or more tables. This is more efficient than calling GetItem multiple times because your application needs only a single network round trip to read the items.

Query   Retrieves all items that have a specific partition key. You must configure the *partition key* value. You can retrieve entire items or only a subset of their attributes. You can apply a condition to the sort key values so that you retrieve only a subset of the data that has the same partition key.

 You can use the Query operation on a table or index if the table or index has both a partition key and a sort key.

Scan   Retrieves all the items in the table or index. You can retrieve entire items or only a subset of their attributes. You can use a filter condition to return only the values that you want and discard the rest.

Updating Data

UpdateItem modifies one or more attributes in an item. You must configure the primary key for the item that you want to modify. You can add new attributes and modify or remove existing attributes. You can also perform conditional updates so that the update is successful only when a user-defined condition is met. You can also implement an atomic counter, which increments or decrements a numeric attribute without interfering with other write requests.

Deleting Data

The following data plane operations enable you to perform delete actions on data in a table:

DeleteItem   Deletes a single item from a table. You must configure the primary key for the item that you want to delete.

BatchDeleteItem   Deletes up to 25 items from one or more tables. This is more efficient than multiple DeleteItem calls, because your application needs only a single network round trip. You can also use BatchWriteItem to add multiple items to one or more tables.

Return Values

In some cases, you may want DynamoDB to return certain attribute values as they appeared before or after you modified them. The PutItem, UpdateItem, and DeleteItem operations have a ReturnValues parameter that you can use to return the attribute values before or after they are modified. The default value for ReturnValues is None, meaning that DynamoDB will not return any information about attributes that were modified.

The following are additional settings for ReturnValues, organized by DynamoDB API operation:

PutItem   The PutItem action creates a new item or replaces an old item with a new item. You can return the item's attribute values in the same operation by using the ReturnValues parameter.

ReturnValues: ALL_OLD

- If you overwrite an existing item, ALL_OLD returns the entire item as it appeared before the overwrite.
- If you write a nonexistent item, ALL_OLD has no effect.

UpdateItem   The most common use for UpdateItem is to update an existing item. However, UpdateItem actually performs an *upsert*, meaning that it will automatically create the item if it does not already exist.

ReturnValues: ALL_OLD

- If you update an existing item, ALL_OLD returns the entire item as it appeared before the update.
- If you update a nonexistent item (upsert), ALL_OLD has no effect.

ReturnValues: ALL_NEW

- If you update an existing item, ALL_NEW returns the entire item as it appeared after the update.
- If you update a nonexistent item (upsert), ALL_NEW returns the entire item.

ReturnValues: UPDATED_OLD

- If you update an existing item, UPDATED_OLD returns only the updated attributes as they appeared before the update.
- If you update a nonexistent item (upsert), UPDATED_OLD has no effect.

ReturnValues: UPDATED_NEW

- If you update an existing item, UPDATED_NEW returns only the affected attributes as they appeared after the update.
- If you update a nonexistent item (upsert), UPDATED_NEW returns only the updated attributes as they appear after the update.

DeleteItem   The DeleteItem deletes a single item in a table by primary key. You can perform a conditional delete operation that deletes the item if it exists, or if it has an expected attribute value.

ReturnValues: ALL_OLD

- If you delete an existing item, ALL_OLD returns the entire item as it appeared before you deleted it.
- If you delete a nonexistent item, ALL_OLD does not return any data.

Requesting Throttle and Burst Capacity

If your application performs reads or writes at a higher rate than your table can support, DynamoDB begins to *throttle* those requests. When DynamoDB throttles a read or write, it returns a ProvisionedThroughputExceededException to the caller. The application can then take appropriate action, such as waiting for a short interval before retrying the request.

The AWS SDKs provide built-in support for retrying throttled requests; you do not need to write this logic yourself. The DynamoDB console displays CloudWatch metrics for your tables so that you can monitor throttled read requests and write requests. If you encounter excessive throttling, consider increasing your table's provisioned throughput settings.

In some cases, DynamoDB uses *burst capacity* to accommodate reads or writes in excess of your table's throughput settings. With burst capacity, unexpected read or write requests can succeed where they otherwise would be throttled. Burst capacity is available on a best-effort basis, and DynamoDB does not verify that this capacity is always available.

Amazon DynamoDB Secondary Indexes: Global and Local

A *secondary index* is a data structure that contains a subset of attributes from a table. The index uses an alternate key to support Query operations in addition to making queries against the primary key. You can retrieve data from the index using a Query. A table can have multiple secondary indexes, which give your applications access to many different Query patterns.

You can create one or more secondary indexes on a table. DynamoDB does not require indexes, but indexes give your applications more flexibility when you query your data. After you create a secondary index on a table, you can read or scan data from the index in much the same way as you do from the table.

DynamoDB supports the following kinds of indexes:

Global secondary index   A *global secondary index* is one with a partition key and sort key that can be different from those on the table.

Local secondary index   A *local secondary index* is one that has the same partition key as the table but a different sort key.

    You can define up to five global secondary indexes and five local secondary indexes per table. You can also scan an index as you would a table.

Figure 14.1 shows a local secondary index for a DynamoDB table of forum posts. The local secondary index allows you to query based on the date and time of the last post to a subject, as opposed to the subject itself.

FIGURE 14.1   Amazon DynamoDB indexes

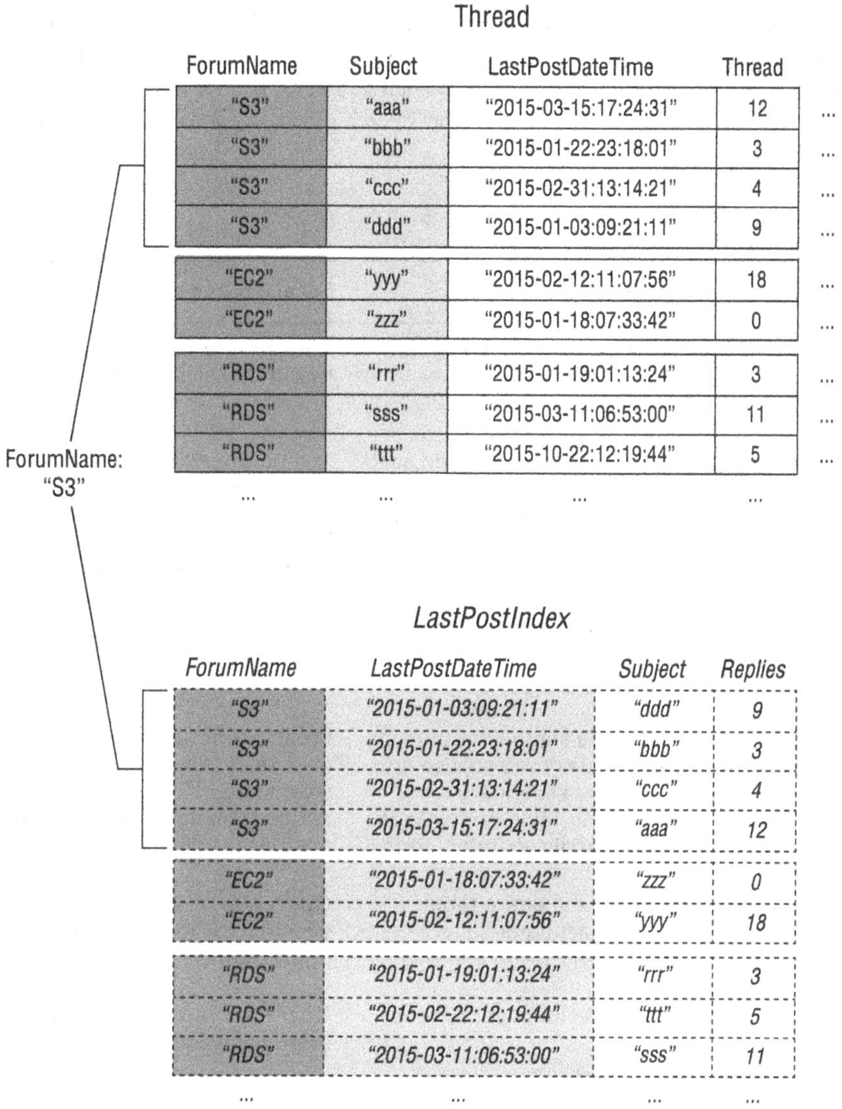

Thread

ForumName	Subject	LastPostDateTime	Thread	
"S3"	"aaa"	"2015-03-15:17:24:31"	12	...
"S3"	"bbb"	"2015-01-22:23:18:01"	3	...
"S3"	"ccc"	"2015-02-31:13:14:21"	4	...
"S3"	"ddd"	"2015-01-03:09:21:11"	9	...
"EC2"	"yyy"	"2015-02-12:11:07:56"	18	...
"EC2"	"zzz"	"2015-01-18:07:33:42"	0	...
"RDS"	"rrr"	"2015-01-19:01:13:24"	3	...
"RDS"	"sss"	"2015-03-11:06:53:00"	11	...
"RDS"	"ttt"	"2015-10-22:12:19:44"	5	...
...	...	...	...	

ForumName: "S3"

LastPostIndex

ForumName	LastPostDateTime	Subject	Replies
"S3"	"2015-01-03:09:21:11"	"ddd"	9
"S3"	"2015-01-22:23:18:01"	"bbb"	3
"S3"	"2015-02-31:13:14:21"	"ccc"	4
"S3"	"2015-03-15:17:24:31"	"aaa"	12
"EC2"	"2015-01-18:07:33:42"	"zzz"	0
"EC2"	"2015-02-12:11:07:56"	"yyy"	18
"RDS"	"2015-01-19:01:13:24"	"rrr"	3
"RDS"	"2015-02-22:12:19:44"	"ttt"	5
"RDS"	"2015-03-11:06:53:00"	"sss"	11
...	...	...	...

Every secondary index is associated with exactly one table from which it obtains its data; it is the *base table* for the index. DynamoDB maintains indexes automatically. When you add, update, or delete an item in the base table, DynamoDB makes the change to the item in any indexes that belong to that table. When you create an index, you configure which attributes copy (project) from the base table to the index. At a minimum, DynamoDB projects the key attributes from the base table into the index.

When you create an index, you define an *alternate key* (partition key and sort key) for the index. You also define the attributes that you want to project from the base table into the index. DynamoDB copies these attributes into the index along with the primary key attributes from the base table. You can Query or Scan the index like a table.

Consider your application's requirements when you determine which type of index to use. Table 14.2 shows the main differences between a global secondary index and a local secondary index.

TABLE 14.2 Global vs. Secondary Indexes

Characteristic	Global Secondary Index	Local Secondary Index
Key Schema	The primary key can be simple (partition key) or composite (partition key and sort key).	The primary key must be composite (partition key and sort key).
Key Attributes	The index partition key and sort key (if present) can be any base table attributes of type string, number, or binary.	The partition key of the index is the same attribute as the partition key of the base table. The sort key can be any base table attribute of type string, number, or binary.
Size Restrictions Per Partition Key Value	No size restrictions.	No size restrictions.
Online Index Operations	Create at the same time that you create a table. You can also add a new global secondary index to an existing table or delete an existing global secondary index.	Create at the same time that you create a table. You cannot add a local secondary index to an existing table, nor can you delete any local secondary indexes that currently exist.
Queries and Partitions	Query over the entire table, across all partitions.	Query over a single partition, as specified by the partition key value in the query.
Read Consistency	Query on eventual consistency only.	Query eventual consistency or strong consistency.
Provisioned Throughput Consumption	Every global secondary index has its own provisioned throughput settings for read and write activity. Queries, scans, and updates consume capacity units from the index, not from the base table.	Query or scan consumes read capacity units from the base table. Writes and write updates consume write capacity units from the base table.
Projected Attributes	Queries or scans can only request the attributes that project into the index. DynamoDB will *not* fetch any attributes from the table.	Queries or scans can request attributes that do not project into the index. DynamoDB will automatically fetch those attributes from the table.

If you write an item to a table, you do not have to configure the attributes for any global secondary index sort key. A table with many global secondary indexes incurs higher costs for write activity than tables with fewer indexes. For maximum query flexibility, you can create up to five global secondary indexes and up to five local secondary indexes per table.

To create more than one table with secondary indexes, you must do so sequentially. Create the first table and wait for it to become active, then create the next table and wait for it to become active, and so on. If you attempt to create more than one table with a secondary index at a time, DynamoDB responds with a LimitExceededException error.

For each secondary index, you must configure the following:

Type of index   The type of index to be created can be either a global secondary index or a local secondary index.

Name of index   The naming rules for indexes are the same as those for table. The name must be unique for the base table, but you can use the same name for indexes that you associate with different base tables.

Index key schema   Every attribute in the index key schema must be a top-level attribute of type string, number, or binary. Other data types, including documents and sets, are not allowed. Other requirements for the key schema depend on the type of index:

> **Global secondary index**   For a global secondary index, the partition key can be any scalar attribute of the base table. A sort key is optional, and it can be any scalar attribute of the base table.

> **Local secondary index**   For a local secondary index, the partition key must be the same as the base table's partition key, and the sort key must be a non-key base table attribute.

Additional attributes   These attributes are in addition to the table's key attributes, which automatically project into every index. You can project attributes of any data type, including scalars, documents, and sets.

> **Global secondary index**   For a *global secondary index, you must configure read and write capacity unit settings.* These provisioned throughput settings are independent of the base table's settings.

> **Local secondary index**   *For a local secondary index, you do not need to configure read and write capacity unit settings.* Any read and write operations on a local secondary index draw from the provisioned throughput settings of its base table.

To generate a detailed list of secondary indexes on a table, use the DescribeTable operation. DescribeTable returns the name, storage size, and item counts for every secondary index on the table. These values refresh approximately every six hours.

Use the Query or Scan operation to access the data in a secondary index. You configure the *base table name, index, attributes to return in the results,* and any *condition expressions* or *filters* that you want to apply. DynamoDB returns the results in ascending or descending order.

When you delete a table, all indexes associated with that table are deleted.

Global Secondary Indexes

Some applications may need to perform many kinds of queries, using a variety of different attributes as query criteria. To support these requirements, you can create one or more global secondary indexes and then issue query requests against these indexes.

To illustrate, Figure 14.2 displays the GameScores table, which tracks users and scores for a mobile gaming application. Each item in GameScores has a partition key (UserId) and a sort key (GameTitle). Figure 14.2 shows the organization of the items.

FIGURE 14.2 Game scores

GameScores

UserId	GameTitle	TopScore	TopScoreDateTime	Wins	Losses	
"101"	"Galaxy Invaders"	5842	"2015-09-15:17:24:31"	21	72	...
"101"	"Meteor Blasters"	1000	"2015-10-22:23:18:01"	12	3	...
"101"	"Starship X"	24	"2015-08-31:13:14:21"	4	9	...
"102"	"Alien Adventure"	192	"2015-07-12:11:07:56"	32	192	...
"102"	"Galaxy Invaders"	0	"2015-09-18:07:33:42"	0	5	...
"103"	"Attack Ships"	3	"2015-10-19:01:13:24"	1	8	...
"103"	"Galaxy Invaders"	2317	"2015-09-11:06:53:00"	40	3	...
"103"	"Meteor Blasters"	723	"2015-10-19:01:13:24"	22	12	...
"103"	"Starship X"	42	"2015-07-11:06:53:00"	4	19	...
...	...	...	...	...	...	

To write a leaderboard application to display top scores for each game, you could generate a query that specifies the key attributes (UserId and GameTitle). While this would be efficient for the application to retrieve data from GameScores based on GameTitle only, it would need to use a Scan operation. As you add more items to the table, Scan operations of all the data becomes slow and inefficient, making it difficult to answer questions based on Figure 14.2, such as the following:

- What is the top score ever recorded for the game Meteor Blasters?
- Which user had the highest score for Galaxy Invaders?
- What was the highest ratio of wins versus losses?

To better implement queries on non-key attributes, create a global secondary index. A global secondary index contains a selection of attributes from the base table, but you organize them by a primary key that is different from that of the table. The index key does not require any of the key attributes from the table, nor does it require the same key schema as a table.

Every global secondary index must have a partition key and can have an optional sort key. The index key schema can be different from the base table schema. You could have a table with a simple primary key (partition key) and create a global secondary index with a composite primary key (partition key and sort key) or vice versa. The index key attributes can consist of any top-level string, number, or binary attributes from the base table but not other scalar types, document types, and set types.

 You can project other base table attributes into the index. When you query the index, DynamoDB can retrieve these projected attributes efficiently; however, global secondary index queries cannot fetch attributes from the base table. *In a DynamoDB table, each key value must be unique.* However, the key values in a global secondary index do not need to be unique. A global secondary index tracks data items only where the key attribute or attributes actually exist.

Attribute Projections

A *projection* is the set of attributes the secondary index copies from a table. While the partition key and sort key of the table project into the index, you can also project other attributes to support your application's Query requirements. When you query an index, DynamoDB accesses any attribute in the projection as if those attributes were in a table of their own.

When you create a secondary index, configure the attributes that project into the index. DynamoDB provides the following options:

KEYS_ONLY   Each item in the index consists only of the table partition key and sort key values, plus the index key values, and this results in the smallest possible secondary index.

INCLUDE   Each item in the index consists only of the table partition key and sort key values plus the index key values, and it includes other non-key attributes that you configure.

ALL   Includes all attributes from the source table, including other non-key attributes that you configure. Because the table data is duplicated in the index, an ALL projection results in the largest possible secondary index.

When you choose the attributes to project into a global secondary index, consider the provisioned throughput costs and the storage costs:

- Before accessing a few attributes with the lowest possible latency, consider projecting only those attributes into a global secondary index. The smaller the index, the less it costs to store it and the lower your write costs will be.

- If your application will frequently access non-key attributes, consider projecting those attributes into a global secondary index. The additional storage costs for the global secondary index offset the cost of performing frequent table scans.

- When you're accessing most of the non-key attributes frequently, project these attributes, or even the entire base table, into a global secondary index. This provides maximum flexibility; however, your storage cost would increase or even double.

- If your application needs to query a table infrequently but must perform many writes or updates against the data in the table, consider projecting KEYS_ONLY. The global secondary index would be of minimal size but would still be available for query activity.

Querying a Global Secondary Index

Use the Query operation to access one or more items in a global secondary index. The query must specify the *name of the base table*, the *name of the index*, the *attributes* the query results return, and any query *conditions* that you want to apply. DynamoDB can return the results in ascending or descending order.

Consider the following example in which a query requests game data for a leaderboard application:

```
{
    "TableName": "GameScores",
    "IndexName": "GameTitleIndex",
    "KeyConditionExpression": "GameTitle = :v_title",
    "ExpressionAttributeValues": {
        ":v_title": {"S": "Meteor Blasters"}
    },
    "ProjectionExpression": "UserId, TopScore",
    "ScanIndexForward": false
}
```

In this query, the following actions occur:

- DynamoDB accesses GameTitleIndex, using the GameTitle partition key to locate the index items for Meteor Blasters. All index items with this partition key are next to each other for rapid retrieval.

- Within this game, DynamoDB uses the index to access the UserID and TopScore for this game.

- The query results return in descending order, as the ScanIndexForward parameter is set to false.

Scanning a Global Secondary Index

You can use the Scan operation to retrieve the data from a global secondary index. Provide the *base table name* and the *index name* in the request. With a Scan operation, DynamoDB reads the data in the index and returns it to the application. You can also request only some of the data and to discard the residual data. To do this, use the `FilterExpression` parameter of the `Scan` operation.

Synchronizing Data between Tables and Global Secondary Indexes

DynamoDB automatically synchronizes each global secondary index with its base table. When an application writes or deletes items in a table, any global secondary indexes on that table update asynchronously by using an eventually consistent model. Though applications seldom write directly to an index, understand the following the implications of how DynamoDB maintains these indexes:

- When you create a global secondary index, you configure one or more index key attributes and their data types.

- When you write an item to the base table, the data types for those attributes must match the index key schema's data types.

- When you put or delete items in a table, the global secondary indexes on that table update in an eventually consistent fashion.

Long Global Index Propagations

Under normal conditions, changes to the table data propagate to the global secondary indexes within a fraction of a second. However, if an unlikely failure scenario occurs, longer propagation delays may occur. Because of this, your applications need to anticipate and handle situations where a query on a global secondary index returns results that are not current.

Considerations for Provisioned Throughput of Global Secondary Indexes

When you create a global secondary index, you must configure read and write capacity units for the workload that you expect on that index. The provisioned throughput settings of a global secondary index are separate from those of its base table. A `Query` operation on a global secondary index consumes read capacity units from the index, not the base table.

When you put, update, or delete items in a table, the global secondary indexes on that table are updated. These index updates consume write capacity units from the index, not from the base table.

To view the provisioned throughput settings for a global secondary index, use the `DescribeTable` operation, and detailed information about the table's global secondary indexes return.

> If you query a global secondary index and exceed its provisioned read capacity, your request throttles. If you perform heavy write activity on the table but a global secondary index on that table has insufficient write capacity, then the write activity on the table throttles.
>
> To avoid potential throttling, the provisioned write capacity for a global secondary index should be equal to or greater than the write capacity of the base table because new updates write to both the base table and global secondary index.

Read Capacity Units

Global secondary indexes support eventually consistent reads, each of which consume one-half of a *read capacity unit*. For example, a single global secondary index query can retrieve up to 8 KB (2 × 4 KB) per read capacity unit. For global secondary index queries, DynamoDB calculates the provisioned read activity in the same way that it does for queries against tables, except that the calculation is based on the sizes of the index entries instead of the size of the item in the base table. The number of read capacity units is the sum of all projected attribute sizes across all returned items; the result is then rounded up to the next 4-KB boundary.

The maximum size of the results returned by a Query operation is 1 MB; this includes the sizes of all of the attribute names and values across all returned items.

For example, if a global secondary index contains items with 2,000 bytes of data and a query returns 8 items, then the total size of the matching items is 2,000 bytes × 8 items = 16,000 bytes; this is then rounded up to the nearest 4-KB boundary. Because global secondary index queries are eventually consistent, the total cost is 0.5 × (16 KB/4 KB), or two read capacity units.

Write Capacity Units

When you add, update, or delete an item in a table and a global secondary index is affected by this, then the global secondary index consumes provisioned write capacity units for the operation. The total provisioned throughput cost for a write consists of the sum of the write capacity units consumed by writing to the base table and those consumed by updating the global secondary indexes. If a write to a table does not require a global secondary index update, then no write capacity is consumed from the index.

For a table write to succeed, the provisioned throughput settings for the table and all of its global secondary indexes must have enough write capacity to accommodate the write; otherwise, the write to the table will throttle.

Factors Affecting Cost of Writes

The cost of writing an item to a global secondary index depends on the following factors:

- If you write a new item to the table that defines an indexed attribute or you update an existing item to define a previously undefined indexed attribute, one write operation is required to put the item into the index.

- If an update to the table changes the value of an indexed key attribute (from A to B), two writes are required—one to delete the previous item from the index and another write to put the new item into the index.

- If an item was present in the index, but a write to the table caused the indexed attribute to be deleted, one write is required to delete the old item projection from the index.

- If an item is not present in the index before or after the item is updated, there is no additional write cost for the index.

- If an update to the table changes the value of only projected attributes in the index key schema but does not change the value of any indexed key attribute, then one write is required to update the values of the projected attributes into the index.

All of these factors assume that the size of each item in the index is less than or equal to the 1-KB item size for calculating write capacity units. Larger index entries require additional write capacity units. Minimize your write costs by considering which attributes your queries must return and projecting only those attributes into the index.

Considerations for Storing Global Secondary Indexes

When an application writes an item to a table, DynamoDB automatically copies the correct subset of attributes to any global secondary indexes in which those attributes should appear. Your account is charged for storing the item in the base table and also for storing attributes in any global secondary indexes on that table.

The amount of space used by an index item is the sum of the following:

- Size in bytes of the base table primary key (partition key and sort key)

- Size in bytes of the index key attribute

- Size in bytes of the projected attributes (if any)

- 100 bytes of overhead per index item

To estimate the storage requirements for a global secondary index, estimate the average size of an item in the index and then multiply by the number of items in the base table that have the global secondary index key attributes.

If a table contains an item for which a particular attribute is not defined but that attribute is defined as an index partition key or sort key, DynamoDB does not write any data for that item to the index.

Managing Global Secondary Indexes

Global secondary indexes require you to create, describe, modify, delete, and detect index key violations.

Creating a Table with Global Secondary Indexes

To create a table with one or more global secondary indexes, use the CreateTable operation with the GlobalSecondaryIndexes parameter. For maximum query flexibility, create up to *five* global secondary indexes per table. *Specify one attribute to act as the index partition key*. You can specify another attribute for the index sort key. It is not necessary for either of these key attributes to be the same as a key attribute in the table.

Each index key attribute must be a scalar of type string, number, or binary, and cannot be a document or a set. You can project attributes of any data type into a global secondary index, including scalars, documents, and sets. You must also provide ProvisionedThroughput settings for the index, consisting of ReadCapacityUnits and WriteCapacityUnits. These provisioned throughput settings are separate from those of the table but behave in similar ways.

Viewing the Status of Global Secondary Indexes on a Table

To view the status of all the global secondary indexes on a table, use the DescribeTable operation. The GlobalSecondaryIndexes portion of the response shows all indexes on the table, along with the current status of each (IndexStatus).

The IndexStatus for a global secondary index is as follows:

Creating Index is currently being created, and it is not yet available for use.

Active Index is ready for use, and the application can perform Query operations on the index.

Updating Provisioned throughput settings of the index are being changed.

Deleting Index is currently being deleted, and it can no longer be used.

When DynamoDB has finished building a global secondary index, the index status changes from Creating to Active.

Adding a Global Secondary Index to an Existing Table

To add a global secondary index to an existing table, use the UpdateTable operation with the GlobalSecondaryIndexUpdates parameter, and provide the following information:

- An *index name*, which must be unique among all of the indexes on the table.
- The *key schema* of the index. Configure *one* attribute for the index *partition key*. You can configure another attribute for the index *sort key*. It is not necessary for either of these key attributes to be the same as a key attribute in the table. The data types for each schema attribute must be scalar: string, number, or binary.
- The attributes to project from the table into the index include the following:

  KEYS_ONLY Each item in the index consists of only the table partition key and sort key values, plus the index key values.

  INCLUDE In addition to the attributes described in KEYS_ONLY, the secondary index includes other non-key attributes that you configure.

  ALL The index includes all attributes from the source table.

- The provisioned throughput settings for the index, consisting of ReadCapacityUnits and WriteCapacityUnits. These provisioned throughput settings are separate from those of the table.

You can create only *one* global secondary index per UpdateTable operation, and you cannot cancel a global secondary index creation process.

Resource Allocation

DynamoDB allocates the compute and storage resources to build the index. During the
resource allocation phase, the IndexStatus attribute is CREATING and the Backfilling
attribute is false. Use the DescribeTable operation to retrieve the status of a table and all
of its secondary indexes.

While the index is in the resource allocation phase, you cannot delete its parent table,
nor can you modify the provisioned throughput of the index or the table. You cannot add
or delete other indexes on the table; however, you can modify the provisioned throughput
of these other indexes.

Backfilling

For each item in the table, DynamoDB determines which set of attributes to write to the
index based on its projection (KEYS_ONLY, INCLUDE, or ALL). It then writes these attributes
to the index. During the backfill phase, DynamoDB tracks items that you add, delete, or
update in the table and the attributes in the index.

During the backfilling phase, the IndexStatus attribute is CREATING and the
Backfilling attribute is true. Use the DescribeTable operation to retrieve the status of a
table and all of its secondary indexes.

While the index is backfilling, you cannot delete its parent table. However, you can still
modify the provisioned throughput of the table and any of its global secondary indexes.

When the index build is complete, its status changes to Active. You are not able to
query or scan the index until it is Active.

Restrictions and Limitations of Backfilling

During the backfilling phase, some writes of violating index items may succeed while others are rejected. This can occur if the data type of an attribute value does not match the
data type of an index key schema data type or if the size of an attribute exceeds the maximum length for an index key attribute.

Index key violations do not interfere with global secondary index creation; however,
when the index becomes Active, the violating keys will not be present in the index. After
backfilling, all writes to items that violate the new index's key schema will be rejected.
To detect and resolve any key violations that may have occurred, run the Violation Detec-
tor tool after the backfill phase completes.

While the resource allocation and backfilling phases are in progress, the index is in the
CREATING state. During this time, DynamoDB performs read operations on the table; you
are not charged for this read activity.

You cannot cancel an in-flight global secondary index creation.

Detecting and Correcting Index Key Violations

Throughout the backfill phase of the global secondary index creation, DynamoDB examines each item in the table to determine whether it is eligible for inclusion in the index, because noneligible items cause index key violations. In these cases, the items remain in the table, but the index will not have a corresponding entry for that item.

An *index key violation* occurs if:

- There is a *data type mismatch* between an attribute value and the index key schema data type. For example, in Figure 14.1, if one of the items in the GameScores table had a TopScore value of type "string," and you add a global secondary index with a number-type partition key of TopScore, the item from the table would violate the index key.

- An attribute value from the table exceeds the maximum length for an index key attribute. The *maximum length of a partition key is 2,048 bytes*, and the *maximum length of a sort key is 1,024 bytes*. If any of the corresponding attribute values in the table exceed these limits, the item from the table violates the index key.

If an index key violation occurs, the backfill phase continues without interruption; however, *any violating items are not included in the index*. After the backfill phase completes, all writes to items that violate the new index's key schema will be rejected.

Deleting a Global Secondary Index from a Table

You use the UpdateTable operation to delete a global secondary index. While the global secondary index is being deleted, there is *no effect* on any read or write activity in the parent table, and you can still modify the provisioned throughput on other indexes. You can delete only one global secondary index per UpdateTable operation.

When you delete a table (DeleteTable), all of the global secondary indexes on that table are deleted.

Local Secondary Indexes

Some applications query data by using only the base table's primary key; however, there may be situations where an *alternate sort key* would be helpful. To give your application a choice of sort keys, create one or more local secondary indexes on a table and issue Query or Scan requests against these indexes.

For example, Figure 14.3 is useful for an application such as discussion forums. The figure shows how the items in the table would be organized.

FIGURE 14.3 Forum thread table

Thread

ForumName	Subject	LastPostDateTime	Replies	
"S3"	"aaa"	"2015-03-15:17:24:31"	12	...
"S3"	"bbb"	"2015-01-22:23:18:01"	3	...
"S3"	"ccc"	"2015-02-31:13:14:21"	4	...
"S3"	"ddd"	"2015-01-03:09:21:11"	9	...
"EC2"	"yyy"	"2015-02-12:11:07:56"	18	...
"EC2"	"zzz"	"2015-01-18:07:33:42"	0	...
"RDS"	"rrr"	"2015-01-19:01:13:24"	3	...
"RDS"	"sss"	"2015-03-11:06:53:00"	11	...
"RDS"	"ttt"	"2015-10-22:12:19:44"	5	...
...	...	...	...	

DynamoDB stores all items with the same partition key value contiguously. In this example, given a particular ForumName, a Query operation could immediately locate the threads for that forum. Within a group of items with the same partition key value, the items are sorted by sort key value. If the sort key (Subject) is also provided in the Query operation, DynamoDB can narrow the results that are returned, such as returning the threads in the S3 forum that have a Subject beginning with the letter a.

Requests may require more complex data-access patterns, such as the following:

- Which forum threads receive the most views and replies?
- Which thread in a particular forum contains the largest number of messages?
- How many threads were posted in a particular forum, within a particular time period?

To answer these questions, the Query action would not be sufficient. Instead, you must scan the entire table. For a table with millions of items, this would consume a large amount of provisioned read throughput and time. However, you can configure one or more local secondary indexes on non-key attributes, such as Replies or LastPostDateTime.

A *local secondary index* maintains an *alternate sort key* for a given partition key value. A local secondary index also contains a copy of some, or all, of the attributes from its base table. You configure which attributes project into the local secondary index when you create the table. *The data in a local secondary index is organized by the same partition key as the base table but with a different sort key.* This enables you to access data items efficiently across this different dimension. For greater Query or Scan flexibility, create up to five local secondary indexes per table.

If an application locates the threads that have been posted within the last three months but lacks a local secondary index, the application must scan the entire thread table and discard any posts that were not listed within the specified time frame. With a local secondary index, a Query operation could use LastPostDateTime as a sort key and find the data quickly.

Figure 14.4 shows a local secondary index named LastPostIndex. The partition key is the same as that of the Thread table (see Figure 14.3), but the sort key is LastPostDateTime.

FIGURE 14.4   Last post index

LastPostIndex

ForumName	LastPostDateTime	Subject
"S3"	"2015-01-03:09:21:11"	"ddd"
"S3"	"2015-01-22:23:18:01"	"bbb"
"S3"	"2015-02-31:13:14:21"	"ccc"
"S3"	"2015-03-15:17:24:31"	"aaa"
"EC2"	"2015-01-18:07:33:42"	"zzz"
"EC2"	"2015-02-12:11:07:56"	"yyy"
"RDS"	"2015-01-19:01:13:24"	"rrr"
"RDS"	"2015-02-22:12:19:44"	"ttt"
"RDS"	"2015-03-11:06:53:00"	"sss"
...	...	...

Every local secondary index must meet the following conditions:

- The partition key is the same as that of its base table.
- The sort key consists of exactly one scalar attribute.
- The sort key of the base table projects into the index, where it acts as a non-key attribute.

In Figure 14.4, the partition key is ForumName, and the sort key of the local secondary index is LastPostDateTime. In addition, the sort key value from the base table (Subject) projects into the index, but it is not a part of the index key. If an application needs a list that is based on ForumName and LastPostDateTime, it can issue a Query request against LastPostIndex. The query results sort by LastPostDateTime and can return in ascending or descending order. The query can also apply key conditions, such as returning only items that have a LastPostDateTime within a particular time span.

Every local secondary index automatically contains the partition and sort keys from its base table, so you can project non-key attributes into the index. When you query the index, DynamoDB can retrieve these projected attributes efficiently. When you query a local secondary index, the Query operation can also retrieve attributes that do not project into the index. DynamoDB automatically collects these attributes from the base table but at a greater latency and with higher provisioned throughput costs.

For any local secondary index, you can store up to 10 GB of data per distinct partition key value.

Creating a Local Secondary Index

To create one or more local secondary indexes on a table, use the LocalSecondaryIndexes parameter of the CreateTable operation. You create local secondary indexes when you create the table. When you delete a table, any local secondary indexes on that table are also deleted. *Configure one non-key attribute to act as the sort key of the local secondary index.* The local secondary indexes attribute is scalar and includes string, number, binary, document types, and set types. You can project attributes of any data type into a local secondary index.

For tables with local secondary indexes, there is a 10-GB size limit per partition key value. A table with local secondary indexes can store any number of items, as long as the total size for any one partition key value does not exceed 10 GB.

Querying a Local Secondary Index

In a DynamoDB table, the combined partition key value and sort key value for each item must be unique. However, in a local secondary index, the sort key value does not need to be unique for a given partition key value. If there are multiple items in the local secondary index that have the same sort key value, a Query operation returns all items with the same partition key value. In the response, the items that the query locates do not return in any particular order.

You can query a local secondary index using eventually consistent or strongly consistent reads. To configure which type of consistency you want, use the ConsistentRead parameter of the Query operation. A strongly consistent read from a local secondary index returns the latest updated values. If the Query operation must collect additional attributes from the base table, those attributes will be consistent with respect to the index.

Scanning a Local Secondary Index

You can use the Scan function to retrieve all data from a local secondary index. Provide the *base table name* and the *index name* in the request. With a Scan function, DynamoDB reads the data in the index and returns it to the application. You can also scan for specific data to return and discard the other data using the FilterExpression parameter of the Scan API.

Item Writes and Local Secondary Indexes

DynamoDB automatically keeps all local secondary indexes synchronized with their respective base tables. Applications seldom write directly to an index. However, understand the implications of how DynamoDB maintains these indexes.

When you create a local secondary index, configure an attribute to serve as the sort key for the index and configure a data type for that attribute. Whenever you write an item to the base table, if the item defines an index key attribute, its type must match the index key schema's data type.

There is no requirement for a one-to-one relationship between the items in a base table and the items in a local secondary index. This behavior can be advantageous for many applications, because a table with many local secondary indexes incurs higher costs for write activity than tables with fewer indexes.

Provisioned Throughput for Local Secondary Indexes

When you create a table in DynamoDB, you provision read and write capacity units for the table's expected workload, which includes read and write activity on the table's local secondary indexes.

Read Capacity Units

When you query a local secondary index, the number of read capacity units consumed depends on how you access the data. As with table queries, an index query can use eventually consistent reads or strongly consistent reads, depending on the value of ConsistentRead. One strongly consistent read consumes one read capacity unit, but an eventually consistent read consumes only half of that. By choosing eventually consistent reads, you can reduce your read capacity unit charges.

For index queries that request only index keys and projected attributes, DynamoDB calculates the provisioned read activity in the same way that it does for queries against tables. However, the calculation is based on the sizes of the index entries instead of the size of the item in the base table. The number of read capacity units is the sum of all projected attribute sizes across all items returned. The result is then rounded up to the next 4-KB boundary.

For index queries that read, attributes do not project into the local secondary index, and DynamoDB must collect those attributes from the base table in addition to reading the projected attributes from the index. These collections occur when you include any non-projected [per DynamoDB documentation] attributes in the Select or ProjectionExpression parameters of the Query operation. Fetching causes additional latency in query responses, and it incurs a higher provisioned throughput cost. In addition to the reads from the local secondary index, you are charged for read capacity units for every base table item fetched. This charge is for reading each entire item from the table, not only the requested attributes.

The maximum size of the results returned by a Query operation is 1 MB. This includes the sizes of all of the attribute names and values across all items returned. However, if a query against a local secondary index causes DynamoDB to fetch item attributes from the base table, the maximum size of the data in the results may be lower. In this case, the result size is the sum of the following factors:

- The size of the matching items in the index, rounded up to the next 4 KB

- The size of each matching item in the base table, with each item individually rounded up to the next 4 KB

Using this formula, the maximum size of the results returned by a Query operation is still 1 MB.

Example 2: Query Read Capacity Units for Local Secondary Index

A table has items the size of 300 bytes. There is a local secondary index on that table, but only 200 bytes of each item projects into the index. If you query this index, the query requires table fetches for each item, and the query returns four items. DynamoDB sums up the following:

- Size of the matching items in the index: 200 bytes × 4 items = 800 bytes; this rounds up to 4 KB.

- Size of each matching item in the base table: (300 bytes, rounds up to 4 KB) × 4 items = 16 KB.

The total size of the data in the result is therefore 20 KB.

Write Capacity Units

When you add, update, or delete items in a table, the local secondary indexes consume provisioned write capacity units for the table. The total provisioned throughput cost for a write is the sum of write capacity units consumed by the write to the table and those consumed by the update of the local secondary indexes.

The cost of writing an item to a local secondary index depends on the following factors:

- If you write a new item to the table that defines an indexed attribute or you update an existing item to define a previously undefined indexed attribute, one write operation is required to put the item into the index.

- If an update to the table changes the value of an indexed key attribute (from A to B), two writes are required, one to delete the previous item from the index and another write to put the new item into the index.

- If an item was present in the index but a write to the table caused the indexed attribute to be deleted, one write is required to delete the old item projection from the index.

- If an item is not present in the index before or after the item update, there is no additional write cost for the index.

All of these factors assume that the size of each item in the index is less than or equal to the 1-KB item size for calculating write capacity units. Larger index entries require additional write capacity units. You can minimize your write costs by considering which attributes your queries must return and project only those attributes into the index.

Storage for Local Secondary Indexes

When an application writes an item to a table, DynamoDB automatically copies the correct subset of attributes to any local secondary indexes in which those attributes should appear. Your account is charged for storing the item in the base table and also for storing attributes in any local secondary indexes on that table.

The amount of space used by an index item is the sum of the following elements:

- Size in bytes of the base table primary key (partition and sort key)
- Size in bytes of the index key attribute
- Size in bytes of the projected attributes (if any)
- 100 bytes of overhead per index item

To estimate the storage requirements for a local secondary index, estimate the average size of an item in the index and then multiply by the number of items in the base table.

If a table contains an item where a particular attribute is not defined but that attribute is defined as an index sort key, then DynamoDB does not write any data for that item to the index.

Amazon DynamoDB Streams

Amazon DynamoDB Streams captures data modification events in DynamoDB tables. The data about these events appear in the stream in near real time and in the order that the events occurred.

Each event represents a stream record. When you enable a stream on a table, DynamoDB captures information about every modification to data items in the table. The stream captures an image of the entire item, including all of its attributes. A *stream record* contains information about a data modification to a single item in a DynamoDB table including the primary key attributes of the items. You can configure the stream so that the stream records capture additional information, such as the "before" and "after" images of modified items. Finally, a stream record is written when an item is deleted from the table, and each stream record also contains the name of the table, the event timestamp, and other metadata.

 NOTE   Stream records have a lifetime of 24 hours, after which they are deleted automatically from the stream.

A DynamoDB stream is a time-ordered flow of information of item-level modifications (create, update, or delete) to items in a DynamoDB table.

DynamoDB Streams does the following:

- Each stream record appears exactly *once* in the stream.
- For each item that is modified in a DynamoDB table, the stream records appear in the *same sequence* as the actual modifications to the item.

Many applications benefit from the ability to capture changes to items stored in a DynamoDB table when such changes occur. The following are common scenarios:

- An application in one AWS Region modifies the data in a Amazon DynamoDB table. A second application in another AWS Region reads these data modifications and writes the data to another table, creating a replica that stays in sync with the original table.
- A popular mobile app modifies data in a DynamoDB table at the rate of thousands of updates per second. Another application captures and stores data about these updates, providing near-real-time usage metrics for the mobile app.
- A global multiplayer game has a multi-master topology, storing data in multiple AWS Regions. Each master stays in sync by consuming and replaying the changes that occur in the remote regions.
- An application automatically sends notifications to the mobile devices of all friends in a group as soon as one friend uploads a new picture.
- A new customer adds data to a DynamoDB table. This event invokes another application that sends a welcome email to the new customer.

Whenever an application creates, updates, or deletes items in the table, Amazon DynamoDB Stream writes a stream record with the primary key attribute, or attributes, of the items that were modified. A stream record contains information about a data modification to a single item in a DynamoDB table. Applications can access this log and view the data items as they appeared before and after they were modified, in near real time.

 DynamoDB Streams writes stream records in near-real time, so you can build applications that consume these streams and act based on the contents.

DynamoDB Cross-Region Replication

You can create tables that automatically replicate across two or more AWS Regions with full support for multi-master writes. Using cross-region replication, you can build fast, massively scaled applications for a global user base without having to manage the replication process.

DynamoDB Stream Endpoints

AWS maintains separate endpoints for DynamoDB and DynamoDB Streams. To work with database tables and indexes, your application must access a DynamoDB endpoint. To read and process DynamoDB Streams records, your application must access a DynamoDB Streams endpoint in the same AWS Region.

Figure 14.5 shows the DynamoDB endpoint flow.

FIGURE 14.5   DynamoDB Streams endpoints

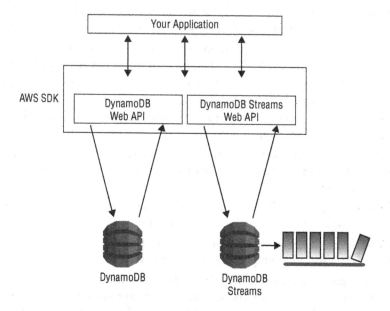

The naming convention for DynamoDB Streams endpoints is streams.dynamodb.<region>.amazonaws.com. For example, if you use the endpoint dynamodb.us-west-2.amazonaws.com to access DynamoDB, use the endpoint streams.dynamodb.us-west-2.amazonaws.com to access DynamoDB Streams.

The AWS SDKs provide separate clients for DynamoDB and DynamoDB Streams. Depending on your requirements, your application can access a DynamoDB endpoint, a DynamoDB Streams endpoint, or both at the same time. To connect to both endpoints, your application must instantiate two clients: one for DynamoDB and one for DynamoDB Streams.

Enabling a Stream

You can enable a stream on a new table when you create it, enable or disable a stream on an existing table, or change the settings of a stream. DynamoDB Streams operates asynchronously, so there is no performance impact on a table if you enable a stream.

You can also use the CreateTable or UpdateTable APIs to enable or modify a stream. The StreamSpecification parameter determines how the stream is configured:

StreamEnabled   Specifies whether a stream for the table is enabled (true) or disabled (false)

StreamViewType   Specifies the information that will be written to the stream whenever data in the table is modified:

KEYS_ONLY   Only the key attributes of the modified item

NEW_IMAGE   The entire item as it appears after it was modified

OLD_IMAGE   The entire item as it appeared before it was modified

NEW_AND_OLD_IMAGES   Both the new and the old images of the item

You can enable or disable a stream at any time. However, if you attempt to enable a stream on a table that already has a stream, you will receive a `ResourceInUseException`. If you attempt to disable a stream on a table that does not have a stream, you will receive a `ValidationException`.

When you set `StreamEnabled` to `true`, DynamoDB creates a new stream with a unique stream descriptor. If you disable and then re-enable a stream on the table, a new stream is created with a different stream descriptor.

The *Amazon Resource Name* (ARN) uniquely identifies every stream. The following is an example of defining an ARN for a stream on a DynamoDB table named `TestTable`:

```
arn:aws:dynamodb:us-west-2:111122223333:table/TestTable/stream/
2015-05-11T21:21:33.291
```

To determine the latest stream descriptor for a table, issue a DynamoDB `DescribeTable` request and look for the `LatestStreamArn` element in the response.

Reading and Processing a Stream

To read and process a stream, your application must connect to a DynamoDB Streams endpoint and issue API requests. A stream consists of *stream records*. Each stream record represents a single data modification in the DynamoDB table to which the stream belongs. Each stream record is assigned a sequence number, reflecting the order in which the record was published to the stream.

Stream records are organized into groups called *shards*. Each shard acts as a container for multiple stream records and contains information required for accessing and iterating through these records. The stream records within a shard are removed automatically after 24 hours. If you disable a stream, any shards that are open are closed.

Shards are ephemeral, meaning that they can be both created and deleted automatically as necessary. Any shard can automatically split into multiple new shards, and a shard may split in response to high levels of write activity on its parent table to enable applications to process records from multiple shards in parallel.

It is equally possible for a parent shard to have only one child shard. Because shards have a parent-and-children lineage, an application must always process a parent shard before it processes a child shard. This ensures that the stream records process in the correct order.

If you use the DynamoDB Streams *Kinesis Adapter*, this processing is handled for you. Your application processes the shards and stream records in the correct order, and it automatically handles new or expired shards and shards that split while the application is running.

Figure 14.6 shows the relationship between a stream, shards in the stream, and stream records in the shards.

FIGURE 14.6   Stream and shard relationship

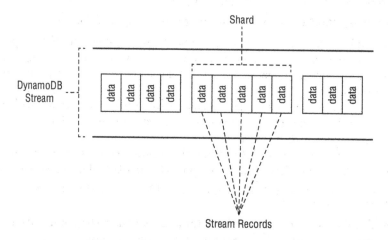

To access a stream and process the stream records, do the following:

1. Identify the unique ARN of the stream that you want to access.

2. Determine which shard or shards in the stream contain the stream records of interest.

3. Access the shard or shards and retrieve the stream records that you want.

   If you perform a PutItem or UpdateItem operation that does not change any data in an item, then DynamoDB Streams will not write a stream record for that operation.

   No more than two processes should be reading from the same stream's shard at the same time. Having more than two readers per shard may result in throttling.

Read Capacity for DynamoDB Streams

DynamoDB is available in multiple AWS Regions around the world. Each region is independent and isolated from other AWS Regions. For example, a table called *People* in the us-east-2 Region and a table named *People* in the us-west-2 Region are two entirely separate tables.

Every AWS Region consists of multiple, distinct locations called *Availability Zones*. Each Availability Zone is isolated from failures in other Availability Zones and provides inexpensive, low-latency network connectivity to other Availability Zones in the same region. This allows rapid replication of your data among multiple Availability Zones in a region.

When an application writes data to a DynamoDB table and receives an HTTP 200 response (OK), all copies of the data are updated. The data is eventually consistent across all storage locations, usually within one second or less.

Eventually consistent reads   DynamoDB supports eventually consistent reads and strongly consistent reads. When you read data from a DynamoDB table, the response may not reflect the results of a recently completed write operation and may include some stale data. If you repeat your read request after a short period, the response returns the latest data.

Strongly consistent reads   DynamoDB uses eventually consistent reads unless you specify otherwise. Read operations, such as GetItem, query, and Scan, provide a ConsistentRead parameter. If you set this parameter to true, DynamoDB uses strongly consistent reads during the operation. When you request a strongly consistent read, DynamoDB returns a response with the most up-to-date data, reflecting the updates from all prior write operations that were successful. A strongly consistent read may not be available if there is a network delay or outage.

DynamoDB Streams API

The DynamoDB Streams API provides the following operations:

ListStreams   Returns a list of stream descriptors for the current account and endpoint, or you can request only the stream descriptors for a particular table name.

DescribeStream   Returns information about a stream, such as its ARN, and where your application can begin to read the first few stream records. The output includes a list of shards associated with the stream, including the shard IDs.

GetShardIterator   Returns a shard iterator, which describes a location within a shard, to retrieve the records from the stream. You can request that the iterator provide access to the oldest point, the newest point, or a particular point in the stream.

GetRecords   Retrieves one or more stream records by using a given shard iterator. Provides the shard iterator returned from a GetShardIterator request.

Data Retention Limit for DynamoDB Streams

All data in DynamoDB Streams is subject to a 24-hour lifetime. You can retrieve and analyze the last 24 hours of activity for any given table; however, data older than 24 hours is susceptible to trimming (removal) at any moment.

If you disable a stream on a table, the data in the stream continues to be readable for 24 hours. After this time, the data expires, and the stream records are deleted automatically. There is no mechanism for manually deleting an existing stream; you must wait until the retention limit expires (24 hours) and all of the stream records are deleted.

AWS Lambda Triggers in DynamoDB Streams

DynamoDB integrates with AWS Lambda, so you can create *triggers* (code that executes automatically) that automatically respond to events in DynamoDB Streams. With triggers, you can build applications that react to data modifications in DynamoDB tables.

Example 3: DynamoDB Table Update Using AWS Lambda and Amazon Resource Name

In Figure 14.2, you have a mobile gaming app that writes to a *GameScores* table. Whenever the TopScore attribute of the *GameScores* table updates, a corresponding stream record writes to the table's stream. This event triggers a Lambda function that posts a congratulatory message on a social media network.

If you enable DynamoDB Streams on a table, you can associate the stream Amazon ARN with a Lambda function that you write. Immediately after an item in the table is modified, a new record appears in the table's stream. Lambda polls the stream and invokes your Lambda function synchronously when it detects new stream records.

The Lambda function can perform any actions that you configure, such as sending a notification or initiating a workflow. For instance, you can write a Lambda function to copy each stream record to persistent storage, such as Amazon Simple Storage Service (Amazon S3), to create a permanent audit trail of write activity in your table.

Query so you can create *triggers* that automatically respond to events in DynamoDB Streams. With triggers, you can build applications that react to data modifications in DynamoDB tables.

If you enable DynamoDB Streams on a table, you can associate the stream ARN with a Lambda function that you write. Immediately after an item in the table is modified, a new record appears in the table's stream. Lambda polls the stream and invokes your Lambda function synchronously when it detects new stream records.

Example 4: Lambda Email Trigger

A *Customers* table, such as the one shown in Figure 14.7, contains customer information for a company. If you want to send a "welcome" email to each new customer, enable a stream on that table and then associate the stream with a Lambda function. The Lambda function executes whenever a new stream record appears, but it processes only new items added to the Customers table. For any item that has an EmailAddress attribute, the Lambda function invokes *Amazon Simple Email Service* (Amazon SES) to send an email to that address. In Figure 14.7, the last customer, Craig Roe, will not receive an email because he does not have an EmailAddress.

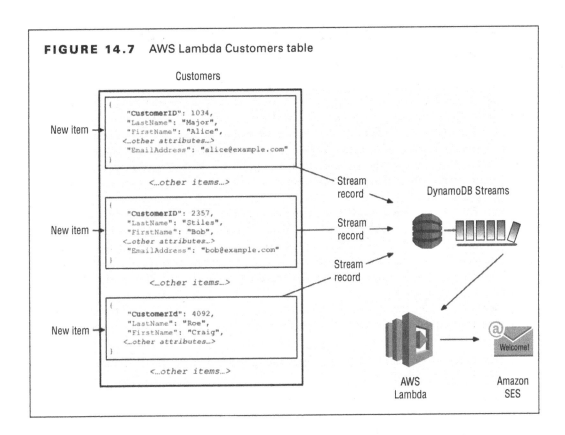

FIGURE 14.7   AWS Lambda Customers table

Amazon DynamoDB Auto Scaling

Amazon DynamoDB automatic scaling actively manages throughput capacity for tables and global secondary indexes. With automatic scaling, you can define a range (upper and lower limits) for read and write capacity units and define a target utilization percentage within that range. DynamoDB automatic scaling seeks to maintain your target utilization, even as your application workload increases or decreases.

With DynamoDB automatic scaling, a table or a global secondary index can increase its provisioned read and write capacity to handle sudden increases in traffic without throttling. When the workload decreases, DynamoDB automatic scaling can decrease the throughput so that you do not pay for unused provisioned capacity.

If you use the AWS Management Console to create a table or a global secondary index, DynamoDB automatic scaling is enabled by default. You can manage automatic scaling settings at any time by using the console, the AWS CLI, or one of the AWS SDKs.

Managing Throughput Capacity Automatically with AWS Auto Scaling

Many database workloads are cyclical in nature or are difficult to predict in advance. In a social networking application, where most of the users are active during daytime hours, the database must be able to handle the daytime activity. But there is no need for the same levels of throughput at night. If a new mobile gaming app is experiencing rapid adoption and becomes too popular, the app could exceed the available database resources, resulting in slow performance and unhappy customers. These situations often require manual intervention to scale database resources up or down in response to varying usage levels.

DynamoDB uses the *AWS Application Auto Scaling* service to adjust provisioned throughput capacity dynamically in response to actual traffic patterns. This enables a table or a global secondary index to increase its provisioned read and write capacity to handle sudden increases in traffic, without throttling. When the workload decreases, Application Auto Scaling decreases the throughput so that you do not pay for unused provisioned capacity.

Application Auto Scaling does not scale down your provisioned capacity if the consumed capacity of your table becomes zero. To scale down capacity manually, perform one of the following actions:

- Send requests to the table until automatic scaling scales down to the minimum capacity.

- Change the policy and reduce the maximum provisioned capacity to the same size as the minimum provisioned capacity.

With Application Auto Scaling, you can create a scaling policy for a table or a global secondary index. The scaling policy specifies whether you want to scale read capacity or write capacity (or both), and the minimum and maximum provisioned capacity unit settings for the table or index.

The scaling policy also contains a target utilization that is the percentage of consumed provisioned throughput at a point in time. Application Auto Scaling uses a target tracking algorithm to adjust the provisioned throughput of the table (or index) upward or downward in response to actual workloads so that the actual capacity utilization remains at or near your target utilization.

DynamoDB automatic scaling also supports global secondary indexes. Every global secondary index has its own provisioned throughput capacity, separate from that of its base table. When you create a scaling policy for a global secondary index, Application Auto Scaling adjusts the provisioned throughput settings for the index to ensure that its actual utilization stays at or near your desired utilization ratio, as shown in Figure 14.8.

FIGURE 14.8   DynamoDB Auto Scaling

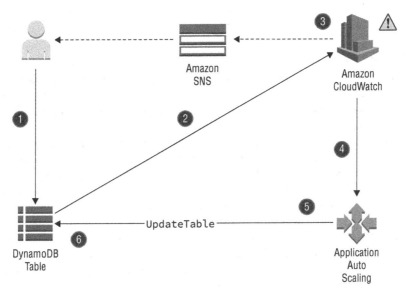

How DynamoDB Auto Scaling Works

The steps in Figure 14.8 summarize the automatic scaling process:

1. Create an Application Auto Scaling policy for your DynamoDB table.

2. DynamoDB publishes consumed capacity metrics to Amazon CloudWatch.

3. If the table's consumed capacity exceeds your target utilization (or falls below the target) for a specific length of time, CloudWatch triggers an alarm. You can view the alarm on the AWS Management Console and receive notifications using Amazon Simple Notification Service (Amazon SNS).

4. The CloudWatch alarm invokes Application Auto Scaling to evaluate your scaling policy.

5. Application Auto Scaling issues an UpdateTable request to adjust your table's provisioned throughput.

6. DynamoDB processes the UpdateTable request, increasing or decreasing the table's provisioned throughput capacity dynamically so that it approaches your target utilization.

DynamoDB automatic scaling modifies provisioned throughput settings only when the actual workload stays elevated or depressed for a sustained period of several minutes. The

Application Auto Scaling target tracking algorithm seeks to keep the target utilization at or near your chosen value over the long term. Sudden, short-duration spikes of activity are accommodated by the table's built-in burst capacity.

Burst Capacity

DynamoDB provides some flexibility in your per-partition throughput provisioning by providing *burst capacity*. Whenever you are not fully using a partition's throughput, Amazon DynamoDB reserves a portion of that unused capacity for later bursts of throughput to handle usage spikes.

DynamoDB currently retains up to 5 minutes (300 seconds) of unused read and write capacity. During an occasional burst of read or write activity, these extra capacity units can be consumed quickly—even faster than the per-second provisioned throughput capacity that you have defined for your table. However, do not rely on burst capacity being available at all times, as DynamoDB can also consume burst capacity for background maintenance and other tasks without prior notice.

To enable DynamoDB automatic scaling, you create a scaling policy. This *scaling policy* specifies the table or global secondary index that you want to manage, which capacity type to manage (read or write capacity), the upper and lower boundaries for the provisioned throughput settings, and your target utilization.

When you create a scaling policy, Application Auto Scaling creates a pair of CloudWatch alarms on your behalf. Each pair represents your upper and lower boundaries for provisioned throughput settings. These CloudWatch alarms are triggered when the table's actual utilization deviates from your target utilization for a sustained period of time.

When one of the CloudWatch alarms is triggered, Amazon SNS sends you a notification (if you have enabled it). The CloudWatch alarm then invokes Application Auto Scaling, which notifies DynamoDB to adjust the table's provisioned capacity upward or downward, as appropriate.

Considerations for DynamoDB Auto Scaling

Before you begin using DynamoDB automatic scaling, be aware of the following:

- DynamoDB automatic scaling can increase read capacity or write capacity as often as necessary in accordance with your automatic scaling policy. All DynamoDB limits remain in effect.

- DynamoDB automatic scaling does not prevent you from manually modifying provisioned throughput settings. These manual adjustments do not affect any existing CloudWatch alarms that are related to DynamoDB automatic scaling.

- If you enable DynamoDB automatic scaling for a table that has one or more global secondary indexes, AWS highly recommends that you also apply automatic scaling uniformly to those indexes. You can apply this by choosing *Apply same settings* to global secondary indexes in the AWS Management Console.

Provisioned Throughput for DynamoDB Auto Scaling

If you are not using DynamoDB automatic scaling, you must manually define your throughput requirements. *Provisioned throughput* is the maximum amount of capacity that an application can consume from a table or index. If your application exceeds your provisioned throughput settings, it is subject to request throttling.

Example 5: Determining the Provisioned Throughput Setting

Suppose that you want to read 80 items per second from a table, where the items are 3 KB in size, and you want strongly consistent reads with each read requiring one provisioned read capacity unit. To determine this, divide the item size of the operation by 4 KB and then round up to the nearest whole number:

3 KB/4 KB = 0.75, or 1 read capacity unit

Knowing this, you must set the table's provisioned read throughput to 80 read capacity units:

1 read capacity unit per item × 80 reads per second = 80 read capacity units

If you want to write 100 items per second to your table, and the items are 512 bytes in size, each write requires one provisioned write capacity unit. To determine this, divide the item size of the operation by 1 KB and then round up to the nearest whole number:

512 bytes/1 KB = 0.5, or 1

To accomplish this, set the table's provisioned write throughput to 100 write capacity units:

1 write capacity unit per item × 100 writes per second = 100 write capacity units

---

Partitions and Data Distribution

DynamoDB stores data in partitions. A *partition* is an allocation of storage for a table, backed by solid-state drives (SSDs) and automatically replicated across multiple Availability Zones within an AWS Region. Partition management is handled entirely by DynamoDB, so you do not have to manage partitions yourself. When you create a table, the initial status of the table is CREATING. During this phase, DynamoDB allocates sufficient partitions to the table so that it can handle your provisioned throughput requirements. You can begin writing and reading table data after the table status changes to ACTIVE.

DynamoDB allocates additional partitions to a table in the following situations:

- If you increase the table's provisioned throughput settings beyond what the existing partitions can support
- If an existing partition fills to capacity and more storage space is required

Partition management occurs automatically in the background, and it is transparent to your applications. Your table remains available throughout and fully supports your provisioned throughput requirements. Global secondary indexes in DynamoDB are also composed of partitions. The data in a global secondary index is stored separately from the data in its base table, but index partitions behave similarly to table partitions.

Data Distribution: Partition Key

If your table has a simple primary key (partition key only), DynamoDB stores and retrieves each item based on its partition key value. To write an item to the table, DynamoDB uses the value of the partition key as input to an internal hash function. The output value from the hash function determines the partition in which the item will be stored. To read an item from the table, you must configure the partition key value for the item. DynamoDB uses this value as input to its hash function, yielding the partition in which the item can be found.

Figure 14.9 shows a table named *Pets*, which spans multiple partitions. The table's primary key is AnimalType (only this key attribute is shown). DynamoDB uses its hash function to determine where to store a new item, in this case based on the hash value of the string Dog. The items are not stored in sorted order. Each item's location is determined by the hash value of its partition key.

FIGURE 14.9   Data distribution and partition

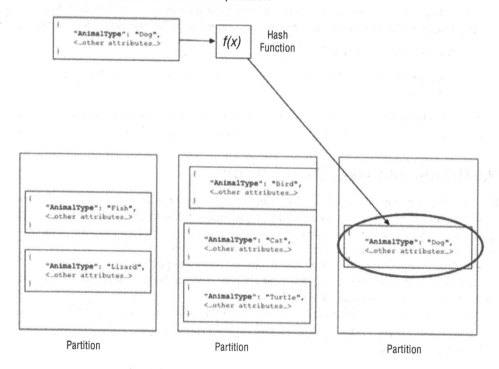

DynamoDB is optimized for uniform distribution of items across a table's partitions, regardless of the number of partitions. Choose a partition key with a large number of distinct values relative to the number of items in the table.

Data Distribution: Partition Key and Sort Key

If the table has a composite primary key (partition key and sort key), DynamoDB calculates the hash value of the partition key in the same way, but it stores the items with the same partition key value physically close together, ordered by sort key value.

To write an item to the table, DynamoDB calculates the hash value of the partition key to determine which partition should contain the item. In that partition, there could be several items with the same partition key value, so DynamoDB stores the item among the others with the same partition key in ascending order by sort key.

To read an item from the table, configure both the partition key value and sort key value. DynamoDB calculates the partition key's hash value, yielding the partition in which the item can be found.

You can read multiple items from the table in a single Query operation, if the desired items have the same partition key value. DynamoDB returns all items with that partition key value. You can apply a condition to the sort key that only returns items within a certain range of values.

Optimistic Locking with Version Number

Optimistic locking is a strategy to ensure that the client-side item that you are updating or deleting is the same as the item in DynamoDB. If you use this strategy, then all writes on your database are protected from being accidentally overwritten.

DynamoDB global tables use a "last writer wins" reconciliation between concurrent updates. If you use Global Tables, last writer policy wins. In this case, the locking strategy does not work as expected.

With optimistic locking, each item has an attribute that acts as a version number. If you retrieve an item from a table, the application records the version number of that item. You can update the item, but only if the version number on the server side has not changed. If there is a version mismatch, then someone else has modified the item before you did, and the update attempt fails because you have an outdated version of the item. If this happens, you retrieve the current item and then attempt to update it again.

To support optimistic locking, the AWS SDK for Java provides the @Amazon DynamoDBVersionAttribute annotation. In the mapping class for your table, designate one property to store the version number and mark it using the annotation. When you save an object, the corresponding item in the DynamoDB table has an attribute that stores the version number. The Amazon DynamoDBMapper assigns a version number when you first save the object, and it automatically increments the version number each time you update the item. Your update or delete requests succeed only if the client-side object version matches the corresponding version number of the item in the Amazon DynamoDB table.

`ConditionalCheckFailedException` occurs if the following conditions are true:

- You use optimistic locking with `@Amazon DynamoDBVersionAttribute`, and the version value on the server is different from the value on the client side.

- You configure your own conditional constraints while saving data by using Amazon `DynamoDBMapper` with Amazon `DynamoDBSaveExpression`, and these constraints failed.

Disabling Optimistic Locking

To disable optimistic locking, change the Amazon `DynamoDBMapperConfig.SaveBehavior` enumeration value from `UPDATE` to `CLOBBER`. Do this by creating an Amazon `DynamoDBMapperConfig` instance that skips version checking and then use this instance for your requests. You can also set locking behavior for a specific operation only. For example, the following Java snippet uses the `DynamoDBMapper` to save a catalog item. It specifies `DynamoDBMapperConfig.SaveBehavior` by adding the optional `DynamoDBMapperConfig` parameter to the save method.

```
DynamoDBMapper mapper = new DynamoDBMapper(client);

// Load a catalog item.
CatalogItem item = mapper.load(CatalogItem.class, 101);
item.setTitle("This is a new title for the item");
...
// Save the item.
mapper.save(item,
    new DynamoDBMapperConfig(
        DynamoDBMapperConfig.SaveBehavior.CLOBBER));
```

DynamoDB Tags

You can label DynamoDB resources with tags. *Tags* allow you to categorize your resources in different ways: by purpose, owner, environment, or other criteria. Tags help you to identify a resource quickly based on the tags that you have assigned to it, and they help you to see your AWS bills broken down by tags.

Tables that have tags automatically tag local secondary indexes and global secondary indexes. Currently, you cannot tag DynamoDB Streams. AWS offerings and services, such as Amazon EC2, Amazon S3, DynamoDB, and more, support tags. Efficient tagging can provide cost insights by enabling you to create reports across services that carry a specific tag.

Tag Restrictions

Each tag consists of a key and a value, both of which you define. Each DynamoDB table can have only one tag with the same key, so if you attempt to add an existing tag (the same key), the existing tag value updates to the new value.

The following restrictions apply:

- Tag keys and values are case-sensitive.
- The maximum key length is 128 Unicode characters, and the maximum value length is 256 Unicode characters. The allowed character types are letters, white space, and numbers, plus the following special characters: + - = . _ : /.
- The maximum number of tags per resource is 50.
- The AWS-assigned tag names and values are automatically assigned the aws: prefix, which you cannot manually assign.
- AWS-assigned tag names do not count toward the tag limit of 50.
- User-assigned tag names have the prefix user: in the cost allocation report.
- You cannot tag a resource at the same time that you create it.

 Tagging is a separate action that you can perform only after you create the resource. You cannot backdate the application of a tag.

DynamoDB Items

A DynamoDB *item* is a collection of attributes that is uniquely identifiable among all other entities in the table, and each item has a *name* and a *value*. An attribute value can be a scalar, a set, or a document type. Each table contains zero or more items. For example, in a *People* table, each item represents a person, and in a "cars" table, each item represents one vehicle. Items in DynamoDB are similar to rows, records, or tables in other database systems, but in DynamoDB, there is no limit to the number of items that you can store in a table.

Atomic Counters

You can use the UpdateItem operation to implement an *atomic counter*, which is a numeric attribute that increments, unconditionally, without interfering with other write requests. With an atomic counter, the updates are not independent, and the numeric value increments each time that you call UpdateItem.

You can use an atomic counter to track the number of visitors to a website. In this case, your application would increment a numeric value, regardless of its current value. If an UpdateItem operation fails, the application may retry the operation. This would risk updating the counter twice, but most can tolerate a slight overcounting or undercounting of website visitors.

An atomic counter would not be appropriate where overcounting or undercounting cannot be tolerated, as in a banking application. In this case, it is safer to use a conditional update instead of an atomic counter.

 All write requests are applied in the order in which they were received.

Conditional Writes

By default, the DynamoDB write operations (`PutItem`, `UpdateItem`, `DeleteItem`) are uncon-
ditional. Each of these operations overwrites an existing item that has the specified primary
key. DynamoDB supports *conditional writes* for these operations. A conditional write succeeds only if the item attributes meet one or more expected conditions; otherwise, it returns
an error.

Conditional writes are helpful in many situations, including cases in which multiple
users attempt to modify the same item. You may want a `PutItem` operation to succeed only
if there is not already an item with the same primary key. Alternatively, you could prevent
an `UpdateItem` operation from modifying an item if one of its attributes has a certain value.
Consider Figure 14.10 in which two users (Alice and Bob) are working with the same item
from a DynamoDB table.

FIGURE 14.10   Conditional write success

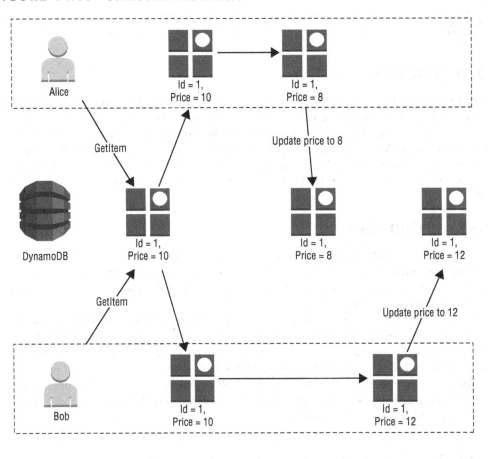

Suppose that Alice updates the Price attribute to 8.

```
aws dynamodb update-item \
    --table-name ProductCatalog \
    --key '{"Id":{"N":"1"}}' \
    --update-expression "SET Price = :newval" \
    --expression-attribute-values file://expression-attribute-values.json
```

The arguments for --expression-attribute-values write to the file
expression-attribute-values.json.

```
{
    ":newval":{"N":"8"}
}
```

Now suppose that Bob issues a similar UpdateItem request later but changes the Price
to 12. For Bob, the --expression-attribute-values parameter looks like this:

```
{
    ":newval":{"N":"12"}
}
```

Bob's request succeeds, but Alice's earlier update is lost.

To request a conditional PutItem, DeleteItem, or UpdateItem, you configure a condition
expression. A *condition expression* is a string containing attribute names, conditional operators, and built-in functions where the entire expression must evaluate to true; otherwise,
the operation fails.

Now consider Figure 14.11, showing how conditional writes would prevent Alice's
update from being overwritten.

Alice first attempts to update Price to 8 but only if the current Price is 10.

```
aws dynamodb update-item \
    --table-name ProductCatalog \
    --key '{"Id":{"N":"1"}}' \
    --update-expression "SET Price = :newval" \
    --condition-expression "Price = :currval" \
    --expression-attribute-values file://expression-attribute-values.json
```

The arguments for --expression-attribute-values write to the file
expression-attribute-values.json.

```
{
    ":newval":{"N":"8"},
    ":currval":{"N":"10"}
}
```

FIGURE 14.11   Conditional write success

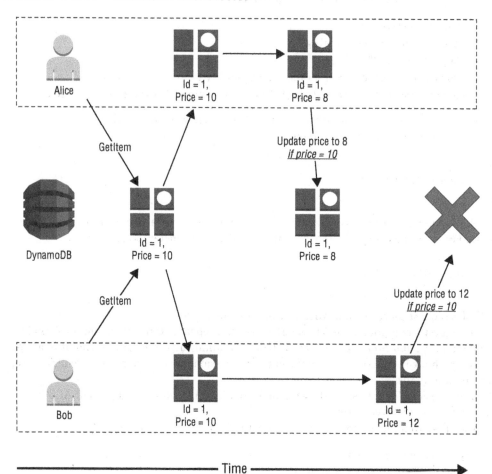

Alice's update succeeds because the condition evaluates to true.

Next, Bob attempts to update the Price to 12 but only if the current Price is 10. For Bob, the --expression-attribute-values parameter looks like the following:

```
{
    ":newval":{"N":"12"},
    ":currval":{"N":"10"}
}
```

Because Alice has previously changed the Price to 8, the condition expression evaluates to false and Bob's update fails.

Time to Live

Time to Live (TTL) for DynamoDB enables you to define when items in a table expire so that they can be automatically deleted from the database.

AWS provides TTL at no extra cost to you as a way to reduce both storage usage and the cost of storing irrelevant data without using provisioned throughput. With TTL enabled on a table, you can set a timestamp for deletion on a per-item basis and limit storage usage to only those records that are relevant.

TTL is useful if you have continuously accumulating data that loses relevance after a specific time, such as session data, event logs, usage patterns, and other temporary data. If you have sensitive data that must be retained only for a certain amount of time according to contractual or regulatory obligations, TTL helps you to make sure that data is removed promptly and on schedule.

Enabling Time to Live

When you enable TTL on a table, a background job checks the TTL attribute of items to determine whether they are expired. TTL compares the current time in epoch time format to the time stored in the Time to Live attribute of an item. If the epoch time value stored in the attribute is less than the current time, the item is marked as expired and later deleted.

 The epoch time format is the number of seconds elapsed since 12:00:00 a.m. on January 1, 1970, UTC.

DynamoDB deletes expired items on a best-effort basis to ensure availability of throughput for other data operations. DynamoDB typically deletes expired items within 48 hours of expiration. The exact duration within which an item is deleted after expiration is specific to the nature of the workload and the size of the table.

Items that have expired but not deleted still show up in reads, queries, and scans. These items can be updated, and successful updates to change or remove the expiration attribute will be honored. As items are deleted, they are immediately removed from local secondary and global secondary indexes in the same eventually consistent way as a standard delete operation.

Before Using Time to Live

Before you enable TTL on a table, consider the following:

- Make sure that any existing timestamp values in the specified Time to Live attribute are correct and in the right format.
- Items with an expiration time greater than five years in the past are not deleted.
- If data recovery is a concern, back up your table.
- For a 24-hour recovery window, use DynamoDB Streams.
- For a full backup, use AWS Data Pipeline.

- Use the AWS CloudFormation to set TTL when you create a DynamoDB table.

- Use Identity and Access Management (IAM) policies to prevent unauthorized updates to the TTL attribute or configuration of the TTL feature. If you allow access to only specified actions in your existing IAM policies, ensure that your policies update to allow `DynamoDB:UpdateTimeToLive` for roles that need to enable or disable TTL on tables.

- Consider whether you must complete any post-processing of deleted items. The stream's records of TTL deletes are marked, and you use AWS Lambda function to monitor the records.

When your program sends a request, DynamoDB attempts to process it. If the request is successful, DynamoDB returns an HTTP success status code (`200 OK`), along with the results from the requested operation.

If the request is unsuccessful, DynamoDB returns an error. Each error has three components:

- An HTTP status code (such as 400)

- An exception name (such as `ResourceNameNotFound`)

- An error message (such as `Requested resource not found: Table: tablename not found`)

The AWS SDKs resolve propagating errors in your application so that you can take appropriate action. For example, in a Java program, write try-catch logic to handle a `ResourceNotFoundException`.

Error Handling in Your Application

For your application to run smoothly, you must add logic to catch and respond to errors. Typical approaches include using try-catch blocks or if-then statements. The AWS SDKs perform their own retries and error checking. If you encounter an error while using one of the AWS SDKs, the error code and description help you troubleshoot it. You may also see a `Request ID` in the response, which can be helpful when working with AWS Support to diagnose an issue.

Error Retries and Exponential Backoff

Numerous components on a network, such as DNS servers, switches, load balancers, and others, can return error responses anywhere in the life of a given request. The usual technique for dealing with these error responses in a networked environment is to implement retries in the client application. This technique increases the reliability of the application and reduces operational costs for the developer.

As each AWS SDK automatically implements retry logic, you can modify the retry parameters to suit your needs. For example, consider a Java application that requires a fail-fast strategy with no retries allowed in case of an error. With the AWS SDK for Java, you could use the ClientConfiguration class and provide a maxErrorRetry value of 0 to turn off the retries.

If you are not using an AWS SDK, attempt to retry original requests that receive server errors (*5xx*). However, client errors (*4xx*), other than a ThrottlingException or a ProvisionedThroughputExceededException, indicate the need to revise the request itself or to correct the problem before trying again.

In addition to simple retries, each AWS SDK implements the *exponential backoff algorithm* for better flow control. The concept behind exponential backoff is to use progressively longer waits between retries for consecutive error responses. For example, you can set the wait to up to 50 milliseconds before the first retry, up to 100 milliseconds before the second retry, up to 200 milliseconds before third retry, and so on.

However, if the request has not succeeded after a minute, the request size may exceed your provisioned throughput and not the request rate. Set the maximum number of retries to stop at around one minute. If the request is not successful, investigate your provisioned throughput options.

Capacity Units Consumed by Conditional Writes

If a ConditionExpression generates an evaluation of false during a conditional write, DynamoDB consumes write capacity from the table. If the item does not currently exist in the table, DynamoDB consumes one write capacity unit. If the item does exist, then the number of write capacity units consumed depends on the size of the item. A failed conditional write of a 1-KB item would consume one write capacity unit. If the item were twice that size, the failed conditional write would consume two write capacity units.

A failed conditional write returns a ConditionalCheckFailedException. When this occurs, you will not receive information in the response about the write capacity that was consumed. However, you can view the ConsumedWriteCapacityUnits metric for the table in Amazon CloudWatch.

To return the number of write capacity units consumed during a conditional write, you use the ReturnConsumedCapacity parameter with the following attributes:

Total   Returns the total number of write capacity units consumed.

Indexes   Returns the total number of write capacity units consumed with subtotals for the table and any secondary indexes that were affected by the operation.

None   No write capacity details are returned (default).

 Write operations consume only write capacity units; they do not consume read capacity units.

Unlike a global secondary index, a local secondary index shares its provisioned throughput capacity with its table. Read and write activity on a local secondary index consumes provisioned throughput capacity from the table.

Configuring Item Attributes

This section describes how to refer to item attributes in an expression and projection expression. You can work with any attribute, even if it is deeply nested within multiple lists and maps.

Item Attributes

You can work with any attribute in an expression, even if it is deeply nested within multiple lists and maps.

Top-Level Attributes

If an attribute is not embedded within another attribute, the attribute is top level. Top-level attributes include the following:

- Id
- Title
- Description
- BicycleType
- Brand
- Price
- Color
- ProductCategory
- InStock
- QuantityOnHand
- RelatedItems
- Pictures
- ProductReviews
- Comment
- Safety.Warning

All of the top-level attributes are scalars, except for Color (list), RelatedItems (list), Pictures (map), and ProductReviews (map).

Nested Attributes

A nested attribute is embedded within another attribute. To access a nested attribute, you use *dereference operators*:

- [n] for list elements
- .(dot) for map elements

Accessing List Elements

The dereference operator for a list element is [n], where n is the element number. List elements are zero-based, so [0] represents the first element in the list, [1] represents the second, and so on. For example:

- `MyList[0]`
- `AnotherList[12]`
- `ThisList[5][11]`

The element `ThisList[5]` is itself a nested list. Therefore, `ThisList[5][11]` refers to the twelfth element in that list.

The number within the square brackets must be a non-negative integer. Therefore, the following expressions are invalid:

- `MyList[-1]`
- `MyList[0.4]`

Accessing Map Elements

The dereference operator for a map element is a dot (.). Use a dot as a separator between elements in a map. For example:

- `MyMap.nestedField`
- `MyMap.nestedField.deeplyNestedField`

Document Paths

In an expression, you use a document path to tell DynamoDB where to find an attribute. For a top-level attribute, the document path is the attribute name. For a nested attribute, you construct the document path by using dereference operators.

The following are examples of document paths:

- Top-level *scalar* attribute: `ProductDescription`.
- Top-level *list* attribute returns the entire list, not only some of the elements: `RelatedItems`.
- Third element from the `RelatedItems` list (remember that list elements are zero-based): `RelatedItems[2]`.
- Front-view *picture* of the product: `Pictures.FrontView`.
- All of the five-star reviews: `ProductReviews.FiveStar`.
- First of the five-star reviews: `ProductReviews.FiveStar[0]`.

You can use any attribute name in a document path if the first character is a–z or A–Z and the second character (if present) is a–z, A–Z, or 0–9. If an attribute name does not meet this requirement, define an expression attribute name as a placeholder.

The maximum depth for a document path is 32. Therefore, the number of dereference operators in a path cannot exceed this limit.

Expressions

In DynamoDB, you can use *expressions* to denote the attributes that you want to read from an item. To indicate any conditions that must be met (conditional update) and to indicate how the attributes are to be updated, you can also use expressions when writing an item.

 NOTE For backward-compatibility, DynamoDB also supports conditional parameters that do not use expressions. New applications should use expressions instead of the legacy parameters.

Item Projection Expressions

To read data from a table, use operations such as GetItem, Query, or Scan. DynamoDB returns *all* of the item attributes by default. To acquire select attributes, use a projection expression.

A *projection expression* is a string that identifies the attributes that you want to collect. To retrieve a single attribute, specify its name. For multiple attributes, the names must be comma-separated.

The following are examples of projection expressions:

- Single top-level attribute:
  Title

- Three top-level attributes; DynamoDB retrieves the entire Color set:
  Title, Price, Color

- Four top-level attributes' DynamoDB returns the entire contents of RelatedItems and ProductReviews:
  Title, Description, RelatedItems, ProductReviews

Attribute Names in a Projection Expression

You can use any attribute name in a projection expression, where the first character is a–z or A–Z and the second character (if present) is a–z, A–Z, or 0–9. If an attribute name does not meet this requirement, you must define an expression attribute name as a placeholder.

Expression Attribute Names

An *expression attribute name* is a placeholder that you use in an expression as an alternative to an actual attribute name. An expression attribute name must begin with a # and be followed by one or more alphanumeric characters. There are several situations in which you use expression attribute names.

Reserved words On certain occasions, you might need to write an expression containing an attribute name that conflicts with a DynamoDB reserved word. Refer to https://docs.aws.amazon.com/amazondynamodb/latest/developerguide/ReservedWords.html.

Example 6: Reserved Words

```
aws dynamodb get-item \
  --table-name ProductCatalog \
  --key '{"Id":{"N":"123"}}' \
  --projection-expression "Comment"
```

 If an attribute name begins with a number or contains a space, a special character, or a reserved word, then you *must* use an expression attribute name to replace that attribute's name in the expression.

Attribute names containing dots In an expression, a dot (.) is interpreted as a separator character in a document path. However, DynamoDB also enables you to use a dot character as part of an attribute name, which can be ambiguous. To illustrate, suppose that you want to retrieve the Safety.Warning attribute from a table.

To work around this, replace Comment with an expression attribute name, such as #c. The # (pound sign) is required, and it indicates that this is a placeholder for an attribute name. Suppose that you want to access Safety.Warning by using a projection-expression:

```
aws dynamodb get-item \
  --table-name ProductCatalog \
  --key '{"Id":{"N":"123"}}' \
  --projection-expression "Safety.Warning"
```

DynamoDB returns an empty result, rather than the expected string ("Always wear a helmet") when DynamoDB interprets a dot in an expression as a document path separator. In this case, you must define an expression attribute names (such as #sw) as a substitute for Safety.Warning. Use the following projection-expression:

```
aws dynamodb get-item \
  --table-name ProductCatalog \
  --key '{"Id":{"N":"123"}}' \
  --projection-expression "#sw" \
  --expression-attribute-names '{"#sw":"Safety.Warning"}'
```

DynamoDB would then return the correct result.

Nested attributes   Suppose that you want to access the nested attribute ProductReviews. OneStar, using the following projection-expression:

```
aws dynamodb get-item \
  --table-name ProductCatalog \
  --key '{"Id":{"N":"123"}}' \
  --projection-expression "ProductReviews.OneStar"
```

The result contains all of the one-star product reviews, which is expected.

But what if you want to use a projection-expression attribute instead? For example, you want to define #pr1star as a substitute for ProductReviews.OneStar:

```
aws dynamodb get-item \
  --table-name ProductCatalog \
  --key '{"Id":{"N":"123"}}' \
  --projection-expression "#pr1star" \
  --expression-attribute-names '{"#pr1star":"ProductReviews.OneStar"}'
```

DynamoDB returns an empty result instead of the expected map of one-star reviews when DynamoDB interprets a dot in an expression attribute value as a character within an attribute's name. When DynamoDB evaluates the expression attribute name #pr1star, it determines that ProductReviews.OneStar refers to a *scalar attribute*, which is not what was intended.

The correct approach is to define an expression-attribute-names attribute for each element in the document path:

#pr: ProductReviews

#1star: OneStar

You then use #pr.#1star for the projection expression:

```
aws dynamodb get-item \
  --table-name ProductCatalog \
  --key '{"Id":{"N":"123"}}' \
  --projection-expression "#pr.#1star" \
  --expression-attribute-names '{"#pr":"ProductReviews", "#1star":"OneStar"}'
```

DynamoDB returns the correct result.

Repeat attribute names   Expression attribute names are helpful when you must refer to the same attribute name repeatedly. For example, consider the following expression for retrieving reviews from a ProductCatalog item:

```
aws dynamodb get-item \
  --table-name ProductCatalog \
  --key '{"Id":{"N":"123"}}' \
  --projection-expression "ProductReviews.FiveStar, ProductReviews.ThreeStar,
ProductReviews.OneStar"
```

To make this more concise, replace `ProductReviews` with an expression attribute name, such as #pr. The revised expression looks like the following:

```
aws dynamodb get-item \
   --table-name ProductCatalog \
   --key '{"Id":{"N":"123"}}' \
   --projection-expression "#pr.FiveStar, #pr.ThreeStar, #pr.OneStar" \
   --expression-attribute-names '{"#pr":"ProductReviews"}'
```

If you define an expression attribute name, you must use it consistently throughout the entire expression. Also, you cannot omit the # symbol.

Expression Attribute Values

If you must compare an attribute with a value, define an expression attribute value as a placeholder. *Expression attribute values* are substitutes for the actual values that you want to compare. These are values that you might not know until runtime. Use expression attribute values with condition expressions, update expressions, and filter expressions. An expression attribute value must begin with a colon (:) followed by one or more alphanumeric characters.

For example, you want to return all of the `ProductCatalog` items that are available in black and cost $500 or less. You could use a `Scan` operation with a `filter-expression`, as in this AWS CLI example:

```
aws dynamodb scan \
   --table-name ProductCatalog \
   --filter-expression "contains(Color, :c) and Price <= :p" \
   --expression-attribute-values file://values.json
```

The arguments for `--expression-attribute-values` are stored in the file `values.json`:

```
{
  ":c": { "S": "Black" },
  ":p": { "N": "500" }
}
```

 Because a Scan operation reads every item in a table, avoid using Scan with large tables. The filter expression is applied to the Scan results, and items that do not match the filter expression are discarded.

If you define an `expression-attribute-values` attribute, you must use it consistently throughout the entire expression. Also, you cannot omit the colon (:) symbol.

Condition Expressions

To manipulate data in a DynamoDB table, use the `PutItem`, `UpdateItem`, and `DeleteItem` operations. You can also use `BatchWriteItem` to perform multiple `PutItem` or `DeleteItem` operations in a single call.

For these data manipulation operations, configure a condition expression to determine which items to modify. If the condition expression evaluates to true, the operation succeeds; otherwise, the operation fails.

The following AWS CLI examples include condition expressions that use the ProductCatalog table. The partition key for this table is Id; there is no sort key. The PutItem operation

creates a sample ProductCatalog item in the examples:

```
aws dynamodb put-item \
   --table-name ProductCatalog \
   --item file://item.json
```

The arguments for --item are stored in the file item.json.

```
{
   "Id": {"N": "456" },
   "ProductCategory": {"S": "Sporting Goods" },
   "Price": {"N": "650" }
}
```

Update Expressions

To update an existing item in a table, use the UpdateItem operation, provide the key of the item that you want to update, and use an update expression, indicating the attributes that you want to modify and the values that you want to assign to them.

An *update expression* specifies how UpdateItem modifies the attributes of an item, such as setting a scalar value or removing elements from a list or a map. An update expression consists of one or more clauses. Each clause begins with a SET, REMOVE, ADD, or DELETE keyword. You can include any of these clauses in an update expression, in any order. *However, each action keyword can appear only once.* Each clause contains one or more actions, separated by commas.

Each of the following actions represents a data modification:

SET Updates the expression to add one or more attributes to an item. If any of these attributes already exists, it is overwritten by the new value.

REMOVE Updates the expression to remove one or more attributes from an item. To perform multiple Remove actions, separate the attributes by commas and use Remove to delete individual elements from a list.

ADD Updates the expression to add a new attribute and its values or values to an item. If the attribute already exists, then the behavior of ADD depends on the attribute's data type:

- If the attribute is a number and the value you are adding is also a number, then the value is mathematically added to the existing attribute. If the value is a negative number, then it is subtracted from the existing attribute.

- If the attribute is a set, and the value you are adding is also a set, then the value is appended to the existing set.

DELETE Deletes the expression.

Example 7: Update Expression

```
update-expression ::=
    [ SET action [, action] ... ]
    [ REMOVE action [, action] ...]
    [ ADD action [, action] ... ]
    [ DELETE action [, action] ...]
```

Working with Queries

The Query operation finds items based on primary key values. You can query any table or secondary index that has a composite primary key (a partition key and a sort key).

You must provide the name of the partition key attribute and a single value for that attribute. Query returns all the items with that partition key value. You can provide a sort key attribute and use a comparison operator to refine the search results.

Key Condition Expression

To specify the search criteria, use a key condition expression. A *key condition expression* is a string that determines the items to be read from the table or index. You must configure the partition key name and value as an equality condition.

You can use any attribute name in a key condition expression as long as the first character is a–z or A–Z and the second character (if present) is a–z, A–Z, or 0–9.

In addition, the attribute name must not be a DynamoDB reserved word. If an attribute name does not meet these requirements, then define an expression attribute name as a placeholder.

For items with a given partition key value, DynamoDB stores these items close together, sorted by the sort key value. In an aws dynamodb Query operation, DynamoDB retrieves the items in sorted order and then processes the items using KeyConditionExpression and any FilterExpression that might be present. At that point, the aws dynamodb query results are sent to the client.

An aws dynamodb query operation generally returns a result set. If no matching items are found, the result set is empty. Query results sort by the sort key value. If the data type of the sort key is Number, the results return in numeric order; otherwise, the results are returned in the order of UTF-8 bytes. The sort order is ascending by default. If you want to reverse the order, set the ScanIndexForward parameter to false. A single Query operation can retrieve a maximum of 1 MB of data. This limit applies before any FilterExpression is applied to the results. If LastEvaluatedKey is present in the response and it is non-null, then paginate the result set.

Example 8: Query Thread Table for *ForumName* (Partition Key)

```
aws dynamodb query \
  --table-name Thread \
  --key-condition-expression "ForumName = :name" \
  --expression-attribute-values '{":name":{"S":"Amazon DynamoDB"}}'
```

Filter Expressions for *Query*

You can use a filter expression to refine the Query results further. A *filter expression* determines which items within the aws dynamodb query results return. All other results are discarded. *A filter expression is applied after an aws dynamodb query finishes, but before the results are returned.* Therefore, a query consumes the same amount of read capacity, regardless of whether a filter expression is used. An aws dynamodb query operation can retrieve a maximum of 1 MB of data. This limit applies before the filter expression is evaluated. A filter expression cannot contain partition key or sort key attributes. Configure those attributes in the key condition expression, not the filter expression.

Example 9: *Query* the Thread Table for Partition Key and Sort Key

```
aws dynamodb query \
  --table-name Thread \
  --key-condition-expression "ForumName = :fn" \
  --filter-expression "#v >= :num" \
  --expression-attribute-names '{"#v": "Views"}' \
  --expression-attribute-values file://values.json
```

Read Consistency for *Query*

A Query operation performs eventually consistent reads by default. This means that the Query results might not reflect changes as the result of recently completed PutItem or UpdateItem operations. If you require strongly consistent reads, set the ConsistentRead parameter to true in the Query request.

DynamoDB Encryption at Rest

DynamoDB offers fully managed encryption at rest. DynamoDB encryption at rest provides enhanced security by encrypting your data at rest. The service uses an AWS Key Management Service (AWS KMS) managed encryption key for DynamoDB. This functionality reduces the operational burden and complexity involved in protecting sensitive data.

Enable encryption for any tables that contain sensitive data. You can enable encryption at rest using the AWS Management Console, AWS CLI, or the DynamoDB API.

> You can enable encryption at rest only when you create a *new* DynamoDB table. You cannot enable encryption at rest on an existing table. *After encryption at rest is enabled, you cannot disable it.*

How Encryption Works

DynamoDB encryption at rest provides an additional layer of data protection by securing your data from unauthorized access to the underlying storage. Organizational and industry policies, or government regulations and compliance requirements, might require the use of encryption at rest to protect your data. You can use encryption to increase the data security of the applications that you deploy to the cloud.

With encryption at rest, you can enable encryption for all of your DynamoDB data at rest, including the data that is persisted in your DynamoDB tables, local secondary indexes, and global secondary indexes. Encryption at rest encrypts your data by using 256-bit AES encryption, also known as AES-256 encryption. It works at the table level and encrypts both the base table and its indexes.

Encryption at rest automatically integrates with AWS KMS for managing the service default key to encrypt your tables. If a service default key does not exist when you create your encrypted DynamoDB table, AWS KMS automatically creates a new key. Encrypted tables that you create in the future use this key. AWS KMS combines secure, highly available hardware and software to provide a key management system scaled for the cloud.

Using the same AWS KMS service default key that encrypts the table, the following elements are also encrypted:

- DynamoDB base tables
- Local secondary indexes
- Global secondary indexes

After you encrypt your data, DynamoDB handles decryption of your data transparently with minimal impact on performance. You do not need to modify your applications to use encryption.

> DynamoDB cannot read your table data unless it has access to the service default key stored in your AWS KMS account. DynamoDB uses envelope encryption and key hierarchy to encrypt data. Your AWS KMS encryption key is used to encrypt the root key of this key hierarchy.

DynamoDB does not call AWS KMS for every DynamoDB operation. The key refreshes once every 5 minutes per client connection with active traffic.

Considerations for Encryption at Rest

Before you enable encryption at rest on a DynamoDB table, consider the following:

- When you enable encryption for a table, all the data stored in that table is encrypted. You cannot encrypt only a subset of items in a table.

- DynamoDB uses a service default key for encrypting all of your tables. If this key does not exist, it is created for you. Remember, you cannot disable service default keys.

- Encryption at rest encrypts data only while it is static (at rest) on a persistent storage media. If data security is a concern for data in transit or data in use, you must take the following additional measures:

   Data in transit: Protect your data while it is actively moving over a public or private network by encrypting sensitive data on the client side or by using encrypted connections, such as HTTPS, Secure Socket Layer (SSL), Transport Layer Security (TLS), and File Transfer Protocol Secure (FTPS).

   Data in use: Protect your data before sending it to DynamoDB by using client-side encryption.

   On-demand backup and restore: You can use on-demand backup and restore with encrypted tables, and you can create a backup of an encrypted table. The table that is restored with this backup has encryption enabled.

Currently, you cannot enable encryption at rest for DynamoDB Streams. If encryption at rest is a compliance/regulatory requirement, turn off DynamoDB Streams for encrypted tables.

IAM Policy Conditions for Fine-Grained Access Control

When you grant permissions in DynamoDB, you can configure conditions that determine how a permissions policy takes effect. In DynamoDB, you can specify conditions when granting permissions by using an IAM policy. For example, you can set the following configurations:

- Grant permissions to allow users read-only access to certain items and attributes in a table or a secondary index.

- Grant permissions to allow users write-only access to certain attributes in a table, based on the identity of that user.

   In DynamoDB, you can specify conditions in an IAM policy by using condition keys.

Examples of Permissions

In addition to controlling access to DynamoDB API actions, you can also control access to individual data items and attributes. For example, you can do the following:

- Grant permissions on a table but restrict access to specific items in that table based on certain primary key values. An example might be a social networking application for games, where all users' game data is stored in a single table, but no users can access data items that they do not own, as shown in Figure 14.12.

FIGURE 14.12 Granting permissions on a table

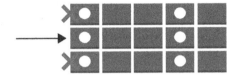

- Hide information so that only a subset of attributes is visible to the user. An example might be an application that displays flight data for nearby airports based on the user's location. Airline names, arrival and departure times, and flight numbers are displayed. However, attributes such as pilot names or number of passengers are hidden, as shown in Figure 14.13.

FIGURE 14.13 Hiding information on a table

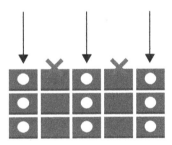

To implement this kind of fine-grained access control, write an IAM permissions policy that specifies conditions for accessing security credentials and the associated permissions and then apply the policy to IAM users, groups, or roles. Your IAM policy can restrict access to individual items in a table, access to the attributes in those items, or both at the same time.

 You can use web identity federation to control access by users who are authenticated by Login with Amazon, Facebook, or Google.

Use the *IAM condition element* to implement a fine-grained access control policy. By adding a condition element to a permissions policy, you can allow or deny access to items and attributes in DynamoDB tables and indexes, based on your particular business requirements.

For example, in Figure 14.1, the game lets players select from and play a variety of games. The application uses a DynamoDB table named GameScores to track high scores and other user data. Each item in the table is uniquely identified by a user ID and the name of the game that the user played. The GameScores table has a primary key consisting of a partition key (UserId) and sort key (GameTitle). Users have access only to game data associated with their user ID. A user who wants to play a game must belong to an IAM role named GameRole, which has a security policy attached to it.

To manage user permissions in this application, you could write a permissions policy such as the following:

```
{
  "Version": "2012-10-17",
  "Statement": [
    {
      "Sid": "AllowAccessToOnlyItemsMatchingUserID",
      "Effect": "Allow",
      "Action": [
        "dynamodb:GetItem",
        "dynamodb:BatchGetItem",
        "dynamodb:Query",
        "dynamodb:PutItem",
        "dynamodb:UpdateItem",
        "dynamodb:DeleteItem",
        "dynamodb:BatchWriteItem"
      ],
      "Resource": [
        "arn:aws:dynamodb:us-west-2:123456789012:table/GameScores"
      ],
      "Condition": {
        "ForAllValues:StringEquals": {
          "dynamodb:LeadingKeys": [
            "${www.amazon.com:user_ID}"

          ],
          "dynamodb:Attributes": [
            "UserId",
            "GameTitle",
            "Wins",
            "Losses",
```

```
            "TopScore",
            "TopScoreDateTime"
        ]
      },
      "StringEqualsIfExists": {
        "dynamodb:Select": "SPECIFIC_ATTRIBUTES"
      }
    }
  }
 ]
}
```

In addition to granting permissions for specific DynamoDB actions (Action element) on the GameScores table (Resource element), the Condition element uses the condition keys specific to DynamoDB that limit the permissions as follows:

dynamodb:LeadingKeys   This condition key enables users to access only the items where the partition key value matches their user ID. This ID, ${www.amazon.com:user_ID}, is a substitution variable.

dynamodb:Attributes   This condition key limits access to the specified attributes so that only the actions listed in the permissions policy can return values for these attributes. In addition, the StringEqualsIfExists clause ensures that the application provides a list of specific attributes to act upon, and that the application cannot request all attributes.

When an IAM policy is evaluated, the result is either true (access is allowed) or false (access is denied). If any part of the Condition element is false, the entire policy evaluates to false and access is denied.

If you use dynamodb:Attributes, you must configure the names of all the *primary key* and *index key attributes* for the table and any secondary indexes that the policy lists. Otherwise, DynamoDB is unable to use these key attributes to perform the requested action.

Configure Conditions with Condition Keys

AWS provides a set of predefined condition keys for all AWS offerings and services that support IAM for access control. For example, use the aws:SourceIp condition key to check the requester's IP address before allowing an action to be performed.

Condition keys are case-sensitive.

Table 14.3 displays the DynamoDB service-specific condition keys that apply to DynamoDB.

TABLE 14.3 DynamoDB Condition Keys

DynamoDB Condition Key	Description
dynamodb:LeadingKeys	Represents the first key attribute of a table and is the partition key for a simple primary key (partition key) or a composite primary key (partition key and sort key). In addition, you must use the ForAllValues modifier when using LeadingKeys in a condition.
dynamodb:Select	Represents the Select parameter of a Query or Scan request using the following values: ▪ ALL_ATTRIBUTES ▪ ALL_PROJECTED_ATTRIBUTES ▪ SPECIFIC_ATTRIBUTES ▪ COUNT
dynamodb:Attributes	Represents a list of the attribute names in a request or the attributes that return from a request. Attributes values are named the same way and have the same meaning as the parameters for certain DynamoDB API actions: ▪ AttributesToGet Used by: BatchGetItem, GetItem, Query, Scan ▪ AttributeUpdates Used by: UpdateItem ▪ Expected Used by: DeleteItem, PutItem, UpdateItem ▪ Item Used by: PutItem ▪ ScanFilter Used by: Scan
dynamodb:ReturnValues	Represents the ReturnValues parameter of a request: ▪ ALL_OLD ▪ UPDATED_OLD ▪ ALL_NEW ▪ UPDATED_NEW ▪ NONE
dynamodb:ReturnConsumedCapacity	Represents the ReturnConsumedCapacity parameter of a request: ▪ TOTAL ▪ NONE

On-Demand Backup and Restore

You can create on-demand backups and enable point-in-time recovery for your DynamoDB tables. DynamoDB on-demand backups enable you to create full backups of your tables for long-term retention and archival for regulatory compliance. You can back up and restore your DynamoDB table data anytime either in the AWS Management Console or as an API call. Backup and restore actions execute with zero impact on table performance or availability.

On-demand backup and restore scales without degrading the performance or availability of your applications. With this distributed technology, you can complete backups in seconds regardless of table size. You can create backups that are consistent across thousands of partitions without worrying about schedules or long-running backup processes. All backups are cataloged, discoverable, and retained until explicitly deleted.

In addition, on-demand backup and restore operations do not affect performance or API latencies. Backups are preserved regardless of table deletion. You can create table backups using the console, the AWS CLI, or the DynamoDB API.

The backup and restore functionality works in the same AWS Region as the source table. DynamoDB on-demand backups are available at no additional cost beyond the normal pricing that is associated with the backup storage size.

Backups

When you create an on-demand backup, a time marker of the request is cataloged. The backup is created asynchronously by applying all changes until the time of the request to the last full table snapshot. Backup requests process instantaneously and become available for restore within minutes. Each time you create an on-demand backup, the entire table data is backed up. You can make an unlimited number of on-demand backups.

All backups in DynamoDB work without consuming any provisioned throughput on the table. DynamoDB backups do not enable causal consistency across items; however, the skew between updates in a backup is usually much less than a second. While a backup is in progress, you cannot perform certain operations, such as pausing or canceling the backup action, deleting the source table of the backup, or disabling backups on a table. However, you can use AWS Lambda functions to schedule periodic or future backups.

 DynamoDB backups also include global secondary indexes, local secondary indexes, streams, and provisioned read and write capacity, in addition to the data.

Restores

A table restores without consuming any provisioned throughput on the table. The destination table is set with the same provisioned read capacity units and write capacity units as the source table, as recorded at the time that you request the backup. The restore process also restores the local secondary indexes and the global secondary indexes.

You can only restore the entire table data to a new table from a backup. Restore times vary based on the size of the DynamoDB table that is being restored. You can write to the restored table only after it becomes active, and you cannot overwrite an existing table during a restore operation. You can use IAM policies for access control.

Point-in-Time Recovery

You can enable *point-in-time recovery* (PITR) and create on-demand backups for your DynamoDB tables. Point-in-time recovery helps protect your DynamoDB tables from accidental write or delete operations. With point-in-time recovery, you do not have to worry about creating, maintaining, or scheduling on-demand backups. DynamoDB maintains incremental backups of your table. In addition, point-in-time operations do not affect performance or API latencies. You can enable point-in-time recovery using the AWS Management Console, AWS CLI, or the DynamoDB API.

How Point-in-Time Recovery Works

When it is enabled, point-in-time recovery provides continuous backups until you explicitly turn it off. After you enable point-in-time recovery, you can restore to any point in time within `EarliestRestorableDateTime` and `LatestRestorableDateTime`. `LatestRestorableDateTime` is typically 5 minutes before the current time. The point-in-time recovery process always restores to a new table. For `EarliestRestorableDateTime`, you can restore your table to any point in time during the last 35 days. The retention period is a fixed 35 days (five calendar weeks) and cannot be modified. Any number of users can execute up to four concurrent restores (any type of restore) in a given account.

When you restore using point-in-time recovery, DynamoDB restores your table data to a new table and to the state based on the selected date and time (`day:hour:minute:second`). In addition to the data, the following are also included on the newly restored table using point-in-time recovery:

- Global secondary indexes
- Local secondary indexes
- Provisioned read and write capacity
- Encryption settings

After restoring a table, you must manually set up the following on the restored table:

- Scaling policies
- IAM policies
- Amazon CloudWatch metrics and alarms
- Tags
- Stream settings
- TTL settings
- Point-in-time recovery settings

Considerations for Point-in-Time Recovery

Before you enable point-in-time recovery on a DynamoDB table, consider the following:

- If you disable point-in-time recovery and then later re-enable it on a table, reset the start time for which you can recover that table. As a result, you can only immediately restore that table using the `LatestRestorableDateTime`.

- If you must recover a deleted table that had point-in-time recovery enabled, you must contact AWS Support to restore that table within the 35-day recovery window.

- You can enable point-in-time recovery on each local replica of a global table. When you restore the table, the backup restores to an independent table that is not part of the global table.

- You can enable point-in-time recovery on an encrypted table.

- AWS CloudTrail logs all console and API actions for point-in-time recovery to enable logging, continuous monitoring, and auditing.

Amazon ElastiCache

Amazon ElastiCache is a web service that makes it easy to set up, manage, and scale distributed in-memory cache environments on the AWS Cloud. It provides a high-performance, resizable, and cost-effective in-memory cache while removing the complexity associated with deploying and managing a distributed cache environment.

You can use ElastiCache to store the application state. Applications often store session data in memory, but this approach does not scale well. To address scalability and provide a shared data storage for sessions that can be accessible from any individual web server, abstract the HTTP sessions from the web servers themselves. A common solution is to leverage an *in-memory key-value* store. ElastiCache supports the following open-source in-memory caching engines:

- *Memcached* is an open source, high-performance, distributed memory object caching system that is widely adopted by and protocol-compliant with ElastiCache.

- *Redis* is an open source, in-memory data structure store that you can use as a database cache and message broker. ElastiCache supports Master/Slave replication and Multi-AZ replication that you can use to achieve cross-Availability Zone redundancy.

ElastiCache is an in-memory cache. Caching frequently used data is one of the most important performance optimizations that you can make in your applications. Compared to retrieving data from an in-memory cache, querying a database is a much more expensive operation. By storing frequently accessed data in-memory, you can greatly improve the speed and responsiveness of read-intensive applications. For instance, application state for a web application can be stored in an in-memory cache, as opposed to storing state data in a database.

While key-value data stores are fast and provide submillisecond latency, the added network latency and cost are the drawbacks. An added benefit of leveraging key-value stores is that they can also cache any data, not only HTTP sessions, which helps boost the overall performance of your applications.

Considerations for Choosing a Distributed Cache

One consideration when choosing a distributed cache for session management is determining the number of nodes necessary to manage the user sessions. You can determine this number by how much traffic is expected and how much risk is acceptable. *In a distributed session cache, the sessions are divided by the number of nodes in the cache cluster. In the event of a failure, only the sessions that are stored on the failed node are affected.* If reducing risk is more important than cost, adding additional nodes to reduce further the percentage of stored sessions on each node may be ideal even when fewer nodes are sufficient.

Another consideration may be whether the sessions must be replicated. Some key-value stores offer replication through read replicas. If a node fails, the sessions are not entirely lost. Whether replica nodes are important in your individual architecture may inform you as to which key-value store you should use. ElastiCache offerings for in-memory key-value stores include ElastiCache for Redis, which supports replication, and ElastiCache for Memcached, which does not support replication.

There are a number of ways to store sessions in key-value stores. Many application frameworks provide libraries that can abstract some of the integration required to Get/Set those sessions in memory. In other cases, you can write your own session handler to persist the sessions directly.

ElastiCache makes it easy to deploy, operate, and scale an in-memory cache in the cloud. ElastiCache improves the performance of web applications by enabling you to retrieve information from fast, managed, in-memory caches instead of relying entirely on slower disk-based databases.

Use Memcached if you require the following:

- Use a simple data model
- Run large nodes with multiple cores or threads
- Scale out or scale in
- Partition data across multiple shards
- Cache objects, such as a database

Use Redis if you require the following:

- Work with complex data types
- Sort or rank in-memory datasets
- Persist the key store
- Replicate data from the primary to one or more read replicas for read-intensive applications

- Automate failover if the primary node fails
- Publish and subscribe (pub/sub): the client is informed of events on the server
- Back up and restore data

Use Table 14.4 to determine which product best fits your needs.

TABLE 14.4 Memcached or Redis

Capability	Memcached	Redis
Simple cache to offload DB burden	✓	✓
Ability to scale horizontally	✓	
Multithreaded performance	✓	
Advanced data types		✓
Sorting/ranking datasets		✓
Pub/sub capability		✓
Multi-AZ with auto-failover		✓
Persistence		✓

ElastiCache Terminology

This section describes some of the key terminology that ElastiCache uses.

Nodes

A *node* is the smallest building block of an ElastiCache deployment. A node is a fixed-size chunk of secure, network-attached RAM. Each node runs an instance of Memcached or Redis, depending on which you select when you create the cluster.

Clusters

Each ElastiCache deployment consists of one or more nodes in a *cluster*. When you create a cluster, you may choose from many different nodes based on the requirements of both your solution case and your capacity. One Memcached cluster can be as large as 20 nodes. Redis clusters consist of a single node; however, you can group multiple clusters into a Redis replication group.

The individual node types are derived from a subset of the Amazon EC2 instance type families, such as t2, m3, and r3. The *t2* cache node family is ideal for development and low-volume applications with occasional bursts, but certain features may not be available. The *m3* family is a mix of memory and compute, whereas the *r3* family is optimized for memory-intensive workloads.

Based on your requirements, you may decide to have a few large nodes or many smaller nodes in your cluster or replication group. As demand for your application fluctuates, you may add or remove nodes over time. Each node type has a preconfigured amount of memory, with a small portion of that memory reserved for both the caching engine and operating system.

Though it is unlikely, always plan for the possible failure of an individual cache node. For a Memcached cluster, decrease the impact of the failure of a cache node by using a larger number of nodes with a smaller capacity instead of a few large nodes.

If ElastiCache detects the failure of a node, it provisions a replacement and then adds it back to the cluster. During this time, your database experiences increased load because any requests that would have been cached now need to be read from the database. For Redis clusters, ElastiCache detects failures and replaces the primary node. If you enable a Multi-AZ replication group, a read replica automatically is promoted to primary automatically to primary.

Replication group   A *replication group* is a collection of Redis clusters with one primary read/write cluster and up to five secondary, read-only clusters called *read replicas*. Each read replica maintains a copy of the data from the primary cluster. Asynchronous replication mechanisms keep the read replicas synchronized with the primary cluster. Applications can read from any cluster in the replication group. Applications can write only to the primary cluster. Read replicas enhance scalability and guard against data loss.

Endpoint   An *endpoint* is the unique address your application uses to connect to an ElastiCache node or cluster. Memcached and Redis have the following characteristics with respect to endpoints:

- A Memcached cluster has its own endpoint and a configuration endpoint.

- A standalone Redis cluster has an endpoint to connect to the cluster for both reads and writes.

- A Redis replication group has two types of endpoints.

  - The *primary endpoint* connects to the primary cluster in the replication group.

  - The *read endpoint* points to a specific cluster in the replication group.

Cache Scenarios

ElastiCache caches data as key-value pairs. An application can retrieve a value corresponding to a specific key. An application can store an item in cache by a specific key, value, and an expiration time. *Time to live* (TTL) is an integer value that specifies the number of seconds until the key expires.

A *cache hit* occurs when an application requests data from the cache, the data is both present and not expired in the cache, and it returns to the application. A *cache miss* occurs if an application requests data from the cache, and it is not present in the cache (returning a null). In this case, the application requests and receives the data from the database and then writes the data to the cache.

Strategies for Caching

The strategy or strategies that you want to implement for populating and maintaining your cache depend on what data you are caching and the access patterns to that data. For example, you would likely not want to use the same strategy for a top-10 leaderboard on a gaming site, Facebook posts, and trending news stories.

Lazy Loading

Lazy loading loads data into the cache only when necessary. Whenever your application requests data, it first makes the request to the ElastiCache cache. If the data exists in the cache and it is current, ElastiCache returns the data to your application. If the data does not exist in the cache or the data in the cache has expired, your application requests the data from your data store, which returns the data to your application. Your application then writes the data received from the store to the cache so that it can be retrieved more quickly the next time that it is requested.

Advantages of Lazy Loading

- Only requested data is cached.

  Because most data is never requested, lazy loading avoids filling up the cache with data that is not requested.

- Node failures are not fatal.

  When a new, empty node replaces a failed node, the application continues to function, though with increased latency. As requests are made to the new node, each missed cache results in a query of the database and adding the data copy to the cache so that subsequent requests are retrieved from the cache.

Disadvantages of Lazy Loading

- There is a cache miss penalty.

  Each cache miss results in three trips:

  1. Initial request for data from the cache
  2. Querying of the database for the data
  3. Writing the data to the cache

  This can cause a noticeable delay in data getting to the application.

- Stale data.

  The application may receive stale data because another application may have updated the data in the database behind the scenes.

  Figure 14.14 summarizes the advantages and disadvantages of lazy loading.

FIGURE 14.14   Lazy loading caching

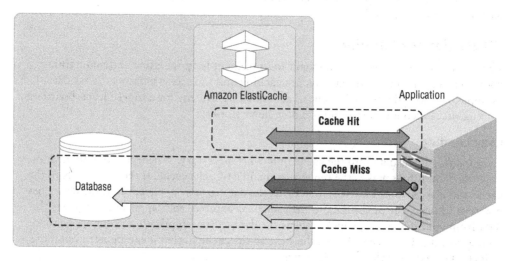

Write-Through

The *write-through* strategy adds data or updates data in the cache whenever data is written to the database.

Advantages of Write-Through

- The data in the cache is never stale.

  Because the data in the cache updates every time it is written to the database, the data in the cache is always current.

Disadvantages of Write-Through

- Write penalty

  Every write involves two trips: a write to the cache and a write to the database.

- Missing data

  When a new node is created either to scale up or replace a failed node, the node does not contain all data. Data continues to be missing until it is added or updated in the database. In this scenario, you might choose to use a lazy caching approach to repopulate the cache.

- Unused data

  Because most data is never read, there can be a lot of data in the cluster that is never read.

- Cache churn

  The cache may be updated often if certain records are updated repeatedly.

Data Access Patterns

Retrieving a flat key from an in-memory cache is faster than the most performance-tuned database query. Analyze the access pattern of the data before you determine whether you should store it in an in-memory cache.

Example 10: Cache Static Elements

An example of data to cache is a list of products in a catalog. For a high-volume web application, the list of products could be returned thousands of times per second. Though it may seem like a good idea to cache the most frequently requested items, your application may also benefit from caching items that are not frequently accessed.

You should not store certain data elements in an in-memory cache. For instance, if your application produces a unique page on every request, you probably do not want to cache the page results. However, though the page is different every time, it makes sense to cache the aspects of the page that are static.

Scaling Your Environment

As your workloads evolve over time, you can use ElastiCache to change the size of your environment to meet the requirements of your workloads. To meet increased levels of write or read performance, expand your cluster horizontally by adding cache nodes. To scale your cache vertically, select a different cache node type.

Scale horizontally   ElastiCache functionality enables you to scale the size of your cache environment horizontally. This functionality differs depending on the cache engine you select. With Memcached, you can partition your data and scale horizontally to 20 nodes or more. A Redis cluster consists of a single cache node that handles read and write transactions. You can create additional clusters to include a Redis replication group. Although you can have only one node handle write commands, you can have up to five read replicas handle read-only requests.

Scale vertically   The ElastiCache service does not directly support vertical scaling of your cluster. You can create a new cluster with the desired cache node types and begin redirecting traffic to the new cluster.

Understand that a new Memcached cluster starts empty. By comparison, you can initialize a Redis cluster from a backup.

Replication and Multi-AZ

Replication is an effective method for providing speedy recovery if a node fails and for serving high quantities of read queries beyond the capacities of a single node. ElastiCache clusters running Redis support both. In contrast, cache clusters running Memcached are standalone in-memory services that do not provide any data redundancy-protection services. Cache clusters running Redis support the notion of replication groups. A *replication group* consists of up to six clusters, with five of them designated as read replicas. By using a replication group, you can scale horizontally by developing code in the application to offload reads to one of the five replicas.

Multi-AZ Replication Groups

With ElastiCache, you can provision a *Multi-AZ replication group* that allows your application to raise the availability and reduce the loss of data. Multi-AZ streamlines the procedure of dealing with a failure by automating the replacement and failover from the primary node.

If the primary node goes down or is otherwise unhealthy, Multi-AZ selects a replica and promotes it to become the new primary; then a new node is provisioned to replace the failed one. ElastiCache updates the DNS entry of the new primary node to enable your application to continue processing without any changes to the configuration of the application and with only minimal disruption. ElastiCache replication is handled asynchronously, meaning that there will be a small delay before the data is available on all cluster nodes.

Backup and Recovery

ElastiCache clusters that run Redis support *snapshots*. Use *snapshots* to persist your data from your in-memory key-value stores to disk. Each snapshot is a full clone of the data that you can use to recover to a specific point in time or to create a copy for other purposes. Snapshots are not available to clusters that use the Memcached caching engine. This is because Memcached is a purely in-memory, key-value store, and it always starts empty. ElastiCache uses the native backup capabilities of Redis and generates a standard Redis database backup file, which is stored in Amazon S3.

Snapshots need memory and compute resources to perform, and this can possibly have a performance impact in heavily used clusters. ElastiCache attempts different backup techniques depending on the amount of memory currently available. As a best practice, set up a replication group and perform the snapshot against one of the read replicas instead of creating the snapshot against the primary node. You can automate the creation of snapshots on a schedule, or you can manually initiate a snapshot. Additionally, you can configure a window when a snapshot will be completed and then configure how many days of backups you want to save. Manual snapshots are stored indefinitely until you delete them.

It does not matter whether the snapshot was created manually or automatically. You can use the snapshot to provision a new cluster. The new cluster has the same configuration as the source cluster by default, but you can override these settings. You can also restore a snapshot from the *.rdb file that is generated from any other Redis compatible cluster. The Redis *.rdb file is a binary representation of the in-memory store. This binary file is sufficient to restore the Redis state completely.

Control Access

The primary way to configure access to your ElastiCache cluster is by restricting connectivity to your cluster through a security group. You can define a security group and add one or more inbound rules that restrict the source traffic. When a cache cluster is deployed inside a virtual private cloud, every node is assigned a private IP address within one or more subnets that you choose. You cannot access individual nodes from the internet or from Amazon EC2 instances outside of the Amazon Virtual Private Cloud (Amazon VPC). You can use the access control lists (ACLs) to constrain network inbound traffic.

Access to manage the configuration and infrastructure of the cluster is controlled separately from access to the actual Memcached or Redis service endpoint. Using the IAM service, you can define policies that control which AWS users can manage the ElastiCache infrastructure.

The ability to configure the cluster and govern the infrastructure is handled independently from access to the actual cache cluster endpoint, which is managed by using the IAM service. Using IAM, you can set up policies that determine which users can manage the ElastiCache infrastructure.

Amazon Simple Storage Service

There are situations when storing state requires the storage of larger files. This may be the case when your application deals with user uploads or interim results of batch processes. In such cases, consider using Amazon Simple Storage Service (Amazon S3) as your store.

Amazon S3 is storage for the internet. It is designed to make web-scale computing easier for developers. Amazon S3 has a simple web services interface that you can use to store and retrieve any amount of data, at any time, from anywhere on the web. The service aims both to maximize benefits of scale and to pass those benefits on to developers.

Amazon S3 Core Concepts

Amazon S3 is a stateless application that does not save client data that generates in one session for use in the next session with that client. Each session starts as if it was the first time, and responses are not dependent on data from a previous session. This means that the server does not store any state about the client session. Instead, the session data is stored on the client and passed to the server as requested.

Buckets

A *bucket* is a container for objects stored in Amazon S3. Every object is contained in a bucket. For example, if the object named photos/car.jpg is stored in the anitacrandle bucket, then it is addressable using the URL http://anitacrandle.s3.amazonaws.com/photos/car.jpg.

Buckets serve several purposes:

- They organize the Amazon S3 namespace at the highest level.
- They identify the account responsible for storage and data transfer charges.
- They play a role in access control.
- They serve as the unit of aggregation for usage reporting.

Creating a Bucket

Amazon S3 provides APIs for creating and managing buckets. By default, you can create up to 100 buckets in each of your accounts. If you need more buckets, increase your bucket limit by submitting a service limit increase.

When you create a bucket, provide a name for the bucket, and then choose the AWS Region where you want to create the bucket. You can store any number of objects in a bucket.

Create a bucket by using any of the following methods:

- Amazon S3 console
- Programmatically, using the AWS SDKs

When using the AWS SDKs, first create a client and then use the client to deliver a request to create a bucket. When you create the client, you can configure an AWS Region. US East (N. Virginia) is the default region. You can also configure an AWS Region in your request to create the bucket.

If you create a client specific to the US East (N. Virginia) Region, the client uses this endpoint to communicate with: Amazon S3: s3.amazonaws.com. You can use this client to create a bucket in any AWS Region in your create bucket request. If you do not specify a region, Amazon S3 creates the bucket in the US East (N. Virginia) Region. If you select an AWS Region, Amazon S3 creates the bucket in the specified region. If you create a client specific to any other AWS Region, it maps to the region-specific endpoint: s3-. amazonaws.com. For example, if you create a client and specify the us-east-2 Region, it maps to the following region-specific endpoint: s3-us-east-2.amazonaws.com.

Regions

You can choose the geographical region where Amazon S3 stores the buckets that you create. You might choose a region to optimize latency, minimize costs, or address regulatory requirements. Objects stored in a region never leave the region unless you explicitly transfer them to another region. For example, objects stored in the EU (Ireland) Region never leave it.

Objects   *Objects* are the principal items stored in Amazon S3. Objects consist of object data and metadata. The data part is opaque to Amazon S3. The metadata is a set of name-value pairs that characterize the object. These include certain default metadata, such as the date last modified and standard HTTP metadata, such as Content-Type. It is also possible for you to configure custom metadata at the time of object creation.

A *key (name)* and a *version ID* uniquely identify an object within a bucket.

Keys   A *key* is the unique identifier for an object within a bucket. Every object in a bucket has exactly one key. Because the combination of a bucket, key, and version ID uniquely identifies each object, Amazon S3 is like a basic data map between bucket + key + version and the object itself. Every object in Amazon S3 can be uniquely addressed through the combination of the web service endpoint, bucket name, key, and, optionally, a version. Figure 14.15 displays one object with a key and ID.

FIGURE 14.15   Object with key and ID

Versioning Enabled

Versioning   *Versioning* is a way to keep multiple variations of an object in the same bucket. You can use versioning to preserve, retrieve, and restore every version of every object stored in your Amazon S3 bucket. With versioning, you can recover from both unintended user actions and application failures.

In Figure 14.16, you can have two objects with the same key, but different version IDs, such as photo.gif (version 111111) and photo.gif (version 121212).

Versioning-enabled buckets allow you to recover objects from accidental deletion or overwrite. For instance:

- If you delete an object, instead of removing it permanently, Amazon S3 inserts a delete marker, which becomes the current object version. You can restore the previous version.

- You can delete object versions whenever you want.

FIGURE 14.16 Same key, different version

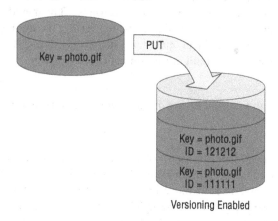

Versioning Enabled

In addition, you can also define lifecycle configuration rules for objects that have a well-defined lifecycle to request Amazon S3 to expire current object versions or permanently remove noncurrent object versions. When your bucket is version-enabled or versioning is suspended, the lifecycle configuration actions work as follows:

- The expiration action applies to the current object version. Instead of deleting the current object version, Amazon S3 retains the current version as a noncurrent version by adding a delete marker, which then becomes the current version.

- The NoncurrentVersionExpiration action applies to noncurrent object versions, and Amazon S3 permanently removes these object versions. You cannot recover permanently removed objects.

A Delete request has the following use cases:

- When versioning is enabled, a simple Delete request cannot permanently delete an object. Instead, Amazon S3 inserts a delete marker in the bucket, and that marker becomes the current version of the object with a new ID.

- When you send a Get request for an object whose current version is a delete marker, Amazon S3 treats it as though the object has been deleted (even though it has not been erased) and returns a 404 error. Figure 14.17 shows that a simple Delete request does not actually remove the specified object. Instead, Amazon S3 inserts a delete marker.

FIGURE 14.17   Delete marker

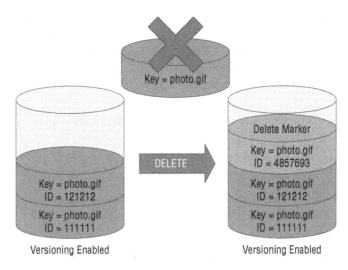

- To permanently delete versioned objects, you must use DELETE Object versionId. Figure 14.18 shows that deleting a specified object version permanently removes that object.

FIGURE 14.18   Permanent delete

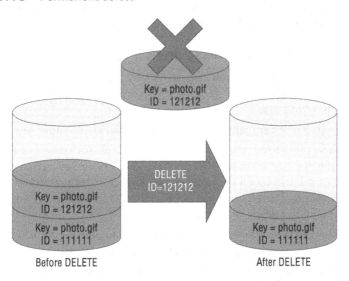

- If you overwrite an object, it results in a new object version in the bucket. You can restore the previous version.

Accessing a Bucket

Use the Amazon S3 console to access your bucket. You can perform almost all bucket operations without having to write any code. If you access a bucket programmatically, Amazon S3 supports the RESTful architecture wherein your buckets and objects are resources, each with a resource Uniform Resource Identifier (URI) that uniquely identifies the resource.

Amazon S3 supports both path-style URLs and virtual hosted-style URLs to access a bucket:

- In a virtual hosted-style URL, the bucket name is part of the domain name in the URL. Here's an example:

  `http://bucket.s3.amazonaws.com`

  `http://bucket.s3-aws-region.amazonaws.com`

- In a path-style URL, the bucket name is not part of the domain (unless you use a region-specific endpoint). Here's an example:

  US East (N. Virginia) Region endpoint: `http://s3.amazonaws.com/bucket`

  Region-specific endpoint: `http://s3-aws-region.amazonaws.com/bucket`

In a path-style URL, the endpoint you use must match the AWS Region where the bucket resides. For example, if your bucket is in the South America (São Paulo) Region, you must use the `http://s3-saeast-1.amazonaws.com/bucket` endpoint.

> Because you can access buckets by using either path-style or virtual hosted-style URLs, as a best practice, AWS recommends that you create buckets with DNS-compliant bucket names.

Bucket Restrictions and Limitations

The account that created the bucket owns it. By default, you can create up to 100 buckets in each of your accounts. If you need additional buckets, increase your bucket limit by submitting a service limit increase.

- Bucket ownership is not transferable; however, if a bucket is empty, you can delete it.

  After a bucket is deleted, the name becomes available for reuse, but the name may not be available for you to reuse for various reasons. For instance, another account could provision a bucket with the same name. Also, it might take some time before the name can be reused. Therefore, if you want to use the same bucket name after emptying the bucket, do not delete the bucket.

- There is no limit to the number of objects that you can store in a bucket and no difference in performance whether you use many buckets or only a few.

  Moreover, you can store all of your objects in one bucket, or you can arrange all of your objects across multiple buckets.

- You cannot create a bucket within another bucket.

- The high-availability engineering of Amazon S3 is focused on GET, PUT, LIST, and DELETE operations.

Because bucket operations work against a centralized, global resource space, it is not appropriate to create or delete buckets on the high-availability code path of your application. It is better to create or delete buckets in a separate initialization or setup routine that you run less often.

 If your solution is designed to create buckets automatically, develop a naming convention for your buckets that creates buckets that are globally unique. Also, make sure that your solution logic can create a different bucket name if a bucket name is already taken.

Rules for Naming Buckets

After you create an S3 bucket, you cannot change the bucket name, so choose the name wisely.

The following are the rules for naming S3 buckets in all AWS Regions:

- Bucket names must be unique across all existing bucket names in Amazon S3.
- Bucket names must comply with DNS naming conventions.
- Bucket names must be between 3 and 63 characters long.
- Bucket names must not contain uppercase characters or underscores.
- Bucket names must start with a lowercase letter or number.
- Bucket names must be a series of one or more labels. Use a single period (.) to separate adjacent labels. Bucket names can contain lowercase letters, numbers, and hyphens. Each label must start and end with a lowercase letter or a number.
- Bucket names must not be formatted as an IP address (for example, 192.168.4.5).
- When you use virtual hosted-style buckets with SSL, the SSL wildcard certificate only matches buckets that do not contain periods. To work around this, use HTTP, or write your own certificate verification logic. AWS recommends that you do not use periods (".") in bucket names when using virtual hosted-style buckets.

Working with Amazon S3 Buckets

Amazon S3 is cloud storage for the internet. To upload your data, such as images, videos, and documents, you must first create a bucket in one of the AWS Regions. You can then upload any number of objects to the bucket.

Amazon S3 is set up with buckets and objects as resources, and it includes APIs to interact with its resources. For instance, you can use the Amazon S3 API to create a bucket and then put objects in the bucket. Additionally, you can use the Amazon S3 web console to execute these actions. The console uses the Amazon S3 APIs to deliver requests to Amazon S3.

An Amazon S3 bucket name is globally unique regardless of the AWS Region in which you create the bucket. Configure the name at the time that you create the bucket. Amazon S3 creates buckets in a region that you choose. To minimize latency, reduce costs, or address regulatory requirements, choose any AWS Region that is geographically close to you.

The following are the most common operations executed through the API:

Create a bucket   Create and name the bucket where you will store your objects.

Write an object   Store data by creating or writing over an object. When you write an object, configure a unique key in the namespace of your bucket. Configure any access control that you want on the object.

Read an object   Retrieve data. You can download data through HTTP or BitTorrent.

Delete an object   Delete data.

List keys   List the keys contained in one of your buckets. You can filter the key list based on a prefix.

Make requests   Amazon S3 is a REST service. You can send requests to Amazon S3 using the REST API or the AWS SDK wrapper libraries. These libraries wrap the underlying Amazon S3 REST API, simplifying your programming tasks.

Every interaction with Amazon S3 is either authenticated or anonymous. Authentication is a process of verifying the identity of the requester trying to access an AWS offering. Authenticated requests must include a signature value that authenticates the request sender. The signature value is, in part, generated from the requester's AWS access keys (access key ID and secret access key).

If you are using the AWS SDK, the libraries compute the signature from the keys you provide. However, if you make direct REST API calls in your application, you must write the code to compute the signature and then add it to the request.

Deleting or Emptying a Bucket

It is easy to delete an empty bucket. However, in certain situations, you may need to delete or empty a bucket that contains objects. In other situations, you may choose to empty a bucket instead of deleting it. This section explains various options that you can use to delete or empty a bucket that contains objects.

You can delete a bucket and its content programmatically using the AWS SDKs. You can also use lifecycle configuration on a bucket to empty its content and then delete the bucket. There are additional options, such as using Amazon S3 console and AWS CLI, but there are limitations on these methods based on the number of objects in your bucket and the bucket's versioning status.

Deleting a Bucket Using Lifecycle Configuration

You can configure lifecycle on your bucket to expire objects. Amazon S3 then deletes expired objects. You can add lifecycle configuration rules to expire all or a subset of objects with a specific key name prefix. For example, to remove all objects in a bucket, set a lifecycle rule to expire objects one day after creation.

If your bucket has versioning enabled, you can also configure the rule to expire noncurrent objects. After Amazon S3 deletes all of the objects in your bucket, you can delete the bucket or keep it. If you want to only empty the bucket but not delete it, remove the lifecycle configuration rule you added to empty the bucket so that any new objects you create in the bucket remain in the bucket.

Object Lifecycle Management

To manage your objects so that they are stored cost-effectively throughout their life, configure their lifecycle policy. A *lifecycle policy* is a set of rules that designates actions that Amazon S3 applies to a group of objects. There are two types of actions:

Transition actions   Designate when objects transition from one storage class to another. For instance, you might decide to transition objects to the STANDARD_IA storage class 45 days after you created them, or archive objects to the GLACIER storage class six months after you created them.

Expiration actions   Designate when objects expire. Amazon S3 deletes expired objects on your behalf.

When to Use Lifecycle Configuration

Set up lifecycle configuration rules for objects that have a clear-cut lifecycle. For example, set up configuration rules for these types of situations:

- If you upload logs periodically to a bucket, your solution may need access to them for a week or so. When you no longer need access to them, you may want to remove them.

- Some objects are frequently accessed for a specific period. When that period is over, they are sporadically accessed. You may not need real-time access to these objects, but your business or regulations might require that you archive them for a specific period. After that, you can delete them.

- You might upload certain types of data to Amazon S3 primarily for archival purposes. For instance, you might archive digital media, healthcare and financial data, database backups, and data that you must retain for regulatory compliance.

With lifecycle configuration policies, you can instruct Amazon S3 to transition objects to less expensive storage classes, archive them for later, or remove them altogether.

Bucket Configuration Options

Amazon S3 supports various options to configure your bucket. For example, you can configure your bucket for website hosting, managing the lifecycle of objects in the bucket, and enabling all access to the bucket. Amazon S3 supports subresources for you to store, and it manages the bucket configuration information. Using the Amazon S3 API, you can create and manage these subresources. You can also use the Amazon S3 console or the AWS SDKs.

Amazon S3 Consistency Model

Amazon S3 provides read-after-write consistency for PUT requests of new objects in your S3 bucket in all regions. However, if you make a HEAD or GET request to the key name (to determine whether the object exists) before creating the object, Amazon S3 provides eventual consistency for read-after-write.

Amazon S3 offers eventual consistency for overwriting PUT and DELETE requests in all regions.

Updates to a single key are atomic. For example, if you PUT to an existing key, a subsequent read might return the old data or the updated data, but it will not write corrupted or partial data.

Amazon S3 achieves high availability by replicating data across multiple servers within Amazon's data centers. If a PUT request is successful, your data is safely stored. However, information about the changes must replicate across Amazon S3, which can take time, so you might observe the following behaviors:

- A process writes a new object to Amazon S3 and immediately lists keys within its bucket. Until the change is fully propagated, the object might not appear in the list.

- A process replaces an existing object and immediately attempts to read it. Until the change is fully propagated, Amazon S3 might return the prior data.

- A process deletes an existing object and immediately attempts to read it. Until the deletion is fully propagated, Amazon S3 might return the deleted data.

- A process deletes an existing object and immediately lists keys within its bucket. Until the deletion is fully propagated, Amazon S3 might list the deleted object.

Amazon S3 does not currently support object locking. If two PUT requests are simultaneously made to the same key, the request with the latest timestamp takes effect. If this is an issue, build an object-locking mechanism into your application. Updates are key-based; there is no way to make atomic updates across keys. For example, you cannot make the update of one key dependent on the update of another key unless you design this functionality into your application.

Table 14.5 describes the characteristics of eventually consistent reads and consistent reads.

TABLE 14.5   Amazon S3 Reads

Eventually Consistent Read	Consistent Read
▪ Stale reads possible	▪ No stale reads
▪ Lowest-read latency	▪ Potential higher-read latency
▪ Highest-read throughput	▪ Potential lower-read throughput

Bucket Policies

Bucket policies are a centralized way to control access to buckets and objects based on numerous conditions, such as operations, requesters, resources, and aspects of the request. The policies are written using the IAM policy language and enable centralized management of permissions.

Individuals and companies can use bucket policies. When companies register with Amazon S3, they create an account. Thereafter, the company becomes synonymous with the account. Accounts are financially responsible for the Amazon resources they (and their employees) create. Accounts grant bucket policy permissions and assign employees permissions based on a variety of conditions. For instance, an account could create a policy that grants a user read access in the following cases:

- From a particular S3 bucket
- From an account's corporate network
- During the weekend

An account can allow one user limited read and write access, while allowing other users to create and delete buckets. An account could allow several field offices to store their daily reports in a single bucket, allowing each office to write only to a certain set of names (e.g., Texas/* or Alabama/*) and only from the office's IP address range.

Unlike ACLs, which can add (grant) permissions only on individual objects, policies can grant or deny permissions across all (or a subset) of objects within a bucket. With one request, an account can set the permissions of any number of objects in a bucket. An account can use wildcards (similar to regular expression operators) on Amazon Resource Names (ARNs) and other values so that an account can control access to groups of objects that begin with a common prefix or end with a given extension, such as .doc.

Only the bucket owner is allowed to associate a policy with a bucket. Policies, written in the IAM policy language, allow or deny requests based on the following:

- Amazon S3 bucket operations (such as PUT Bucket acl) and object operations (such as PUT Object, or GET Object)
- Requester
- Conditions specified in the policy

An account can control access based on specific Amazon S3 operations, such as GetObject, GetObjectVersion, DeleteObject, or DeleteBucket.

The conditions can be such things as IP addresses, IP address ranges in Classless Inter-Domain Routing (CIDR) notation, dates, user agents, HTTP referrer, and transports, such as HTTP and HTTPS.

Amazon S3 Storage Classes

Amazon S3 offers a variety of *storage classes* devised for different scenarios. Among these storage classes are *Amazon S3 STANDARD* for general-purpose storage of frequently accessed data; *Amazon S3 STANDARD_IA* (Infrequent Access) for long-lived, but less frequently accessed data; and *GLACIER* for long-term archival purposes.

Storage Classes for Frequently Accessed Objects

Amazon S3 provides storage classes for performance-sensitive use cases (millisecond access time) and frequently accessed data. Amazon S3 provides the following storage classes:

STANDARD   *Standard* is the default storage class. If you do not specify the storage class when uploading an object, Amazon S3 assigns the STANDARD storage class.

REDUCED_REDUNDANCY   The *Reduced Redundancy Storage* (RRS) storage class is designed for noncritical, reproducible data that you can store with less redundancy than the STANDARD storage class.

Regarding durability, RRS objects have an average annual expected loss of 0.01 percent of objects. If an RRS object is lost, when requests are made to that object, Amazon S3 returns a 405 error.

The STANDARD storage class is more cost-effective than the REDUCED_ REDUNDANCY storage class; therefore, AWS recommends that you do not use the RRS storage class.

Storage Classes for Infrequently Accessed Objects

The STANDARD_IA and ONEZONE_IA storage classes are designed for data that is long-lived and infrequently accessed. STANDARD_IA and ONEZONE_IA objects are available for millisecond access (similar to the STANDARD storage class). Amazon S3 charges a fee for retrieving these objects; thus, they are most appropriate for infrequently accessed data.

Possible use cases for STANDARD_IA and ONEZONE_IA are as follows:

- For storing backups
- For older data that is accessed infrequently but that still requires millisecond access

---

STANDARD_IA and ONEZONE_IA Storage Classes

The STANDARD_IA and ONEZONE_IA storage classes are suitable for objects larger than 128 KB that you plan to store for at least 30 days. If an object is less than 128 KB, Amazon S3 charges you for 128 KB. If you delete an object before the 30-day minimum, you are charged for 30 days.

These storage classes differ as follows:

STANDARD_IA   Objects stored using this storage class are stored redundantly across multiple, geographically distinct Availability Zones (similar to the STANDARD storage class). STANDARD_IA objects are resilient to data loss of an Availability Zone. This storage class provides more availability, durability, and resiliency than the ONEZONE_IA class.

ONEZONE_IA   Amazon S3 stores the object data in only one Availability Zone, which makes it less expensive than STANDARD_IA. However, the data is not resilient to the physical loss of the Availability Zone resulting from disasters, such as earthquakes and floods. The ONEZONE_IA storage class is as durable as STANDARD_IA, but it is less available and less resilient.

To determine when to use a particular storage class, follow these recommendations:

STANDARD_IA   Use for your primary copy (or only copy) of data that cannot be regenerated.

ONEZONE_IA   Use if you can regenerate the data if the Availability Zone fails.

GLACIER Storage Class

You use the *GLACIER* storage class to archive data where access is infrequent. Objects that you archive are not available for real-time access. The GLACIER storage class offers the same durability and resiliency as the STANDARD storage class.

When you store objects in Amazon S3 with the GLACIER storage class, Amazon S3 uses the low-cost Amazon Simple Storage Service Glacier (Amazon S3 Glacier) service to store these objects. Though the objects are stored in Amazon S3 Glacier, these remain Amazon S3 objects that are managed in Amazon S3, and they cannot be accessed directly through Amazon S3 Glacier.

At the time that you create an object, it is not possible to specify GLACIER as the storage class. The way that GLACIER objects are created is by uploading objects first using STANDARD as the storage class. You can transition these objects to the GLACIER storage class by using lifecycle management.

 You must restore the GLACIER objects to access them.

Setting the Storage Class of an Object

Amazon S3 APIs offer support for setting or updating the storage class of objects. When you create a new object, configure its storage class. For example, when you create objects with the PUT Object, POST Object, and Initiate Multipart Upload APIs, add the x-amz-storageclass request header to configure a storage class. If you do not add this header, Amazon S3 uses STANDARD, the default storage class.

You can also change the storage class of an object that is already stored in Amazon S3 by making a copy of the object using the PUT Object - Copy API. Copy the object in the same bucket with the same key name, and configure request headers as follows:

- Set the x-amz-metadata-directive header to COPY.
- Set the x-amz-storage-class to the storage class that you want to use.

In a versioning-enabled bucket, you cannot change the storage class of a specific version of an object. When you copy it, Amazon S3 gives it a new version ID. You can direct Amazon S3 to change the storage class of objects by adding a lifecycle configuration to a bucket.

Amazon S3 Default Encryption for S3 Buckets

Amazon S3 default encryption provides a way to set the default encryption behavior for an Amazon S3 bucket. You can set default encryption on a bucket so that all objects are encrypted when they are stored in the bucket. The objects are encrypted using server-side encryption with either Amazon S3 managed keys (SSE-S3) or AWS KMS managed keys (SSE-KMS).

When you use server-side encryption, Amazon S3 encrypts an object before saving it to disk in its data centers and then decrypts the object when you download it.

Protecting Data Using Encryption

Data protection refers to protecting data while in transit (as it travels to and from Amazon S3), and at rest (while it is stored on disks in Amazon S3 data centers). You can protect data in transit by using SSL or by using client-side encryption with the following options of protecting data at rest in Amazon S3:

Use server-side encryption   You request Amazon S3 to encrypt your object before saving it on disks in its data centers and then decrypt the object when you download it.

Use client-side encryption   You can encrypt data on the client side and upload the encrypted data to Amazon S3 and then manage the encryption process, the encryption keys, and related tools.

Protecting Data Using Server-Side Encryption

Server-side encryption is about data encryption at rest; that is, Amazon S3 encrypts your data at the object level as it writes it to disks in its data centers and decrypts it for you when you access it. As long as you authenticate your request and you have access permissions, there is no difference in the way that you access encrypted or unencrypted objects. For example, if you share your objects using a presigned URL, that URL works the same way for both encrypted and unencrypted objects.

Consider the following mutually exclusive options, depending on how you choose to manage the encryption keys:

Use server-side encryption with Amazon S3 Managed Keys (SSE-S3)   Each object is encrypted with a unique key employing strong multifactor encryption. As an additional safeguard, it encrypts the key itself with a master key that it regularly rotates. Amazon S3 server-side encryption uses one of the strongest block ciphers available, 256-bit Advanced Encryption Standard (AES-256), to encrypt your data.

Use server-side encryption with AWS KMS Managed Keys (SSE-KMS)   SSE-KMS is similar to SSE-S3, but with additional benefits and charges for using this service. There are separate permissions for the use of an envelope key (that is, a key that protects your data's encryption key) that provides added protection against unauthorized access of your objects in Amazon S3.

SSE-KMS also provides you with an audit trail of when your key was used and by whom. Additionally, you can create and manage encryption keys yourself or use a default key that is unique to you, the service you are using, and the region in which you are working.

Use server-side encryption with customer-provided keys (SSE-C)   You manage the encryption keys, and Amazon S3 manages the encryption as it writes to disks. You also manage decryption when you access your objects.

NOTE   When you list objects in your bucket, the list API will return a list of all objects, regardless of whether they are encrypted.

Working with Amazon S3 Objects

Amazon S3 is a simple key-value store designed to store as many objects as you want. Store these objects in one or more buckets. An object consists of the following:

Key   The key is the name that you assign to an object. The object key is used to retrieve the object.

Version ID   Within a bucket, a key and version ID uniquely identify an object. The version ID is a string that Amazon S3 generates when you add an object to a bucket.

Value   The information being stored. An object value can be any sequence of bytes. Objects can range in size from 0 to 5 terabytes (TB).

Metadata   A set of key-value pairs with which you can store information about the object. You can assign metadata, referred to as *user-defined metadata*, to your objects in Amazon S3. Amazon S3 also assigns system metadata to these objects, which it uses for managing objects.

Subresources   Amazon S3 uses the subresource mechanism to store object-specific additional information. Because subresources are subordinates to objects, they are always associated with an entity, such as an object or a bucket.

Access control information   You can control access to the objects that you store in Amazon S3. Amazon S3 supports both the resource-based access control, such as an access control list (ACL) and bucket policies, and user-based access control.

Object Keys and Metadata

Each Amazon S3 object is composed of several parts. These parts include the data, a key, and metadata. An *object key* (or key name) uniquely identifies the object in a bucket. *Object metadata* is a set of name-value pairs. You can set the object metadata at the time that you upload an object. However, after you upload the object, you cannot modify object metadata. The only way to modify object metadata after it has been uploaded is to create a copy of the object.

When you upload an object, set the key name, which uniquely identifies the object in that bucket. As an example, in the Amazon S3 console, when you select a bucket, a list of objects that reside in your bucket is displayed. These names are the object keys. The name for a key is a sequence of Unicode characters whose UTF-8 encoding is limited to 1,024 bytes.

If you anticipate that your workload against Amazon S3 will exceed 100 requests per second, follow the Amazon S3 key naming guidelines for best performance.

Object Key Naming Guidelines

Though you can use any UTF-8 characters in an object key name, the following best practices for key naming help ensure maximum compatibility with other applications. Each application might parse special characters differently. The following guidelines help you maximize compliance with DNS, web-safe characters, XML parsers, and other APIs.

The following character sets are generally safe for use in key names:

- a–z
- A–Z
- 0–9
- _ (underscore)
- – (dash)
- . (period)
- ! (exclamation point)
- * (asterisk)
- ' (apostrophe)
- , (comma)

    The following are examples of valid object key names:

    - `2your-customer`
    - `your.great_photos-2018/jane/yourvacation.jpg`
    - `videos/2018/graduation/video1.wmv`

The Amazon S3 data model is a flat structure: you create a bucket, and the bucket stores objects. There is no hierarchy of sub-buckets or subfolders; however, you can infer logical hierarchy by using key name prefixes and delimiters as the Amazon S3 console does. The Amazon S3 console supports the concept of folders.

Object Metadata

There are two kinds of object metadata: system metadata and user-defined metadata.

System-Defined Metadata

For each object stored in a bucket, Amazon S3 maintains a set of system metadata. Amazon S3 processes this system metadata as needed. For example, Amazon S3 maintains the object creation date and size metadata, and it uses this information as part of object management.

There are two categories of system metadata.

- Metadata, such as object creation date, is system controlled where only Amazon S3 can modify the value.
- Other system metadata are examples of system metadata whose values you control.

    If your bucket is configured as a website, sometimes you might want to redirect a page request to another page or an external URL. In this case, a webpage is an object in your bucket. Amazon S3 stores the page redirect value as system metadata whose value you control.

When you create objects, you can configure values of these system metadata items or update the values when you need to.

Table 14.6 lists system-defined metadata and whether you can modify it.

TABLE 14.6   System-Defined Metadata

Name	Description	Modifiable
Content-Length	Size of object in bytes.	No
Last-Modified	The object creation date or last modified date, whichever is the latest.	No
Content-MD5	The base64-encoded 128-bit MD5 digest of the object.	No
x-amz-server-side-encryption	Indicates whether server-side encryption is enabled for the object and whether that encryption is from the AWS Key Management Service (SSE-KMS) or from AWS managed encryption (SSE-S3).	Yes
x-amz-version-ID	Object version. When you enable versioning on a bucket, Amazon S3 assigns a version number to objects added to the bucket.	No
x-amz-delete-marker	In a bucket that has versioning enabled, this Boolean marker indicates whether the object is a delete marker.	No
x-amz-storage-class	Storage class used for storing the object.	Yes
x-amz-websiteredirect-location	Redirects requests for the associated object to another object in the same bucket, or to an external URL.	Yes
x-amz-server-sideencryption-aws-kmskey-ID	If x-amz-server-side-encryption is present and has the value of aws:kms, this indicates the ID of the AWS KMS master encryption key that was used for the object.	Yes
x-amz-server-sideencryption-customeralgorithm	Indicates whether server-side encryption with customer-provided encryption keys (SSE-C) is enabled.	Yes

User-Defined Metadata

When uploading an object, you can also attach metadata to the object. Provide this optional information as a key-value pair when you deliver a PUT or POST request to create the object. When you upload objects using the REST API, the optional user-defined metadata names must begin with x-amz-meta- to distinguish them from other HTTP headers. When you retrieve the object using the REST API, this prefix is returned. User-defined metadata is a set of key-value pairs. Amazon S3 stores user-defined metadata keys in lowercase.

Object Tagging

You can use object tagging as a way to categorize your objects. Each tag is a key-value pair. The following are tagging examples:

- Suppose that an object contains protected health information (PHI) data. You might tag the object by using the following key-value pair:

    PHI=True

- Suppose that you store project files in your S3 bucket. You might tag these objects with a key called Project, and the following value:

    Project=Aqua

- You can set up multiple tags to an object, as shown in the following:

    Project=Y
    Classification=sensitive

You can add tags to new objects and existing objects. Note the following:

- You can associate up to 10 tags with an object. Tags associated with an object must have unique tag keys.
- A tag key can be up to 128 Unicode characters in length, and tag values can be up to 256 Unicode characters in length.
- Key and values are case-sensitive.

Object key name prefixes also enable you to categorize storage. However, prefix-based categorization is one-dimensional. Consider the following object key names:

- images/photo1.jpg
- projects/accountingproject/document.pdf
- project/financeproject/document2.pdf

These key names have the prefixes images/, projects/accountingproject/, and projects/financeproject/. These prefixes enable one-dimensional categorization; that is, everything under a prefix is one category. For example, the prefix projects/accountingproject identifies all documents related to the project accountingproject.

Tagging creates another dimension. If you want photo1 in the project financeproject category, tag the object accordingly. In addition to data classification, tagging offers the following additional benefits:

- Object tags enable fine-grained access control of permissions. For instance, you could grant an IAM user permissions to read-only objects with certain tags.

- Object tags enable fine-grained object lifecycle policies where you can configure tag-based filters, in addition to key name prefixes, in a lifecycle policy.

- When using Amazon S3 analytics, you can configure filters to group objects together for analysis by object tags, by key name prefix, or by both prefix and tags.

- You can customize Amazon CloudWatch metrics to display information by specific tag filters.

 Though it is acceptable to use tags to label objects that contain confidential information, the tags themselves should not contain any confidential data.

Operations on Objects

Amazon S3 enables you to store (POST and PUT), retrieve (GET), and delete (DELETE) objects. You can retrieve an entire object or a portion of an object. If you have enabled versioning on the bucket, you can retrieve a specific version of the object. You can also retrieve a sub-resource associated with your object and update it where applicable. You can make a copy of your existing object.

Depending on the size of the object, consider the following when uploading or copying a file:

Uploading objects   You can upload objects of up to 5 GB in size in a single operation. If your object is larger than 5 GB, use the multipart upload API. By using the multipart upload API, you can upload objects up to 5 TB each.

Copying objects   The Copy operation creates a copy of an object that is already stored in Amazon S3. You can create a copy of your object up to 5 GB in size in a single atomic operation. However, for copying an object greater than 5 GB, use the multipart upload API.

Getting Objects

You can retrieve objects directly from Amazon S3. The following options are available to you when retrieving objects:

Retrieve an entire object   A single GET operation can return the entire object stored in Amazon S3.

Retrieve object in parts   Use the Range HTTP header in a GET request to retrieve a specific range of bytes in an object stored in Amazon S3. Resume fetching other parts of the object when your application is ready. This ability to resume the download is useful when you need only portions of your object data. It is also useful where network connectivity is poor, and you must react to failures.

When you retrieve an object, its metadata is returned in the response headers. There are situations when you want to override certain response header values returned in a GET response. For example, you might override the Content-Disposition response header value in your GET request. To override these values, use the REST GET Object API to specify query string parameters in your GET request.

The AWS SDKs for Java, .NET, and PHP also provide necessary objects that you can use to specify values for these response headers in your GET request. When retrieving objects that are stored encrypted using server-side encryption, you must provide appropriate request headers.

Sharing an Object with Others

All objects uploaded to Amazon S3 are private by default. Only the object owner has permission to access these objects. However, the object owner can choose to share objects with others by generating a presigned URL, using their own security credentials, to grant time-limited permission to interact with the objects.

When you create a presigned URL for your object, you must provide your security credentials, specify a bucket name and an object key, specify the HTTP method (GET to download the object), and specify both the expiration date and the time. The presigned URLs are valid only for the specified duration.

Anyone who receives the presigned URL can then access the object. For example, if you have an image in your bucket and both the bucket and object are private, you can share the image with others by generating a presigned URL. You can generate a presigned URL programmatically using the AWS SDK for Java and .NET.

Anyone with valid security credentials can create a presigned URL. However, to access an object successfully, only someone who has permission to perform the operation that the presigned URL is based upon can create the presigned URL.

Uploading Objects

Depending on the size of the data that you are uploading, Amazon S3 provides the following options:

Upload objects in a single operation   Use a single PUT operation to upload objects up to 5 GB in size. For objects that are up to 5 TB in size, use the multipart upload API.

Upload objects in parts   The multipart upload API is designed to improve the upload experience for larger objects. Upload these object parts independently, in any order, and in parallel.

AWS recommends that you use multipart uploading in the following ways:

- If you are uploading large objects over a stable high-bandwidth network, use multipart uploading to maximize the use of your available bandwidth by uploading object parts in parallel for multithreaded performance.

- If you are uploading over a spotty network, use multipart uploading to increase resiliency to network errors by avoiding upload restarts. When using multipart uploading, you must retry uploading only parts that are interrupted during the upload. You do not need to restart uploading your object from the beginning.

When uploading an object, you can request that Amazon S3 encrypt it before saving it to disk and decrypt it when you download it.

Uploading Objects Using Multipart Upload API

Use multipart upload to upload a single object as a set of parts. Each part is a contiguous portion of the object's data. You can upload these object parts independently and in any order. If transmission of any part fails, you can retransmit that part without affecting other parts. After all parts of your object are uploaded, Amazon S3 assembles these parts and then creates the object. When your object size reaches 100 MB, consider using multipart uploads instead of uploading the object in a single operation.

Using multipart upload provides the following advantages:

Improved throughput   You can upload parts in parallel to improve throughput.

Quick recovery from any network issues   Smaller part size minimizes the impact of restarting a failed upload resulting from a network error.

Pause and resume object uploads   You can upload object parts over time. Once you initiate a multipart upload, there is no expiry; you must explicitly complete or abort the multipart upload.

Begin an upload before you know the final object size   You can upload an object as you are creating it.

Copying Objects

The Copy operation creates a copy of an object that is already stored in Amazon S3. You can create a copy of your object up to 5 GB in a single atomic operation. However, to copy an object that is greater than 5 GB, you must use the multipart upload API.

Using the Copy operation, you can do the following:

- Create additional copies of objects.
- Rename objects by copying them and then deleting the original ones.
- Move objects across Amazon S3 locations (for example, us-west-1 and EU).
- Change object metadata.

Each Amazon S3 object has metadata. It is a set of name-value pairs. You can set object metadata at the time you upload it. After you upload the object, you cannot modify object metadata. The only way to modify object metadata is to make a copy of the object and then set the metadata. In the Copy operation, you set the same object as the source and target.

Each object has metadata, which can be system metadata or user-defined. Users control some of the system metadata, such as storage class configuration to use for the object and configure server-side encryption. When you copy an object, both user-controlled system metadata and user-defined metadata are also copied. Amazon S3 resets the system-controlled metadata. For example, when you copy an object, Amazon S3 resets the creation date of the copied object. You do not need to set any of these values in your copy request.

When you copy an object, you might decide to update several metadata values. For example, if your source object is configured to use standard storage, you might choose to use RRS for the object copy. You might also decide to alter user-defined metadata values present on the source object. If you choose to update any of the object's user-configurable metadata (system- or user-defined) during the copy, then you must explicitly specify all of the user-configurable metadata present on the source object in your request, even if you are changing only one of the metadata values.

 If the source object is archived in Amazon S3 Glacier (the storage class of the object is GLACIER), you must first restore a temporary copy before you can copy the object to another bucket.

When you copy objects, you can request that Amazon S3 save the target object encrypted using an AWS KMS encryption key, an Amazon S3 managed encryption key, or a customer-provided encryption key. Accordingly, you must configure encryption information in your request. If the copy source is an object that is stored in Amazon S3 using server-side encryption with a customer-provided key, then provide encryption information in your request so that Amazon S3 can decrypt the object for copying.

 Copying objects across locations incurs bandwidth charges.

Listing Object Keys

You can list Amazon S3 object keys by prefix. By choosing a common prefix for the names of related keys and marking these keys with a special character that delimits hierarchy, you can use the list operation to select and browse keys in a hierarchical fashion. This can be likened to how files are stored in directories within a file system.

Amazon S3 exposes a list operation that enables you to enumerate the keys contained in a bucket. Keys are selected for listing by bucket and prefix. For instance, suppose that you have a bucket named dictionary that contains a key for every English word. You might make a call to list all of the keys in that bucket that start with the letter q. List results are returned in UTF-8 binary order. Whether you use the SOAP or REST list operations does not matter because they both return an XML document that has the names of matching keys and data about the object identified by each key.

 SOAP support over HTTP is deprecated, but it is still available over HTTPS. New Amazon S3 features do not support SOAP. AWS recommends that you use either the REST API or the AWS SDKs.

Groups of keys that share a prefix terminated by a special delimiter can be rolled up by that common prefix for the purposes of listing. This enables applications to organize and browse their keys hierarchically, much like how you would organize your files into directories in a file system. For example, to extend the dictionary bucket to contain more than only English words, you might form keys by prefixing each word with its language and a delimiter, such as Spanish/logical. Using this naming scheme and the hierarchical listing feature, you could retrieve a list of only Spanish words. You could also browse the top-level list of available languages without having to cycle through all the lexicographically intervening keys.

Listing Keys Hierarchically Using a Prefix and Delimiter

The prefix and delimiter parameters limit the kind of results the List operation returns. The prefix parameter limits results to only those keys that begin with the specified prefix, and the delimiter parameter causes the list to roll up all keys that share a common prefix into a single summary list result.

The purpose of the prefix and delimiter parameters is to help you organize and browse your keys hierarchically. To do this, first choose a delimiter for your bucket, such as slash (/), that does not occur in any of your anticipated key names. Next, construct your key names by concatenating all containing levels of the hierarchy, separating each level with the delimiter.

For example, if you were storing information about cities, you might naturally organize them by continent, then by country, and then by province or state. Because these names do not usually contain punctuation, you might select slash (/) as the delimiter. The following examples use a slash (/) delimiter:

- Europe/Spain/Madrid
- North America/Canada/Quebec/Bordeaux
- North America/USA/Texas/San Antonio
- North America/USA/Texas/Houston

If you stored data for every city in the world in this manner, it would become awkward to manage a flat key namespace. By using Prefix and Delimiter response elements with the list operation, you can use the hierarchy to list your data. For example, to list all of the states in the United States, set Delimiter='/' and Prefix='North America/USA/'. To list all of the provinces in Canada for which you have data, set Delimiter='/' and Prefix='North America/Canada/'.

Iterating Through Multipage Results

Because buckets can contain a virtually unlimited number of objects and keys, the entire results of a list operation can be large. To manage large result sets, the Amazon S3 API supports pagination to break them into multiple responses. Each list keys response returns a page of up to 1,000 keys with an indicator that illustrates whether the response is truncated. Send a series of list keys requests until you have retrieved all of the keys.

Deleting Objects

Amazon S3 provides several options for deleting objects from your bucket. You can delete one or more objects directly from your S3 bucket. If you want to delete a single object, you can use the Amazon S3 Delete API. If you want to delete multiple objects, you can use the Amazon S3 Multi-Object Delete API, which enables you to delete up to 1,000 objects with a single request. The Multi-Object Delete operation requires a single query string Delete parameter to distinguish it from other bucket POST operations.

When deleting objects from a bucket that is not version-enabled, provide only the object key name. However, when deleting objects from a version-enabled bucket, provide the version ID of the object to delete a specific version of the object.

Deleting Objects from a Version-Enabled Bucket

If your bucket is version-enabled, then multiple versions of the same object can exist in the bucket. When working with version-enabled buckets, the DELETE API enables the following options:

Specify a nonversioned delete request   Specify only the object's key, not the version ID. In this case, Amazon S3 creates a delete marker and returns its version ID in the response. This makes your object disappear from the bucket.

Specify a versioned delete request   Specify both the key and a version ID. In this case, the following two outcomes are possible:

- If the version ID maps to a specific object version, then Amazon S3 deletes the specific version of the object.

- If the version ID maps to the delete marker of that object, Amazon S3 deletes the delete marker. This causes the object to reappear in your bucket.

Performance Optimization

This section discusses Amazon S3 best practices for optimizing performance.

Request Rate and Performance Considerations

Amazon S3 scales to support high request rates. If your request rate grows steadily, Amazon S3 automatically partitions your buckets as needed to support higher request rates. However, if you expect a rapid increase in the request rate for a bucket to more than 300 PUT/LIST/DELETE requests per second or more than 800 GET requests per second, AWS recommends that you open a support case to prepare for the workload and avoid any temporary limits on your request rate.

If your requests are typically a mix of GET, PUT, DELETE, or GET Bucket (List Objects), choose the appropriate key names for your objects to ensure better performance by providing low-latency access to the Amazon S3 index. It also ensures scalability regardless of the number of requests that you send per second. If the bulk of your workload consists of GET requests, AWS recommends using the Amazon CloudFront content delivery service.

> The Amazon S3 best practice guidelines apply only if you are routinely processing 100 or more requests per second. If your typical workload involves only occasional bursts of 100 requests per second and fewer than 800 requests per second, you do not need to follow these recommendations.

Workloads with Different Request Types

When you are uploading a large number of objects, you might use sequential numbers or date-and-time values as part of the key names. For instance, you might decide to use key names that include a combination of the date and time, as shown in the following example, where the prefix includes a timestamp:

```
demobucket/2018-31-05-16-00-00/order1234234/receipt1.jpg
demobucket/2018-31-05-16-00-00/order3857422/receipt2.jpg
demobucket/2018-31-05-16-00-00/order1248473/receipt2.jpg
demobucket/2018-31-05-16-00-00/order8474937/receipt2.jpg
demobucket/2018-31-05-16-00-00/order1248473/receipt3.jpg
...
demobucket/2018-31-05-16-00-00/order1248473/receipt4.jpg
demobucket/2018-31-05-16-00-00/order1248473/receipt5.jpg
demobucket/2018-31-05-16-00-00/order1248473/receipt6.jpg
demobucket/2018-31-05-16-00-00/order1248473/receipt7.jpg
```

The way these keys are named presents a performance problem. To get a better understanding of this issue, consider the way that Amazon S3 stores key names. Amazon S3 maintains an index of object key names in each AWS Region. These keys are stored in UTF-8 binary ordering across multiple partitions in the index. The key name dictates where (or which partition) the key is stored in. In this case, where you use a sequential prefix such as a timestamp, or an alphabetical sequence, would increase the chances that Amazon S3 targets a specific partition for a large number of your keys, overwhelming the I/O capacity of the partition. However, if you introduce randomness in your key name prefixes, the key names, and therefore the I/O load, distribute across more than one partition.

If you anticipate that your workload will consistently exceed 100 requests per second, avoid sequential key names. If you must use sequential numbers or date-and-time patterns in key names, add a random prefix to the key name. The randomness of the prefix more evenly distributes key names across multiple index partitions.

The guidelines for the key name prefixes also apply to the bucket names. When Amazon S3 stores a key name in the index, it stores the bucket names as part of the key name (demobucket/object.jpg).

One way to introduce randomness to key names is to add a hash string as a prefix to the key name. For instance, you can compute an MD5 hash of the character sequence that you plan to assign as the key name. From the hash, select a specific number of characters and add them as the prefix to the key name.

> A hashed prefix of three or four characters should be sufficient. AWS strongly recommends using a hexadecimal hash as the prefix.

GET-Intensive Workloads

If your workload consists mostly of sending GET requests, then in addition to the preceding guidelines, consider using Amazon CloudFront for performance optimization.

Integrating CloudFront with Amazon S3 enables you to deliver content with low latency and a high data transfer rate. You will also send fewer direct requests to Amazon S3, which helps to lower your costs.

Suppose that you have a few objects that are popular. CloudFront fetches those objects from Amazon S3 and caches them. CloudFront can then serve future requests for the objects from its cache, reducing the number of GET requests it sends to Amazon S3.

Storing Large Attribute Values in Amazon S3

Amazon DynamoDB currently limits the size of each item that you store in a table to 400 KB. If your application needs to store more data in an item than the DynamoDB size limit permits, store the large attributes as an object in Amazon S3. You can then store the Amazon S3 object identifier in your item.

You can also use the object metadata support in Amazon S3 to store the primary key value of the corresponding table item as Amazon S3 object metadata. Doing this provides a link back to the parent item in DynamoDB, which helps with maintenance of the Amazon S3 objects.

Example 11: Store Large Attribute Values in Amazon S3

Suppose that you have a table that stores product data, such as item price, description, book authors, and dimensions for other products. If you want to store an *image* of each product that was too large to fit in an *item*, use Amazon S3 images as an item in DynamoDB.

When implementing this strategy, remember the following limitations and restrictions:

- DynamoDB does not support transactions that cross Amazon S3 and DynamoDB. Therefore, your application must deal with any failures, which could include cleaning up orphaned Amazon S3 objects.

- Amazon S3 limits the length of object identifiers. You must organize your data in a way that does not generate excessively long object identifiers or violate other Amazon S3 constraints.

Amazon Elastic File System

Amazon Elastic File System (Amazon EFS) provides simple, scalable file storage for use with Amazon EC2. With Amazon EFS, storage capacity is elastic, growing and shrinking automatically as you add and remove files so your applications have the storage they need when they need it. The simple web services interface helps you create and configure file systems quickly and easily. The service manages all of the file storage infrastructure, meaning that you can avoid the complexity of deploying, patching, and maintaining complex file system configurations, such as situations where it must facilitate user uploads or interim results of batch processes. By placing those files in a shared storage layer, it helps you to avoid the introduction of stateful components.

Amazon EFS supports the Network File System versions 4.0 and 4.1 (NFSv4) protocol, so the applications and tools that you use today work seamlessly with Amazon EFS. Multiple Amazon EC2 instances can access an Amazon EFS file system at the same time, providing a common data source for workloads and applications running on more than one instance or server.

The service is highly scalable, highly available, and highly durable. Amazon EFS stores data and metadata across multiple Availability Zones in a region, and it can grow to petabyte scale, drive high levels of throughput, and allow massively parallel access from Amazon EC2 instances to your data.

Amazon EFS provides file system access semantics, such as strong data consistency and file locking. Amazon EFS also allows you to control access to your file systems through Portable Operating System Interface (POSIX) permissions.

Amazon EFS supports two forms of encryption for file systems: encryption in transit and encryption at rest. You can enable encryption at rest when creating an Amazon EFS file system. If you do, all of your data and metadata is encrypted. You can enable encryption in transit when you mount the file system.

Amazon EFS is designed to provide the throughput, input/output operations per second (IOPS), and low latency needed for a broad range of workloads. With Amazon EFS, throughput and IOPS scale as a file system grows, and file operations are delivered with consistent, low latencies.

How Amazon EFS Works

Figure 14.19 shows an example of VPC accessing an Amazon EFS file system. In this example, Amazon EC2 instances in the VPC have file systems mounted.

Amazon EFS provides file storage in the AWS Cloud. With Amazon EFS, you can create a file system, mount the file system on an Amazon EC2 instance, and then read and write data to and from your file system. You can mount an Amazon EFS file system in your VPC through the NFSv4 protocol.

FIGURE 14.19 VPC accessing an Amazon EFS

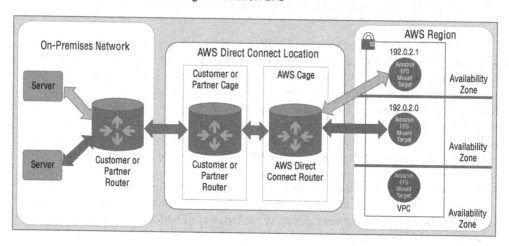

You can access your Amazon EFS file system concurrently from Amazon EC2 instances in your Amazon VPC so that applications that scale beyond a single connection can access a file system. Amazon EC2 instances running in multiple Availability Zones within the same region can access the file system so that many users can access and share a common data source.

However, there are restrictions. You can mount an Amazon EFS file system on instances in only one VPC at a time. Both the file system and VPC must be in the same AWS Region.

To access your Amazon EFS file system in a VPC, create one or more mount targets in the VPC. A *mount target* provides an IP address for an NFSv4 endpoint at which you can mount an Amazon EFS file system. Mount your file system using its DNS name, which resolves to the IP address of the Amazon EFS mount target in the same Availability Zone as your EC2 instance. You can create one mount target in each Availability Zone in a region. If there are multiple subnets in an Availability Zone in your Amazon VPC, create a mount target in one of the subnets, and all EC2 instances in that Availability Zone share that mount target.

Mount targets themselves are designed to be highly available. When designing your application for both high availability and the ability to failover to other Availability Zones, keep in mind that the IP addresses and DNS for your mount targets in each Availability Zone are static. After mounting the file system via the mount target, use it like any other POSIX-compliant file system.

You can mount your Amazon EFS file systems on your on-premises data center servers when connected to your Amazon VPC with AWS Direct Connect (DX). You can mount your Amazon EFS file systems on on-premises servers to migrate datasets to Amazon EFS, enable cloud-bursting scenarios, or back up your on-premises data to Amazon EFS.

You can mount Amazon EFS file systems on Amazon EC2 instances or on-premises through a DX connection.

How Amazon EFS Works with AWS Direct Connect

Using an Amazon EFS file system mounted on an on-premises server, you can migrate on-premises data into the AWS Cloud hosted in an Amazon EFS file system. You can also take advantage of bursting. This means that you can move data from your on-premises servers into Amazon EFS, analyze it on a fleet of Amazon EC2 instances in your Amazon VPC, and then store the results permanently in your file system or move the results back to your on-premises server.

Consider the following when using Amazon EFS with DX:

- Your on-premises server must have a Linux-based operating system. AWS recommends Linux kernel version 4.0 or later.

- For the sake of simplicity, AWS recommends mounting an Amazon EFS file system on an on-premises server using a mount target IP address instead of a DNS name.

- AWS Virtual Private Network (AWS VPN) is not supported for accessing an Amazon EFS file system from an on-premises server.

You can use any one of the mount targets in your Amazon VPC as long as the subnet of the mount target is reachable by using the DX connection between your on-premises server and Amazon VPC. To access Amazon EFS from an on-premises server, you must add a rule to your mount target security group to allow inbound traffic to the NFS port (2049) from your on-premises server.

In Amazon EFS, a file system is the primary resource. Each file system has properties such as ID, creation token, creation time, file system size in bytes, number of mount targets created for the file system, and the file system state.

Amazon EFS also supports other resources to configure the primary resource. These include mount targets and tags:

Mount Target

- To access your file system, create mount targets in your Amazon VPC. Each mount target has the following properties:
  - Mount target ID
  - Subnet ID where it is created
  - File system ID for which it is created
  - IP address at which the file system may be mounted
  - Mount target state

    You can use the IP address or the DNS name in your mount command.

Tags

- To help organize your file systems, assign your own metadata to each of the file systems that you create. Each tag is a key-value pair.

Each file system has a DNS name of the following form:

`file-system-ID.efs.aws-region.amazonaws.com`

You can configure this DNS name in your mount command to mount the Amazon EFS file system.

Suppose that you create an efs-mount-point subdirectory in your home directory on your EC2 instance or on-premises server. Use the mount command to mount the file system. For example, on an Amazon Linux AMI, you can use following mount command:

```
$ sudo mount -t nfs -o nfsvers=4.1,rsize=1048576,wsize=1048576,hard,timeo=600,
retrans=2,noresvport file-system-DNS-name:/ ~/efs-mount-point
```

You can think of mount targets and tags as *subresources* that do not exist without being associated with a file system.

Amazon EFS provides API operations for you to create and manage these resources. In addition to the create and delete operations for each resource, Amazon EFS also supports a describe operation that enables you to retrieve resource information. The following options are available for creating and managing these resources:

- Use the Amazon EFS console.

- Use the Amazon EFS command line interface (CLI).

You can also manage these resources programmatically as follows:

Use the AWS SDKs   The AWS SDKs simplify your programming tasks by wrapping the underlying Amazon EFS API. The SDK clients also authenticate your requests by using access keys that you provide.

Call the Amazon EFS API directly from your application   If you cannot use the SDKs, you can make the Amazon EFS API calls directly from your application. However, if you use this option, you must write the necessary code to authenticate your requests.

Authentication and Access Control

You must have valid credentials to make Amazon EFS API requests, such as creating a file system. In addition, you must also have permissions to create or access resources. By default, when you use the account root user credentials, you can create and access resources owned by that account. However, AWS does not recommend using account root user credentials. In addition to creating or accessing resources, you must grant permissions to any AWS IAM users and roles you create in your account.

Data Consistency in Amazon EFS

Amazon EFS provides the open-after-close consistency semantics that applications expect from NFS. In Amazon EFS, write operations are durably stored across Availability Zones when an application performs a synchronous write operation (for example, using the open Linux command with the O_DIRECT flag, or the fsync Linux command) and when an application closes a file.

Amazon EFS provides stronger consistency than open-after-close semantics, depending on the access pattern. Applications that perform synchronous data access and perform non-appending writes have read-after-write consistency for data access.

Creating an IAM User

Services in AWS, such as Amazon EFS, require that you provide credentials when you access them so that the service can determine whether you have permissions to access its resources. AWS recommends that you do not use the AWS account credentials of your account to make requests. Instead, create an IAM user, and grant that user full access. AWS refers to these users as administrators. You can use the administrator credentials, instead of AWS account credentials, to interact with AWS and perform tasks, such as creating a bucket, creating users, and granting them permissions.

For all operations, such as creating a file system and creating tags, a user must have IAM permissions for the corresponding API action and resource. You can perform any Amazon EFS operations using the AWS account credentials of your account. However, using AWS account credentials is not considered a best practice. If you create IAM users in your account, you can give them permissions for Amazon EFS actions with user policies. Additionally, you can use roles to grant cross-account permissions.

Creating Resources for Amazon EFS

Amazon EFS provides elastic, shared file storage that is POSIX-compliant. The file system that you create supports concurrent read and write access from multiple Amazon EC2 instances, and it is accessible from all of the Availability Zones in the AWS Region where it is created. You can mount an Amazon EFS file system on EC2 instances in your Amazon VPC through the Network File System versions 4.0 and 4.1 protocol (NFSv4).

As an example, suppose that you have one or more EC2 instances launched in your Amazon VPC. You want to create and use a file system on these instances. To use Amazon EFS file systems in the VPC, follow these steps:

1. **Create an Amazon EFS file system.** When creating a file system, AWS recommends that you consider using the Name tag, because its value appears in the console, making the file easier to identify. You can also add other optional tags to the file system.

2. **Create mount targets for the file system.** To access the file system in your Amazon VPC and mount the file system to your Amazon EC2 instance, you must create mount targets in the VPC subnets.

3. **Create security groups.** Both an Amazon EC2 instance and mount target must have associated security groups. These security groups act as a virtual firewall that controls the traffic between them. You can use the security group that you associated with the mount target to control inbound traffic to your file system by adding an inbound rule to the mount target security group that allows access from a specific EC2 instance. Then you can mount the file system only on that EC2 instance.

Creating a File System

You can use the Amazon EFS console, or the AWS CLI, to create a file system. You can also use the AWS SDKs to create file systems programmatically.

Using File Systems

Amazon EFS presents a standard file system interface that supports semantics for full file system access. Using NFSv4.1, you can mount your Amazon EFS file system on any Amazon EC2 Linux-based instance. Once mounted, you can work with the files and directories as you would with a local file system. You can also use AWS DataSync to copy files from any file system to Amazon EFS.

After you create the file system and mount it on your EC2 instance, you should be aware of several rules to use it effectively. For example, when you first create the file system, there is only *one root directory* at /. By default, only the *root user* (UID 0) has read-write-execute permissions. For other users to modify the file system, the root user must explicitly grant them access.

NFS-Level Users, Groups, and Permissions

Amazon EFS file system objects have a Unix-style mode associated with them. This value defines the permissions for performing actions on that object, and users familiar with Unix-style systems can understand how Amazon EFS manages these permissions.

Further, on Unix-style systems, users and groups are mapped to numeric identifiers, which Amazon EFS uses to represent file ownership. A single owner and a single group own file system objects, such as files or directories on Amazon EFS. Amazon EFS uses these numeric IDs to check permissions when a user attempts to access a file system object.

User and Group ID Permissions on Files and Directories within a File System

Files and directories in an Amazon EFS file system support standard Unix-style read/write/execute permissions based on the user ID and group ID asserted by the mounting NFSv4.1 client. When a user tries to access files and directories, Amazon EFS checks their user ID and group IDs to determine whether the user has permission to access the objects. Amazon EFS also uses these IDs as the owner and group owner for new files and directories that the user creates. Amazon EFS does not inspect user or group names—it uses only the numeric identifiers.

When you create a user on an EC2 instance, you can assign any numeric UID and GID to the user. The numeric user IDs are set in the /etc/passwd file on Linux systems. The numeric group IDs are in the /etc/group file. These files define the mappings between names and IDs. Outside of the EC2 instance, Amazon EFS does not perform any authentication of these IDs, including the root ID of 0.

If a user accesses an Amazon EFS file system from two different EC2 instances, depending on whether the UID for the user is the same or different on those instances, you may observe different behavior. If the user IDs are the same on both EC2 instances, Amazon EFS considers them the same user, regardless of the EC2 instance they use. The user experience when accessing the file system is the same from both EC2 instances. If the user IDs are not the same on both EC2 instances, Amazon EFS considers them to be different users, and the user experience will not be the same when accessing the Amazon EFS file system from the two different EC2 instances. If two different users on different EC2 instances share an ID, Amazon EFS considers them the same user.

Deleting an Amazon EFS File System

File system deletion is a permanent action that destroys the file system and any data in it. Any data that you delete from a file system is gone, and you cannot restore the data.

  Always unmount a file system before you delete it.

Managing Access to Encrypted File Systems

Using Amazon EFS, you can create encrypted file systems. Amazon EFS supports two forms of encryption for file systems: encryption in transit and encryption at rest. Any key management that you must perform is related only to encryption at rest. Amazon EFS automatically manages the keys for encryption in transit. If you create a file system that uses encryption at rest, data and metadata are encrypted at rest.

Amazon EFS uses AWS KMS for key management. When you create a file system using encryption at rest, specify a customer master key (CMK). The CMK can be aws/elasticfilesystem (the AWS managed CMK for Amazon EFS), or it can be a CMK that you manage. File data, the contents of your files, is encrypted at rest using the CMK that you specified when you created your file system.

The AWS managed CMK for your file system is used as the master key for the metadata in your file system; for instance, file names, directory names, and directory contents. You are responsible for the CMK used to encrypt your file data (the contents of your files) at rest. Moreover, you are responsible for the management of who has access to your CMKs and the contents of your encrypted file systems. IAM policies and AWS KMS control these permissions. IAM policies control a user's access to Amazon EFS API actions. AWS KMS key policies control a user's access to the CMK that you specified when the file system was created.

As a key administrator, you can both import external keys and modify keys by enabling, disabling, or deleting them. The state of the CMK that you specified (when you created the file system with encryption at rest) affects access to its contents. To provide users access to the contents of an encrypted at rest file system, the CMK must be in the enabled state.

Amazon EFS Performance

Amazon EFS file systems are spread across an unconstrained number of storage servers, allowing file systems to expand elastically to petabyte scale. The distribution also allows them to support massively parallel access from Amazon EC2 instances to your data. Because of this distributed design, Amazon EFS avoids the bottlenecks and limitations inherent to conventional file servers.

This distributed data storage design means that multithreaded applications and applications that concurrently access data from multiple Amazon EC2 instances can drive substantial levels of aggregate throughput and IOPS. Analytics and big data workloads, media processing workflows, content management, and web serving are examples of these applications.

Additionally, Amazon EFS data is distributed across multiple Availability Zones, providing a high level of availability and durability.

Performance Modes

To support a wide variety of cloud storage workloads, Amazon EFS offers two performance modes: General Purpose and Max I/O. At the time that you create your file system, you select a file system's performance mode. There are no additional charges associated with the two performance modes. Your Amazon EFS file system is billed and metered the same, irrespective of the performance mode chosen. You cannot change an Amazon EFS file system's performance mode after you have created the file system.

General Purpose performance mode   AWS recommends the General Purpose performance mode for the majority of your Amazon EFS file systems. General Purpose is ideal for latency-sensitive use cases, such as web serving environments, content management systems, home directories, and general file serving. If you do not choose a performance mode when you create your file system, Amazon EFS selects the General Purpose mode for you by default.

Max I/O performance mode   File systems in the Max I/O mode can scale to higher levels of aggregate throughput and operations per second with a trade-off of slightly higher latencies for file operations. Highly parallelized applications and workloads, such as big data analysis, media processing, and genomics analysis can benefit from this mode.

Throughput Scaling in Amazon EFS

Throughput on Amazon EFS scales as a file system grows. Because file-based workloads are typically spiky, driving high levels of throughput for short periods of time and low levels of throughput the rest of the time, Amazon EFS is designed to burst to high throughput levels for periods of time.

All file systems, regardless of size, can burst to 100 MB/s of throughput, and those larger than 1 TB can burst to 100 MB/s per TB of data stored in the file system. For example, a 10-TB file system can burst to 1,000 MB/s of throughput (10 TB × 100 MB/s/TB). The portion of time a file system can burst is determined by its size, and the bursting model is designed so that typical file system workloads will be able to burst virtually any time they need to.

Amazon EFS uses a credit system to determine when file systems can burst. Each file system earns credits over time at a baseline rate that is determined by the size of the file system, and it uses credits whenever it reads or writes data. The baseline rate is 50 MB/s per TB of storage (equivalently, 50 KB/s per GB of storage).

Accumulated burst credits give the file system permission to drive throughput above its baseline rate. A file system can drive throughput continuously at its baseline rate. Whenever the file system is inactive or when it is driving throughput below its baseline rate, the file system accumulates burst credits.

Summary

In this chapter, stateless applications are defined as those that do not require knowledge of previous individual interactions and do not store session information locally. Stateless application design is beneficial because it reduces the risk of loss of session information or critical data. It also improves user experience by reducing the chances that context-specific data is lost if a resource containing session information becomes unavailable. To accomplish this, AWS customers can use Amazon DynamoDB, Amazon ElastiCache, Amazon Simple Storage Service (Amazon S3), and Amazon Elastic File System (Amazon EFS).

DynamoDB is a fast and flexible NoSQL database service that is used by applications that require consistent, single-digit millisecond latency at any scale. In stateless application design, you can use DynamoDB to store and rapidly retrieve session information. This separates session information from application resources responsible for processing user interactions. For example, a web application can use DynamoDB to store user shopping carts. If an application server becomes unavailable, the users accessing the application do not experience a loss of service.

To further improve speed of access, DynamoDB supports global secondary indexes and local secondary indexes. A secondary index contains a subset of attributes from a table and uses an alternate key to support custom queries. A local secondary index has the same partition key as a table but uses a different sort key. A global secondary index has different partition and sort keys.

DynamoDB uses read and write capacity units to determine cost. A single read capacity unit represents one strongly consistent read per second (or two eventually consistent reads per second) for items up to 4 KB in size. A single write capacity unit represents one write per second for items up to 1 KB in size. Items larger than these values consume additional read or write capacity.

ElastiCache enables you to quickly deploy, manage, and scale distributed in-memory cache environments. With ElastiCache, you can store application state information in a shared location by using an in-memory key-value store. Caches can be created using either Memcached or Redis caching engines. Read and write operations to a backend database can be time-consuming. Thus, ElastiCache is especially effective as a caching layer for heavy-use applications that require rapid access to backend data. You can also use ElastiCache to store HTTP sessions, further improving the performance of your applications.

ElastiCache offers various scalability configurations that improve access times and availability. For example, read-heavy applications can use additional cache cluster nodes to respond to queries. Should there be an increase in demand, additional cluster nodes can be scaled out quickly.

There are some differences between the available caching engines. AWS recommends that you use Memcached for simple data models that may require scaling and partitioning/sharding. Redis is recommended for more complex data types, persistent key stores, read-replication, and publish/subscribe operations.

In certain situations, storing state information can involve larger file operations (such as file uploads and batch processes). Amazon S3 can support millions of operations per second on trillions of objects through a simple web service. Through simple integration, developers can take advantage of the massive scale of object storage.

Amazon S3 stores objects in buckets, which are addressable using unique URLs (such as http://johnstiles.s3.amazonaws.com/). Buckets enable you to group similar objects and configure access control policies for internal and external users. Buckets also serve as the unit of aggregation for usage reporting. There is no limit to the number of objects that can be stored in a bucket, and there is no performance difference between using one or multiple buckets for your web application. The decision to use one or more buckets is often a consideration of access control.

Amazon S3 buckets support versioning and lifecycle configurations to maintain the integrity of objects and reduce cost. Versioning ensures that any time an object is modified and uploaded to a bucket, it is saved as a new version. Authorized users can access previous versions of objects at any time. In versioned buckets, a delete operation places a marker on the object (without deleting prior versions). Conversely, you must use a separate operation to fully remove an object from a versioned bucket. Use lifecycle configurations to reduce cost by automatically moving infrequently accessed objects to lower-cost storage tiers.

Amazon EFS provides simple, scalable file storage for use with multiple concurrent Amazon EC2 instances or on-premises systems. In stateless design, having a shared block storage system removes the risk of loss of data in situations where one or more instances become unavailable.

Exam Essentials

Understand block storage vs. object storage.   The difference between block storage and object storage is the fundamental unit of storage. With block storage, each file saved to the drive is composed of blocks of a specific size. With object storage, each file is saved as a single object regardless of size.

Understand when to use Amazon Simple Storage Service and when to use Amazon Elastic Block Storage or Amazon Elastic File System.   This is an architectural decision based on the type of data that you are storing and the rate at which you intend to update that data. Amazon Simple Storage Service (Amazon S3) can hold any type of data, but Amazon S3 would not be a good choice for a database or any rapidly changing data types.

Understand Amazon S3 versioning.   Once Amazon S3 versioning is enabled, you cannot disable the feature—you can only suspend it. Also, when versioning is activated, items that are deleted are assigned a delete marker and are not accessible. The deleted objects are still in Amazon S3, and you will continue to incur charges for storing them.

Know how to control access to Amazon S3 objects. IAM policies specify which actions are allowed or denied on specific AWS resources. Amazon S3 bucket policies are attached only to Amazon S3 buckets. Amazon S3 bucket policies specify which actions are allowed or denied for principals on the bucket to which the bucket policy is attached.

Know how to create or select a proper primary key for an Amazon DynamoDB table. DynamoDB stores data as groups of attributes, known as *items*. Items are similar to rows or records in other database systems. DynamoDB stores and retrieves each item based on the primary key value, which must be unique. Items are distributed across 10 GB storage units, called *partitions* (physical storage internal to DynamoDB). Each table has one or more partitions. DynamoDB uses the partition key value as an input to an internal hash function. The output from the hash function determines the partition in which the item is stored. The hash value of its partition key determines the location of each item. All items with the same partition key are stored together. Composite partition keys are ordered by the sort key value. If the collection size grows bigger than 10 GB, DynamoDB splits partitions by sort key.

Understand how to configure the read capacity units and write capacity units properly for your tables. When you create a table or index in DynamoDB, you must specify your capacity requirements for read and write activity. By defining your throughput capacity in advance, DynamoDB can reserve the necessary resources to meet the read and write activity your application requires while ensuring consistent, low-latency performance.

One read capacity unit (RCU) represents one strongly consistent read per second, or two eventually consistent reads per second, for an item up to 4 KB in size. If you need to read an item that is larger than 4 KB, DynamoDB must consume additional RCUs. The total number of RCUs required depends on the item size and whether you want an eventually consistent or strongly consistent read.

One write capacity unit (WCU) represents one write per second for an item up to 1 KB in size. If you need to write an item that is larger than 1 KB, DynamoDB must consume additional WCUs. The total number of WCUs required depends on the item size.

Understand the use cases for DynamoDB streams. A DynamoDB stream is an ordered flow of information about changes to items in an DynamoDB table. When you enable a stream on a table, DynamoDB captures information about every modification to data items in the table. Whenever an application creates, updates, or deletes items in the table, DynamoDB Streams writes a stream record with the primary key attributes of the items that were modified. A stream record contains information about a data modification to a single item in a DynamoDB table. You can configure the stream so that the stream records capture additional information, such as the before and after images of modified items.

Know what secondary indexes are and when to use a local secondary index versus a global secondary index and the differences between the two. A global secondary index is an index with a partition key and a sort key that can be different from those on the base table.

A global secondary index is considered *global* because queries on the index can span all of the data in the base table, across all partitions. A local secondary index is an index that has the same partition key as the base table, but a different sort key. A local secondary index is *local* in the sense that every partition of a local secondary index is scoped to a base table partition that has the same partition key value.

Know the operations that can be performed using the DynamoDB API. Know the more common DynamoDB API operations: CreateTable, UpdateTable, Query, Scan, PutItem, GetItem, UpdateItem, DeleteItem, BatchGetItem, and BatchWriteItem. Understand the purpose of each operation and be familiar with some of the parameters and limitations for the batch operations.

Be familiar with handling errors when using DynamoDB. Understand the differences between 400 error codes and 500 error codes and how to handle both classes of errors. Also, understand which techniques to use to mitigate the different errors. In addition, you should understand what causes a ProvisionedThrouphputExceededException error and what you can do to resolve the issue.

Understand how to configure your Amazon S3 bucket to serve as a static website. To host a static website, you configure an Amazon S3 bucket for website hosting and then upload your website content to the bucket. This bucket must have public read access. It is intentional that everyone has read access to this bucket. The website is then available at the AWS Region specific website endpoint of the bucket.

Be familiar with the Amazon S3 API operations. Be familiar with the API operations, such as PUT, GET, SELECT, and DELETE. Understand how having versioning enabled affects the behavior of the DELETE operation. You should also be familiar with the situations that require a multipart upload and how to use the associated API.

Understand the differences among the different Amazon S3 storage classes. The storage classes are Standard, Infrequent Access (IA), Glacier, and Reduced Redundancy. Understand the differences and why you might choose one storage class over the other and knowing the consequences of those choices.

Know how to use Amazon ElastiCache. Improve the performance of your application by deploying ElastiCache clusters as a part of your application and offloading read requests for frequently accessed data. Use the lazy loading caching strategy in your solution to first check the cache for your query results before checking the database.

Understand when to choose one specific cache engine over another. ElastiCache provides two open source caching engines. You are responsible for choosing the engine that meets your requirements. Use Redis when you must persist and restore your data, you need multiple replicas of your data, or you are seeking advanced features and functionality, such as sort and rank or leaderboards. Redis supports these features natively. Alternatively, you can use Memcached when you need a simpler, in-memory object store that can be easily partitioned and horizontally scaled.

Resources to Review

AWS Database Blog:

> https://aws.amazon.com/blogs/database/

Amazon DynamoDB Blog:

> https://aws.amazon.com/blogs/aws/tag/amazon-dynamo-db/

Best Practices for Amazon DynamoDB:

> https://docs.aws.amazon.com/amazondynamodb/latest/developerguide/
> best-practices.html

Amazon DynamoDB Read Consistency:

> https://docs.aws.amazon.com/amazondynamodb/latest/developerguide/
> HowItWorks.ReadConsistency.html

Amazon ElastiCache for Redis User's Guide:

> https://docs.aws.amazon.com/AmazonElastiCache/latest/red-ug/WhatIs.html

Amazon ElastiCache Tutorials and Videos:

> https://docs.aws.amazon.com/AmazonElastiCache/latest/red-ug/
> Tutorials.html

Performance at Scale with Amazon ElastiCache (Whitepaper):

> https://d0.awsstatic.com/whitepapers/performance-at-scale-with-
> amazon-elasticache.pdf

Amazon ElastiCache FAQs:

> https://aws.amazon.com/elasticache/faqs/

Amazon VPCs and ElastiCache Security:

> https://docs.aws.amazon.com/AmazonElastiCache/latest/mem-ug/VPCs.html

Amazon Simple Storage Service Developer Guide:

> https://docs.aws.amazon.com/AmazonS3/latest/dev/Welcome.html

Getting Started with Amazon Simple Storage Service:

> https://docs.aws.amazon.com/AmazonS3/latest/gsg/GetStartedWithS3.html

AWS Storage Services Overview (Whitepaper):

> https://d1.awsstatic.com/whitepapers/Storage/
> AWS%20Storage%20Services%20Whitepaper-v9.pdf

Projects on AWS: Host a Static Website:

> https://aws.amazon.com/getting-started/projects/host-static-
> website/?trk=gs_card

Amazon S3 Frequently Asked Questions:

> https://aws.amazon.com/s3/faqs/?nc=sn&loc=6

Deep Dive on Amazon S3 & Amazon Glacier Storage
Management (Video):

> https://www.youtube.com/watch?v=SUWqDOnXeDw

What is Cloud Object Storage?

> https://aws.amazon.com/what-is-cloud-object-storage/

When to Choose Amazon EFS:

> https://aws.amazon.com/efs/when-to-choose-efs/

Amazon EFS FAQs:

> https://aws.amazon.com/efs/faq/

Amazon Elastic File System: Choosing Between the Different Throughput and
Performance Modes (Whitepaper):

> https://d1.awsstatic.com/whitepapers/Storage/amazon_efs_choosing_
> between_different_performance_and_throughput.pdf

Deep Dive on Amazon EFS (Video):

> https://www.youtube.com/watch?v=LWiAwIa2H7c&feature=youtu.be

Exercises

Create an Amazon ElastiCache Cluster Running Memcached

In this exercise, you will create an Amazon ElastiCache cluster using the Memcached
engine.

1. Sign in to the AWS Management Console, and open the ElastiCache console at
   https://console.aws.amazon.com/elasticache/.

2. To create a new ElastiCache cluster, begin the launch and configuration
   process.

3. For **Cluster engine**, choose **Memcached** and configure the cluster name, number of
   nodes, and node type.

4. (Optional) Configure the security group and maintenance window as needed.

5. Review the cluster configuration, and begin provisioning the cluster. Connect to the
   cluster with any Memcached client by using the DNS name of the cluster.

You have now created your first ElastiCache cluster.

EXERCISE 14.2

Expand the Size of a Memcached Cluster

In this exercise, you will expand the size of an existing Amazon ElastiCache Memcached cluster.

1. Launch a Memcached cluster by following the steps in the previous exercise.

2. Navigate to the Amazon ElastiCache dashboard, and view the configuration of your existing cluster.

3. View the list of nodes that are currently being used, and then add one new node by increasing the number of nodes.

4. Apply the changes to the configuration, and wait for the new node to finish provisioning.

5. Confirm that the new node has been provisioned, and connect to the node using a Memcached client.

You have horizontally scaled an existing ElastiCache cluster by adding a new cache node.

EXERCISE 14.3

Create and Attach an Amazon EFS Volume

In this exercise, you will create a new Amazon EFS volume and attach it to a running instance.

1. While signed in to the AWS Management Console, open the Amazon EC2 console at https://console.aws.amazon.com/ec2.

   If you don't see a running Linux instance, launch a new instance.

2. Open the Amazon EFS service dashboard. Choose **Create File System**.

3. Select the Amazon VPC where your Linux instance is running.

4. Accept the default mount targets, and make a note of the security group ID assigned to the targets.

5. Choose any settings, and then create the file system.

6. Assign the same default security group used by the file system to your Linux instance.

(continued)

7. Log in to the console of the Linux instance, and install the NFS client on the Amazon EC2 instance. For Amazon Linux, use the following command:

```
sudo yum install -y nfs-utils
```

8. Create a new directory on your Amazon EC2 instances, such as awsdev: `sudo mkdir awsdev`.

9. Mount the file system using the DNS name:

```
sudo mount -t nfs4 -o nfsvers=4.1,rsize=1048576,wsize=1048576,hard,timeo=600,
retrains=2 fs-12341234.efs.region-1.amazonaws.com:/ awsdev
```

You have mounted the Amazon EFS volume to the instance.

EXERCISE 14.4

Create and Upload to an Amazon S3 Bucket

In this exercise, you will create an Amazon S3 bucket and upload and publish files of the bucket.

1. While signed in to the AWS Management Console, open the Amazon S3 console at https://console.aws.amazon.com/s3/.

2. Choose **Create bucket**.

3. On the **Name and region** page, enter a globally unique name for your bucket and select the appropriate AWS Region. Accept all of the remaining default settings.

4. Choose **Create the bucket**.

5. Select your bucket.

6. Upload data files to the new Amazon S3 bucket:

   a. Choose **Upload**.

   b. In the **Upload - Select Files** wizard, choose **Add Files** and choose a file that you want to share publicly.

   c. Choose **Next**.

7. To make the file available to the general public, on the **Set Permissions** page, under **Manage Public Permissions**, grant everyone read access to the object.

8. Review and upload the file.

9. Select the object name to go to the properties screen. Select and open the URL for the file in a new browser window.

You should see your file in the S3 bucket.

EXERCISE 14.5

Create an Amazon DynamoDB Table

In this exercise, you will create an DynamoDB table.

1. While signed in to the AWS Management Console, open the DynamoDB console at `https://console.aws.amazon.com/dynamodb/`.

2. Choose **Create Table** and then do the following:

    a. In **Table**, enter the table name.

    b. For **Primary key**, in the **Partition** field, type `Id`.

    c. Set the **data type** to `String`.

3. Retain all the remaining default settings and choose **Create**.

You have created a DynamoDB table.

EXERCISE 14.6

Enable Amazon S3 Versioning

In this exercise, you will enable Amazon S3 versioning, which prevents objects from being accidentally deleted or overwritten.

1. While signed in to the AWS Management Console, open the Amazon S3 console at `https://console.aws.amazon.com/s3/`.

2. In the **Bucket name** list, choose the name of the bucket for which you want to enable versioning.

    If you don't have a bucket, follow the steps in Exercise 14.4 to create a new bucket.

3. Choose **Properties**.

4. Choose **Versioning**.

5. Choose **Enable versioning**, and then choose **Save**.

Your bucket is now versioning enabled.

EXERCISE 14.7

Create an Amazon DynamoDB Global Table

In this exercise, you will create a DynamoDB global table.

1. While signed in to the AWS Management Console, open the Amazon S3 console at `https://console.aws.amazon.com/dynamodb`.

2. Choose a region for the source table for your DynamoDB global table.

3. In the navigation pane on the left side of the console, choose **Create Table** and then do the following:

   a. For **Table name**, type **Tables**.

   b. For **Primary key**, choose an appropriate primary key. Choose **Add sort key**, and type an appropriate sort key. The data type of both the partition key and the sort key should be strings.

4. To create the table, choose **Create**.

   This table will serve as the first replica table in a new global table, and it will be the prototype for other replica tables that you add later.

5. Select the **Global Tables** tab, and then choose **Enable streams**. Leave the **View type** at its default value (New and old images).

6. Choose **Add region**, and then choose another region where you want to deploy another replica table. In this case, choose **US West (Oregon)** and then choose **Continue**. This will start the table creation process in US West (Oregon).

   The console will check to ensure that there is no table with the same name in the selected region. (If a table with the same name does exist, then you must delete the existing table before you can create a new replica table in that region.)

   The **Global Table** tab for the selected table (and for any other replica tables) will show that the table is replicated in multiple regions.

7. Add another region so that your global table is replicated and synchronized across the United States and Europe. To do this, repeat step 6, but this time specify **EU (Frankfurt)** instead of US West (Oregon).

You have created a DynamoDB global table.

EXERCISE 14.8

Enable Cross-Region Replication

In this exercise, you will enable cross-region replication of the contents of the original bucket to a new bucket in a different region.

1. While signed into the AWS Management Console, open the Amazon S3 console at https://console.aws.amazon.com/s3/.

2. Create a new bucket in a different region from the bucket that you created in Exercise 14.4. Enable versioning on the new bucket (see Exercise 14.6).

3. Choose **Management**, choose **Replication**, and then choose **Add rule**.

4. In the **Replication rule** wizard, under **Set Source**, choose **Entire Bucket**.

5. Choose **Next**.

6. On the **Set destination** page, under **Destination bucket**, choose your newly-created bucket.

7. Choose the storage class for the target bucket. Under **Options**, select **Change the storage class for the replicated objects**. Select a storage class.

8. Choose **Next**.

9. For IAM, on the **Configure options** page, under **Select** role, choose **Create new role**.

10. Choose **Next**.

11. Choose **Save**.

12. Load a new object in the source bucket.

    The object appears in the target bucket.

You have enabled cross-region replication, which can be used for compliance and disaster recovery.

EXERCISE 14.9

Create an Amazon DynamoDB Backup Table

In this exercise, you will create a DynamoDB table backup.

1. While signed into the AWS Management Console, open the DynamoDB console at https://console.aws.amazon.com/dynamodb/.

2. Choose one of your existing tables. If there are no tables, follow the steps in Exercise 14.7 to create a new table.

(continued)

3. On the **Backups** tab, choose **Create Backup**.

4. Type a name for the backup name of the table you are backing. Then choose **Create** to create the backup.

   While the backup is being created, the backup status is set to Creating. After the backup is finalized, the backup status changes to Available.

You have created a backup of a DynamoDB table.

Restoring an Amazon DynamoDB Table from a Backup

In this exercise, you will restore a DynamoDB table by using the backup created in the previous exercise.

1. While signed in to the AWS Management Console, navigate to the DynamoDB console at https://console.aws.amazon.com/dynamodb/.

2. In the navigation pane on the left side of the console, choose **Backups**.

3. In the list of backups, choose the backup that you created in the previous step.

4. Choose **Restore Backup**.

5. Type a table name as the new table name. Confirm the backup name and other backup details. Then choose **Restore table** to start the restore process.

   The table that is being restored is shown with the status Creating. After the restore process is finished, the status of your new table changes to Active.

You have performed the restoration of a DynamoDB table from a backup.

Review Questions

1. Which of the following is the maximum Amazon DynamoDB item size limit?

   A. 512 KB

   B. 400 KB

   C. 4 KB

   D. 1,024 KB

2. Which of the following is true when using Amazon Simple Storage Service (Amazon S3)?

   A. Versioning is enabled on a bucket by default.

   B. The largest size of an object in an Amazon S3 bucket is 5 GB.

   C. Bucket names must be globally unique.

   D. Bucket names can be changed after they are created.

3. Which of the following is *not* a deciding factor when choosing an AWS Region for your bucket?

   A. Latency

   B. Storage class

   C. Cost

   D. Regulatory requirements

4. Which of the following features can you use to protect your data at rest within Amazon DynamoDB?

   A. Fine-grained access controls

   B. Transport Layer Security (TLS) connections

   C. Server-side encryption provided by the DynamoDB service

   D. Client-side encryption

5. You store your company's critical data in Amazon Simple Storage Service (Amazon S3). The data must be protected against accidental deletions or overwrites. How can this be achieved?

   A. Use a lifecycle policy to move the data to Amazon S3 Glacier.

   B. Enable MFA Delete on the bucket.

   C. Use a path-style URL.

   D. Enable versioning on the bucket.

6. How does Amazon Simple Storage Service (Amazon S3) object storage differ from block and file storage? (Select TWO.)

   A. Amazon S3 stores data in fixed blocks.

   B. Objects can be any size.

   C. Objects are stored in buckets.

   D. Objects contain both data and metadata.

7. What is the lifetime of data in an Amazon DynamoDB stream?

   A. 14 days

   B. 12 hours

   C. 24 hours

   D. 4 days

8. How many times does each stream record in Amazon DynamoDB Streams appear in the stream?

   A. Twice

   B. Once

   C. Three times

   D. This value can be configured.

9. Versioning is a means of keeping multiple variants of an object in the same bucket. You can use versioning to preserve, retrieve, and restore every version of every object stored in your Amazon S3 bucket. With versioning, you can easily recover from both unintended user actions and application failures. Which of the following is *not* a versioning state of a bucket?

   A. Versioning paused

   B. Versioning disabled

   C. Versioning suspended

   D. Versioning enabled

10. Your team has built an application as a document management system that maintains metadata on millions of documents in a DynamoDB table. When a document is retrieved, you want to display the metadata beside the document. Which DynamoDB operation can you use to retrieve metadata attributes from a table?

   A. QueryTable

   B. UpdateTable

   C. Search

   D. Scan

11. Which of the following objects are good candidates to store in a cache? (Select THREE.)

   A. Session state

   B. Shopping cart

   C. Product catalog

   D. Bank account balance

12. Which of the following cache engines does Amazon ElastiCache support? (Select TWO.)

   A. Redis

   B. MySQL

   C. Couchbase

   D. Memcached

13. How many nodes can you add to an Amazon ElastiCache cluster that is running Redis?

    A. 100

    B. 5

    C. 20

    D. 1

14. What feature does Amazon ElastiCache provide?

    A. A highly available and fast indexing service for querying

    B. An Amazon Elastic Compute Cloud (Amazon EC2) instance with a large amount of memory and CPU

    C. A managed in-memory caching service

    D. An Amazon EC2 instance with Redis and Memcached already installed

15. When designing a highly available web solution using stateless web servers, which services are suitable for storing session-state data? (Select THREE.)

    A. Amazon CloudFront

    B. Amazon DynamoDB

    C. Amazon CloudWatch

    D. Amazon Elastic File System (Amazon EFS)

    E. Amazon ElastiCache

    F. Amazon Simple Queue Service (Amazon SQS)

16. Which AWS database service is best suited for nonrelational databases?

    A. Amazon Simple Storage Service Glacier (Amazon S3 Glacier)

    B. Amazon Relational Database Service (Amazon RDS)

    C. Amazon DynamoDB

    D. Amazon Redshift

17. Which of the following statements about Amazon DynamoDB table is true?

    A. Only one local secondary index is allowed per table.

    B. You can create global secondary indexes only when you are creating the table.

    C. You can have only one global secondary index.

    D. You can create local secondary indexes only when you are creating the table.

Chapter 15

Monitoring and Troubleshooting

**THE AWS CERTIFIED DEVELOPER –
ASSOCIATE EXAM TOPICS COVERED IN
THIS CHAPTER MAY INCLUDE, BUT ARE
NOT LIMITED TO, THE FOLLOWING:**

Domain 5: Monitoring and Troubleshooting

✓ **5.1 Write code that can be monitored.**

  Content may include the following:

  ▪ Monitoring basics

  ▪ Using Amazon CloudWatch

  ▪ Using AWS CloudTrail

✓ **5.2 Perform root cause analysis on faults found in
testing or production.**

  Content may include the following:

  ▪ Using AWS X-Ray to troubleshoot application issues

Introduction to Monitoring and Troubleshooting

Monitoring the applications and services you build is vital to the success of any information technology (IT) organization. With the AWS Cloud, you can leverage monitoring resources to drive business decisions such as what resources to create, improve, optimize, and secure.

Traditional approaches to monitoring do not scale for cloud architectures. Large systems can be difficult to set up, configure, and scale. These efforts are compounded by the trend away from monolithic installations toward service-oriented architecture (SOA), microservices, and serverless architectures. Monitoring modern IT systems is proportionally difficult. When working on a monolithic application, you can add logging statements and troubleshoot with breakpoints. However, applications today are spread across multiple systems over large networks that make it difficult to track the health of systems and react to issues. For example, using logging statements to monitor execution time and error rates of AWS Lambda functions can become difficult as your infrastructure grows and spreads across multiple AWS Regions.

The AWS Cloud provides fully managed services to help you implement monitoring solutions that are reliable, scalable, and secure. AWS offers services to help you monitor, log, and analyze your applications and infrastructure. In this section, you explore Amazon CloudWatch, AWS CloudTrail, and AWS X-Ray. Figure 15.1 shows the AWS monitoring services available.

FIGURE 15.1   Various monitoring services on AWS

Amazon
CloudWatch

AWS
CloudTrail

AWS
X-Ray

Monitoring Basics

Before you explore these services, consider why they are essential. As a developer, you are designing systems to provide IT or business solutions to a customer. Success is measured by the effective application of software to business objectives. What are some of the metrics that you must track over time to ensure that these objectives are being met?

Choosing Metrics

AWS takes the approach of "working backward" from the customer. You can accomplish this by starting with the customer and tracing the underlying components that affect the customer's experience. This provides a foundation for identifying which metrics to monitor, as they correlate directly to the customer experience. Frequently, the top characteristics that directly affect the customer experience are performance and cost. Changes to either have a direct impact on how customers perceive the software they use.

Deciding which metrics to monitor requires that you answer several crucial questions.

Performance and Cost

Question: Are my customers having a good experience with the services or systems that that I provide?

The phrase *good experience* can be broken down into measurable metrics, such as request latency, time to first byte, error rates, and more. Metrics, such as instance CPU utilization or network bytes in/out, however, may not be representative of the customer experience.

It is good practice to measure any metric that directly affects customers using your software or system. The second question to ask is: "What is the overall cost of my system?" Increases in performance often correlate directly to increases in cost. With unlimited money, it would be easy to design a system that scales infinitely in response to customer usage. However, this is never a reality. Instead, you need to measure the performance of your system to determine what is acceptable performance based on the usage at any point in time. This is the case when metrics that are not customer-facing often take precedence.

Trends

Question: How can I use monitoring to predict changes in customer demand?

With the agility and elasticity of the AWS Cloud, this can be especially useful. Monitoring and measuring customer demand over time allows you to scale your infrastructure predictively to meet changes in customer demand without having to purchase more resources than are necessary. For example, suppose that you have a web application that runs on three Amazon Elastic Compute Cloud (Amazon EC2) instances during the day. In the evenings, demand increases significantly for several hours before decreasing again late at night. On weekends, your application sees almost no traffic. With historical information obtained through monitoring, you can design your application to scale out across more Amazon EC2 instances during the evenings and scale in on the weekends when there is little demand. Predictive scaling occurs before customer demand changes, ensuring a smooth experience while new resources are created and brought online.

Troubleshooting and Remediation

Question: Where do problems occur?

As Werner Vogels, VP and CTO of AWS, once said, "Everything fails all the time." No system is impervious to failure. By gathering potentially relevant information ahead of time, it becomes easier to determine causes for failure. By collecting this information, you can reduce mean time between failure (MTBF), mean time to resolution (MTTR), and other key operational performance metrics.

Learning and Improvement

Question: "Can you detect or prevent problems in the future?"

By evaluating operational metrics over time, you can reveal patterns and common issues in your systems.

> When choosing metrics, align them closely to your business processes to provide a better customer experience. For example, suppose that you have an application running in AWS Elastic Beanstalk. Unknown to you, the application has a memory leak. Without tracking memory utilization over time, you will not have insight into why customers are experiencing degraded performance. If your Elastic Beanstalk environment is configured to scale out based on CPU utilization, it is possible that no new instances are launched to serve customer requests. In this case, the memory leak prevents new requests from being processed, causing a drop in CPU utilization. Without comprehensive tracking of system performance, issues such as this can go unnoticed until system-wide outages occur.

These factors impact what is referred to as the health of your systems. As a developer and contributor, you are not only responsible for the code that you develop but also for the operational health of these services. It is vital to align operational and health metrics properly with customer expectations and experiences.

Amazon CloudWatch

Amazon CloudWatch is a monitoring and metrics service that provides you with a fully managed system to collect, store, and analyze your metrics and logs. By using CloudWatch, you can create notifications on changes in your environment.

Typical use cases include the following:

- Infrastructure monitoring and troubleshooting
- Resource optimization
- Application monitoring
- Logging analytics
- Error reporting and notification

CloudWatch enables you to collect and store monitoring and operations data from logs, metrics, and events that run on AWS and on-premises resources. To ensure that your applications run smoothly, you can use CloudWatch to perform the following tasks:

- Set alarms
- Visualize logs and metrics
- Automate recovery from errors
- Troubleshoot issues
- Discover insights that enable you to optimize your resources

How Amazon CloudWatch Works

CloudWatch acts as a *metrics repository*, storing metrics and logs from various sources. These metrics can come from AWS resources using built-in or custom metrics. Figure 15.2 illustrates the role of CloudWatch in operational health.

FIGURE 15.2   Diagram of Amazon CloudWatch

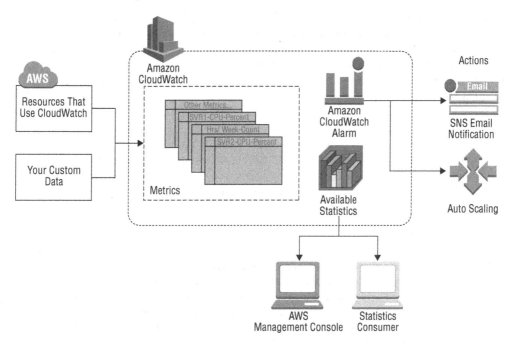

CloudWatch can process these metrics into statistics that are made available through the CloudWatch console, AWS APIs, the AWS Command Line Interface (AWS CLI), and AWS software development kits (AWS SDKs). Using CloudWatch, you can display graphs, create alarms, or integrate with third-party solutions.

Amazon CloudWatch Metrics

To understand CloudWatch better, especially how data is collected and organized, review the following terms.

Built-In Metrics

A *metric* is a set of time-series data points that you publish to CloudWatch. For example, a commonly monitored metric for Amazon EC2 instances is CPU utilization. Data points can come from multiple systems, both AWS and on-premises. You can also define custom metrics based on data specific to your system. A metric is identified uniquely by a namespace, a name, and zero or more dimensions.

Namespace

A *namespace* is a collection of metrics or a container of related metrics; for example, namespaces used by AWS offerings or services that all start with AWS. Amazon EC2 uses the AWS/EC2 namespace. As a developer, you can create namespaces for different components of your applications, such as front-end, backend, and database components.

Name

A *name* for a given metric defines the attribute or property that you are monitoring; for example, CPU Utilization in the AWS/EC2 namespace. The AWS/EC2 namespace contains various metrics that are important to monitoring the health of Amazon EC2 resources, such as CPU Utilization, Disk I/O, Network I/O, or Status Check. You can also create custom metrics for attributes, such as request latency, HTTP 400/500 response codes, and throttling.

Dimension

A *dimension* is a name/value pair used to define a metric uniquely. For example, for the namespace AWS/EC2 and name/metric CPUUtilization, the dimension might be InstanceId. For a fleet of Amazon EC2 instances, you can measure CPUUtilization as one metric for multiple dimensions (one for each instance). You can use the dimensions to structure and organize the data points you gather.

When you're creating metrics, consider defining namespaces that align with your different services and assigning dimensions as important metrics that describe the health of that service. For example, if you have a front-end web fleet running NGINX servers, then dimensions, such as requests-per-second, response time, active connections, and response codes, could help you determine what configuration changes would optimize system performance.

Data Points

When data is published to CloudWatch, it is pushed in sets of data points. Each data point contains information such as the timestamp, value, and unit of measurement.

Timestamp

Timestamps are dateTime objects with the complete date and time; for example, 2016-10-31T23:59:59Z. Although not required, AWS recommends formatting times as Coordinated Universal Time (UTC).

Value

The *value* is the measurement for the data point.

Unit

A *unit* of measurement is used to label your data. This offers a better understanding of what the value represents. Example units include Bytes, Seconds, Count, and Percent. If you do not specify a unit in CloudWatch, your data point units are designated as None.

CloudWatch stores this data based on the *retention period*, which is the length of time to keep data points available. Data points are stored in CloudWatch based on how often the data points are published.

- Data points with a published frequency less than 60 seconds are available for 3 hours. These data points are high-resolution custom metrics.
- Data points with a published frequency of 60 seconds (1 minute) are available for 15 days.
- Data points with a published frequency of 300 seconds (5 minutes) are available for 63 days.
- Data points with a published frequency of 3,600 seconds (1 hour) are available for 455 days (15 months).

From these data points, CloudWatch can calculate statistics to provide you with insight into your application, service, or environment. In the next section, you will discover how CloudWatch calculates and organizes these statistics.

Statistics

CloudWatch provides statistics based on metric data provided to the service. *Statistics* are aggregations of data points over specified periods of time for specified metrics. A *period* is the length of time, in seconds. Periods can be defined in values of 1, 5, 10, 30, or any multiple of 60 seconds (up to 86,400 seconds, or 1 day). The available statistics in CloudWatch include the following:

- Minimum (Min), the lowest value recorded over the specified period
- Maximum (Max), the highest value recorded over the specified period
- Sum, the total value of the samples added together over the specified period
- Average (Avg), the Sum divided by the SampleCount over the specified period
- SampleCount, the number of data points used in the calculation over the specified period
- pNN, percentile statistics for tracking metric outliers

Statistics can be used to gain insight into the health of your application and to help you determine the correct settings for various configurations. For example, you may want to implement automatic scaling on your fleet of Amazon EC2 instances in order to avoid having to launch and terminate instances manually. To do so, you must configure an Auto Scaling group. Configuration settings for an Auto Scaling group include the minimum, desired, and maximum number of instances to run in your account. By monitoring statistics over time, you can determine the minimum and maximum number of instances needed to support the average, minimum, and maximum workload.

CloudWatch statistics provide a powerful way to process large amounts of metrics at scale and present insightful data that is easy to consume. Now that you understand how CloudWatch metrics work and are organized, explore the metrics available.

Aggregations

CloudWatch aggregates metrics according to the period of time you specify when retrieving statistics. When you request this statistic, you also can have CloudWatch filter the data points based on the dimensions of the metrics. For example, in Amazon DynamoDB, metrics are fetched across all DynamoDB operations. You can specify a filter on the dimension operations to exclude specific operations, such as GetItem requests. CloudWatch does not aggregate data across regions.

Available Metrics

Table 15.1 describes the available metrics for Elastic Load Balancing resources. To discover all of the available metrics, refer to the AWS documentation.

TABLE 15.1   Elastic Load Balancing Metrics

Namespace	AWS/ELB AWS/ApplicationELB AWS/NetworkELB
Dimensions	LoadBalancerName: name of the load balancer
Key metrics	▪ HealthyHostCount: number of responding backend servers ▪ RequestCount: number of IPv4 and IPv6 requests ▪ ActiveConnectionCount: total number of concurrent active connections from clients

Table 15.2 describes the available Amazon EC2 metrics.

TABLE 15.2 Amazon EC2 Metrics

Namespace	AWS/EC2
Dimensions	• `InstanceId`: identifier of a particular Amazon EC2 instance • `InstanceType`: type of Amazon EC2 instance, such as t2.micro, m4.large
Key metrics	• `CPUUtilization`: percentage of vCPU utilization on the instance • `DiskReadOps, DiskWriteOps`: number of operations per second on attached disk • `DiskReadBytes, DiskWriteBytes`: volume of bytes to transfer on attached disk • `NetworkIn, NetworkOut`: number of bytes sent or received by network interfaces • `NetworkPacketsIn, NetworkPacketsOut`: number of packets sent or received by network interfaces

 Amazon EC2 does not report memory utilization to CloudWatch. This is because memory is allocated in full to an instance by the underlying host. Memory consumption is visible only to the guest operating system (OS) of the instance. However, you can report memory utilization to CloudWatch using the CloudWatch agent.

Table 15.3 describes the AWS Auto Scaling group metrics.

TABLE 15.3 AWS Auto Scaling Groups

Namespace	AWS/AutoScaling
Dimensions	AutoScalingGroupName: name of the Auto Scaling group
Key metrics	• `GroupMinSize, GroupMaxSize, GroupDesiredCapacity`: minimum, maximum, and desired size of the Auto Scaling group • `GroupInServiceInstances`: number of instances up and running in the Auto Scaling group • `GroupTotalInstances`: total number of instances in the Auto Scaling group, regardless of state

Table 15.4 describes the Amazon Simple Storage Service (Amazon S3) metrics.

TABLE 15.4   Amazon S3 Metrics

Namespace	AWS/S3
Dimensions	▪ BucketName: name of a specific Amazon S3 bucket ▪ StorageType: the Amazon S3 storage class (STANDARD, STANDARD_IA, and GLACIER storage classes) of the bucket
Key metrics	▪ BucketSizeBytes: total size, in bytes, of data stored in an Amazon S3 bucket ▪ NumberOfObjects: total number of objects stored in an Amazon S3 bucket ▪ AllRequests: total number of requests made to an Amazon S3 bucket

Table 15.5 describes the Amazon DynamoDB metrics.

TABLE 15.5   Amazon DynamoDB Metrics

Namespace	AWS/DynamoDB
Dimensions	▪ TableName: name of Amazon DynamoDB table ▪ Operation: limits metrics to either a particular operation (PutItem, GetItem, UpdateItem, DeleteItem, Query, Scan, BatchGetItem) or BatchWriteITem
Key metrics	▪ ConsumedReadCapacityUnits, ConsumedWriteCapacityUnits: total number of read and write capacity units consumed ▪ ThrottledRequests: requests to DynamoDB that exceed the provisioned throughput limits on a resource (such as a table or an index) ▪ ReadThrottleEvents: requests to DynamoDB that exceed the provisioned read capacity units for a table or a global secondary index ▪ WriteThrottleEvents: requests to DynamoDB that exceed the provisioned write capacity units for a table or a global secondary index ▪ ReturnedBytes: size of response returned in request ▪ ReturnedItemCount: number of items returned in request

Table 15.6 describes the Amazon API Gateway metrics.

TABLE 15.6   Amazon API Gateway Metrics

Namespace	AWS/ApiGateway
Dimensions	▪ ApiName: filters out metrics for a particular API
	▪ ApiName, Method, Resource, Stage: filters out metrics for a particular API, method, resource, and stage
	▪ ApiName, Stage: filters out metrics for a particular deployed stage of an API
Key metrics	▪ 4XXError: number of HTTP 400 errors
	▪ 5XXError: number of HTTP 500 errors
	▪ Latency: time between when Amazon API Gateway receives a request and when it responds to the client

Table 15.7 describes the AWS Lambda metrics.

TABLE 15.7   AWS Lambda Metrics

Namespace	AWS/Lambda
Dimensions	FunctionName: name of your AWS Lambda function
Key metrics	▪ Invocations: number of executions of your AWS Lambda function
	▪ Errors: number of executions in which your AWS Lambda function failed
	▪ Duration: total time for each execution of your AWS Lambda function

Table 15.8 describes the Amazon Simple Queue Service (Amazon SQS) metrics.

TABLE 15.8   Amazon SQS Metrics

Namespace	AWS/SQS
Dimensions	QueueName: name of the Amazon SQS queue
Key metrics	<ul><li>ApproximateNumberOfMessagesVisible: number of messages currently available for retrieval</li><li>ApproximateNumberOfMessagesNotVisible: number of messages currently being processed, or messages that are inflight (Visibility Timeout is still active)</li><li>NumberOfMessagesDeleted: number of messages that have been deleted</li></ul>

Amazon SQS does not report the total number of messages in the queue. You can find this value by adding ApproximateNumberOfMessagesVisible and ApproximateNumberOfMessagesNotVisible.

Table 15.9 describes the Amazon Simple Notification Service (Amazon SNS) metrics.

TABLE 15.9   Amazon SNS Metrics

Namespace	AWS/SNS
Dimensions	TopicName: name of the Amazon SNS topic
Key metrics	<ul><li>NumberOfMessagesPublished: number of messages sent to an SNS topic</li><li>NumberOfNotificationsDelivered: number of messages that were successfully delivered to subscribers</li><li>NumberOfNotificationsFailed: number of messages that were unsuccessfully delivered to subscribers</li></ul>

Custom Metrics

In addition to the built-in metrics that AWS provides, CloudWatch also supports custom metrics that you can publish from your systems. This section includes some commands that you can use to publish metrics to CloudWatch.

High-Resolution Metrics

With custom metrics, you have two options for resolution (the time interval between data points) for your metrics. You can use *standard resolution* for data points that have a granularity of one minute or *high resolution* for data points that have a granularity of less than one second. By default, most metrics delivered by AWS services have standard resolution.

Publishing Metrics

CloudWatch supports multiple options when you publish metrics. You can publish them as single data points, statistics sets, or zero values. Single data points are optimal for most telemetry. However, statistics sets are recommended for values with high-resolution data points in which you are sampling multiple times per minute. *Statistics sets* are sets of calculated values, such as minimum, maximum, average, sum, and sample count, as opposed to individual data points. The value 0 is for applications that have periods of inactivity, where no data is sent. The following are some sample scripts using the AWS CLI to publish data points.

USING THE AWS CLI TO PUBLISH SINGLE DATA POINTS

The following commands each publish a single data point under the Metric Name PageViewCount to the Namespace MyService with respective values and timestamps. You are not required to create a metric name or namespace. CloudWatch is aware of the data points to a metric or creates a new metric if it does not exist.

```
aws cloudwatch put-metric-data \
      --metric-name PageViewCount \
      --namespace MyService \
      --value 2 \
      --timestamp 2018-10-20T12:00:00.000Z

aws cloudwatch put-metric-data \
      --metric-name PageViewCount \
      --namespace MyService \
      --value 4 \
      --timestamp 2018-10-20T12:00:01.000Z

aws cloudwatch put-metric-data \
      --metric-name PageViewCount \
      --namespace MyService \
      --value 5 \
      --timestamp 2018-10-20T12:00:02.000Z
```

USING THE AWS CLI TO PUBLISH STATISTICS SETS

The following command publishes a statistic set to the metric-name PageViewCount to the namespace MyService, with values for various statistics (Sum 11, Minimum 2, Maximum 5), and SampleCount 3 with the corresponding timestamp:

```
aws cloudwatch put-metric-data \
      --metric-name PageViewCount \
      --namespace MyService \
      --statistic-values Sum=11,Minimum=2,Maximum=5,SampleCount=3 \
      --timestamp 2018-10-14T12:00:00.000Z
```

USING THE AWS CLI TO PUBLISH THE VALUE ZERO

The following command publishes a single data point with the value 0 to the metric-name PageViewCount to the namespace MyService with the corresponding timestamp:

```
aws cloudwatch put-metric-data \
      --metric-name PageViewCount \
      --namespace MyService \
      --value 0 \
      --timestamp 2018-10-14T12:00:00.000Z
```

Retrieving Statistics for a Metric

After you publish data to CloudWatch, you may want to retrieve statistics for a specified metric of a given resource.

USING THE AWS CLI TO RETRIEVE STATISTICS FOR A METRIC

This command retrieves the Sum, Max, Min, Average, and SampleCount statistics for the metric-name PageViewCount to the namespace MyService with a period interval of 60 seconds between the start-time and end-time. This means that CloudWatch will aggregate data points in one-minute intervals to calculate statistics.

```
aws cloudwatch get-metric-statistics \
      --namespace MyService \
      --metric-name PageViewCount \
      --statistics "Sum" "Maximum" "Minimum" "Average" "SampleCount" \
      --start-time 2018-10-20T12:00:00.000Z \
      --end-time 2018-10-20T12:05:00.000Z \
      --period 60
```

Example output from this command displays a single data point for the Metric
PageViewCount.

```
{
    "Datapoints": [
        {
            "SampleCount": 3.0,
            "Timestamp": "2016-10-20T12:00:00Z",
            "Average": 3.6666666666666665,
            "Maximum": 5.0,
            "Minimum": 2.0,
            "Sum": 11.0,
            "Unit": "None"
        }
    ],
    "Label": "PageViewCount"
}
```

Amazon CloudWatch Logs

Though most commercial standard applications already produce some form of logging,
most modern applications are deployed in distributed or service-oriented architectures.
Collecting and processing these logs can be a challenge as a system grows and expands
across multiple regions. Centralized logging using CloudWatch Logs can overcome this
challenge. With CloudWatch Logs, you can set up a central log storage location to ingest
and process logs at scale.

Log Aggregation

Setting up centralized logging with CloudWatch Logs is a straightforward process. The
first step is to install and configure the CloudWatch agent, which is used to collect custom
logs and metrics from Amazon EC2 instances or on-premises servers. You can choose
which log files you want to ingest by pointing to the locations using a JavaScript Object
Notation (JSON) configuration file. The second step is to configure AWS Identity and
Access Management (IAM) roles or users to grant permission for the agent to publish
logs into CloudWatch. In addition to the CloudWatch agent, you can also send metrics to
CloudWatch using the AWS CLI, AWS SDK, or AWS API.

Because you are collecting logs from multiple sources, CloudWatch organizes your logs
into three conceptual levels: groups, streams, and events.

Log Groups

A *log group* is collection of log streams. For example, if you have a service that consists of a
cluster of multiple machines, a log group would be a container for the logs from each of the
individual instances.

Log Streams

A *log stream* is a sequence of log events such as a single log file from one of your instances.

Log Events

A *log event* is a record of some activity from an application, process, or service. This is analogous to a single line in a log file.

CloudWatch stores log events based on your retention settings, which are assigned at the log group. The default configuration is to store log data in Amazon CloudWatch Logs indefinitely. You are charged for any data stored in CloudWatch Logs in addition to data transferred out of the service. You can export CloudWatch Logs to Amazon S3 for long-term storage, which is valuable when regulations require long-term log retention. Long-term retention can be combined with Amazon S3 lifecycle policies to archive data to Amazon S3 Glacier for additional cost savings.

Log Searches

With centralized logging on CloudWatch Logs, you do not need to search through hundreds of individual servers to find a problem. After logs are ingested into CloudWatch Logs, you can search for logs through a central location using metric filters.

Metric Filters

A *metric filter* is a text pattern used to parse log data for specific events. As an example, consider the log in Table 15.10.

TABLE 15.10   Example Log

Line	Log Event
1	[ERROR] Caught IllegalArgumentException
2	[ERROR] Unhandled Exception
3	Another message
4	Exiting with ERRORCODE: -1
5	[WARN] Some message
6	[ERROR][WARN] Some other message

To look for occurrences of the ERROR event, you use ERROR as your metric filter, as illustrated in Table 15.11. CloudWatch will search for that term across the logs.

TABLE 15.11   Example Metric Filters

Metric Filter	Description
""	Matches all log events.
"ERROR"	Matches log events containing the term "ERROR."
	Based on the events in the example log in Table 15.10, this metric filter would find lines 1–3 and 6.
"ERROR" - "EXITING"	Matches log events containing the term "ERROR" except "EXITING."
	Based on the events in the example log in Table 15.10, this metric filter would find lines 1, 2, and 6.
"ERROR Exceptions"	Matches log events containing both terms "ERROR" and "Exceptions." This filter is an AND function.
	Based on the events in the example log in Table 15.10, this metric filter would find lines 1 and 2.
"?ERROR ?WARN"	Matches log events containing either the term "ERROR" or "WARN." This filter is an OR function.
	Based on the event in the example log in Table 15.10, this metric filter would find lines 1, 2, 4, and 6.

If your logs are structured in JSON format, CloudWatch can also filter object properties. Consider the following example JSON log.

Example AWS CloudTrail JSON Log Event

```
{
    "user": {
        "id": 1,
        "email": "Admin@example.com"

    },
    "users": [
        {
         "id": 2,
         "email": "John.Doe@example.com"

        },
        {
         "id": 3,
         "email": "Jane.Doe@example.com"
```

```
        }
    ],
    "actions": [
        "GET",
        "PUT",
        "DELETE"
    ],
    "coordinates": [
        [0, 1, 2],
        [4, 5, 6],
        [7, 8, 9]
    ]
}
```

You can create a metric filter that selects and compares certain properties of this event, as shown in Table 15.12.

TABLE 15.12   Example JSON Metric Filters

JSON Metric Filter	Description
{ ($.user.id = 1) && ($.users[0] .email = "John.Doe@example.com") }	Check that the property user.id equals 1 and the first user's email is John.Doe@example.com. The preceding log event would be returned.
{ ($.user.id = 2 && $.users[0] .email = "John.Doe@exmple.com") || $.actions[2] = "GET" }	Check that the property user.id equals 2 and the first user's email is John.Doe@example.com or the second action is GET. The preceding example would not be returned, because the second action is PUT, not GET.

Log Processing

Instead of having to write additional code to add monitoring to your application, CloudWatch can process logs that you already generate and provide valuable metrics. Using the example from the previous section, the same metric filter can be used to generate metrics corresponding to the number of occurrences of the term ERROR in your logs.

Amazon CloudWatch Alarms

After data points are established in CloudWatch, either as metrics or as logs (from which you generate metrics), you can set *alarms* to monitor your metrics and trigger actions in response to changes in state. CloudWatch alarms have three possible states: OK, ALARM, and INSUFFICIENT_DATA. Table 15.13 defines each alarm state.

TABLE 15.13 Alarm States

State	Description
OK	The metric or expression is within the defined threshold.
ALARM	The metric or expression is outside of the defined threshold.
INSUFFICIENT_DATA	The alarm has just started, the metric is not available, or not enough data is available for the metric to determine the alarm state.

An ALARM state may not indicate a problem. It means that the given metric is outside the defined threshold. For example, you have two alarms for Auto Scaling groups: one for high CPU utilization and one for low CPU utilization. During normal use, both alarms should be OK, indicating that you have adequate capacity to handle the current workload. If your workload changes, the high CPU utilization metric threshold may be breached, sending the corresponding alarm into ALARM state. With an Auto Scaling group, the alarm's state change triggers a scale-out event, adding capacity to your infrastructure.

Using Amazon CloudWatch Alarms

When you create an alarm, specify three settings that determine when the alarm should change states: the threshold, period, and data points on which you want to notify, as described in Table 15.14.

TABLE 15.14 Alarm Settings

Setting	Description
Period	The length of time (in seconds) to evaluate the metric or expression to create each individual data point for an alarm. If you choose one minute as the period, there is one data point every minute.
Evaluation Period	The number of the most recent periods, or data points, to evaluate when determining alarm state.
Data Points to Alarm	The number of data points within the evaluation period that must breach the specified threshold to cause the alarm to go to the ALARM state. These data points do not have to be consecutive.

Figure 15.3 illustrates how an alarm works based on configuration settings.

FIGURE 15.3   Alarm evaluation

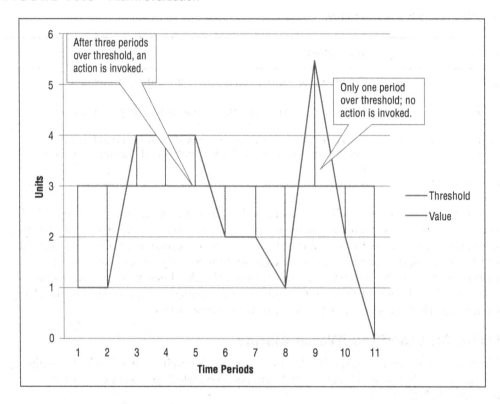

The figure illustrates a threshold configured to the value 3 (in blue), a period set to 3, and data points in red. Notice how the settings drive the alarm occurrence. Even though the data points breach the threshold after the third period, it is not sustained for the required three periods to be in an ALARM state. Only after the fifth period would the alarm change to an ALARM state (the upper threshold is breached for three periods). Between the fifth and sixth period, the data points drop below the threshold. However, because the state has not dropped below the threshold for three periods, it does not change to an OK state until the eighth period. It remains in the OK state past the ninth period because three consecutive periods exceeding the threshold are necessary for the alarm state to change.

Alarms can trigger Amazon EC2 actions and EC2 Auto Scaling actions. CloudWatch can leverage Amazon SNS or Amazon SQS for alarm state notifications, both of which provide numerous integrations with other AWS services.

Exercise caution when creating email notifications for alarms in your environment. This can lead to many unnecessary emails to you or your team. Ultimately, these notifications get filtered as spam or result in "notification fatigue." Evaluate your alarms and the metrics you are monitoring to determine whether notifications are necessary. If they are only status updates, set notifications sparingly.

Amazon CloudWatch Dashboards

CloudWatch offers a convenient way to observe operational metrics for all of your applications. *CloudWatch dashboards* are customizable pages in the CloudWatch console that you can use to monitor resources in a single view (see Figure 15.4).

FIGURE 15.4 Amazon CloudWatch dashboard

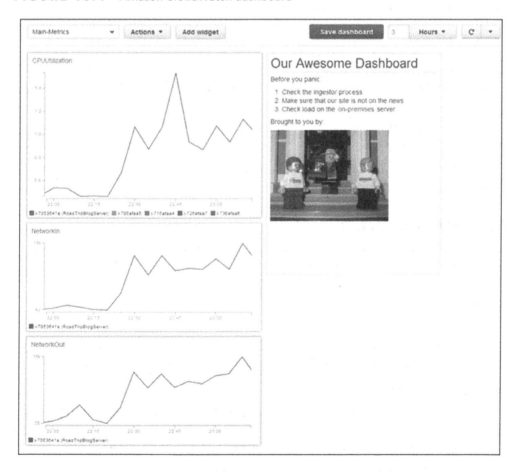

CloudWatch dashboards provide customizable status pages in the CloudWatch console. These status pages can be used to monitor resources across multiple regions and on-premises in a consolidated view using widgets. Each widget can be customized to present information in CloudWatch in a user-friendly way so that educated decisions can be made based on the current status of your system.

AWS CloudTrail

All actions in your AWS account are composed of API calls, regardless of the origin (the AWS Management Console or programmatic/scripted actions). As you create resources in your account, API calls are being made to AWS services in different regions around the world. *AWS CloudTrail* is a fully managed service that continuously monitors and records API calls and stores them in Amazon S3. You can use these logs to troubleshoot and resolve operational issues, meet and verify regulatory compliance, and monitor or alarm on specific events in your account. CloudTrail supports most AWS services, making it easy for IT and security administrators to analyze activity in accounts. IT auditors can also use log files as compliance aids.

CloudTrail helps answer the following five key questions about monitoring access:

- Who made the API call?
- When was the API call made?
- What was the API call?
- Which resources were acted upon in the API call?
- Where was the origin of the API call?

AWS CloudTrail Events

A *CloudTrail event* is any single API activity in an AWS account. This activity can be an action triggered by any of the following:

- AWS IAM user
- AWS IAM role
- AWS service

CloudTrail tracks two types of events: management events and data events. Events are recorded in the region where the action occurred, except for global service events.

Management Events

Management events give insight into operations performed on AWS resources, such as the following examples:

Configuring security: An example is attaching a policy to an IAM role.

Configuring routing rules: An example is adding inbound security group rules.

Data Events

Data events give insight into operations that store data in (or extract data from) AWS resources, such as the following examples:

Amazon S3 object activity: Examples are GetObject and PutObject operations.

AWS Lambda function executions: These use the InvokeFunction operation.

By default, CloudTrail tracks the last 90 days of API history for management events. The following is example output for a CloudTrail event:

```
{
    "Records": [{
        "eventVersion": "1.01",
        "userIdentity": {
            "type": "IAMUser",
            "principalId": "AIDAJDPLRKLG7UEXAMPLE",
            "arn": "arn:aws:iam::123456789012:user/Alice",
            "accountId": "123456789012",
            "accessKeyId": "AKIAIOSFODNN7EXAMPLE",
            "userName": "Alice",
            "sessionContext": {
                "attributes": {
                    "mfaAuthenticated": "false",
                    "creationDate": "2014-03-18T14:29:23Z"
                }
            }
        },
        "eventTime": "2014-03-18T14:30:07Z",
        "eventSource": "cloudtrail.amazonaws.com",
        "eventName": "StartLogging",
        "awsRegion": "us-west-2",
        "sourceIPAddress": "198.162.198.64",
        "userAgent": "signin.amazonaws.com",
        "requestParameters": {
            "name": "Default"
        },
        "responseElements": null,
        "requestID": "cdc73f9d-aea9-11e3-9d5a-835b769c0d9c",
        "eventID": "3074414d-c626-42aa-984b-68ff152d6ab7"
    },
    ... additional entries ...
    ]
```

This event provides the following information:

- The user who made the request from the userIdentityField. In this example, it is the IAM user Alice.

- When the request was made (the eventTime). In this case, it is 2014-03-18T14:30:07Z.

- Where the request was made (the sourceIPAddress). In this case, it is 198.162.198.64.

- The action the request is trying to perform (the eventName). In this case, it is the StartLogging operation.

As a security precaution, you can use events such as this example to configure alerts when an IAM user attempts to sign in to the AWS Management Console too many times.

Global Service Events

Some AWS services allow you to create, modify, and delete resources from any region. These are referred to as *global services*. Examples of global services include the following:

- IAM

- AWS Security Token Service (AWS STS)

- Amazon CloudFront

- Amazon Route 53

Global services are logged as occurring in US East (N. Virginia) Region. Any trails created in the CloudTrail console log global services by default, which are delivered to the Amazon S3 bucket for the trail.

Trails

If you need long-term storage of events (for example, for compliance purposes), you can configure a trail of events as log files in CloudTrail. A trail is a configuration that enables delivery of CloudTrail events to an Amazon S3 bucket, Amazon CloudWatch Logs, and Amazon CloudWatch Events. When you configure a trail, you can filter the events that you want to be delivered.

AWS X-Ray

The services covered so far are centered on the concept of using logs as monitoring and troubleshooting tools. Developers often write code, test the code, and inspect the logs. If there are errors, they may add breakpoints, run the test again, and add log statements. This works well in small cases, but it becomes cumbersome as teams, software, and infrastructure grow. Traditional troubleshooting and debugging processes do not work well at scaling across multiple services. Troubleshooting cross-service and cross-region interactions can be especially difficult when different systems use varying log formats.

AWS X-Ray is a service that collects data about requests served by your application. It provides tools you can use to view, filter, and gain insights into that data to identify issues and opportunities for optimization.

AWS X-Ray Use Cases

X-Ray helps developers build, monitor, and improve applications. Use cases include the following:

- Identifying performance bottlenecks
- Pinpointing specific service issues
- Identifying errors
- Identifying impact to users

X-Ray integrates with the AWS SDK, adding traces to track your application requests as they are generated and received from various services.

Tracking Application Requests

To understand better how X-Ray works, consider the example service shown in Figure 15.5. In this service, the front-end fleet relies on a backend API, which is built using API Gateway, which acts as proxy to Lambda. Lambda then uses Amazon DynamoDB to store data.

FIGURE 15.5 Microservice example

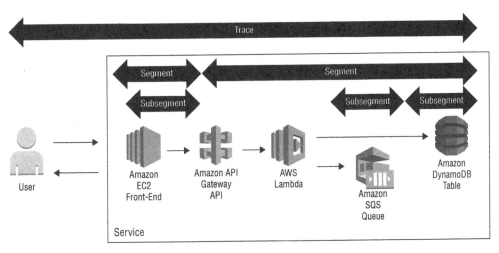

X-Ray can track a user request using a trace, segment, and subsegment.

Trace   A *trace* is the path of a request through your application. This is the end-to-end request from the client—from its entry into your environment to the backend and back to the user. A trace ID is passed through the AWS services with the request so that X-Ray can collate related segments.

Segment   A *segment* is data from a particular service. When a segment is reported to X-Ray, a trace ID is reported. Segments are analogous to links in a chain whereby the chain is the request generated by the user. In the example microservice, two segments correspond to two services: the front-end service and the backend API.

Subsegment   A *subsegment* identifies the underlying API calls made from a particular service. Subsegments are collated into segments. In this scenario, the backend API sends requests to Amazon DynamoDB and Amazon SQS.

From these components of a request, X-Ray compiles the traces into a service graph that describes the components and their interactions needed to complete a request. A *service graph* is a visual representation of the services and resources that make up your application. Figure 15.6 shows an example of a service graph.

FIGURE 15.6   Example service graph for an application

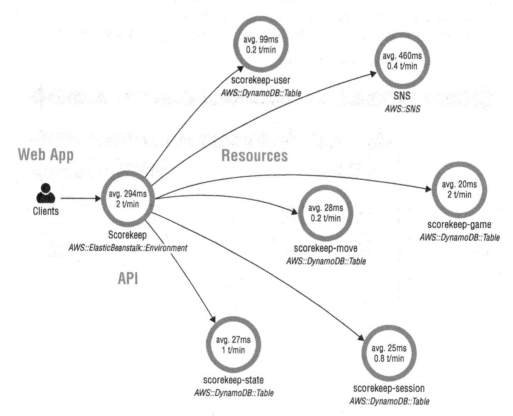

The service graph provides an overview of the health of various aspects of your system, such as average latencies and request rates between your services and dependent resources. The colored circles also show the ratio of different response codes, as listed in Table 15.15.

TABLE 15.15 AWS X-Ray Service Graph Status Codes

Color	Status Code
Purple	Throttling or HTTP 5XX codes
Orange	Client-side or HTTP 4XX codes
Red	Fault application failure
Green	OK or HTTP 2XX codes

X-Ray provides a convenient way for you to view system performance and to identify problems or bottlenecks in your applications. However, it does not provide auditing capabilities or the tracking of all requests to a system. X-Ray collects a statistically significant number of requests to a system so that meaningful insights can be provided. These insights enable you to focus on troubleshooting a particular service or improvements to a specific component of your application.

Summary

AWS provides multiple options for monitoring and troubleshooting your applications. As you have discovered, AWS services help you manage logs from various systems, either running on the cloud or on-premises, create triggers that notify you about application health and issues in your infrastructure, and build applications with modern debugging tools for distributed applications. These services overcome the difficulties of creating a centralized logging solution.

Exam Essentials

Know what Amazon CloudWatch is and why it is used. CloudWatch is the service used to aggregate, analyze, and alert on metrics generated by other AWS services. It is used to monitor the resources you create in AWS and the on-premises infrastructure. You can use CloudWatch to store logs from your applications and trigger actions in response to events.

Know what common metrics are available for Amazon Elastic Compute Cloud (Amazon EC2) in Amazon CloudWatch.   Amazon EC2 metrics in CloudWatch include the following:

- `CPUUtilization`
- `DiskReadOps`
- `DiskReadBytes`
- `DiskWriteOps`
- `DiskWriteBytes`
- `NetworkIn`
- `NetworkOut`
- `StatusCheckFailed`

Amazon EC2 does not report OS-level metrics such as memory utilization.

Understand the difference between high-resolution and standard-resolution metrics. High-resolution metrics are delivered in a period of less than one minute. Standard-resolution metrics are delivered in a period greater than or equal to one minute.

Know what AWS CloudTrail is and why it is used.   CloudTrail is used to monitor API calls made to the AWS Cloud for various services. CloudTrail helps IT administrators, IT security administrators, DevOps engineers, and auditors to enable compliance and the monitoring of access to AWS resources within an account.

Know what AWS CloudTrail tracks automatically.   By default, CloudTrail tracks the last 90 days of activity. These events are limited to management events with create, modify, and delete API calls.

Understand the difference between AWS CloudTrail management and data events. Management events are operations performed on resources in your AWS account. Data events are operations performed on data stored in AWS resources. Examples are creating or deleting objects in Amazon S3 and inserting or updating items in an Amazon DynamoDB table.

Know what AWS X-Ray is and why it is used.   X-Ray is a service that collects data about your application requests, including the various subservices or systems that perform tasks to complete a request. X-Ray is commonly used to help developers find bottlenecks in distributed applications and monitor the health of various components in their services.

Know the basics of AWS X-Ray and how it helps troubleshoot applications.   X-Ray records requests by initiating a trace ID with the origin of the request. This trace ID is added as a header to the request that propagates to various services. If you enable the X-Ray SDK in your applications, X-Ray submits telemetry and the request as segments for each service and subsegments for downstream services upon which you depend. Using these traces, X-Ray collates the data to view request performance metrics, such as latency and error rates. The data can then be used to create a graph of your application and its dependencies and the health of any requests your application might make.

Resources to Review

Launch your application with the AWS Startup Kit:

https://aws.amazon.com/blogs/startups/launch-your-app-with-the-aws-startup-kit/

AWS re:Invent 2018: Monitor All Your Things: Amazon CloudWatch in Action with BBC (DEV302):

https://www.youtube.com/watch?v=uuBuc60AcVY

Create a CloudWatch Dashboard:

https://docs.aws.amazon.com/AmazonCloudWatch/latest/monitoring/create_dashboard.html

What is Amazon CloudWatch?

https://docs.aws.amazon.com/AmazonCloudWatch/latest/monitoring/WhatIsCloudWatch.html

Using Amazon CloudWatch Alarms:

https://docs.aws.amazon.com/AmazonCloudWatch/latest/monitoring/AlarmThatSendsEmail.html

Using Amazon CloudWatch Metrics:

https://docs.aws.amazon.com/AmazonCloudWatch/latest/monitoring/working_with_metrics.html

AWS re:Invent 2018: Augmenting Security Posture and Improving Operational Health with AWS CloudTrail (SEC323):

https://www.youtube.com/watch?v=YWzmoDzzg4U

What is Amazon CloudWatch Logs?

https://docs.aws.amazon.com/AmazonCloudWatch/latest/logs/WhatIsCloudWatchLogs.html

SID 341: Using AWS CloudTrail Logs for Scalable, Automated Anomaly Detection:

https://github.com/aws-samples/aws-cloudtrail-analyzer-workshop

What Is AWS CloudTrail?

https://docs.aws.amazon.com/awscloudtrail/latest/userguide/cloudtrail-user-guide.html

CloudTrail Concepts:

https://docs.aws.amazon.com/awscloudtrail/latest/userguide/cloudtrail-concepts.html

AWS X-Ray Sample Application:

https://docs.aws.amazon.com/xray/latest/devguide/xray-scorekeep.html

AWS re:Invent 2017: Monitoring Modern Applications: Introduction to AWS X-Ray (DEV204):

> https://www.youtube.com/watch?v=kFsIZsaqpzE

AWS X-Ray Service Graph:

> https://docs.aws.amazon.com/xray/latest/devguide/xray-concepts
> .html#xray-concepts-servicegraph

AWS CloudTrail Event History Now Available to All Customers:

> https://aws.amazon.com/about-aws/whats-new/2017/08/aws-cloudtrail-event-
> history-now-available-to-all-customers/

Exercises

EXERCISE 15.1

Create an Amazon CloudWatch Alarm on an Amazon S3 Bucket

It is common to monitor the storage usage of your Amazon S3 buckets and trigger notifications when there is a large increase in storage used. In this exercise, you will use the AWS CLI to configure an Amazon CloudWatch alarm to trigger a notification when more than 1 KB of data is uploaded to an Amazon S3 bucket.

If you need directions while completing this exercise, see "Using Amazon CloudWatch Alarms" here:

> https://docs.aws.amazon.com/AmazonCloudWatch/latest/monitoring/
> AlarmThatSendsEmail.html

1. Create an Amazon S3 bucket in your AWS account. For instructions, see this page:

    > https://docs.aws.amazon.com/AmazonS3/latest/user-guide/
    > create-bucket.html

2. Open the Amazon CloudWatch console at https://console.aws.amazon.com/cloudwatch/.

3. Select Alarms ➢ Create Alarm.

4. Choose Select Metric.

    a. Select the All Metrics tab.

    b. Expand AWS Namespaces.

    c. Select S3.

    d. Select Storage Metrics.

    e. Select a metric where BucketName matches the name of the Amazon S3 bucket that you created and where Metric Name is BucketSizeBytes.

5.   Choose Select Metric.

6.   Under Alarm Details:

   a.   For Name, enter **S3 Storage Alarm**.

   b.   For the comparator, select >= (greater than or equal to).

   c.   Set the value to 1000 for 1 KB.

7.   Under Actions:

   a.   For Whenever This Alarm, select State Is ALARM.

   b.   For Send Notification To, select New List.

   c.   For Name, enter **My S3 Alarm List**.

   d.   For Email List, enter your email address.

8.   Choose Create Alarm.

The alarm is created in your account. If you already have data in your Amazon S3 bucket, it is switched from Insufficient Data to Alarm state. Otherwise, try uploading several files to your bucket to monitor changes in alarm state.

To delete the alarm, follow these steps:

1.   Open the Amazon CloudWatch console at https://console.aws.amazon.com/ cloudwatch/.

2.   Select Alarms.

3.   Select the alarm you want to delete.

4.   For Actions, select Delete.

In this exercise, you created an Amazon CloudWatch alarm to notify administrators when large files are uploaded to Amazon S3 buckets in your account.

EXERCISE 15.2

Enable an AWS CloudTrail Trail on an Amazon S3 Bucket

1.   In this exercise, you will set up access logs to an Amazon S3 bucket in your account to monitor activity.Create an Amazon S3 bucket in your AWS account.

   For instructions on how to do so, see the following:

   https://docs.aws.amazon.com/AmazonS3/latest/user-guide/ create-bucket.html

2.   Open the AWS CloudTrail console at https://console.aws.amazon.com/ cloudtrail/.

(*continued*)

3. Select Create Trail.

4. Set Trail name to **s3_logs**.

5. Under Management Events, select None.

6. Under Data Events, select Add S3 Bucket.

7. For S3 bucket, enter your Amazon S3 bucket name.

8. Under Storage Location, for Create A New S3 bucket, select Yes.

9. For Name, enter a name for your Amazon S3 bucket.

10. Choose Create.

In this exercise, you enabled AWS CloudTrail to record data events and store corresponding logs to an Amazon S3 bucket.

Create an Amazon CloudWatch Dashboard

In this exercise, you will create an Amazon CloudWatch dashboard to see graphed metric data.

1. Open the Amazon CloudWatch console at https://console.aws.amazon.com/cloudwatch/.

2. In the navigation pane, select Dashboards.

3. Choose Create Dashboard.

4. For Dashboard Name, enter a name for your dashboard.

5. Select Create Dashboard.

6. In the modal window, select the Line graph.

7. Choose Configure.

8. From the available metrics, select one or more metrics that you want to monitor.

9. Choose Create Widget.

10. To add more widgets, choose Add Widget and repeat steps 6 through 9 for other widget types.

11. Choose Save Dashboard.

In this exercise, you created an Amazon CloudWatch dashboard to create graphs of important metric data for resources in your account.

Review Questions

1. You are required to set up dynamic scaling using Amazon CloudWatch alarms.

   Which of the following metrics could you monitor to trigger Auto Scaling events to scale out and scale in your instances?

   A. High CPU utilization to trigger scale-in action, and low CPU utilization to trigger scale-out action

   B. High CPU utilization to trigger scale-out action, and low CPU utilization to trigger scale-in action

   C. High latency to trigger a scale-in action, and low latency to trigger a scale-out action

   D. None of the above

2. What is the length of time that metrics are stored for a data point with a period of 300 seconds (5 minutes) in Amazon CloudWatch?

   A. The data point is stored for 3 hours.

   B. The data point is stored for 15 days.

   C. The data point is stored for 30 days.

   D. The data point is stored for 63 days.

   E. The data point is stored for 455 days (15 months).

3. Which of the following does an AWS CloudTrail event *not* provide?

   A. Who made the request

   B. When the request was made

   C. What request is being made

   D. Why the request was made

   E. Which resource was acted on

4. You must set up centralized logging for an application and create a cost-effective way to archive logs for compliance purposes.

   Which is the best solution?

   A. Install the Amazon CloudWatch agent on your servers to ingest the logs and store them indefinitely.

   B. Configure Amazon CloudWatch to ingest logs from your application servers.

   C. Install the Amazon CloudWatch agent on your servers to ingest the logs and set a new retention period for logs with regular exports to Amazon S3 for archival.

   D. None of the above.

5. Which of the following options allow logs and metrics to be ingested into Amazon CloudWatch? (Select THREE.)

   A. Install the Amazon CloudWatch agent and configure it to ingest logs.

   B. Execute API operations to push metrics to Amazon CloudWatch.

   C. Configure Amazon CloudWatch to pull logs from servers.

   D. Use the AWS CLI to push metrics to Amazon CloudWatch.

6. The following are Apache HTTP access logs.

   Which filter pattern would select events matching 404 errors?

   ```
   127.0.0.1 - - [24/Sep/2013:11:49:52 -0700] "GET /index.html HTTP/1.1" 404 287
   127.0.0.1 - - [24/Sep/2013:11:49:52 -0700] "GET /index.html HTTP/1.1" 404 287
   127.0.0.1 - - [24/Sep/2013:11:50:51 -0700] "GET /~test/ HTTP/1.1" 200 3
   127.0.0.1 - - [24/Sep/2013:11:50:51 -0700] "GET /favicon.ico HTTP/1.1" 404 308
   127.0.0.1 - - [24/Sep/2013:11:50:51 -0700] "GET /favicon.ico HTTP/1.1" 404 308
   127.0.0.1 - - [24/Sep/2013:11:51:34 -0700] "GET /~test/index.html HTTP/1.1" 200 3
   ```

   A. 4xx

   B. 400

   C. 404

   D. None of the above

7. You build an application and enable AWS X-Ray tracing. You analyze the service graph and determine that the application requests to Amazon DynamoDB are not performing well and a majority of the issues are purple.

   What kind of problem is your application experiencing?

   A. Throttling

   B. Error

   C. Faults

   D. OK

8. Which AWS service enables you to monitor resources and gather statistics, such as CPU utilization, from a single "pane of glass" interface?

   A. AWS CloudTrail logs

   B. Amazon CloudWatch alarms

   C. Amazon CloudWatch dashboards

   D. Amazon CloudWatch Logs

9. By default, what is the number of days of AWS account activity that you can view, search, and download from the AWS CloudTrail event history?

   A. 30 days

   B. 60 days

   C. 75 days

   D. 90 days

10. Which of the following is not able to access AWS CloudTrail data?

    A. AWS CLI

    B. AWS Management Console

    C. AWS CloudTrail API

    D. None of the above

11. In AWS CloudTrail, which of the following are management events? (Select TWO.)

    A. Adding a row to an Amazon DynamoDB table

    B. Modifying an Amazon S3 bucket policy

    C. Uploading an object to an Amazon S3 bucket

    D. Creating an Amazon Relational Database Service (Amazon RDS) database instance

    E. Sending a notification to Amazon Simple Notification Service (Amazon SNS)

12. Suppose that you have a custom web application running on an Amazon Elastic Compute Cloud (Amazon EC2) instance.

    What steps are needed to configure this instance to send custom application logs to Amazon CloudWatch Logs? (Select THREE.)

    A. Install the Amazon CloudWatch Logs agent.

    B. Attach an Elastic IP address to your Amazon EC2 instance.

    C. Configure the agent to send specific logs.

    D. Start the agent.

    E. Install the AWS Systems Manager agent.

13. Which of the following are not supported Amazon CloudWatch alarm actions?

    A. AWS Lambda functions

    B. Amazon Simple Notification Service (Amazon SNS) topics

    C. Amazon Elastic Compute Cloud (Amazon EC2) actions

    D. EC2 Auto Scaling actions

14. Which of the following Amazon Elastic Compute Cloud (Amazon EC2) metrics is not directly available through Amazon CloudWatch metrics?

    A. CPU utilization

    B. Network traffic in/out

    C. Disk I/O

    D. Memory (RAM) utilization

15. Which of the following is the correct Amazon CloudWatch metric namespace for Amazon Elastic Compute Cloud (Amazon EC2) instances?

    A. AWS/EC2

    B. Amazon/EC2

    C. AWS/EC2Instance

    D. Amazon/EC2Instance

Chapter

16

Optimization

**THE AWS CERTIFIED DEVELOPER –
ASSOCIATE EXAM TOPICS COVERED IN
THIS CHAPTER MAY INCLUDE, BUT ARE
NOT LIMITED TO, THE FOLLOWING:**

Domain 3: Development with AWS Services

✓ **3.4   Write code that interacts with AWS services by using
APIs, SDKs, and AWS CLI.**

Content may include the following:

- Programming AWS APIs

Domain 4: Refactoring

✓ **4.1   Optimize application to best use AWS services
and features.**

Content may include the following:

- Cost optimization
- Performance optimization
- Best practices for achieving optimization

Domain 5: Monitoring and Troubleshooting

✓ **5.1   Write code that can be monitored.**

Content may include the following:

- Tools for cost monitoring
- Tools for performance monitoring

Introduction to Optimization

Creating a software system is a lot like constructing a building. If the foundation is not solid, structural problems can undermine the integrity and function of the building. The AWS Well-Architected Tool helps you understand the pros and cons of decisions that you make while building systems on AWS. By using the tool, you will learn architectural best practices for designing and operating reliable, secure, efficient, and cost-effective systems in the AWS Cloud. When architecting technology solutions, if you neglect the five pillars of operational excellence, security, reliability, performance efficiency, and cost optimization, it can become challenging to build a system that delivers on your expectations and requirements. Incorporating these pillars into your architecture helps you to produce stable and efficient systems.

This chapter covers some of the best practices and considerations in designing systems with the most effective use of services and resources to achieve business outcomes at a minimal cost and maintain the optimal performance efficiency.

Cost Optimization: Everyone's Responsibility

All teams help manage cloud costs, and cost optimization is everyone's responsibility. Make sure that costs are known from beginning to end, at every level, and from executives to engineers. Ensure that project owners and budget holders know what their upfront and ongoing costs are. Business decision makers must track costs against budgets and understand return on investment (ROI).

Encourage everyone to track their cost optimization daily so that they can establish a habit of efficiency and see the daily impact of their cost savings over time.

Developers' and engineers' contributions are a significant part of the organization's success. Every engineer can be a cost engineer. Engineers should design the code to consume resources only when needed, control the utilization, build sizing into architecture, and tag the resources to optimize usage.

Tagging

By tagging your AWS resources, you can assign custom metadata to instances, images, and other resources. For example, you can categorize resources by owner, purpose, or environment, which helps you organize them and assign cost accountability. When you apply tags to your AWS resources and activate the tags, AWS adds this information to the Cost and Usage reports.

Follow Mandatory Cost Tagging

An effective tagging strategy gives you improved visibility and monitoring, helps you create accurate chargeback and showback models, and extract more granular and precise insights into usage and spending by applications and teams. The following tag categories help you achieve these goals:

Environment   Distinguishes among development, test, and production infrastructure. Specifying an environment tag reduces analysis time, post-processing, and the need to maintain a separate mapping file of production versus nonproduction accounts.

Application ID   Identifies resources that are related to a specific application for easy tracking of spending changes and that turn off at the end of projects.

Automation Opt-In/Opt-Out   Indicates whether a resource should be included in an automated activity such as starting, stopping, or resizing instances.

Cost Center/Business Unit   Identifies the cost center or business unit associated with a resource, typically for cost allocation and tracking.

Owner   Used to identify who is responsible for the resource. This is typically the technical owner. If needed, you can add a separate business owner tag. You can specify the owner as an email address. Using email addresses supports automated notifications to both the technical and business owners as required (for example, if the resource is a candidate for elasticity or right sizing).

Tag on Creation

You can make tagging a part of your build process and automate it with AWS management tools, such as AWS Elastic Beanstalk and AWS OpsWorks.

The following AWS CLI sample adds two tags, CostCenter and environment, for an Amazon Machine Image (AMI) and an instance:

```
aws ec2 create-tags --resources ami-1a2b3c4d i-1234567890abcdef0 --tags
Key=CostCenter,Value=123    Key=environment,Value=Production
```

You can execute management tasks at scale by listing resources with specific tags and then executing the appropriate actions. For example, you can list all the resources with the tag and value of environment:test; then, for each of the resources, delete or terminate the resource. This is useful for automating shutdown or removal of a test environment at the end of the working day. Running reports on tagged and, more importantly, untagged resources enables greater compliance with internal cost management policies.

Enforce Tag Use

Using AWS Identity and Access Management (IAM) policies, you can enforce tag use to gain precise control over access to resources, ownership, and accurate cost allocation.

The following example policy allows a user to create an Amazon Elastic Block Store (Amazon EBS) volume only if the user applies the tags (Costcenter and environment) that are defined in the policy using the qualifier ForAllValues. If the user applies any tag that is not included in the policy, the action is denied. To enforce case sensitivity, use the condition aws:TagKeys as follows:

```
Effect: Allow
Action: 'ec2:CreateVolume'
Resource: 'arn:aws:ec2:us-east-1:123456789012:volume/*'
Condition:
    StringEquals:
        'aws:RequestTag/costcenter': '115'
        'aws:RequestTag/environment': prod
    'ForAllValues:StringEquals':
        'aws:TagKeys':
            - Costcenter
            - environment
```

Tagging Tools

The following tools help you manage your tags:

AWS Tag Editor—Finds resources with search criteria (including missing and misspelled tags) and enables you to edit tags from the AWS Management Console

AWS Config—Identifies resources that do not comply with tagging policies

Capital One's Cloud Custodian (open source)—Ensures tagging compliance and remediation

Reduce AWS Usage

Set a continuous practice to review your consumption of AWS resources, and understand the factors that contribute to cost. Use various AWS monitoring tools to provide visibility, control, and cost optimization. Implement the best practice of oversight to make sure that you are not overspending. Following the DevOps phase, use dashboards to view the estimated costs of your AWS usage, top services that you use most, and the proportion of your costs to which each service contributed. If your monthly bill increases, make sure that it is for the right reason (business growth) and not the wrong reason (waste).

Delete Unnecessary EBS Volumes

Stopping an Amazon Elastic Compute Cloud (Amazon EC2) instance leaves any attached Amazon Elastic Block Store (Amazon EBS) volumes operational. You continue to incur charges for these volumes until you delete them.

Stop Unused Instances

Stop instances used in development and production during hours when these instances are not in use and then start them again when their capacity is needed. Assuming a 50-hour workweek, you can save 70 percent of costs by automatically stopping dev/test/production instances during nonbusiness hours.

Delete Idle Resources

Consider the following best practices to reduce costs associated with AWS idle resources, such as unattached Amazon EBS volumes and unused Elastic IP addresses:

- The easiest way to reduce operational costs is to turn off instances that are no longer being used. If you find instances that have been idle for more than two weeks, it's safe to stop or even terminate them.

- Terminating an instance, however, automatically deletes attached EBS volumes and requires effort to re-provision if the instance is needed again. If you decide to delete an EBS volume, consider storing a snapshot of the volume so that it can be restored later if needed.

- Spin up instances to test new ideas. If the ideas work, keep the instance for further refinement. If not, spin it down.

- An Elastic IP address does not incur charges as long as it is associated with an Amazon EC2 instance. If an Elastic IP address is not used, you can avoid charges by releasing the IP address. After you release an IP address, you cannot provision that same Elastic IP address again.

Update Outdated Resources

As AWS releases new services and features, it is a best practice to review your existing architectural decisions to ensure that they remain cost effective and stay evergreen. As your requirements change, be aggressive in decommissioning resources, components, and work-loads that you no longer require.

Delete Unused Keys

Each customer master key (CMK) that you create in AWS Key Management Service (AWS KMS), regardless of whether you use it with KMS-generated key material or key material imported by you, incurs a cost you until you delete it. Before deleting a CMK, you might want to know how many ciphertexts were encrypted under that key. Knowing how a CMK was used in the past might help you decide whether you will need it in the future by using AWS CloudTrail usage logs. After you are sure that you want to delete a CMK in AWS KMS, schedule the key deletion.

Delete Old Snapshots

If your architecture suggests a backup policy that takes EBS volume snapshots daily or weekly, then you will quickly accumulate snapshots. To reduce storage costs, check for "stale" snapshots—ones that are more than 30 days old—and delete them. Deleting a snapshot has no effect on the volume. You can use the AWS Management Console or AWS Command Line Interface (AWS CLI) for this purpose.

Right Sizing

Right sizing is the process of matching instance types and sizes to performance and capacity requirements at the lowest possible cost. To achieve cost optimization, right sizing must become an ongoing process within your organization. Even if you right size workloads initially, performance and capacity requirements can change over time, which can result in underused or idle resources. New projects and workloads require additional cloud resources. Therefore, if there is no periodic check on right sizing, overprovisioning is the likely outcome.

AWS provides APIs, SDKs, and features that allow resources to be modified as demands change.

The following are examples of how you can change the instance type to match performance and capacity requirements:

- On Amazon Elastic Compute Cloud (Amazon EC2), you can perform a stop-and-start to allow a change of instance size or instance type.

- On Amazon EBS, you can increase volume size or adjust performance while volumes are still in use to improve performance through increased input/output operations per second (IOPS) or throughput or to reduce cost by changing the type of volume.

Select the Right Use Case

As you monitor current performance, identify the following usage needs and patterns so that you can take advantage of potential right-sizing options:

Steady state   The load remains constant over time, making forecasting simple. Consider using Reserved Instances to gain significant savings.

Variable, but predictable   The load changes on a predictable schedule. Consider using AWS Auto Scaling.

Dev, test, production   Development, testing, and production environments can usually be turned off outside of work hours.

Temporary   Temporary workloads that have flexible start times and can be interrupted are good candidates for Spot Instances instead of On-Demand Instances.

Select the Right Instance Family

When you launch an instance, the instance type that you specify determines the hardware of the host computer used for your instance. Each instance type offers different compute, memory, and storage capabilities, and they are grouped in instance families based on these capabilities. Depending on the AWS offering, you can determine the right instance family for your infrastructure.

Amazon Elastic Cloud Compute

Amazon Elastic Cloud Compute (Amazon EC2) provides a wide selection of instances, which gives you flexibility to right size CPU and memory needs for your compute resources to match capacity needs at the lowest cost. Following are the different options for CPU, memory, and network resources:

General purpose (includes A1, T2, M3, and M4 instance types)   A1 instances deliver significant cost savings and are ideally suited for scale-out workloads, such as web servers, containerized microservices, caching fleets, and distributed data stores. T2 instances are a low-cost option that provides a small amount of CPU resources that can be increased in short bursts when additional cycles are available. They are well suited for lower throughput applications, such as administrative applications or low-traffic websites. M3 and M4 instances provide a balance of CPU, memory, and network resources, and they are ideal for running small and midsize databases, more memory-intensive data processing tasks, caching fleets, and backend servers.

Compute optimized (includes the C3 and C4 instance types)   This family has a higher ratio of virtual CPUs to memory than the other families and the lowest cost per virtual CPU of all of the Amazon EC2 instance types. Consider compute-optimized instances first if you are running CPU-bound, scale-out applications, such as front-end fleets for high-traffic websites, on-demand batch processing, distributed analytics, web servers, video encoding, and high-performance science and engineering applications.

Memory optimized (includes the X1, R3, and R4 instance types)   Designed for memory-intensive applications, these instances have the lowest cost per GiB of RAM of all Amazon EC2 instance types. Use these instances if your application is memory-bound.

Storage optimized (includes the I3 and D2 instance types)   Optimized to deliver tens of thousands of low-latency, random input/output operations per second (IOPS) to applications. Storage-optimized instances are best for large deployments of NoSQL databases. I3 instances are designed for I/O-intensive workloads and equipped with super-efficient NVMe SSD storage. These instances can deliver up to 3.3 million IOPS in 4-KB blocks and up to 16 GB per second of sequential disk throughput. D2 or dense storage instances are designed for workloads that require high sequential read and write access to large datasets such as Hadoop, distributed computing, massively parallel processing data warehousing, and log-processing applications.

Accelerated computing (includes the P2, G3, and F1 instance types)   Provides access to hardware-based compute accelerators, such as graphics processing units (GPUs) or field programmable gate arrays (FPGAs). Accelerated-computing instances enable more parallelism for higher throughput on compute-intensive workloads.

Amazon Relational Database Service

Similar to Amazon EC2 instances, Amazon Relational Database Service (Amazon RDS) provides options to choose from database instances that are optimized for memory, performance, and I/O.

Standard performance (includes the M3 and M4 instance types)   Designed for general-purpose database workloads that do not run many in-memory functions. This family has the most options for provisioning increased IOPS.

Burstable performance (includes T2 instance types)   For workloads that require burstable performance capacity.

Memory optimized (includes the R3 and R4 instance types)   Optimized for in-memory functions and big data analysis.

Select the Right Instance Compatibility

You can right size an instance by migrating to a different model within the same instance family or by migrating to another instance family. When you're migrating within the same instance family, consider vCPU, memory, network throughput, and ephemeral storage.

Virtualization type   The instances must have the same Linux Amazon Machine Image (AMI) virtualization type (PV AMI versus HVM) and platform (Amazon EC2-Classic versus Amazon EC2-VPC).

Network   Instances unsupported in Amazon EC2-Classic must be launched in a virtual private cloud (VPC).

Platform   If the current instance type supports 32-bit AMIs, make sure to select a new instance type that also supports 32-bit AMIs (not all Amazon EC2 instance types do).

Using Instance Reservations

Amazon EC2 provides several purchasing options to enable you to optimize your costs based on your needs.

AWS Pricing for Reserved Instances

Amazon EC2 Reserved Instances allow you to commit to usage parameters. To unlock an hourly rate that is up to 75 percent lower than On-Demand pricing, you can commit to a one-year or three-year duration at the time of purchase.

There are three payment options for Reserved Instances:

No Upfront   No upfront payment is required, and Reserved Instances are billed monthly. This requires a good payment history with AWS.

Partial Upfront   A portion of the cost is paid upfront, and the remaining hours in the term are billed at a discounted hourly rate, regardless of whether the RI is being used.

All Upfront   Full payment is made at the start of the term, with no other costs or additional hourly charges incurred for the remainder of the term, regardless of hours used.

Amazon EC2 Reservations

Amazon EC2 Reserved Instances provide a reservation of resources and capacity when used in a specific Availability Zone within an AWS Region:

- With Reserved Instances, you commit to a period of usage (one or three years) and save up to 75 percent over equivalent On-Demand hourly rates.

- For applications that have steady state or predictable usage, Reserved Instances can provide significant savings compared to using On-Demand Instances, without requiring a change to your workload.

Convertible Reserved Instances

Convertible Reserved Instances are provided for a one-year or three-year term, and they enable conversion to different families, new pricing, different instance sizes, different platforms, or tenancy during the period. Use Convertible Reserved Instances when you are uncertain about instance needs in the future, but you are still committed to using Amazon EC2 instances for a three-year term in exchange for a significant discount.

Suppose that you own an Amazon EC2 Reserved Instance for a c4.8xlarge for three years. This Reserved Instance applies to any usage of a Linux/Unix c4 instance with shared tenancy in the same region as the Reserved Instance, such as 1 c4.8xlarge instance, 2 c4.4xlarge instances, or 16 c4.large instances, during this term. This adds flexibility to match the new needs of your workloads:

- There are no limits to how many times you perform an exchange, as long as the target Convertible Reserved Instance is of an equal or higher value than the Convertible Reserved Instances that you are exchanging.

- Exchanging Convertible Reserved Instances is free of charge, but you might need to pay a true-up cost if the value is lower than the value of the Reserved Instances for which you're exchanging. For example, you can convert C3 Reserved Instances to C4 Reserved Instances to take advantage of a newer instance type, or you can convert C4 Reserved Instances to M4 Reserved Instances if your application requires more memory. You can also use Convertible Reserved Instances to take advantage of Amazon EC2 price reductions over time.

Reserved Instance Marketplace

Use the *Reserved Instance Marketplace* to sell your unused Reserved Instances and buy Reserved Instances from other AWS customers. As your needs change throughout the course of your term, the AWS Marketplace provides an option to buy Reserved Instances for shorter terms and with a wider selection of prices.

Amazon Relational Database Service Reservations

Reserved DB instances are not physical instances; they are a billing discount applied to the use of certain on-demand DB instances in your account. Discounts for reserved DB instances are tied to instance type and AWS Region.

All Reserved Instance types are available for Amazon Aurora, MySQL, MariaDB, PostgreSQL, Oracle, and SQL Server database engines.

- Reserved Instances can also provide significant cost savings for mission-critical applications that run on Multi-AZ database deployments for higher availability and data durability. Reserved Instances can minimize your costs up to 69 percent over On-Demand rates when used in steady state.

- Most production applications require database servers to be available 24/7. Consider using Reserved Instances to gain substantial savings if you are currently using On-Demand Instances.

- Any usage of running DB instances that exceeds the number of applicable Reserved Instances you have purchased are charged the On-Demand rate. For example, if you own three Reserved Instances with the same database engine and instance type (or instance family, if size flexibility applies) in a given region, the billing system checks each hour to determine how many total instances you have running that match those parameters. If it is three or fewer, you are charged the Reserved Instance rate for each instance running that hour. If more than three are running, you are charged the On-Demand rate for the additional instances.

- With size flexibility, your Reserved Instance's discounted rate is automatically applied to usage of any size in the instance family (using the same database engine) for the MySQL, MariaDB, PostgreSQL, and Amazon Aurora database engines and the "Bring your own license" (BYOL) edition of the Oracle database engine. For example, suppose that you purchased a db.m4.2xlarge MySQL Reserved Instance in US East (N. Virginia). The discounted rate of this Reserved Instance can automatically apply to two db.m4.xlarge MySQL instances without you needing to do anything.

- The Reserved Instance discounted rate also applies to usage of both Single-AZ and Multi-AZ configurations for the same database engine and instance family.

  Suppose that you purchased a db.r3.large PostgreSQL Single-AZ Reserved Instance in EU (Frankfurt). The discounted rate of this Reserved Instance can automatically apply to 50 percent of the usage of a db.r3.large PostgreSQL Multi-AZ instance in the same region.

Using Spot Instances

Amazon EC2 Spot Instances offer spare compute capacity in the AWS Cloud at steep discounts compared to On-Demand Instances.

You can use Spot Instances to save up to 90 percent on stateless web applications, big data, containers, continuous integration/continuous delivery (CI/CD), high performance computing (HPC), and other fault-tolerant workloads. Or, scale your workload throughput by up to 10 times and stay within the existing budget.

Spot Fleets

Use *Spot Fleets* to request and manage multiple Spot Instances automatically, which provides the lowest price per unit of capacity for your cluster or application, such as a batch-processing job, a Hadoop workflow, or an HPC grid computing job. You can include the instance types that your application can use. You define a target capacity based on your application needs (in units, including instances, vCPUs, memory, storage, or network throughput) and update the target capacity after the fleet is launched. Spot Fleets enable you to launch and maintain the target capacity and to request resources automatically to replace any that are disrupted or manually terminated.

To ensure that you have instance capacity, you can include a request for On-Demand capacity in your Spot Fleet request. If there is capacity, the On-Demand request is fulfilled. If there is capacity and availability, the balance of the target capacity is fulfilled as Spot.

The following example specifies the desired target capacity as 10, of which 5 must be On-Demand capacity. Spot capacity is not specified; it is implied in the balance of the target capacity minus the On-Demand capacity. If there is available Amazon EC2 capacity and availability, Amazon EC2 launches 5 capacity units as On-Demand and 5 capacity units (10–5=5) as Spot.

```
{
"IamFleetRole":"arn:aws:iam::1234567890:role/aws-ec2-spot-fleet-tagging-role",
"AllocationStrategy":"lowestPrice",
"TargetCapacity":10,
"SpotPrice":null,
"ValidFrom":"2018-04-04T15:58:13Z",
"ValidUntil":"2019-04-04T15:58:13Z",
"TerminateInstancesWithExpiration": true,
"LaunchSpecifications":[],
"Type":"maintain",
"OnDemandTargetCapacity":5,
"LaunchTemplateConfigs":[
    {
"LaunchTemplateSpecification":{
"LaunchTemplateId": "lt-0dbb04d4a6abcabcabc",
```

```
"Version": "2"
      },
"Overrides": [
        {
"InstanceType": "t2.medium",
"WeightedCapacity": 1,
"SubnetId": "subnet-d0dc51fb"
        }
      ]
    }
  ]
}
```

Amazon EC2 Fleets

With a single API call, *Amazon EC2 Fleet* enables you to provision compute capacity across different instance types, Availability Zones, and across On-Demand, Reserved Instances, and Spot Instances purchase models to help optimize scale, performance, and cost.

By default, Amazon EC2 Fleet launches the On-Demand option that is at the lowest price. For Spot Instances, Amazon EC2 Fleet provides two allocation strategies: lowest price and diversified. The lowest-price strategy allows you to provision Spot Instances in pools that provide the lowest price per unit of capacity at the time of the request. The diversified strategy allows you to provision Spot Instances across multiple Spot pools, and you can maintain your fleet's target capacity to increase application.

Design for Continuity

With Spot Instances, you avoid paying more than the maximum price you specified. If the Spot price exceeds your maximum willingness to pay for a given instance or when capacity is no longer available, your instance is terminated automatically (or stopped or hibernated, if you opt for this behavior on a persistent request).

Spot offers features, such as termination notices, persistent requests, and spot block duration, to help you better track and control when Spot Instances can run and terminate (or stop or hibernate).

Using Termination Notices

If you need to save state, upload final log files, or remove Spot Instances from an Elastic Load Balancing load balancer before interruption, you can use termination notices, which are issued 2 minutes before interruption.

If your instance is marked for termination, the termination notice is stored in the instance's metadata 2 minutes before its termination time. The notice is accessible at `http://169.254.169.254/latest/meta-data/spot/termination-time`. The notice includes the time when the shutdown signal will be sent to the instance's operating system.

Relevant applications on Spot Instances should poll for the termination notice at 5-second intervals, which gives the application almost the entire 2 minutes to complete any needed processing before the instance is terminated and taken back by AWS.

Using Persistent Requests

You can set your request to remain open so that a new instance is launched in its place when the instance is interrupted. You can also have your Amazon EBS–backed instance stopped upon interruption and restarted when Spot has capacity at your preferred price.

Using Block Durations

You can also launch Spot Instances with a fixed duration (Spot blocks, 1–6 hours), which are not interrupted as the result of changes in the Spot price. Spot blocks can provide savings of up to 50 percent.

You submit a Spot Instance request and use the new BlockDuration parameter to specify the number of hours that you want your instances to run, along with the maximum price that you are willing to pay.

You can submit a request of this type by running the following command:

```
$ aws ec2 request-spot-instances \
    block-duration-minutes 360 \
    instance-count 2 \
    spot-price "0.25"
:
```

Alternatively, you can call the RequestSpotInstances function.

Minimizing the Impact of Interruptions

Because the Spot service can terminate Spot Instances without warning, it is important to build your applications in a way that allows you to make progress even if your application is interrupted. There are many ways to accomplish this, including the following:

Adding checkpoints   Add checkpoints that save your work periodically, for example, to an Amazon EBS volume. Another approach is to launch your instances from Amazon EBS–backed AMI.

Splitting up the work   By using Amazon Simple Queue Service (Amazon SQS), you can queue up work increments and track work that has already been done.

Using AWS Auto Scaling

Using AWS Auto Scaling, you can scale workloads in your architecture. It automatically increases the number of resources during the demand spikes to maintain performance and decreases capacity when demand lulls to reduce cost. AWS Auto Scaling is well-suited for applications that have stable demand patterns and for ones that experience hourly, daily, or weekly variability in usage. AWS Auto Scaling is useful for applications that show steady demand patterns and that experience frequent variations in usage.

Amazon EC2 Auto Scaling

Amazon EC2 Auto Scaling helps you scale your Amazon EC2 instances and Spot Fleet capacity up or down automatically according to conditions that you define. AWS Auto Scaling is generally used with Elastic Load Balancing to distribute incoming application traffic across multiple Amazon EC2 instances in an AWS Auto Scaling group. AWS Auto Scaling is triggered using scaling plans that include policies that define how to scale (manual, schedule, and demand spikes) and the metrics and alarms to monitor in Amazon CloudWatch.

CloudWatch metrics are used to trigger the scaling event. These metrics can be standard Amazon EC2 metrics, such as CPU utilization, network throughput, Elastic Load Balancing observed request and response latency, and even custom metrics that might originate from application code on your Amazon EC2 instances.

You can use Amazon EC2 Auto Scaling to increase the number of Amazon EC2 instances automatically during demand spikes to maintain performance and decrease capacity during lulls to reduce costs.

Dynamic Scaling

The *dynamic scaling* capabilities of Amazon EC2 Auto Scaling refers to the functionality that automatically increases or decreases capacity based on load or other metrics. For example, if your CPU spikes above 80 percent (and you have an alarm set up), Amazon EC2 Auto Scaling can add a new instance dynamically, reducing the need to provision Amazon EC2 capacity manually in advance. Alternatively, you could set a target value by using the new Request Count Per Target metric from Application Load Balancer, a load balancing option for the Elastic Load Balancing service. Amazon EC2 Auto Scaling will then automatically adjust the number of Amazon EC2 instances as needed to maintain your target.

Scheduled Scaling

Scaling based on a schedule allows you to scale your application ahead of known load changes, such as the start of business hours, thus ensuring that resources are available when users arrive, or in typical development or test environments that run only during defined business hours or periods of time.

You can use APIs to scale the size of resources within an environment (vertical scaling). For example, you could scale up a production system by changing the instance size or class. This can be achieved by stopping and starting the instance and selecting the different instance size or class. You can also apply this technique to other resources, such as EBS volumes, which can be modified to increase size, adjust performance (IOPS), or change the volume type while in use.

Fleet Management

Fleet management refers to the functionality that automatically replaces unhealthy instances in your application, maintains your fleet at the desired capacity, and balances instances across Availability Zones. Amazon EC2 Auto Scaling fleet management ensures that your application is able to receive traffic and that the instances themselves are working properly. When AWS Auto Scaling detects a failed health check, it can replace the instance automatically.

Instances Purchasing Options

With Amazon EC2 Auto Scaling, you can provision and automatically scale instances across purchase options, Availability Zones, and instance families in a single application to optimize scale, performance, and cost. You can include Spot Instances with On-Demand and Reserved Instances in a single AWS Auto Scaling group to save up to 90 percent on compute. You have the option to define the desired split between On-Demand and Spot capacity, select which instance types work for your application, and specify preferences for how Amazon EC2 Auto Scaling should distribute the AWS Auto Scaling group capacity within each purchasing model.

Golden Images

A *golden image* is a snapshot of a particular state of a resource, such as an Amazon EC2 instance, Amazon EBS volumes, and an Amazon RDS DB instance. You can customize an Amazon EC2 instance and then save its configuration by creating an Amazon Machine Image (AMI). You can launch as many instances from the AMI as you need, and they will all include those customizations. A golden image results in faster start times and removes dependencies to configuration services or third-party repositories. This is important in auto-scaled environments in which you want to be able to launch additional resources in response to changes in demand quickly and reliably.

AWS Auto Scaling

AWS Auto Scaling monitors your applications and automatically adjusts capacity of all scalable resources to maintain steady, predictable performance at the lowest possible cost. Using AWS Auto Scaling, you can set up application scaling for multiple resources across multiple services in minutes.

AWS Auto Scaling automatically scales resources for other AWS services, including Amazon ECS, Amazon DynamoDB, Amazon Aurora, Amazon EC2 Spot Fleet requests, and Amazon EC2 Scaling groups.

If you have an application that uses one or more scalable resources and experiences variable load, use AWS Auto Scaling. A good example would be an ecommerce web application that receives variable traffic throughout the day. It follows a standard three-tier architecture with Elastic Load Balancing for distributing incoming traffic, Amazon EC2 for the compute layer, and Amazon DynamoDB for the data layer. In this case, AWS Auto Scaling scales one or more Amazon EC2 Auto Scaling groups and DynamoDB tables that are powering the application in response to the demand curve.

AWS Auto Scaling continually monitors your applications to make sure that they are operating at your desired performance levels. When demand spikes, AWS Auto Scaling automatically increases the capacity of constrained resources so that you maintain a high quality of service.

AWS Auto Scaling bases its scaling recommendations on the most popular scaling metrics and thresholds used for AWS Auto Scaling. It also recommends safe guardrails for scaling by providing recommendations for the minimum and maximum sizes of the resources. This way, you can get started quickly and then fine-tune your scaling strategy over time, allowing you to optimize performance, costs, or balance between them.

The *predictive scaling* feature uses machine learning algorithms to detect changes in daily and weekly patterns, automatically adjusting their forecasts. This removes the need for the manual adjustment of AWS Auto Scaling parameters as cyclicality changes over time, making AWS Auto Scaling simpler to configure, and provides more accurate capacity provisioning. Predictive scaling results in lower cost and more responsive applications.

DynamoDB Auto Scaling

DynamoDB automatic scaling uses the AWS Auto Scaling service to adjust provisioned throughput capacity dynamically on your behalf in response to actual traffic patterns. This enables a table or a global secondary index to increase its provisioned read and write capacity to handle sudden increases in traffic without throttling. When the workload decreases, AWS Auto Scaling decreases the throughput so that you don't pay for unused provisioned capacity.

Amazon Aurora Auto Scaling

Amazon Aurora automatic scaling dynamically adjusts the number of Aurora Replicas provisioned for an Aurora DB cluster. Aurora automatic scaling is available for both Aurora MySQL and Aurora PostgreSQL. Aurora automatic scaling enables your Aurora DB cluster to handle sudden increases in connectivity or workload. When the connectivity or workload decreases, Aurora automatic scaling removes unnecessary Aurora Replicas so that you don't pay for unused provisioned DB instances.

Amazon Aurora Serverless is an on-demand, automatic scaling configuration for the MySQL-compatible edition of Amazon Aurora. An Aurora Serverless DB cluster automatically starts up, shuts down, and scales capacity up or down based on your application's needs. Aurora Serverless provides a relatively simple, cost-effective option for infrequent, intermittent, or unpredictable workloads.

Accessing AWS Auto Scaling

There are several ways to get started with AWS Auto Scaling. You can set up AWS Auto Scaling through the AWS Management Console, with the AWS CLI, or with AWS SDKs.

You can access the features of AWS Auto Scaling using the AWS CLI, which provides commands to use with Amazon EC2 and Amazon CloudWatch and Elastic Load Balancing.

To scale a resource other than Amazon EC2, you can use the Application Auto Scaling API, which allows you to define scaling policies to scale your AWS resources automatically or schedule one-time or recurring scaling actions.

Using Containers

Containers provide a standard way to package your application's code, configurations, and dependencies into a single object. Containers share an operating system installed on the server and run as resource-isolated processes, ensuring quick, reliable, and consistent deployments, regardless of environment.

Containers provide process isolation that lets you granularly set CPU and memory utilization for better use of compute resources.

Containerize Everything

Containers are a powerful way for developers to package and deploy their applications. They are lightweight and provide a consistent, portable software environment for applications to run and scale effortlessly anywhere.

Use Amazon Elastic Container Service (Amazon ECS) to build all types of containerized applications easily, from long-running applications and microservices to batch jobs and machine learning applications. You can migrate legacy Linux or Windows applications from on-premises to the AWS Cloud and run them as containerized applications using Amazon ECS.

Amazon ECS enables you to use containers as building blocks for your applications by eliminating the need for you to install, operate, and scale your own cluster management infrastructure. You can schedule long-running applications, services, and batch processes using Docker containers. Amazon ECS maintains application availability and allows you to scale your containers up or down to meet your application's capacity requirements. Amazon ECS is integrated with familiar features like Elastic Load Balancing, EBS volumes, virtual private cloud (VPC), and AWS Identity and Access Management (IAM). Use APIs to integrate and use your own schedulers or connect Amazon ECS into your existing software delivery process.

Containers without Servers

AWS Fargate technology is available with Amazon ECS. With Fargate, you no longer have to select Amazon EC2 instance types, provision and scale clusters, or patch and update each server. You do not have to worry about task placement strategies, such as binpacking or host spread, and tasks are automatically balanced across Availability Zones. Fargate manages the availability of containers for you. You define your application's requirements, select Fargate as your launch type in the AWS Management Console or AWS CLI, and Fargate takes care of all of the scaling and infrastructure management required to run your containers.

For developers who require more granular, server-level control over the infrastructure, Amazon ECS EC2 launch type enables you to manage a cluster of servers and schedule placement of containers on the servers.

Using Serverless Approaches

Serverless approaches are ideal for applications whereby load can vary dynamically. Using a serverless approach means no compute costs are incurred when there is no user traffic, while still offering instant scale to meet high demand, such as a flash sale on an ecommerce site or a social media mention that drives a sudden wave of traffic. All of the actual hardware and server software are handled by AWS.

Benefits gained by using AWS Serverless services include the following:

- No need to manage servers
- No need to ensure application fault tolerance, availability, and explicit fleet management to scale to peak load
- No charge for idle capacity

You can focus on product innovation and rapidly construct these applications:

- Amazon S3 offers a simple hosting solution for static content.
- AWS Lambda, with Amazon API Gateway, supports dynamic API requests using functions.
- Amazon DynamoDB offers a simple storage solution for session and per-user state.
- Amazon Cognito provides a way to handle user registration, authentication, and access control to resources.
- AWS Serverless Application Model (AWS SAM) can be used by developers to describe the various elements of an application.
- AWS CodeStar can set up a CI/CD toolchain with a few clicks.

Compared to traditional infrastructure approaches, an application is also often less expensive to develop, deliver, and operate when it has been architected in a serverless fashion. The serverless application model is generic, and it applies to almost any type of application from a startup to an enterprise.

Here are a few examples of application use cases:

- Web applications and websites
- Mobile backends
- Media and log processing

- IT automation
- AWS IoT Core backends
- Web hooked systems
- Chatbots
- Clickstream and other near real-time streaming data processes

Optimize Lambda Usage

AWS Lambda provides the cloud-logic layer, and with Lambda you can run code for virtually any type of application or backend service, all with zero administration. A variety of events can trigger Lambda functions, enabling developers to build reactive, event-driven systems without managing infrastructure. When there are multiple, simultaneous events, Lambda scales by running more copies of the function in parallel, responding to each individual trigger. As a result, there is no possibility of an idle server or container. The problem of wasted infrastructure expenditures is eliminated by design in architectures that use Lambda functions.

Serverless applications are typically composed of one or more Lambda functions; therefore, monitor the execution duration and configuration of your functions closely.

Consider the following recommendations for optimizing Lambda functions:

Optimal memory size   The memory usage for your function is determined per invocation and can be viewed in CloudWatch Logs. By analyzing the Max Memory Used: field in the Invocation report, you can determine whether your function needs more memory or whether you over-provisioned your function's memory size.

Language runtime performance   If your application use case is both latency-sensitive and susceptible to incurring the initial invocation cost frequently (spiky traffic or infrequent use), then recommend one of the interpreted languages, such as Node.js or Python.

Optimizing code   Much of the application performance depends on your logic and dependencies. Pay attention to reusing the objects and using global/static variables. Keep live or reuse HTTP/session connections, and use default network environments as much as possible.

Optimizing Storage

AWS storage services are optimized for different storage scenarios—there is no single data storage option that is ideal for all workloads. When evaluating your storage requirements, consider data storage options for each workload separately.

To optimize the storage, you must first understand the performance levels of your workloads. Conduct a performance analysis to measure input/output operations per second, throughput, quick access to your data, durability, sensitivity, size, and budget.

Amazon offers three broad categories of storage services: object, block, and file storage. Each offering is designed to meet a different storage requirement, which gives you flexibility to find the solution that works best for your storage scenarios.

Object Storage

Amazon Simple Storage Service (Amazon S3) is highly durable, general-purpose object storage that works well for unstructured datasets such as media content.

There are multiple tiers of storage: hot, warm, or cold data. In terms of pricing, the colder the data, the cheaper it is to store, and the costlier it is to access when needed.

Standard (STANDARD)   This is the best storage option for data that you frequently access. Amazon S3 delivers low latency and high throughput, and it is ideal for use cases such as cloud applications, dynamic websites, content distribution, gaming, and data analytics.

Amazon S3 Standard – Infrequent Access (STANDARD_IA)   Use this storage option for data that you access less frequently, such as long-term backups and disaster recovery. It offers cheaper storage over time, but higher charges to retrieve or transfer data.

Amazon S3 Intelligent-Tiering (INTELLIGENT_TIERING)   This storage class is designed to optimize the cost by moving data to the most cost-effective access tier automatically without degrading the performance of the application. If an object in the infrequent access tier is accessed, it is automatically moved back to the frequent access tier.

Amazon S3 One Zone-Infrequent Access (ONEZONE_IA)   This storage class provides a lower-cost option for infrequently accessed data that requires rapid access. The data is stored in only one Availability Zone (AZ), and it saves up to 20 percent of storage costs as compared to STANDARD_IA. Use this option for storing secondary backups of on-premises data or data that can be easily recreated.

Amazon S3 Glacier (GLACIER)   This option is designed for long-term storage of infrequently accessed data, such as end-of-lifecycle, compliance, or regulatory backups. Different methods of data retrieval are available at various speeds and cost. Retrieval can take from a few minutes to several hours.

Amazon S3 Glacier Deep Archive (DEEP_ARCHIVE)   This is the lowest-cost class designed for long-term retention of rarely accessed data. Data will be retained for 7–10 years and may be accessed about once or twice a year. When you need the data, you can retrieve it within 12 hours. This storage is ideal for maintaining backups of historical regulatory or compliance data and disaster recovery backups.

Block Storage

Amazon Elastic Block Store (Amazon EBS) volumes provide a durable block-storage option for use with Amazon EC2 instances. Use Amazon EBS for data that requires long-term persistence and quick access at assured levels of performance. There are two types of block storage: solid-state drive (SSD) storage and hard disk drive (HDD) storage.

SSD storage is optimized for transactional workloads wherein performance is closely tied to IOPS. Choose from two SSD volume options:

General Purpose SSD (gp2)   Designed for general use and offers a balance between cost and performance.

Provisioned IOPS SSD (io1)   Best for latency-sensitive workloads that require specific minimum-guaranteed IOPS. With io1 volumes, you pay separately for Provisioned IOPS, so unless you need high levels of Provisioned IOPS, gp2 volumes are a better match at lower cost.

HDD storage is designed for throughput-intensive workloads, such as data warehouses and log processing. There are two types of HDD volumes:

Throughput Optimized HDD (st1)   Best for frequently accessed, throughput-intensive workloads.

Cold HDD (sc1)   Designed for less frequently accessed, throughput-intensive workloads.

File Storage

Amazon Elastic File System (Amazon EFS) provides simple, scalable file storage for use with Amazon EC2 instances. Amazon EFS supports any number of instances at the same time. Amazon EFS is designed for workloads and applications such as big data, media-processing workflows, content management, and web serving.

Amazon S3 and Amazon EFS allocate storage based on your usage, and you pay for what you use. However, for EBS volumes, you are charged for provisioned (allocated) storage regardless of whether you use it or not. The key to keeping storage costs low without sacrificing required functionality is to maximize the use of Amazon S3 when possible and use more expensive EBS volumes with provisioned I/O only when application requirements demand it.

Optimize Amazon S3

Perform analysis on data access patterns, create inventory lists, and configure lifecycle policies. Identifying the right storage class and moving less frequently accessed Amazon S3 data to cheaper storage tiers yields considerable savings. For example, by moving data from the STANDARD to STANDARD_IA storage class, you can save up to 60 percent (on a per-gigabyte basis) of Amazon S3 pricing. By moving data that is at the end of its lifecycle and accessed on rare occasions from Amazon S3 Glacier, you can save up to 80 percent of Amazon S3 pricing.

Storage Management Tools/Features

The following sections detail some of the tools that help to determine when to transition data to another storage class.

Cost Allocation S3 Bucket Tags

To track the storage cost or other criteria for individual projects or groups of projects, label your Amazon S3 buckets using cost allocation tags. A *cost allocation tag* is a key-value pair that you associate with an S3 bucket. To manage storage data most effectively, you can use these tags to categorize your S3 objects and filter on these tags in your data lifecycle policies.

Amazon S3 Analytics: Storage Class Analysis

Use this feature to analyze storage access patterns to help you decide when to transition the right data to the right storage class. This feature observes data access patterns to help you determine when to transition less frequently accessed STANDARD storage to the STANDARD_IA storage class.

After storage class analysis observes the infrequent access patterns of a filtered set of data over a period of time, you can use the analysis results to help you improve your lifecycle policies. You can configure storage class analysis to analyze all the objects in a bucket. Alternatively, you can configure filters to group objects together for analysis by common prefix (that is, objects that have names that begin with a common string), by object tags, or by both prefix and tags. You'll most likely find that filtering by object groups is the best way to benefit from storage class analysis.

You can use the Amazon S3 console, the s3:PutAnalyticsConfiguration REST API, or the equivalent from the AWS CLI or AWS SDKs to configure storage class analysis.

Amazon S3 Inventory

This tool audits and reports on the replication and encryption status of your S3 objects on a weekly or monthly basis. This feature provides CSV output files that list objects and their corresponding metadata, and it lets you configure multiple inventory lists for a single bucket, organized by different Amazon S3 metadata tags. You can also query Amazon S3 inventory through standard SQL by using Amazon Athena, Amazon Redshift Spectrum, and other tools, such as Presto, Apache Hive, and Apace Spark.

Amazon CloudWatch

Amazon S3 can also publish storage, request, and data transfer metrics to Amazon CloudWatch. Storage metrics are reported daily, are available at one-minute intervals for granular visibility, and can be collected and reported for an entire bucket or a subset of objects (selected via prefix or tags).

Use Amazon S3 Select

Amazon S3 Select enables applications to retrieve only a subset of data from an object by using simple SQL expressions. By using Amazon S3 Select to retrieve only the data needed by your application, you can achieve drastic performance increases—in many cases, you can get as much as a 400 percent improvement.

Following is a Python sample code snippet that shows how to retrieve columns from an object containing data in CSV format. This code snippet retrieves the city and airport code, where country name is similar to "United States." If you have column headers and you set the `FileHeaderInfo` to `Use`, you can identify columns by name in the SQL expression.

```
result = s3.select_object_content(
        Bucket=example-bucket-us-west-2',
        Key='sample-data/airportCodes.csv',
        ExpressionType='SQL',
        Expression="select s.city, s.code from s3object s where" \
                "s.\"Country (Name)\" like '%United States%'",
        InputSerialization = {'CSV': {"FileHeaderInfo": "Use"}},
        OutputSerialization = {'CSV': {}},
:
```

Use Amazon Glacier Select

Amazon Glacier Select unlocks an opportunity to query your archived data easily. With Glacier Select, you can filter directly against an Amazon S3 Glacier object by using standard SQL statements.

It works like any other retrieval job, except for having an additional set of parameters (`SelectParameters`) that you can pass in an initiate job request.

The following is an example of a Python code snippet that shows how to pass an SQL expression under `SelectParameters`:

```
jobParameters = {
    "Type": "select", "ArchiveId": "ID",
    "Tier": "Expedited",
    "SelectParameters": {
        "InputSerialization": {"csv": {}},
        "ExpressionType": "SQL",
        "Expression": "SELECT * FROM archive WHERE _5='498960'",
        "OutputSerialization": {
            "csv": {}
        }
    }
}
```

With both Amazon S3 Select and Glacier Select, you can lower your costs and uncover more insights from your data, regardless of which storage tier it is in.

Optimize Amazon EBS

With Amazon EBS, you are paying for provisioned capacity and performance—even if the volume is unattached or has low write activity. To optimize storage performance and costs for Amazon EBS, monitor volumes periodically to identify ones that are unattached or appear to be underutilized or overutilized, and adjust provisioning to match actual usage.

Check Configuration

Follow these configuration guidelines

- To achieve the best performance consistently, launch instances as EBS optimized. For instances that are not EBS-optimized by default, you can enable EBS optimization when you launch the instances or enable EBS optimization after the instances are running.

  To enable this feature, you can use either the Amazon EC2 console or AWS Tools. For AWS CLI, use ebs-optimized with the command run-instances to enable EBS optimization when launching and with the command modify-instance-attribute to enable EBS optimization for a running instance.

- Choose an EBS-optimized instance that provides more dedicated EBS throughput than your application needs; otherwise, the Amazon EBS to Amazon EC2 connection becomes a performance bottleneck.

- New EBS volumes receive their maximum performance the moment that they are available and do not require initialization. However, storage blocks on volumes that were restored from snapshots must be initialized before you can access the block. This preliminary action takes time and can cause a significant increase in the latency of an I/O operation the first time each block is accessed.

- To achieve a higher level of performance for a file system than you can provision on a single volume, create a RAID 0 (zero) array. Consider using RAID 0 when I/O performance is more important than fault tolerance. For example, you could use it with a heavily used database where data replication is already set up separately.

Use Monitoring Tools

AWS offers tools that help you optimize block storage.

Amazon CloudWatch

Amazon CloudWatch automatically collects a range of data points for EBS volumes, and you can then set alarms on volume behavior.

Consider the following important metrics:

BurstBalance When your burst bucket is depleted, volume I/O credits (for gp2 volumes) or volume throughput credits (for st1 and sc1 volumes) are throttled to the baseline. Check the BurstBalance value to determine whether your volume is being throttled for this reason.

VolumeQueueLength If your I/O latency is higher than you require, check VolumeQueueLength to make sure that your application is not trying to drive more IOPS than you have provisioned. If your application requires a greater number of IOPS than your volume can provide, consider using a larger gp2 volume with a higher base performance level or an io1 volume with more Provisioned IOPS to achieve faster latencies.

VolumeReadBytes, VolumeWriteBytes, VolumeReadOps, VolumeWriteOps HDD-backed st1 and sc1 volumes are designed to perform best with workloads that take advantage of the 1,024 KiB maximum I/O size. To determine your volume's average I/O size, divide `VolumeWriteBytes` by `VolumeWriteOps`. The same calculation applies to read operations. If the average I/O size is below 64 KiB, increasing the size of the I/O operations sent to an st1 or sc1 volume should improve performance.

AWS Trusted Advisor

AWS Trusted Advisor is another way for you to analyze your infrastructure to identify unattached, underutilized, and overutilized EBS volumes.

Delete Unattached Amazon EBS Volumes

To find unattached EBS volumes, look for volumes that are *available*, which indicates that they are not attached to an Amazon EC2 instance. You can also look at network throughput and IOPS to determine whether there has been any volume activity over the previous two weeks, or you can look up the last time the EBS volume was attached. If the volume is in a nonproduction environment, hasn't been used in weeks, or hasn't been attached in a month, there is a good chance that you can delete it.

Before deleting a volume, store an Amazon EBS snapshot (a backup copy of an EBS volume) so that the volume can be quickly restored later if needed.

Resize or Change the EBS Volume Type

Identify volumes that are underutilized and downsize them or change the volume type. Monitor the read/write access of EBS volumes to determine whether throughput is low. If you have a current-generation EBS volume attached to a current-generation Amazon EC2 instance type, you can use the elastic volumes feature to change the size or volume type or (for an SSD io1 volume) adjust IOPS performance without detaching the volume.

Follow these tips:

- For General Purpose SSD gp2 volumes, optimize for capacity so that you're paying only for what you use.

- With Provisioned IOPS SSD io1 volumes, pay close attention to IOPS utilization rather than throughput, since you pay for IOPS directly. Provision 10–20 percent above maximum IOPS utilization.

- You can save by reducing Provisioned IOPS or by switching from a Provisioned IOPS SSD io1 volume type to a General Purpose SSD gp2 volume type.

- If the volume is 500 GB or larger, consider converting to a Cold HDD sc1 volume to save on your storage rate.

Delete Stale Amazon EBS Snapshots

If you have a backup policy that takes EBS volume snapshots daily or weekly, you will quickly accumulate snapshots. Check for stale snapshots that are more than 30 days old and delete them to reduce storage costs. Deleting a snapshot has no effect on the volume.

Optimizing Data Transfer

Optimizing data transfer ensures that you minimize data transfer costs. Review your user presence if global or local and how the data gets located in order to reduce the latency issues.

- Use *Amazon CloudFront*, a global content delivery network (CDN), to locate data closer to users. It caches data at edge locations across the world, which reduces the load on your resources. By using CloudFront, you can reduce the administrative effort in delivering content automatically to large numbers of users globally, with minimum latency. Depending on your application types, distribute your entire website, including dynamic, static, streaming, and interactive content through CloudFront instead of scaling out your infrastructure.

- *Amazon S3 transfer acceleration* enables fast transfer of files over long distances between your client and your S3 bucket. Transfer acceleration leverages Amazon CloudFront globally distributed edge locations to route data over an optimized network path. For a workload in an S3 bucket that has intensive GET requests, you should use Amazon S3 with CloudFront.

- When uploading large files, use *multipart uploads* with multiple parts uploading at once to help maximize network throughput. Multipart uploads provide the following advantages:

  - *Improved throughput*—You can upload parts in parallel to improve throughput.

  - *Quick recovery from any network issues*—Smaller part size minimizes the impact of restarting a failed upload due to a network error.

  - *Pause and resume object uploads*—You can upload object parts over time. After you initiate a multipart upload, there is no expiry; you must explicitly complete or abort the multipart upload.

  - *Begin an upload before you know the final object size*—You can upload an object as you are creating it.

- Using *Amazon Route 53*, you can reduce latency for your users by serving their requests from the AWS Region for which network latency is lowest. Amazon Route 53 latency-based routing lets you use Domain Name System (DNS) to route user requests to the AWS Region that will give your users the fastest response.

Caching

Caching improves application performance by storing frequently accessed data items in memory so that they can be retrieved without accessing the primary data store. Cached information might include the results of I/O-intensive database queries or the outcome of computationally intensive processing.

When the result set is not found in the cache, the application can calculate it or retrieve it from a database of expensive, slowly mutating third-party content and store it in the cache for subsequent requests.

Amazon ElastiCache

Amazon ElastiCache is a web service that makes it easy to deploy, operate, and scale an in-memory cache in the cloud. It supports two open-source, in-memory caching engines: Memcached and Redis.

- The *Memcached* caching engine is popular for database query results caching, session caching, webpage caching, API caching, and caching of objects such as images, files, and metadata. Memcached is also a great choice to store and manage session data for internet-scale applications in cases wherein persistence is not critical.

- *Redis* caching engine is a great choice for implementing a highly available in-memory cache to decrease data access latency, increase throughput, and ease the load off your relational or NoSQL database and application. Redis has disk persistence built in, and you can use it for long-lived data.

Lazy loading is a good caching strategy whereby you populate the cache only when an object is requested by the application, keeping the cache size manageable. Apply a lazy caching strategy anywhere in your application where you have data that is going to be read often but written infrequently. In a typical web or mobile app, for example, a user's profile rarely changes but is accessed throughout the application.

Amazon DynamoDB Accelerator (DAX)

Amazon DynamoDB Accelerator (DAX) is a fully managed, highly available, in-memory cache for Amazon DynamoDB. This feature delivers performance improvements from milliseconds to microseconds, for high throughput. DAX adds in-memory acceleration to your DynamoDB tables without requiring you to manage cache invalidation, data population, or clusters.

DAX is ideal for applications that require the fastest possible response time read operations but that are also cost-sensitive and require repeated reads against a large set of data. For example, consider an ecommerce system that has a one-day sale on a popular product that would sharply increase the demand or a long-running analysis of regional weather data that could temporarily consume all of the read capacity in a DynamoDB table. Naturally, these would negatively impact other applications that must access the same data.

Relational Databases and Amazon DynamoDB

Traditional *relational database management system (RDBMS)* platforms store data in a normalized relational structure that reduces hierarchical data structures to a set of common elements that are stored across multiple tables.

RDBMS platforms use an ad hoc query language (generally a flavor of SQL) to generate or materialize views of the normalized data to support application-layer access patterns.

A relational database system does not scale well for the following reasons:

- It normalizes data and stores it on multiple tables that require multiple queries to write to disk.

- It generally incurs the performance costs of an Atomicity, Consistency, Isolation, Durability (ACID)–compliant transaction system.

- It uses expensive joins to reassemble required views of query results.

For this reason, when your business requires a low-latency response to high-traffic queries, taking advantage of a NoSQL system generally makes technical and economic sense. Amazon DynamoDB helps solve the problems that limit relational system scalability by avoiding them.

DynamoDB scales well for these reasons:

- Schema flexibility lets Amazon DynamoDB store complex hierarchical data within a single item.

- Composite key design lets it store related items close together on the same table.

The following are some recommendations for maximizing performance and minimizing throughput costs when working with Amazon DynamoDB.

Apply NoSQL Design

NoSQL design requires a different mind-set than RDBMS design. For an RDBMS, you can create a normalized data model without thinking about access patterns. You can then extend it later when new questions and query requirements arise.

NoSQL design is different:

- For DynamoDB, by contrast, design your schema after you know the questions it needs to answer. Understanding the business problems and the application use cases up front is essential.

- Maintain as few tables as possible in an Amazon DynamoDB application. Most well-designed applications require only one table.

Keep Related Data Together

Keeping related data in proximity has a major impact on cost and performance. Instead of distributing related data items across multiple tables, keep related items in your NoSQL system as close together as possible.

Keep Fewer Tables

In general, maintain as few tables as possible in an Amazon DynamoDB application. Most well-designed applications require only one table, unless there is a specific reason for using multiple tables.

Distribute Workloads Evenly

The optimal usage of a table's provisioned throughput depends on the workload patterns of individual items and the partition key design.

Designing Partition Keys

The more distinct partition key values that your workload accesses, the more those requests are spread across the partitioned space. In general, you use your provisioned throughput more efficiently as the ratio of partition key values accessed to the total number of partition key values increases.

Table 16.1 provides a comparison of the provisioned throughput efficiency of some common partition key schemas.

TABLE 16.1   Samples of Partition Key Distributions

Partition Key Value	Uniformity
User ID, where the application has many users	Good
Status code, where there are only a few possible status codes	Bad
Item creation date, rounded to the nearest time period (for example, day, hour, or minute)	Bad
Device ID, where each device accesses data at relatively similar intervals	Good
Device ID, where even if there are many devices being tracked, one is by far more popular than all the others	Bad

If a single table has only a small number of partition key values, consider distributing your write operations across more distinct partition key values. Structure the primary key elements to avoid one "hot" (heavily requested) partition key value that slows the overall performance.

For example, consider a table with a composite primary key. The partition key represents the item's creation date, rounded to the nearest day. The sort key is an item identifier. On a given day, say 2014-07-09, all of the new items are written to that single partition key value (and corresponding physical partition).

If the table fits entirely into a single partition (considering growth of your data over time) and if your application's read and write throughput requirements don't exceed the read and write capabilities of a single partition, your application won't encounter any unexpected throttling because of partitioning.

Implementing Write Sharding

One better way to distribute writes across a partition key space in DynamoDB is to expand the space. One strategy for distributing loads more evenly across a partition key space is to add a random number or a calculated hash suffix to the end of the partition key values. Then you can randomize the writes across the larger space. A randomizing strategy can greatly improve write throughput.

For example, in the case of a partition key that represents today's date in the Order table, suppose that each item has an accessible OrderId attribute and that you most often need to find items by OrderId in addition to date. Before your application writes the item to the table, it could calculate a hash suffix based on the OrderId (similar to OrderId, modulo 200, + 1) and append it to the partition key date. The calculation might generate a number between 1 and 200 that is fairly evenly distributed, similar to what the random strategy produces.

With this strategy, the writes are spread evenly across the partition key values and thus across the physical partitions. You can easily perform a GetItem operation for a particular item and date because you can calculate the partition key value for a specific OrderId value.

Upload Data Efficiently

Typically, when you load data from other data sources, Amazon DynamoDB partitions your table data on multiple servers. You get better performance if you upload data to all the allocated servers simultaneously.

For example, suppose that you want to upload user messages to a DynamoDB table that uses a composite primary key with UserID as the partition key and MessageID as the sort key.

You can distribute your upload work by using the sort key to load one item from each partition key value, then another item from each partition key value, and so on.

Every upload in this sequence uses a different partition key value, keeping more DynamoDB servers busy simultaneously and improving your throughput performance.

Use Sort Keys for Version Control

Many applications need to maintain a history of item-level revisions for audit or compliance purposes and to be able to retrieve the most recent version easily.

For each new item, create two copies of the item. One copy should have a version-number prefix of zero (for example, v0) at the beginning of the sort key, and one should have a version-number prefix of one (for example, v001_).

Every time the item is updated, use the next higher version prefix in the sort key of the updated version and copy the updated contents into the item with the version prefix of zero. This means that the latest version of any item can be located easily by using the zero prefix.

Keep the Number of Indexes to a Minimum

Create secondary indexes on attributes that are queried often. Indexes that are seldom used contribute to increased storage and I/O costs without improving application performance.

Choose Projections Carefully

Because secondary indexes consume storage and provisioned throughput, keep the size of the index as small as possible. Also, the smaller the index, the greater the performance advantage compared to querying the full table. Project only the attributes that you regularly request. Every time you update an attribute that is projected in an index, you incur the extra cost of updating the index as well.

Optimize Frequent Queries to Avoid Fetches

To get the fastest queries with the lowest possible latency, project all of the attributes that you expect those queries to return. In particular, if you query a local secondary index for attributes that are not projected, Amazon DynamoDB automatically fetches those attributes from the table, which requires reading the entire item from the table. This introduces latency and additional I/O operations that you can avoid.

Use Sparse Indexes

For any item in a table, Amazon DynamoDB writes a corresponding index entry only if the index sort key value is present in the item. If the sort key doesn't appear in every table item, the index is said to be sparse.

Sparse indexes are useful for queries over a small subsection of a table. It's faster and less expensive to query that index than to scan the entire table.

For example, suppose that you have a table in which you store all of your customer orders with the following key attributes:

Partition key: `CustomerId`

Sort key: `OrderId`

To track open orders, you can insert the `OrderOpenDate` attribute set to the date on which each order was placed and then delete it after the order is fulfilled. If you then create an index on `CustomerId` (partition key) and `OrderOpenDate` (sort key), only those orders with `OrderOpenDate` defined appear in it. That way, when you query the sparse index, the items returned are the orders that are unfulfilled and sorted by the date on which each order was placed.

Avoid Scans as Much as Possible

In general, `Scan` operations are less efficient than other operations in DynamoDB. A *Scan operation* scans the entire table or secondary index. It then filters out values to provide the result you want.

If possible, avoid using a `Scan` operation on a large table or index with a filter that removes many results. Also, as a table or index grows, the `Scan` operation slows down. The `Scan` operation examines every item for the requested values and can use up the provisioned throughput for a large table or index in a single operation.

This usage of capacity units by a scan prevents other potentially more important requests for the same table from using the available capacity units. As a result, you'll likely get a `ProvisionedThroughputExceeded` exception for those requests.

For faster response times, design your tables and indexes so that your applications can use `Query` instead of `Scan`. (For tables, you can also consider using the `GetItem` and APIs.) `GetItem` is highly efficient because it provides direct access to the physical location of the item.

Monitoring Costs

When you measure and monitor your users and applications and combine the data you collect with data from AWS monitoring tools, you can perform a gap analysis that tells you how closely aligned your system utilization is to your requirements. By working continually to minimize this utilization gap, you can ensure that your systems are cost effective.

Over time, you can continue to reduce cost with continuous monitoring and tagging. Similar to application development, cost optimization is an iterative process. Because your application and its usage will evolve over time and because AWS iterates frequently and regularly releases new options, it is important to evaluate your solution continuously.

Cost Management Tools

AWS provides tools to help you identify those cost-saving opportunities and keep your resources right-sized. Use these tools to help you access, organize, understand, control, and optimize your costs.

AWS Trusted Advisor

AWS Trusted Advisor is an online tool that provides you with real-time guidance to help you provision your resources following AWS best practices.

Whether you're establishing new workflows or developing applications, or as part of ongoing improvements, take advantage of the recommendations provided by Trusted Advisor on a regular basis. By reviewing the recommendations, you can look for opportunities to save money.

Here are some Trusted Advisor checks that help you determine how to reduce your bill:

- Low utilization of Amazon EC2 instances
- Idle resources, such as load balancers and Amazon RDS DB instances
- Underutilized Amazon EBS volumes and Amazon Redshift clusters
- Unassociated Elastic IP addresses
- Optimization, lease expiration—Amazon Reserved Instances
- Inefficiently configured Amazon Route 53 latency record sets

AWS Cost Explorer

Use the *AWS Cost Explorer* tool to dive deeper into your cost and usage data to identify trends, pinpoint cost drivers, and detect anomalies. It includes Amazon EC2 usage reports, which let you analyze the cost and usage of your Amazon EC2 instances over the last 13 months. You can analyze your cost and usage data in aggregate (such as total costs and usage across all accounts) down to granular details (for example, m2.2xlarge costs within the Dev account tagged *"project: GuardDuty"*).

AWS Cost Explorer built-in reports include the following:

Monthly Costs by AWS Service   Allows you to visualize the costs and usage associated with your top five cost-accruing AWS services and gives you a detailed breakdown on all services in the table view. The reports let you adjust the time range to view historical data going back up to 12 months to gain an understanding of your cost trends.

Amazon EC2 Monthly Cost and Usage   Lets you view all AWS costs over the past two months, in addition to your current month-to-date costs. From there, you can drill down into the costs and usage associated with particular linked accounts, regions, tags, and more.

Monthly Costs by Linked Account   Allows you to view the distribution of costs across your organization.

Monthly Running Costs   Provides an overview of all running costs over the past three months and provides forecasted numbers for the coming month with a corresponding confidence interval. This report gives you good insight into how your costs are trending and helps you plan ahead.

AWS Cost Explorer Reserved Instance Reports include the following:

RI Utilization Report   Visualize the degree to which you are using your existing resources and identify opportunities to improve your Reserved Instance cost efficiencies. The report shows how much you saved by using Reserved Instances, how much you overspent on Reserved Instances, and your net savings from purchasing Reserved Instances during the selected time range. This helps you to determine whether you have purchased too many Reserved Instances.

RI Coverage Report   Discover how much of your overall instance usage is covered by Reserved Instances so that you can make informed decisions about when to purchase or modify a Reserved Instance to ensure maximum coverage. These show how much you spent on On-Demand Instances and how much you might have saved had you purchased more reservations. The report enables you to determine whether you have under-purchased Reserved Instances.

AWS Cost Explorer API

Use *AWS Cost Explorer API* to query your cost and usage data programmatically (using AWS CLI or AWS SDKs). You can query for aggregated data such as total monthly costs or total daily usage. You can also query for granular data, such as the number of daily write operations for Amazon DynamoDB database tables in your production environment. All of the AWS

SDKs greatly simplify the process of signing requests and save you a significant amount of time when compared with using the AWS Cost Explorer API.

You can access your Amazon EC2 Reserved Instance purchase recommendations programmatically through the AWS Cost Explorer API. Recommendations for Reserved Instance purchases are calculated based on your past usage and indicate opportunities for potential cost savings.

The following example retrieves recommendations for Partial Upfront Amazon EC2 instances with a three-year term based on the last 60 days of Amazon EC2 usage.

Here's the AWS CLI command:

```
aws ce get-reservation-purchase-recommendation --service "Amazon Redshift"
--lookback-period-in-days SIXTY_DAYS --term-in-years THREE_YEARS --payment-
option PARTIAL_UPFRONT
```

Here's the output:

```
{
    "Recommendations": [],
    "Metadata": {
        "GenerationTimestamp": "2018-08-08T15:20:57Z",
        "RecommendationId": "00d59dde-a1ad-473f-8ff2-iexample3330b"
    }
}
```

AWS Budgets

With *AWS Budgets*, you can set custom budgets that alert you when your costs or usage exceed (or are forecasted to exceed) your budgeted amount. You can also use AWS Budgets to set Reserved Instance utilization or coverage targets and receive alerts when your utilization drops below the threshold you define. Reserved Instance alerts support Amazon EC2, Amazon RDS, Amazon Redshift, and Amazon ElastiCache reservations.

Budgets can be tracked at the monthly, quarterly, or yearly level, and you can customize the start and end dates. You can further refine your budget to track costs associated with multiple dimensions, such as AWS service, linked account, tag, and others. You can send budget alerts through email or Amazon Simple Notification Service (Amazon SNS) topic. For example, you can set notifications that alert you if you accrue 80, 90, and 100 percent of your actual budgeted costs in addition to a notification that alerts you if you are forecasted to exceed your budget.

AWS Cost and Usage Report

The *AWS Cost and Usage Report* tracks your AWS usage and provides estimated charges associated with that usage. You can configure this report to present the data hourly or daily. It is updated at least once a day until it is finalized at the end of the billing period. The AWS Cost and Usage report gives you the most granular insight possible into your costs and usage, and it is the source of truth for the billing pipeline. It can be used to develop advanced custom metrics using business intelligence, data analytics, and third-party cost optimization tools.

The AWS Cost and Usage report is delivered automatically to an S3 bucket that you specify, and it can be downloaded directly from there (standard Amazon S3 storage rates apply). It can also be ingested into Amazon Redshift or uploaded to Amazon QuickSight.

Amazon CloudWatch

Amazon CloudWatch is a monitoring service for AWS Cloud resources and the applications you run on AWS. You can use Amazon CloudWatch to collect and track metrics and log files, set alarms, and automatically react to changes in your AWS resources. You can create an alarm to perform one or more of the following actions based on the value of the metric:

- Automatically stop or terminate Amazon EC2 instances that have gone unused or underutilized for too long
- Stop your instance if it has an EBS volume as its root device

For example, you may run development or test instances and occasionally forget to shut them off. You can create an alarm that is triggered when the average CPU utilization percentage has been lower than 10 percent for 24 hours, signaling that it is idle and no longer in use. You can create a group of alarms that first sends an email notification to developers whose instance has been underutilized for 8 hours and then terminates that instance if its utilization has not improved after 24 hours.

Amazon CloudWatch Events deliver a near real-time stream of system events that describe changes in AWS resources. Using simple rules, you can route each type of event to one or more targets, such as Lambda functions, Amazon Kinesis streams, and Amazon SNS topics.

AWS Cost Optimization Monitor

AWS Cost Optimization Monitor is an automated reference deployment solution that processes detailed billing reports to provide granular metrics that you can search, analyze, and visualize in a customizable dashboard. The solution uploads detailed billing report data automatically to Amazon Elasticsearch Service (Amazon ES) for analysis and leverages its built-in support for Kibana, enabling you to visualize the first batch of data as soon as it's processed.

The default dashboard is configured to show specific cost and usage metrics. All of these metrics, as listed here, were selected based on best practices observed across AWS customers:

- Amazon EC2 Instances Running per Hour
- Total Cost
- Cost by Tag Key: Name
- Cost by Amazon EC2 Instance Type
- Amazon EC2 Elasticity
- Amazon EC2 Hours per Dollar Invested

Cost Optimization: Amazon EC2 Right Sizing

Amazon EC2 Right Sizing is an automated AWS reference deployment solution that uses managed services to perform a right-sizing analysis and offer detailed recommendations for more cost-effective instances. The solution analyzes two weeks of utilization data to provide detailed recommendations for right sizing your Amazon EC2 instances.

Monitoring Performance

After you have implemented your architecture, monitor its performance so that you can remediate any issues before your customers are aware of them. Use monitoring metrics to raise alarms when thresholds are breached. The alarm can trigger automated action to work around any components with poor performance.

AWS provides tools that you can use to monitor the performance, reliability, and availability of your resources on the AWS Cloud.

Amazon CloudWatch

Amazon CloudWatch is essential to performance efficiency, which provides system-wide visibility into resource utilization, application performance, and operational health.

You can create an alarm to monitor any Amazon CloudWatch metric in your account. For example, you can create alarms on an Amazon EC2 instance CPU utilization, Elastic Load Balancing request latency, Amazon DynamoDB table throughput, or Amazon SQS queue length.

In the following example, AWS CLI is used to create an alarm to send an Amazon SNS email message when CPU utilization exceeds 70 percent:

```
aws cloudwatch put-metric-alarm --alarm-name cpu-mon --alarm-description
"Alarm when CPU exceeds 70 percent" --metric-name CPUUtilization --namespace
AWS/EC2 --statistic Average --period 300 --threshold 70 --comparison-operator
GreaterThanThreshold  --dimensions "Name=InstanceId,Value=i-12345678"
--evaluation-periods 2 --alarm-actions arn:aws:sns:us-east-
1:111122223333:MyTopic --unit Percent
```

Here are a few examples of when and how alarms are sent:

- Sends an email message using Amazon SNS when the average CPU use of an Amazon EC2 instance exceeds a specified threshold for consecutive specified periods

- Sends an email when an instance exceeds 10 GB of outbound network traffic per day

- Stops an instance and sends a text message (SMS) when outbound traffic exceeds 1 GB per hour

- Stops an instance when memory utilization reaches or exceeds 90 percent so that application logs can be retrieved for troubleshooting

AWS Trusted Advisor

AWS Trusted Advisor inspects your AWS environment and makes recommendations that help to improve the speed and responsiveness of your applications.

The following are a few Trusted Advisor checks to improve the performance of your service. The Trusted Advisor checks your service limits, ensuring that you take advantage of provisioned throughput, and monitors for overutilized instances:

- Amazon EC2 instances that are consistently at high utilization can indicate optimized, steady performance, but this check can also indicate that an application does not have enough resources.

- Provisioned IOPS (SSD) volumes that are attached to an Amazon EC2 instance that is not Amazon EBS–optimized. Amazon EBS volumes are designed to deliver the expected performance only when they are attached to an EBS-optimized instance.

- Amazon EC2 security groups with a large number of rules.

- Amazon EC2 instances that have a large number of security group rules.

- Amazon EBS magnetic volumes (standard) that are potentially overutilized and might benefit from a more efficient configuration.

- CloudFront distributions for alternate domain names with incorrectly configured DNS settings.

    Some HTTP request headers, such as Date or User-Agent, significantly reduce the cache hit ratio. This increases the load on your origin and reduces performance because CloudFront must forward more requests to your origin.

Summary

In this chapter, you learned about the following:

- Cost-optimizing practices
- Right sizing your infrastructure
- Optimizing using Reserved Instances, Spot Instances, and AWS Auto Scaling
- Optimizing storage and data transfer
- Optimizing using NoSQL database (Amazon DynamoDB)
- Monitoring your costs and performance
- Tools, such as AWS Trusted Advisor, Amazon CloudWatch, and AWS Budgets

Achieving an optimized system is a continual process. An optimized system uses all the provisioned resources efficiently and achieves your business goal at the lowest price point. Engineers must know the cost of deploying resources and how to architect for cost optimization. Practice eliminating the waste and bring accountability in every step of the build process. Use mandatory cost tags on all of your resources to gain precise insights into usage. Define IAM policies to enforce tag usage, and use tagging tools, such as AWS Config and AWS Tag Editor, to manage tags. Be cost-conscious, reduce the usage by terminating unused instances, and delete old snapshots and unused keys.

Right size your infrastructure by matching instance types and sizes, and set periodic checks to ensure that the initial provision remains optimum as your business changes over time. With Amazon EC2, you can choose the combination of instance types and sizes most appropriate for your applications. Amazon RDS instances are also optimized for memory, performance, and I/O.

Amazon EC2 Reserved Instances provide you with a significant discount (up to 75 percent) compared to On-Demand Instance pricing. Using Convertible Reserved Instances, you can change instance families, OS types, and tenancies while benefitting from Reserved Instance pricing. Reserved Instance Marketplace allows you to sell the unused Reserved Instances or buy them from other AWS customers, usually at lower prices and shorter terms. With size flexibility, discounted rates for Amazon RDS Reserved Instances are automatically applied to the usage of any size within the instance family.

Spot Instances provide an additional option for obtaining compute capacity at a reduced cost and can be used along with On-Demand and Reserved Instances. Spot Fleets enable you to launch and maintain the target capacity and to request resources automatically to replace any that are disrupted or manually terminated. Using the termination notices and persistent requests in your application design help to maintain continuity as the result of interruptions.

AWS Auto Scaling automatically scales if your application experiences variable load and uses one or more scalable resources, such as Amazon ECS, Amazon DynamoDB, Amazon Aurora, Amazon EC2 Spot requests, and Amazon EC2 scaling groups. Predictive Scaling uses machine learning models to forecast daily and weekly patterns. Amazon EC2 Auto Scaling enables you to scale in response to demand and known load schedules. It supports the provisioning of scale instances across purchase options, Availability Zones, and instance families to optimize performance and cost.

Containers provide process isolation and improve the resource utilization. Amazon ECS lets you easily build all types of containerized applications and launch thousands of containers in seconds with no additional complexity. With AWS Fargate technology, you can manage containers without having to provision or manage servers. It enables you to focus on building and running applications, not the underlying infrastructure.

AWS Lambda takes care of receiving events or client invocations and then instantiates and runs the code. That means there's no need to manage servers. Serverless services have built-in automatic scaling, availability, and fault tolerance. These features allow you to focus on product innovation and rapidly construct applications, such as web applications, websites, web-hooked systems, chatbots, and clickstream.

AWS storage services are optimized to meet different storage requirements. Use the Amazon S3 analytics feature to analyze storage access patterns to help you decide when to transition the right data to the right storage class and to yield considerable savings. Monitor Amazon EBS volumes periodically to identify ones that are unattached or appear to be underutilized or overutilized, and adjust provisioning to match actual usage.

Optimizing data transfer ensures that you minimize data transfer costs. Use options such as Amazon CloudFront, Amazon S3 transfer acceleration, and Amazon Route 53 to let data reach Regions faster and reduce latency issues.

NoSQL database systems like Amazon DynamoDB use alternative models for data management, such as key-value pairs or document storage. DynamoDB enables you to offload the administrative burdens of operating and scaling a distributed database so that you don't have to worry about hardware provisioning, setup and configuration, replication, software patching, or cluster scaling. Follow best practices, such as distributing data evenly, effective partition and sort keys usage, efficient data scanning, and using sparse indexes for maximizing performance and minimizing throughput costs, when working with Amazon DynamoDB.

AWS provides several tools to help you identify those cost-saving opportunities and keep your resources right-sized. AWS Trusted Advisor inspects your AWS environment to identify idle and underutilized resources and provides real-time insight into service usage to help you improve system performance and save money. Amazon CloudWatch collects and tracks metrics, monitors log files, sets alarms, and reacts to changes in AWS resources automatically. AWS Cost Explorer checks patterns in AWS spend over time, projects future costs, identifies areas that need further inquiry, and provides Reserved Instance recommendations.

Optimization is an ongoing process. Always stay current with the pace of AWS new releases, and assess your existing design solutions to ensure that they remain cost-effective.

Exam Essentials

Know the importance of tagging.   By using tags, you can assign metadata to AWS resources. This tagging makes it easier to manage, search for, and filter resources in billing reports and automation activities and when setting up access controls.

Know about various tagging tools and how to enforce the tag rules.   With AWS Tag Editor, you can add tags to multiple resources at once, search for the resources that you want to tag, and then add, remove, or edit tags for the resources in your search results. AWS Config identifies resources that do not comply with tagging policies. You can use IAM policy conditions to force the usage of tags while creating the resources.

Know the fundamental practices in reducing the usage.   Follow the best practices of cost optimization in every step of your build process, such as turning off unused resources, spinning up instances only when needed, and spinning them down when not in use. Use tagging to help with the cost allocation. Use Amazon EC2 Spot Instances, Amazon EC2, and Reserved Instances where appropriate, and use alerts, notifications, and cost-management tools to stay on track.

Know the various usage patterns for right sizing.   By understanding your business use case and backing up the analysis with performance metrics, you can choose the most appropriate options, such as steady state; variable; predictable, but temporary; and development, test, and production usage.

Know the various instance families for right sizing and the corresponding use cases. Amazon EC2 provides a wide selection of instances to match capacity needs at the lowest cost and comes with different options for CPU, memory, and network resources. The families include General Purpose, Compute Optimized, Memory Optimized, Storage Optimized, and Accelerated Computing.

Know Amazon EC2 Auto Scaling benefits and how this feature can make your solutions more optimized and highly available. AWS Auto Scaling is a fast, easy way to optimize the performance and costs of your applications. It makes smart scaling decisions based on your preferences, automatically maintains performance even when your workloads are periodic, unpredictable, and continuously changing.

Know how to create a single AWS Auto Scaling group to scale instances across different purchase options. You can provision and automatically scale Amazon EC2 capacity across different Amazon EC2 instance types, Availability Zones, and On-Demand, Reserved Instances, and Spot purchase options in a single AWS Auto Scaling group. You can define the desired split between On-Demand and Spot capacity, select which instance types work for your application, and specify preferences for how Amazon EC2 Auto Scaling should distribute the AWS Auto Scaling group capacity within each purchasing model.

Know how block, object, and file storages are different. Block storage is commonly dedicated, low-latency storage for each host, and it is provisioned with each instance. Object storage is developed for the cloud, has vast scalability, is accessed over the web, and is not directly attached to an instance. File storage enables accessing shared files as a file system.

Know key CloudWatch metrics available to measure the Amazon EBS efficiency and how to use them. CloudWatch metrics are statistical data that you can use to view, analyze, and set alarms on the operational behavior of your volumes. Depending on your needs, set alarms and response actions that correspond to each data point. For example, if your I/O latency is higher than you require, check the metric VolumeQueueLength to make sure that your application is not trying to drive more IOPS than you have provisioned. Review and learn more about the available metrics that help optimize the block storage.

Know tools and features that help in efficient data transfer. Using Amazon CloudFront, you can locate data closer to users and reduce administrative efforts to minimize data transfer costs. Amazon S3 Transfer Acceleration enables fast data transfer over an optimized network path. Use the multipart upload file option while uploading a large file to improve network throughput.

Know key differences between RDBMS and NoSQL databases to design efficient solutions using Amazon DynamoDB. Schema flexibility and the ability to store related items together make DynamoDB a solution for solving problems associated with changing business needs and scalability issues unlike relational databases.

Know the importance of distributing the data evenly when designing DynamoDB tables. Use provisioned throughput more efficiently by making the partition key more distinct. That way, data spreads throughout the provisioned space. Use the sort key with the partition key to make a unique key to achieve better performance while uploading data simultaneously.

Know the different ways to read data from DynamoDB tables to avoid scans.   DynamoDB provides Query and Scan actions to read data from a table and does not support table joins. DynamoDB provides the GetItem action for retrieving an item by its primary key. GetItem is highly efficient because it provides direct access to the physical location of the item. The scan always scans the entire table and can consume large amounts of system resources.

Know the AWS Cost Management tools and their features.   AWS provides tools to help you manage, monitor, and, ultimately, optimize your costs. Use AWS Cost Explorer for deeper dives into the cost drivers. Use AWS Trusted Advisor to inspect your AWS infrastructure to identify overutilized or idle resources. AWS Budgets enables you to set custom cost and usage budgets and receive alerts when budgets approach or exceed the limits. There are a wide range of tools to explore, such as AWS Cost Optimization – Amazon EC2 Right Sizing, and monitoring tools to identify additional savings opportunities.

Know how the AWS Trusted Advisor features help in saving costs and improving the performance of your solutions.   AWS Trusted Advisor scans your AWS environment, compares it to AWS best practices, and makes recommendations for saving money, improving system performance, and more. Cost Optimization recommendations highlight unused and underutilized resources. Performance recommendations help to improve the speed and responsiveness of your applications.

Know how to evaluate the reporting details in the AWS Cost Explorer default reports.   Cost Explorer provides you with default reports: Cost and Usage reports and Reserved Instance reports. Cost and Usage reports include your daily costs and monthly costs by service, listing the top five services. These reports help you to determine whether you have purchased too many Reserved Instances. The Reserved Instance Coverage reports show how many of your instance hours are covered by Reserved Instances, how much you spent on On-Demand Instances, and how much you might have saved had you purchased more reservations. This enables you to determine whether you have under-purchased Reserved Instances.

Know how to extract recommendations using AWS Cost Explorer API.   The Cost Explorer API allows you to use either AWS CLI or SDKs to query your cost and usage data. You can query for aggregated data, such as total monthly costs or total daily usage. You can also query for granular data, such as the number of daily write operations for DynamoDB database tables in your production environment.

Know all of the Amazon CloudWatch metrics and how to set alarms.   With Amazon CloudWatch, you can observe CPU utilization, network throughput, and disk I/O, and match the observed peak metrics to a new and cheaper instance type. You choose a CloudWatch metric and threshold for the alarm to watch. The alarm turns into the alarm state when the metric breaches the threshold for a specified number of evaluation periods. Use the Amazon CloudWatch console, AWS CLI, or AWS SDKs for creating or managing alarms.

Know how AWS Lambda integrates with other AWS serverless services to build cost-effective solutions.   AWS Lambda provides the cloud-logic layer and integrates seamlessly with the other serverless services to build virtually any type of application or backend service. For example, Amazon S3 automatically triggers Lambda functions when an object is created, copied, or deleted. Lambda functions can process Amazon SQS messages.

Resources to Review

AWS Well-Architected Framework (Whitepaper):

> https://d1.awsstatic.com/whitepapers/architecture/AWS_Well-Architected_
> Framework.pdf

Cost Optimization Pillar–AWS Well-Architected Framework (Whitepaper):

> https://d1.awsstatic.com/whitepapers/architecture/AWS-Cost-
> Optimization-Pillar.pdf

Performance Efficiency Pillar–AWS Well-Architected Framework (Whitepaper):

> https://d0.awsstatic.com/whitepapers/architecture/AWS-Performance-
> Efficiency-Pillar.pdf

Cost Management in the AWS Cloud (Whitepaper):

> https://d1.awsstatic.com/whitepapers/aws-tco-2-cost-management.pdf

Architecting for the Cloud–AWS Best Practices (Whitepaper):

> https://d1.awsstatic.com/whitepapers/AWS_Cloud_Best_Practices.pdf

Creating a Culture of Cost Transparency and Accountability (Whitepaper):

> https://d1.awsstatic.com/whitepapers/cost-optimization-transparency-
> accountability.pdf

Maximizing Value with AWS (Whitepaper):

> https://d1.awsstatic.com/whitepapers/total-cost-of-operation-benefits-
> using-aws.pdf

Laying the Foundation: Setting Up Your Environment for Cost Optimization (Whitepaper):

> https://docs.aws.amazon.com/whitepapers/latest/cost-optimization-
> laying-the-foundation/introduction.html

Right Sizing: Provisioning Instances to Match Workloads (Whitepaper):

> https://d1.awsstatic.com/whitepapers/cost-optimization-right-sizing.pdf

AWS Storage Optimization (Whitepaper):

> https://docs.aws.amazon.com/whitepapers/latest/cost-optimization-
> storage-optimization/introduction.html

AWS Storage Services Overview (Whitepaper):

> https://d1.awsstatic.com/whitepapers/AWS Storage Services
> Whitepaper-v9.pdf

Optimizing Enterprise Economics with Serverless Architectures (Whitepaper):

https://d0.awsstatic.com/whitepapers/optimizing-enterprise-economics-serverless-architectures.pdf

Serverless Architectures with AWS Lambda (Whitepaper):

https://d1.awsstatic.com/whitepapers/serverless-architectures-with-aws-lambda.pdf

Cloud Storage with AWS:

https://aws.amazon.com/products/storage/

Tagging Your Amazon EC2 Resources:

https://docs.aws.amazon.com/AWSEC2/latest/UserGuide/Using_Tags.html

Amazon EC2 Instance Types:

https://aws.amazon.com/ec2/instance-types/

Amazon EC2 Reserved Instances:

https://aws.amazon.com/ec2/pricing/reserved-instances/

Amazon RDS Reserved Instances:

https://aws.amazon.com/rds/reserved-instances/

Amazon EC2 Spot Instances:

https://aws.amazon.com/ec2/spot/

AWS Auto Scaling:

https://aws.amazon.com/blogs/aws/category/auto-scaling/

Containers on AWS:

https://aws.amazon.com/containers/services/

Automatic Scaling for Spot Fleet:

https://docs.aws.amazon.com/AWSEC2/latest/UserGuide/spot-fleet-automatic-scaling.html

Using Amazon Aurora Auto Scaling with Aurora Replicas:

https://docs.aws.amazon.com/AmazonRDS/latest/AuroraUserGuide/Aurora.Integrating.AutoScaling.html

Amazon Elastic Container Service:

https://docs.aws.amazon.com/ecs/index.html#lang/en_us.

Best Practices for DynamoDB:

https://docs.aws.amazon.com/amazondynamodb/latest/developerguide/best-practices.html

AWS Trusted Advisor:

https://aws.amazon.com/premiumsupport/technology/trusted-advisor/.

Analyzing Your Costs with Cost Explorer:

> https://docs.aws.amazon.com/awsaccountbilling/latest/aboutv2/
> ce-what-is.html

Using Amazon CloudWatch Alarms:

> https://docs.aws.amazon.com/AmazonCloudWatch/latest/monitoring/
> AlarmThatSendsEmail.html

AWS re:Invent 2014 | (ENT302) Cost Optimization on AWS (Video):

> https://www.youtube.com/watch?v=mqY8xfKU5yE

Exercises

 Before you begin this task, you must first create an SNS topic (name: myHighCpuAlarm) and subscribe to it.

EXERCISE 16.1

Set Up a CPU Usage Alarm Using AWS CLI

In this exercise, you will use the AWS CLI to create a CPU usage alarm that sends an email message using Amazon SNS when the CPU usage exceeds 70 percent.

1. Set up an SNS topic with the name **myHighCpuAlarm** and subscribe to it. For more information, see this article:

    https://docs.aws.amazon.com/AmazonCloudWatch/latest/monitoring/US_
    SetupSNS.html

2. Create an alarm using the put-metric-alarm command as follows:

```
aws cloudwatch put-metric-alarm \
    --alarm-name cpu-mon \
    --alarm-description "Alarm when CPU exceeds 70%" \
    --metric-name CPUUtilization \
    --namespace AWS/EC2 \
    --statistic Average \
    --period 300 \
    --threshold 70 \
    --comparison-operator GreaterThanThreshold \
    --dimensions Name=InstanceId,Value=i-12345678 \
    --evaluation-periods 2 \
    --alarm-actions arn:aws:sns:us-east-1:111122223333:myHighCpuAlarm \
    --unit Percent
```

For Windows, replace the backslash (\) Unix continuation character at the end of each line with a caret (^).

3. Test the alarm by forcing an alarm state change using the set-alarm-state command.

   a. Change the alarm state from INSUFFICIENT_DATA to OK.

   aws cloudwatch set-alarm-state --alarm-name cpu-mon --state-reason "initializing" --state-value OK

   b. Change the alarm state from OK to ALARM.

   aws cloudwatch set-alarm-state –alarm-name cpu-mon --state-reason "initializing" --state-value ALARM

   c. Check that you have received an email notification about the alarm.

Using AWS CLI, you created a CPU alarm that sends an email notification when CPU usage exceeds 70 percent. You tested it by manually changing its alarm state to ALARM.

EXERCISE 16.2

Modify Amazon EBS Optimization for a Running Instance

In this exercise, you will use the Amazon EC2 console to enable the optimization for a running instance by modifying its Amazon EBS optimized instance attribute.

1. Open the Amazon EC2 console at https://console.aws.amazon.com/ec2/.

2. In the navigation pane, click **Instances**, and select the instance.

3. Choose **Actions** ➢ **Instance State** ➢ **Stop**.

4. In the **Confirmation** dialog box, choose **Yes** ➢ **Stop**.

   It can take a few minutes for the instance to stop.

5. With the instance still selected, choose **Actions** ➢ **Instance Settings** and then choose **Change Instance Type**.

6. In the **Change Instance Type** dialog box, do one of the following:

   a. If the instance type of your instance is Amazon EBS–optimized, **EBS-optimized** is selected by default, and you cannot change it. Choose **Cancel**.

   b. If the instance type of your instance supports Amazon EBS optimization, choose **EBS-optimized** ➢ **Apply**.

(continued)

EXERCISE 16.2 *(continued)*

   c. If the instance type of your instance does not support Amazon EBS optimization, select an instance type from **Instance Type** that supports Amazon EBS optimization and then choose **EBS-optimized** ➢ **Apply**.

7. Choose **Actions** ➢ **Instance State** ➢ **Start**.

You enabled the EBS optimization feature for a running Amazon EC2 instance using AWS Console.

 When you stop an instance, the data on any instance store volumes is erased. To keep data in instance store volumes, back it up to persistent storage.

EXERCISE 16.3

Create an AWS Config Rule

In this exercise, using the AWS Management Console, you will create an AWS Config rule to monitor whether Elastic IP addresses are attached to Amazon EC2 instances.

1. Create an Elastic IP address to be used as part of this exercise, but do not attach it to any Amazon EC2 instance. See the following for instructions:

https://docs.aws.amazon.com/AWSEC2/latest/UserGuide/elastic-ip-addresses-eip.html#using-instance-addressing-eips-releasing

2. Open the AWS Config console at https://console.aws.amazon.com/config/.

3. Choose **Get Started Now**.

4. On the **Settings** page, for **Resource types to record**, select **All resources**.

5. For **Amazon S3 Bucket**, select the Amazon S3 bucket to which AWS Config sends configuration history and configuration snapshot files.

6. For **Amazon SNS Topic**, select whether AWS Config streams information by selecting the **Stream configuration changes and notifications to an Amazon SNS topic**.

7. For **Topic Name**, type a name for your SNS topic.

8. For **Bucket Name**, type a name for your Amazon S3 bucket.

9. For **AWS Config role**, choose the IAM role that grants AWS Config permission to record configuration information and send this information to Amazon S3 and Amazon SNS.

10. Choose **Create AWS Config service-linked role**, and then **Next**.

11. On the **AWS Config Role** page, in the search bar, enter **eip** to find a specific rule from the list.

12. Select the **eip-attached** rule.

13. Choose **Next** and then **Confirm**.

AWS Config will run this rule against your resources. The rule flags the unattached EIP as non-compliant.

14. Delete the AWS Config rule.

15. Release the Elastic IP address. See the following for instructions:

`https://docs.aws.amazon.com/AWSEC2/latest/UserGuide/elastic-ip-addresses-eip.html#using-instance-addressing-eips-releasing`

From the AWS Config console, you used AWS Config to create a rule to determine whether an Elastic IP address is attached to an Amazon EC2 instance.

EXERCISE 16.4

Create a Launch Configuration and an AWS Auto Scaling Group, and Schedule a Scaling Action

In this exercise, using AWS Management Console, you will create a launch configuration and AWS Auto Scaling policy, and verify the scheduled scaling action.

1. To create a launch configuration, complete the following steps:

    a. Open the Amazon EC2 console at `https://console.aws.amazon.com/ec2/`.

    b. On the navigation pane, under **AWS Auto Scaling**, choose **Launch Configurations**. On the next page, choose **Create launch configuration**.

    c. On the **Choose AMI** page, select your custom AMI.

    d. On the **Choose Instance Type** page, select a hardware configuration for your instance and choose **Next: Configure details**. Configure the remaining details.

    e. On the **Configure Details** page, do the following:

        (i) For **Name**, type a name for your launch configuration.

        (ii) For **Advanced Details, IP Address Type**, select **Assign a public IP address to every instance**.

    f. Choose **Skip to review**.

    g. On the **Review** page, choose **Edit security groups**. Follow the instructions to choose an existing security group, and then choose **Review**.

    h. On the **Review** page, choose **Create launch configuration**.

(continued)

   i. For **Select an existing key pair or create a new key pair** page, select one of the listed options.

   j. Select the acknowledgment check box, and then choose **Create launch configuration**.

2. To create an AWS Auto Scaling group, complete the following steps:

   a. Select **Create an AWS Auto Scaling group using this launch configuration**.

   b. On the **Create AWS Auto Scaling Group** page, follow these steps:

      (i) For **Group name**, enter a name for your AWS Auto Scaling group.

      (ii) For **Group size**, enter **1** as the initial number of instances for your AWS Auto Scaling group.

      (iii) For **Network**, select the default VPC.

      (iv) For **Subnet**, select one or more subnets from the listed subnets.

   c. Choose **Next: Configure scaling policies.**

   d. On the **Configure scaling policies** page, select **Keep this group at its initial size** and then choose **Review.**

   e. On the **Review** page, choose **Create AWS Auto Scaling group.**

   f. On the **AWS Auto Scaling group creation status** page, choose **Close**.

3. To schedule an AWS Auto Scaling action and verify that it's working, complete the following steps:

   a. Select your AWS Auto Scaling group.

   b. On the **Schedule Actions** tab, select **Create Scheduled Action**.

   c. On **Schedule Action** page, follow these steps:

      (i) For **Name**, type name of the action.

      (ii) For **Max**, type **2**.

      (iii) For **Desired Capacity**, type **2**.

      (iv) For **Start Time**, select current day in Date (UTC), and type current UTC time + 2 minutes.

   d. Select **Save**.

   e. Select the **Instances** tab, refresh the tab in the next two minutes, and observe that a new Amazon EC2 instance was created.

In this exercise, you created a launch configuration and an AWS Auto Scaling group using the launch group that you just created. To test whether automatic scaling is working, you added a Scaling action to launch a new Amazon EC2 instance by increasing capacity. You also verified that a new instance was added to the current capacity.

Review Questions

1. You are developing an application that will run across dozens of instances. It uses some components from a legacy application that requires some configuration files to be copied from a central location and held on a volume local to each of the instances. You plan to modify your application with a new component in the future that will hold this configuration in Amazon DynamoDB. Which storage option should you use in the interim to provide the lowest cost and the lowest latency for your application to access the configuration files?

   A. Amazon S3

   B. Amazon EBS

   C. Amazon EFS

   D. Amazon EC2 instance store

2. Similar to SQL, Amazon DynamoDB provides several operations for reading the data. Which operation is the most efficient way to retrieve a single item?

   A. Query

   B. Scan

   C. GetItem

   D. Join

3. AWS Trusted Advisor offers a rich set of best practice checks and recommendations across five categories: cost optimization, security, fault tolerance, performance, and service limits. Which of the following checks is NOT under Cost and Performance categories?

   A. Amazon EBS Provisioned IOPS (SSD) volume attachment configuration

   B. Amazon CloudFront header forwarding and cache hit ratio

   C. Amazon EC2 Availability Zone balance

   D. Unassociated Elastic IP address

4. Which of the following common partition schemas includes a partition key design that distributes I/O requests evenly across partitions and uses provisioned I/O capacity of an Amazon DynamoDB table efficiently?

   A. Status code, where there are only a few possible status codes

   B. User ID, where the application has many users

   C. Item creation date, rounded to the nearest time period

   D. Device ID, where even if there are many devices tracked, one is by far more popular than all the others

5. You are developing an application that consists of a set of Amazon EC2 instances hosting a web layer and a database hosting a MySQL instance. You are required to add a layer that can be used to ensure that the most frequently accessed data from the database is fetched in a faster and more efficient manner. Which of the following can be used to store the frequently accessed data?

    A. Amazon Simple Queue Service (Amazon SQS) queue

    B. Amazon Simple Notification Service (Amazon SNS) topic

    C. Amazon CloudFront distribution

    D. Amazon ElastiCache instance

6. You have an application deployed to the AWS platform. The application makes requests to an Amazon Simple Storage Service (Amazon S3) bucket. After monitoring the Amazon CloudWatch metrics, you notice that the number of GET requests has suddenly spiked. Which of the following can be used to optimize Amazon S3 cost and performance?

    A. Add Amazon ElastiCache in front of the S3 bucket.

    B. Use Amazon DynamoDB instead of Amazon S3.

    C. Place an Amazon CloudFront distribution in front of the S3 bucket.

    D. Place an Elastic Load Balancing load balancer in front of the S3 bucket.

7. You are writing an application that will store data in an Amazon DynamoDB table. The ratio of read operations to write operations will be 1,000 to 1, with the same data being accessed frequently. Which feature or service should you enable on the DynamoDB table to optimize performance and minimize costs?

    A. Amazon DynamoDB Auto Scaling

    B. Amazon DynamoDB cross-region replication

    C. Amazon DynamoDB Streams

    D. Amazon DynamoDB Accelerator

8. A developer is migrating an on-premises web application to the AWS Cloud. The application currently runs on a 32-processor server and stores session state in memory. On Mondays, the server runs at 80 percent CPU utilization, but at only about 5 percent CPU utilization at other times. How should the developer change the code to optimize running in the AWS Cloud?

    A. Store session state on the Amazon EC2 instance store.

    B. Encrypt the session state in memory.

    C. Store session state in an Amazon ElastiCache cluster.

    D. Compress the session state in memory.

9. A company is using an ElastiCache cluster in front of their Amazon RDS instance. The company would like you to implement logic into the code so that the cluster retrieves data from Amazon RDS only when there is a cache miss. Which strategy can you implement to achieve this?

   A. Error retries

   B. Lazy loading

   C. Exponential backoff

   D. Write-through

10. Your application will be hosted on an Amazon EC2 instance, which will be part of an AWS Auto Scaling group. The application must fetch the private IP of the instance. Which of the following can achieve this?

    A. Query the instance metadata.

    B. Query the instance user data.

    C. Have the application run `ifconfig`.

    D. Have an administrator get the IP address from the Amazon EC2 console.

11. You just developed code in AWS Lambda that uses recursive functions. You see some throttling errors in the metrics. Which of the following should you do to resolve the issue?

    A. Use API Gateway to call the recursive code.

    B. Use versioning for the recursive function.

    C. Place the recursive function in a separate package.

    D. Avoid using recursive code in your function.

12. A production application is making calls to an Amazon Relational Database Service (Amazon RDS) instance. The application's reporting module is experiencing heavy traffic, causing performance issues. How can the application be optimized to alleviate this issue?

    A. Move the database to Amazon DynamoDB, and point the reporting module to the new DynamoDB table.

    B. Enable Multi-AZ for the database, and point the reporting module to the secondary database.

    C. Enable read replicas for the database, and point the reporting module to the read replica.

    D. Place an Elastic Load Balancing load balancer in front of the reporting part of the application.

13. Your application uses Amazon S3 buckets. You have users in other countries accessing objects in those buckets. What can you do to reduce latency for those users outside of your country?

    A. Host a static website.

    B. Change the storage class.

    C. Enable cross-region replication.

    D. Enable encryption.

14. You have an application that uploads objects to Amazon S3 between 200–500 MB. The process takes longer than expected, and you want to improve the performance of the application. Which of the following would you consider?

    A. Enable versioning on the bucket.

    B. Use the multipart upload API.

    C. Write the items in batches for better performance.

    D. Create multiple threads to upload the objects.

15. You must bootstrap your application script to instances that are launched inside an AWS Auto Scaling group. Which is the most optimal way to achieve this?

    A. Create a Lambda function to install the script.

    B. Place a scheduled task on the instance that starts on boot.

    C. Place the script in the instance user data.

    D. Place the script in the instance metadata.

Appendix

Answers to Review Questions

Chapter 1: Introduction to AWS Cloud API

1. **B.** The specific credentials include the access key ID and secret access key. If the access key is valid only for a short-term session, the credentials also include a session token.

    AWS uses the user name and passwords for working with the AWS Management Console, not for working with the APIs. Data encryption uses the customer master keys, not API access.

2. **C.** Most AWS API services are regional in scope. The service is running and replicating your data across multiple Availability Zones within an AWS Region. You choose a regional API endpoint either from your default configuration or by explicitly setting a location for your API client.

3. **A.** The AWS SDK relies on access keys, not passwords. The best practice is to use AWS Identity and Access Management (IAM) credentials and not the AWS account credentials. Comparing IAM users or IAM roles, only IAM users can have long-term security credentials.

4. **C.** Although you can generate IAM users for everyone, this introduces management overhead of a new set of long-term credentials. If you already have an external directory of your organization's users, use IAM roles and identity federation to provide short-term, session-based access to AWS.

5. **A.** The permissions for `DynamoDBFullAccess` managed policy grant access to *all* Amazon DynamoDB tables in your account. Write a custom policy to scope the access to a specific table. You can update the permissions of a user independently from the lifecycle of the table. DynamoDB does not have its own concept of users, but it uses the AWS API and relies on IAM.

6. **B.** You can view or manage your AWS resources with the console, AWS CLI, or AWS SDK. The core functionality of each SDK is powered by a common set of web services on the backend. Most AWS services are isolated by AWS Region.

7. **B.** If you look closely at the URL, the AWS Region string is incorrectly set as `us-east-1a`, which is specific to the Availability Zone. An AWS Region string ends in a number, and the correct configuration is `us-east-1`. If the error was related to API credentials, you would receive a more specific error related to credentials, such as `AccessDenied`.

8. **B.** This policy allows access to the `s3:ListBucket` operation on `example_bucket` as a specific bucket. This does not grant access to operations on the objects within the bucket. IAM is granular. The date in the `Version` attribute is a specific version of the IAM policy language and not an expiration.

9. **D.** The long-term credentials are not limited to a single AWS Region. IAM is a global service, and IAM user credentials are valid across different AWS Regions. However, when the API call is made, a signing key is derived from the long-term credentials, and that signing key is scoped to a region, service, and day.

10. B. The `AssumeRole` method of the AWS Security Token Service (AWS STS) returns the security credentials for the role that include the access key ID, secret access key, and session token. AWS Key Management Service (AWS KMS) is not used for API signing. The identity provider may provide a SAML assertion, but AWS STS generates the AWS API credentials.

11. D. The `DynamoDBReadOnlyAccess` policy is a built-in policy that applies to the resource * wildcard, which means that it applies to any and all DynamoDB tables accessible from the account regardless of when those tables were created. Because IAM policies are related to the IAM user, not the access key, rotating the key does not affect the policy. IAM policies are also global in scope, so you do not need a custom one per AWS Region. You can add IAM users to IAM groups but not IAM roles. Instead, roles must be assumed for short-term sessions.

12. B. The IAM trust policy defines the principals who can request role credentials from the AWS STS. Access policies define what API actions can be performed with the credentials from the role.

13. C. You can define an IAM user for your new team member and add the IAM user to an IAM group to inherit the appropriate permissions. The best practice is *not* to use *AWS account root user* credentials. Though you can use AWS Directory Service to track users, this answer is incomplete, and the AWS KMS is not related to permissions. Roles can be assumed only for short-term sessions—there are no long-term credentials directly associated with the role.

14. C. The AWS API backend is accessed through web service calls and is operating system– and programming language–agnostic. You do not need to do anything special to enable specific programming languages other than downloading the appropriate SDK.

15. B. The primary latency concern is for customers accessing the data, and there are no explicit dependencies on existing infrastructure in the United States. Physically locating the application resources closer to these users in Australia reduces the distance that the information must travel and therefore decreases the latency.

Chapter 2: Introduction to Compute and Networking

1. B. You launch Amazon Elastic Compute Cloud (Amazon EC2) instances into specific subnets that are tied to specific Availability Zones. You can look up the Availability Zone in which you have launched an Amazon EC2 instance. While an Availability Zone is part of a region, this answer is not the most specific. You do not get to choose the specific data center, and edge locations do not support EC2.

2. B. When you stop an Amazon EC2 instance, its public IP address is released. When you start it again, a new public IP address is assigned. If you require a public IP address to be persistently associated with the instance, allocate an Elastic IP address. SSH key pairs and security group rules do not have any built-in expiration, and SSH is enabled as a service by default. It is available even after restarts. Security groups do not expire.

3. A. A restricted rule that allows RDP from only certain IP addresses may block your request if you have a new IP address because of your location. Because you are trying to connect to the instance, verify that an appropriate inbound rule is set as opposed to an outbound rule. For many variants of Windows, RDP is the default connection mechanism, and it defaults to enabled even after a reboot.

4. A, D. The NAT gateway allows outbound requests to the external API to succeed while preventing inbound requests from the internet. Configuring the security group to allow only inbound requests from your web servers allows outbound requests to succeed because the default rule for the security group allows outbound requests to the APIs that your web service needs. Option B is incorrect because security group rules cannot explicitly deny traffic; they can only allow it. Option C is incorrect because network ACLs are stateless, and this rule would prevent all of the replies to your outbound web requests from entering the public subnet.

5. C. You are in full control over the software on your instance. The default user that was created when the instance launched has full control over the guest operating system and can install the necessary software. Instance profiles are unrelated to the software on the instance.

6. D. You can query the Amazon EC2 metadata service for this information. Networking within the Amazon Virtual Private Cloud (Amazon VPC) is based on private IP addresses, so this rules out options A and B. Because the metadata service is available, you are not required to use a third-party service, which eliminates option C.

7. A. You can implement user data to execute scripts or directives that install additional packages. Even though you can use Amazon Simple Storage Service (Amazon S3) to stage software installations, there is no special bucket. You have full control of EC2 instances, including the software. AWS KMS is unrelated to software installation.

8. A. Amazon EC2 instances are resizable. You can change the RAM available by changing the instance type. Option B is incorrect because you can change this attribute only when the instance is stopped. Although option C is one possible solution, it is not required. Option D is incorrect because the RAM available on the host server does not change the RAM allocation for your EC2 instance.

9. A. AWS generates the default password for the instance and encrypts it by using the public key from the Amazon EC2 key pair used to launch the instance. You do not select a password when you launch an instance. You can decrypt this with the private key. IAM users and IAM roles are not for providing access to the operating system on the Amazon EC2 instance.

10. A, B, E. For an instance to be directly accessible as a web server, you must assign a public IP address, place the instance in a public subnet, and ensure that the inbound security group rules allow HTTP/HTTPS. A public subnet is one in which there is a direct route to an internet gateway. Option C defines a private subnet. Because security groups are stateful, you are not required to set the outbound rules—the replies to the inbound request are automatically allowed.

11. A, D. You can use an AMI as a template for launching any number of Amazon EC2 instances. AMIs are available for various versions of Windows and Linux. Option B is false because AMIs are local to the region in which they were created unless they are explicitly copied. Option C is false because, in addition to AWS-provided AMIs, there are third-party AMIs in the marketplace, and you can create your own AMIs.

12. B, D. Option B is true; Amazon Elastic Block Store (Amazon EBS) provides persistent storage for all types of EC2 instances. Option D is true because hardware accelerators, such as GPU and FGPA, are accessible depending on the type of instance. Option A is false because instance store is provided only for a few Amazon EC2 instance types. Option C is incorrect because Amazon EC2 instances can be resized after they are launched, provided that they are stopped during the resize. Hardware accelerators, such as GPU and FGPA, are accessible depending on the type of instance.

13. B, D. Only instances in the running state can be started, stopped, or rebooted.

14. D. Both the web server and the database are running on the same instance, and they can communicate locally on the instance. Option A is incorrect because security groups apply to only network traffic that leaves the instance. Option C is incorrect because network ACLs apply only to traffic leaving a subnet. Similarly, option B is incorrect because the public IP address is required for inbound requests from the internet but is not necessary for requests local to the same instance.

15. C. A public subnet is one in which there is a route that directs internet traffic (0.0.0.0/0) to an internet gateway. None of the other routes provides a direct route to the internet, which is required to be a public subnet.

16. D. A private subnet that allows outbound internet access must provide an indirect route to the internet. This is provided by a route that directs internet traffic to a NAT gateway or NAT instance. Option C is incorrect because a route to an internet gateway would make this a public subnet with a direct connection to the internet. The remaining options do not provide access to the internet.

17. D. Amazon VPC Flow Logs have metadata about each traffic flow within your Amazon VPC and show whether the connection was accepted or rejected. The other responses do not provide a log of network traffic.

18. C. Amazon CloudWatch is the service that tracks metrics, including CPU utilization for an Amazon EC2 instance. The other services are not responsible for tracking metrics.

19. B. EBS volumes provide persistent storage for an Amazon EC2 instance. The data is persisted until the volume is deleted and therefore persists on the volume when the instance is stopped.

20. F. You can install any software you want on an Amazon EC2 instance, including any interpreters required to run your application code.

21. B, C. Web requests are typically made on port 80 for HTTP and port 443 for HTTPS. Because security groups are stateful, you must set only the inbound rule. Options A and D are unnecessary because the security group automatically allows the outbound replies to the inbound requests.

22. B, D. The customer is responsible for the guest operating system and above. Options C and E fall under AWS responsibility. AWS is responsible for the virtualization layer, underlying host machines, and all the way down to the physical security of the facilities.

Chapter 3: Hello, Storage

1. D. Amazon EC2 instance store is directly attached to the instance, which will give you the lowest latency between the disk and your application. Instance store is also provided at no additional cost on instance types that have it available, so this is the lowest-cost option. Additionally, since the data is being retrieved from somewhere else, it can be copied back to an instance as needed.

Option A is incorrect because Amazon S3 cannot be directly mounted to an Amazon EC2 instance.

Options B and C are incorrect because Amazon EBS and Amazon Elastic File System (Amazon EFS) would be a higher-cost option with higher latency than instance store.

2. D, E. Objects are stored in buckets and contain both data and metadata.

Option A is incorrect because Amazon S3 is object storage, not block storage.

Option B is incorrect because objects are identified by a URL generated from the bucket name, service region endpoint, and key name.

Option C is incorrect because Amazon S3 object can range in size from a minimum of 0 bytes to a maximum of 5 TB.

3. B. The volume is created immediately, but the data is loaded lazily, meaning that the volume can be accessed upon creation, and if the data being requested has not yet been restored, it will be restored upon first request.

Options A and C are incorrect because it does not matter what the size of the volume is or the amount of the data that is stored on the volume. Lazy loading will get data upon first request as needed while the volume is being restored.

Option D is incorrect because an Amazon EBS-optimized instance provides additional, dedicated capacity for Amazon EBS I/O. This minimizes contention, but it does not increase or decrease the amount of time before the data is made available while restoring a volume.

4. A, B, D. Option C is incorrect because Amazon S3 is accessible through a URL. Amazon EFS is an AWS service that can be mounted to the file system of multiple Amazon EC2 instances. Amazon S3 can be accessible to multiple EC2 instances, but not through a file system mount.

Option E is incorrect because, unlike Amazon EBS volumes, storage in a bucket does not need to be pre-allocated and can grow in a virtually unlimited manner.

5. A, C. Amazon Simple Storage Service Glacier is optimized for long-term archival storage and is not suited to data that needs immediate access or short-lived data that is erased within 90 days.

6. B. Option B is correct because pre-signed URLs allow you to grant time-limited permission to download objects from an Amazon S3 bucket.

Option A is incorrect because static web hosting requires world-read access to all content.

Option C is incorrect because AWS IAM policies do not know who are the authenticated users of your web application, as these are not IAM users.

Option D is incorrect because logging can help track content loss, but not prevent it.

7. A, D. Option A is correct because the data is automatically replicated within an availability zone.

Option D is correct because Amazon EBS volumes persist when the instance is stopped.

Option B is incorrect. There are no tapes in the AWS infrastructure.

Option C is incorrect because Amazon EBS volumes can be encrypted upon creation and used by an instance in the same manner as if they were not encrypted.

8. C. The Max I/O performance mode is optimized for applications where tens, hundreds, or thousands of EC2 instances are accessing the file system. It scales to higher levels of aggregate throughput and operations per second with a trade-off of slightly higher latencies for file operations.

Option A is incorrect because the General-Purpose performance mode in Amazon EFS is appropriate for most file systems, and it is the mode selected by default when you create a file system. However, when you need concurrent access from 10 or more instances to the file system, you may need to increase your performance.

Option B is incorrect. This is an option to increase I/O throughput for Amazon EBS volumes by connecting multiple volumes and setting up RAID 0 to increase overall I/O.

Option D is incorrect. Changing to a larger instance size will increase your cost for compute, but it will not improve the performance for concurrently connecting to your Amazon EFS file system from multiple instances.

9. A, B, D. Options A, B, and D are required, and optionally you can also set a friendly CNAME to the bucket URL.

Option C is incorrect because Amazon S3 does not support FTP transfers.

Option E is incorrect because HTTP does not need to be enabled.

10. C. A short period of heavy traffic is exactly the use case for the bursting nature of general-purpose SSD volumes—the rest of the day is more than enough time to build up enough IOPS credits to handle the nightly task.

Option A is incorrect because to set up a Provisioned IOPS SSD volume to handle the peak would mean overprovisioning and spending money for more IOPS than you need during off-peak time.

Option B is incorrect because instance stores are not durable.

Option D is incorrect because magnetic volumes cannot provide enough IOPS.

11. C, D, E. Option A is incorrect because you store data in Amazon S3 Glacier as an archive. You upload archives into vaults. Vaults are collections of archives that you use to organize your data. Amazon S3 stores data in objects that live in buckets.

Option B is incorrect because archives are identified by system-created archive IDs, not key names like in S3.

12. A. Amazon EFS supports one to thousands of Amazon EC2 instances connecting to a file system concurrently.

Options B and C are incorrect because Amazon EBS and Amazon EC2 instance store can be mounted only to a single instance at a time.

Option D is incorrect because Amazon S3 does not provide a file system connection, but rather connectivity over the web. It cannot be mounted to an instance directly.

13. B. There is no delay in processing when commencing a snapshot.

Options A and C are incorrect because the size of the volume or the amount of the data that is stored on the volume does not matter. The volume will be available immediately.

Option D is incorrect because an Amazon EBS-optimized instance provides additional, dedicated capacity for Amazon EBS I/O. This minimizes contention, but it does not change the fact that the volume will still be available while taking a snapshot.

14. B, C, E. Amazon S3 bucket policies can specify a request IP range, an AWS account, and a prefix for objects that can be accessed.

Options A and D are incorrect because bucket policies cannot be restricted by company name or country of origin.

15. B, D. Option B is incorrect because Amazon S3 cannot be mounted to an Amazon EC2 instance like a file system.

Option D is incorrect because Amazon S3 should not serve as primary database storage because it is object storage, not transactional block-based storage. Databases are generally stored on disk in one or more large files. If you needed to change one row in a database, the entire database file would need to be updated in Amazon S3, and every time you needed to access a record, you'd need to download the whole database.

16. B, C, E. Option A is incorrect because static web hosting does not restrict data access. You can host a website on Amazon S3, but the bucket must have public read access, so everyone in the world will have read access to this bucket.

Option B is correct because creating a presigned URL for an object optionally allows you to share objects with others.

Option C is correct because Amazon S3 access control lists (ACLs) enable you to manage access to buckets and objects, defining which AWS accounts or groups are granted access and the type of access.

Option D is incorrect because using an Amazon S3 lifecycle policy does not restrict data access. Lifecycle policies can be used to define actions for Amazon S3 to take during an object's lifetime (for example, transition objects to another storage class, archive them, or delete them after a specified period of time).

Option E is correct because a bucket policy is a resource-based AWS IAM policy that allows you to grant permission to your Amazon S3 resources for other AWS accounts or IAM users.

17. C, E. Option A is incorrect because even though you get increased redundancy with using cross-region replication, that does not protect the object from being deleted.

Option B is incorrect because vault locks are a feature of Amazon S3 Glacier, not a feature of Amazon S3.

Option D is incorrect because a lifecycle policy would move the object to Amazon Glacier, moving it out of your intended storage in S3 and reducing the time to access the data, and it does not prevent it from being deleted once it arrives in Amazon S3 Glacier.

C and E are correct. Versioning protects data against inadvertent or intentional deletion by storing all versions of the object, and MFA Delete requires a one-time code from a multi-factor authentication (MFA) device to delete objects.

18. C. To track requests for access to your bucket, enable access logging. Each access log record provides details about a single access request, such as the requester, bucket name, request time, request action, response status, and error code (if any). Access log information can be useful in security and access audits. It can also help you learn about your customer base and understand your Amazon S3 bill.

19. A, B, D. Option A is correct because cross-region replication allows you to replicate data between distance AWS Regions to satisfy these requirements.

Option B is correct because this can minimize latency in accessing objects by maintaining object copies in AWS Regions that are geographically closer to your users.

Option D is correct because you can maintain object copies in both regions, allowing lower latency by bringing the data closer to the compute.

Option C is incorrect because cross-region replication does not protect against accidental deletion.

Option E is incorrect because Amazon S3 is designed for 11 nines of durability for objects in a single region. A second region does not significantly increase durability.

20. C. If data must be encrypted before being sent to Amazon S3, client-side encryption must be used.

Options A, B, and D are incorrect because they use server-side encryption. This will only encrypt the data at rest in Amazon S3, not prior to transit to Amazon S3.

21. B. Data is automatically replicated across at least three Availability Zones within a single region.

Option A is incorrect because you can optionally choose to replicate data to other regions, but that is not done by default.

Option C is incorrect because versioning is optional, and data in Amazon S3 is durable regardless of turning on versioning.

Option D is incorrect because there are no tapes in the AWS infrastructure.

Chapter 4: Hello, Databases

1. B, D, E. Amazon Relational Database Service (Amazon RDS) manages the work involved in setting up a relational database, from provisioning the infrastructure capacity to installing the database software. After your database is up and running, Amazon RDS automates common administrative tasks, such as performing backups and patching the software that powers your database. Option A is incorrect. Because Amazon RDS provides native database access, you interact with the relational database software as you normally would. This means that you're still responsible for managing the database settings that are specific to your application. Option C is incorrect. You need to build the relational schema that best fits your use case and are responsible for any performance tuning to optimize your database for your application's workflow and query patterns.

2. B. Amazon Neptune is a fast, reliable, fully managed graph database to store and manage highly connected datasets. Option A is incorrect because Amazon Aurora is a managed SQL database that is meant for transactional workloads that are ACID-compliant. Option C is incorrect because this is a managed NoSQL database service, which is meant for more key-value datasets with no relationships. Option D is incorrect because Amazon Redshift is a data warehouse that can be used for running analytical queries (OLAP) on data warehouses that are petabytes in scale.

3. B. NoSQL databases, such as Amazon DynamoDB, excel at scaling to hundreds of thousands of requests with key-value access to user profile and session. Option A is incorrect because the session state is typically suited for small amounts of data, and DynamoDB can scale more effectively with this type of dataset. Option C is incorrect because Amazon Redshift is a data warehouse service that is used for analytical queries on petabyte scale datasets, so it would not be a good solution. Option D is incorrect because DynamoDB provides scale, whereas MySQL on Amazon EC2 eventually becomes bottlenecked. Additionally, NoSQL databases are much faster and more scalable for this type of dataset.

4. A. 1 RCU = One strongly consistent read per second of 4 KB.

   15 KB is four complete chunks of 4 KB (4 × 4 = 16).

   So you need 25 × 4 = 100 RCUs.

5. C. 1 RCU = Two eventually consistent reads per second of 4 KB.

   15 KB is four complete chunks of 4 KB (4 × 4 = 16).

   So you need (25 × 4) / 2 = 50 RCUs.

6. D. 1 WCU = 1 write per second of 1 KB (1024 bytes).

   512 bytes uses one complete chunk of 1 KB (512/1024 = 0.5, rounded up to 1).

   So you need 100 × 1 = 100 WCUs.

7. B. Amazon DynamoDB Accelerator (DAX) is a write-through caching service that quickly integrates with DynamoDB with a few quick code changes. DAX will seamlessly intercept the API call, and your caching solution will be up and running in a short amount of

time. Option A is incorrect because you could implement your own solution; however, this would likely take a significant amount of development time. Option C is incorrect because your company would like to get the service up and running quickly. Implementing Redis on Amazon EC2 to meet your application's needs would take additional time. Option D is incorrect for many of the same reasons as option C, as time is a factor here. Additionally, your company would like to refrain from managing more EC2 instances, if possible.

8. B. With Amazon ElastiCache, only Redis can be run in a high-availability configuration. Option A is incorrect because this would add complexity to your architecture. It would also likely introduce additional latency, as the company is already using Amazon RDS. Option C is incorrect because ElastiCache for Memcached does not support a high-availability configuration. Option D is incorrect because DAX is a caching mechanism that is used for DynamoDB, not Amazon RDS.

9. C. Amazon Redshift is the best option. It is a managed AWS data warehouse service that allows you to scale up to petabytes worth of data, which would definitely meet their needs. Option A is incorrect because Amazon RDS cannot store that much data; the limit of Amazon RDS for Aurora is 64 TB. Option B is incorrect because DynamoDB is not meant for analytical-type queries—it is meant for simple queries and key-value pair data, which is more transactional based. You can query based on only the partition and sort key in DynamoDB. Option D is incorrect because Amazon ElastiCache is a caching solution that is meant for temporary data. However, you could store queries that ran in Amazon Redshift inside ElastiCache. This would improve the performance of frequently run queries, but by itself is not a solution.

10. A. Scans are less efficient than queries. When possible, always use queries with DynamoDB. Option B is incorrect because doing nothing isn't a good solution; the problem is unlikely to go away. Option C is incorrect because a strongly consistent read would actually be a more expensive query in terms of compute and cost. Strongly consistent reads cost twice as much as eventually consistent reads. Option D is incorrect because the concern is with reading data, not writing data. WCUs are write capacity units.

Chapter 5: Encryption on AWS

1. B, D, E. Option A is incorrect because data can be encrypted in any location (on-premises or in the AWS Cloud). Option C is incorrect because encryption keys should be stored in a secured hardware security module (HSM). Option B is correct because there must be data to encrypt in order to use an encryption system. Option D is correct because tools and a process must be in place to perform encryption. Option E is correct because encryption requires a defined algorithm.

2. A, C. Option B is incorrect because KMI does not have a concept of a data layer. Option D is incorrect because KMI does not have a concept of an encryption layer. Option A is correct because the storage layer is responsible for storing encryption keys. Option C is correct because the management layer is responsible for allowing authorized users to access the stored keys.

3. A, C, D. Option A is correct because this is a common method to offload the responsibility of key storage while maintaining customer-owned management processes. Option C is correct because customers can use this approach to fully manage their keys and KMI. Option D is correct because AWS Key Management Service (AWS KMS) supports both encryption and KMI. Option B is incorrect because this would imply significant overhead to manage the storage while not providing customer benefits.

4. D. Option A is incorrect; with SSE-S3, Amazon S3 is responsible for encrypting the objects, not AWS KMS. Option B is incorrect because the customer provides the key to the Amazon S3 service. Option C is incorrect because the question specifically states that server-side encryption is used. Option D is correct because none of the other options listed server-side encryption with AWS KMS (SSE-KMS), whereby AWS KMS manages the keys.

5. B. Option A is incorrect. AWS KMS does not currently support asymmetric encryption. Option B is correct because AWS CloudHSM supports both asymmetric and symmetric encryption. Options C and D are incorrect because CloudHSM supports asymmetric encryption.

6. A, B. Option A is correct because AWS KMS uses AES-256 as its encryption algorithm. Option B is correct because CloudHSM supports a variety of symmetric encryption options. Options C and D are incorrect because AWS KMS and CloudHSM support symmetric encryption options.

7. C. Option A is incorrect because the organization does *not* want to manage any of the encryption keys. With AWS KMS, it will have to create customer master keys (CMKs). Option B is incorrect because by using customer-provided keys, the organization would have to manage the keys. Option C is correct because Amazon S3 manages the encryption keys and performs rotations periodically. Option D is incorrect because SSE-S3 provides this option.

8. C. Option A is incorrect because AWS KMS provides a centralized key management dashboard; however, this feature does not leverage CloudHSM. Option B is incorrect because you want to use AWS KMS *with* CloudHSM and not use it as a replacement for AWS KMS. Option C is correct because custom key stores allow AWS KMS to store keys in an CloudHSM cluster. Option D is incorrect because S3DistCp is a feature for Amazon Redshift whereby it copies data from Amazon S3 to the cluster.

9. A. Option A is correct because AWS KMS provides the simplest solution with little development time to implement encryption on an Amazon EBS volume. Option B is incorrect because even though you can use open source or third-party tooling to encrypt volumes, there would be some setup and configuration involved. Using CloudHSM would also require some configuration and setup, so option C is incorrect. Option D is incorrect because AWS KMS enables you to encrypt Amazon EBS volumes.

10. D. Options A, B, and C are incorrect because AWS KMS integrates with all these services.

Chapter 6: Deployment Strategies

1. **D.** Option D is correct because AWS CodePipeline is a continuous delivery service for fast and reliable application updates. It allows the developer to model and visualize the software release process. CodePipeline automates your build, test, and release process when there is a code change.

   Option A is incorrect because AWS CodeCommit is a secure, highly scalable, managed source control service that hosts private Git repositories.

   Option B is incorrect because AWS CodeDeploy automates code deployments to any instance and handles the complexity of updating your applications.

   Option C is incorrect because AWS CodeBuild compiles source code, runs tests, and produces ready-to-deploy software packages.

2. **A, B, C, D.** A, B, C, and D are correct because you can use them all to create a web server environment with AWS Elastic Beanstalk.

   Option E is incorrect because AWS Lambda is an event-driven, serverless computing platform that runs code in response to events. Lambda automatically manages the computing resources required by that code.

3. **C.** Elastic Beanstalk supports Java, Node.js, and Go, so options A, B, and D are incorrect. It does not support Objective C, so option C is the correct answer.

4. **A.** Elastic Beanstalk deploys application code and the architecture to support an environment for the application to run.

5. **A, C.** Elastic Beanstalk supports Linux and Windows. No support is available for an Ubuntu-only operating system, Fedora, or Jetty.

6. **A, B.** Elastic Beanstalk can run Amazon EC2 instances and build queues with Amazon SQS.

7. **A, B.** Elastic Beanstalk can access Amazon S3 buckets and connect to Amazon RDS databases. It cannot install Amazon GuardDuty agents or create or manage Amazon WorkSpaces.

8. **C.** By using IAM policies, you can control access to resources attached to users, groups, and roles.

9. **B, C.** Elastic Beanstalk creates a service role to access AWS services and an instance role to access instances.

10. **C.** Elastic Beanstalk runs at no additional charge. You incur charges only for services deployed.

11. **D.** Charges are incurred for all accounts that use the allocated resources.

12. **C.** An existing Amazon RDS instance is deleted if the environment is deleted. There is no auto-retention of the database instance. You must create a snapshot to retain the data and to restore the database.

Chapter 7: Deployment as Code

1. **A.** Options B and D are incorrect because the deployment is already in progress, and this would not be possible if the AWS CodeDeploy agent had not been installed and running properly. The CodeDeploy agent sends progress reports to the CodeDeploy service. The service does not attempt to query instances directly, and the Amazon EC2 API does not interact with instances at the operating system level. Thus, option C is incorrect, and option A is correct.

2. **B.** Option B is correct because the ApplicationStop lifecycle event occurs before any new deployment files download. For this reason, it will not run the first time a deployment occurs on an instance. Option C is incorrect, as this is a valid lifecycle event. Option A is incorrect. Option D is incorrect because lifecycle hooks are not aware of the current state of your application. Lifecycle hook scripts execute any listed commands.

3. **A.** Option B requires precise timing that would be overly burdensome to add to a CI/CD workflow. Option C would not include edge cases where both sources are updated within a small time period and would require separate release cadences for both sources. Option D is incorrect, as AWS CodePipeline supports multiple sources. When multiple sources are configured for the same pipeline, the pipeline will be triggered when any source is updated.

4. **C.** Option A is incorrect because storing large binary objects in a Git-based repository can incur massive storage requirements. Any time a binary object is modified in a repository, a new copy is saved. Comparing cost to Amazon S3 storage, it is more expensive to take this approach. By building the binary objects into an Amazon Machine Image (AMI), you are required to create a new AMI any time changes are made to the objects; thus, option B is incorrect. Option D and E introduce unnecessary cost and complexity into the solution. By using both an AWS CodeCommit repository and Amazon S3 archive, the lowest cost and easiest management is achieved.

5. **D.** Option A is incorrect because rolling deployments without an additional batch would result in less than 100 percent availability, as one batch of the original set of instances would be taken out of circulation during the deployment process. Option B is incorrect because if you add an additional batch, it would ensure 100 percent availability at the lowest cost but would require a longer update process than replacing all instances at once. Option C is incorrect because, by default, blue/green deployments will leave the original environment intact, accruing charges until it is manually deleted. Option D is correct as immutable updates would result in the fastest deployment for the lowest cost. In an immutable update, a new Auto Scaling group is created and registered with the load balancer. Once health checks pass, the existing Auto Scaling group is terminated.

6. **D.** Option C is incorrect because Amazon S3 does not have a concept of service roles. When a pipeline is initiated, it is done in response either to a change in a source or when a previous change is released by an authorized AWS IAM user or role. However, after the pipeline has been initiated, the AWS CodePipeline service role is used to perform pipeline actions. Thus, options A and B are incorrect. Option D is correct, because the pipeline's service role requires permissions to download objects from Amazon S3.

7. B. Option A is incorrect because this output is used only in the CodeBuild console. Option D is incorrect because CodeBuild natively supports this functionality. Though option C would technically work, CodeBuild supports output artifacts in the buildspec.yml specification. The BuildSpec includes a files directive to indicate any files from the build environment that will be passed as output artifacts. Thus, option B is correct.

8. C. Option A is incorrect because a custom build environment would expose the secrets to any user able to create new build jobs using the same environment. Option B is also incorrect. Though uploading the secrets to Amazon S3 would provide some protection, administrators with Amazon S3 access may still be able to view the secrets. Option D is incorrect because AWS does not recommend storing sensitive information in source control repositories, as it is easily viewed by anyone with access to the repository. Option D is correct. By encrypting the secrets with AWS KMS and storing them in AWS Systems Manager Parameter Store, you ensure that the keys are protected both at rest and in transit. Only AWS IAM users or roles with permissions to both the key and parameter store would have access to the secrets.

9. A. Options B, C, D, and E are incorrect. AWS Lambda functions can execute as part of a pipeline only with the Invoke action type.

10. A, B. Options D and E are incorrect because FIFO/LIFO are not valid pipeline action configurations. Option C is incorrect because pipeline stages support multiple actions. Pipeline actions can be specified to occur both in series and in parallel within the same stage. Thus, options A and B are correct.

11. D. Option A is incorrect because it will only create or update a stack, not delete the existing stack. Option B is incorrect because the desired actions are in the wrong order. Option C is incorrect because the final action, "Replace a failed stack," is not needed. Option D is correct. Only two actions are required. First, the stack must be deleted. Second, the replacement stack can be created. Unless otherwise required, however, both actions can be essentially accomplished by using one "Create or update a stack" action.

12. D. Option A is incorrect. AWS CodeCommit is fully compatible with existing Git tools, and it also supports authentication with AWS Identity and Access Management (IAM) credentials. Options B and C are incorrect. These are the only protocols over which you can interact with a repository. You can use the CodeCommit credential helper to convert an IAM access key and secret access key to valid Git credentials for SSH and HTTPS authentication. Thus, option D is correct.

13. C. Options A, B, and D are all valid Amazon Simple Notification Service (Amazon SNS) notification event sources for CodeCommit repositories. Option C is correct because Amazon SNS notifications cannot be configured to send when a commit is made to a repository.

14. C, E. Options A, B, and D are incorrect because these action types do not support CodeBuild projects. Options C and E are correct because CodeBuild projects can be executed in a pipeline as part of build and test actions.

15. D. Environment variables in CodeBuild projects are not encrypted and are visible using the CodeBuild API. Thus, options A, B, and C are incorrect. If you need to pass sensitive information to build containers, use Systems Manager Parameter Store instead. Thus, option D is correct.

16. A. Because AWS does not have the ability to create or destroy infrastructure in customer data centers, options B, C, and D are incorrect. Option A is correct because on-premises instances support only in-place deployments.

17. C. Options A and B are incorrect because AWS CodeDeploy will not modify files on an instance that were not created by a deployment. Option D is incorrect because this approach could result in failed deployments because of missing settings in your configuration file. Option C is correct. By default, CodeDeploy will not remove files that it does not manage. This is maintained as a list of files on the instance.

18. C. Option A is incorrect because function versions cannot be modified after they have been published. Option B is also incorrect because function version numbers cannot be changed. Aliases can be used to point to different function versions; however, the alias itself cannot be overwritten (it is a pointer to a function version). Thus, option D is incorrect. AWS Lambda does not support in-place deployments. This is because, after a function version has been published, it cannot be updated. Option C is correct.

19. C. AWS CodePipeline requires that every pipeline contain a source stage and at least one build or deploy stage. Thus, the minimum number of stages is 2.

20. C. Option A is not correct because deleting the old revisions will temporarily resolve the issue. However, future deployments will continue to consume disk space. The same reasoning applies to options B and D, which are also temporary solutions to the problem. The CodeDeploy agent configuration file includes a number of useful settings. Among these, a limit can be set on how many revisions to store on an instance at any point in time. Thus, option C is correct.

Chapter 8: Infrastructure as Code

1. D. Only the Resources section of a template is required. If this section is omitted, AWS CloudFormation has no resources to manage. However, a template does not require Parameters, Metadata, or AWSTemplateFormatVersion. Thus, options A, B, C, and E are incorrect.

2. E. The return value of the Ref intrinsic function for an AWS::ElasticLoadBalancing::LoadBalancer resource is the load balancer name, which is not valid in a URL, so option A is incorrect. Since the application server instances are in a private subnet, neither will have a public DNS name; thus, option B is incorrect. Option C uses incorrect syntax for the Ref intrinsic function. Option D attempts to output a URL for the database instance. Thus, option E is correct.

3. A, C, D. If account limits were preventing the launch of additional instances, the stack creation process would fail as soon as AWS CloudFormation attempts to launch the instance (the Amazon EC2 API would return an error to AWS CloudFormation in this case). Thus, option B is incorrect. Any issues preventing the instance from calling cfn-signal and sending a success/failure message to AWS CloudFormation would cause the creation policy to time out. Thus, options A, C, and D are correct answers.

4. C. Option A is incorrect because AWS CloudFormation does not monitor the status of your database and would not be able to determine whether the database is corrupted. It also does not track whether there are currently running transactions before attempting updates. Thus, option E is incorrect. If an invalid update is submitted, the stack generates an error message when attempting the database update. Thus, option D is incorrect. Though option B would work, it is not needed to remove the database from the stack and manage it separately. Option C is correct because an AWS CloudFormation service role extends the default timeout value for stack actions to allow you to manage resources with longer update periods.

5. A. Custom resource function permissions are obtained by a function execution role, not the service role invoking the stack update; thus, option B is incorrect. When the AWS Lambda function corresponding to a custom resource no longer exists, the custom resource will fail to update immediately; thus, option C is incorrect. However, if the custom resource function is executed but does not provide a response to the AWS CloudFormation service endpoint, the resource times out with the aforementioned error. Thus, option A is correct.

6. A. AWS CloudFormation processes transformations by creating a change set, which generates an AWS CloudFormation supported template. Without the AWS::Serverless transform, AWS CloudFormation cannot process the AWS SAM template. For any stack in your account, the current template can be downloaded using the get-stack-template AWS CLI command. This command will return templates as processed by AWS CloudFormation; thus, option B is incorrect. Option C is also incorrect, because the original template is not saved before executing the transform. Option D is also incorrect, as AWS CloudFormation saves the current template for all stacks.

7. E. AWS SAM supports other AWS CloudFormation resources, and it is not limited to defining only AWS::Serverless::* resource types; thus, option D is incorrect, and option A is correct. However, the AWS::Serverless transform will not automatically associate serverless functions with AWS::ApiGateway::RestApi resources. The transform will automatically associate any functions with the serverless API being declared, or it will create a new one when the transform is executed. Thus, option B is also correct. Option C is also correct because AWS Serverless also supports Swagger definitions to outline the endpoints of your OpenAPI specification.

8. A. The cfn-init helper script is used to define which packages, files, and other configurations will be performed when an instance is first launched. The cfn-signal helper script is used to signal back to AWS CloudFormation when a resource creation or update has completed, so options B and C are incorrect. Option D is incorrect because cfn-update, is not a valid helper script. The cfn-hup helper script performs updates on an instance when its parent stack is updated. Thus, option A is correct.

9. C. Wait conditions accept only one signal and will not track additional signals from the same resource; thus, options A and B are incorrect. WaitCount is an invalid option type, so option D is incorrect. Option C is correct because creation policies enable you to specify a count and timeout.

10. A. Options B and C will affect resources in your account. Option D would let you see the syntax differences between two template versions, but this does not indicate what type of updates will happen on the resources themselves. Thus, option D is incorrect. Change sets create previews of infrastructure changes without actually executing them. After reviewing the changes that will be performed, the change set can be executed on the target stack.

11. B. Option A is incorrect, as this is a supported feature of nested stacks. Option C creates a circular dependency between the parent and child stacks (the parent stack needs to import the value from the child stack, which cannot be created until the parent begins creation). Option D is incorrect because cross-stack references are not possible without exporting and importing outputs. Option B uses intrinsic functions to access resource properties in the same manner as any other stack resource.

12. B. AWS CloudFormation does not assume full administrative control on your account, and it requires permissions to interact with resources you own. AWS CloudFormation can operate using a service role; however, this must be explicitly passed as part of the stack operation. Otherwise, it will execute with the same permissions as the user performing the stack operation. Thus, option B is the correct answer.

13. C. Because the reference to the Amazon DynamoDB table is made as part of an arbitrary string (the function code), AWS CloudFormation does not recognize this as a dependency between resources. To prevent any potential errors, you would need to declare explicitly that the function depends on the table. Thus, option C is correct.

14. E. Replacing updates results in the deletion of the original resource and the creation of a replacement. AWS CloudFormation creates the replacement first with a new physical ID and verifies it before deleting the original. Because of this, option E is correct (all of the above).

15. B, C. Option A is incorrect, as it states that no interruption will occur. Options D and E are not valid update types. Replacing updates delete the original resource and provision a replacement. Updates with some interruption have resource downtime, but the original resource is not replaced. Thus, options B and C are correct.

16. A. The export does not need to be removed from the stack before it can be deleted, so option B is incorrect. Options C and D are also incorrect, as the stack does not need to be deleted. However, the stack cannot be deleted until any other stacks that import the value remove the import. Thus, option A is correct.

17. B, D, E. If a stack update fails for any reason, the next state would be UPDATE_ROLLBACK_IN_PROGRESS, which must occur before the rollback fails or completes. A stack that is currently updating can either complete the update, fail to update, or complete and clean up old resources. Thus, options B, D, and E are correct.

18. B. Because the stack status shows the update has completed, you know that the update did not fail. This means that options A and D are incorrect. When a stack updates and resources are created, they will not be deleted unless the update fails. Thus, option C is incorrect. Old resources that are no longer required are removed during the cleanup phase. Thus, option B is correct.

19. A, C. AWS CloudFormation currently supports JSON and YAML template formats only.

20. E. AWS CloudFormation provides a number of benefits over procedural scripting. The risk of human error is reduced because templates are validated by AWS CloudFormation before deployment. Infrastructure is repeatable and versionable using the same process as application code development. Individual users provisioning infrastructure need a reduced scope of permissions when using AWS CloudFormation service roles. Thus, option E is correct.

21. B. Option C is incorrect because, though on-premises servers can be part of a custom resource's workflow, they do not receive requests directly. Options D and E are incorrect because specific actions are not declared in custom resource properties. Option A is incorrect because AWS services themselves do not process custom resource requests. Specifically, Amazon SNS topics and AWS Lambda functions can act as recipients to custom resource requests. Thus, option B is correct.

22. C. Options A and B are incorrect because they would require interacting with other AWS services using the AWS CLI. For certain situations, such as running arbitrary commands in Amazon EC2 instance user data scripts, this would work. However, not all resource types have this ability. Option D is incorrect, as this is a built-in functionality of AWS CloudFormation. Option C is correct because any data that is declared in a custom resource response is accessible to the remainder of the template using the `Fn::GetAtt` intrinsic function.

Chapter 9: Configuration as Code

1. E. You can raise all of the limits listed by submitting a limit increase request to AWS Support.

2. D. Option A is incorrect because instances do not attempt to download new cookbooks when performing Chef runs. Option B is incorrect because AWS OpsWorks Stacks does not have a concept of cookbook caching. Option C is incorrect because lifecycle events do not allow you to specify cookbook versions. Option D is correct because after updating a custom cookbook repository, any currently online instances will not automatically receive the updated cookbooks. To upload the modified cookbooks to the instances, you must first run the `Update Custom Cookbooks` command.

3. B. Options A, C, and D are incorrect because OpsWorks Stacks provides integration with Elastic Load Balancing to handle automatic registration and deregistration. Option B is correct as the Elastic Load Balancing layers for OpsWorks Stacks automatically register instances when they come online and deregister them when they move to a different state. You can also enable connection draining to prevent deregistration until any active sessions end.

4. A, B. Option C is incorrect because changing the cluster capacity will not affect service scaling. Option D is incorrect because submitting a replacement will result in the same behavior. If there are insufficient resources to launch replacement tasks when a service updates, Amazon Elastic Container Service (Amazon ECS) will continue to attempt to launch the tasks until it is able to do so. If you increase the cluster size, additional resources add to the pool to allow the new task to start. After it has done so, the old task will terminate. After it terminates, the cluster can scale back to its original size. If the downtime of this service does not concern you, set the minimum in-service percentage to 0 percent to allow Amazon ECS to terminate the currently running task before it launches the new one. Thus, options A and B are correct.

5. B. Options A, C, and D are incorrect because no other parties have access to the underlying clusters in AWS Fargate. When you use the Fargate launch type, AWS provisions and manages underlying cluster instances for your containers. You do not need to manage maintenance and patching. Thus, option B is correct.

6. A. Option B is incorrect, as this is a matter of personal preference. Option C is also incorrect because instances can be stopped and started individually, not only in layers at a time. Option D is incorrect because the configure lifecycle event runs on all instances in a stack, regardless of layer. Assigning recipes is performed at the layer level, meaning that all instances in the same layer will run the same configuration code. Organizing instances into layers based on purpose removes the need to add complex conditional logic. Thus, option A is correct.

7. C. Option A is incorrect because AWS OpsWorks Stacks does not include a central Chef Server. Option B is incorrect because storing recipes as part of an AMI would introduce considerable complexity for regular recipe code updates. Option D is incorrect because Amazon EC2 is not a valid storage location for cookbooks. A custom cookbook repository location is configured for a stack. When instances in the stack are first launched, they will download cookbooks from this location and run them as part of lifecycle events. Thus, option C is correct.

8. A. Option B is incorrect because you cannot associate a single Amazon RDS database instance with multiple stacks at the same time. Option C is incorrect because this approach would require manual snapshotting and data migration that is not necessary. Option D is incorrect. Migration of database instances between stacks is a common workflow. To migrate an Amazon RDS layer, you must remove it from the first layer before you add it to the second. Thus, option A is correct.

9. C. Option A is incorrect because 24/7 instances are normally recommended for constant demand. Option B is incorrect because load-based instances are recommended for variable, unpredictable demand changes. Option D is incorrect because On-Demand is an Amazon ECS instance type, not an OpsWorks Stacks instance type. You configure time-based instances to start and stop on a specific schedule. AWS recommends this for a predictable increase in workload throughout a day. Thus, option C is correct.

10. B. Option A is incorrect because 24/7 instances are normally recommended for constant demand. Option C is incorrect because time-based instances are recommended for changes in load that are predictable over time. Option D is incorrect because Spot is an Amazon ECS instance type, not an OpsWorks Stacks instance type. Option B is correct because load-based instances are recommended for unpredictable changes in demand.

11. A. Option B is incorrect because the Amazon ECS service role is used to create and manage AWS resources on behalf of the customer. Option C is incorrect because AWS Systems Manager is not part of Amazon ECS. Option D is incorrect because Amazon ECS automates the process of stopping and starting containers within a cluster. The Amazon ECS agent is responsible for all on-instance tasks such as downloading container images and starting or stoping containers. Thus, option A is correct.

12. B. Option A is incorrect. Though high availability is a tenet of SOA, it is not a requirement. Option C is incorrect because SOA does not define how development teams are organized. Option D is incorrect because SOA does not define what should or should not be procured from vendors. Service-oriented architecture involves using containers to implement discrete application components separately from one another to ensure availability and durability of each component. Thus, option B is correct.

13. D. A single task definition can describe up to 10 containers to launch at a time. To launch more containers, you need to create multiple task definitions. Task definitions should group containers by similar purpose, lifecycle, or resource requirements. Thus, option D is correct.

14. A. Option B is incorrect because PAT cannot be configured within your VPC (it must be configured using a proxy instance of some kind). Option C is incorrect because containers can be configured to bind to a random port instead of a specific one. Dynamic host port mapping allows you to launch multiple copies of the same container listening on different ports. Classic Load Balancers do not support dynamic host port mapping. Thus, option D is incorrect. Option A is correct because the Application Load Balancer is then responsible for mapping requests on one port to each container's specific port.

15. A. Options B and C are incorrect because they do not consider the Availability Zone of each cluster instance when placing tasks. Option D is incorrect because least cost is not a valid placement policy. The spread policy distributes tasks across multiple availability zones and cluster instances. Thus, option A is correct.

Chapter 10: Authentication and Authorization

1. D. You need to use a third-party IdP as the confirmation of identity. Based on that confirmation, a policy can be assigned. Option A is incorrect because roles cannot be assigned to users outside of your account. Option B is incorrect because you cannot assign an IAM user ID to a user that is external to AWS. Option C is incorrect because it makes provisioning an identity a manual process.

2. D. An identity provider (IdP) answers the question "Who are you?" Based on this answer, policies are assigned. Those policies control the level of access to the AWS infrastructure and applications (if using AWS for managed services).

Option A is incorrect; it is one of the functions of a service provider—to control access to applications. Option B is incorrect; policies are used to control access to APIs, which is how access to the AWS infrastructure is controlled. Option C is incorrect; identity providers do no error checking on policy assignment.

3. A. Where possible, using multi-factor authentication (MFA) minimizes the impact of lost or compromised credentials. Option B is incorrect in that embedding credentials is both a security risk and makes credential administration much more difficult. Option C would decrease the opportunity for misuse. It would not address any misuse that was a result of internal users. Option D is a good step but not as secure as option A.

4. D. If you want to use Security Assertion Markup Language (SAML) as an identity provider (IdP), use SAML 2.0. With Amazon Cognito, you can use Google (option A), Microsoft Active Directory (option B), and your own identity store (option C) as identity providers.

5. C. By using AWS Cloud services, such as Amazon Cognito, you are able to view the API calls in AWS CloudTrail. Amazon CloudWatch Logs are generated if you are using Amazon Cognito to control access to AWS resources. Option A is incorrect as AWS can act as an IdP for non-AWS services. Option B is incorrect in that Amazon CloudWatch allows you to monitor the creation and modification of identity pools. It will not show activity. Option D is incorrect because the service provider assigns the policies, not the identity provider (IdP).

6. A, C. AD Connecter is easy to set up, and you continue to use the existing AD console to do configuration changes on Active Directory. Option B is incorrect because you cannot connect to multiple Active Directory domains with AD Connector, only a single one. AD Connector requires a one-to-one relationship with your on-premises domains. You can use AD Connector for AWS-created applications and services. Option D is incorrect because AD Connector is used to support AWS services.

7. A. To use AWS Single Sign-On (AWS SSO), you must set up AWS Organizations Service and enable all the features. AWS SSO uses Microsoft Active Directory (either AWS Managed Microsoft Active Directory or Active Directory Connector [AD Connector] but not Simple Active Directory). AWS SSO does not support Amazon Cognito. Option B is incorrect because AWS SSO does not use SAML. Options C and D are incorrect because you do not need to deploy either Simple AD or Amazon Cognito as a prerequisite for using AWS SSO.

8. C. Option C is correct because `GetFederationToken` returns a set of temporary security credentials (consisting of an access key ID, a secret access key, and a security token) for a federated user. You call the `GetFederationToken` action using the long-term security credentials of an IAM user. This is appropriate in contexts where those credentials can be safely stored, usually in a server-based application. Option D is incorrect because `GetSessionToken` provides only temporary security credentials. Option A is incorrect because AssumeRole is shorter lived (the default is 60 minutes; can be extended to 720 minutes). Options B and D are incorrect because `GetUserToken` and `GetSessionToken` are nonexistent APIs.

9. B. Because it is a managed service, you are not able to access the Amazon EC2 instances directly running AWS Managed Microsoft AD. AWS Managed Microsoft AD provides for daily snapshots, monitoring, and the ability to sync with an existing on-premises Active Directory.

10. A. Amazon Active Directory Connector (AD Connector) allows you to use your existing RADIUS-based multi-factor authentication (MFA) infrastructure to provide authentication.

Chapter 11: Refactor to Microservices

1. B. Option B is correct because a `Parallel` state enables you to execute several different execution paths at the same time in parallel. This is useful if you have activities or tasks that do not depend on each other and can execute in parallel. This can make your workflow complete faster. Option A is incorrect because it executes only one of the branches, not all. Option C is incorrect because it can execute one task, not multiple. Option D is incorrect because it waits and does not execute any tasks.

2. B. The messages move to the dead-letter queue if they have met the `Maximum Receives` parameter (the number of times that a message can be received before being sent to a dead-letter queue) and have not been deleted.

3. A. Amazon Simple Queue Service (Amazon SQS) attributes supports 256 KB messages. Refer to Table 11.2, Table 11.3, and Table 11.4.

4. B. Option B is correct because to send a message larger than 256 KB, you use Amazon SQS to save the file in Amazon S3 and then send a link to the file on Amazon SQS. Option A is incorrect because using the technique in option B, this is possible. Option C is incorrect because AWS Lambda cannot push messages to Amazon SQS that exceed the size limit of 256 KB. Option D is incorrect because it does not address the question.

5. C. Option C is correct if you need to send messages to other users. Create an Amazon SQS queue and subscribe all the administrators to this queue. Configure an Amazon CloudWatch event to send a message on a daily cron schedule into the Amazon SQS queue. Option A is not correct because Amazon SQS queues do not support subscriptions. Option B is not correct because the message is sent without any status information. Option D is not correct because AWS Lambda does not allow sending outgoing email messages on port 22. Email servers use port 22 for outgoing messages. Port 22 is blocked on Lambda as an antispam measure.

6. A. Amazon SNS supports the same attributes and parameters as Amazon SQS. Refer to Table 11.2, Table 11.3, and Table 11.4.

7. D. Option D is correct because there is no limit on the number of consumers as long as they stay within the capacity of the stream, which is based on the number of shards. For a single shard, the capacity is 2 MB of read or five transactions per second. Options A and B are incorrect because there is no limit on the number of consumers that can consume from the stream. Option C is incorrect because together the consumers can consume only 2 MB per second or five transactions per second.

8. C. Option C is correct because Amazon Kinesis Data Streams is a service for ingesting large amounts of data in real time and for performing real-time analytics on the data. Option A is not correct because you use Amazon SQS to ingest events, but it does not provide a way to aggregate them in real time. Option B is incorrect because Amazon SNS is a notification service that does not support ingesting. Option D is incorrect because Amazon Kinesis Data Firehose provides analytics; however, it has a latency of at least 60 seconds.

9. A. Options B, C, and D are incorrect because there are no guarantees about where the records for Washington and Wyoming will be relative to each other. They could be on the same shard, or they could be on different shards. Option A is correct because the records for Washington will not be distributed across multiple shards.

10. E. Option E is correct because all the options from A through D are correct. Options A, B, C, and D are all valid options for writing Amazon Kinesis Data Streams producers.

Chapter 12: Serverless Compute

1. D. Option D is correct because it enables the company to keep their existing AWS Lambda functions intact and create new versions of the AWS Lambda function. When they are ready to update the Lambda function, they can assign the PROD alias to the new version. Option A is possible; however, this adds a lot of unnecessary work, because developers would have to update all of their code everywhere. Option B is incorrect because moving regions would require moving all other services or introducing latency into the architecture, which is not the best option. Option C is possible; however, creating new AWS accounts for each application version is not a best practice, and it complicates the organization of such accounts unnecessarily.

2. B. At the time of this writing, the maximum amount of memory for a Lambda function is 3008 MB.

3. A. At the time of this writing, the default timeout value for a Lambda function is 3 seconds. However, you can set this to as little as 1 second or as long as 300 seconds.

4. C. Options A, B, and D are all viable answers; however, the question asks what is the best *serverless* option. Lambda is the only serverless option in this scenario; therefore, option C is the best answer.

5. D. At the time of this writing, the maximum execution time for a Lambda function is 300 seconds (5 minutes).

6. A. At the time of this writing, Ruby is not supported for Lambda functions.

7. A. At the time of this writing, the default limit for concurrent executions with Lambda is set to 1000. This is a soft limit that can be raised. To do this, you must open a case through the AWS Support Center page and send a Server Limit Increase request.

8. C. There are two types of policies with Lambda: a function policy and an execution policy, or AWS role. A function policy defines which AWS resources are allowed to invoke your function. The execution role defines which AWS resources your function can access. Here, the function is invoked successfully, but the issue is that the Lambda function does not have access to process objects inside Amazon S3. Option A is not correct because a function policy is responsible for invoking or triggering the function; here, the function is invoked and executes properly. Option B is not correct, as the scenario states that the trust policy is valid. The execution policy or AWS role is responsible for providing Lambda with access to other services; thus, the correct answer is option C.

9.   A. Option A is correct because Lambda automatically retries failed executions for asynchronous invocations. You can also configure Lambda to forward payloads that were not processed to a DLQ, which can be an Amazon SQS queue or Amazon SNS topic. Option B is incorrect because a VPC network is an AWS service that allows you to define your own network in the AWS Cloud. Option C is incorrect because this is dealing with concurrency issues, and here you have no problems with Lambda concurrency. Additionally, concurrency is enabled by default with Lambda. Option D is incorrect because Lambda does support SQS.

10.   C. Option C is correct because the environment variables enable you to pass settings dynamically to your function code and libraries without changing your code. Option A is not correct, because dead-letter queries are used for events that could not be processed by Lambda and need to be investigated later. Option B is not correct because it can be done. Option D is incorrect because this can be accomplished through environment variables.

Chapter 13: Serverless Applications

1.   D. Option A is incorrect. While AWS CloudFormation can help you provision infrastructure, AWS Serverless Application Model (AWS SAM) is optimized for deploying AWS serverless resources by making it easy to organize related components and resources that operate on a single stack; therefore, option A is not the best answer. Option C is incorrect because AWS OpsWorks is managed by Puppet or Chef, which you can use to deploy infrastructure. However, these are not the optimal answers given that you are specifically looking for serverless technologies. The same is true for Ansible in option B. Option D is correct because AWS SAM is an open-source framework that you can use to build serverless applications on AWS.

2.   B. CORS is responsible for allowing cross-site access to your APIs. Without it, you will not be able to call the Amazon API Gateway service. You use a stage to deploy your API, and a resource is a typed object that is part of your API's domain. Each resource may have an associated data model and relationships to other resources and can respond to different methods. Option A is incorrect because you do need to enable CORS. Option B is correct because CORS is responsible for allowing one server to call another server or service. For more information on CORS, see: `https://developer.mozilla.org/en-US/docs/Web/HTTP/CORS`. Option C is incorrect, as deploying a stage allows you to deploy your API. Option D is incorrect, as a resource is where you can define your API, but it is not yet deployed to a stage and "live."

3.   A, C. There are three benefits to serverless stacks: no server management, flexible scaling, and automated high availability. Costs vary case by case. For these reasons, option A and option C are the best answers.

4.   D. Option A is incorrect; API Gateway only supports HTTPS endpoints. Option B is incorrect because API Gateway does not support creating FTP endpoints. Option C is incorrect; API Gateway does not support SSH endpoints. API Gateway only creates HTTPS endpoints.

5. C. Option A is incorrect because Amazon CloudFront supports a variety of sources, including Amazon S3. Option B is incorrect, because serverless applications contain both static and dynamic data. Additionally, CloudFront supports both static and dynamic data. Option C is correct because CloudFront supports a variety of origins. For the serverless stack, it supports Amazon S3. Option D is incorrect because Amazon S3 is a valid origin for CloudFront.

6. D. Option A, option B, and option C are each not the only language/platform supported. Option D is correct because all of these languages/platforms are supported.

7. C. Option C is correct because Amazon Cognito supports SMS-based MFA.

8. D. Options A, B, and C are incorrect because Amazon Cognito supports device tracking and remembering.

9. A. Option A is correct because the events property allows you to assign Lambda to an event source. Option B is incorrect because handler is the function handler in an Lambda function. Option C is incorrect because context is the context object for a Lambda function. Option D is incorrect because runtime is the language that your Lambda function runs as.

10. D. Option A is incorrect. You can run React in an AWS service. Option B is incorrect. You can run your web server with Amazon S3. With option C, you do not need to load balance Lambda functions because Lambda scales automatically. Option D is correct. You can run a fully dynamic website in a serverless fashion. You can also use JavaScript frameworks such as Angular and React. The NoSQL database may need to be refactored to run in Amazon DynamoDB.

Chapter 14: Stateless Application Patterns

1. B. Option B is correct because the maximum size of an item in an DynamoDB table is 400 KB. Option C is incorrect because 4 KB is the capacity of a strongly consistent read per second, or two eventually consistent reads per second, for an item up to 4 KB in size. Option D is incorrect because 1,024 KB is not the size limit of an DynamoDB item. The maximum item size is 400 KB.

2. C. Option C is correct because when creating a new bucket, the bucket name must be globally unique. Option A is incorrect because versioning is disabled by default. Option B is incorrect because the maximum size for an object stored in Amazon S3 is 5 TB, not 5 GB. Option D is incorrect because you cannot change a bucket name after you have created the bucket.

3. B. Option B is correct because storage class is the only factor that is not considered when determining which region to choose. Option A is incorrect because latency is a factor when choosing a bucket region. Option C is incorrect because prices are different between regions; thus, you might consider cost when choosing a bucket region. Option D is incorrect because you may be required to store your data in a bucket in a particular region based on legal requirements or compliance.

4. C. Option C is correct because the recommended technique for protecting your table data at rest is the server-side encryption. Option A is incorrect because fine-grained access controls are a mechanism for providing access to resources and API calls, but the mechanism is not used to encrypt or protect data at rest. Option B is incorrect because TLS protects data in transit, not data at rest. Option D is incorrect because client-side encryption is applied to data before it is transmitted from a user device to a server.

5. D. Option D is correct because versioning-enabled buckets enable you to recover objects from accidental deletion or overwrite. Option A is incorrect because lifecycle policies are used to transition data to a different storage class and do not protect objects against accidental overwrites or deletions. Option B is incorrect because enabling MFA Delete on the bucket requires an additional method of authentication before allowing a deletion. Option C is incorrect because using a path-style URL is unrelated to protecting overwrites or accidental deletions.

6. C, D. Options C and D are correct because Amazon S3 stores objects in buckets, and each object that is stored in a bucket is made up of two parts: the object itself and the metadata. Option A is incorrect because Amazon S3 stores data as objects, not in fixed blocks. Option B is incorrect because the size limit of an object is 5 TB.

7. C. Option C is correct because DynamoDB Streams captures a time-ordered sequence of item-level modifications in any DynamoDB table, and the service stores this information in a log for up to 24 hours. Options A, B, and D are incorrect because 24 hours is the maximum time that data persists on an Amazon DynamoDB stream.

8. B. Option B is correct because DynamoDB Streams ensures that each stream record appears exactly once in the stream. Options A and C are incorrect because each stream record appears exactly once. Option D is incorrect because you cannot set the retention period.

9. A. Option A is correct because your bucket can be in only one of three versioning states: versioning-enabled, versioning-disabled, or versioning-suspended. Thus, versioning-paused is a state that is not a valid configuration. Options A, B, and C are incorrect—they are all valid bucket states for versioning.

10. A. Option A is correct because QueryTable is the DynamoDB operation used to find items based on primary key values. Option B is incorrect because UpdateTable is the DynamoDB operation used to modify the provisioned throughput settings, global secondary indexes, or DynamoDB Streams settings for a given table. Option C is incorrect because DynamoDB does not have a Search operation. Option D is incorrect because Scan is the DynamoDB operation used to read every item in a table.

11. A, B, C. Option D is incorrect because when compared to the other options, a bank balance is not likely to be stored in a cache; it is probably not data that is retrieved as frequently as the others are fetched. Options A, B, and C are all better data candidates to cache because multiple users are more likely to access them repeatedly. Although, you could also cache the bank account balance for shorter periods if the database query is not performing well.

12. A, D. Options A and D are correct because Amazon ElastiCache supports both the Redis and Memcached open-source caching engines. Option B is incorrect because MySQL is not a caching engine—it is a relational database engine. Option C is incorrect because Couchbase is a NoSQL database and not one of the caching engines that ElastiCache supports.

13. C. Option C is correct because the default limit is 20 nodes per cluster.

14. C. Option C is correct because ElastiCache is a managed in-memory caching service. Option A is incorrect because the description aligns more closely to the Elasticsearch Service. Option B is incorrect because this is not an accurate description of the ElastiCache service. Option D is incorrect because, as a managed service, ElastiCache does not manage Amazon EC2 instances.

15. B, D, E. Option B is correct because DynamoDB is a NoSQL low-latency transactional database that you can use to store state. Option D is correct because Amazon Elastic File System (Amazon EFS) is an elastic file system that you can also use to store state. Option E is correct because ElastiCache is an in-memory cache that is also a good solution for storing state. Option A is incorrect because Amazon CloudFront is a content delivery network that is used more for object caching, not in-memory caching. Option C is incorrect because Amazon CloudWatch is a metric repository and does not provide any kind of user-accessible storage. Option F is incorrect because Amazon SQS is used for exchanging messages.

16. C. Option C is correct because Amazon DynamoDB is a nonrelational database that delivers reliable performance at any scale. Option A is incorrect because Amazon S3 Glacier is for data archiving and long-term backup. It is also an object store and not a database store. Option B is incorrect because Amazon RDS is designed for relational workloads. Option D is incorrect because Amazon Redshift is a data warehousing service.

17. D. Option D is correct because local secondary indexes on a table are created when the table is created. Options A and C are incorrect because you can have five local secondary indexes or five global secondary indexes per table. Option B is incorrect because you can create global secondary indexes after you have created the table.

Chapter 15: Monitoring and Troubleshooting

1. B. Option A is incorrect because you do not want to scale in to reduce your capacity when you are experiencing a high load. Option C is incorrect because you do not want to scale in to reduce your capacity when your application is taking a long time to respond. Option D is incorrect because metrics are required for triggering AWS Auto Scaling events. Option B is correct because scaling out should occur when more resources are being consumed than normal, and scaling in should occur when less resources are being consumed.

2. D. Options A, B, C, and D are all incorrect because data points with a period of 300 seconds are stored for 63 days in Amazon CloudWatch.

3. D. Option A is incorrect because AWS CloudTrail events show who made the request. Option B is incorrect because CloudTrail shows when the request was made, and option C is incorrect because CloudTrail shows what was requested. Option E is incorrect because CloudTrail shows what resource was acted on. Option D is correct because CloudTrail can provide no insight into why a request was made.

4. C. Option A would work; however, it is not the most cost-effective way because logs stored in CloudWatch cost more than logs stored in Amazon S3. Option B is incorrect because CloudWatch cannot ingest logs without access to your servers. Option C is correct because archiving logs from CloudWatch to Amazon S3 reduces overall data storage costs.

5. A, B, D. Option C is incorrect because CloudWatch has no way to access data in your applications or servers. You must push the data either by using the CloudWatch SDK or AWS CLI or by installing the CloudWatch agent. Option A is correct because the Cloud-Watch agent is required to send operating system and application logs to CloudWatch. Option B is likewise correct because metrics logs are sent to CloudWatch using the `PutMetricData` and `PutLogEvents` API actions. Option D is also correct because the AWS CLI can be used to send metrics to CloudWatch using the `put-metric-data` and `put-log-events` commands.

6. C. Options A and B are incorrect because the strings must match a filter pattern equal to 404. Option C is correct because 404 matches the error code present in the example logs.

7. A. AWS X-Ray color-codes the response types you get from your services. For 4XX, or client-side errors, the circle is orange. Thus, option B is incorrect. Application failures or faults are red, and successful responses, or 2XX, are green. Thus, options C and D are incorrect. For throttling, or 5XX series errors, the circle is purple. Thus, option A is correct.

8. C. Option A is incorrect because CloudTrail logs list security-related events and do not provide a dashboard feature. Option B is incorrect because CloudWatch alarms are used to notify you when something isn't operating based on your specifications. Option D is incorrect because Amazon CloudWatch Logs are for sending and storing server logs to the CloudWatch service; however, you could use these logs to create a metric and then place it on the CloudWatch dashboard. Option C is the correct answer. Use CloudWatch dashboards to create a single interface where you can monitor all the resources.

9. D. CloudTrail stores the CloudTrail event history for 90 days; however, if you would like to store this information permanently, you can create an CloudTrail trail, which stores the logs in Amazon S3.

10. D. Option C is incorrect because the `LookupEvents` API action can be used to query event data. Options A and B are also incorrect because the AWS CLI and the AWS Management Console use the same CloudTrail APIs to query event data. Thus, option D is correct.

11. B, D. Management events are operations performed on resources in your AWS account. Data events are operations performed on data stored in AWS resources. For example, modifying an object in Amazon S3 would qualify as a data event, and changing a bucket policy would qualify as a management event. Because options A, C, and E involve sending or receiving data, not modifying or creating AWS resources, they are data events. Thus, options B and D are correct.

12. A, C, D. When installing the CloudWatch Logs agent, no additional networking configuration is required as long as your instance can reach the CloudWatch API endpoint. Therefore, option B is incorrect. You can use AWS Systems Manager to install and start the agent, but it is not required to install the Systems Manager agent alongside the CloudWatch Logs agent; thus, option E is incorrect. When installing the agent, you must configure the specific logs to send. The agent must be started before new log data is sent to CloudWatch Logs.

13. A. CloudWatch alarms support triggering actions in Amazon EC2, EC2 Auto Scaling, and Amazon SNS. Thus, options B, C, and D are incorrect. It is possible to trigger AWS Lambda functions from an alarm, but only by first sending the alarm notification to an Amazon SNS topic. Thus, option A is correct.

14. D. CPU, network, and disk activity are metrics that are visible to the underlying host for an instance. Thus, options A, B, and C are incorrect. Because memory is allocated in a single block to an instance and is managed by the guest OS, the underlying host does not have visibility into consumption. This metric would have to be delivered to CloudWatch as a custom metric by using the agent. Thus, option D is correct.

15. A. No namespace starts with an Amazon prefix; therefore, options B and D are incorrect. Option C is incorrect because namespaces are specific to a service (Amazon EC2), not a resource (an instance). Option A is correct because the Amazon EC2 service uses the AWS prefix, followed by EC2.

Chapter 16: Optimization

1. D. Amazon EC2 instance store is directly attached to the instance, which gives you the lowest latency between the disk and your application. Instance store is also provided at no additional cost on instance types that have it available, so this is the lowest-cost option. Additionally, because the data is being retrieved from somewhere else, it can be copied back to an instance as needed. Option A is incorrect because Amazon S3 cannot be directly mounted to an Amazon EC2 instance. Options B and C are incorrect because Amazon EBS and Amazon EFS would be higher-cost options, with a higher latency than an instance store.

2. C. GetItem retrieves a single item from a table. This is the most efficient way to read a single item because it provides direct access to the physical location of the item. Options A and B are incorrect. Query retrieves all the items that have a specific partition key. Within those items, you can apply a condition to the sort key and retrieve only a subset of the data. Query provides quick, efficient access to the partitions where the data is stored. Scan retrieves all of the items in the specified table, and it can consume large amounts of system resources based on the size of the table. Option D is incorrect. DynamoDB is a nonrelational NoSQL database, and it does not support table joins. Instead, applications read data from one table at a time.

3. C. Option C is a fault-tolerance check. By launching instances in multiple Availability Zones in the same region, you help protect your applications from a single point of failure. Options A and B are performance checks. Provisioned IOPS volumes in the Amazon EBS are designed to deliver the expected performance only when they are attached to an Amazon EBS optimized instance. Some headers, such as Date or User-Agent, significantly reduce the cache hit ratio (the proportion of requests that are served from a CloudFront edge cache). This increases the load on your origin and reduces performance because CloudFront must forward more requests to your origin. Option D is a cost check. Elastic IP addresses are static IP addresses designed for dynamic cloud computing. A nominal charge is imposed for an Elastic IP address that is not associated with a running instance.

4. B. Options A, C, and D are incorrect because partition keys used in these options could cause "hot" (heavily requested) partition keys because of lack of uniformity. Design your application for uniform activity across all logical partition keys in the table and its secondary indexes. Use distinct values for each item.

5. D. Option A is incorrect because SQS is a messaging service. Option B is incorrect because SNS is a notification service. Option C is incorrect because CloudFront is a web distribution service. Option D is correct because ElastiCache improves the performance of your application by retrieving data from high throughput and low latency in-memory data stores. For details, see https://aws.amazon.com/elasticache.

6. C. Option C is correct because CloudFront optimizes performance if your workload is mainly sending GET requests. There are also fewer direct requests to Amazon S3, which reduces cost. For details, see https://docs.aws.amazon.com/AmazonS3/latest/dev/request-rate-perf-considerations.html.

7. D. Option A is incorrect because AWS Auto Scaling is optimal for unpredictable workloads. Option B is incorrect because cross-region replication is better for disaster recovery scenarios. Option C is incorrect because DynamoDB streams are better suited to stream data to other sources. Option D is correct because Amazon DynamoDB Accelerator (DAX) provides fast in-memory performance. For details, see https://docs.aws.amazon.com/amazondynamodb/latest/developerguide/DAX.html.

8. C. Option A is incorrect because EC2 instance store is too volatile to be optimal. Option B is incorrect because this is a security solution and will not impact performance positively. Option C is correct because ElastiCache is ideal for handling session state. You can abstract the HTTP sessions from the web servers by using Redis and Memcached. Option D is incorrect because compression is not the optimal solution given the choices. For details, see https://aws.amazon.com/caching/session-management/.

9. B. Option B is correct because lazy loading only loads data into the cache when necessary. This avoids filling up the cache with data that isn't requested. Options A, C, and D are

incorrect because they do not match the requirement of the question. For details, see https://docs.aws.amazon.com/AmazonElastiCache/latest/mem-ug/Strategies.html.

10. A. Option A is correct because information about the instance, such as private IP, is stored in the instance metadata. Option B is incorrect because private IP information is not stored in the instance user data. Option C is incorrect because running ifconfig is manual and not automated. Option D is incorrect because it is not clear on what type of instance the application is running. For details, see https://docs.aws.amazon.com/AWSEC2/latest/UserGuide/ec2-instance-metadata.html.

11. D. Options A, B, and C are incorrect because they are not recommended best practices. Option D is correct because it is one of the recommendations in the best practices documentation, "Avoid using recursive code." For details, see https://docs.aws.amazon.com/lambda/latest/dg/best-practices.html.

12. C. Option A is incorrect because changing the entire architecture is not ideal. Option B is incorrect because Multi-AZ is used for fault tolerance. Option C is correct because loads can be reduced by routing read queries from your application to the read replica. Option D is incorrect because using an Elastic Load Balancing load balancer will not reduce the query load. For details, see https://aws.amazon.com/rds/details/read-replicas/.

13. C. Option A is incorrect because this is relevant only when you need a static website. Option B is incorrect because changing the storage class does not help with latency. Option C is correct because cross-region replication maintains object copies in regions that are geographically closer to your users, reducing latency. Option D is incorrect because encryption is necessary only for securing data at rest. For details, see https://docs.aws.amazon.com/AmazonS3/latest/dev/crr.html.

14. B. Options A, C, and D are incorrect because they are not optimal for handling large object uploads to Amazon S3. Option B is correct because a multipart upload enables you to upload large objects in parts to Amazon S3. For details, see https://docs.aws.amazon.com/AmazonS3/latest/dev/mpuoverview.html.

15. C. Option A is incorrect because this is not the optimal approach for bootstrapping. Option B is incorrect because, while possible, bootstrapping in the user data is optimal. Option C is correct because instance user data is used to perform common automated configuration tasks and run scripts after boot. Option D is incorrect because bootstrapping is done in instance user data, not instance metadata. For details, see https://docs.aws.amazon.com/AWSEC2/latest/UserGuide/user-data.html.

Index

B

Comprehensive Online Learning Environment

Register to gain one year of FREE access to the online interactive learning environment and test bank to help you study for your AWS Certified Developer - Associate exam— included with your purchase of this book!

The online test bank includes the following:

- **Assessment Test** to help you focus your study to specific objectives
- **Chapter Tests** to reinforce what you've learned
- **Practice Exams** to test your knowledge of the material
- **Digital Flashcards** to reinforce your learning and provide last-minute test prep before the exam
- **Searchable Glossary** to define the key terms you'll need to know for the exam

Go to http://www.wiley.com/go/sybextestprep to register and gain access to this comprehensive study tool package.

Register and Access the Online Test Bank

To register your book and get access to the online test bank, follow these steps:

1. Go to bit.ly/SybexTest.
2. Select your book from the list.
3. Complete the required registration information, including answering the security verification to prove book ownership. You will be emailed a PIN code.
4. Follow the directions in the email or go to https://www.wiley.com/go/sybextestprep.
5. Enter the PIN code you received and click the "Activate PIN" button.
6. On the Create an Account or Login page, enter your username and password, and click Login. A "Thank you for activating your PIN!" message will appear. If you don't have an account already, create a new account.
7. Click the "Go to My Account" button to add your new book to the My Products page.